Early Western Civilization

Source Readings

Robert Cleve
California State University, Northridge

KENDALL/HUNT PUBLISHING COMPANY
4050 Westmark Drive   Dubuque, Iowa 52002

Contents

Chapter 4: Ancient Rome

Preface

College courses in Western Civilization traditionally treat a succession of societies, beginning, in the third millennium B.C., with a narrow view of the ancient near eastern civilization of Sumer and expanding that view, through the ancient, medieval and modern ages, into the wide vista of the 21st century "world village." This is normally a one year program. The first half of that study involves the history of the peoples of the ancient Near East, Egypt, Greece and the Roman civilization of the Mediterranean basin. This book attempts to provide the student with a very brief sampling of primary sources for those ages.

What are primary sources? Simply stated, primary sources are the raw material of history. The term includes a wide variety of materials: literature, documents, coins, letters artifacts, art objects, etc. The historian evaluates this material and constructs a picture of our past. The result is the narrative story of history contained in the course textbook. Obviously, such a construction is subjective and open to controversy—in the final analysis it is only the historian's opinion. Therefore, the serious student owes it to him/herself to look beyond the textbook to the primary sources.

The selections of primary sources contained in this book are chiefly drawn from ancient literature and they are only a minute sample. They have been carefully selected to give you, the student, a brief exposure to the timeless ideas of the our past, the ideas that made us what we are. However, do not assume, simply because these sources are primary, or simply because they were written many centuries ago, that they are more objective then the secondary source of your textbook. The authors of these ancient histories, letters and documents were also human and they were also driven by the same motives and biases that drive the modern historian. Thus, you must approach these selections with the same caution, suspicion and mistrust that you give to secondary material. Always question everything. Even the choosing of the selections for inclusion in this book was unavoidably made with a certain bias and subjectivity. Another historian would have chosen differently. Of course, this kind of controversy is the life blood of history. It is what drives the historical process.

Nevertheless, these primary sources provide an enhanced view of the history of early Western Civilization, an insight not possible from secondary sources alone. This is important. It provides the student with the ability to make at least a partially independent judgment of the objectivity of the secondary material.

Chapter 1

Ancient Mesopotamia

Ishtar Lion Gate Bas Relief, Ishtar Lion Gate, Istanbul, Turkey

Epic of Gilgamesh

The Epic of Gilgamesh, written about 2600 B.C., involves the gods in human activities. Gilgamesh is probably a historical figure who ruled the city of Uruk. The story deals with a profound theme, the human protest against death. In the end Gilgamesh must accept the reality of his own mortality. There is no escape. Thus, this epic is an expression of the pessimism that pervaded all of Mesopotamian culture. Because King Gilgamesh, drives his subjects too hard, they appeal to the gods for help. The gods decide that a man of Gilgamesh's immense vigor and strength requires a rival with similar attributes with whom he could contend. The creation goddess, Aruru, is instructed to create a man worthy of Gilgamesh. From clay she fashions Enkidu in the image of Anu, the god of the heavens and father of all the gods. Enkidu is a powerful man who roams with the animals and destroys traps set by hunters, one of whom appeals to King Gilgamesh. The two of them, accompanied by a harlot, find Enkidu at a watering place frequented by animals. The harlot removes her clothes and seduces Enkidu, who spends a week with her, oblivious to everything else. After this encounter, the bond between Enkidu and the animals is broken. He now enters civilization and is befriended by Gilgamesh. The two heroes become inseparable friends and experience many adventures together. During one adventure they slay the terrible monster of the cedar forest, Humbaba.

Returning to Uruk after the encounter with Humbaba, Gilgamesh washes away the grime of battle and dons his royal clothes; thus arrayed he attracts the goddess of love, Ishtar, patroness of Uruk, who proposes marriage, but because of Ishtar's previous marriages and infidelities, Gilgamesh refuses. Ishtar falls into a bitter rage and appeals to her father, the god Anu, to unleash the fearful Bull of Heaven on Gilgamesh. However, Gilgamesh and Enkidu together slay the beast. To avenge the deaths of Humbaha and the Bull of Heaven, the gods decide that Enkidu shall die. In the following passage. Enkidu dreams of his impending death and the House of Darkness, from which no one returns.

When the daylight came Enkidu got up and cried to Gilgamesh, "O my brother, such a dream I had last night. Anu, Enlil, Ea and heavenly Shamash took counsel together, and Anu said to Enlil, 'Because they have killed the Bull of Heaven, and because they have killed Humbaba who guarded the Cedar Mountain one of the two must die.' . . ."

So Enkidu lay stretched out before Gilgamesh; his tears ran down in streams and he said to Gilgamesh, "O my brother, so dear as you are to me, brother, yet they will take me from you." Again he said, 'I must sit down on the threshold of the dead and never again will I see my dear brother with my eyes." . . .

. . .In bitterness of spirit he poured out his heart to his friend. "It was I who cut down the cedar, I who leveled the forest, I who slew Humbaba and now see what has become of me. Listen, my friend, this is the dream I dreamed last night. The heavens roared, and earth rumbled back an answer; between them stood I before an awful being, the somber-faced man-bird; he had directed on me his purpose. His was a vampire face, his foot was a lion's foot, his hand was an eagle's talon. He fell on me and his claws were in my hair, he held me fast and I smothered; then he transformed me so that my arms became wings covered with feathers. He turned his stare towards me, and he led me away to the palace of Irkalla, the Queen of Darkness, to the house from which none who enters ever returns, down the road from which there is no coming back.

"There is the house whose people sit in darkness; dust is their food and clay their meat. They are clothed like birds with wings for covering, they see no light, they sit in darkness. I entered the house of dust and I saw the kings of the earth, their crowns put away for ever; rulers and princes, all those who once wore kingly crowns and ruled the world in the days of old. They who had stood in the place of the gods like Anu and Enlil, stood now like servants to fetch baked meats in the house of dust, to carry cooked meat and cold water from the water-skin. In the house of dust which I entered were high priests and acolytes, priests of the incantation and of ecstasy; there were servers of the temple, and there was Etana, that king of Kish whom the eagle carried to heaven in the days of old. I saw also Samuqan, god of cattle, and there was Ereshkigal the Queen of the Underworld; and Belit-Sheri squatted in front of her, she who is recorder of the gods and keeps the book of death. She held a tablet from which she read. She raised her head, she saw me and spoke: 'Who has brought this one here?' Then I awoke like a man drained of blood who wanders alone in a waste of rushes; like one whom the bailiff has seized and his heart pounds with terror."

Gilgamesh had peeled off his clothes, he listened to his words and wept quick tears, Gilgamesh listened and his tears flowed. . .

This day on which Enkidu dreamed came to an end and he lay stricken with sickness. One whole day he lay on his bed and his suffering increased. He said to Gilgamesh, the friend on whose account he had left the wilderness, "Once I ran for you, for the water of life, and I now have nothing." A second day he lay on his bed and Gilgamesh watched over him but the sickness increased. A third day he lay on his bed, he called out to Gilgamesh, rousing him up. Now he was weak and his eyes were blind with weeping. Ten days he lay and his suffering increased, eleven and twelve days he lay on his bed of pain. Then he called to Gilgamesh, 'My friend, the great goddess cursed me and I must die in shame. I shall not die like a man fallen in battle; I feared to fall, but happy is the man who falls in the battle, for I must die in shame." And Gilgamesh wept over Enkidu. With the first light of dawn he raised his voice and said to the counselors of Uruk:

"Hear me, great ones of Uruk,
I weep for Enkidu, my friend,
Bitterly moaning like a woman mourning
I weep for my brother.
O Enkidu, my brother,
You were the axe at my side,
My hand's strength, the sword in my belt,
The shield before me.

A glorious robe, my fairest ornament;
An evil Fate has robbed me.

All the people of Eridu
Weep for you Enkidu.

What is this sleep which holds you now?
You are lost in the dark and cannot hear me.

He touched his heart but it did not beat, nor did he lift his eyes again. When Gilgamesh touched his heart it did not beat. So Gilgamesh laid a veil, as one veils the bride, over his friend. He began to rage like a lion, like a lioness robbed of her whelps. This way and that he paced round the bed, he tore out his hair and strewed it around. He dragged off his splendid robes and flung them down as though they were abominations.

In the first light of dawn Gilgamesh cried out, "I made you rest on a royal bed. you reclined on a couch at my left hand, the princes of the earth kissed your feet. I will cause all the people of Uruk to weep over you and raise the dirge of the dead. The joyful people will stoop with sorrow; and when you have gone to the earth I will let my hair grow long for your sake, I will wander through the wilderness in the skin of a lion." The next day also, in the first light, Gilgamesh lamented; seven days and seven nights he wept for Enkidu. until the worm fastened on him. Only then he gave him up to the earth, for the Anunnaki, the judges [of the dead], had seized him.

In his despair, Gilgamesh is confronted with the reality of his own death. Yearning for eternal life, he seeks Utnapishtim, legendary king of the city of Shurrupok, a man to whom the gods had granted everlasting life.

Bitterly Gilgamesh wept for his friend Enkidu; he wandered over the wilderness as a hunter, he roamed over the plains; in his bitterness he cried. "How can I rest, how can I be at peace? Despair is in my heart. What my brother is now, that shall I be when I am dead. Because I am afraid of death I will go as best I can to find Utnapishtim whom they call the Faraway, for he has entered the assembly of the gods." So Gilgamesh traveled over the wilderness, he wandered over the grasslands, a long journey, in search of Utnapishtim, whom the gods took after the deluge; and they set him to live in the land of Dilmun, in the garden of the sun; and to him alone of men they gave everlasting life.

In the garden of the gods, Gilgamesh speaks with Siduri, the divine winemaker, who tells him that his search for eternal life is hopeless.

". . . My friend who was very dear to me and who endured dangers beside me, Enkidu my brother, whom I loved, the end of mortality has overtaken him. I wept for him seven days and nights till the worm fastened on him. Because of my brother I am afraid of death, because of my brother I stray through the wilderness and cannot rest. But now, young woman, maker of wine, since I have seen your face do not let me see the face of death which I dread so much."

She answered, "Gilgamesh. where are you hurrying to? You will never find that life for which you are looking. When the gods created man they allotted to him death, but life they retained in their own keeping. As for you, Gilgamesh, fill your belly with good things; day and night, night and day, dance and be merry, feast and rejoice. Let your clothes be fresh, bathe yourself in water, cherish the little child that holds your hand, and make your wife happy in your embrace; for this too is the lot of man."

But Gilgamesh said to Siduri, the young woman, "How can I be silent, how can I rest, when Enkidu whom I love is dust, and I too shall die and be laid in the earth. You live by the sea-shore and look into the heart of it; young woman, tell me now, which is the way to Utnapishtim, the son of Ubara-Tutu? What directions are there for the passage; give me. oh, give me directions. I will cross the Ocean if it is possible: if it is not I will wander still farther in the wilderness.

Siduri instructs Gilgamesh how to reach Utnapishtim. Ferried across the "waters of death" by a boatman, Gilgamesh meets Utnapishtim. But he, too, cannot give Gilgamesh the eternal life for which he yearns.

. . . "Oh father Utnapishtim, you who have entered the assembly of the gods, I wish to question you concerning the living and the dead, how shall I find the life for which I am searching?"

Utnapishtim said, "There is no permanence. Do we build a house to stand for ever, do we seal a contract to hold for all time? Do brothers divide an inheritance to keep for ever, does the flood-time of rivers endure? It is only the nymph of the dragon-fly who sheds her larva and sees the sun in his glory. From the days of old there is no permanence. The sleeping and the dead, how alike they are, they are like a painted death. What is there between the master and the servant when both have fulfilled their doom? When the Anunnaki, the judges, come together, and Mammetun the mother of destinies, together they decree the fates of men. Life and death they allot but the day of death they do not disclose."

The tale concludes with one of the many Near Eastern flood stories that preceded the account of Noah in Genesis.

The Babylonian Story of the Flood 2

There are a number of Mesopotamian versions of the story of a great flood that destroyed the world. The oldest of these versions is in Sumerian and is told as part of a story of the beginnings of things, leading from creation to earliest dynasties, and are thus part of the oldest traditions of Mesopotamia, while the latest version is embodied in the great Babylonian epic, recounting the adventures of a semi-mythical hero Gilgamesh. This epic, known to us from numerous fragments in the library of Ashurbanapal, is a composite production containing a number of independent tales, loosely strung together, and all brought into connection with the favorite hero Gilgamesh. Some of the tales embody dimmed historical traditions centering around the ancient city of Uruk, while others are nature myths, associated with occurrences in nature and in which the gods appear as the actors. The epic in its final form comprised twelve tablets, corresponding to the months of the year, with at least some of the episodes told on tablets the number of which in the series is correlated to the season of the year to which the myth belongs. Thus on the sixth tablet marking the end of the summer season, there is told the story of Gilgamesh's rejection of the marriage offer of the goddess Ishtar—symbolizing the loss of nature's charms. In the same way, the Deluge story is recounted in the eleventh tablet, corresponding to the month when the rainy season is at its height and the winter storms reach their climax. Gilgamesh himself, however, has nothing to do with the Deluge. He is somewhat artificially introduced into it by the accident of his encountering the hero who has escaped the general destruction of mankind. Gilgamesh, smitten with painful disease as a punishment for the insult offered to the goddess Ishtar, and fearing death, wanders about in search of healing and to secure immortality. He learns of a remote ancestor Utnapishtim, who has been granted the gift of immortal life. After long and weary wanderings with many adventures he at last finds himself face to face with Utnapishtim, whose name signifies "He who has experienced life." Amazed to find Utnapishtim looking like an ordinary mortal, Gilgamesh asks Utnapishtim how he came to secure immortality. In reply, Utnapishtim tells him the story of a great deluge which destroyed mankind, and from which he and his family were rescued through the contrivance of Ea, the god of humanity. The Deluge was suggested, as was the picture of primeval chaos, by the climatic conditions prevailing in the Euphrates Valley, which before the perfection of an elaborate canal system experienced a destructive overflow at each recurring rainy and stormy season. The tradition of a particularly destructive flood entailing much loss of life may have been an additional factor in giving to the deluge myth its definite form. The eleventh tablet of the Gilgamesh epic begins as follows:

Source: *The Civilization of Babylonia and Assyria* by Morris Jastrow, Jr. (J.P. Lippincott Company, 1915).

"Gilgamesh speaks to him, to Utnapishtim, the far-removed:
'I gaze at thee, Utnapishtim!
Thy appearance is not different. As I am, so art thou.
And thou are not different. As I am, so art thou.
Thou art completely ready for the fray.
. . .thou hast placed upon thee.
(Tell me) how thou didst enter into the assembly of the gods and secure life."

In reply Utnapishtim tells the following story:

"I will reveal to thee, Gilgamesh, a secret story,
And the decision of the gods I will tell thee.
The city Shuruppak, a city which thou knowest,
(The one that) lies on the Euphrates,
That city was old, and the gods thereof
Induced the great gods to bring a cyclone over it;
It was planned (?) by their father Anu,
(By) their counselor, the warrior Enlil,
(By) their herald Ninib,
(By) their leader En-nugi.
The lord of brilliant vision, Ea, was with them.
He repeated their decision to the reed-hut.[1]
'Reed-hut, reed-hut, wall, wall,
Reed-hut, hear! Wall, give ear!
O man of Shuruppak, son of Ubara-Tutu,
Break up the house, build a ship,
Abandon your property, seek life!
Throw aside your possession and preserve life!
Bring into the ship seed of all living things!
The ship that thou shalt build,
Let its dimensions be measured, (so that)
Its breadth and length be made to correspond.
On a level with the deep, provide it with a covering."

In another version the name of the hero of the Deluge is given as Atrakhasis, signifying "the very clever one." This alternate name is introduced also at the end of our version of the tale, where Ea says that he sent Atrakhasis a dream which the latter correctly understood. Evidently two traditions of the manner in which the hero of

---

1. Refers to the hut in which Utnapishtim lives. This points to the primitive conditions which existed at the time the deluge occurred.

the deluge was warned of the coming destruction were current. Both were embodied in our tale, which thus is revealed as itself a composite production. Utnapishtim continues his narrative:

"I understood and spoke to Ea, my lord:
(The command) of my lord which thou hast commanded,
As I have understood (it), I will carry out.
(But what) shall I answer the city, the people, and the elders?
Ea opened his mouth and spoke:
Spoke to me, his servant.
'(As answer) thus speak to them:
(Know that) Enlil has conceived hatred towards me,
So that I can no longer dwell (in your city).
(On) Enlil's territory I dare no longer set my face.
Therefore, I go to the "deep" to dwell with Ea, my lord.
Over you he will cause blessing to rain down.
(Catch of) bird, catch of fish,'
And . . . rich crops."

At this point the tablet is defective. Utnapishtim must have told Gilgamesh how he completed the ship, first drawing a plan and building according to it. Thereupon the text proceeds:

"On the fifth day, I designed its outline.
According to the plan (?), the walls were to be ten Gar[2] high.
Correspondingly, ten Gar the measure of its width.
I determined upon its shape (and) drew it.
I weighted it six-fold.
I divided (the superstructure?) into seven parts.
Its interior I divided into nine parts.
Water-plugs I constructed in the interior.
I selected a pole and added accessories.
Six Sar of asphalt I poured on the outer wall.
Three Sar of pitch (I poured) on the inner wall.
Three Sar the workmen carried away in their baskets.[3] Of oil,
Beside one Sar of oil which was used for the sacrifices,
The boatman secreted two Sar of oil.[4]

---

2. A Gar is 12 cubits. A cubit was based on the distance from elbow to the tip of the middle finger, about 18 inches. Thus a Gar was about 18 feet and the "wall" of the ship was to be 180 feet high. A very impressive structure indeed.
3. That is "graft," material taken by the workmen.
4. More graft.

Utnapishtim then proceeds:

"All that I had I loaded on her.
All that I had of silver I loaded on her.
All that I had of gold I loaded on her.
All that I had of living beings of all kinds I loaded on her.
I brought to the ship all my family and household;
Cattle of the field, beasts of the field, all the workmen I brought on board."

The ship draws water to two-thirds of its bulk. The description of the storm which now follows is one of the finest passages in the narrative.

"Shamash had fixed the time,
'When the rulers of darkness (?) at evening time shall cause a terrific rain-storm,
Step into the ship and close the door!'
The fixed time approached,
When the rulers of darkness (?) at evening time were to cause a terrific rain-storm.
I recognized the symptoms of (such) a day,
A day, for the appearance of which I was in terror.
I entered the ship and closed the door.
To steer the ship, to Puzur-Kurgal, the boatman,
I entrusted the palace[5] together with its cargo.
As morning dawned,
There arose on the firmament of heaven black clouds,
Adad thundered therein;
Nabu and Lugal marched in advance,
Ira[6] tears out the ship's pole.
Ninib marches, commanding the attack,
The Anunnaki[7] lift torches,
Illuminating the land with their sheen,
Adad's roar reaches to heaven,
All light is changed to darkness.

One day the hurricane raged
Storming furiously.
Coming like a combat over men.
Brother sees not brother:

---

5. The designation of the ship as "the place" is an indication of its large size, with its many stories and compartments.
6. The god of pestilence.
7. A collective name for the minor gods.

Those in heaven[8] do not know one another.
The gods are terrified at the cyclone,
They flee and mount to the heaven of Anu;[9]
The gods crouch like dogs in an enclosure.
Ishtar cries aloud like one in birth throes,
The mistress of the gods howls aloud:
'That day be turned to clay,[10]
When I in the assembly of the gods decreed evil;
That I should have decreed evil in the assembly of the gods!
For the destruction of my people should have ordered a combat!
Did I bring forth my people,
That like fish they should fill the sea?'
All of the Anunnaki weep with her.
The gods sit down, depressed and weeping.
Their lips are closed
Six days and nights
The storm, cyclone (and) hurricane continued to sweep over the land.
When the seventh day approached, the hurricane and cyclone ceased the combat,
After having fought like warriors (?).
The sea grew quiet, the evil storm abated, the cyclone was restrained.
I looked at the day and the roar had quieted down.
And all mankind had turned to clay.
Like an enclosure . . . had become.
I opened a window and light fell on my face,
I bowed down and sat down (and) wept,
Tears flowed over my face.
I looked in all directions of the sea.
At a distance of twelve (miles)[11] an island appeared.
At mount Nisir the ship stood still.
Mount Nisir took hold of the ship so that it could not move.
One day, two days, Mount Nisir,
Three days, four days, Mount Nisir,
Five days, six days, Mount Nisir.
When the seventh day arrived,
I sent forth a dove letting it free.
The dove went hither and thither;
Not finding a resting-place, it came back.
I sent forth a swallow, letting it free.

---

8. The gods in general.
9. To the highest part of heaven.
10. That is, be cursed with destruction.
11. Or "after a space of twelve double hours."

The swallow went hither and thither.
Not finding a resting-place, it came back.
I sent forth a raven, letting it free.
The raven went and saw the decrease of the waters.
It ate, croaked (?), but did not turn back.
Then I let (all) out to the four regions (and) brought an offering.
I brought a sacrifice on the mountain top.
Seven and seven *adagur* jars I arranged.
Beneath them I strewed reeds, cedar wood and myrtle.
The gods smelled the odor,
The gods smelled the sweet odor.
The gods like flies gathered around the sacrificer."

The gods now realize what havoc had been wrought by their decision and begin to regret it. Ishtar, more particularly as the mother goddess, bitterly laments the destruction of mankind.

"As soon as the mistress of the gods[12] arrived,
She raised on high the large necklace (?) which Anu had made according to his art.
'Ye gods, as surely as I will not forget these precious stones at my neck,
So I will remember these days—never to forget them.
Let the gods come to the sacrifice,
But let Enlil not come to the sacrifice.
Because without reflection he brought on the cyclone,
And decreed destruction for my people.'
As soon as Enlil arrived,
He saw the ship, and Enlil was enraged.
Filled with anger at the Igigi.[13]
'Who now has escaped with his life?
No man was to survive the destruction!
Ninib opened his mouth and spoke,
Spoke to the warrior Enlil,
'Who except Ea can plan any affair?
Ea indeed knows every order.'
Ea opened his mouth and spoke,
Spoke to the warrior Enlil:
'Thou art the leader (and) warrior of the gods.
But why didst thou, without reflection, bring on the cyclone?
On the sinner impose his sin,

---

12. Ishtar
13. Here a collective name for the gods, though generally designating, like Anunnaki, a lower group of divine beings.

On the evil-doer impose his evil,
But be merciful not to root out completely, be considerate not (to destroy altogether)!
Instead of bringing on a cyclone,
Lions might have come and diminished mankind.
Instead of bringing on a cyclone,
Jackals might have come and diminished mankind.
Instead of bringing on a cyclone,
Famine might have come and overwhelmed the land.
Instead of bringing on a cyclone,
Ira might have come and destroyed the land.
I did not reveal the oracle of the great gods,
I sent Atrakhasis a dream and he understood the oracle of the gods.
Now take counsel for him.'"

Enlil is moved by this eloquent appeal and is reconciled. He himself accords immortal life to Utnapishtim and his wife, and with this act the story ends.

"Enlil mounted the ship,
Took hold of my hand and led me up,"
Led me up and caused my wife to kneel at my side,
Touched our foreheads, stepped between us (and) blessed us.
'Hitherto Utnapishtim was a man;
Now Utnapishtim and his wife shall be on a level with the gods.
Utnapishtim shall dwell in the distance, at the confluence of the streams.'
Then they took me and settled me at the confluence of the streams."

The remainder of the tablet is taken up with Gilgamesh's sojourn with Utnapishtim and his wife who care for the weary wanderer. He is refreshed by a deep sleep, is given guidance for a safe return across the waters of death which he had to pass in order to reach the dwelling place of Utnapishtim, but the hero returns without having secured from his remote ancestor any hint of how to attain the gift of immortal life. The story merely shows that some favorite of the gods may escape the general fate of mankind, but that is all. Immortality is the privilege of the gods. Man must be resigned to his fate, to pass to Aralu, the general gathering place of the dead after life has fled, and there to lie inactive but conscious, imprisoned in a dark and gloomy prison, time without end.

The Law Code of Hammurabi

The last major period (roughly 2000–1600 B.C.) in the early history of Mesopotamia is commonly called the Old Babylonian period because of the importance of the First Dynasty of Babylon, and especially of Hammurabi (ca. 1792–1750 B.C.), the outstanding member of that dynasty. This turbulent period was characterized by political instability, chronic economic depression, and extremes of wealth and poverty. Incessant wars to maintain the balance of power, fought by continually shifting coalitions of city-states, beset the land together with resurgent oligarchy. Temporary respite from the latter evil was at times provided by strong rulers, like Hammurabi, who temporarily united all of Mesopotamia under the sway of Babylon.

Of major interest are the social reforms promulgated by these stronger rulers of the Old Babylonian period. In broad reference to their work as social reformers, these rulers commonly employed the phrase, "I have established freedom," meaning the removal of abuses from the oppressed and the restoration and safeguarding of their rights. In part, these reformers viewed social justice as a return to "the divinely decreed way of life of former days," or what was now termed kittum, "truth," the fixed and invariable body of law upon which society had been founded, the creation of the gods who had entrusted it to the ruler's care. But greater emphasis was placed on a new, dynamic type of law that had emerged as a supplement to kittum. Called misharum, literally "rightings" and hence translated "equity," "justice," or "righteousness," this new law was of human origin, the work of a true legislator. Promulgated as "judgments" and "decisions" of the ruler, these misharu-acts sought to alleviate the injustices produced by the economic and social dislocations of the Old Babylonian period for which kittum had no specific remedy. The distinction between these two types of law, which are found in all civilizations, was briefly stated by Hammurabi in calling himself "the king of justice (misharum), to whom Shamash has committed truth "kittum."

While many misharu-acts only proclaimed the remission of various obligations, including indebtedness, and, at times, the freeing of persons enslaved for debt, others comprised extensive collections of remedial legislation. The best known and only virtually complete example of the latter "codes" (there are four from the Old Babylonian period and one from the preceding Third Dynasty of Ur) is that of Hammurabi. Its prologue and epilogue set forth the divine commission which Hammurabi received from the gods to secure the general welfare, while the nearly three hundred individual laws, touching on a wide variety of abuses,

Source: *The Code of Hammurabi* by Robert F. Harper, trans. (Chicago, University of Chicago Press, 1904).

justify Hammurabi's claim of having acted "like a real father to his people . . . [who] has established prosperity . . . and given good government to the land."

PROLOGUE

When the lofty Anu, king of the Anunnaki gods, and Enlil, lord of heaven and earth, he who determines the destiny of the land, committed the rule of all mankind to Marduk, the chief son of Ea; when they made him great among the Igigi gods; when they pronounced the lofty name of Babylon; when they made it famous among the quarters of the world and in its midst established an everlasting kingdom whose foundations were firm as heaven and earth—at that time, Anu and Enlil named me, Hammurabi, the exalted prince, the worshiper of the gods, to cause justice to prevail in the land, to destroy the wicked and the evil, to prevent the strong from oppressing the weak, to go forth like the sun over the black-headed people, to enlighten the land and to further the welfare of the people. Hammurabi, the shepherd named by Enlil, am I, who brought about plenty and abundance; . . . obedient to the mighty Shamash; . . . who rebuilt [the temple] Ebabbar for Shamash, his helper; . . . the powerful king, the sun of Babylon, who caused light to go forth over the lands of Sumer and Akkad; the king who caused the four quarters of the world to render obedience; the favorite of Ishtar, am I.

When Marduk sent me to rule the people and to bring help to the country, I established law and justice in the language of the land and promoted the welfare of the people. At that time (I decreed):

THE ADMINISTRATION OF JUSTICE

1. If a man brings an accusation against another man, charging him with murder, but cannot prove it, the accuser shall be put to death.

3. If a man bears false witness in a case, or does not establish the testimony that he has given, if that case is a case involving life, that man shall be put to death.

4. If he bears (false) witness concerning grain or money, he shall himself bear the penalty imposed in that case.

5. If a judge pronounces a judgment, renders a decision, delivers a verdict duly signed and sealed, and afterward alters his judgment, they shall call that judge to account for the alteration of the judgment which he has pronounced, and he shall pay twelve-fold the penalty in that judgment; and, in the assembly, they shall expel him from his seat of judgment, and with the judges in a case he shall not take his seat.

PROPERTY

9. If a man who has lost anything finds that which was lost in the possession of (another) man, and the man in whose possession the lost property is found says, "It was sold to me, I purchased it in the presence of witnesses"; and the owner of the lost property says, "I will bring witnesses to identify my lost property"; if the purchaser produces the seller who has sold it to him and the witnesses in whose presence he purchased it, and the owner of the lost property produces witnesses to identify his lost property, the judges shall consider their evidence. The witnesses in whose presence the purchase was made and the witnesses to identify the lost property shall give their testimony in the presence of god. The seller shall be put to death as a thief; the owner of the lost property shall recover his loss; the purchaser shall recover from the estate of the seller the money which he paid out.

10. If the purchaser does not produce the seller who sold it to him and the witnesses in whose presence he purchased it, and if the owner of the lost property produces witnesses to identify his lost property, the purchaser shall be put to death as a thief. The owner of the lost property shall recover his lost property.

11. If the (alleged) owner of the lost property does not produce witnesses to identify his lost property, he has attempted fraud, he has stirred up strife, he shall be put to death.

22. If a man practices robbery and is captured, that man shall be put to death.

23. If the robber is not captured, the man who has been robbed shall, in the presence of god, make an itemized statement of his loss, and the city and the governor in whose province and jurisdiction the robbery was committed shall compensate him for whatever was lost.

24. If it is a life (that is lost), the city and governor shall pay one mina [about one pound] of silver to his heirs.

IRRIGATION

53. If a man neglects to maintain his dike and does not strengthen it, and a break is made in his dike and the water carries away the farmland, the man in whose dike the break has been made shall replace the grain which has been damaged.

54. If he is not able to replace the grain, they shall sell him and his goods and the farmers whose grain the water has carried away shall divide (the results of the sale).

55. If a man opens his canal for irrigation and neglects it and the water carries away an adjacent field, he shall pay out grain on the basis of the adjacent field.

56. If a man opens up the water and the water carries away the improvements of an adjacent field, he shall pay out ten *gur* of grain per *bur* [of damaged land].

LOANS AND INTEREST

88. If a merchant lends grain at interest, for one *gur* [300 *sila*] he shall receive one hundred *sila* as interest [33 1/3 per cent]; if he lends money at interest, for one shekel of silver he shall receive one-fifth of a shekel as interest [20 per cent].

90. If a merchant increases the interest on grain above one hundred *sila* for one *gur*, or the interest on silver above one-fifth of a shekel (per shekel), and takes this interest, he shall forfeit whatever he lent.

94. If a merchant lends grain or silver at interest and when he lends it at interest he gives silver by the small weight and grain by the small measure but when he gets it back he gets silver by the large weight and grain by the large measure, the merchant shall forfeit whatever he lent.

104. If a merchant gives to an agent grain, wool, oil, or goods of any kind with which to trade, the agent shall write down the value and return (the money) to the merchant. The agent shall take a sealed receipt for the money which he gives to the merchant.

105. If the agent is careless and does not take a receipt for the money which he has given to the merchant, the money not receipted for shall not be placed to his account.

108. If a wine seller does not take grain for the price of a drink but takes money by the large weight, or if she makes the measure of drink smaller than the measure of grain, they shall call that wine seller to account and throw her into the water.

109. If bad characters gather in the house of a wine seller and she does not arrest those bad characters and bring them to the palace, that wine seller shall be put to death.

110. If a priestess who is not living in a convent opens a wine shop or enters a wine shop for a drink, they shall burn that woman.

DEBT SLAVERY

117. If a man is in debt and sells his wife, son, or daughter, or binds them over to service, for three years they shall work in the house of their purchaser or master; in the fourth year they shall be given their freedom.

118. If he binds over to service a male or female slave and lets the time (of redemption) expire and the merchant transfers or sells such slave, there is no cause for complaint.

MARRIAGE AND THE FAMILY

128. If a man takes a wife and does not arrange a contract for her, that woman is not a wife.

129. If the wife of a man is caught lying with another man, they shall bind them and throw them into the water. If the husband of the woman wishes to spare his wife, then the king shall spare his servant.

131. If a man has accused his wife but she has not been caught lying with another man, she shall take an oath in the name of god and return to her house.

136. If a man deserts his city and flees and afterwards his wife enters into another house, if that man returns and wishes to take back his wife, the wife of the fugitive shall not return to her husband because he hated his city and fled.

138. If a man wishes to divorce his wife who has not borne him children, he shall give her money to the amount of her marriage price and he shall make good to her the dowry which she brought from her father's house and then he may divorce her.

141. If the wife of a man who is living in his house sets her face to go out and plays the part of a fool, neglecting her house and belittling her husband, they shall call her to account; and if her husband says, "I divorce her," he may let her go. On her departure nothing shall be given to her for her divorce. If her husband says, "I will not divorce her," her husband may marry another woman. The first woman shall dwell in the house of her husband as a maidservant.

142. If a woman hates her husband and says, "You may not possess me, the city council shall inquire into her case; and if she has been careful and without reproach and her husband has been going about and greatly belittling her, that woman has no blame. She may take her dowry and go to her father's house.

143. If she has not been careful but has gadded about, neglecting her house and belittling her husband, they shall throw that woman into the water.

145. If a man takes a wife and she does not present him with children and he sets his face to take a concubine, that man may take a concubine and bring her into his house. That concubine shall not rank with his wife.

146. If a man takes a wife and she gives a maidservant to her husband, and that maidservant bears children and afterwards claims equal rank with her mistress because she has borne children, her mistress may not sell her, but she may reduce her to bondage and count her among the slaves.

148. If a man has married a wife and a disease has seized her, if he is determined to marry a second wife, he shall marry her. He shall not divorce the wife whom the disease has seized. In the home they made together she shall dwell, and he shall maintain her as long as she lives.

150. If a man gives to his wife a field, garden, house, or goods and delivers to her a sealed deed, after (the death of) her husband her children cannot enter a claim against her. The mother may will her estate to her son whom she loves, but to an outsider she may not.

159. If a man, who has brought a gift to the house of his father-in-law and has paid the marriage price, looks with longing upon another woman and says to his father-in-law, "I will not marry your daughter," the father of the daughter shall take to himself whatever was brought to him.

160. If a man has brought a gift to the house of his father-in-law and has paid the marriage price and the father of the daughter says, "I will not give you my daughter," he shall double the amount that was brought to him and return it.

162. If a man takes a wife and she bears him children and that woman dies, her father may not lay claim to her dowry. Her dowry belongs to her children.

165. If a man presents a field, garden, or house to his favorite son and writes for him a sealed deed, after the father dies, when the brothers divide (the estate), he shall take the present which the father gave him, but otherwise they shall divide the goods of the father's estate equally.

168. If a man sets his face to disinherit his son and says to the judges, "I will disinherit my son," the judges shall inquire into his record, and if the son has not committed a crime sufficiently grave to cut him off from sonship, the father may not cut off his son from sonship.

170. If a man's wife bears him children and his maidservant bears him children, and the father during his lifetime says to the children which the maidservant bore him, "My children," and reckons them with the children of his wife, after the father dies the children of the wife and the children of the maidservant shall divide the goods of the father's estate equally. The son of the wife shall have the right of choice at the division.

ADOPTION

185. If a man takes in his own name a young boy as a son and rears him, one may nor bring claim for that adopted son.

191. If a man, who has taken a young boy as a son and reared him, establishes his own house and acquires children, and sets his face to cut off the adopted son, that son shall not go off empty-handed. The father who reared him shall give to him of his goods one-third the portion of a son and then he shall go. He may not give to him (any portion) of field, garden, or house.

PERSONAL INJURY AND MANSLAUGHTER

195. If a son strikes his father, they shall cut off his hand.

196. If a man destroys the eye of another man, they shall destroy his eye.

197. If he breaks another man's bone, they shall break his bone.

198. If he destroys the eye of a client or breaks the bone of a client, he shall pay one mina of silver.

199. If he destroys the eye of a man's slave or breaks a bone of a man's slave, he shall pay one-half his price.

200. If a man knocks out a tooth of a man of his own rank, they shall knock out his tooth.

201. If he knocks out a tooth of a client, he shall pay one-third mina of silver.

206. If a man strikes another man in a quarrel and wounds him, he shall swear, "I struck him without intent," and he shall pay for the physician.

207. If he dies as the result of the blow, he shall swear (as above), and if the man was a free man, he shall pay one-half mina of silver.

208. If he was a client, he shall pay one-third mina of silver.

PHYSICIAN'S FEES AND MALPRACTICE

215. If a physician operates on a man for a severe wound with a bronze lancet and saves the man's life, or if he opens an abscess (in the eye) of a man with a bronze lancet and saves that man's eye, he shall receive ten shekels of silver.

216. If he is a client, he shall receive five shekels.

217. If he is a man's slave, the owner of the slave shall give two shekels of silver to the physician.

218. If a physician operates on a man for a severe wound with a bronze lancet and causes the man's death, or opens an abscess (in the eye) of a man with a bronze lancet and destroys the man's eye, they shall cut off his hand.

219. If a physician operates on a slave of a client for a severe wound with a bronze lancet and causes his death, he shall restore a slave of equal value.

221. If a physician sets a broken bone for a man or cures a sprained tendon, the patient shall give five shekels of silver to the physician.

222. If he is a client, he shall give three shekels of silver.

223. If he is a man's slave, the owner shall give two shekels of silver to the physician.

BUILDING REGULATIONS

228. If a builder builds a house for a man and completes it, he shall give him two shekels of silver per *sar* of house as his fee.

229. If a builder builds a house for a man and does not make its construction sound, and the house which he has built collapses and causes the death of the owner of the house, the builder shall be put to death.

233. If a builder builds a house for a man and does not make its construction sound, and a wall cracks, that builder shall strengthen that wall at his own expense.

WAGE REGULATIONS

257. If a man hires a field laborer, he shall pay him eight *gur* of grain per year.

258. If a man hires a herdsman, he shall pay him six *gur of* grain per year.

268. If a man hires an ox to thresh, twenty *sila* of grain is its [daily] hire.

269. If a man hires an ass to thresh, ten *sila* of grain is its hire.

271. If a man hires oxen, a wagon, and a driver, he shall pay 180 *sila* of grain per day.

273. If a man hires a laborer, from the beginning of the year until the fifth month he shall pay six

she of silver per day; from the sixth month till the end of the year he shall pay five *she* of silver per day.

274. If a man hires an artisan, the [daily] wage of a [potter?] is five *she* of silver; the wage of a bricklayer is five *she* of silver; the wage of a tailor is five *she* of silver; the wage of a stone-cutter is [. . .] *she* of silver; the wage of a jeweler is [. . .] *she* of silver; the wage of a smith is [. . .] *she* of silver; the wage of a carpenter is four *she* of silver; the wage of a leather worker is [. . .] *she* of silver; the wage of a basket maker is [. . .] *she* of silver; the wage of a builder is [. . .] *she* of silver.

EPILOGUE

(These are) the just laws which Hammurabi, the wise king, established and by which he gave the land stable support and good government. Hammurabi, the perfect king, am I. I was not careless, nor was I neglectful of the black-headed people, whose rule Enlil presented and Marduk delivered to me. . . .

The great gods called me, and I am the guardian shepherd whose scepter is just and whose beneficent shadow is spread over my city. In my bosom I carried the people of the land of Sumer and Akkad; under my protection they prospered; I governed them in peace; in my wisdom I sheltered them.

In order that the strong might not oppress the weak, that justice be given to the orphan and the widow, in Babylon, the city whose turrets Anu and Enlil raised, in Esagila, the temple whose foundations are firm as heaven and earth, for the pronouncing of judgments in the land, for the rendering of decisions for the land, and to give justice to the oppressed, my weighty words I have written upon my monument, and in the presence of my image as king of justice have I established it.

The king who is preeminent among kings am I. My words are precious, my wisdom is unrivaled. By the command of Shamash, the great judge of heaven and earth, may I make justice to shine forth on the land. By the order of Marduk, my lord, may no one scorn my statutes, may my name be remembered with favor in Esagila forever.

Let any oppressed man, who has a cause, come before my image as king of justice! Let him read the inscription on my monument! Let him give heed to my weighty words! And may my monument enlighten him as to his cause and may he understand his case! May he set his heart at ease! (and he will exclaim): "Hammurabi indeed is a ruler who is like a real father to his people; he has given reverence to the words of Marduk, his lord; he has obtained victory for Marduk in north and south; he has made glad the heart of Marduk, his lord; he has established prosperity for the people for all time and given good government to the land."

In the days that are yet to come, for all future time, may the king who is in the land observe the words of justice which I have written upon my monument! May he not alter the judgments of the land which I have pronounced, or the decisions of the country which I have rendered! May he not scorn my statutes! If that man have wisdom, if he wish to give his land good government, let him give attention to the words which I have written upon my monument! And may this monument enlighten him as to procedure and administration, the judgments which I have pronounced, and the decisions which I have rendered for the land! And let him rightly rule his black-headed people; let him pronounce judgments for them and render for them decisions! Let him root out the wicked and the evil from his land! Let him promote the welfare of his people!

Hammurabi, the king of justice [*misharum*], to whom Shamash has committed truth [*kittum*], am I. My words are weighty; my deeds are unrivaled; only to the fool are they vain; to the wise they are worthy of every praise.

Love Song to King Shu-Suen

Shu-Suen was the penultimate king of the famous Third Dynasty of Ur. The love song to him, of which we here give the first stanzas, is placed in the mouth of his young and impatient bride. Who she was does not appear, but it is tempting to identify her with Shu-Suen's concubine Kubatum, who figures in another love song which has the form of a dialogue with the king. These two songs and two others that look as if they might be from the same hand stand, so far, alone in Sumerian literature; they were probably the work of a gifted woman at Shu-Suen's court, either Kubatum herself or a girl in her entourage. That her work appealed to Sumerian taste may be gathered from the fact that it was still copied by scribes in Nippur some three hundred years later. From Nippur, about 1700 B.C. or earlier.

Youth of my heart, my beloved one,
O that to sweeten still more
your charms, which are sweetness,
are honey—

Lad of my heart, my beloved one,
O that to sweeten still more
your charms, which are sweetness,
are honey.

You, my own warrior, might march against me—
I would flee before you, youth,
into the bed.

O that you, my own warrior, might march against me—
I would flee before you, lad,
into the bed.

O that you might treat me, youth, with all sweetness,
my sweet and darling one,
with whom I would speak (words of) honey,
on the quilt of the bed
we would rejoice in your charm
and all your sweetness.

O that you might treat me, lad, with all sweetness
my sweet and darling one,
with whom I would speak (words of) honey—
youth, I am in love with you.

The Pious Sufferer 5

The sense of guilt as expressed in much Mesopotamian literature leads naturally to the problem as to the cause of suffering in this world, especially the suffering endured by those who are not conscious of any wrong-doing. The penitent himself confesses at times that he does not know what deity he has offended, which implies that he also does not know wherein his guilt consists. The impossibility of fathoming the ways of the gods is suggested in the frequent outburst of despair "how long, how long yet, O lord," introduced at times like a refrain in the appeal for forgiveness and release, as well as in such utterances that no one really has certain knowledge—"no one has understanding." This thought carried further leads to a doubt whether the gods have the same standards as prevail in human society. At least the question is raised, and in the face of the fact, too evident to be concealed, that the wicked often flourish in this world, whereas those who lead blameless lives are weighed down with sickness, distress, and misfortune of all kinds, there must have been many a thinker who struggled with the problem that lies at the basis of the Biblical Book of Job—the reason for the existence of evil in a world controlled by powers who are supposed to be kindly disposed. The pious Babylonian had an answer ready at hand. The gods were kind and gracious as long as one did not offend them, but there were the demons lurking everywhere, ready to pounce on their victims unawares—particularly the demons of the various diseases that destroy one's vitality. But the further question would still arise—why do the gods, superior to the demons, allow the latter to maim at will and strike the guilty and guiltless alike, and why are those whose wickedness is apparent permitted to escape?

The tragedy of life, with its woes and hardships, and the impossibility of penetrating the mysteries of the universe, are brought out with considerable force in a composition, Babylonian in origin, which has come down to us in several fragments from the library of Ashurbanapal and from the literary section of the temple at Sippar. The poem, for such it is, is in the form of a lament of an individual Tabi-utul-Enlil, whose home is Nippur and who appears to have been a ruler in that place. He speaks of himself as obedient to the gods, concerned for his salvation, careful in his doings, and yet, despite all this, he has been smitten with painful disease affecting every part of his body, for which he can find no relief, and the cause of which he has been unable to ascertain. He is not conscious of guilt, and the priests to whom he applied offered neither help nor consolation. The story is made the occasion of philosophical reflections on the fate of man, on his helplessness in suffering and his weakness in combating the ills to which human flesh is heir. These reflections constitute the value of the composition, and give it an exceptional place among the productions of Babylonian literature. Unfortunately it is only preserved in part. It consisted of four tablets of approximately 120 lines each, but of the total only about one-third are preserved and many of these lines are imperfect. Fortunately, by a careful study it is possible to follow the general course of the composition. The preserved portions, moreover, include two passages which belong to the finest specimen of Babylonian literature, noteworthy both in thought and in eloquent diction.

Source: *The Civilization of Babylonia and Assyria* by Morris Jastrow, Jr. (J.P. Lippincott Company, 1915).

In the first tablet, beginning with the praise of "lord of wisdom"—originally no doubt Enlil of Nippur, but transferred in the course of further redaction to Marduk, the head of the later Babylonian pantheon, we have a description of the evil that has overwhelmed Tabi-utul-Enlil which reads, so far as preserved, as follows:

(My eyeballs he obscured, bolting them as with) a lock
(My ears he bolted), like those of a deaf person.
A king—I have been changed into a slave,
As a madman (my) companions maltreat me.
Send me help from the pit dug (for me)!
At the cry of my lament, open a hole for him (?),
By day—deep sighs, at night—weeping,
The month—cries, the year—distress."

The second tablet opens with a reflection on the sadness of life's experiences and the difficulty of penetrating the ways of the gods to ascertain how to please them; and as in the case of Job, the reflections are interspersed with laments about his own forlorn condition.

"I had reached and passed the allotted time of life;
Whithersoever I turned—evil upon evil.
Misery had increased, justice was gone,
I cried to my god, but he did not show me his countenance;
I prayed to my goddess, but she did not raise her head.
The diviner-priest could not determine the future by an inspection,
The necromancer did not through an offering justify my suit,
The zakiku-priest I appealed to, but he revealed nothing,
The chief exorciser did not by (his) rites release me from the ban.
The like of this had never been seen;
Whithersoever I turned, trouble was in pursuit."

His punishment seems inexplicable to him, as he proceeds to set forth how he always endeavored to perform his duties towards the gods and men punctiliously.

"As though I had not always set aside the portion for the god,
And had not invoked the goddess at the meal,
Had not bowed my face, and brought my tribute,
As though I were one in whose mouth supplication and prayer were not constant,
Who had set aside the day of the god, neglected the new-moon festival,
Been negligent, spurned their images,
Not taught his people fear and reverence,

Not invoked his god, eaten of his (the god's) food;
Neglected his goddess, and did not offer to her a libation.
With the oppressor who has forgotten his lord,
Who has profaned the sacred name of his god, am I rated.
(Whereas) I thought only of supplication and prayer;
Prayer was my practice, sacrificing my law,
The day of worship of the gods the joy of my heart,
The day of devotion to the goddess more (to me) than riches;
Royal prayer—that was my joy;
Its celebration—my delight.
I taught my country to guard the name of the god,
To honor the name of the goddess I accustomed my people.
The glorification of the king I made like unto that of a god,
And in the fear of the palace I instructed the people.
I thought that such things were pleasing to a god."

Despite all this, the pious ruler was smitten with disease and accordingly he indulges in the gloomy thought that the ways of the gods are mysterious. One can never be certain of pleasing them. The fate of man is uncertain. Joy changes to grief suddenly, and apparently without cause or reason.

"What, however, seems good to oneself, to a god is displeasing,
What is spurned by oneself finds favor with a god;
Who is there that can grasp the will of the gods in heaven!
The plan of a god full of mystery (?)—who can understand it?
How can mortals learn the way of a god?
He who was alive yesterday is dead today;
In an instant he is cast into grief, of a sudden he is crushed;
For a moment he sings and plays,
In a twinkling he wails like a mourner.
Like opening and closing,[1] their (mankind's) spirit changes;
If they are hungry they are like a corpse,
Have they had enough, they consider themselves equal to their god;
If things go well, they prate of mounting to heaven,
If they are in distress, they speak of descending into Irkalla."[2]

The sufferer reverts to his sufferings and describes how the demons of disease have laid him low.

---

1. Explained in the commentary "like day and night."
2. One of the terms of the neither world.

"An evil demon has come out of his (lair);
From yellowish, the sickness became white.[3]
It struck my neck and crushed my back,
It bent my high stature like a poplar;
Like a plant of the marsh, I was uprooted, thrown on my back.
Food became bitter and putrid,
The malady dragged on its course.
Though without food, hunger diminished (?);
The sap of my blood (he[4] drained).
Nourishment was withheld. . .
My flesh was wasted, my body grew wan.
I took to my bed, unable to leave the couch.
The house became my prison;
As fetters for my body, my hands were powerless,
As pinions for my person, my feet were stretched out,
My discomfiture was painful, the pain severe.
A strap of many twists has struck me,
A sharply-pointed spear pierced me.
All day the pursuer followed me,
At night he granted me no respite whatever,
As though wrenched, my joints were torn apart,
My limbs were shattered and rendered helpless.
In my stall I passed the night like an ox,
I was saturated like a sheep in my excrements;
The disease of my joints baffled the chief exorciser,
And my omens were obscure to the diviner,
The exorciser could not interpret the character of my disease,
And the limit of my malady the diviner could not fix.
No god came to my aid, taking me by the hand,
No goddess had compassion for me, coming to my side.
The grave was open, my burial prepared,
Though not yet dead, the lamentation was over.
The people of my land had already said 'alas' over me."[5]
My enemy heard it and his face shone;
As the joyful tidings were announced to him his liver rejoiced,
I knew it was the day when my whole family,
Resting under the protection of their deity would be in (distress.)[6]

---

3. The color of the skin at first yellow becomes pale.
4. The sickness, the demon.
5. As over a dead person.
6. Two obscure lines, the general sense of which is that he felt the end was near.

The sufferer, paralyzed, bed-ridden, totally helpless, blind, deaf, unable to take food, racked with unceasing pain, was thus brought to the brink of despair. All hope had fled and his friends and family already mourned him as dead. The third tablet beginning

"His hand is 'heavy, I can no longer endure it,"

evidently continued the plaint but soon passed on to an account of a dream sent to the sufferer in which Ur-Bau, described as "a strong hero decked with a crown" appears and apparently gives him a reassuring message from Marduk (originally Enlil) that he will be released from his sufferings. It is to be regretted that this portion of the composition is so badly preserved, for it must have contained the reason why Marduk decided to come to the relief of the pious sufferer. We are left to conjecture why, but it is plausible to assume that Marduk is seized with pity and recognizes that Tabi-utul-Enlil did not merit the punishment sent to him. Perhaps it was even suggested that the sufferings were sent as a trial of his piety, though this in default of direct evidence must not be regarded as more than a conjecture. At all events, Tabi-utul-Enlil is healed, and we are given a vivid picture of how, as a result of his final appeal to Marduk, the demons of disease are driven away by a mighty storm.

"He sent a mighty storm to the foundation of heaven,
To the depths of the earth he drove it.
He drove back the evil demon into the abyss.[7]
The nameless Utukku he drove into his mountain house.[8]
He confounded Labartu,[9] forcing him back into the mountain.
On the tide of the sea he swept away the ague.[10]
He tore out the root of my disease like a plant.
The bad sleep,[11] (disturbing?) my rest, filled and darkening the heavens as with smoke.
The aches and groans like (those of) a lion (?),
He stirred up as in a storm and filled the earth,
The violent headache[12] which overthrows (the strong [?]),
He tore out . . . and bathed me with the dew of the night.
My eyeballs which were covered with a veil of night,"[13]

---

7. Literally Apsu, here perhaps intended as a designation of the depths of the earth whence the demons rise up.
8. Literally "his E-Kur," here a designation of the dwelling place of the demons in the mountains.
9. One of the demons.
10. Shuruppu, "chills and fever," here personified, as were all diseases.
11. The nightmare, also personified as a demon.
12. Again personified as in the medical texts.
13. Cataract in meant.

Through a mighty wind he drove away (the veil) and made them shine brilliantly.
My ears which had been closed and bolted as those of a deaf person,
He removed their deafness and opened their hearing.
My nose which through the force of the fever was choked up,
He healed the hurt so that I could breathe again.
My lips which had been closed through exhausted strength,
He reduced their swelling (?) and loosened their bonds.
My mouth which had been covered, so that with difficulty (?) (I uttered sounds),
He purified, like copper he made it shine.
My teeth which had been seized so that they were (pressed) together,[14]
He opened a space between them and strengthened their base.[15]
The tongue which was swollen so that I could not move it,
He took away its coating (?) so that speech returned.
The throat which was compressed, closed up like that of a corpse,
He healed so that my breast resounded like a flute.
My spittle which had been shut off so that it could not come forth,[16]
He loosened the bonds, opening them like a door.

To the opulent[17] who had been reduced to starvation, enchained like a guilty one,
He brought food and provided drink.
My neck which had been twisted and bent low,
He made erect and like a cedar raised up.
He made my stature like one of perfect strength,
Like one released from a demon, he polished my nails.
He cured me of scurvy, healed me of the itch (?).
My knees that had been fettered like those of a bird of the gorge,[18]

My entire body he restored,
He wiped away the blemish, making it[19] resplendent,
The oppressed stature regained its splendor,
On the banks of the stream where judgment is held over men[20]
The brand of slavery was removed, the fetters taken off."

Thus one trace after the other of the complicated series of diseases from which he was suffering was removed till he was entirely restored to his former vigor. The composition closes with the enforcement of the lesson never to despair of divine help.

---

14. The teeth were pressed together as in lockjaw.
15. He fixed them firm in their sockets.
16. Like Job he was unable to swallow or spit out his saliva.
17. Though a king with all things at his command, he is wasted like one dying of famine, since he could not eat nor drink.
18. He could not walk.
19. The body.
20. Referring to the ceremony of cleansing from sin by immersion into a stream.

"Let him who sins against E-sagila,[21] let him learn from me,
Into the jaw of the lion, about to devour me, Marduk inserted a bit.
Marduk has seized the snare (?) of my pursuer, has encompassed his lair."

In this strain no doubt the poem continued to the close—in illustration of the lesson to be derived from Tabi-utul-Enlil's terrible yet marvelous experience. Like the Biblical poem, detailing Job's sufferings and the discourse of the problem involved, our composition ends in a kind of non sequitur. The problem is not solved, at least not to our satisfaction, for the just and innocent continue to suffer. The consolation, however, remains that the mercy of the gods in the end never fails. Even though one may be already in the jaws of death, a god if he be so inclined as was Marduk, or as was Enlil, the god of Nippur, in the original form of the story, can still save one. Though diviners and exorcisers fail, Marduk can intervene directly and restore the wasted body to perfect vigor. So all ends happily—at least for Tabi-utul-Enlil. Yet the question remains, why do the innocent suffer?

---

21. The name of Marduk's temple at Babylon, here used for the god.

Letters 6

An urgent request for money to settle a promissory note.

To Ibi-Nin-Shubur speaks as follows Yauin-iturna. May Shamash and Marduk grant you life!
I am responsible for a note for (the purchase of) a female slave. Now that the time of the payment of that note has arrived the agent is pressing me. Therefore, I am sending Arad-Innanna to you. Give him three shekels of silver due from yon and two shekels of your own money to he charged against me and properly attested in Babylon. Be sure to give Arad-Innanna the conrrect amount. Do not detain Arad-Innanna[1] and please fix up the transaction with him correctly.

A letter with three commissions.

To Etiatim speaks as follows, Ili'u-Shamash.
May Shamash and Marduk grant you life! I am well. (1) It is impossible (for me) to come to see you. I am obliged to go to Gatana. (2) The she-ass and a young one of good breed, let the butcher kill for me. The young one I got from Belanu, son of Sin-turrim, for 5 1/2 shekels of silver. Two shekels of silver I gave him. Three and one half shekels of silver give him. Do not give him more or less. Let him weigh the silver for me.[2] (3) As to the one female slave which I left with you, do not put her to service.[3] Sell her for silver on my account. Hand over 7 1/2 Ka of sesame and take a receipt for 2 Gur. One Gur you have received, and this leaves one Gur.

Military report to an Assyrian king of the submission of certain places in a mountainous region, and a request for further orders.

To the king my lord, your servant Ashur-bel-danin, greeting to the king, my lord! The people of Ushkha and the people of Kuda against whom the king my lord sent me have submitted to the authority of the king my lord. Cities which since the days of Shamash have never been subjected, now with the aid of the guard at my disposal I subdued completely. Those once dependent remain dependent, those (once,) troops remain troops of the king.[4] The entire mountain district now recognizes (the authority) of the king. May the heart of the king my lord rejoice! The troops at my disposal I shall retain that they may act as a guard.

Source: *The Civilization of Babylonia and Assyria* by Morris Jastrow, Jr. (J.P. Lippincott Company, 1915).

Regarding the people of Muma who have not (yet) submitted themselves, (and) have not accepted the authority of the king and with whom there has been no intercourse,[5] let the king send me his orders.

Letter of the court physician to the king, replying to a complaint of the king that his physician has failed to cure him.

The king my Lord continues to declare 'the state of this sickness of mine you do not recognize, you do not bring about a cure.' Now I confess that hitherto I did not understand this rheumatism,[6] but now I seal this letter to send it to the king my Lord. Let it be read to the king my Lord and properly understood. When it reaches the king my Lord let a physician . . . carry out the accompanying directions. Let the king apply this liniment.[7] If the king does this, this fever will soon leave the king my Lord. A second and a third time this liniment should be applied to the king my Lord. The king must see to this. If it please the king, let it be done in the morning. This disease is in the blood. Let them bring the king *silbani*,[8] as was twice done already, and let it be vigorously done. I shall come to inform myself, and as soon as the perspiration flows freely from the king, my Lord, I will send to the king, my Lord, something to apply to the king's neck. With a salve which I shall send the king let the king be rubbed at the appointed time.

Letter of Arad-Nana, the court physician, regarding a case of hemorrhages of the nose from which the king's son is suffering.

To the king my Lord, your servant Arad-Nana. Hearty greetings to the king, my Lord. May Ninib and Gula grant the king, my Lord, happiness and health.

Hearty greetings to the king's son. The treatment which we prescribe for him is to be given every two-thirds of a double hour during the day[9]. . .

In regard to the bleeding of the nose about which the Rab-Mugi [a high official] has reported to me that yesterday toward evening there was much bleeding, those dressings are not properly

---

1. Send him back as soon as possible.
2. To make sure that the exact amount is given.
3. Literally "do not subdue her," evidently in the sense of not to use her for slave service, but to sell her.
4. A characteristic Assyrian boast, voicing the confidence in the military supremacy of Assyria. As a matter of fact, however, rebellions against Assyrian authority were constantly taking place.
5. That is, no negotiations for terms of submission have been as yet opened.
6. Literally "the sickness of the muscles."
7. Evidently the wash or liniment was sent with the letter.
8. Dried licorice root, but in this passage a liniment or a massage treatment appears to be intended.
9. The Mesopotamians divided the full day into twelve double hours. As a survival of this method based on sexagesimal system, we still have only twelve numerals on our watch dials and divide the day and night each into twelve hours, instead of counting the hours of a full day consecutively from one to twenty four, as is now done by military and some others. Every two-thirds of a double hour would therefore be every eighty minutes. The following lines are obscure and are therefore omitted.

applied; they have been placed upon the alae of the nose, obstructing the breathing, while at the same time the blood flows into the mouth. Let the nose be plugged up to the back so that air will be held off, and the bleeding will cease. If it please the king I will come to look at it to-morrow. Meanwhile may I hear good news.

Three Creation Stories

1. THE ENUMA ELISH

The Enuma Elish (which are the first two words of the epic and mean "When on High") is the creation myth of ancient Mesopotamia. This is the Babylonian version of a much older Sumerian myth and originally the chief figure of the myth was Enlil, the Sumerian storm god. When Babylon conquered the rest of Mesopotamia and established the Old Babylonian Empire around 1800 B.C., it became necessary to explain how the local god of Babylon, Marduk, had now become supreme among the gods. Therefore, the older Sumerian myth of creation was retold and Marduk was substituted for Enlil.

When on high the heaven had not been named,[1]
Firm ground below had not been called by name,
Naught but primordial Apsu, their begetter,
(And) Mummu[2] Tiamat, she who bore them all,
Their waters commingling as a single body;[3]
No reed hut had been matted, no marsh land had appeared,
When no gods whatever had been brought into being,
Un-named, their destinies yet undermined—
Then it was that the gods were emerged from within them.
Lahmu and Lahamu were came forth, were called by name,
Before they had grown in age and statue.
Anshar and Kishar were shaped, more mighty than the others.
They extended the days, added on the years.
Anu was their heir, rival of his father;
Verily, Anu, Anshar's first-born, was his equal.
Anu sired his image Nudimmud.[4]
This Nudimmud was the master of his father,[5]
Of broad wisdom, understanding, mighty in strength,

Pritchard, J.B.; *Ancient Near Eastern Texts Relating to the Old Testament*, Copyright © 1950, 1955, 1969, renewed 1978 by Princeton University Press. Reprinted by permission of Princeton University Press.

Mightier by far than his grandfather, Anshar.
He had no rival among the gods, his brothers.
The divine brothers[6] banded together,
They disturbed Tiamat as they rushed here and there,
Indeed, they distraught and tormented Tiamat
By their boisterous mirth in the dwelling of Heaven.
Apsu could not diminish their clamor
And Tiamat was dumbfounded at their ways.
Their doings were loathsome to him.
Offensive and overbearing were their ways.
Then Apsu, the begetter of great gods,
Cried out, addressing Mummu, his vizier:
"O Mummu, my vizier, who rejoices my spirit,
Come hither and let us go to Tiamat!"
They went and sat down before Tiamat,
Exchanging counsel about the gods, their off-spring.
Apsu, opening his mouth,
Said unto radiant Tiamat:
"Their ways are truly abominable unto me.
By day I find no relief, nor repose by night.
I will destroy, I will wreck their ways,
That quite may be restored. Let us have rest!"
As soon as Tiamat heard this,
She was troubled and called out to her husband.
She cried out, as she raged all alone,
Injecting woe into her mood:
"What? Should we destroy that which we have produced?
Their ways indeed are most troublesome, but let us practice kindness!"
Then answered Mummu, giving counsel to Apsu;
Rude and ungracious was Mummu's advice:
"Destroy, my father, their rebellious ways.
Then shall you have relief by day and rest by night!"
When Apsu heard this, his face grew luminous
Because of the evil he planned against his godly sons.

---

1. I.e., had not been created. The ancients believed that naming a thing was, in itself, an act of creation.
2. Probably an epithet in the sense of "mother." Not to be confused with the vizier Mummu who is mentioned later.
3. I.e., the fresh waters (Apsu) and the salt waters (Tiamat) have not been separated yet.
4. Another name of Ea (=Enki), the god of the earth and water.
5. This motif of the younger gods becoming more powerful than the older gods, and eventually supplanting them, is central to almost all of the mythological cycles of the Near East and the Eastern Mediterranean. It represents what may be yought of as the ultimate "generation gap." Here this theme also symbolizes the process of creation, because the forces of nature (the gods) become more differentiated and defined.
6. I.e., the younger gods.

He embraced Mummu by the neck
As he sat down on his knees to kiss him.
Now whatever they had plotted between them,
Was repeated unto the gods, their first-born.
When the gods heard this, they were astonished,
Then lapsed into silence and remained speechless.
Superior in wisdom, accomplished and resourceful,
Ea, the all-wise, saw through their design.
Made artful his spell against it, surpassing and holy.
He recited it and made it subsist in the deep,
As he poured sleep upon him. Sound asleep he lay.
When he had made Apsu lie prone, deep in sleep,
Mummu, the advisor, was powerless to stir.
He[7] loosened Apsu's band, tore off his tiara,
Removed his halo and put it on himself.
Having constrained Apsu, he slew him.
Mummu he bound and locked.
Having thus upon Apsu established his ascendance,
He laid hold of Mummu, holding him by the nose-rope.
After Ea had vanquished and tramped down his foes,
Had assured his triumph over his enemies,
In profound peace he rested in his sacred chamber,
He named it "Apsu," for shrines he assigned it.
He founded his cult in that same place.
Ea and Damkina, his wife, dwelled there in splendor.
In the chamber of fates, the house of destinies,
A god was engendered, most able and wisest of gods.
In the heart of holy Apsu was Marduk created.
He who begot him was Ea, his father.

Now Tiamat renewed the conflict and created an army of monsters. This time even the great Ea could not withstand the attack and the gods decided to ask the young Marduk to defend them against Tiamat.

Lord Anshar, father of the gods, rose up in grandeur,
And having pondered in his heart, he said to the Anunnaki:[8]
"He whose strength is potent shall be our avenger,
He who is sharp in battle, Marduk, the hero!"
Ea called Marduk into his secluded presence.
Giving counsel, he told him what was in his heart.

---

7. "He" refers to Ea, not Mummu.
8. A complex concept that is taken here to mean "the attendant deities."

Marduk came forth, the wisest of the gods, your son,
His heart prompted him to face Tiamat.
He opened his mouth, saying to me:
"If indeed as your avenger,
I am to vanquish Tiamat and save your lives,
Convene the assembly and proclaim supreme my destiny!
When jointly in Ubshukinna[9] you sat down rejoicing,
Let my word, instead of yours, determine the fates.
What I may bring into being shall be unchangeable;
Neither dismissed nor replaced shall be the command of my lips!"
Now hasten hither and promptly fix for him your decrees,
That he may go forth to face your mighty foe!

They erected for him a ample throne.
Facing his fathers, he sat down, presiding.
"You are the most honored of the great gods,
Your decree is unrivaled, your command is Anu.[10]
You, Marduk are the most honored of the great gods,
Your decree is unrivaled, your word is Anu.
From this day unchangeable shall be your pronouncement.
To raise or bring low—these shall be in your hand.
Your utterance shall be true, your command shall be unimpeachable.
No one among the gods shall transgress your bounds!
Adornment being wanted for the seats of the gods,
Let the place of their shrines ever be in your place.
O Marduk, you are indeed our avenger.
We have granted you kingship over the entire universe.
Your word shall be supreme when you sit in assembly.
Your weapons shall not fail; they shall smash your foes!
O lord, spare the life of him who trusts you,
But pour out the life[11] of the god who seized evil."
Having placed in their midst a piece of cloth,
They addressed themselves to Marduk, their first-born
"Lord, truly your decree is first among gods.
Say but to wreck or create; it shall be.
Open your mouth; the cloth will vanish!
Speak again, and the cloth shall be whole!"
At the word emerged from his mouth the cloth vanished.
He spoke again, his fathers, saw the outcome of his word,

---

9. The assembly hall of the gods.
10. That is, has the authority of Anu, who was formerly the chief god.
11. This expression is taken from the shedding of blood, which was considered by the Babylonians to be the basis of life.

When the gods, his fathers, saw the outcome of his word,
Joyfully they paid homage: "Marduk is king!"
They conferred on him scepter, throne, and vestment;
They gave him unequaled weapons that ward off the foes:
"Go and terminate the life of Tiamat.
May the winds bear her blood to places undisclosed."
Marduk's destiny thus fixed, the gods, his fathers,
Caused him to go the way of success and achievement.
He constructed a bow, marked it as his weapon,
Attached thereto the arrow, grasped it in his right hand;
He raised the mace, grasped it in his right hand;
He hung bow and quiver at his side.
In front of him he sat the lightening,
He filled his body with blazing flame.
He then made a net to enfold Tiamat,
He stationed the four winds that nothing of her might escape,
The South Wind, the North Wind, the East Wind, the West Wind.
Close to his side he held the net, the gift of his father, Anu.
He brought forth Imhullu "the Evil Wind," the Whirlwind, the Hurricane,
The Fourfold Wind, the Sevenfold Wind, the Cyclone, the Matchless Wind;
Then he sent forth the seven winds he had brought forth.
To sir up the inside of Tiamat they rose up behind him.
Then the lord raised up the flood-storm, his mighty weapon.
He mounted the storm-chariot irresistible and terrifying.
He harnessed and yoked to it a team-of-four,
The Killer, the Relentless, the Trampler, the Swift.
Sharp were their poison bearing teeth.
They were versed in ravage, skilled in destruction.
On his right he posted the Smiter, fearsome in battle,
On the left the Combat, which repels all the zealous.
His cloak was an armor of terror,
His head was turbaned with his fearsome halo.
The lord went forth and followed his course,
He set his face Towards the raging Tiamat.
He held a spell between his lips;
A plant to put out poison was grasped in his hand.
Then they milled about him, the gods milled about him,
The gods, his fathers, milled about him, the gods milled about him.
The lord approached to scan the inside of Tiamat,
(And) of Kingu, her consort, the scheme to perceive.
As Marduk looks on, Kingu's course becomes upset,
His will is distracted and his maneuvers are confused.
And when the gods, his helpers, who marched at his side,

Saw the valiant hero, blurred became their vision.
Without turning her neck, Tiamat emitted a cry,
Molding savage defiance in her lips:
"Too important are you for the lord of the gods to rise up against you!
Is it in their place that they have gathered, or in your place?"
Thereupon the lord raised his mighty weapon, the flood storm,
And to enraged Tiamat he spoke the following words:
"Why have you risen, why have you arrogantly exalted?
You have charged your own heart to stir up conflict,
[. . .]¹² sons reject their own fathers,
While you, who have born them, has foresworn love!
You have appointed Kingu as your consort,
Conferring upon him the rank of Anu, not rightfully his,
Against Anshar, king of the gods, you seek evil;
Against the gods, my fathers, you have confirmed your wickedness.
Though you have drawn up your forces, readied your weapons,
Stand alone, that I and you may meet in single combat!"
When Tiamat head this,
She was like one possessed; she took leave of her senses.
In fury Tiamat cried out aloud.
To the roots of her legs shook both together.
She recites a charm, keeps casting her spell,
While the gods of battle sharpen their weapons.
Tiamat and Marduk, wisest of gods then joined battle,
They strove in single combat, locked in conflict.
The lord spread out his net to enfold her,
He let loose in her face The Evil Wind, which followed behind.
When Tiamat opened her mouth to consume him,
He drove in the Evil Wind and she could not close her lips.
As the fierce winds encumbered her belly,
Her body was distended and her mouth was wide open.
He released an arrow, it tore her belly,
It cut through her insides, splitting her heart.
Having subdued her, he blotted out her life.
He threw down her carcass and stood upon it.
After he had slain Tiamat, the leader,
Her band was shattered, her troupe broken up;¹³
And her helpers, the gods who marched at her side,
Trembled with terror and turned their backs,

---

12. [. . .] represents a fragment of the text which has been lost.
13. The following lines divide Tiamat's forces into three categories: (1) the gods who had gone over to Tiamat, (2) the eleven kinds of monsters which Tiamat had created, and Kingu, Tiamat's new husband and general.

In order to save and preserve their lives.
Encircled tightly, they could not escape.
He made them captives and he smashed their weapons.
They found themselves ensnared in the net;
Thrown into cells, they were filled with wailing;
Bearing his wrath, they were held imprisoned.
And the eleven creatures which she had charged with awe,
The band of demons that marched before her,
He cast into fetters, their hands [. . .].
For all their resistance, he trampled them underfoot.
And Kingu, who had been made chief among them,
He bound and accounted him to Uggae.[14]
He took from him the Tables of Fate, not rightfully his,
Sealed them with a seal and fastened them on his own breast.
When he had vanquished and subdued his adversaries,
Had [. . .] the vainglorious foe,
Had wholly established Anshar's triumph over the foe,
Nudimmud's desire had achieved, valiant Marduk
Strengthened his hold on the vanquished gods,
And turned back to Tiamat whom he had bound.
The lord trampled on the legs of Tiamat,
With his unsparing mace he crushed her skull.
When the arteries of her blood he had severed,
The North Wind bore it to places undisclosed.
On seeing this, his fathers were joyful and jubilant,
They brought gifts of homage to him.
Then the lord paused to view her dead body,
That he might divide the monster and do artful works.
He split her like a shellfish into two parts:
Half of her he sat up as the ceiling of the sky,
He pulled down the bar and posted guards.
He ordered them not to allow her waters to escape.
He crossed the heavens and surveyed the regions.
He squared Apsu's quarter, the abode of Nudimmud,
As the lord measured the dimensions of Apsu.
The Great Abode, its likeness, he fixed as Esharra,[15]
The Great Abode, Esharra, which he made the firmament.
Anu, Enlil, and Ea he made occupy their places.
He constructed stations for the gods,
Aligning their astral likenesses as constellations.

---

14. The god of death.
15. Poetic name for the earth, which the Babylonians visualized as the dome of Apsu.

He determined the year by assigning the zones:
He set up three constellations for each of the twelve months.
After defining the days of the years by means of astrological figures,
He founded the station of Nebiru[16] to determine their divine bands,
That none might transgress or fall short.
Alongside it he set up the stations of Enlil and Ea.
Having opened up the gates on both sides,[17]
He strengthened the locks to the left and the right.
In her belly he established the zenith.
The moon he caused to shine, the night to him entrusting.
He appointed him a creature of the night to signify the days:
"Monthly, without cease, from designs with a crown.
At the month's very start, rising over the land,
You shall have luminous horns to signify six days,
On the seventh day reaching a half-crown.
At full moon stand in opposition in mid-month.
When the sun overtakes you at the base of heaven,
Diminish your crown and retrogress in light.
At the time of disappearance approach you the course of the sun,
And on the twenty-ninth you again stand in opposition to the sun."

"It was Kingu who contrived the uprising,
And caused Tiamat to rebel, and join battle."
They bound him, holding him before Ea.
They imposed on him his guilt and severed his blood vessels.
Out of his blood they fashioned humankind.
He[18] imposed upon it the service and let free the gods.
After Ea, the wise, had created humankind,
Had imposed upon it the service of the gods—
That toil was beyond human comprehension;
As artfully planned by Marduk, did Nudimmud create it—
Marduk, the king of the gods divided
All the Anunnaki[19] above and below.
He assigned them to Anu to guard his instructions.
Three hundred in the heavens he stationed as a guard.

---

16. The planet Jupiter.
17. The gates of East and West through which the sun was believe to pass.
18. Ea.
19. Here, Anunnaki refers to the underworld gods.

2. THE THEOLOGY OF MEMPHIS

This is a remarkable document, because it appears to anticipate, as early as 3000 B.C., the Biblical New Testament Logos doctrine and the First Principle concept of Greek classical philosophy. It has survived because Pharaoh Shabaka (715–664), of Twenty-fifth Dynasty, ordered the ancient text, which was written on some perishable material, probably papyrus, to be inscribed in stone.

Narmer, the founder of the First Dynasty, established his capital at Memphis. Consequently, the local god of that city, Ptah, soon came to be regarded as the chief of the Egyptian pantheon. It seemed quite logical to the ancient Egyptians that if Memphis was now ruling over Egypt then the local god of Memphis must occupy a position of priority over the other gods. A similar process occurred later during the Eighteenth Dynasty, when Thebes became the capital of Egypt and the patron deity of Thebes, Amun, acquired the attributes of Re, to become Amun-Re.

The purpose of the Theology of Memphis is too explain how and why Ptah occupies the position of supremacy among the gods. The most unusual feature of the Memphite theology, however, is that Ptah creates the universe through the power of his mind or thought, not in the usual physical way of the creator gods of antiquity. Thus, the things of this world are merely the objective forms of divine thought and Ptah is the source of that divine will.

Live the Horus:[20] Who Prospers the Two Lands;[21] the Two Goddesses:[22] Who prospers the Two Lands; the Horus of Gold: Who Prospers the Two Lands; the King of Upper and Lower Egypt: Nefer-ka-Re; the Son of Re:[23] Sha-[ba-ka], beloved of Ptah-South-of-His-Wall[24], living like Re forever. His majesty copied this text anew in the House of his father Ptah-South-of-His-Wall. Now his majesty had found (it) as (something) which the ancestors had made but which was worm-eaten. It was unknown from beginning to end. Then [his majesty] copied [it] anew, (so that) it is better than its state formerly, in order that his name might endure and his memorial be made to last in the House of his father Ptah-South-of-His-Wall in the course of eternity, through that which the Son of Re: [Sha-ba-ka] did for his father Ptah-tenen,[25] so that he might be given life forever . . .

The Ennead[26] gathered themselves to him,[27] and he judged Horus and Seth.[28] He prevented them from quarreling (further), and he made Seth the King of Upper Egypt in the land of Upper Egypt, at the place where he was (born), *Su*. Then Geb made Horus the King of Lower Egypt in the land of Lower Egypt, at the place where his father[29] was drowned, Pezshet-Tawi. Thus Horus stood in (one) place, and Seth stood in (another) place, and they were reconciled about the Two Lands. . .

Words spoken (by) Geb (to) Seth: "Go to the place in which thou wert born." Seth—Upper Egypt.

Words spoken (by) Geb (to) Horus: "Go to the place which thy father was drowned." Horus—Lower Egypt.

Words spoken (by) Geb (to) Horus and Seth: "I have judged you." Lower and Upper Egypt.

(But it became) ill in the heart of Geb that the portion of Horus was (only) equal to the portion of Seth. So Geb gave his (entire) inheritance to Horus, that is, the son of his son, his first born . . . (Thus) Horus stood over the (entire) land. Thus this land was united, proclaimed with the great name: "Ta-tenen, South-of-His-Wall, the Lord of Eternity."[30] The two other Great Sorceresses[31] grew up in this land. So it was that Horus appeared as King of Upper and Lower Egypt, who united the Two Lands in Wall Nome,[32] in the place in which the Two Lands are united.

It happened that reed and papyrus were set at the great double door of the House of Ptah.[33] That means Horus and Seth, who were reconciled and united, so that they associated and their quarreling ceased in the place which they *reached*, being joined in the House of Ptah, "the balance of the Two Lands," in which Upper and Lower Egypt have been weighed. . .

The gods who came into being as Ptah:—[34]

Ptah who is upon the Great throne. . .

Ptah-Nun, the father who [begot] Atum;

Ptah-Naunet, the mother who bore Atum;[35]

---

20. The king of Egypt, here identified with the sky-god Horus.

21. Upper and Lower Egypt.

22. Isis and Nepphths.

23. Egyptian kings were also believed to be the sons of the sun-god Re. It did not insult the Egyptian sense of logic to identify the king with more than one god at the same tim, anymore than it insults the sense of logic of modern Christians to identify the One Godhead as a Trinity of divine figures.

24. Every important Egyptian god has many identifying epithets. "South of His Wall" is only one of many names by which Ptah is known.

25. The name of Ptah as the primordial creator god.

26. The original family of nine gods, in four generations: (1) Atum, the creator god; (2) Shu, god of air, and Tefnut, goddess of moisture; (3) Geb, god of earth, and Nut, goddesses of the sky; (4) the gods Osiris and Seth, and the goddesses Isis and Nephthys.

27. The earth god, Geb.

28. Reference to the legendary contest between Horus (son of Osiris) and Seth, in which Geb decided which of them should rule Egypt.

29. The god Osiris, the son of Geb and father of Horus.

30. Names of Ptah.

31. The crowns of Upper and Lower Egypt.

32. The province, or nome, in which Memphis was located was named "White Wall."

33. The intertwining plants tutelary plants of Upper and Lower Egypt, symbolizing the union of the two parts of Egypt.

34. Who have their form in Ptah.

35. Ptah was conceived of as both Nun, the primordial water, and his consort Nannet. In these capacities he brought forth Atum, the creator god of the more ancient Heliopolitan theology.

Ptah the Great, that is, the heart and tongue of the Ennead;

[Ptah] . . . who gave birth to the gods . . .[36]

There came into being as the heart[37] and there came into being as tongue[38] (something) in the form of Atum. The mighty Great One is Ptah, who transmitted [*life* to all gods], as well as (to) their *ka's*,[39] though this heart, by which Horus became Ptah, and through this tongue, by which Thoth became Ptah.[40]

(Thus) it happened that the heart and tongue gained control over [every] (other) member of the body, by teaching that he is in every body and in every mouth of all gods, all men, [all] cattle, all creeping things, and (everything) that lives, by thinking and commanding everything that he wishes.[41]

His Ennead is before him in (the form of) teeth and lips. That is (the equivalent of) the semen and hands of Atum. Whereas the Ennead (of Ptah), however, is the teeth and lips in this mouth, which pronounced the name of everything, from which Shu and Tefnut[42] came forth, and which was the fashioner of the Ennead.[43]

The sight of the eyes, the hearing of the ears, and the smelling of the air by the nose, they report to the heart. It is this which causes every completed (concept) to come forth, and it is the tongue which announces what the heart thinks.[44]

Thus all the gods were formed and his Ennead was completed. Indeed, all the divine order[45] really came into being through what the heart thought and the tongue commanded. Thus the *ka*-spirits were made and the *hemsut*-spirits were appointed, they who make all provisions and all nourishment, by this speech. (*Thus justice was given to*) him who does what is liked, (*and injustice to*) him who does what is disliked. Thus life was given to him who has peace and death was given to him who has sin. Thus were made all work and all crafts, the action of the arms, the movements of the legs, and the activity of every member, in conformance with (this) command which the heart thought, which came forth through the tongue, and which gives value to everything.

(Thus) it happened that is was said of Ptah: "He who made all and brought the gods into being." He is indeed Ta-tenen,[46] who brought forth the gods, for everything came forth from him, nourishment and provisions, the offerings of the gods, and every good thing. Thus it was discovered and understood that his strength is greater than (that of the other) gods. And so Ptah was

---

36. The text is fragmented here, though it is clear that three other forms of Ptah are mentioned.
37. The heart was believed to be the seat of the mind or intelligence.
38. The spoken word or authoritative. The ancients always attempted to use a concrete word to express an abstract thought or idea.
39. Ka was the vital force, or personality.
40. The gods Horus and Thoth (the god of wisdom and the scribe of the gods) are equated with the organs of thought and speech.
41. Ptah, as the mind and speech of the universe, has transmitted his divine power into all living things.
42. Atum's children.
43. A distinction is made here between the act of creation of Atum, accomplished in the ordinary physical way, and the creation of Ptah, through the agency of mind and speech.
44. This is rather similar concept to the Biblical "let there be" creation by divine command.
45. Literally, "every word of the god."
46. The name of Ptah in his capacity of creator-god.

satisfied,[47] after he made everything, as well as all the divine order. He had formed the gods, he had made cities, he had formed nomes, he had put the gods in their shrines, he had established their offerings, he had founded their shrines, he had made their bodies like that (with which) their hearts were satisfied. So the gods entered into their bodies of every (kind of) wood, of every (kind of) stone, of every (kind of) clay,[48] or everything which might grew upon him,[49] in which they had their form. So all the gods, as wells as their *ka's* gathered themselves to him, content and associated with the Lord of the Two Lands.

The Great Seat,[50] which *rejoices* the heart of the gods, which is in the House of Ptah, *the mistress of all life*, is the Granary of the God,[51] through which the sustenance of the Two Lands is prepared, because of the fact that Osiris drowned in his water,[52] while Isis and Nephthys watched. They saw him and they *were distressed at* him. Horus commanded Isis and Nephthys *repeatedly* that they lay hold on Osiris and prevent his drowning. They turned their (heads) in time. So they brought him to land.[53] He entered the mysterious portals in the glory of the lords of eternity, in the steps of him who shines forth on the horizon, on the ways of Re in the Great Seat. He joined with the court and associated with the gods of Ta-tenen Ptah, the lord of years.

Thus Osiris came to be in the land in the "House of the Sovereign" on the north side of this land, which he had reached. His son Horus appeared as King of Upper Egypt and appeared as King of Lower Egypt, in the embrace of his father Osiris, together with the gods who were in front of him and who were behind him.

3. The Creation Story From Genesis

The traditions upon which the Book of Genesis is based are obviously of great antiquity. The story of the creation, like other events in the history of the Hebrew people, was no doubt transmitted orally for many generations before being committed to writing. Tradition long held that Moses was the author of Genesis; but scholarship has since shown this to be impossible. The book as it now stands is a composite of various sources. The unknown author or authors sometimes included multiple accounts of the same event, and did not always resolve minor inconsistencies. It is now believed that three main sources were employed in the composition of Genesis: the "J" source, in which God is called "Yahweh" (Jahweh), originating in

---

47. Or, "so Ptah rested."
48. It is important to understand (contrary to modern thinking) that these images of wood, stone and clay were not the gods themselves, but merely places where they might appear.
49. Upon Ptah in his form as the land rising out of the primordial waters.
50. Ptah's throne in his temple at Memphis.
51. The god is Ptah Ta-tenen, whose throne is the granary which keeps Egypt alive.
52. Osiris was murdered by his brother Seth, who threw the corpse into the Nile river. After a long search, Isis, his sister and wife, found the body and restored it to life. Thereafter Osiris reigned over the realm of the dead. The son of Osiris and Isis was Horus, who later contended with Seth for the rule over Egypt (see chart above).
53. Osiris was originally a god of vegetation. The bringing ashore of his body at this place is given as the explanation for Memphis's position as granary (i.e., capital) of Egypt.

the tenth or ninth century B.C.; the "F" source, in which the word for God is "Elohim," slightly later in date. and the P or Priestly source, from about the fifth century B.C. The book as we now have it was probably substantially complete by the fifth century B.C.

According to the Genesis story, creation was effected by one God, who is eternal; creation was a purposeful event; and evil in the world is the punishment for disobedience to God.

Chapter 1

1. In the beginning God created the heaven and the earth.

2. And the earth was without form, and void; and darkness was upon the face of the deep. And the Spirit of God moved upon the face of the waters.

3. And God said, Let there be light: and there was light.

4. And God saw the light, that it was good: and God divided the light from the darkness.

5. And God called the light Day, and the darkness he called Night. And the evening and the morning were the first day.

6. And God said, Let there be a firmament in the midst of the waters, and let it divide the waters from the waters.

7. And God made the firmament, and divided the waters which were under the firmament from the waters which were above the firmament: and it was so.

8. And God called the firmament Heaven. And the evening and the morning were the second day.

9. And God said, Let the waters under the heaven be gathered together unto one place, and let the dry land appear: and it was so.

10. And God called the dry land Earth; and the gathering together of the waters called he Seas: and God saw that it was good.

11. And God said, Let the earth bring forth grass, the herb yielding seed, and the fruit tree yielding fruit after his kind, whose seed is in itself, upon the earth: and it was so.

12. And the earth brought forth grass, and herb yielding seed after his kind, and the tree yielding fruit, whose seed was in itself, after his kind: and God saw that it was good.

13. And the evening and the morning were the third day.

14. And God said, Let there be lights in the firmament of the heaven to divide the day from the night; and let them be for signs, and for seasons, and for days, and years:

15. And let them be for lights in the firmament of the heaven to give light upon the earth: and it was so.

16. And God made two great lights; the greater light to rule the day, and the lesser light to rule the night: he made the stars also.

17. And God set them in the firmament of the heaven to give light upon the earth.

18. And to rule over the day and over the night, and to divide the light from the darkness: and God saw that it was good.

19. And the evening and the morning were the fourth day.

20. And God said, Let the waters bring forth abundantly the moving creature that hath life, and fowl that may fly above the earth in the open firmament of heaven.

21. And God created great whales, and every living creature that moveth, which the waters brought forth abundantly, after their kind, and every winged fowl after his kind: and God saw that it was good.

22. And God blessed them, saying, Be fruitful, and multiply, and fill the waters in the seas, and let fowl multiply in the earth.

23. And the evening and the morning were the fifth day.

24. And God said, Let the earth bring forth the living creature after his kind, cattle, and creeping thing, and beast of the earth after his kind: and it was so.

25. And God made the beast of the earth after his kind, and cattle after their kind, and every thing that creepeth upon the earth after his kind: and God saw that it was good.

26. And God said, Let us make man in our image, after our likeness: and let them have dominion over the fish of the sea, and over the fowl of the air, and over the cattle, and over all the earth, and over every creeping thing that creepeth upon the earth.

27. So God created man in his own image, in the image of God created he him; male and female created he them.

28. And God blessed them, and God said unto them, Be fruitful, and multiply, and replenish the earth, and subdue it: and have dominion over the fish of the sea, and over the fowl of the air, and over every living thing that moveth upon the earth.

29. And God said, Behold, I have given you every herb bearing seed, which is upon the face of all the earth, and every tree, in the which is the fruit of a tree yielding seed; to you it shall be for meat.

30. And to every beast of the earth, and to every fowl of the air, and to every thing that creepeth upon the earth, wherein there is life, I have given every green herb for meat: and it was so.

31. And God saw every thing that he had made, and, behold, it was very good. And the evening and the morning were the sixth day.

Chapter 2

1. Thus the heavens and the earth were finished, and all the host of them.

2. And on the seventh day God ended his work which he had made; and he rested on the seventh day from all his work which he had made.

3. And God blessed the seventh day and sanctified it: because that in it he had rested from all his work which God created and made.

4. These are the generations of the heavens and of the earth when they were created, in the day that the Lord God made the earth and the heavens,

5. And every plant of the field before it was in the earth, and every herb of the field before it grew: for the Lord God had not caused it to rain upon the earth, and there was not a man to till the ground.

6. But there went up a mist from the earth, and watered the whole face of the ground.

7. And the Lord God formed man of the dust of the ground, and breathed into his nostrils the breath of life; and man became a living soul.

8. And the Lord God planted a garden eastward in Eden; and there he put the man whom he had formed.

9. And out of the ground made the Lord God to grow every tree that is pleasant to the sight, and good for food; the tree of life also in the midst of the garden, and the tree of knowledge of good and evil.

10. And a river went out of Eden to water the garden; and from thence it was parted, and became into four heads.

11. The name of the first is Pison: that is it which compasseth the whole land of Havilah, where there is gold;

12. And the gold of that land is good: there is bdellium and the onyx stone.

13. And the name of the second river is Gihon: the same is it that compasseth the whole land of Ethiopia.

14. And the name of the third river is Hiddekel: that is it which goeth toward the east of Assyria. And the fourth river is Euphrates.

15. And the Lord God took the man, and put him into the garden of Eden to dress it and to keep it.

16. And the Lord God commanded the man, saying, Of every tree of the garden thou mayest freely eat:

17. But of the tree of the knowledge of good and evil, thou shalt not eat of it: for in the day that thou eatest thereof thou shalt surely die.

18. And the Lord God said, It is not good that the man should be alone; I will make him an help meet for him.

19. And out of the ground the Lord God formed every beast of the field, and every fowl of the air; and brought them unto Adam to see what he would call them: and whatsoever Adam called every living creature, that was the name thereof.

20. And Adam gave names to all cattle, and to the fowl of the air, and to every beast of the field; but for Adam there was not found an help meet for him.

21. And the Lord God caused a deep sleep to fall upon Adam, and he slept; and he took one of his ribs, and closed up the flesh instead thereof;

22. And the rib, which the Lord God had taken from man, made he a woman, and brought her unto the man.

23. And Adam said, This is now bone of my bones, and flesh of my flesh: she shall be called Woman, because she was taken out of Man.

24. Therefore shall a man leave his father and his mother, and shall cleave unto his wife: and they shall be one flesh.

25. And they were both naked, the man and his wife, and were not ashamed.

Chapter 2

Ancient Egypt

The Great Pyramids, Giza, Egypt.

The Pyramid Texts 8

The Pyramid Texts are carved on the walls of the sarcophagus chambers and adjoining rooms and corridors that together form the royal burial suites inside the pyramids of Saqqara. They were discovered in 1881 in five of the Saqqara pyramids; those of Unas, the last king of the Fifth Dynasty, and of Kings Teti, Pepi I, Mernere, and Pepi II, the principal kings of the Sixth Dynasty.

Since the 1920s some additional texts were found in the pyramids of the three queens of Pepi II, and in the pyramid of King Ibi of the Eighth Dynasty.

Taken together they constitute a corpus of incantations, the purpose of which is to promote the resurrection and well being of the deceased kings. As carved on the walls, the incantations are clearly separated from one another by means of an introductory term and by dividing lines. Thus they form distinct, self-contained "utterances." The oldest group, that in the pyramid of Unas, consists of 228 utterances.

The utterances translated here are drawn from the pyramid of Unas. The central theme and purpose of the Pyramid Texts is the resurrection of the dead king and his ascent to the sky. The principal stages of his dramatic conquest of eternal life are: (1) the awakening in the tomb from the sleep of death; (2) the ascent to the sky; (3) and the admission to the company of the immortal gods. These stages are envisioned with a variety of detail, and joined to them are ancillary themes. Thus numerous texts are concerned with purification and with the offering of food and drink, and the texts of this type were originally recited by the priests during the several stages of the king's burial and in the subsequent funerary cult performed at the pyramid. Other texts, such as the spells against snakes, come from the sphere of daily life. Yet others are primarily speculative and concerned with envisioning the realm of the gods.

The utterances vary greatly in length. By and large, the short ones are unified and consistent, while the long ones tend to be repetitious and diffuse. This also means that the compositions most successful as poetry will be found among the shorter texts. All Pyramid Texts are composed in the "orational style," a recitative that depends for its effects on a strong regular rhythm. Here and there, when suffused with feeling and imagination, the incantations attain the heightened intensity which is the universal hallmark of poetry.

UTTERANCE 217

The king joins the sun-god[1]

Re-Atum, this Unas comes to you,
A spirit[2] indestructible
Who lays claim to the place of the four pillars!
Your son comes to you, this Unas comes to you,
May you cross the sky united in the dark,
May you rise in lightland, the place in which you shine!
Seth, Nephthys, go proclaim to Upper Egypt's gods
And their spirits:

Step-Pyramid, Saqqara, Egypt.

---

1. The utterance consists of four parts in each of which the king announces his arrival in the sky to the sun-god and commands certain gods, associated with the four cardinal points, to broadcast his coming to the four sides of the universe. The symmetry of the composition is heightened by repetitions and relieved by variations.
2. The word rendered "spirit" and "spirits" is *akh* in the singular and plural forms.

"This Unas comes, a spirit indestructible,
If he wishes you to die, you will die,
If he wishes you to live, you will live!"
Re-Atum, this Unas comes to you,
A spirit indestructible
Who lays claim to the place of the four pillars!
Your son comes to you, this Unas comes to you,
May you cross the sky united in the dark,
May you rise in lightland, the place in which you shine!
Osiris, Isis, go proclaim to Lower Egypt's gods
And their spirits:
"This Unas comes, a spirit indestructible,
Like the morning star above Hapy,
Whom the water-spirits worship;
Whom he wishes to live will live,
Whom he wishes to die will die!"

Re-Atum, this Unas comes to you,
A spirit indestructible
Who lays claim to the place of the four pillars!
Your son comes to you, this Unas comes to you,
May you cross the sky united in the dark,
May you rise in lightland, the place in which you shine!
Thoth, go proclaim to the gods of the west
And their spirits:
"This Unas comes, a spirit indestructible,
Decked above the neck as Anubis,
Lord of the western height,
He will count hearts, he will claim hearts,
Whom he wishes to live will live,
Whom he wishes to die will die!"

Re-Atum, this Unas comes to you,
A spirit indestructible
Who lays claim to the place of the four pillars!
Your son comes to you, this Unas comes to you,
May you cross the sky united in the dark,
May you rise in lightland, the place in which you shine!
Horus, go proclaim to the powers of the east
And their spirits:
"This Unas comes, a spirit indestructible,
Whom he wishes to live will live,
Whom he wishes to die will die!"

Re-Atum, your son comes to you,
Unas comes to you,
Raise him to you, hold him in your arms,
He is your son, of your body, forever!

UTTERANCES 273–274

The king feeds on the gods

Sky rains, stars darken,
The vaults quiver, earth's bones tremble,
The [planets] stand still
At seeing Unas rise as power,
A god who lives on his fathers,
Who feeds on his mothers!

Unas is master of cunning
Whose mother knows not his name;
Unas's glory is in heaven,
His power is in lightland;
Like Atum, his father, his begetter,
Though his son, he is stronger than he!

The forces of Unas are behind him,
His helpers[3] are under his feet,
His gods on his head, his serpents on his brow,
Unas's lead-serpent is on his brow,
Soul-searcher whose flame consumes,
Unas's neck is in its place.

Unas is the bull of heaven
Who rages in his heart,
Who lives on the being of every god,
Who eats their entrails
When they come, their bodies full of magic
From the Isle of Flame.[4]

Unas is one equipped who has gathered his spirits,
Unas has risen as Great One, as master of servants,

---

3. His ksw and hmwst, the male and female personifications of the faculties.
4. The Isle of Flame is an often mentioned part of the celestial topography.

He will sit with his back to Geb,
Unas will judge with Him-whose-name-is-hidden
On the day of slaying the eldest.[5]
Unas is lord of offerings who knots the cord,
Who himself prepares his meal,

Unas is he who eats men, feeds on gods,
Master of messengers who sends instructions:
It is Horn-grasper [in Kehau] who lassoes them for Unas,
It is Serpent Raised-head who guards, who holds them for him,[6]
It is He-upon-the-willows who binds them for him.
It is Khons, slayer of lords, who cuts their throats for Unas,
Who tears their entrails out for him,
He the envoy who is sent to punish.
It is Shesmu[7] who carves them up for Unas,
Cooks meals of them for him in his dinner-pots.

Unas eats their magic, swallows their spirits:
Their big ones are for his morning meal,
Their middle ones for his evening meal,
Their little ones for his night meal,
And the oldest males and females for his fuel.
The Great Ones in the northern sky light him fire
For the kettles' contents with the old ones' thighs,
For the sky-dwellers serve Unas,
And the pots are scraped for him with their women's legs.

He has encompassed the two skies,
He has circled the two shores;
Unas is the great power that overpowers the powers,
Unas is the divine hawk, the great hawk of hawks,
Whom he finds on his way he devours whole.
Unas's place is before all the nobles in lightland,
Unas is god, oldest of the old,
Thousands serve him, hundreds offer to him,
Great-Power rank was given him by Orion, father of gods.

---

5. An obscure passage which has been variously rendered.
6. Three divinities will catch and bind the king's victims: a "grasper of horns," a serpent, and
hry trwt, whom Sethe rendered as "he who is over the reddening," i.e., the blood. This demon only binds the victims,
however, the slaughter being subsequently done by Khons. Hence I take *trwt* to be the word for "willows," and "he upon
the willows" to be the demon who binds the victims with willow branches.
7. After Khons has slain the gods, Shesmu, the god of the oil and wine press, cooks them.

Unas has risen again in heaven,
He is crowned as lord of lightland.
He has smashed bones and marrow,
He has seized the hearts of gods,
He has eaten the Red, swallowed the Green.
Unas feeds on the lungs of the wise,
Likes to live on hearts and their magic;
Unas abhors licking the coils of the Red
But delights to have their magic in his belly.

The dignities of Unas will not be taken from him,
For he has swallowed the knowledge of every god;
Unas's lifetime is forever, his limit is eternity
In his dignity of "If-he-likes-he-does if-he-hates-he-does-not,"
As he dwells in lightland for all eternity.
Lo, their power is in Unas's belly,
Their spirits are before Unas as broth of the gods,
Cooked for Unas from their bones.
Lo, their power is with Unas,
Their shadows (are taken) from their owners,
For Unas is of those who risen is risen, lasting lasts.
Not can evildoers harm Unas's chosen seat
Among the living in this land for all eternity!

A Spell from the Coffin Texts 9

Beginning in the First Intermediate Period, it became customary to inscribe the coffins of non-royal well-to-do persons with spells designed to protect the dead against the dangers of the netherworld and to bring about an afterlife modeled on that of the divine king. Like the king, the common man (and woman) now desired to rise up to the sky and to join the gods. Along with these grandiose wishes, the texts spell out more ordinary concerns and fears, such as the fear to suffer hunger and thirst, and the wish to be united with one's family.

In inspiration, the Coffin Texts descend directly from the Pyramid Texts, and some of their spells are direct borrowings. But the bulk of the material is new and reflects its non-royal origin. As a corpus, the Coffin Texts are far less coherent than the Pyramid Texts, for they lack a unifying point of view. Inspired by a reliance on magic, they lack the humility of prayer and the restraints of reason. Oscillating between grandiose claims and petty fears, they show the human imagination at its most abstruse. Fear of death and longing for eternal life have been brewed in a sorcerer's cauldron from which they emerge as magic incantations of the most phrenetic sort. The attempt to overcome the fear of death by usurping the royal claims to immortality resulted in delusions of grandeur which accorded so little with the observed facts of life as to appear paranoid.

Now and then a more reasonable attitude prevails, as in the first part of the spell here translated. It consists of a speech of the sun-god Re, in which the god takes credit for four good deeds which he did at the time of creation. In listing the four deeds the god makes two assertions of prime importance: that he created all men as equals; and that it was not he who taught mankind to do wrong; rather, people do wrong of their own volition. This portion of the text is much above the usual level. The remainder is a typical Coffin Text spell, a grandiose claim that the dead will win entry into heaven and will be the equal of the sun-god.

The spell was used on a number of coffins, and the translation draws on the several versions as found side by side in de Buck's masterly edition.[1]

Words spoken by Him-whose-names-are-hidden, the All-Lord, as he speaks before those who silence the storm, in the sailing of the court:[2]

Hail in peace! I repeat to you the good deeds which my own heart did for me from within the serpent-coil,[3] in order to silence strife. I did four good deeds within the portal of lightland:

I made the four winds, that every man might breathe in his time. This is one of the deeds.

I made the great inundation, that the humble might benefit by it like the great. This is one of the deeds.

I made every man like his fellow; and I did not command that they do wrong. It is their hearts that disobey what I have said. This is one of the deeds.

I made that their hearts are not disposed to forget the West, in order that sacred offerings he made to the gods of the nomes. This is one of the deeds.

I have created the gods from my sweat, and the people from the tears of my eye.[4]

The dead speaks

I shall shine[5] and be seen every day as a dignitary of the All-Lord, having given satisfaction to the Weary-hearted.[6]

I shall sail rightly in my bark, I am lord of eternity in the crossing of the sky.

I am not afraid in my limbs, for Hu and Hike[7] overthrow for me that evil being.

I shall see lightland, I shall dwell in it. I shall judge the poor and the wealthy.

I shall do the same for the evil-doers; for mine is life, I am its lord, and the scepter will not be taken from me.

I have spent a million years with the Weary-hearted, the son of Geb, dwelling with him in one place; while hills became towns and towns hills, for dwelling destroys dwelling.[8]

I am lord of the flame who lives on truth; lord of eternity maker of joy, against whom that worm shall not rebel.

I am he who is in his shrine, master of action who destroys the storm; who drives off the serpents of many names when he goes from his shrine.

---

1. A. de Buck, *The Egyptian Coffin Texts*, ed. A. de Buck and A.H. Gardner. 7 vols. Chicago, 1935–1961, VII.461–471 and 262.

2. *Sgrw nln* might be either the active or the passive participle; the passive participle means: "those stilled from tumult." In the active sense it would refer to the gods who accompany the sun-god. *Smwt* are the courtiers, or entourage, of Re.

3. The serpent-dragon Aapophis who symbolized the lurking dangers of the world.

4. The word play on *rmt*, "people," and *rmyt*, "tears," which occurs a number of times as an allusion to the creation of mankind.

5. Here begins the spell that is put in the mouth of the dead. In four of the versions it is cast in the first person, and in two version in the third.

6. An epithet of Osiris. The meaning seems to be that the dead must first satisfy Osiris, the ruler of the dead, before he can join the sun-god.

7. The personification of effective speech and of magic.

8. The claims get successively grander until the dead speaks as if he were the sun-god himself. That this identification is intended is shown by the explanatory remark with which the spell ends.

Lord of the winds who announces the northwind, rich in names in the mouth of the Ennead.
Lord of lightland, maker of light, who lights the sky with his beauty.

I am he in his name! Make way for me, that I may see Nun and Amun! For I am that equipped spirit (akh) who passes by the [guards]. They do not speak for fear of Him-whose-name-is-hidden, who is in my body. I know him, I do not ignore him! I am equipped and effective in opening his portal!

As for any person who knows this spell, he will be like Re in the eastern sky, like Osiris in the netherworld. He will go down to the circle of fire, without the flame touching him ever!

The Book of the Dead

The Book of the Dead, or, "the coming forth by day," as the Egyptians called it, was a large compilation of spells designed to bring about the resurrection of the dead person and his safety in the afterlife. It is the direct successor of the Middle Kingdom Coffin Texts, which were derived from the Pyramid Texts. Like the Pyramid Texts and the Coffin Texts, the Book of the Dead reflects ritual acts performed during and after the burial. Gathered into a collection and inscribed on papyrus scrolls, the spells acquired the form of a mass-produced book that could be purchased by anyone. The prospective owner merely had to have his name and titles inserted in a ready-made scroll, or he could have a copy made to order. The finished scroll was buried with its owner, either placed on the sarcophagus, or on the body itself, or in a special container.

At the beginning of the New Kingdom, the Book of the Dead was still in the process of formation. It achieved its final form in the Saite period (the Twenty-Sixth Dynasty), when all its spells were put into a fixed sequence of chapters. Modern scholarship has added numbers to the chapters; the total number of chapters presently known is 192. No individual scroll contains all the chapters. In their fixed sequence the chapters offer a certain degree of order but no precise plan or progression.

The texts are written in cursive hieroglyphs and are accompanied by illustrations, or vignettes, drawn in ink of various colors. Like those of the Pyramid Texts and Coffin Texts, the spells of the Book of Dead vary greatly in length. One of the longest, and the most famous, is Chapter 125, the Judgment of the Dead. The chapter's principal illustration is the scene that shows the weighing of the dead person's heart on the scales before an assembly of gods who are presided over by Osiris. The selection of Book of the Dead texts given here is designed to lead up to Chapter 125 through a small sampling of a few major themes in a number of short spells selected to serve as background against which to view the climactic judgment scene.

It is evident that the Book of the Dead is a book of magic. In all periods of ancient Egyptian culture magic was considered a legitimate tool; and in the confrontation with death the magical approach attained its most luxuriant growth. That is to say, magical means were not felt to be inimical to piety. If not inimical, the reliance on magical means was nevertheless distinct from the humble approach to the gods which informs the prayers.

No other nation of the ancient world made so determined an effort to vanquish death and win eternal life. Individual thinkers might increasingly lose faith in the promise of eternal life, and might adopt attitudes of resignation and even skepticism. But the majority appear to have clung to the hope of a bodily afterlife and to a reliance on magic as the means to achieve it. Eternal life had come to be conceived in the most grandiose terms: the dead were to become godlike and join the company of the gods. Yet when combined with the ethical concept of a judgment in the hereafter, the magical approach could not but be contrary to morality and piety. It is thus no accident that the positive virtues taught in the Instructions *and affirmed in the* Autobiographies *are almost all given the form of negative statements in Chapter 125: the dead delivers a long recitation of sins not committed in order to pass the judgment of the gods. Magic and morality are here yoked together, but they remain incompatible.*

CHAPTER 23

The Opening of the Month

Formula for opening N's mouth[1] for him in the necropolis. He shall say:

My mouth is opened by Ptah[2],
My mouth's bonds are loosed by my city-god.
Thoth[3] has come fully equipped with spells,
He looses the bonds of Seth from my mouth.
Atum[4] has given me my hands,
They are placed as guardians.

My mouth is given to me,
My mouth is opened by Ptah
With that chisel of metal
With which he opened the mouth of the gods.
I am Sakhmet-Wadjet[5] who dwells in the west of heaven,
I am Sahyt among the souls of On.

---

1. The name and title of the deceased are given. The opening of the mouth was an important ritual that was performed before statues and before mummies prior to their burial.
2. Originally the local god of Memphis, but by the Pyramid Age he assumed the position of creator god. See *The Theology of Memphis.*
3. Thoth, depicted as a crouching baboon, was the lord of the moon, the "lord of time" and "reckoner of years." He invented writing. As a protector of Osiris he was also a helper of the dead.
4. The creator god of Heliopolis. He was a personification of the primeval chaos from which issued all that exists. In the creation story, he appears as the primeval hill. In the *Book of the Dead*, Chapter 175, Atum addresses Osiris concerning the end of the world and announces that he will destroy all that he has made and turn himself back into the primeval serpent.
5. Together with her husband Ptah and her son Nefertem, Sekhmet made up the Memphite triad. Her name meant "the mighty one' and her nature was that of a goddess of war. Wadjet was the name of the goddess of Buto in the delta and meant "papyrus-colored one." The cobra was her sacred animal.

As for any spells, any spells spoken against me,
The gods shall rise up against them,
The entire Ennead, the entire Ennead!

Chapter 30B

The Heart as Witness

Formula for not letting the heart of N oppose him in the necropolis. He shall say:

O my heart of my mother,[6]
O my heart of my mother,
O my heart of my being!
Do not rise up against me as witness,
Do not oppose me in the tribunal,
Do not rebel against me before the guardian of the scales!

You are my *ka*[7] within my body,
The Khnum[8] who prospers my limbs.
Go to the good place prepared for us,
Do not make my name stink before them,
The magistrates who put people in their places!
If it's good for us it's good for the judge,
It pleases him who renders judgment.
Do not invent lies before the god.
Before the great god, the lord of the west,
Lo, your uprightness brings vindication!

Chapter 105

An Address to the Ka

Formula to appease the *ka* to be said by N.

Hail to you, my *ka*, my helper!
Behold, I have come before you,

---

6. I.e., the person's very own heart, which he had since birth.
7. The ka was the term for the creative and preserving power of life. It was the individual's vitality, vital force, personality, etc.
8. Khnum was the guardian of the source of the Nile. In southern Egypt he was a creator god, the "father of fathers, the mother of mothers."

Risen, animated, mighty, healthy!
I have brought incense to you,
To purify you with it,
To purify your sweat with it.

Whatever evil speech I made,
Whatever evil deed I did,
Be it removed from me!
For mine is that green amulet,
Fastened to the neck of Re,
That makes the lightlanders green.
My ka greens like theirs,
My *ka's* food is as theirs.

O Weigher on the scales,
May *maat*[9] rise to the nose of Re that day!
Do not let my head be removed from me!
For mine is an eye that sees,
An ear that hears;
For I am not an ox for slaughter,
I shall not be an offering for those above!
Let me pass by you, I am pure,
Osiris has vanquished his foes!

CHAPTER 125

The Judgment of the Dead

The Declaration of Innocence

(1) To be said on reaching the Hall of the Two Truths[10] so as to purge N of any sins committed and to see the face of every god:

Hail to you, great God, Lord of the Two Truths!
I have come to you, my Lord,
I was brought to see your beauty.

---

9. The goddess *Maat* was the personification of the basic laws of all existence; she embodied the concepts of law, truth and world order. Without *Maat* life was impossible for she was Re's food and drink.
10. *Maat* in duel form.

I know you, I know the names of the forty-two gods,[11]
Who are with you in the Hall of the Two Truths,
Who live by warding off evildoers,
Who drink of their blood,
On that day of judging characters before Wennofer.[12]
Lo, your name is "He-of-Two-Daughters,"
(And) "He-of-Maat's-Two-Eyes."
Lo, I come before you,
Bringing Maat to you,
Having repelled evil for you.

I have not done crimes against people,
I have not mistreated cattle,
I have not sinned in the Place of Truth.[13]
I have not known what should not be known,[14]
I have not done any harm.
I did not begin a day by exacting more than my due,
My name did not reach the bark of the mighty ruler.
I have not blasphemed a god,
I have not robbed the poor.
I have not done what the god abhors,
I have not maligned a servant to his master.
I have not caused pain,
I have not caused tears.
I have not killed,
I have not ordered to kill,
I have not made anyone suffer.
I have not damaged the offerings in the temples,
I have not depleted the loaves of the gods,
I have not stolen the cakes of the dead.
I have not copulated nor defiled myself.
I have not increased nor reduced the measure,
I have not diminished the arura,
I have not cheated in the fields.
I have not added to the weight of the balance,
I have not falsified the plummet of the scales.
I have not taken milk from the mouth of children,
I have not deprived cattle of their pasture.

---

11. The dead person insists that he knows the names of the gods. Knowing their names meant having power over them.
12. A name of Osiris.
13. A term for temple and necropolis.
14. Literally, "I have not known what is not."

I have not snared birds in the reeds of the gods,
I have not caught fish in their ponds.
I have not held back water in its season,
I have not dammed a flowing stream,
I have not quenched a needed fire.
I have not neglected the days of meat offerings,
I have not detained cattle belonging to the god,
I have not stopped a god in his procession.
I am pure, I am pure, I am pure, I am pure!
I am pure as is pure that great heron in Hnes.
I am truly the nose of the Lord of Breath,
Who sustains all the people,
On the day of completing the Eye[15] in On,
In the second month of winter, last day,
In the presence of the lord of this land.
I have seen the completion of the Eye in On!
No evil shall befall me in this land,
In this Hall of the Two Truths;
For I know the names of the gods in it,
The followers of the great God!

The Declaration to the Forty-two Gods[16]

O Wide-of-stride who comes from On: I have not done evil.
O Flame-grasper who comes from Kheraha: I have not robbed.
O Long-nosed who comes from Khmun:[17] I have not coveted.
O Shadow-eater who comes from the cave: I have not stolen.
O Savage-faced who comes from Rostau: I have not killed people.
O Lion-Twins who come from heaven: I have not trimmed the measure.
O Flint-eyed who comes from Khem: I have not cheated.
O Fiery-one who comes backward: I have not stolen a god's property.
O Bone-smasher who comes from Hnes: I have not told lies.
O Flame-thrower who comes from Memphis: I have not seized food.
O Cave-dweller who comes from the west: I have not sulked.
O White-toothed who comes from Lakeland:[18] I have not trespassed.
O Blood-eater who comes from slaughter-place: I have not slain sacred cattle.
O Entrail-eater who comes from the tribunal: I have not extorted.
O Lord of Maat who comes from Maaty: I have not stolen bread rations.
O Wanderer who comes from Bubastis: I have not spied.

---

15. The Horus Eye.
16. Most of the forty-two gods are minor demons, only a few are major gods.
17. Thoth of Hermopolis in the shape of the long-nosed Ibis.
18. Sobk, the crocodile-god of the Fayyum.

O Pale-one who comes from On: I have not prattled.

O Villain who comes from Anjdty: I have contended only for my goods.

O Fiend who comes from slaughter-house: I have not committed adultery.

O Examiner who comes from Mm's temple: I have not defiled myself.

O Chief of the nobles who comes from Imu: I have not caused fear.

O Wrecker who comes from Huy: I have not trespassed.

O Disturber who comes from the sanctuary: I have not been violent.

O Child who comes from the nome of On: I have not been deaf to Maat.

O Foreteller who comes from Wensi: I have not quarreled.

O Bastet who comes from the shrine: I have not winked.

O Backward-faced who comes from the pit: I have not copulated with a boy.

O Flame-footed who comes from the dusk: I have not been false.

O Dark-one who comes from darkness: I have not reviled.

O Peace-bringer who comes from Sais: I have not been aggressive.

O Many-faced who comes from Djefet: I have not had a hasty heart.

O Accuser who comes from Utjen: I have not attacked and reviled a god.

O Horned-one who comes from Siut: I have not made many words.

O Nefertem who comes from Memphis: I have not sinned, I have not done wrong.

O Timeless-one who comes from Djedu: I have not made trouble.

O Willful-one who comes from Tjebu: I have not Fwadedl in water.

O Flowing-one who comes from Nun: I have not raised my voice.

O Commander of people who comes from his shrine: I have not cursed a god.

O Benefactor who comes from Huy: I have not been boastful.

O Nehebkau who comes from the city: I have not been haughty.

O High-of-head who comes from the cave: I have not wanted more than I had.

O Captor who comes from the graveyard: I have not cursed god in my town.

The Address to the Gods

Hail to you, gods!
I know you, I know your names.
I shall not fall in fear of you,
You shall not accuse me of crime to this god whom you follow!
No misfortune shall befall me on your account!
You shall speak rightly about me before the All-Lord,
For I have acted rightly in Egypt.
I have not cursed a god,
I have not been faulted.
Hail to you, gods in the Hall of the Two Truths,
Who have no lies in their bodies,
Who live on *maat* in On,
Who feed on their rightness before Horus in his disk.
Rescue me from Babi, who feeds on the entrails of nobles,
On that day of the great reckoning.

Behold me, I have come to you,
Without sin, without guilt, without evil,
Without a witness against me,
Without one whom I have wronged.
I live on *maat*, I feed on *maat*,
I have done what people speak of,
What the gods are pleased with,
I have contented a god with what he wishes.
I have given bread to the hungry,
Water to the thirsty,
Clothes to the naked,
A ferryboat to the boatless.
I have given divine offerings to the gods,
Invocation-offerings to the dead.
Rescue me, protect me,
Do not accuse me before the great god!

I am one pure of mouth, pure of hands,
One to whom "welcome" is said by those who see him;
For I have heard the words spoken by the Donkey and the Cat,
In the house of the Open-mouthed;
I was a witness before him when he cried out,
I saw the splitting of the ished-tree in Rostau.
I am one who is acquainted with the gods,
One who knows what concerns them.
I have come here to bear witness to *maat*,
To set the balance in right position among the dead.
O you who are high upon your standard,
Lord of the *atef*-crown,
Who is given the name "Lord of Breath":[19]
Rescue me from your messengers,
Who inflict wounds,
Who mete out punishment,
Who have no compassion,
For I have done *maat* for the Lord of *maat!*
I am pure,
My front is pure,
My rear is pure,
My middle has been in the well of maat,
No limb of mine is unclean.
I have washed in the well of the South,

---

19. Osiris is meant.

I have halted at the town of the North,
In the meadow of the grasshoppers,
Where the crew of Re bathes by day and by night,
Where the gods enjoy passing by day and by night.

The First Interrogation

"Let him come," they say to me,
"Who are you?" they say to me,
"What is your name?" they say to me.
"I am the stalk of the papyrus,
He-who-is-in-the-moringa[20] is my name.
"Where have you passed by?" they say to me,
"I have passed by the town north of the moringa."
"What have you seen there?"
"The Leg and the Thigh."
"What did you say to them?"
"I have witnessed the acclaim in the land of the Fenkhu."
"What did they give you?"
A firebrand and a faience column."
"What did you do with them?"
"I buried them on the shore of the pool Maaty,
At the time of the evening meal."
"What did you find there on the shore of the pool Maaty?"
"A scepter of flint whose name is 'Breath-giver'."
"What did you do to the firebrand and the faience column,
When you had buried them?"
"I lamented over them,
I took them up,
I extinguished the fire,
I broke the column,
Threw it in the pool."[21]
"Come then, enter the gate of this Hall of the Two Truths,
For you know us."

The Second Interrogation

"I shall not let you enter through me,"
Says the beam of this gate,
"Unless you tell my name.
"'Plummet-of-the-Place-of-Truth' is your name.

---

20. Epithet of Osiris.
21. Most of the questions and answers refer to the mysteries of Osiris.

"I shall not let you enter through me,"
Says the right leaf of this gate,
"Unless you tell my name."
"'Scale-pan-that-carries-maat' is your name.
"I shall not let you enter through me"
Says the left leaf of this gate,
"Unless you tell my name."
"'Scale-pan-of-wine' is your name.
"I shall not let you pass over me,
Says the threshold of this gate,
"Unless you tell my name."
"'Ox-of-Geb' is your name."
"I shall not open for you,"
Says the bolt of this gate,
"Unless you tell my name."
"'Toe-of-his-mother' is your name.
"I shall not open for you,"
Says the bolt-clasp of this gate,
"Unless you tell my name."
"'Eye-of-Sobk-Lord-of-Bakhu' is your name."
"I shall not open for you,
I shall not let you enter by me,"
Says the keeper of this gate,
"Unless you tell my name.
"'Breast-of-Shu-given-him-to-guard-Osiris' is your name."
"We shall not let you pass over us,"
Say the cross-timbers,
"Unless you tell our name."
"'Offspring-of-Renenutet' is your name."
"You know us, pass over us.

"You shall not tread upon me,
Says the floor of this hall.
"Why not, since I am pure?"
"Because we do not know your feet,
With which you tread on us;
Tell them to me.
"'Who-enters-before-Mm' is the name of my right foot,
"'*Wnpt*[22]-of-Nephthys' is the name of my left foot."
"Tread upon us, since you know us."
"I shall not announce you,"

---

22. An unknown word.

Says the guard of the Hall,
"Unless you tell my name."
"'Knower-of-hearts Examiner-of-bellies' is your name."
"To which god present shall I announce you?"
"Tell it to the Interpreter of the Two Lands."
"Who is the Interpreter of the Two Lands?"
"It is Thoth."

"Come," says Thoth,
"Why have you come?"
"I have come here to report."
"What is your condition?"
"I am free of all wrongdoing,
I avoided the strife of those in their day,
I am not one of them."
"To whom shall I announce you?"
"To him whose roof is of fire,
Whose walls are living cobras,
The floor of whose house is in the flood."
"Who is he?"
"He is Osiris."
"Proceed, you are announced,
The Eye is your bread,
The Eye is your beer,
The Eye is your offering on earth,"
So says he to me.

Instructions for use

This is the way to act toward the Hall of the Two Truths. A man says this speech when he is pure, clean, dressed in fresh clothes, shod in white sandals, painted with eye-paint, anointed with the finest oil of myrrh. One shall offer to him beef, fowl, incense, bread, beer, and herbs. And you make this image in drawing on a clean surface in red [paint] mixed with soil on which pigs and goats have not trodden.

He for whom this scroll is recited will prosper, and his children will prosper. He will be the friend of the king and his courtiers. He will receive bread, beer, and a big chunk of meat from the altar of the great god. He will not be held back at any gate of the west. He will be ushered in with the kings of Upper and Lower Egypt. He will be a follower of Osiris.

Effective a million times.

The Instruction of Ptahhotep

11

This long work has survived in four copies, three of which are written on papyrus rolls while the fourth, containing only the beginning, is on a wooden tablet. The only complete version is that of Papyus Prisse of the BibliothÈque Nationale, which dates from the Middle Kingdom. The other two papyri, both in the British Museum, are from the Middle and New Kingdoms, respectively. The wooden tablet, Carnarvon Tablet I in the Cairo Museum, also dates from the New Kingdom. The version of P. Prisse differs considerably from that of the other three copies. The translation here given reproduces excerpts from the text of P. Prisse only.

The work consists of thirty-seven maxims framed by a prologue and an epilogue. Each maxim is developed as a unit of at least four, and rarely more than twelve, sentences and clauses. Some themes and topics recur several times, an indication of their importance in the scale of values.

Taken together, the thirty-seven maxims do not amount to a comprehensive moral code, nor are they strung together in any logical order. But they touch upon the most important aspects of human relations and they focus on the basic virtues. The cardinal virtues are self-control, moderation, kindness, generosity, justice, and truthfulness tempered by discretion. These virtues are to be practiced alike toward all people. No martial virtues are mentioned. The ideal man is a man of peace.

THE INSTRUCTION OF PTAHHOTEP

Instruction of the Mayor of the city, the Vizier Ptahhotep, under the Majesty of King Isesi, who lives for all eternity. The mayor of the city, the vizier Ptahhotep, said:

O king, my lord!
Age is here, old age arrived,
Feebleness came, weakness grows,

(so) [Childlike] one sleeps all day.
Eyes are dim, ears deaf,
Strength is waning through weariness,
The mouth, silenced, speaks not,
The heart, void, recalls not the past,
The bones ache throughout.
Good has become evil, all taste is gone,
What age does to people is evil in everything.
The nose, clogged, breathes not,
[Painful] are standing and sitting.

May this servant be ordered to make a staff of old age,[1]
So as to tell him the words of those who heard,
The ways of the ancestors,
Who have listened to the gods.
May such be done for you,
So that strife may be banned from the people,
And the Two Shores may serve you!
Said the majesty of this god:
Instruct him then in the sayings of the past,
May he become a model for the children of the great,
May obedience enter him,
And the devotion of him who speaks to him,
No one is born wise.

Beginning of the formulations of excellent discourse spoken by the Prince, Count, God's Father, God's beloved, Eldest Son of the King, of his body, Mayor of the city and Vizier, Ptahhotep, in instructing the ignorant in knowledge and in the standard of excellent discourse, as profit for him who will hear, (so) as woe to him who would neglect them. He spoke to his son:

1. Don't be proud[2] of your knowledge,
Consult the ignorant and the wise;
The limits of art are not reached,
No artist's skills are perfect;
Good speech is more hidden than greenstone,
Yet may be found among maids at the grindstones.

---

1. "Staff of old age" is a metaphor for son or successor.
2. Literally, "Do not let your heart he big." Ptahhotep distinguishes between *ꜣs-ib*, "big-hearted," in the sense of "proud, arrogant," and *wr-ib*, "great-hearted," in the sense of 'high-minded, magnanimous." Elsewhere this distinction is not made; for example the courtier Tjetji calls himself *ꜥs n ib-f*, which is of course "great of heart" in the positive sense.

2. If you meet a disputant in action,
A powerful man, superior to you,
Fold your arms, bend your back,
To flout him will not make him agree with you.
Make little of the evil speech
By not opposing him while he's in action;
He will be called an ignoramus,
Your self-control will match his pile (of words).

3. If you meet a disputant in action
Who is your equal, on your level,
You will make your worth exceed his by silence,
While he is speaking evilly,
There will be much talk by the hearers,
Your name will be good in the mind of the magistrates.

4. If you meet a disputant in action,
A poor man, not your equal,
Do not attack him because he is weak,
Let him alone, he will confute himself.
Do not answer him to relieve your heart,
Do not vent yourself[3] against your opponent,
Wretched is he who injures a poor man,
One will wish to do what you desire,
You will beat him through the magistrates' reproof.

7. If you are one among guests
At the table of one greater than you,
Take what he gives as it is set before you;
Look at what is before you,
Don't shoot many glances at him,
Molesting him offends the *ka*.
Don't speak to him until he summons,
One does not know what may displease;
Speak when he has addressed you,
Then your words will please the heart.
The nobleman, when he is behind food,[4]
Behaves as his ka commands him;

---

3. Literally, "Do not wash your heart." "To wash the heart" (*i'ib*) is to relieve the heart of feelings, be they of anger or of joy. In *Peasant*, the hunter "washes his heart" by indulging in the joy of killing animals. When the heart is "washed" it is "appeased," as in *Sinuhe*.
4. The Egyptian says "behind food" rather than "before food."

He will give to him whom he favors,
It is the custom when night has come.
It is the *ka* that makes his hands reach out
The great man gives to the chosen man;
Thus eating is under the counsel of god,
A fool is who complains of it.

9. If you plow and there's growth in the field,
And god lets it prosper in your hand,
Do not boast at your neighbors' side,
One has great respect for the silent man:
Man of character is man of wealth.
If he robs he is like a crocodile in court.[5]
Don't impose on one who is childless,
Neither decry nor boast of it;[6]
There is many a father who has grief,
And a mother of children less content than another;
It is the lonely whom god fosters,
While the family man prays for a follower.

11. Follow your heart as long as you live,
Do no more than is required,
Do not shorten the time of "follow-the-heart,"
Trimming its moment offends the *ka*.
Don't waste time on daily cares
Beyond providing for your household;
When wealth has come, follow your heart,
Wealth does no good if one is glum!

12. If you are a man of worth
And produce a son by the grace of god,
If he is straight, takes after you,
Takes good care of your possessions,
Do for him all that is good,
He is your son, your *ka* begot him,
Don't withdraw your heart from him.
But an offspring can make trouble:
If he strays, neglects your counsel,
Disobeys all that is said,
His mouth spouting evil speech,

---

5. This sentence appears to be out of place here.
6. I.e., neither decry childlessness nor boast of having children.

Punish him for all his talk!
They hate him who crosses you,
His guilt was fated in the womb;
He whom they guide can not go wrong,
Whom they make boatless can not cross.[7]

14. If you are among the people,
Gain supporters through being trusted;
The trusted man who does not vent his belly's speech,
He will himself become a leader.
A man of means—what is he like?
Your name is good, you are not maligned,
Your body is sleek, your face benign,
One praises you without your knowing.
He whose heart obeys his belly
Puts contempt of himself in place of love,
His heart is bald, his body unanointed;
The great-hearted is god-given,
He who obeys his belly belongs to the enemy.[8]

16. If you are a man who leads,
Whose authority reaches wide,
You should do outstanding things,
Remember the day that comes after.
No strife will occur in the midst of honors,
But where the crocodile enters hatred arises.

17. If you are a man who leads,
Listen calmly to the speech of one who pleads;
Don't stop him from purging his body
Of that which he planned to tell.
A man in distress wants to pour out his heart
More than that his case be won.
About him who stops a plea
One says: "Why does he reject it ?"
Not all one pleads for can be granted,
But a good hearing soothes the heart.

---

7. The idea that the gods determine a man's character and fate was not developed to the point where it would have overwhelmed the sense of free will and personal responsibility.

8. This maxim contrasts the "heart" as the seat of reason with the "belly" as the seat of unreasoning feelings, desires, and appetites. But elsewhere in the text "belly" and "heart" are used interchangeably

18. If you want friendship to endure
In the house you enter
As master, brother, or friend,
In whatever place you enter,
Beware of approaching the women!
Unhappy is the place where it is done,
"Unwelcome" is he who intrudes on them.
A thousand men are turned away from their good:
A short moment like a dream,
Then death comes for having known them.
Poor advice is "shoot the opponent,"
When one goes to do it the heart rejects it.
He who fails through lust of them,
No affair of his can prosper.

19. If you want a perfect conduct,
To be free from every evil,
Guard against the vice of greed:
A grievous sickness without cure,
There is no treatment for it.
It embroils fathers, mothers,
And the brothers of the mother,
It parts wife from husband;
It is a compound of all evils,
A bundle of all hateful things.
That man endures whose rule is rightness,
Who walks a straight line;
He will make a will by it,
The greedy has no tomb.

20. Do not be greedy in the division[9]
Do not covet more than your share;
Do not be greedy toward your kin,
The mild has a greater claim than the harsh.
Poor is he who shuns his kin,
He is deprived of [interchange],[10]
Even a little of what is craved
Turns a quarreler into an amiable man.

---

9. I.e., in the sharing of inheritance.
10. *Sw m int mdt* looks like yet another idiom that we do not understand; the context suggests social intercourse, conversation.

21. When you prosper and found your house,
And love your wife with ardor,
Fill her belly, clothe her back,
Ointment soothes her body.
Gladden her heart as long as you live,
She is a fertile field for her lord.
Do not contend with her in court,
Keep her from power, restrain her—
Her eye is her storm when she gazes—
Thus will you make her stay in your house.
————————[11]

22. Sustain your friends with what you have,
You have it by the grace of god;
Of him who fails to sustain his friends
One says, "a selfish *ka*."
One plans the morrow but knows not what will be,
The (right) *ka* is the *ka* by which one is sustained.
If praiseworthy deeds are done,
Friends will say, "welcome!"
One does not bring supplies to town,
One brings friends when there is need.

23. Do not repeat calumny,
Nor should you listen to it,
It is the spouting of the hot-bellied.
Report a thing observed, not heard,
If it is negligible, don't say anything,
He who is before you recognizes worth.
If a seizure is ordered and carried out,
Hatred will arise against him who seizes;
Calumny is like a dream against which one covers the face.

24. If you are a man of worth
Who sits in his master's council,
Concentrate on excellence,
Your silence is better than chatter.
Speak when you know you have a solution,
It is the skilled who should speak in council;
Speaking is harder than all other work,
He who understands it makes it serve.

---

11. The final three sentences are obscure.

25. If you are mighty, gain respect through knowledge
And through gentleness of speech.
Don't command except as is fitting,
He who provokes gets into trouble.
Don't be haughty, lest you be humbled,
Don't be mute, lest you be chided.
When you answer one who is fuming,
Avert your face, control yourself.
The flame of the hot-heart[12] sweeps across,
He who steps gently, his path is paved.
He who frets all day has no happy moment,
He who's gay all day can't keep house.
_____[13]

28. If you are a magistrate of standing,
Commissioned to satisfy the many,
Hew a straight line
When you speak don't lean to one side,
Beware lest one complain:
"Judges, he distorts the matter!"
And your deed turns into a judgment (of you).

30. If you are great after having been humble,
Have gained wealth after having been poor
In the past, in a town which you know,
Knowing so your former condition,
Do not put trust in your wealth,
Which came to you as gift of god;
So that you will not fall behind one like you,
To whom the same has happened.

31. Bend your back to your superior,
Your overseer from the palace;
Then your house will endure in its wealth,
Your rewards in their right place.
Wretched is he who opposes a superior,
One lives as long as he is mild,
Baring the arm does not hurt it.[14]
Do not plunder a neighbor's house,

_____

12. See note 3 above.
13. The final lines are obscure.
14. I.e., stretching the arm out of the sleeve in a gesture of greeting.

Do not steal the goods of one near you,
Lest he denounce you before you are heard.
A quarreler is a mindless person,
If he is known as an aggressor
The hostile man will have trouble in the neighborhood.

33. If you probe the character of a friend,
Don't inquire, but approach him,
Deal with him alone,
So as not to suffer from his manner.
Dispute with him after a time,
Test his heart in conversation;
If what he has seen escapes him,[15]
If he does a thing that annoys you,
Be yet friendly with him, don't attack;
Be restrained, don't let fly,
Don't answer [hostility] with hostility,
Neither part from him nor attack him;
His time does not fail to come,
One does not escape what is fated.

34. Be generous as long as you live,
What leaves the storehouse does not return;
It is the food to be shared which is coveted,
One whose belly is empty is an accuser;
One deprived becomes an opponent,
Don't have him for a neighbor.
Kindness is a man's memorial
For the years after the function.

35. Know your helpers, then you prosper,
Don't be mean toward your friends,
They are one's watered field,
And greater then one's riches,
For what belongs to one belongs to another.
The character of a son-of-man is profit to him;[16]
Good nature is a memorial.

---

15. Does this mean "forgetful" or "indiscreet"?

16. "Son-of-man" here and elsewhere in the sense of "wellborn," is well known. The parallel expressions in Hebrew and Aramaic had the same connotation.

Be a Scribe 12

Numerous papyri and ostraca of Ramesside date testify to the existence of a school system that taught young boys to become professional scribes and hence civil servants. Not all instruction took place in schools. Many of the texts suggest a personal form of teaching in which a senior official guided a young man who had completed his basic schooling and was already a member of the bureaucracy.

Writing was taught by making the pupils copy a variety of compositions: literary works that were highly esteemed, and basic genres such as letters, hymns, prayers, and of course, instructions in wisdom. Through copying, taking down dictation, and memorizing the students acquired the basic skills of reading and writing and the more advanced knowledge of grammar, orthography, vocabulary, and composition. Furthermore, it could be hoped that the moral teachings propounded in the didactic texts would help to form the characters of the young scribes.

Through being used as teaching materials, all literary works, as well as actual letters and documents dealing with business and legal matters, became school texts. But the school system also gave rise to a specific genre of texts which reflected the educational process and the relation between teacher and pupil. These were works composed by teachers and pupils which in turn became models to be copied. Their contents revolved around three main themes: 1. The teacher's advice to the student, exhorting him to diligence and warning against dissipation. 2. The praise of the scribe's profession as one superior to all others. 3. The grateful replies of the student who lauds his teacher and wishes him wealth and happiness.

Letter-writing was an important feature of scribal activity. Hence the copying of real letters and the composition of model letters played a large part in the instruction. Even the texts devoted to the teacher-pupil theme were often cast in the form of letters.

In the papyri that have survived, different kinds of texts, used in the schools, were often copied out one after another regardless of their content. Thus works that had originated in specific situations of life, such as business letters, came to be side by side with model compositions invented by teachers and students. But now and then a scribe made a "book" by selecting compositions on related themes and putting them in a meaningful order. Such a book is Papyrus Lansing. It is a schoolbook in the specific sense, for it is devoted to the theme "Be a scribe."

The book treats the typical topics of the teacher-pupil relation in a sequence of eleven sections: 1. Address. 2–4. Praise of the scribal profession and exhortations to the pupil. 5–6. The miseries of other professions.

7. Additional advice and exhortations. 8. The special hardships of the soldier's life. 9–11. The pupil praises his teacher. The final section of Papyrus Lansing contains a letter which is not connected with the "book."

1. TITLE

[Beginning of the instruction in letter-writing made by the royal scribe and chief overseer of the cattle of Amen-Re, King of Gods, Nebmare-nakht] for his apprentice, the scribe Wenemdiamun.

2. PRAISE OF THE SCRIBE'S PROFESSION

[The royal scribe] and chief overseer of the cattle of Amen-[Re, King of Gods, Nebmare-nakht speaks to the scribe Wenemdiamun].[Apply yourself to this] noble profession. "Follower of Thoth" is the good name of him who exercises it.——————. He makes friends with those greater than he. Joyful——————. Write with your hand, read with your mouth. Act according to my words. ——————, my heart is not disgusted. ——————. —————— to my instructing you. You will find it useful. —————— [with bread and] beer. You will be advanced by your superiors. You will be sent on a mission ——————. Love writing, shun dancing; then you become a worthy official. Do not long for the marsh thicket.[1] Turn your back on throw stick and chase. By day write with your fingers; recite by night. Befriend the scroll, the palette. It pleases more than wine. Writing for him who knows it is better than all other professions. It pleases more than bread and beer, more than clothing and ointment. It is worth more than an inheritance in Egypt, than a tomb in the west.

3. ADVICE TO THE UNWILLING PUPIL

Young fellow, how conceited you are! You do not listen when I speak. Your heart is denser than a great obelisk, a hundred cubits high, ten cubits thick. When it is finished and ready for loading, many work gangs draw it. It hears the words of men; it is loaded on a barge. Departing from Yebu it is conveyed, until it comes to rest on its place in Thebes.[2]

So also a cow is bought this year, and it plows the following year. It learns to listen to the herdsman; it only lacks words. Horses brought from the field, they forget their mothers. Yoked they go up and down on all his majesty's errands. They become like those that bore them, that stand in the stable. They do their utmost for fear of a beating.

But though I beat you with every kind of stick, you do not listen. If I knew another way of doing it, I would do it for you, that you might listen. You are a person fit for writing, though you

---

1. The marsh thicket signifies the joys of hunting and fishing.
2. The simile is mixed. It begins as a criticism of the pupil's heart (i.e., mind) which is "dense," and proceeds to describe the finished stone obelisk which fulfills its function, in contrast with the idle pupil who does not.

have not yet known a woman. Your heart discerns, your fingers are skilled, your mouth is apt for reciting.

Writing is more enjoyable than enjoying a basket of *b3y*³ and beans; more enjoyable than a mother's giving birth, when her heart knows no distaste. She is constant in nursing her son; her breast is in his mouth every day. Happy is the heart (of) him who writes; he is young each day.

4. The Idle Scribe is Worthless

The royal scribe and chief overseer of the cattle of Amen-Re, King of Gods, Nebmare-nakht, speaks to the scribe Wenemdiamun, as follows. You are busy coming and going, and don't think of writing. You resist listening to me; you neglect my teachings.

You are worse than the goose of the shore, that is busy with mischief. It spends the summer destroying the dates, the winter destroying the seed-grain. It spends the balance of the year in pursuit of the cultivators. It does not let seed be cast to the ground without snatching it in its fall. One cannot catch it by snaring. One does not offer it in the temple. The evil, sharpeyed bird that does no work!

You are worse than the desert antelope that lives by running. It spends no day in plowing. Never at all does it tread on the threshing-floor. It lives on the oxen's labor, without entering among them. But though I spend the day telling you "Write," it seems like a plague to you. Writing is very pleasant! —————.

5. All Occupations Are Bad Except That of the Scribe

See for yourself with your own eye. The occupations lie before you.⁴

The washer-man's day is going up, going down. All his limbs are weak, (from) whitening his neighbors' clothes every day, from washing their linen.

The maker of pots is smeared with soil, like one whose relations have died. His hands, his feet are full of clay; he is like one who lives in the bog.

The cobbler mingles with vats. His odor is penetrating. His hands are red with madder, like one who is smeared with blood. He looks behind him for the kite, like one whose flesh is exposed.

The watchman⁵ prepares garlands and polishes vase-stands. He spends a night of toil just as one on whom the sun shines.

---

3. An unknown word
4. All occupations except that of the scribe are derided and ridiculed through exaggerated and farcical descriptions of their hardships.
5. The word is obscure but the context suggests a man who guards and cleans the temple at night and makes it ready for the morning service.

The merchants travel downstream and upstream. They are as busy as can be, carrying goods from one town to another. They supply him who has wants. But the tax collectors carry off the gold, that most precious of metals.

The ships' crews from every house (of commerce), they receive their loads. They depart from Egypt for Syria, and each man's god is with him. (But) not one of them says: "We shall see Egypt again!"

The carpenter who is in the shipyard carries the timber and stacks it. If he gives today the output of yesterday, woe to his limbs! The shipwright stands behind him to tell him evil things.

His outworker who is in the fields, his is the toughest of all the jobs. He spends the day loaded with his tools, tied to his tool-box. When he returns home at night, he is loaded with the tool-box and the timbers, his drinking mug, and his whetstones.

The scribe, he alone, records the output of all of them. Take note of it!

6. The Misfortunes of the Peasant

Let me also expound to you the situation of the peasant, that other tough occupation. [Comes] the inundation and soaks him ——————, he attends to his equipment. By day he cuts his farming tools; by night he twists rope. Even his midday hour he spends on farm labor. He equips himself to go to the field as if he were a warrior. The dried field lies before him; he goes out to get his team. When he has been after the herdsman for many days, he gets his team and comes back with it. He makes for it a place in the field. Comes dawn, he goes to make a start and does not find it in its place. He spends three days searching for it; he finds it in the bog. He finds no hides on them; the jackals have chewed them. He comes out, his garment in his hand, to beg for himself a team.

When he reaches his field he finds (it) broken up. He spends time cultivating, and the snake is after him. It finishes off the seed as it is cast to the ground. He does not see a green blade. He does three plowings with borrowed grain. His wife has gone down to the merchants and found nothing for barter. Now the scribe lands on the shore. He surveys the harvest. Attendants are behind him with staffs, Nubians with clubs. One says (to him): "Give grain." "There is none. He is beaten savagely. He is bound, thrown in the well, submerged head down. His wife is bound in his presence. His children are in fetters. His neighbors abandon them and flee. When it's over, there's no grain.

If you have any sense, be a scribe. If you have learned about the peasant, you will not be able to be one. Take note of it!

7. Be a Scribe

The scribe of the army and commander[6] of the cattle of the house of Amun, Nebmare-nakht, speaks to the scribe Wenemdiamun, as follows. Be a scribe! Your body will be sleek; your hand

---

6. A joking alteration of the teacher's title.

will be soft. You will not flicker like a flame, like one whose body is feeble. For there is not the bone of a man in you. You are tall and thin. If you lifted a load to carry it, you would stagger, your legs would tremble. You are lacking in strength; you are weak in all your limbs; you are poor in body.

Set your sight on being a scribe; a fine profession that suits you. You call for one; a thousand answer you. You stride freely on the road. You will not be like a hired ox. You are in front of others.

I spend the day instructing you. You do not listen! Your heart is like an (empty) room. My teachings are not in it. Take their meaning to yourself!

The marsh thicket is before you each day, as a nestling is after its mother. You follow the path of pleasure; you make friends with revellers. You have made your home in the brewery, as one who thirsts for beer. You sit in the parlor with an idler.[7] You hold the writings in contempt. You visit the prostitute. Do not do these things! What are they for? They are of no use. Take note of it!

8. THE SCRIBE DOES NOT SUFFER LIKE THE SOLDIER

Furthermore. Look, I instruct you to make you sound; to make you hold the palette freely. To make you become one whom the king trusts; to make you gain entrance to treasury and granary. To make you receive the ship-load at the gate of the granary. To make you issue the offerings on feast days. You are dressed in fine clothes; you own horses. Your boat is on the river; you are supplied with attendants. You stride about inspecting. A mansion is built in your town. You have a powerful office, given you by the king. Male and female slaves are about you. Those who are in the fields grasp your hand, on plots that you have made. Look, I make you into a staff of life! Put the writings in your heart, and you will be protected from all kinds of toil. You will become a worthy official.

Do you not recall the (fate of) the unskilled man? His name is not known. He is ever burdened (like an ass carrying) in front of the scribe who knows what he is about.

Come, (let me tell) you the woes of the soldier, and how many are his superiors: the general, the troop-commander, the officer who leads, the standard-bearer, the lieutenant, the scribe, the commander of fifty, and the garrison-captain. They go in and out in the halls of the palace, saying: "Get laborers!" He is awakened at any hour. One is after him as (after) a donkey. He toils until the Aten sets in his darkness of night. He is hungry, his belly hurts; he is dead while yet alive. When he receives the grain-rations having been released from duty, it is not good for grinding.

He is called up for Syria. He may not rest. There are no clothes, no sandals. The weapons of war are assembled at the fortress of Sile. His march is uphill through mountains. He drinks water every third day; it is smelly and tastes of salt. His body is ravaged by illness. The enemy comes, surrounds him with missiles, and life recedes from him. He is told: "Quick, forward, valiant soldier! Win for yourself a good name!" He does not know what he is about. His body is weak, his

---

7. "He whose back is turned to his job."

legs fail him. When victory is won, the captives are handed over to his majesty, to be taken to Egypt. The foreign woman faints on the march; she hangs herself (on) the soldier's neck. His knapsack drops, another grabs it while he is burdened with the woman. His wife and children are in their village; he dies and does not reach it. If he comes out alive, he is worn out from marching. Be he at large, be he detained, the soldier suffers. If he leaps and joins the deserters, all his people are imprisoned. He dies on the edge of the desert, and there is none to perpetuate his name. He suffers in death as in life. A big sack is brought for him; he does not know his resting place.

Be a scribe, and be spared from soldiering! You call and one says: "Here I am." You are safe from torments. Every man seeks to raise himself up. Take note of it!

9. The Pupil Wishes to Build a Mansion for His Teacher

Furthermore. (To) the royal scribe and chief overseer of the cattle of Amen-Re, King of Gods, Nebmare-nakht. The scribe Wenemdiamun greets his lord: In life, prosperity, and health! This letter is to inform my lord. Another message to my lord. I grew into a youth at your side. You beat my back; your teaching entered my ear. I am like a pawing horse. Sleep does not enter my heart by day; nor is it upon me at night. (For I say): I will serve my lord just as a slave serves his master.

I shall build a new mansion for you (on) the ground of your town, with trees (planted) on all its sides. There are stables within it. Its barns are full of barley and emmer, wheat, cumin dates, hrw-bik, gmnn, beans, lentils, coriander, peas, seed-grain, 'dn, flax, herbs, reeds, rushes, *ybr, istpn,* dung for the winter, alfa grass, reeds, *rdmt* grass, produced by the basketful. Your herds abound in draft animals, your cows are pregnant. I will make for you five aruras of cucumber beds to the south.

10. The Teacher has Built a Mansion

Raia[8] has built a beautiful mansion; it lies opposite Edjo. He has built it on the border. It is reconstructed like a work of eternity. It is planted with trees on all sides. A channel was dug in front of it. The lapping of waves sounds in one's sleep. One does not tire of looking at it. One is gay at its door and drunk in its halls. Handsome doorposts of limestone, carved and chiseled. Beautiful doors, freshly carved. Walls inlaid with lapis lazuli.

Its barns are supplied with grain, are bulging with abundance. Fowl yard and aviary are filled with geese; byres filled with cattle. A bird pool full of geese; horses in the stable. Barges, ferryboats, and new cattle boats are moored at its quay. Young and old, the poor have come to live around it. Your provisions last; there is abundance for all who come to you.

You walk about on new lands and high lands without limit. Their grain is more abundant than the pond water that was there before. Crews land at the quay to make festive the barns with count-

---

8. Nickname of Nebmare-nakht.

less heaps for the Lord of Thebes. Its west side is a pond for snaring geese of all kinds, a resort of hunters from the very beginning. One of its ponds has more fish than a lake. Its *ḥ*-birds are like marsh birds.

Happiness dwells within. No one says, "If only!" Many stables are around it, and grazing fields for cattle. Goats abound, kids caper; the many shorthorns are lowing. There are glens rich in green plants in summer and in winter. Fish abound in their basins: bulti-fish, *sn'*-fish, *dss*-fish. The fish are more plentiful than the sands of the shore; one cannot reach the end of them.

Amun himself established it. The plantations are his in truth. You sit in their shade; you eat their fruit. Garlands are made for you of their branches; you are drunken with their wines. Boats are built for you of their pines, a chariot of their *t3g3*-trees. You flourish and prosper every day. The sustenance of Amun is with you, O Raia, chief overseer of the cattle of Amun!

11. An Encomium of the Teacher

You are nimble-handed with the censer, before the Lord of Gods at his every appearance.[9]

You are father of the god in command of the mysteries, with censer in your right, byssus in your left; the censer in your fist blesses your lord.

You are a noble priest in the House of Ptah, versed in all the mysteries in the House of the Prince.

You are the burial priest of Kamutef, chief seer of Re in Thebes, offerer of his oblations.

You are swift-footed at the Sokar-feast, drawing Egypt's people to your lord with the flail.

You are graceful with the libation vase, pouring, censing, and calling the praises.

You are nimble-handed when you circulate the offerings, foremost in calling the daily praises.

You are he who holds the Eye of Mut, mistress of heaven, on the first day of her procession in Ashru.

You are the water-pourer of Khons in Thebes, on the day of circulating offerings in the House of the Prince.

You are wise in planning, skilled in speech; farseeing at all times; what you do succeeds.

You are a judge of hearts; you resemble the Ibis; wise in all ways like the Eye and the Ear.[10]

You are the good champion of your people; your great meals overflow like Hapy.

You are rich in food, you know how to proffer it, to all whom you love, like a surging sea.

You are a magistrate who is calm, a son of praised ones; loved by all, and praised by the king.

You are a man of high standing since birth; your house overflows with foods.

You are rich in fields, your barns are full; grain clung to you on the day you were born.

You are rich in teams, your sails are bright; your barges on the deep are like jasper.

You are rich in crews skilled in rowing; their shouts please as they carry and load.

You are one weighty of counsel who weighs his answer; since birth you have loathed coarse language.

---

9. The encomium is metrically structured. Each period begins with *mntk*, "you are," and consists of two, three or four sentences or clauses.

10. Sight and hearing personified as divinities.

You are handsome in body, gracious in manner, beloved of all people as much as Hapy.

You are a man of choice words, who is skilled in saying them; all you say is right, you abhor falsehood.

You are one who sits grandly in your house; your servants answer speedily; beer is poured copiously; all who see you rejoice in good cheer.

You serve your lord, you nourish your people; whatever you say soothes the heart.

You are one who offers the beer-jug and fills the bowl; one beloved of the herdsman[11] when the offering is made.

You are one who directs the jubilees (for) his lord, one who lays the Nine Bows under his feet, one who provides for his army.

The Great Sphinx, Giza, Egypt.

---

11. Literally, "he who drives the calves," that is, the king performing a harvest ceremony.

Love Poems

13

Four manuscripts containing love poems are known. They are: *Papyrus Chester Beatty I; Papyrus Harris 500; a Turin Papyrus fragment; and a fragmentary Cairo Museum Vase.*

In their introductory titles some of the collections are called "sayings," others are called "songs." Calling them "love poems" rather than "love songs" is not meant to deny the probability that many of them were sung, but is designed to emphasize their literary origin. The freshness, immediacy, and universality of these poems should not mislead the reader into believing them to be the spontaneous outpourings of unlettered young lovers. Their style, prosody, and choice of words, all bear the stamp of deliberate, literate artistry.

The form basic to all the poems is the direct first-person speech of either a young man or a young woman. It is a monologue addressed to the speaker's own heart. In the seven stanzas of the first Chester Beatty cycle there is a regular alternation of male and female speakers. The other collections do not have this regularity. The lovers refer to each other as "brother" and "sister," these words being the normal terms of endearment in ancient Egyptian usage, just as "baby," for example, is often used in modern English to refer to a lover.

Though sophisticated in the context of their own times, the poems have the conceptual simplicity and the terseness of language that are the hallmarks of ancient Egyptian literature. That simplicity and terseness must be retained in the translations. Some recent renderings of Egyptian love poems exhibit a typically modern lush and mannered eroticism which is quite alien to the ancient Egyptian. These renderings are so unfaithful to the letter and spirit of the originals as to be undeserving of the name "translations."

From Papyrus Chester Beatty I

A Cycle of Seven Stanzas[1]

Beginning of the sayings of the great happiness

The *One,* the sister without peer,
The handsomest of all!
She looks like the rising morning star

At the start of a happy year.
Shining bright, fair of skin,
Lovely the look of her eyes,
Sweet the speech of her lips,
She has not a word too much.
Upright neck, shining breast,
Hair true lapis lazuli;
Arms surpassing gold,
Fingers like lotus buds.
Heavy thighs, narrow waist,
Her legs parade her beauty;
With graceful step she treads the ground,
Captures my heart by her movements.
She causes all men's necks
To turn about to see her;
Joy has he whom she embraces,
He is like the first of men!
When she steps outside she seems
Like that other *One*![2]

Second Stanza

My *brother* torments my heart with his voice,
He makes sickness take hold of me;
He is neighbor to my mother's house,
And I cannot go to him!
Mother is right in charging him thus:
"Give up seeing her!"
It pains my heart to think of him,
I am possessed by love of him.
Truly, he is a foolish one,
But I resemble him;
He knows not my wish to embrace him,
Or he would write to my mother.
Brother, I am promised to you
By the Gold[3] of women!

---

1. The cycle consists of seven stanzas, each headed by the word "house," which means "stanza," or, "chapter," followed by a numeral. In addition, the first line of each stanza repeats the appropriate numeral, or uses a homophone of the numeral; and the same word recurs as the final word of the stanza. Thus the first stanza begins and ends with the word "one," while the second begins and ends with the word "brother," which is a homophone of the numeral "two," and so on. The stanzas are spoken by a young man and a young woman in alternating sequence.
2. The "One" is the sun, viewed as the sole eye of heaven.
3. Hathor, patroness of love, was called "the gold" or "the golden one."

Come to me that I see your beauty,
Father, Mother will rejoice!
My people will hail you all together,
They will hail you, O my *brother*!

Third Stanza

My heart *devised* to see her beauty
While sitting down in her house;
On the way I met Mehy on his chariot,
With him were his young men.
I knew not how to avoid him:
Should I stride on to pass him?
But the river was the road,
I knew no place for my feet.
My heart, you are very foolish,
Why accost Mehy?
If I pass before him,
I tell him my movements;
Here, I'm yours, I say to him,
Then he will shout my name,
And assign me to the first. . .
Among his *followers*.[4]

Fourth Stanza

My heart flutters hastily,
When I think of my love of you;
It lets me not act sensibly,[5]
It leaps [from] its place.
It lets me not put on a dress,
Nor wrap my scarf around me;
I put no paint upon my eyes,
I'm even not anointed.
"Don't wait, go there," says it to me,
As often as I think of him;
My heart, don't act so stupidly,
Why do you play the fool?

---

4. This whole stanza is unfortunately rather obscure. It has been concluded that Mehy, spelled like the word *mhy*, "flax," is the name of a prince, but his role is enigmatic. Nor is it clear what the consequences of encountering him are, for the phrase *t3 kpyw tpy* is obscure. the speaker of the stanza is the young man, not the young woman. The final *m-ht* hardly matches the beginning *hmt*.
5. Literally, "go about like a person."

Sit still, the brother comes to you,
And many eyes as well![6]
Let not the people say of me:
"A woman fallen through love!"
Be steady when you think of him,
My heart, do not *flutter*!

Fifth Stanza

I *praise* the Golden,[7] I worship her majesty,
I extol the Lady of Heaven;
I give adoration to Hathor,
Laudations to my Mistress!
I called to her, she heard my plea,
She sent my mistress to me;
She came by herself to see me,
O great wonder that happened to me!
I was joyful, exulting, elated,
When they said: "See, she is here!"
As she came, the young men bowed,
Out of great love for her.
I make devotions to my goddess,
That she grant me my sister as gift;
Three days now[8] that I pray to her name,
Five days since she went from me!

Sixth Stanza

I *passed* before his house,
I found his door ajar;
My brother stood by his mother,
And all his brothers with him.
Love of him captures the heart
Of all who tread the path;
Splendid youth who has no peer,
Brother outstanding in virtues!
He looked at me as I passed by,
And I, by myself, rejoiced;
How my heart exulted in gladness,

---

6. I.e., many people will be watching you.
7. Ever since I found "O Golden" in the poem "Calypso's Island" by Archibald MacLeich ("She is not beautiful as you, O Golden") I think it permissible to write "golden" rather than "golden one." (Lichtheim)
8. Literally, "Three days till yesterday."

My brother, at your sight!
If only the mother knew my heart,
She would have understood by now;
O Golden, put it in her heart,
Then will I hurry to my brother!
I will kiss him before his companions,
I would not weep before them;
I would rejoice at their understanding
That you acknowledge me!
I will make a feast for my goddess,
My heart leaps to go;
To let me see my brother tonight,
O happiness in *passing*!

Seventh Stanza

Seven days since I saw my sister,
And sickness invaded me;
I am heavy in all my limbs,
My body has forsaken me.
When the physicians come to me,
My heart rejects their remedies;
The magicians are quite helpless,
My sickness is not discerned.
To tell me "She is here" would revive me!
Her name would make me rise;
Her messengers s coming and going,
That would revive my heart!
My sister is better than all prescriptions,
She does more for me than all medicines;
Her coming to me is my amulet,
The sight of her makes me well!
When she opens her eyes my body is young,
Her speaking makes me strong;
Embracing her expels my malady—
Seven days since she went from me!

FROM PAPYRUS CHESTER BEATTY I

Three Poems

I

O that you came to your sister swiftly!
Like a swift envoy of the king;
The heart of his lord frets for his message,
His heart is anxious to hear it.
All stables are held ready for him,
He has horses at the stations;
The chariot is harnessed in its place,
He may not pause on the road.
When he arrives at his sister's house,
His heart will jubilate!

II

O that you came to (your sister swiftly)!
Like a horse of the king;
Picked from a thousand steeds of all kinds,
The choicest of the stables.
It is singled out in its feed,
Its master knows its paces;
When it hears the sound of the whip,
There's no holding it back.
There's no chief of charioteers
Who could overtake it.
Sister's heart is aware:
He is not far from her!

III

O that you came to your sister swiftly,
Like a bounding gazelle in the wild;
Its feet reel, its limbs are weary,
Terror has entered its body.
A hunter pursues it with his hounds,
They do not see (it in) its dust;
It sees a resting place as a trap
It takes the river as road.
May you attain her hiding-place,
Before your hand is kissed four times;
As you pursue your sister's love,
The Golden gives her to you, my friend!

The Story of Sinuhe

The numerous, if fragmentary, copies of this work testify to its great popularity, and it is justly considered the most accomplished piece of Middle Kingdom prose literature.

The Prince, Count, Governor of the domains of the sovereign in the lands of the Asiatics, true and beloved Friend of the King, the Attendant Sinuhe, says:

I was an attendant who attended his lord, a servant of the royal harem, waiting on the Princess, the highly praised Royal Wife of King Sesostris in Khenemsut, the daughter of King Amenemhet in Kanefru, Nefru, the revered.[1]

Year 30, third month of the inundation, day 7: the god ascended to his horizon. The King of Upper and Lower Egypt, *Sehetepibre*, flew to heaven and united with the sun-disk, the divine body merging with its maker. Then the residence was hushed; hearts grieved; the great portals were shut; the courtiers were head-on-knee; the people moaned.

His majesty, however, had dispatched an army to the land of the Tjemeh, with his eldest son as its commander, the good god Sesostris. He had been sent to smite the foreign lands and to punish those of Tjehenu.[2] Now he was returning, bringing captives of the Tjehenu and cattle of all kinds beyond number. The officials of the palace sent to the western border to let the king's son know the event that had occurred at the court. The messengers met him on the road, reaching him at night. Not a moment did he delay. The falcon flew with his attendants, without letting his army know it.

But the royal sons who had been with him on this expedition had also been sent for. One of them was summoned while I was standing (there). I heard his voice, as he spoke, while I was in the near distance. My heart fluttered, my arms spread out, a trembling befell all my limbs. I removed myself in leaps, to seek a hiding place. I put myself between two bushes, so as to leave the road to its traveler.

I set out southward. I did not plan to go to the residence. I believed there would be turmoil and did not expect to survive it. I crossed Maaty near Sycamore; I reached Isle-of-Snefru.[3] I spent the day there at the edge of the cultivation. Departing at dawn I encountered a man who stood on the road. He saluted me while I was afraid of him. At dinner time I reached "Cattle-Quay." I crossed in a barge without a rudder, by the force of the westwind. I passed to the east of the quarry, at the height of "Mistress of the Red Mountain." Then I made my way northward. I reached the "Walls of the Ruler," which were made to repel the Asiatics and to crush the Sand-farers. I crouched in a bush for fear of being seen by the guard on duty upon the wall.

I set out at night. At dawn I reached Peten. I halted at "Isle-of-Kem-Wer." An attack of thirst overtook me; I was parched, my throat burned. I said, "This is the taste of death." I raised my heart and collected myself when I heard the lowing sound of cattle and saw Asiatics. One of their leaders, who had been in Egypt, recognized me. He gave me water and boiled milk for me. I went with him to his table. What they did for me was good.

Land gave me to land. I traveled to Byblos; I returned to Qedem. I spent a year and a half there. Then Ammunenshi, the ruler of Upper Retenu, took me to him, saying to me: "You will be happy with me; you will hear the language of Egypt." He said this because he knew my character and had heard of my skill, Egyptians who were with him having borne witness for me. He said to me: "Why have you come here? Has something happened at the residence ? "I said to him: "King Sehetepibre departed to the horizon, and one did not know the circumstances." But I spoke in half-truths:[4] "When I returned from the expedition to the land of the Tjemeh, it was reported to me and my heart grew faint. It carried me away on the path of flight, though I had not been talked about; no one had spat in my face; I had not heard a reproach; my name had not been heard in the mouth of the herald. I do not know what brought me to this country; it is as if planned by god. As if a Delta-man saw himself in Yebu, a marsh-man in Nubia."

Then he said to me: "How then is that land without that excellent god, fear of whom was throughout the lands like Sakhmet in a year of plague?" I said to him in reply: "Of course his son has entered into the palace, having taken his father's heritage.

He is a god without peer,
No other comes before him;
He is lord of knowledge, wise planner, skilled leader,
One goes and comes by his will.

He was the smiter of foreign lands,
While his father stayed in the palace,
He reported to him on commands carried out.

---

1. Sinuhe was specifically in the service of Princess Nefru, the wife of Sesostris I, the latter being co-regent at the time of his father's death. Khenemsut and Kanefru are the names of the pyramids of Sesostris I and Amenemhet I.
2. Tjemeh and Tjehenu designated two distinct Libyan peoples who merged in the course of time. In this story the terms are used interchangeably.
3. Sinuhe is traveling south along the edge of the western desert, until he crosses the Nile at a spot the name of which Goedicke explained as "Cattle-Quay." He landed in the vicinity of the "Red Mountain" (today's Gebel al-Ahmar), and only then did he decide to flee the country and hence turned northward.
4. Sinuhe's "half-truths" consist in pretending that the death of the old king was reported to him when in fact he had only overheard a conspiratorial message, and in disclaiming any knowledge of the circumstances.

He is a champion who acts with his arm,
A fighter who has no equal,
When seen engaged in archery,
When joining the melee.

Horn-curber who makes hands turn weak,
His foes can not close ranks;
Keen-sighted he smashes foreheads,
None can withstand his presence.

Wide-striding he smites the fleeing,
No retreat for him who turns him his back;
Steadfast in time of attack,
He makes turn back and turns not his back.

Stouthearted when he sees the mass,
He lets not slackness fill his heart;
Eager at the sight of combat,
Joyful when he works his bow.

Clasping his shield he treads under foot,
No second blow needed to kill;
None can escape his arrow,
None turn aside his bow.

The Bowmen flee before him,
As before the might of the goddess;
As he fights he plans the goal,
Unconcerned about all else.

Lord of grace, rich in kindness,
He has conquered through affection;
His city loves him more than itself,
Acclaims him more than its own god.

Men outdo women in hailing him,
Now that he is king;
Victor while yet in the egg,
Set to be ruler since his birth.

Augmenter of those born with him,
He is unique, god-given;
Happy the land that he rules!

Enlarger of frontiers
He will conquer southern lands,
While ignoring northern lands,
Though made to smite Asiatics and tread on Sand-farers!

"Send to him! Let him know your name as one who inquires while being far from his majesty. He will not fail to do good to a land that will be loyal to him."

He said to me: "Well then, Egypt is happy knowing that he is strong. But you are here. You shall stay with me. What I shall do for you is good."

He set me at the head of his children. He married me to his eldest daughter. He let me choose for myself of his land, of the best that was his, on his border with another land. It was a good land called Yaa. Figs were in it and grapes. It had more wine than water. Abundant was its honey, plentiful its oil. All kinds of fruit were on its trees. Barley was there and emmer, and no end of cattle of all kinds.

Much also came to me because of the love of me; for he had made me chief of a tribe in the best part of his land. Loaves were made for me daily, and wine as daily fare, cooked meat, roast fowl, as well as desert game. For they snared for me and laid it before me, in addition to the catch of my hounds. Many sweets were made for me, and milk dishes of all kinds.

I passed many years, my children becoming strong men, each a master of his tribe. The envoy who came north or went south to the residence stayed with me. I let everyone stay with me. I gave water to the thirsty; I showed the way to him who had strayed; I rescued him who had been robbed. When Asiatics conspired to attack the Rulers of Hill-Countries,[5] I opposed their movements. For this ruler of Retenu made me carry out numerous missions as commander of his troops. Every hill tribe against which I marched I vanquished, so that it was driven from the pasture of its wells. I plundered its cattle, carried off its families, seized their food, and killed people by my strong arm, by my bow, by my movements and my skillful plans. I won his heart and he loved me, for he recognized my valor. He set me at the head of his children, for he saw the strength of my arms.

There came a hero of Retenu,[6]
To challenge me in my tent.
A champion was he without peer,
He had subdued it all.
He said he would fight with me,
He planned to plunder me,
He meant to seize my cattle
At the behest of his tribe.

---

5. Sinuhe is on the side of the *ḥḳ3w ḫ3swt*, the "rulers of mountain-lands," the term from which the name "Hyksos" was derived.
6. In this passage Sinuhe's prose assumes the symmetrical rhythm of poetry.

The ruler conferred with me and I said: "I do not know him; I am not his ally, that I could walk about in his camp. Have I ever opened his back rooms or climbed over his fence? It is envy, because he sees me doing your commissions. I am indeed like a stray bull in a strange herd, whom the bull of the herd charges, whom the longhorn attacks. Is an inferior beloved when he becomes a superior? No Asiatic makes friends with a Delta-man. And what would make papyrus cleave to the mountain? If a bull loves combat, should a champion bull retreat for fear of being equaled? If he wishes to fight, let him declare his wish. Is there a god who does not know what he has ordained, and a man who knows how it will be?"

At night I strung my bow, sorted my arrows, practiced with my dagger, polished my weapons. When it dawned Retenu came. It had assembled its tribes; it had gathered its neighboring peoples; it was intent on this combat.

He came toward me while I waited, having placed myself near him. Every heart burned for me; the women jabbered. All hearts ached for me thinking: "Is there another champion who could fight him?" He <raised> his battle-axe and shield, while his armful of missiles fell toward me. When I had made his weapons attack me, I let his arrows pass me by without effect, one following the other. Then, when he charged me, I shot him, my arrow sticking in his neck. He screamed; he fell on his nose; I slew him with his axe. I raised my war cry over his back, while every Asiatic shouted. I gave praise to Mont, while his people mourned him. The ruler Ammunenshi took me in his arms.

Then I carried off his goods; I plundered his cattle. What he had meant to do to me I did to him. I took what was in his tent; I stripped his camp. Thus I became great, wealthy in goods, rich in herds. It was the god who acted, so as to show mercy to one with whom he had been angry, whom he had made stray abroad. For today his heart is appeased.

A fugitive fled his surroundings—[7]
I am famed at home.
A laggard lagged from hunger—
I give bread to my neighbor.
A man left his land in nakedness—
I have bright clothes, fine linen.
A man ran for lack of one to send—
I am rich in servants.
My house is fine, my dwelling spacious—
My thoughts are at the palace!

Whichever god decreed this flight, have mercy, bring me home! Surely you will let me see the place in which my heart dwells! What is more important than that my corpse be buried in the

---

7. In *Schott Festschrpft*, p. 128, Westendorf gave a new analysis and translation of this beautiful poem which climaxes the account of Sinuhe's career abroad. While it is true that the preposition *n* in all four occurrences here has the meaning "because of," to translate it thus would destroy the attempt to render the poem as a poem. The change of mood, from Sinuhe's exultation over his success to his intense longing for the lost homeland, occurs in the last distich (as Westendorf suggested), and provides the transition to the prayers for return.

land in which I was born! Come to my aid! What if the happy event should occur![8] May god pity me! May he act so as to make happy the end of one whom he punished! May his heart ache for one whom he forced to live abroad! If he is truly appeased today, may he hearken to the prayer of one far away! May he return one whom he made roam the earth to the place from which he carried him off!

May Egypt's king have mercy on me, that I may live by his mercy! May I greet the mistress of the land who is in the palace! May I hear the commands of her children! Would that my body were young again! For old age has come; feebleness has overtaken me. My eyes are heavy, my arms weak; my legs fail to follow. The heart is weary; death is near. May I be conducted to the city of eternity! May I serve the Mistress of All! May she speak well of me to her children; may she spend eternity above me![9]

Now when the majesty of King Kheperkare was told of the condition in which I was, his majesty sent word to me with royal gifts, in order to gladden the heart of this servant like that of a foreign ruler. And the royal children who were in his palace sent me their messages. Copy of the decree brought to this servant concerning his return to Egypt:

Horus: Living in Births; the Two Ladies: Living in Births; the King of Upper and Lower Egypt: *Kheperkare*; the Son of Re: *Sesostris*, who lives forever. Royal decree to the Attendant Sinuhe:

This decree of the King if brought to you to let you know: That you circled the foreign countries, going from Qedem to Retenu, land giving you to land, was the counsel of your own heart. What had you done that one should act against you? You had not cursed, so that your speech would be reproved. You had not spoken against the counsel of the nobles, that your words should have been rejected. This matter—it carried away your heart. It was not in my heart against you. This your heaven in the palace lives and prospers to this day.[10] Her head is adorned with the kingship of the land; her children are in the palace. You will store riches which they give you; you will live on their bounty. Come back to Egypt! See the residence in which you lived! Kiss the ground at the great portals, mingle with the courtiers! For today you have begun to age. You have lost a man s strength. Think of the day of burial, the passing into reveredness.

A night is made for you with ointments and wrappings from the hand of Tait. A funeral procession is made for you on the day of burial; the mummy case is of gold, its head of lapis lazuli. The sky is above you as you lie in the hearse, oxen drawing you, musicians going before you. The dance of the *mww*-dancers is done at the door of your tomb; the offering-list is read to you; sacrifice is made before your offering-stone. Your tomb-pillars, made of white stone, are among (those of) the royal children. You shall not die abroad! Not shall Asiatics inter you. You shall not be wrapped in the skin of a ram to serve as your coffin. Too long a roaming of the earth! Think of your corpse, come back!

This decree reached me while I was standing in the midst of my tribe. When it had been read to me, I threw myself on my belly. Having touched the soil, I spread it on my chest.[11] I strode around my camp shouting: "What compares with this which is done to a servant whom his heart

8. I.e., "what if death should occur while I am still abroad?"
9. In this context the "Mistress of All" could be either the queen or the goddess Nut.
10. The queen is meant.
11. A gesture of humility.

led astray to alien lands? Truly good is the kindness that saves me from death! Your *ka* will grant me to reach my end, my body being at home!"

Copy of the reply to this decree:

The servant of the Palace, Sinuhe, says: In very good peace! Regarding the matter of this flight which this servant did in his ignorance. It is your *ka*, O good god, lord of the Two Lands, which Re loves and which Mont lord of Thebes favors; and Amun lord of Thrones-of-the-Two-Lands, and Sobk-Re lord of Sumenu, and Horus, Hathor, Atum with his Ennead, and Sopdu-Neferbau-Semseru the Eastern Horus, and the Lady of Yemet—may she enfold your head—and the conclave upon the flood, and Min-Horus of the hill-countries, and Wereret lady of Punt, Nut, Haroeris-Re, and all the gods of Egypt and the isles of the sea—may they give life and joy to your nostrils, may they endue you with their bounty, may they give you eternity without limit, infinity without bounds! May the fear of you resound in lowlands and highlands, for you have subdued all that the sun encircles! This is the prayer of this servant for his lord who saves from the West.

The lord of knowledge who knows people knew in the majesty of the palace that this servant was afraid to say it. It is like a thing too great to repeat. The great god, the peer of Re, knows the heart of one who has served him willingly. This servant is in the hand of one who thinks about him. He is placed under his care. Your Majesty is the conquering Horus; your arms vanquish all lands. May then your Majesty command to have brought to you the prince of Meki from Qedem, the mountain chiefs from Keshu, and the prince of Menus from the lands of the Fenkhu. They are rulers of renown who have grown up in the love of you. I do not mention Retenu—it belongs to you like your hounds.

Lo, this flight which the servant made—I did not plan it. It was not in my heart; I did not devise it. I do not know what removed me from my place. It was like a dream. As if a Delta-man saw himself in Yebu, a marsh-man in Nubia. I was not afraid; no one ran after me. I had not heard a reproach; my name was not heard in the mouth of the herald. Yet my flesh crept, my feet hurried, my heart drove me; the god who had willed this flight dragged me away. Nor am I a haughty man. He who knows his land respects men. Re has set the fear of you throughout the land, the dread of you in every foreign country. Whether I am at the residence, whether I am in this place, it is you who covers this horizon.[12] The sun rises at your pleasure. The water in the river is drunk when you wish. The air of heaven is breathed at your bidding. This servant will hand over to the brood which this servant begot in this place. This servant has been sent for! Your Majesty will do as he wishes! One lives by the breath which you give. As Re, Horus, and Hathor love your august nose, may Mont lord of Thebes wish it to live forever!

I was allowed to spend one more day in Yaa, handing over my possessions to my children, my eldest son taking charge of my tribe; all my possessions became his—my serfs, my herds, my fruit, my fruit trees. This servant departed southward. I halted at Horusways. The commander in charge of the garrison sent a message to the residence to let it be known. Then his majesty sent a trusted overseer of the royal domains with whom were loaded ships, bearing royal gifts for the Asiatics who had come with me to escort me to Horusways. I called each one by his name, while every butler was at his task. When I had started and set sail, there was kneading and straining beside me, until I reached the city of Itj-tawy.

---

12. Or: yours is all that the horizon covers.

When it dawned, very early, they came to summon me. Ten men came and ten men went to usher me into the palace. My forehead touched the ground between the sphinxes, and the royal children stood in the gateway to meet me. The courtiers who usher through the forecourt set me on the way to the audience-hall. I found his majesty on the great throne in a kiosk of gold. Stretched out on my belly, I did not know myself before him, while this god greeted me pleasantly. I was like a man seized by darkness. My *ba* was gone, my limbs trembled; my heart was not in my body, I did not know life from death.[13]

His majesty said to one of the courtiers: "Lift him up, let him speak to me." Then his majesty said: "Now you have come, after having roamed foreign lands. Flight has taken its toll of you. You have aged, have reached old age. It is no small matter that your corpse will be interred without being escorted by Bowmen. But don't act thus, don't act thus, speechless though your name was called!" Fearful of punishment I answered with the answer of a frightened man:

"What has my lord said to me, that I might answer it? It is not disrespect to the god! It is the terror which is in my body, like that which caused the fateful flight! Here I am before you. Life is yours. May your Majesty do as he wishes!"

Then the royal daughters were brought in, and his majesty said to the queen: "Here is Sinuhe, come as an Asiatic, a product of nomads!" She uttered a very great cry, and the royal daughters shrieked all together. They said to his majesty: "Is it really he, O king, our lord?" Said his majesty: "It is really he!" Now having brought with them their necklaces, rattles, and sistra, they held them out to his majesty:[14]

Your hands upon the radiance, eternal king,
Jewels of heaven's mistress!
The Gold[15] gives life to your nostrils,
The Lady of Stars enfolds you!

Southcrown fared north, northcrown south,
Joined, united by your majesty's word.
While the Cobra decks your brow,
You deliver the poor from harm.
Peace to you from Re, Lord of Lands!
Hail to you and the Mistress of All!

Slacken your bow, lay down your arrow,
Give breath to him who gasps for breath!
Give us our good gift on this good day,
Grant us the son of northwind, Bowman born in Egypt!

---

13. I.e., he fainted.

14. The princesses hold out the emblems sacred to Hathor and perform a ceremonial dance and a song in which they beg a full pardon for Sinuhe.

15. Epithet of Hathor.

He made the flight in fear of you,
He left the land in dread of you!
A face that sees you shall not pale,
Eyes that see you shall not fear!

His majesty said: "He shall not fear, he shall not dread!" He shall be a Companion among the nobles. He shall be among the courtiers. Proceed to the robing-room to wait on him!" I left the audience-hall, the royal daughters giving me their hands. We went through the great portals, and I was put in the house of a prince. In it were luxuries: a bathroom and mirrors. In it were riches from the treasury; clothes of royal linen, myrrh, and the choice perfume of the king and of his favorite courtiers were in every room. Every servant was at his task. Years were removed from my body. I was shaved; my hair was combed. Thus was my squalor returned to the foreign land, my dress to the Sand-farers. I was clothed in fine linen; I was anointed with fine oil. I slept on a bed. I had returned the sand to those who dwell in it, the tree-oil to those who grease themselves with it.

I was given a house and garden that had belonged to a courtier. Many craftsmen rebuilt it, and all its woodwork was made anew. Meals were brought to me from the palace three times, four times a day, apart from what the royal children gave without a moment's pause.

A stone pyramid was built for me in the midst of the pyramids. The masons who build tombs constructed it. A master draughtsman designed in it. A master sculptor carved in it. The overseers of construction in the necropolis busied themselves with it. All the equipment that is placed in a tomb-shaft was supplied. Mortuary priests were given me. A funerary domain was made for me. It had fields and a garden in the right place, as is done for a Companion of the first rank. My statue was overlaid with gold, its skirt with electrum. It was his majesty who ordered it made. There is no commoner for whom the like has been done. I was in the favor of the king, until the day of landing[16] came.

Colophon: It is done from beginning to end as it was found in writing.

---

16. The day of death. Through its beginning and its ending, the story is given the form of the tomb-autobiography in which the narrator looks back on his completed life.

The Edwin Smith Surgical Papyrus

15

The Edwin Smith Surgical Papyrus is of considerable interest to the intellectual history of mankind. As noted by the translator, James H. Breasted, "Here we find the first scientific observer known to us, and in this papyrus we have the earliest known scientific document." The unknown author, who lived sometime during the Old Kingdom, has written a treatise on surgery in which he inductively draws conclusions from a body of observed facts. In seeking causes, he has separated the natural from the supernatural and is concerned only with the former. And in prescribing treatment he resorts to the use of magic in only one of the forty-eight cases described. A truly scientific attitude is further illustrated in fourteen of the cases he has classified as ailments "not to be treated" but nevertheless has fully described because of their intrinsic interest.

Cases 1 and 8 in particular highlight the remarkable scientific character of this treatise. The physician who "measures to the heart" and "its vessels" by taking the pulse (Case 1) has recognized the relation of the heart to the other parts of the body and has approached the concept of the circulation of the blood. And in Case 8 there is clear insistence that the unknown and mysterious cause of the fracture and partial paralysis in question is not to be considered supernatural ("something entering from outside" as "the breath of an outside god") but natural ("something which his flesh engenders").

The promise of this text was destined to be short-lived, however; with few exceptions, thought in ancient Egypt and in the whole ancient Near East remained in bondage to religion. It is one of the glories of the ancient Greeks that they were the first to make permanent the emancipation of thought from religion and myth.

CASE 1. A WOUND IN THE HEAD PENETRATING TO THE BONE

Examination. If thou examinest a man having a wound in his head, penetrating to the bone of his skull, but not having a gash, thou shouldst palpate his wound: shouldst thou find his skull uninjured, not having a perforation, a split, or a smash in it,

Diagnosis. Thou shouldst say regarding him: "One having a wound in his head, while his wound does not have two lips, [. . .] nor a gash, although it penetrates to the bone of his head. An ailment which I will treat."

Treatment. Thou shouldst bind it with fresh meat the first day and treat afterward with grease, honey and lint every day until he recovers.

Explanatory Gloss A. As for: "Thou examinest a man," it means counting any one [. . .] like counting things with a bushel. For examining is like one's counting a certain quantity with a bushel, or counting something with the fingers, in order to know [. . .]. It is measuring things. . . in order to know the action of the heart. There are canals in it [the heart] to every member. Now if the priests of Sekhmet or any physician put his hands or his fingers upon the head, upon the back of the head, upon the two hands, upon the pulse, upon the two feet, he measures to the heart, because its vessels are in the back of the head and in the pulse; and because its pulsation is in every vessel of every member. He says "measure" regarding his wound because of the vessels to his head and to the back of his head and to his two feet [. . .] his heart in order to recognize the indications which have arisen therein; meaning to measure it in order to know what is befalling therein.

CASE 8. COMPOUND COMMINUTED FRACTURE OF THE SKULL DISPLAYING NO VISIBLE EXTERNAL INJURY

Examination. If thou examinest a man having a smash of his skull, under the skin of his head, while there is nothing at all upon it, thou shouldst palpate his wound. Shouldst thou find that there is a swelling protruding on the outside of that smash which is in his skull, while his eye is askew because of it, on the side of him having that injury which is in his skull; and he walks shuffling with his sole, on the side of him having that injury which is in his skull,

Diagnosis. Thou shouldst distinguish him from one whom something entering from outside has smitten, but simply as one the head of whose shoulder-fork is not released, as well as one whose nails have fallen into the middle of his hand, while he discharges blood from his nostrils and his ears, and he suffers a stiffness in his neck. An ailment not to be treated.

Treatment. His treatment is sitting, until he gains color, and until thou knowest he has reached the decisive point.

Second Examination. Now as soon as thou findest that smash which is in his skull like those corrugations which form on molten copper, and something therein throbbing and fluttering under thy fingers like the weak place of an infant's crown before it knits together—when it has happened there is no throbbing and fluttering under thy fingers, until the brain of his skull is rent open—and he discharges blood from both his nostrils and both his ears, and he suffers with stiffness in his neck,

Second Diagnosis. An ailment not to be treated.

Explanatory Gloss A. As for: "A smash in his skull under the skin of his head, there being no wound at all upon it," it means a smash of the shell of his skull, the flesh of his head being uninjured.

Explanatory Gloss B. As for: "He walks shuffling with his sole," he [the surgeon] is speaking about his walking with his sole dragging, so that it is nor easy for him to walk, when it (the sole) is feeble and turned over, while the tips of his toes are contracted to the ball of his sole, and they [the toes] walk fumbling the ground. He [the surgeon] says: "He shuffles," concerning it.

Explanatory Gloss C. As for: "One whom something entering from outside has smitten" on the side of him having this injury, it means one whom something entering from outside presses, on the side of him having this injury.

Explanatory Gloss D. As for: "Something entering from outside," it means the breath of an outside god or death; not the intrusion of something which his flesh engenders.

Explanatory Gloss E. As for: "One the head of whose shoulder fork is not released, as well as one whose nails have fallen into the middle of his hand," it means that he says: "One to whom the head of his shoulder-fork is not given, and one who does not fall with his nails in the middle of his palm."

CASE 35. A FRACTURE OF THE CLAVICLE

Examination. If thou examinest a man having a break in his collar-bone, and thou shouldst find his collar-bone short and separated from its fellow,

Diagnosis. Thou shouldst say concerning him: "One having a break in his collarbone. An ailment which I will treat."

Treatment. Thou shouldst place him prostrate on his back, with something folded between his shoulder-blades; thou shouldst spread out with his two shoulders in order to stretch apart his collar-bone until that break falls into its place. Thou shouldst make for him two splints of linen, and thou shouldst apply one of them both on the inside of his upper arm and the other on the under side of his upper arm. Thou shouldst bind it with *ymrw,* and treat it afterward with honey every day, until he recovers.

An Egyptian-Hittite Treaty

During Akhenaton's preoccupation with religious reform, much of the Egyptian Empire in the Levant was lost to the Hittites. The pharaohs of the Nineteenth Dynasty to recover their former territories. Ramses II (1290–1224 B.C.) led an expedition into Palestine, resulting in a long bitter war with the Hittites in which neither side could get the upper hand. Both sides were finally, about 1270 B.C., forced to except a treaty of peace and alliance, the earliest known surviving international treaty text. The treaty is a complex one, with provisions for non-aggression, mutual aid against attack, and extradition of political fugitives. Both Hittite and Egyptian versions of the treaty exist, and it is interesting to observe that each of the rival kings, Ramses II and Hattusilis III, claims to have defeated the other in battle and, with reluctance, submits to the appeal of the other for peace. The Egyptian version, excerpted here, is blunt: Hattusilis sent messengers to "beg peace" from Ramses, "who makes his boundary where he will in every land."

Copy of the tablet of silver which the great chief of Hatti, Hattusilis, caused to be brought to Pharaoh by the hand of his messenger Tartesub and his messenger Ramose, in order to beg peace from the Majesty of Usi-ma-Re-serpen-Re, son of Re, Ramesse-mi-Amun [Ramses II]., bull of rulers, who makes his boundary where he will in every land. . . .

PEACE AND BROTHERHOOD

Behold, Hattusilis, the great chief of Hatti, has made himself in a treaty with [Ramses], the great ruler of Egypt, beginning with this day, to cause to be made good peace and good brotherhood between us forever; and he is in brotherhood with me and at peace with me, and I am in brotherhood with him and at peace with him forever.

And since Muwarttallis, the great chief of Hatti, my brother, hastened after his fate, and Hartusilis took his seat as great chief of Hatti on the throne of his father; behold I have become with Ramesse-mi-Amun, the great ruler of Egypt, we being together in our peace and our brotherhood; and it is better than the peace and the brotherhood of formerly, which was in the land.

Behold I, being the great chief of Hatti, am with Ramesse-mi-Amun, the great ruler of Egypt, in good peace and good brotherhood.

And the children of the children of the great chief of Hatti shall be in brotherhood and at peace with the children of the children of Ramesse-mi-Amun, the great ruler of Egypt; they being in our policy of brotherhood and our policy of peace.

And the land of Egypt with the land Hatti shall be at peace and in brotherhood like us forever; and hostilities shall not be made between them forever.

Mutual Nonaggression

And the great chief of Hatti shall not trespass into the land of Egypt forever to take aught from it; and [Ramses], the great ruler of Egypt, shall not trespass into the land of Hatti to take aught from it forever. . .

Temple of Ramses II, Abu Simbel, Egypt.

Mutual Defense

And if another enemy come to the lands of [Ramses], the great ruler of Egypt, and he send to the great chief of Hatti saying, "Come with me as help against him"; the great chief of Hatti shall come to him, the great chief of Hatti shall slay his enemy.

But if it be not the desire of the great chief of Hatti to come, he shall send his troops and his chariotry and shall slay his enemy.

Or if Ramesse-mi-Amun, the great ruler of Egypt, become incensed against servants of his, and they do another offense against him, and he go to slay his enemy; the great chief of Hatti shall act with him to destroy everyone against whom they shall be incensed. . . .

Extradition of Fugitives

If any great man flee from the land of Egypt and he come to the lands of the great chief of Hatti; or a town or a district. . . belonging to the lands of Ramessemi-Amun, the great ruler of Egypt, and they come to the great chief of Hatti: the great chief of Hatti shall not receive them. The great chief of Hatti shall cause them to be brought to [Ramses], the great ruler of Egypt, their lord, on account of it.

Or if one [common] man or two men who are unknown flee . . . and they come to the land of Hatti, they shall be brought to Ramesse-mi-Amun, the great ruler of Egypt. . . .

Divine Witnesses

As for these words of the treaty made by the great chief of Hatti with Ramesse-mi-Amun, the great ruler of Egypt, in writing upon this tablet of silver; as for these words, a thousand gods, male gods and female gods of those of the land of Hatti, together with a thousand gods, male gods and female gods of those of the land of Egypt—they are with me as witnesses hearing these words. . .

As to these words which are upon this tablet of silver of the land of Hatti and of the land of Egypt, as to him who shall not keep them, a thousand gods of the land of Hatti and a thousand gods of the land of Egypt shall destroy his house, his land and his servants. But he who shall keep these words which are on this tablet of silver, be they Hatti, or be they Egyptians, and who do not neglect them, a thousand gods of the land of Hatti and a thousand gods of the land of Egypt will cause him to be healthy and to live, together with his houses and his land and his servants.

Chapter 3

Ancient Greece

The Erechtheum Temple, Acropolis, Athens, Greece.

Herodotus: The Persian Invasion of Greece 17

The Greeks, of course, invented history. Herodotus (ca 484–ca 425 B.C.) of Halicarnassus, a city on the coast of Asia Minor, has been quite correctly awarded the title "the father of history." He wrote the world's first history, which he defined as an "honest attempt to find out what happened, then to explain why it happened." He wrote an account of the Persian War, the conflict between the small disunited Greek city-states and the wealthy, powerful Persian Empire. Herodotus tried to control his mass of accumulated data concerning the subject through personal investigation and rational analysis. He traveled to all the areas about which he wrote and personally consulted the royal achieves of Assyria, Persia and Egypt for material covering at least the previous 150 years or so. He also drew on the memories of those who had participated in the war.

The unifying theme of Herodotus' History is the timeless conflict between East and West, which began with the Trojan War, and seems as relevant today as it did 2,500 years ago. Herodotus constructed his historical narrative from smaller narratives and summaries of events which are often peripheral to his main subject. He was also a consummate story teller, sometimes incorporating mythology and legend into his history as fact. Moreover, at times he exaggerated: for example, he said that Xerxes' invasion force consisted of 2,317,610 men and 1,207 warships, which supported his purpose to insure "that the great and noble actions of the Greeks and Asiatics may not lose their fame." In addition, these huge figures support Herodotus' view of causality in history and point toward his explanation of how a few Greek city-states were able to defeat the powerful Persian Empire that stretched across 3,000 miles and commanded the resources of forty-six nations. His answer was hubris, or over-blown pride, a concept the Greeks understood well. "God tolerates pride in none but himself."

The selections below are from book 7 of Herodotus' History and begin with a description of the preparations of the Persians and the Greeks for war and end with the Battle of Thermopylae, where a small Greek force of 7,000 men met defeat.

From *Herodotus*, translated by A.D. Godley. (Cambridge, Loeb Classical Library, Harvard University Press, 1922).

8. After the conquest of Egypt, purposing now to take in hand the expedition against Athens, Xerxes held an assembly of the noblest among the Persians, convened with special intent, that he might learn their opinions and himself declare his will before them all. When they were assembled, Xerxes spoke to them as follows: "Persians! this is no new law of my bringing in and ordaining, but one that I have received and will obey. As I learn from our eldest, we have never yet remained at peace ever since Cyrus deposed Astyages and we won this our lordship from the Medes. It is the will of heaven; and we ourselves win advantage by our many enterprises. Now of the nations that Cyrus and Cambyses and Darius my father subdued and added to our realm, none need tell you; for well you know them. But for myself, ever since I came to this throne, I have taken thought how best I shall not fall short in this honorable place of those that were before me, nor gain for the Persians a lesser power than they; and my thought persuades me, that we may win not only renown, but a land neither less nor worse, but more fertile, than that which we now possess; and not only so, but vengeance and requital withal. For this cause I have now summoned you together, that I may impart to you my purpose. It is my intent to bridge the Hellespont and lead my army through Europe to Hellas, that I may punish the Athenians for what they have done to the Persians and to my father. You saw that Darius my father was minded to make an expedition against these men. But he is dead, and it was not granted him to punish them; and I, on his and all the Persians' behalf, will never rest till I have taken and burnt Athens, for the unprovoked wrong that its people did to my father and me; first they came to Sardis with our slave Aristagoras the Milesian, and burnt the groves and the temples; and next, how they dealt with us when we landed on their shores and Datis and Artaphrenes were our generals, all of you, I think, know. For these causes then I am resolved to send an army against them; and thus much advantage, as my reckoning shows me, we shall gain thereby: if we subdue those men, and their neighbors who dwell in the land of Pelops the Phrygian, we shall make the borders of Persian territory and of the firmament of heaven to be the same; for no land that the sun beholds will lie on our borders, but I will make all to be one country, when I have passed over the whole of Europe. For, as I learn, there will then be left neither inhabited city, nor nation of men, that is able to meet us in battle, if those of whom I speak are once taken out of our way. Thus they that have done us wrong and they that have done us none will alike bear the yoke of slavery. As for you, this is how you shall best please me: when I declare the time for your coming, every one of you must appear, and with a good will; and whosoever comes with his army best equipped shall receive from me such gifts as are reckoned most precious among us. All this, then, must so be done; but that none may think that I take counsel of myself alone, I lay the matter before you all, and bid him who will to declare his opinion." So spoke Xerxes, and ceased.

9. After him spoke Mardonius, and said: "Sire, you surpass not only all Persians that have been but also all that shall be; for besides that you have dealt excellently and truly with all other matters, you will not suffer the Ionians[1] that dwell in Europe to make a mock of us, which they have no right to do. For it were strange indeed, that we, who have subdued and made slaves of Sacae and Indians and Ethiopians and Assyrians and many other great nations, for no wrong done to the Persians but of mere desire to add to our power—that we, I say, shall not take vengeance on the Greeks for unprovoked wrong-doing. What have we to fear from them? Have they mighty

---

1. To the Persians all Greeks were "Ionians."

hosts or abundance of wealth to affright us? Their manner of fighting we know, and their wealth we know, that it is but little and we have conquered and hold their sons, even those who dwell in our land and are called Ionians and Aeolians and Dorians. I myself have tried conclusions with these men, when by your father's command I marched against them; and I marched as far as Macedonia and well-nigh to Athens itself, yet none came out to meet me in battle. Yet wars the Greeks do wage, and, as I learn, most senselessly they do it, in their wrong-headedness and folly. When they have declared war against each other, they come down to the fairest and most level ground that they can find and there they fight, so that the victors come not off without great harm; and of the vanquished I say not so much as a word, for they are utterly destroyed. Yet speaking as they do the same language, they should end their disputes by the means of heralds and messengers, and by any way rather than fighting; or if needs must that they war against each other, they should discover each where his strongest defense lies, and there make his essay. The Greek custom, then, is no good one; and when I marched as far as the land of Macedonia, it came not into their thoughts to fight. But against you, O king! who shall make war? For you will have at your back the multitudes of Asia, and all your ships; for myself, I think there is not so much boldness in Hellas as that; but if time should show me wrong in my judgment, and those men were foolhardy enough to do battle with us, they would be taught that we are the greatest warriors no earth. But whatsoever betide, let us be ever venturesome; for naught comes of itself, and all men's gains are the fruit of adventure."

10. Thus smoothly Mardonius spoke of Xerxes' opinion, and made an end. The rest of the Persians held their peace, not daring to utter any counsel contrary to that which had been given; then spoke Artabanus the son of Hystaspes, who was the king's uncle, and emboldened thereby. "O king," he said, "if opinions opposite the one to the other be not uttered, it is not possible that choice should find the better, but that one which has been spoken must be followed; but if they be spoken, the better can be found; even as the purity of gold cannot of itself be discerned, but when gold by rubbing is compared with gold,[2] we then discern the better. Now I forbade Darius, your father and my brother, to lead his army against the Scythians, who have no cities anywhere to dwell in. But he, in his hope to subdue the nomad Scythians, would not be guided by me; he led his army, and returned from that expedition with the loss of many gallant men of his host. You, O king! are purposing to lead your armies against men far better than the Scythians—men who are said to be most doughty warriors by sea and land; and it is right that I should show to you what danger lies therein. You will bridge the Hellespont (so you say) and march your army through Europe to Hellas. Now I will suppose that matters have so fallen out that you are worsted either by land or by sea, or even both; for the men are said to be valiant, and well may we guess that it is so, seeing that so great a host, that followed Datis and Artaphrenes to Attica, was destroyed by the Athenians alone.[3] Be it, then, granted that they win not success both by sea and by land; but if they attack with their ships and prevail in a sea-fight, and then sail to the Hellespont and thereafter break your bridge, that, O king, is the hour of peril. It is from no wisdom of my own that I thus conjecture; it is because I know what disaster was that which well-nigh once overtook us, when your father, making a highway over the Thracian Bosporus, and bridging the river

---

2. I.e. rubbing against the touchstone, which would be stained by pure gold.
3. Artabanus here, of course, refers to the Battle of Marathon, 490 B.C.

Ister, crossed over to attack the Scythians. At that time the Scythians used every means of entreating the Ionians, who had been charged to guard the bridges of the Ister, to break the way of passage; and then, if Histiaeus the despot of Miletus had consented to the opinion of the other despots and not withstood it, the power of Persia had perished. Yet it were a thing of dread even in the telling, that one, and he but a man, should hold in his hand all the king's fortunes. Do you then make no plan to run into any such danger, when there is no need therefor, but be ruled by me: for the nonce, dismiss this assembly; and presently, whenever you so please, having first considered the matter by yourself, declare what seems to you best. A well-laid plan is ever to my mind most profitable; for even though it be thwarted later, yet none the less has the plan been good, and it is but chance that has baffled the design; but he that has made a sorry plan has gotten, if fortune favor him, but a chance prize, and none the less has his plan been evil. You see how the god smites with his thunderbolt creatures of greatness more than common, nor suffers them to display their pride, but such as are little move him not to anger; and you see how it is ever on the tallest buildings and trees that his bolts fall; for it is heaven's way to bring low all things of surpassing bigness. Thus a numerous host is destroyed by one that is lesser, the god of his jealousy sending panic fear or thunderbolt among them, whereby they do unworthily perish; for the god suffers pride in none but himself. Now haste is ever the parent of failure, whereof grievous hurts are apt to come; but in waiting there is good, which in due time shall appear, though in the present it seem not so. This, O king, is my counsel to you. But to you I say, Mardonius son of Gobryas! cease from foolish speaking about the Greeks, for they deserve not to be maligned. It is by speaking calumniously of the Greeks that you would hearten the king to send this expedition; and that, methinks, is the end to which you press with all eagerness. Nay, let it not be so. Calumny is a very gross business; there are two in it that do and one that suffers wrong. He that utters the calumny wrongs another, accusing an absent man, and the other does a wrong likewise in that he is over persuaded before he has learnt the whole truth; and he that is absent and hears not what is said of him suffers wrong in the matter, being maligned by the one and condemned by the other. Nay, if an army must by all means be sent against these Greeks, hear me now: Let the king himself abide in the Persian land, and let us two stake our children's lives upon it; then do you lead out the army, choosing what men you will and taking as great an armament as you desire; and if it fare with the king's fortunes as you say it will, let my sons be slain, and myself too with them; but if the issue be as I foretell, let your sons be so treated, and you likewise, if you return. But if you will not submit yourself to this, and will at all hazards lead your army overseas to Hellas, then I think that they who are left behind in this place will hear that Mardonius has wrought great harm to Persia, and is torn asunder by dogs and birds in the land of Athens or of Lacedaemon, if not peradventure ere that on the way thither; and that thus you have learnt what manner of men are they whom you would persuade the king to attack."

11. Thus spoke Artabanus. But Xerxes answered in wrath, "Artabanus, you are my father's brother; that shall save you from receiving the fit reward of foolish words. Yet for your craven lack of spirit I lay upon you this disgrace, that you shall not go with me and my army against Hellas, but abide here with the women; and I myself will accomplish all that I have said, with no help from you. . . ."

19. After this Xerxes, being now intent on the expedition, saw yet a third vision in his sleep, which the Magians[4] interpreted to have regard to the whole earth and to signify that all men should be his slaves. This was the vision: Xerxes thought that he was crowned with an olive bough, the shoots of which spread over the whole earth, and presently the Crown vanished from off his head where it was set. This the Magians interpreted; and of the Persians who had been assembled, every man forthwith rode away to his own governorship and there used all zeal to fulfill the king's behest, each desiring to receive the promised gifts; and thus it was that Xerxes dealt with the mustering of his army, searching out every part of the continent.

20. For full four years[5] from the conquest of Egypt he was equipping his host and preparing all that was needful therefor; and ere the fifth year was completed he set forth on his march with the might of a great multitude. Of all armaments whereof we have knowledge this was by much the greatest, insomuch that none were aught in comparison of it, neither the armament that Darius led against the Scytluians, . . . nor in so far as report tells—the armament led by the sons of Atreus against Troy. . . .

21. All these armaments and whatsoever others have ever been could not together be compared with this single one. For what nation did not Xerxes lead from Asia against Hellas? What water did not fall short of the needs of his host, save only the great rivers? Some supplied him with ships, some were enrolled in his infantry, some were charged with the provision of horsemen, others of horse-bearing transports to follow the army, and others again of warships for the bridges, or of food and ships.

33. After this he prepared to march to Abydos; and meanwhile his men were bridging the Hellespont from Asia to Europe. On the Chersonese which is by the Hellespont here is between the town of Sestus and Madytus a broad head land running out into the sea over against Abydos. . . .[6]

34. Beginning then from Abydos they whose business it was made bridges across to that headland, the Phoenicians one of flaxen cables, and the Egyptians the second, which was of papyrus. From Abydos to the opposite shore it is a distance of seven furlongs.[7] But no sooner had the strait been bridged than a great storm swept down and brake and scattered all that work.

35. When Xerxes heard of that, he was very angry, and gave command that the Hellespont be scourged with three hundred lashes, and a pair of fetters be thrown into the sea; nay, I have heard ere now that he sent branders with the rest to brand the Hellespont. This is certain, that he charged them while they scourged to utter words outlandish and presumptuous: "Thou bitter water," they should say, "our master thus punishes thee, because thou didst him wrong albeit he had done thee none. Yea, Xerxes the king will pass over thee, whether thou wilt or no; it is but just that no man offers thee sacrifice, for thou art a turbid and a briny river." Thus he commanded that the sea should be punished, and that they who had been overseers of the bridging of the Hellespont should be beheaded.

---

4. The hereditary priestly class of the Medes and Persians.

5. 484–481 B.C.

6. Between the modern bays of Zemenik (Sestos) and Kilia: some four miles broad.

7. The modern distence is half as much again, which perhaps can be explained by the erosion of the coasts, due to a current which strikes them near Sestos and rebounds on Abydos.

36. So this was done by those who were appointed to that thankless honor; and new masters of their craft set about making the bridges. The manner of their doing it was as I will show. That they might lighten the strain of the cables, they laid fifty-oared ships and triremes alongside of each other, three hundred and sixty to bear the bridge that was nearest to the Euxine sea, and three hundred and fourteen to bear the other; all lay obliquely to the line of the Pontus and parallel with the current of the Hellespont. Having so laid the ships alongside they let down very great anchors, both from the end of the ship nearest the Pontus to hold fast against the winds blowing from within that sea, and from the other end, towards the west and the Aegean, to hold against the west and south winds. Moreover they left for passage an opening in the line of fifty-oared ships and triremes, that so he that would might be able to voyage to the Pontus, or out of it. Having so done, they stretched the cables from the land, twisting them taut with wooden windlasses; and they did not as before keep the two kinds apart, but assigned for each bridge two cables of flax and four of papyrus. All these were of the same thickness and fair appearance, but the flaxen were heavier in their proportion, a cubit thereof weighing a talent.[8] When the strait was thus bridged, they sawed balks of wood to a length equal to the breadth of the floating supports[9], and laid them in order on the taut cables, and having set them alongside they then made them fast. This done, they heaped brushwood on to the bridge, and when this was all laid in order they heaped earth on it and stamped it down; then they made a fence on either side, lest the beasts of burden and horses should be frightened by the sight of the sea below them.

37. When the bridges and the work at Athos were ready, and the moles at the canal's entrances, that were built to prevent the surf from silting up the entrances of the dug passage, and the canal itself was reported to be now perfectly made, the army then wintered, and at the beginning of spring[10] was ready and set forth from Sardis to march to Abydos. When they had set forth, the sun left his place in the heaven and was unseen, albeit the sky was without clouds and very clear, and the day was turned into night. When Xerxes saw and took note of that, he was moved to think upon it, and asked the Magians what the vision might signify. They declared to him, that the god was showing to the Greeks the desolation of their cities; for the sun (they said) was the prophet of the Greeks, as the moon was theirs. Xerxes rejoiced exceedingly to hear that, and kept on his march.

44. When Xerxes had come to the midst of Abydos, he desired to see the whole of his army; and this he could do, for a lofty seat of white stone had been set up for him on a hill[11] there with that intent, built by the people of Abydos at the king's command. There Xerxes sat, and looked down on the sea-shore, viewing his army and his fleet; and as he viewed them he was fain to see the ships contend in a race. They did so, and the Phoenicians of Sidon won it; and Xerxes was pleased with the race, and with his armament.

45. But when he saw the whole Hellespont hidden by his ships, and all the shores and plains of Abydos thronged with men, Xerxes first declared himself happy, and presently he fell a-weeping.

---

8. About 80 pounds.
9. I.e. the line of ships supporting the cables.
10. Probably about the middle of April, 480 B.C.
11. Probably what is called Mal-Tepe, on the promontory of Nagara.

46. Perceiving that, his uncle Artabanus, who in the beginning had spoken his mind freely and counseled Xerxes not to march against Hellas—Artabanus, I say, marking how Xerxes wept, questioned him and said, "What a distance is there, O king, between your acts of this present and a little while ago: Then you declared your happiness, and now you weep." "Ay verily," said Xerxes; "for I was moved to compassion, when I considered the shortness of all human life, seeing that of all this multitude of men not one will be alive a hundred years hence." "In our life," Artabanus answered, "we have deeper sorrows to bear than that. For short as our lives are, there is no man here or elsewhere so fortunate, that he shall not be constrained, ay many a time and not once only, to wish himself dead rather than alive. Misfortunes so fall upon us and sicknesses so trouble us, that they make life to seem long for all its shortness. Thus is life so sorry a thing that death has come to be a man s most desirable refuge therefrom; the god is seen to be envious therein, after he has given us but a taste of the sweetness of living."

56. Having passed over to Europe, Xerxes viewed his army crossing under the lash; seven days and seven nights it was in crossing, with never a rest. There is a tale that, when Xerxes had now crossed the Hellespont, a man of the Hellespont cried, "O Zeus, why hast thou taken the likeness of a Persian man and changed thy name to Xerxes, leading the whole world with thee to remove Hellas from its place? For that thou mightest have done without these means."

60. What the number of each part of it was I cannot with exactness say; for there is no one who tells us that; but the tale of the whole land army was shown to be a million and seven hundred thousand. The numbering was on this wise—Ten thousand men were collected in one place, and when they were packed together as closely as might be a line was drawn round them; this being drawn, the ten thousand were sent away, and a wall of stones built on the line reaching up to a man's middle; which done, others were brought into the walled space, till in this way all were numbered. . . .

100. When his host had been numbered and marshaled, Xerxes had a desire to ride through and view it. This he presently did; riding in a chariot past the men of each nation, he questioned them, and his scribes wrote all down, till he had gone from end to end of the horse and foot. This done, and the ships being drawn down and launched in the sea, Xerxes alighted from his chariot into a ship of Sidon, sitting wherein under a golden canopy he was carried past the prows of the ships, questioning of them in like manner as of the army and making the answers to be written down. The captains put out as far as four hundred feet from the shore, and there kept the ships anchored in a line, their prows turned landward, and the fighting men on them armed as for war; Xerxes viewed them, passing between the prows and the land.

101. Having passed by all his fleet likewise and disembarked from his ship, he sent for Demaratus[12] son of Ariston, who was marching with him against Hellas, and called and questioned him, saying: "Now, Demaratus, it is my pleasure to ask you what I would fain know. You are a Greek, and, as I am told by you and the other Greeks that converse with me, a man of not the least nor the weakest of Greek cities. Now therefore tell me this: will the Greeks offer me battle and abide my coming? For to my thinking, even if all the Greeks and all the men of the western lands were assembled together, they are not of power to abide my attack, if they be not in

---

12. The exiled king of Sparta.

accord. Nevertheless I would fain learn your mind and hear what you say of them." To this question Demaralus made answer, "O king, must I speak truly, or so as to please you?" Xerxes bade him speak the truth, and said that he would lose none of the king's favor thereby.

102. Hearing that, "O king," said Demaratus, "seeing that you bid me by all means speak the whole truth, and say that which you shall not afterwards prove to be false—in Hellas poverty is ever native to the soil, but courage comes of their own seeking, the fruit of wisdom and strong law; by use of courage Hellas defends herself from poverty and tyranny. Now I say naught but good of all Greeks that dwell in those Dorian lands; yet it is not of all that I would now speak, but only of the Lacedaemonians; and this I say of them; firstly, that they will never accept conditions from you that import the enslaving of Hellas; and secondly, that they will meet you in battle, yea, even though all the rest of the Greeks be on your side. But, for the number of them, ask me not how many these men are, who are like to do as I say; be it of a thousand men, or of more or of fewer than that, their army will fight with you."

103. Hearing that, Xerxes smiled, and said, "A strange saying., Demaratus! that a thousand men should fight with a host so great as mine! I pray you tell me this: you were (you say) these men's king: will you consent at this present to fight with ten men? Yet if the order of your state be such as you define it to be,[13] you, being their king should rightly encounter twice as many according to your laws; for if each of those Greeks is a match for ten men of my army, then it is plain to me that you must be a match for twenty. That were a proof that what you say is true; but if you Greeks who so exalt yourselves are like in stature and all else to yourself and those of your nation who have audience of me, then beware lest the words you have spoken be but idle boasting. Nay, let us look at it by plain reason's light; how should a thousand, or ten thousand, or even fifty thousand, if they be all alike free and not under the rule of one man, withstand so great a host as mine? For grant your Greeks to be five thousand, we should so be more than a thousand to one. For, were they under the rule of one according to our custom, they might from fear of him show a valor greater than natural, and under compulsion of the lash might encounter odds in the field; but neither of these would they do while they were suffered to be free. For myself, I think that even were they equal in numbers it would go hard with the Greeks to fight against the Persians alone. Not so; it is we alone and none others that have this skill whereof you speak, yet even of us not many but a few only; there are some among my Persian spear-men that will gladly fight with three Greeks at once; of this you have no knowledge and do but utter arrant folly.

104. To this Demaratus answered, "O king, I knew from the first that the truth would be unwelcome to you. But since you constrained me to speak as truly as I could, I have told you how it stands with the Spartans. Yet you yourself best know what love I bear them—men that have robbed me of my honorable office and the prerogative of my house, and made me a cityless exile; then it was your father that received me and gave me dwelling and livelihood. It is not then to be thought that a right-minded man will reject from him plain good will, but rather that he will requite it with full affection. But for myself; I will not promise that I can fight with ten men, no, nor with two, and of my own will I would not even fight with one; yet under stress of necessity, or of some great issue to spur me on, I would most gladly fight with one of those men who claim to be each a match for three Greeks. So is it with the Lacedaemonians; fighting singly they are as

---

13. This no doubt alludes to the double portion given to a Spartan king at feasts.

brave as any man living, and together they are the best warriors on earth. Free they are, yet not wholly free; for law is their master, whom they fear much more than your men fear you. This is my proof—what their law bids them, that they do; and its bidding is ever the same, that they must never flee from the battle before whatsoever odds, but abide at their post and there conquer or die. If this that I say seems to you but foolishness, then let me hereafter hold my peace; it is under constraint that I have now spoken. But may your wish, O king! be fulfilled."

105. Thus Demaratus answered; Xerxes made a jest of the matter and showed no anger, but sent him away with all kindness. Having thus conversed with Demaratus, and having appointed Mascames son of Megadostes his viceroy of that same Doriscus, deposing him whom Darius had set there, Xerxes marched his army through Thrace towards Hellas.

131. Xerxes delayed for many days in the parts of Pieria; for a third part of his army was clearing a road over the Macedonian mountains, that all the army might pass by that way to the Perrhaebian country; and now returned the heralds who had been sent to Hellas to demand earth, some empty-handed, some bearing earth and water.

132. Among those who paid that tribute were the Thessalians, Dolopes, Enienes, Perrhaebians, Locrians, Magnesians, Melians, Achaeans of Phthia, Thebans, and all the Boeotians except the men of Thespiae and Plataea. Against all of these the Greeks who declared war with the foreigner entered into a sworn agreement, which was this: that if they should be victorious they would dedicate to the god of Delphi a tithe of the possessions of all Greeks who had of free will surrendered themselves to the Persians. Such was the agreement sworn by the Greeks.

133. But to Athens and Sparta Xerxes sent no heralds to demand earth, and this was the reason: when Darius had before sent men with this same purpose, the demanders were cast at the one city into the Pit[14] and at the other into a well, and bidden to carry thence earth and water to the king. For this cause Xerxes sent no demand. What calamity befell the Athenians for thus dealing with the heralds I cannot say, save that their land and their city was laid waste; but I think that there was another reason for this, and not the aforesaid.[15]

138. The professed intent of the king's march was to attack Athens, but in truth all Hellas was his aim. This the Greeks had long since learnt, but not all of them regarded the matter alike. Those of them that had paid tribute of earth and water to the Persian were of good courage, thinking that the foreigner would do them no harm; but they who had refused tribute were sore afraid, since there were not in Hellas ships enough to do battle with their invader, and the greater part of them had no stomach for grappling with the war, but were making haste to side with the Persian.

139. Here I am constrained perforce to declare an opinion which will be displeasing to most; but I will not refrain from uttering what seems to me to be true. Had the Athenians been panic-struck by the threatened peril and left their own country, or had they not indeed left it but remained and surrendered themselves to Xerxes, none would have essayed to withstand the king by sea. If, then, no man had withstood him by sea, I will show what would have happened by land: though the Peloponnesians had built not one but many walls across the Isthmus for their armor, yet the Lacedaemonians would have been deserted by their allies (these having no choice or free will in the matter, but seeing their cities taken one by one by the foreign fleet), till at last they would

14. Into which criminals condemned to death were thrown.
15. Possibly the burning of the temple at Sardis.

have stood alone; and so standing they would have fought a great fight and nobly perished. Such would have been their fate; or it may be that, when they saw the rest of Hellas siding with the enemy, they would have made terms with Xerxes; and thus either way Hellas would have been subdued by the Persians. For I cannot perceive what advantage could accrue from the walls built across the isthmus, while the king was master of the seas. But as it is, to say that the Athenians were the saviors: of Hellas is to hit the truth. For whichever part they took, that way the balance was like to incline; and by choosing that Hellas should remain free they and none others roused all the rest of the Greeks who had not gone over to the Persians, and did under heaven beat the king off. Nor were they moved to desert Hellas by the threatening oracles that came from Delphi and sorely dismayed them, but they stood firm and were bold to abide the invader of their country.

145. . . .All the Greeks that had the better purpose for Hellas now assembling themselves together and there taking counsel and plighting faith, they resolved in debate to make an end of all their feuds and their wars against each other, from whatever cause arising; and among others that were afoot the greatest was the war between the Athenians and the Aeginetans. Presently, learning that Xerxes was at Sardis with his army, they planned to send men into Asia to spy out the king's doings, and to dispatch messengers, some to Argos, who should make the Argives their brothers in arms against the Persian, some to Gelon son of Dinomenes in Sicily, some to Corcyra, praying aid for Hellas, and some to Crete; for they hoped that since the danger threatened all Greeks alike, all of Greek blood might unite and work jointly for one common end. . . .

146. Being so resolved, and having composed their quarrels, they first sent three men as spies into Asia. These came to Sardis, and took note of the king's army; but they were discovered, and after examination by the generals of the land army they were led away for execution. So they were condemned to die; but when Xerxes heard of it he blamed the judgment of his generals, and sent some of his guards, charging them if they found the spies alive to bring them before him. They were found still living and brought into the king's presence; then Xerxes, having enquired of them the purpose of their coming, bade his guards lead them about and show them all his army, horse and foot; and when the spies should have seen all to their hearts' content, send them away unharmed whithersoever they would go.

147. The reason alleged for his command was this: had the spies been put to death, the Greeks would not so soon have learnt the unspeakable greatness of his power, and the Persians would have done their enemy no great harm by putting three men to death; "but if they return to Hellas," said he, "methinks when the Greeks hear of my power they will before the expedition surrender this peculiar freedom that they have, and so we need not be at pains to march against them." This was like that other saying of Xerxes', when he was at Abydos and saw ships laden with corn sailing out of the Pontus through the Hellespont, voyaging to Aegina and the Peloponnese. They that sat by him, perceiving that they were enemy ships, were for taking them, and looked to the king for him to give the word. But Xerxes asked them whither the ships were sailing; "to your enemies, Sire," said they, "carrying corn." Whereto Xerxes answered, "And are not we too sailing to the same places as they, with corn among all our other provisions? What wrong are they doing us in carrying food thither?"

175. Being come to the Isthmus, the Greeks consulted together how and where they should stand to fight, having regard to what was said by Alexander. The counsel that prevailed was, that

they should guard the pass of Thermopylae; for they saw that it was narrower than the pass into Thessaly and moreover nearer home; and for the path which brought about the fall of those Greeks who fell at Thermopylae, they knew not even that there was one till they came to Thermopylae and learnt of it from the men of Trachis. This pass then they were resolved to guard, and so stay the foreigners' passage into Hellas, while their fleet should sail to Artemisium in the territory of Histiaea. These places are near together, so that each force could be informed of the other's doings; and their nature is as I will now show.

184. Until the whole host reached this place and Thermopylae it suffered no hurt; and calculation proves to me that its numbers were still such as I will now show. The ships from Asia being twelve hundred and seven, the whole multitude of all the nations, which was in them from the first, was two hundred and forty-one thousand and four hundred men, two hundred being reckoned for each ship.[16] On board of all these ships were thirty fighting men of the Persians and Medes and Sacae, over and above the company which each had of native fighters; the sum of this added multitude is thirty-six thousand, two hundred and ten. But to this and to the first number I add the crews of the ships of fifty oars, reckoning each at eighty men, be they more or fewer. Now seeing that, as has already been said, there were collected three thousand of these craft,[17] the number of men in them must be on that showing two hundred and forty thousand. These then were the ship's companies from Asia, and the total sum of them was five hundred and seventeen thousand, six hundred and ten. The footmen were shown to be seven hundred thousand and one hundred in number, and the horsemen eighty thousand; to whom I add the Arabian camel-riders and Libyan charioteers, reckoning them at twenty thousand men. Thus if the forces of sea and land be added together their total sum will be two millions, three hundred and seventeen thousand, six hundred and ten. Thus far I have spoken of the armament that came from Asia itself, without the service-train that followed it and the corn-bearing craft and the companies thereof.

201. King Xerxes, then, lay encamped in that part of Malis which belongs to Trachis, and the Greeks in the midst of the pass: the place where they were is called by most of the Greeks Thermopylae, but by the people of the country and their neighbors Pylae. In these places, then, they lay encamped, Xerxes being master of all that was north[18] Trachis, and the Greeks of all that lay southward towards this part of the mainland.[19]

202. The Greeks that awaited the Persian in that place were these:—Of the Spartans, three hundred men-at-arms; a thousand Tegeans and Mantineans, half from each place; from Orchomenus in Arcadia a hundred and twenty, and a thousand from the rest of Arcadia; besides these Arcadians, four hundred from Corinth, two hundred from Phlius, and eighty Mycenaeans. These were they who had come from Peloponnesus: from Boeotia, seven hundred Thespians and four hundred Thebans.

203. Besides these the whole power of the Opuntian Locrians and a thousand Phocians had been summoned, and came. The Greeks had of their own motion summoned these to their aid, telling them by their messengers that they themselves had come for an advance guard of the rest,

---

16. 200 was the usual complement for a Greek trireme—170 rowers, 30 fighters.
17. But Herodotus' total of 3,000 is only partly composed of 50-oared ships.
18. Actually, west. "Southward" below should be "eastward."
19. I.e. Greece.

that the coming of the remnant of the allies was to be looked for every day, and that the sea was strictly watched by them, being guarded by the Athenians and Aeginetans and all that were enrolled in the fleet; there was naught (they said) for them to fear; for the invader of Hellas was no god, but a mortal man, and there was no mortal, nor ever would be, to whom at birth some admixture of misfortune was not allotted; the greater the man, the greater the misfortune; most surely then he that marched against them, being but mortal, would be disappointed of his hope. Hearing that, the Locrians and Phocians marched to aid the Greeks at Trachis.

204. All these had their generals, each city its own; but he that was most regarded and was leader of the whole army was Leonidas of Lacedaemon, whose descent was from Anaxandrides, Leon, Eurycratides, Anaxandrus, Eurycrates, Polydorus, Alcamenes, Teleclus, Archelaus, Hegesilatis, Doryssus, Leobotes, Echestratus, Agis, Eurysthenes, Aristodemus, Aristomachus, Cleodaeus, Hyllus, Heracles; who was king at Sparta, yet had not looked to be such.

205. For since he had two elder brothers, Cleomenes and Dorieus, he had renounced all thought of the kingship. But when Cleomenes died without male issue, and Dorieus was dead too (having met his end in Sicily), so it came about that the succession fell to Leonidas, because he was older than Anaxandrides' youngest son Cleombrotus, and moreover had Cleomenes' daughter to wife. He now came to Thermopylae, with a picked force of the customary three hundred,[20] and those that had sons and he brought with him too those Thebans whom I counted among the number, whose general was Leontiades son of Eurymachus. Leonidas was at pains to bring these Thebans more than any other Greeks, because they were constantly charged with favoring the Persian part; therefore it was that he summoned them to the war, because he desired to know whether they would send their men with him or plainly refuse the Greek alliance. They sent the men; but they had other ends in view.

206. These, the men with Leonidas, were sent before the rest by the Spartans, that by the sight of them the rest of the allies might be moved to arm, and not like others take the Persian part, as might well be if they learnt that the Spartans were delaying; and they purposed that later when they should have kept the feast of the Carnea,[21] which was their present hindrance, they would leave a garrison at Sparta and march out with the whole of their force and with all speed. The rest of the allies had planned to do the same likewise; for an Olympic festival fell due at the same time as these doings; wherefore they sent their advance guard, not supposing that the war at Thermopylae would so speedily come to an issue.

207. Such had been their intent; but the Greeks at Thermopylae, when the Persian drew near to the entrance of the pass, began to lose heart and debate whether to quit their post or not. The rest of the Peloponnesians were for returning to the Peloponnese and guarding the isthmus; but the Phocians and Locrians were greatly incensed by this counsel, and Leonidas gave his vote for remaining where they were and sending messages to the cities to demand aid, seeing that he and his were too few to beat off the Median host.

208. While they thus debated, Xerxes sent a mounted watcher to see how many they were and what they had in hand; for while he was yet in Thessaly, he had heard that some small army was here gathered, and that its leaders were Lacedaemonians, Leonidas a descendant of Heracles among

---

20. The regular number of the royal bodyguard.
21. The national festival in honor of Apollo, held in September.

them. The horseman rode up to the camp and viewed and overlooked it, yet not the whole; for it was not possible to see those that were posted within the wall which they had restored and now guarded; but he took note of those that were without, whose arms were piled outside the wall, and it chanced that at that time the Lacedaemonians were posted there. There he saw some of the men at exercise, and others combing their hair. Marveling at the sight, and taking exact note of their numbers, he rode back unmolested, none pursuing nor at all regarding him; so he returned and told Xerxes all that he had seen.

209. When Xerxes heard that, he could not understand the truth, namely, that the Lacedaemonians were preparing to slay to the best of their power or be slain; what they did appeared to him laughable; wherefore he sent for Demaratus the son of Ariston who was in his camp, and when he came questioned him of all these matters, that he might understand what it was that the Lacedaemonians were about. "I have told you already," said Demaratus, "of these men, when we were setting out for Hellas; but when you heard, you mocked me, albeit I told you of this which I saw plainly would be the outcome; for it is my greatest endeavor, O king, to speak truth in your presence. Now hear me once more: these men are come to fight with us for the passage, and for that they are preparing; for it is their custom to dress their hair whenever they are about to put their lives in jeopardy. Moreover I tell you, that if you overcome these and what remains behind at Sparta, there is no other nation among men, O king! that will abide and withstand you; now are you face to face with the noblest royalty and city and the most valiant men in Hellas." Xerxes deemed what was said to be wholly incredible, and further enquired of him how they would fight against his army, being so few. "O king," Demaratus answered, "use me as a liar, if the event of this be not what I tell you."

210. Yet for all that Xerxes would not believe him. For the space of four days the king waited, ever expecting that the Greeks would take to flight; but on the fifth, seeing them not withdrawing and deeming that their remaining there was but shamelessness and folly, he was angered, and sent the Medes and Cissians against them, bidding them take the Greeks alive and bring them into his presence. The Medes bore down upon the Greeks and charged them; many fell, but others attacked in turn; and though they suffered grievous defeat yet they were not driven off. But they made it plain to all and chiefly to the king himself that for all their number of human creatures there were few men among them. This battle lasted all the day.

211. The Medes being so roughly handled, they were then withdrawn from the fight, and the Persians whom the king called Immortals attacked in their turn, led by Hydarnes. It was thought that they at least would make short and easy work of the Greeks; but when they joined battle, they fared neither better nor worse than the Median soldiery, fighting as they were in a narrow space and with shorter spears than the Greeks, where they could make no use of their numbers. But the Lacedaemonians fought memorably. They were skilled warriors against unskilled; and it was among their many feats of arms, that they would turn their backs and feign flight; seeing which, the foreigners would pursue after them with shouting and noise; but when the Lacedaemonians were like to be overtaken they turned upon the foreigners, and so rallying overthrew Persians innumerable; wherein some few of the Spartans themselves were slain. So when the Persians, attacking by companies and in every other fashion, could yet gain no inch of the approach, they drew off out of the fight.

212. During these onsets the king (it is said) thrice sprang up in fear for his army from the throne where he sat to view them. Such was then the fortune of the fight, and on the next day the foreigners had no better luck at the game. They joined battle, supposing that their enemies, being so few, were now disabled by wounds and could no longer withstand them, but the Greeks stood arrayed by battalions and nations, and each of these fought in its turn, save the Phocians, who were posted on the mountains to guard the path. So when the Persians found the Greeks in no way different from what the day before had shown them to be, they drew off from the fight.

213. The king being at a loss how to deal with the present difficulty, Epialtes son of Eurydemus, a Malian, came to speak with him, thinking so to receive a great reward from Xerxes, and told him of the path leading over the mountain to Thermopylae; whereby he was the undoing of the Greeks who had been left there. This Epialtes afterwards fled into Thessaly, for fear of the Lacedaemonians; and he being so banished a price was put on his head by the Pylagori when the Amphictyons sat together in their council at Thermopylae; and a long time after that, having returned to Anticyra, he was slain by Athenades, a man of Trachis. It was for another cause that this Athenades slew Epialtes, but he was none the less honored for it by the Lacedaemonians.

219. The Greeks at Thermopylae were warned first by Megistias the seer; who, having examined the offerings, advised them of the death that awaited them in the morning; and presently came deserters, while it was yet night, with news of the circuit made by the Persians; which was lastly brought also by the watchers running down from the heights when day was now dawning. Thereupon the Greeks held a council, and their opinions were divided, some advising that they should not leave their post, and some being contrariwise minded; and presently they parted asunder, these taking their departure and dispersing each to their own cities, and those resolving to remain where they were with Leonidas.

220. It is said indeed that Leonidas himself sent them away, desiring in his care for them to save their lives, but deeming it unseemly for himself and the Spartans to desert that post which they had first come to defend. But to this opinion I the rather incline, that when Leonidas perceived the allies to be faint of heart and not willing to run all risks with him he bade them go their ways, departure being for himself not honorable; if he remained, he would leave a name of great renown, and the prosperity of Sparta would not be blotted out. For when the Spartans enquired of the oracle concerning this war at its very first beginning, the Pythian priestess had prophesied to them that either Lacedaemon should be destroyed of the foreigners, or that its king should perish: which answer was given in these hexameter verses:

Fated it is for you, ye dwellers in wide-wayed Sparta,
Either your city must fall, that now is mighty and famous,
Wasted by Persian men, or the watcher of fair Lacedaemon.
Mourn for a king that is dead, from Heracles' line descended.
Yea, for the foe thou hast nor bulls nor lions can conquer;
Mighty he cometh as Zeus, and shall not be stayed in his coming;
One of the two will he take, and rend his quarry asunder.

Of this (it is my belief) Leonidas bethought himself, and desired that the Spartans alone should have the glory wherefore he chose rather to send the allies away than that the departure of those who went should be the unseemly outcome of divided counsels.

221. In which matter I hold it for one of my strongest proofs, that Megistias the Acarnanian (reputed a descendant of Melampus), who advised the Greeks from the offerings of what should befall them, was past all doubt bidden by Leonidas to depart, lest he should perish with the rest. Yet though thus bidden Megistias himself would not go; he had an only son in the army, and him he sent away instead.

222. So those of the allies who were bidden to go went their ways in obedience to Leonidas, and the Thespians and Thebans alone stayed by the Lacedaemonians; the Thebans indeed against their will and desire, and kept there by Leonidas as hostages; but the Thespians remained with great goodwill. They refused to depart and leave Leonidas and his comrades, but remained there and died with him. Their general was Demophilus son of Diadromes.

223. Xerxes, having at sunrise offered libations, waited till about the hour of marketing and then made his assault, having been so advised by Epialtes; for the descent from the mountain is more direct and the way is much shorter than the circuit and the ascent.[22] So the foreigners that were with Xerxes attacked; but the Greeks with Leonidas, knowing that they went to their death, advanced now much farther than before into the wider part of the strait. For ere now it was the wall of defense that they had guarded, and all the former days they had withdrawn themselves into the narrow way and fought there but now they met their enemies outside the narrows, and many of the foreigners were there slain; for their captains came behind the companies with scourges and drove all the men forward with lashes. Many of them were thrust into the sea and there drowned, and more by far were trodden down bodily by each other, none regarding who it was that perished; for inasmuch as the Greeks knew that they must die by the hands of those who came round the mountain, they put forth the very utmost of their strength against the foreigners, in their recklessness and frenzy.

224. By this time the spears of the most of them were broken, and they were slaying the Persians with their swords. There in that travail fell Leonidas, fighting most gallantly, and with him other famous Spartans, whose names I have learnt for their great worth and desert, as I have learnt besides the names of all the three hundred.[23] There too fell, among other famous Persians, Abrocomes and Hyperanthes, two sons of Darius by Phratagune, daughter of Artanes. This Artanes was brother to king Darius, and son of Hystaspes who was the son of Arsames; and when he gave his daughter in marriage to Darius he dowered her with the whole wealth of his house, she being his only child.

225. So two brothers of Xerxes fell there in the battle; and there was a great struggle between the Persians and Lacedaemonians over Leonidas' body, till the Greeks of their valor dragged it away and four times put their enemies to flight. Nor was there an end of this mellay till the men with Epialtes came up. When the Greeks were aware of their coming, from that moment the face of the battle was changed; for they withdrew themselves back to the narrow part of the way, and passing within the wall they took pose, all save the Thebans, upon the hillock that is in the mouth of the pass, where now stands the stone lion in honor of Leonidas. In that place they defended

---

22. So that the Persians who came by the Anopaea path, leaving the top of the pass at dawn could reach the low ground by mid morning.

23. Leonidas' body was brought to Sparta and buried there in 440 B.C.; a column was erected on his grave bearing the names of the three hundred, which Herodotus probably saw.

themselves with their swords, as many as yet had such, ay and with fists and teeth; till the foreigners overwhelmed them with missile weapons, some attacking them in front and throwing down the wall of defense, and others standing around them in a ring.

226. Thus did the men of Lacedaemon and Thespiae bear themselves. Yet the bravest of them all (it is said) was Dieneces, a Spartan, of whom a certain saying is reported: before they joined battle with the Medes, it was told Dieneces by a certain Trachinian that the enemies were so many, that when they shot with their bows the sun was hidden by the multitude of arrows; whereby being no whit dismayed, but making light of the multitude of the Medes, "Our friend from Trachis," quoth he, "brings us right good news, for if the Medes hide the sun we shall fight them in the shade and not in the sunshine,"

228. All these, and they that died before any had departed at Leonidas' bidding, were buried where they fell, and there is an inscription over them, which is this:

Four thousand warriors, flower of Pelops' land,
Did here against three hundred myriads stand.

This is the inscription common to all ; the Spartans have one for themselves:

Go tell the Spartans, you that pass by,
That here obedient to their words we lie.

That is for the Lacedaemonians, and this for the seer:

Here fought and fell Megistias, hero brave,
Slain by the Medes, who crossed Spercheius' wave
Well knew the seer his doom, but scorned to fly,
And rather chose with Sparta's king to die.

The inscriptions and the pillars were set there in their honor by the Amphictyons, except the epitaph of the diviner Megistias; that inscription was made for him for friendship's sake by Simonides son of Leoprepes.[24]

---

24. As a matter of fact, Simonides composed all three inscriptions; but the epitaph of Megistias was the only one which he made at his own expense.

The Dying Gaul, a Roman copy of a Hellenistic bronze. Capitoline Museum, Rome.

Thucydides: The Peloponnesian War

18

Ancient reconstructions of the life of Thucydides are mostly speculative as almost nothing is known of him except the few details recorded by the historian himself in the text of his Histories: he was an Athenian; he was "young" when he began to write his history in 431 B.C.; he was a strategos in 424 when he lost Amphipolis to Brasidas and was exiled; he was unaware of Conon's restoration of Athenian sea power in 394. Everything else is speculation.

Thucydides wrote a history of the Peloponnesian War between Sparta and Athens, an event he partici-pated in himself and he considered it to rival the wars recorded by Homer and Herodotus, not so much in heroism as in suffering. He improved on the historical method of Herodotus by a more intense concentra-tion on factual accuracy, by the elimination of all romance and myth from his account, by narrowing the focus to the war itself and the politics involving it, and by a closer analysis of the causes of the events. He must not be blamed, therefore, for ignoring the domestic politics of Sparta and Athens, or omitting the kind of ethnographical material found in Herodotus. Neither does he discuss the economic factors of the war. The selections below begin with the famous "Funeral Oration of Pericles," which gives us an ideal-ized view of the Athenian democracy and its empire, and then describe four of the major events of the war.

I. PERICLES' FUNERAL ORATION

Book 2.36. "I shall speak first of our ancestors, for it is right and at the same time fitting, on an occasion like this, to give them this place of honor in recalling what they did. For this land of ours, in which the same people have never ceased to dwell in an unbroken line of successive gen-erations, they by their valor transmitted to our times a free state. And not only are they worthy of our praise, but our fathers still more; for they, adding to the inheritance which they received, acquired the empire we now possess and bequeathed it, not without toil, to us who are alive to-day. And we ourselves here assembled, who are now for the most part still in the prime of life, have further strengthened the empire in most respects, and have provided our city with all re-

From *Thucydides*, translated by Charles Foster Smith (Cambridge, Loeb Classical Library, Harvard University Press, 1919).

sources, so that it is sufficient for itself both in peace and in war. The military exploits whereby our several possessions were acquired, whether in any case it were we ourselves or our fathers that valiantly repelled the onset of war, Barbarian or Hellenic, I will not recall, for I have no desire to speak at length among those who know. But I shall first set forth by what sort of training we have come to our present position, and with what political institutions arid as the result of what manner of life our empire became great, and afterwards proceed to the praise of these men; for I think that on the present occasion such a recital will be not inappropriate and that the whole throng, both of citizens and of strangers, may with advantage listen to it.

2.37. "We live under a form of government which does not emulate the institutions of our neighbors;[1] on the contrary, we are ourselves a model which some follow,[2] rather than the imitators of other peoples. It is true that our government is called a democracy, because its administration is in the hands, not of the few, but of the many; yet while as regards the law all men are on an equality for the settlement of their private disputes, as regards the value set on them it is as each man is in any way distinguished that he is preferred to public honors, not because he belongs to a particular class, but because of personal merits; nor, again, on the ground of poverty is a man barred from a public career by obscurity of rank if he but has it in him to do the state a service. And not only in our public life are we liberal, but also as regards our freedom from suspicion of one another in the pursuits of everyday life; for we do not feel resentment at our neighbor if he does as he likes, nor yet do we put on sour looks which, though harmless, are painful to behold. But while we thus avoid giving offence in our private intercourse, in our public life we are restrained from lawlessness chiefly through reverent fear, for we render obedience to those in authority and to the laws, and especially to those laws which are ordained for the succor of the oppressed and those which, though unwritten, bring upon the transgressor a disgrace which all men recognize.

2.38. "Moreover, we have provided for the spirit many relaxations from toil: we have games[3] and sacrifices regularly throughout the year and homes fitted out with good taste and elegance; and the delight we each day find in these things drives away sadness. And our city is so great that all the products of all the earth flow in upon us, and ours is the happy lot to gather in the good fruits of our own soil with no more home-felt security of enjoyment than we do those of other lands.

2.39. "We are also superior to our opponents in our system of training for warfare, and this in the following respects. In the first place, we throw our city open to all the world and we never by exclusion acts debar any one from learning or seeing anything which an enemy might profit by observing if it were not kept from his sight; for we place our dependence, not so much upon prearranged devices to deceive, as upon the courage which springs from our own souls when we are called to action. And again, in the matter of education, whereas they from early childhood by a laborious discipline make pursuit of manly courage, we with our unrestricted mode of life are

---

1. Alluding to the Spartans, whose institutions were said to have been borrowed from Crete; in fact, throughout the whole speech the contrast is with Spartan conditions.
2. Possible allusion to the embassy sent from Rome in 454 B.C. to examine the laws of Solon (Livy, 3.31).
3. Referring especially to the contests at the chief festivals like the Panathenaea and Dionysia, which by their artistic setting and performance were recreations for the mind and spirit quite as much as physical exercises.

none the less ready to meet any equality of hazard.[4] And here is the proof: When the Lacedaemonians invade our territory they do not come alone but bring all their confederates with them, whereas we, going by ourselves against our neighbors' territory, generally have no difficulty, though fighting on foreign soil against men who are defending their own homes, in overcoming them in battle. And in fact our united forces no enemy has ever yet met, not only because we are constantly attending to the needs of our navy, but also because on land we send our troops on many enterprises; but if they by chance engage with a division of our forces and defeat a few of us, they boast that they have repulsed us all, and if the victory is ours, they claim that they have been beaten by us all. If, then, by taking our ease rather than by laborious training and depending on a courage which springs more from manner of life than compulsion of laws, we are ready to meet dangers, the gain is all ours, in that we do not borrow trouble by anticipating miseries which are not yet at hand, and when we come to the test we show ourselves fully as brave as those who are always toiling; and so our city is worthy of admiration in these respects, as well as in others.

2.40. "For we are lovers of beauty yet with no extravagance and lovers of wisdom yet without weakness. Wealth we employ rather as an opportunity for action than as a subject for boasting; and with us it is not a shame for a man to acknowledge poverty, but the greater shame is for him not to do his best to avoid it. And you will find united in the same persons an interest at once in private and in public affairs, and in others of us who give attention chiefly to business, you will find no lack of insight into political matters. For we alone regard the man who takes no part in public affairs, not as one who minds his own business, but as good for nothing; and we Athenians decide public questions for ourselves[5] or at least endeavor to arrive at a sound understanding of them, in the belief that it is not debate that is a hindrance to action, but rather not to be instructed by debate before the time comes for action. For in truth we have this point also of superiority over other men, to be most daring in action and yet at the same time most given to reflection upon the ventures we mean to undertake with other men, on the contrary, boldness means ignorance and reflection brings hesitation. And they would rightly be adjudged most courageous who, realizing most clearly the pains no less than the pleasures involved, do not on that account turn away from danger. A gain, in nobility of spirit, we stand in sharp contrast to most men; for it is not by receiving kindness, but by conferring it, that we acquire our friends. Now he who confers the favor is a firmer friend, in that he is disposed, by continued goodwill toward the recipient, to keep the feeling of obligation alive in him; but he who owes it is more listless in his friendship, knowing that when he repays the kindness it will count, not as a favor bestowed, but as a debt repaid. And, finally, we alone confer our benefits without fear of consequences, not upon a calculation of the advantage we shall gain, but with confidence in the spirit of liberality which actuates us.

2.41. "In a word, then, I say that our city as a whole is the school of Hellas, and that, as it seems to me, each individual amongst us could in his own person, with the utmost grace and versatility, prove himself self-sufficient in the most varied forms of activity. And that this is no

---

4. Pericles here hints at his policy, outlined elsewhere, of always acting on the defensive when the enemy forces are distinctly superior.

5. In contrast with the Spartans, whose officials made the important decisions.

mere boast inspired by the occasion, but actual truth, is attested by the very power of our city, a power which we have acquired in consequence of these qualities. For Athens alone among her contemporaries, when put to the test, is superior to the report of her, and she alone neither affords to the enemy who comes against her cause for irritation at the character of the foe by whom he is defeated, nor to her subject cause for complaint that his masters are unworthy. Many are the proofs which we have given of our power and assuredly it does not lack witnesses, and therefore we shall be the wonder not only of the men of to-day but of after times; we shall need no Homer to sing our praise nor any other poet whose verses may perhaps delight for the moment but whose presentation of the facts will be discredited by the truth. Nay, we have compelled every sea and every land to grant access to our daring, and have everywhere planted everlasting memorials both of evil to foes and of good to friends.[6] Such, then, is the city for which these men nobly fought and died, deeming it their duty not to let her be taken from them; and it is fitting that every man who is left behind should suffer willingly for her sake.

2.42. "It is for this reason that I have dwelt upon the greatness of our city; for I have desired to show you that we are contending for a higher prize than those who do not enjoy such privileges in like degree, and at the same time to let the praise of these men in whose honor I am now speaking be made manifest by proofs. Indeed, the greatest part of their praise has already been spoken; for when I lauded the city, that was but the praise wherewith the brave deeds of these men and men like them have already adorned her; and there are not many Hellenes whose fame would be found, like theirs, evenly balanced with their deeds. And it seems to me that such a death as these men died gives proof enough of manly courage, whether as first revealing it or as affording its final confirmation. Aye, even in the case of those who in other ways fell short of goodness, it is but right that the valor with which they fought for their country should be set before all else; for they have blotted out evil with good and have bestowed a greater benefit by their service to the state than they have done harm by their private lives. And no one of these men either so set his heart upon the continued enjoyment of wealth as to become a coward, or put off the dreadful day, yielding to the hope which poverty inspires, that if he could but escape it he might yet become rich; but, deeming the punishment of the foe to be more desirable than these things, and at the same time regarding such a hazard as the most glorious of all, they chose, accepting the hazard, to be avenged upon the enemy and to relinquish these other things, trusting to hope the still obscure possibilities of success, but in action, as to the issue that was before their eyes, confidently relying upon themselves. And then when the moment of combat came, thinking it better to defend themselves and suffer death rather than to yield and save their lives, they fled, indeed, from the shameful word of dishonor, but with life and limb stood stoutly to their task, and in the brief instant ordained by fate, at the crowning moment not of fear but of glory, they passed away.

2.43. "And so these men then bore themselves after a manner that befits our city; but you who survive, though you may pray that it be with less hazard, should resolve that you will have a spirit to meet the foe which is no whit less courageous; and you must estimate the advantage of such a spirit not alone by a speaker's words, for he could make a long story in telling you—what you yourselves know as well as he—all the advantages that are to be gained by warding off the foe.

---

6. The reference is to Athenian colonies, which according to the bearing of the natives, had been attended with ill consequences for them (Oreos and Aegina) or good (on the Thracian coast).

Nay rather you must daily fix your gaze upon the power of Athens and become lovers of her, and when the vision of her greatness has inspired you, reflect that all this has been acquired by men of courage who knew their duty and in the hour of conflict were moved by a high sense of honor, who, if ever they failed in any enterprise, were resolved that at least their country should not find herself deserted by their velour, but freely sacrificed to her the fairest offering it was in their power to give. For they gave their lives for the common weal, and in so doing won for themselves the praise which grows not old and the most distinguished of all sepulchres—not that in which they lie buried, but that in which their glory survives in everlasting remembrance, celebrated on every occasion which gives rise to word of eulogy or deed of emulation. For the whole world is the sepulchre of famous men, and it is not the epitaph upon monuments set up in their own land that alone commemorates them, but also in lands not their own there abides in each breast an unwritten memorial of them, planted in the heart rather than graven on stone. Do you, therefore, now make these men your examples, and judging freedom to be happiness and courage to be freedom, be not too anxious about the dangers of war. For it is not those that are in evil plight who have the best excuse for being unsparing of their lives, for they have no hope of better days, but rather those who run the risk, if they continue to live, of the opposite reversal of fortune, and those to whom it makes the greatest difference if they suffer a disaster. For to a manly spirit more bitter is humiliation associated with cowardice than death when it comes unperceived in close company with stalwart deeds and public hopes.

2.44. "Wherefore, I do not commiserate the parents of these men, as many of you as are present here, but will rather try to comfort them. For they know that their lives have been passed amid manifold vicissitudes; and it is to be accounted good fortune when men win, even as these now, a most glorious death—and you a like grief—and when life has been meted out to them to be happy in no less than to die in. It will be difficult, I know, to persuade you of the truth of this, when you will constantly be reminded of your loss by seeing others in the enjoyment of blessings in which you too once took delight; and grief, I know, is felt, not for the want of the good things which a man has never known, but for what is taken away from him after he has once become accustomed to it. But those of you who are still of an age to have offspring should bear up in the hope of other children; for not only to many of you individually will the children that are born hereafter be a cause of forgetfulness of those who are gone, but the state also will reap a double advantage—it will not be left desolate and it will be secure. For they cannot possibly offer fair and impartial counsel who, having no children to hazard, do not have an equal part in the risk.[7] But as for you who have passed your prime, count as gain the greater portion of your life during which you were fortunate and remember that the remainder will be short; and be comforted by the fair fame of these your sons. For the love of honor alone is untouched by age, and when one comes to the ineffectual period of life it is not 'gain' as some say,[8] that gives the greater satisfaction, but honor.

---

7. No one could be a member of the Boule (Council of Five Hundred) until he was thirty, when he was almost certain to be married; and according to Deinarchus, no man was allowed to speak in the Assembly until he had legitimate male issue.
8. Plutarch, *Moralia*, 786b. Simonides replied to those who charged him with love of money, that, deprived by old age of other pleasures, he is still comforted by one, that of gain.

2.45. "But for such of you here present as are sons and brothers of these men, I see the greatness of the conflict that awaits you—for the dead are always praised—and even were you to attain to surpassing virtue, hardly would you be judged, I will not say their equals, but even a little inferior. For there is envy of the living on account of rivalry, but that which has been removed from our path is honored with a goodwill that knows no antagonism.

"If I am to speak also of womanly virtues, referring to those of you who will henceforth be in widowhood, I will sum up all in a brief admonition: Great is your glory if you fall not below the standard which nature has set for your sex, and great also is hers of whom there is least talk among men whether in praise or in blame.

2.46. "I have now spoken, in obedience to the law, such words as I had that were fitting, and those whom we are burying have already in part also received their tribute in our deeds[9] besides, the state will henceforth maintain their children at the public expense until they grow to manhood, thus offering both to the dead and to their survivors a crown of substantial worth as their prize in such contests. For where the prizes offered for virtue are greatest, there are found the best citizens. And now, when you have made due lament, each for his own dead, depart."

II. THE REVOLT OF MITYLENE

A year after Pericles' death, Mitylene, on the island of Lesbos, revolted from the Athenian empire. The revolt was put down and the Athenian assembly voted to make an example of Lesbos in order to discourage future revolts. A ship was dispatched with orders to kill all the men of Mitylene and sell the women and children into slavery. However, Thucydides says: "The next day there was a feeling of repentance; they reflected that the decree was cruel and indiscriminate, to slay a whole city and not the guilty only." The speech below was given by Cleon, the mover of the original motion.

Thucydides poses here the age old question: can a democracy run an empire? Later the Romans gave up their democracy and kept their empire, the Athenians, however, kept their democracy and lost their empire. When this question is applied to the modern world, it deals with U.S. "world leadership." Does America, while keeping its democracy, have the will to retain its world leadership?

Book 3.37. "On many other occasions in the past I have realized that a democracy is incompetent to govern others, but more than ever to-day, when I observe your change of heart concerning the Mytilenaeans. The fact is that, because your daily life is unaffected by fear and intrigue in your relations to each other, you have the same attitude towards your allies also, and you forget that whenever you are led into error by their representations or yield out of pity, your weakness

---

9. I.e. the honors shown them throughout the rest of the ceremony, as contrasted with the words of the eulogist.

involves you in danger and does not win the gratitude of your allies. For you do not reflect that the empire you hold is a despotism imposed upon subjects who, for their part, do intrigue against you and submit to your rule against their will, who render obedience, not because of any kindnesses you may do them to your own hurt, but because of such superiority as you may have established by reason of your strength rather than of their goodwill. But quite the most alarming thing is, if nothing we have resolved upon shall be settled once for all, and if we shall refuse to recognize that a state which has inferior laws that are inviolable is stronger than one whose laws are good but without authority; that ignorance combined with self-restraint is more serviceable than cleverness combined with recklessness; and that simpler people for the most part make better citizens than the more shrewd. The latter always want to show that they are wiser than the laws, and to dominate all public discussions, as if there could never be weightier questions on which to declare their opinions, and as of such consequence of such conduct they generally bring their states to ruin; the former, on the contrary, mistrusting their own insight, are content to be less enlightened than the laws and less competent than others to criticize the words of an able speaker, but being impartial judges rather than interested contestants they generally prosper. Thus, then, we ought to act and not be so excited by eloquence and combat of wits as to advise the Athenian people contrary to our own judgment.

3.38. "As for me, I have not changed my opinion, and I wonder at those who propose to debate again the question of the Mytilenaeans and thus interpose delay, which is in the interest of those who have done the wrong; for thus the edge of the victim's wrath is duller when he proceeds against the offender, whereas the vengeance that follows upon the very heels of the outrage exacts a punishment that most nearly matches the offence. And I wonder, too, who will answer me and undertake to prove that the wrong doings of the Mytilenaeans are beneficial to us but that our misfortunes prove injurious to our allies. Manifestly he must either have such confidence in his powers of speech as to undertake to show that what is universally accepted as true has not been established,[10] or else, incited by gain, will by an elaborate display of specious oratory attempt to mislead you. But in contests of that kind the city bestows the prizes upon others, while she herself undergoes all the risks. And you are yourselves to blame, for your management or these contests is wrong. It is your wont to be spectators of words and hearers of deeds, forming your judgment of future enterprises according as able speakers represent them to be feasible, but as regards accomplished facts, not counting what has been done more credible, because you have seen it, than what you have heard, you are swayed in judgment by those who have made an eloquent invective. You are adepts not only at being deceived by novel proposals but also at refusing to follow approved advice, slaves as you are of each new paradox and scorners of what is familiar. Each of you wishes above all to be an orator himself, or, failing that, to vie with those dealers in paradox by seeming not to lag behind them in wit but to applaud a smart saying before it is out of the speaker's mouth; you are as quick to forestall what is said as you are slow to foresee what will come of it. You seek, one might say, a world quite unlike that in which we live, but give too little heed to that which is at hand. In a word, you are in thrall to the pleasures of the ear and are more like men who sit as spectators at exhibitions of sophists than men who take counsel for the welfare of the state.

---

10. Or, "your absolute resolve has really not been adopted."

3.39. "And it is from these ways that I seek to turn you when I attempt to prove that Mitylene has done you more injury than any single state. I can make allowance for men who resorted to revolt because they were unable to bear your rule or because they were compelled by your enemies to do so; but men who inhabited a fortified island and had no fear of our enemies except by sea, and even there were not without the protection of a force of their own triremes, who moreover were independent and were treated by us with the highest consideration, when these men have acted thus, what else is it but conspiracy and rebellion rather than revolt—for revolt is the work of those who suffer oppression—and a deliberate attempt by taking their stand on the side of our bitterest enemies to bring about our destruction? And yet this is assuredly a more heinous thing than if they had gone to war against us by themselves for the acquisition of power. The calamities of their neighbors who had already revolted from us and been subdued proved no warning to them; nor did the good fortune which they enjoyed make them hesitate to take the perilous step; on the contrary, becoming over confident as to the future, and conceiving hopes which, though greater than their powers, were less than their ambition, they took up arms, presuming to put might before right; for the moment they thought they should prove superior they attacked us unprovoked. And indeed it is the rule, that such states as come to unexpected prosperity most fully and most suddenly, do turn to insolence, whereas men generally find success less precarious when it comes in accordance with reasonable calculations than when it surpasses expectation, and more easily, as it seems, they repel adversity than maintain prosperity. But the Mytilenaeans from the first ought never to have been treated by us with any more consideration than our other allies, and then they would not have broken out into such insolence; for it is human nature in any case to be contemptuous of those who pay court but to admire those who will not yield.

"Let them be punished, therefore, even now, in a manner befitting their crime, and do not put the blame upon the aristocrats and exonerate the common people. For they all alike attacked you, even the commons, who, if they had taken our side, might now have been reinstated in their city; but they thought there was less risk in sharing the dangers of the oligarchs, and so joined them in the revolt. Consider, moreover, your allies: if you inflict upon those who willfully revolt no greater punishment than upon those who revolt under compulsion from our foes, which of them, think you, will not revolt on a slight pretext, when the alternatives are liberty if he succeeds or a fate not irreparable if he fails? We, on the other hand, shall have to risk our money and our lives against each separate state, and when we succeed we shall recover a ruined state and be deprived for the future of its revenue, the source of our strength, whereas if we fail we shall be adding fresh enemies to those we have already, and when we should be resisting our present foes we shall be fighting our own allies.

3.40. "We must not, therefore, hold out to them any hope, either to be secured by eloquence or purchased by money, that they will be excused on the plea that their error was human. For their act was no unintentional injury but a deliberate plot; and it is that which is unintentional which is excusable. Therefore, I still protest, as I have from the first,[11] that you should not reverse your former decision or be led into error by pity, delight in eloquence, or clemency, the three

---

11. Referring to what happened in the assembly of the day before, in which, however, he had urged the action that was taken; its reconsideration was not urged until the present meeting.

influences most prejudicial to a ruling state. For compassion may rightly be bestowed upon those who are likewise compassionate and not upon those who will show no pity in return but of necessity are always enemies. As to the orators who charm by their eloquence, they will have other opportunities of display in matters of less importance, and not where the city for a brief pleasure will pay a heavy penalty while they themselves get a fine fee for their fine speaking. And clemency would better be reserved for those who will afterwards be faithful allies than be shown to those who remain just what they were before and no whit the less our enemies.

"I can sum up what I have to say in a word. If you take my advice, you will do not only what is just to the Mytilenaeans but also at the same time what is expedient for us; but if you decide otherwise, you will not win their gratitude but will rather bring a just condemnation upon yourselves; for if these people had a right to secede, it would follow that you are wrong in exercising dominion. But if, right or wrong, you are still resolved to maintain it, then you must punish these people in defiance of equity as your interests require; or else you must give up your empire and in discreet safety practice the fine virtues you preach. Resolve also to punish them with the same penalty that has already been voted, and that those who have escaped the plot shall not appear to have less feeling than those who framed it, bearing in mind what they would probably have done to you had they won the victory, especially since they were the aggressors. Indeed it is generally those who wrong another without cause that follow him up to destroy him utterly, perceiving the danger that threatens from an enemy who is left alive; for one who has been needlessly injured is more dangerous if he escape than an avowed enemy who expects to give and take.

"Do not, then, be traitors to your own cause, but recalling as nearly as possible how you felt when they made you suffer and how you would then have given anything to crush them, now pay them back. Do not become tender-hearted at the sight of their present distress, nor unmindful of the danger that so lately hung over you, but chastise them as they deserve, and give to your other allies plain warning that whoever revolts shall be punished with death. For if they realize this, the less will you have to neglect your enemies and fight against your own allies."

III. THE CORCYREAN REVOLUTION

The Peloponnesian War was above all a conflict between two ideologies: the conservative, totalitarianism of the Spartans, who were determined to keep democracy as far away from their state as possible. The Peloponnesian League was a confederation of states ruled by oligarchical governments. The ruling classes of these states feared that the democratic influence of Athens would undermine their conservative societies. Sparta, therefore, supported the most conservative elements in the states which it attempted to dominate.

Athens, on the other hand, was the most radically democratic of all the Greek city-states and it always supported the democratic elements in the states that composed its empire, still called the "Delian League." The democrats in these states welcomed Athenian support and protection against their own aristocracies, who they feared were always ready to impose an oligarchy.

Therefore, both sides attempted to inflame class hatred and conflict in the cities of their enemy. This was the origin of the revolt of Mitylene. Earlier, the Athenians formed an alliance with the democratic government of Corcyra, modern Corfu, a state located within the Spartan sphere of influence. This was one of the factors that touched off the Peloponnesian War. In 427, Sparta supported the oligarchic party in Corcyra in a bloody uprising and both Sparta and Athens sent aid to the warring factions. The democrats finally won the day and proceeded to liquidate their opposition. This inspired Thucydides to write the following analysis of the psychology of class warfare.

Book 3.82. To such excesses of savagery did the revolution go; and it seemed the more savage, because it was among the first that occurred for afterwards practically the whole Hellenic world was convulsed, since in each state the leaders of the democratic factions were at variance with the oligarchs, the former seeking to bring in the Athenians, the latter the Lacedaemonians. And while in time of peace they would have had no pretext for asking their intervention, nor any inclination to do so, yet now that these two states were at war, either faction in the various cities, if it desired a evolution, found it easy to bring in allies also, for the discomfiture at one stroke of its opponents and the strengthening of its own cause. And so there fell upon the cities on account of revolutions many grievous calamities, such as happen and always will happen while human nature is the same, but which are severer or milder, and different in their manifestations, according as the variations in circumstances present themselves in each case. For in peace and prosperity both states and individuals have gentler feelings, because men are not then forced to face conditions of dire necessity; but war, which robs men of the easy supply of their daily wants, is a rough schoolmaster and creates in most people a temper that matches their condition.

And so the cities began to be disturbed by revolutions, and those that fell into this state later, on hearing of what had been done before, carried to still more extravagant lengths the invention of new devices, both by the extreme ingenuity of their attacks and the monstrousness of their revenges. The ordinary acceptation of words in their relation to things was changed as men thought fit. Reckless audacity came to be regarded as courageous loyalty to party, prudent hesitation as specious cowardice, moderation as a cloak for unmanly weakness, and to be clever in everything was to do naught in anything. Frantic impulsiveness was accounted a true man's part, but caution in deliberation a specious pretext for shirking. The hot-beaded man was always trusted, his opponent suspected. He who succeeded in a plot was clever, and he who had detected one was still shrewder; on the other hand, he who made it his aim to have no need of such things[12] was a disrupter of party and scared of his opponents. In a word, both he that got ahead of another who intended to do something evil and he that prompted to evil one who had never thought of it were alike commended. Furthermore, the tie of blood was weaker than the tie of party, because the partisan was more ready to dare without demur; for such associations are not entered into for the public good in conformity with the prescribed laws, but for selfish aggrandizement contrary to the established laws. Their pledges to one another were confirmed not so much by divine law as

---

12. I.e. either of plotting or of detecting plots.

by common transgression of the law. Fair words proffered by opponents, if these had the upper hand, were received with caution as to their actions and not in a generous spirit.[13] To get revenge on some one was more valued than never to have suffered injury oneself. And if in any case oaths of reconcilement were exchanged, for the moment only were they binding, since each side had given them merely to meet the emergency, having at the time no other resource; but he who, when the opportunity offered and he saw his enemy off his guard, was the first to pluck up courage, found his revenge sweeter because of the violated pledge than if he had openly attacked, and took into account not only the greater safety of such a course, but also that, by winning through deceit, he was gaining besides the prize of astuteness. And in general it is easier for rogues to get themselves called clever than for the stupid to be reputed good,[14] and they are ashamed of the one but glory in the other.

The cause of all these evils was the desire to rule which greed and ambition inspire, and also, springing from them, that ardor[15] which belongs to men who once have become engaged in factious rivalry. For those who emerged as party leaders in the several cities, by assuming on either side a fair sounding name, the one using as its catch-word "political equality for the masses under the law," the other "temperate aristocracy,"[16] while they pretended to be devoted to the common weal, in reality made it their prize; striving in every way to get the better of each other they dared the most awful deeds, and sought revenges still more awful, not pursuing these within the bounds of justice and the public weal, but limiting them, both parties alike, only by the moment's caprice; and they were ready, either by passing an unjust sentence of condemnation or by winning the upper hand through acts of violence, to glut the animosity of the moment. The result was that though neither had any regard for true piety, yet those who could carry through an odious deed under the cloak of a specious phrase received the higher praise. And citizens who belonged to neither party were continually destroyed by both, either because they would not make common cause with them, or through mere jealousy that they should survive.

3.83. So it was that every form of depravity showed itself in Hellas in consequence of its revolutions, and that simplicity, which is the chief element of a noble nature, was laughed to scorn and disappeared, while mutual antagonism of feeling, combined with mistrust, prevailed far and wide. For there was no assurance binding enough, no oath terrible enough, to reconcile men; but always, if they were stronger, since they accounted all security hopeless, they were rather disposed to take precautions against being wronged than able to trust others. And it was generally those of meaner intellect who won the day; for being afraid of their own defects and of their opponents' sagacity, in order that they might not be worsted in words, and, by reason of their opponents intellectual versatility find themselves unawares victims of their plots, they boldly resorted to deeds. Their opponents, on the other hand, contemptuously assuming that they would be aware in time and that there was no need to secure by deeds what they might have by wit, were taken off their guard and perished in greater numbers.

---

13. Or, "Fair words proffered by their opponents they received, if they had the upper hand, by vigilant action rather than with frank generosity."

14. Or, "And in general men are more willing to called clever rogues than good simpletons."

15. Or, "party spirit."

16. These phrases used in place of the objectionable terms "democracy" and "oligarchy."

3.84. It was in Corcyra, then, that most of these atrocities were first committed—all the acts of retaliation which men who are governed with highhanded insolence rather than with moderation are likely to commit upon their rulers when these at last afford them opportunity for revenge; or such as men resolve upon contrary to justice when they seek release from their accustomed poverty, and in consequence of their sufferings are likely to be most eager for their neighbors' goods and assaults of pitiless cruelty, such as men make, not with a view to gain, but when, being on terms of complete equality with their foe, they are utterly carried away by uncontrollable passion. At this crisis, when the life of the city had been thrown into utter confusion, human nature, now triumphant over the laws, and accustomed even in spite of the laws to do wrong, took delight in showing that its passions were ungovernable, that it was stronger than justice and an enemy to all superiority. For surely no man would have put revenge before religion, and gain before innocence of wrong, had not envy swayed him with her blighting power. Indeed, men do not hesitate, when they seek to avenge themselves upon others, to abrogate in advance the common principles observed in such cases—those principles upon which depends every man's own hope of salvation should he himself be overtaken by misfortune—thus failing to leave them in force against the time when perchance a man in peril shall have need of some one of them.

IV. THE MELIAN DIALOGUE

Melos was the one island in the south Aegean that remained outside the Delian League and neutral at the beginning of the Peloponnesian War. In 416 B.C. the Athenians demanded submission of the Melians and they refused. The island was captured after a six month siege and the punishment was severe: all the men were slaughtered and the women and children sold into slavery. Below, Thucydides presents the dialogue between the Melians and the Athenian envoys who brought the original demand for submission. There is none of the high democratic idealism of the Pericles funeral oration here, only the stark reality of power, which recognizes no limitations from religion, justice or even compassion.

Book 5.84. The next summer Alcibiades sailed to Argos with twenty ships and seized such Argives as seemed to be still open to suspicion and to favor the side of the Lacedaemonians, to the number of three hundred men; and these the Athenians deposited in the adjacent islands over which they had sway. The Athenians also made an expedition against the island of Melos with thirty ships of their own, six Chian and two Lesbian, and twelve hundred Athenian hoplites, three hundred bowmen, and twenty mounted archers, and from their allies and the islanders about fifteen hundred hoplites. Now the Melians are colonists of the Lacedaemonians, and were unwilling to obey the Athenians like the rest of the islanders. At first they remained quiet as neutrals; then when the Athenians tried to force them by ravaging their land, they went to war openly. Accordingly, having encamped in their territory with the forces just mentioned, the Athenian commanders, Cleomedes son of Lycomedes and Teisias son of Teisimachus, before doing any harm to the land, sent envoys to make proposals to the Melians. These envoys the Melians did not bring before the popular assembly, but bade them tell in the presence of the magistrates and the few[17] what they had come for. The Athenian envoys accordingly spoke as follows:

5.85. "Since our proposals are not to be made before the assembly, your purpose being, as it seems, that the people may not hear from us once for all, in an uninterrupted speech, arguments that are seductive and untested,[18] and so be deceived—for we see that it is with this thought that you bring us before the few—do you who sit here adopt a still safer course. Take up each point, and do not you either make a single speech, but conduct the inquiry by replying at once to any statement of ours that seems to be unsatisfactory. And first state whether our proposal suits you."

5.86. The commissioners of the Melians answered: "The fairness of the proposal, that we shall at our leisure instruct one another, is not open to objection, but these acts of war, which are not in the future, but already here at hand, are manifestly at variance with your suggestion. For we see that you are come to be yourselves judges of what is to be said here, and that the outcome of the discussion will in all likelihood be, if we win the debate by the righteousness of our cause and for that very reason refuse to yield, war for us, whereas if we are persuaded, servitude."

5.87. ATH. "Well, if you have met to argue from suspicions about what may happen in the future, or for any other purpose than to consult for the safety of your city in the light of what is present and before your eyes, we may as well stop; but if you have this end in view, we may speak on."

5.88. MEL. "It is natural and pardonable for men in such a position as ours to resort to many arguments and many suppositions. This conference, however, is here to consider the question of our safety; so let the discussion, if it please you, proceed in the way that you propose.

5.89. ATH. "Well, then, we on our part will make use of no fair phrases, saying either that we hold sway justly because we overthrew the Persians, or that we now come against you because we are injured, offering in a lengthy speech arguments that would not be believed; nor, on the other hand, do we presume that you will assert, either that the reason why you did not join us in the war was because you were colonists of the Lacedaemonians, or that you have done us no wrong. Rather we presume that you aim at accomplishing what is possible in accordance with the real thoughts of both of us, since you know as well as we know that what is just is arrived at in human arguments only when the necessity on both sides is equal, and that the powerful exact what they can, while the weak yield what they must."

5.90. MEL. "As we think, at any rate, it is expedient (for we are constrained to speak of expediency, since you have in this fashion, ignoring the principle of justice, suggested that we speak of what is advantageous) that you should not rule out the principle of the common good, but that for him who is at the time in peril what is equitable should also be just, and though one has not entirely proved his point he should still derive some benefit there from. And this is not less for your interest than for our own, inasmuch as you, if you shall ever meet with a reverse, would not only incur the greatest punishment, but would also become a warning example to others."[19]

---

17. Probably the chief governing body, a chamber of Oligarchs, to which the magistrates belonged.

18. I.e. not questioned or put to the proof.

19. I.e. "cruel conduct on your part would justify others in inflicting like punishment upon you should you ever be defeated."

5.91. ATH. "But we on our part, so far as our empire is concerned, even if it should cease to be, do not look forward to the end with dismay. For it is not those who rule over others, as the Lacedaemonians also do—though our quarrel is not now with the Lacedaemonians—that are a terror to the vanquished, but subject peoples who may perchance themselves attack and get the better of their rulers. And as far as that is concerned, you must permit us to take the risk. But that it is for the benefit of our empire that we are here, and also the safety of your city that we now propose to speak, we shall make plain to you, since what we desire is to have dominion over you without trouble to ourselves, and that you should be saved to the advantage of both."

5.92. MEL. "And how could it prove as advantageous for us to become slaves, as it is for you to have dominion?"

5.93. ATH. "Because it would be to your advantage to submit before suffering the most horrible fate, and we should gain by not destroying you."

5.94. MEL. "And so, you mean, you would not consent to our remaining at peace and being friends instead of enemies, but allies of neither combatant?"

5.95. ATM. "No; for your hostility does not injure us so much as your friendship; for in the eyes of our subjects that would be a proof of our weakness, whereas your hatred is a proof of our power.

5.96. MEL. "Do your subjects regard equity in such a way as to put in the same category those that do not belong to you at all and those—your own colonists in most cases and in others revolted subjects—who have been subdued by you?"

5.97. ATH. "As to pleas of justice, they think that neither the one nor the other lacks them, but that those who preserve their freedom owe it to their power, and that we do not attack them because we are afraid. So that, to say nothing of our enlarging our empire, you would afford us security by being subdued, especially if you, an insular power, and weaker than other islanders, should fail to show yourselves superior to a power which is master of the sea."

5.98. MEL. "But do you not think there is security in the other course?[20] For here also it is necessary, just as you force us to abandon all pleas of justice and seek to persuade us to give ear to what is to your own interests, that we, too, tell you what is to our advantage and try to persuade you to adopt it, if that happens to be to your advantage also. How, we say, shall you not make enemies of all who are now neutral, as soon as they look at our case and conclude that some day you will come against them also? And in this what else are you doing but strengthening the enemies you already have, and bringing upon you, against their inclination, others who would never have thought of becoming your enemies?"

5.99. ATH. "Not so, for we do not reckon those as the more dangerous to us who, dwelling somewhere on the mainland and being free men, will defer for a long time taking any precautions against us, but rather those who dwell in some of the islands, both those who, like you, are subject to no control, and those who are already exasperated by tile necessity of submission to our rule. For it is these who are most likely to give way to recklessness and bring both themselves and us into danger which they cannot but foresee."

5.100. MEL. "Surely, then, if you and your subjects brave so great a risk, you in order that you may not lose your empire, and they, who are already your slaves, in order that they may be rid of

---

20. In neutrality, referred to in Chapter 94.

it, for us surely who still have our freedom it would be the height of baseness and cowardice not to resort to every expedient before submitting to servitude."

5.101. ATH. "No, not if you take a sensible view of the matter; for with you it is not a contest on equal terms to determine a point of manly honor, so as to avoid incurring disgrace; rather the question before you is one of self-preservation—to avoid offering resistance to those who are far stronger than you.

5.102. MEL. "But we know that the fortune of war is sometimes impartial and not in accord with the difference in numbers. And for us, to yield is at once to give up hope; but if we make an effort, there is still hope that we may stand erect."

5.103. ATH. "Hope is indeed a solace in danger, and for those who have other resources in abundance, though she may injure, she does not ruin them; but for those who stake their all on a single throw—hope being by nature prodigal—it is only when disaster has befallen that her true nature is recognized, and when at last she is known, she leaves the victim no resource wherewith to take precautions against her in future. This fate, we beg of you, weak as you are and dependent on a single turn of the scale, do not willingly incur; nor make yourselves like the common crowd who, when it is possible still to be saved by human means, as soon as distress comes and all visible grounds of hope fail them, betake themselves to those that are invisible—to divination, oracles, and the like, which, with the hopes they inspire, bring men to ruin."

5.104. MEL. "We, too, be well assured, think it difficult to contend both against your power and against fortune, unless she shall be impartial; but nevertheless we trust that, in point of fortune, we shall through the divine favor be at no disadvantage because we are god-fearing men standing our ground against men who are unjust; and as to the matter of power, that the alliance of the Lacedaemonians will supply what we lack, since that alliance must aid us, if for no other reason, because of our kinship with them and for very shame. So our confidence is not altogether so irrational as you may suppose."

5.105. ATH. "Well, as to the kindness of the divine favor, neither do we expect to fall short of you therein. For in no respect are we departing from men's observances regarding that which pertains to the divine or from their desires regarding that which pertains to themselves, in aught that we demand or do. For of the gods we hold the belief, and of men we know, that by a necessity of their nature wherever they have power they always rule. And so in our case since we neither enacted this law nor when it was enacted were the first to use it, but found it in existence and expect to leave it in existence for all time, so we make use of it, well aware that both you and others, if clothed with the same power as we are, would do the same thing. And so with regard to the divine favor, we have good reason not to be afraid that we shall be at a disadvantage. But as to your expectation regarding the Lacedaemonians, your confident trust that out of shame for-sooth they will aid you—while we admire your simplicity, we do not envy you your folly. We must indeed acknowledge that with respect to themselves and the institutions of their own country, the Lacedaemonians practice virtue in a very high degree; but with respect to their conduct towards the rest of mankind, while one might speak at great length, in briefest summary one may declare that of all men with whom we are acquainted they, most conspicuously, consider what is agreeable to be honorable, and what is expedient just. And yet such an attitude is not favorable to your present unreasonable hope of deliverance."

5.106. MEL. "But we find in this very thing our strongest ground of confidence—that in their own interest the Lacedaemonians will not be willing to betray the Melians who are their colonists, and so incur, on the one hand, the distrust of all the Hellenes who are well-disposed towards them, and, on the other, give aid to their enemies."

5.107. ATH. "Do you not think, then, that self-interest goes hand in hand with security, while justice and honor are practiced with danger—a danger the Lacedaemonians are in general the least disposed to risk?"

5.108. MEL. "Nay, but even the dangers we believe they would be more ready to incur for our sakes, and that they would consider them less hazardous than if incurred for others, inasmuch as we lie close to the Peloponnesus when anything is to be undertaken there and on account of affinity of sentiment are more to be trusted than any others."

5.109. ATH. "But for men who are about to take part in a struggle, that which inspires their confidence is clearly not the good will of those who call them to their aid, but such marked superiority in actual power of achievement as they may possess; and to this superiority the Lacedaemonians give heed rather more than do the rest of mankind. At any rate, they so mistrust their own resources that they always associate themselves with many allies when they attack their neighbors; so that it is not likely they will ever cross over to an island while we are masters of the sea."

5.110. MEL "But there are others whom they might send; besides, the Cretan sea is wide, so that upon it the capture of a hostile squadron by the masters of the sea will be more difficult than it would be to cross over in security for those who wish to elude them. And if they should fail in this attempt they could turn against your territory and against any of the rest of your allies whom Brasidas did not reach; and then you would have to exert yourselves, not for the acquisition of territory that never belonged to you, but for the preservation of your own confederacy, aye, and your own country."

5.111. ATH. "Of these contingencies one or another might indeed happen; but they would not be new to our experience, and you yourselves are not unaware that the Athenians have never in a single instance withdrawn from a siege through fear of any foe. However, we cannot but reflect that, although you said that you would take counsel concerning your deliverance, you have not in this long discussion advanced a single argument that ordinary men[21] would put their confidence in if they expected to be delivered. On the contrary, your strongest grounds for confidence are merely cherished hopes whose fulfillment is in the future, whereas your present resources are too slight, compared with those already arrayed against you, for any chance of success. And you exhibit a quite unreasonable attitude of mind if you do not even now, after permitting us to withdraw, come to some decision that is wiser than your present purpose. For surely you will not take refuge in that feeling which most often brings men to ruin when they are confronted by dangers that are clearly foreseen and therefore disgraceful—the fear of such disgrace. For many men, though they can still clearly foresee the dangers into which they are drifting, are lured on by the power of a seductive word—the thing called disgrace—until, the victims of a phrase, they are indeed plunged, of their own act, into irretrievable calamities, and thus incur in addition a disgrace that is more disgraceful, because associated with folly rather than with misfortune. Such a course you

---

21. I.e. men who expect to be saved by human means, not by divine intervention.

will avoid, if you take wise counsel, and you will not consider it degrading to acknowledge your-selves inferior to the most powerful state when it offers you moderate terms—to become allies, keeping your own territory but paying tribute—and, when a choice is given you of war or safety, not to hold out stubbornly for the worse alternative. Since those who, while refusing to submit to their equals, yet comport themselves wisely towards their superiors and are moderate towards their inferiors—these, we say, are most likely to prosper. Consider, then, once more after our withdrawal, and reflect many times in your deliberations that your fatherland is at stake, your one and only fatherland, and that upon one decision only will depend her fate for weal or woe.

5.112. So the Athenians retired from the conference; and the Melians, after consulting together in private, finding themselves of much the same opinion as they had expressed before, answered as follows "Men of Athens, our opinion is no other than it was at first, nor will we in a short moment rob of its liberty a city which has been inhabited already seven hundred years; but trust-ing to the fortune which by divine favor has preserved her hitherto, and to such help as men, even the Lacedaemonians, can give, we shall try to win our deliverance. But we propose to you that we be your friends, but enemies to neither combatant, and that you withdraw from our ter-ritory, after making such a truce as may seem suitable for both of us."

5.113. Such was the answer of the Melians; and the Athenians, as they were quitting the con-ference, said: "Then, as it seems to us, judging by the result of these deliberations of yours, you are the only men who regard future events as more certain than what lies before your eyes, and who look upon that which is out of sight, merely because you wish it, as already realized. You have staked your all, putting your trust in the Lacedaemonians, in fortune and in fond hopes; and with your all you will come to ruin."

5.114. So the Athenian envoys returned to the army; and their generals, as the Melians would not yield, immediately commenced hostilities, and drew a wall round about the city of Melos, distributing the work among the several states. Afterwards, leaving some of their own troops and of their allies to keep guard both by land and by sea, they withdrew with the greater part of the army, while the rest remained behind and besieged the place.

5.115. About the same time the Argives invaded Phliasia; but being ambushed by the Phliasians and the Argive exiles they lost about eighty men. Also the Athenians at Pylos took much booty from the Lacedaemonians; but even this did not move the Lacedaemonians to renounce the treaty and make war upon them. They made proclamation, however, that any one of their own people who wished might make reprisals upon the Athenians. The Corinthians also went to war with the Athenians on account of some private differences; but the rest of tile Peloponnesians kept quiet. The Melians, too, took the part of the Athenian wall over against the market-place by a night assault; then having slain some of the men and brought in grain and as many other neces-saries as they could, they withdrew and kept quiet. After that the Athenians maintained a better watch. So the summer ended.

5.116. The following winter the Lacedaemonians were on the point of invading Argive terri-tory, but as the sacrifices for crossing the boundaries were not favorable they returned home. On account of this intention on the part of the Lacedaemonians, the Argives, suspecting certain men in their city, seized some of them, but the rest escaped. About the same time the Melians again at another point took a part of the Athenian encompassing wall, the garrison not being numerous. But later, in consequence of these occurrences, another force came from Athens, of which

Philocrates son of Demeas was commander, and the Melians, being now closely besieged—some treachery, too, having made its appearance among them—capitulated to the Athenians on the condition that these should determine their fate. The Athenians thereupon slew all the adult males whom they had taken and made slaves of the children and women. But the place they then peopled with new settlers from Athens, sending thither at a later time five hundred colonists.

V. THE SICILIAN EXPEDITION

*Thucydides' **History of the Peloponnesian War** reaches its tragic climax with the description of the Athenian expedition to Sicily in 425–413 B.C. The goal of the project was to bring the Peloponnesian League to its knees through economic pressure. The Athenians believed this could be accomplish through the conquest of the populous island of Sicily, the source of much of their enemies food supply and markets. At this point, the ambition of the Athenians knew no limits: in the words of Thucydides they believed they were strong enough "to conquer the whole world." Indeed their attitude approached the level viewed by the Greeks as hubris, pride so arrogant that was an offense to the gods.*

The blame for the failure of the mission, at least according to Thucydides, was the folly of the Athenian masses, inflamed by the demagogues, often viewed as the fatal flaw in a democracy by the Greek philosophers. In the words of Thucydides, with Pericles, "what was nominally a democracy became in his hands government by the first citizen. With Pericles' successors it was different. More on a level with one another, and each grasping at supremacy, they ended by committing even the conduct of the state affairs to the whims of the multitude. This, as might have been expected in a large imperial state, produced a host of blunders, among them the Sicilian expedition. . ."

The selections below describe that ill-fatted expedition.

Book 4.24. So much Nicias said, thinking that he would deter the Athenians by the multitude of his requirements, or, if he should be forced to make the expedition, he would in this way set out most safely. They, however, were not diverted from their eagerness for the voyage by reason of the burdensomeness of the equipment, but were far more bent upon it; and the result was just the opposite of what he had expected; for it seemed to them that he had given good advice, and that now certainly there would be abundant security. And upon all alike there fell an eager desire to sail—upon the elders, from a belief that they would either subdue the places they were sailing against, or that at any rate a great force could suffer no disaster; upon those in the flower of their age, through a longing for far-off sights and scenes, in good hopes as they were of a safe return; and upon the great multitude—that is, the soldiers—who hoped not only to get money for the present,[22] but also to acquire additional dominion which would always be an inexhaustible source of pay. And so, on account of the exceeding eagerness of the majority, even if anyone was not satisfied, he held his peace, in the fear that if he voted in opposition he might seem to be disloyal to the state.

4.30. After that, when it was already midsummer, the departure for Sicily was made. Orders had been given beforehand for most of the allies, as well as for the provision-ships and smaller boats and all the rest of the armament that went with them, to assemble at Corcyra, with the intention that from there they should all cross the Ionian Gulf to the promontory of Lapygia in one body. But the Athenians themselves and the allies that were present went down to the Piraeus at dawn on a day appointed and proceeded to man the ships for the purpose of putting to sea. And with them went down also all the general throng, everyone, we may almost say, that was in the city, both citizens and strangers, the natives to send off each their own, whether friends or kinsmen or sons, going at once in hope and with lamentations—hope that they would make conquests in Sicily, lamentations that they might never see their friends again, considering how long was the voyage from their own land on which they were being sent. And at this crisis, when under impending dangers they were now about to take leave of one another, the risks came home to them more than when they were voting for the expedition; but still their courage revived at the sight of their present strength because of the abundance of everything they saw before their eyes. The strangers on the other hand and the rest of the multitude had come for a spectacle, in the feeling that the enterprise was noteworthy and surpassing belief.

Book 7.50. Meanwhile Gylippus and Sicanus had returned to Syracuse. Sicanus had failed to win over Agrigentum, for while he was still at Gela the party at Agrigentum that was friendly to the Syracusans had been driven out; but Gylippus brought with him a large additional force from Sicily as well as the hoplites that had been sent on board the merchant-ships from the Peloponnesus the preceding spring, and had reached Selinus on their way from Libya. It seems that they had been driven out of their course to Libya, where the Cyrenacans had given them two triremes and pilots for their voyage; as they sailed alone the shore of Libya they had joined forces with the Euesperitae, who were being besieged by the Libyans, and had defeated the latter; and sailing thence along the coast to Neapolis, an emporium of the Carthaginians, from which place the distance to Sicily is shortest—two days and one night—and from there crossing to Sicily, they arrived at Selinus. As soon as these reinforcements arrived, the Syracusans began their preparations to attack the Athenians again on both elements—by sea and by land. The Athenian generals, on the other hand, seeing that the enemy had been reinforced by a fresh army, while their own situation was not only not improving, but on the contrary was daily growing worse in all respects, and especially through the distress caused by the sickness among the troops, repented that they had not moved away before. And since even Nicias no longer opposed as earnestly as before, but only urged that the matter be not openly put to a vote, they sent out word as secretly as possible to all the officers for a departure by sea from the camp, and that they should be ready whenever the signal should be given. But after all was ready and when they were about to make their departure, the moon, which happened then to be at the full, was eclipsed.[23] And most of the Athenians,

---

22. Or, "the great multitude and the soldiers were hoping to get money for the present."
23. August 27, 413 B.C.

taking the incident to heart, urged the generals to wait. Nicias also, who was somewhat too much given to divination and the like, refused even to discuss further the question of their removal until they should have waited thrice nine days, as the soothsayers prescribed. Such, then, was the reason why the Athenians delayed and stayed on. . .

7.71. And the armies on the shore on both sides, so long as the fighting at sea was evenly balanced, underwent a mighty conflict and tension of mind, the men of Sicily being ambitious to enhance the glory they had already won, while the invaders were afraid that they might fare even worse than at present. For the Athenians their all was staked upon their fleet, and their fear for the outcome like unto none they had ever felt before; and on account of the different positions which they occupied on the shore they necessarily had different views of the fighting.[24] For since the spectacle they were witnessing was near at hand and not all were looking at the same point at the same time, if one group saw the Athenians prevailing anywhere, they would take heart and fall to invoking the gods not to rob them of their safe return; while those whose eyes fell upon a portion that was being defeated uttered shrieks of lamentation, and by the mere sight of what was going on were more cowed in spirit than the men who were actually fighting. Others, again, whose gaze was fixed on some part of the field where the battle was evenly balanced, on account of the long-drawn uncertainty of the conflict were in a continual state of most distressing suspense, their very bodies swaying, in the extremity of their fear, in accord with their opinion of the battle; for always they were within a hair's breadth of escaping or of perishing. And in the same Athenian army one might hear, so long as the combatants were fighting on equal terms, every kind of cry at the same time—wailing, shouting, "We are winning," "We are beaten," and all the divers kinds of cries that a great army in great danger would be constrained to utter. The men also on board the Athenian ships were affected in a similar way, until at last the Syracusans and their allies, after the fighting had been maintained a long time, routed the Athenians and pressing on triumphantly, with loud cries and exhortations, pursued them to the land. Thereupon as regards the naval force such ships as had not been captured in the deep water were driven to shore, some to one place, some to another, and the men tumbled out of the ships and rushed for the camp; as for the army on land, their emotions were no longer at variance, but with one impulse all broke forth into wailing and groaning, being scarcely able to bear what was happening, and ran along the shore, some to the ships, in order to help their comrades, some to what remained of their wall, in order to guard it; while still others, and these the greater number, were now concerned only about themselves and how they might be saved. And at the moment there reigned a consternation greater than any fear felt before. These men had now suffered a fate not unlike that which they had themselves inflicted upon the Lacedaemonians at Pylos; for when their fleet had been destroyed there, the men who had crossed over to the island were also as good as lost to them. And so at the present time the Athenians could have no hope of getting safely away by land unless something quite extraordinary should happen.

7.75. After this, when it seemed to Nicias and Demosthenes that adequate preparations had been made, the departure of the army at last took place—on the third day following the sea-fight. And it was terrible, not in one aspect only of their fortunes, in that they were going away after

---

24. Or, "For since the Athenians had their all staked upon the ships, there was fear for the outcome like to none they had ever felt, and on this account they necessarily had different views of the sea-fighting."

losing all their ships, and, in place of high hopes, with danger threatening both themselves and their State, but also in that, on the abandonment of their camp, it fell to the lot of each man to see things that were painful both to sight and mind. The corpses were still unburied, and whenever a man saw one of his own friends lying dead, he was plunged into grief commingled with fear; and the living who were being left behind, wounded or sick, far more than the dead seemed piteous to the living, and were more wretched than those that had perished. For turning to entreaty and lamentation, they drove the men to distraction; begging to be taken along and calling aloud upon each one if they saw anywhere a comrade or a kinsman, clinging to their tent-mates now going away and following after them as long as they were able, and then, when the bodily strength of one or another failed, falling behind, though not without faint appeals to the gods and lamentations; so that the whole army, being filled with grief and in such perplexity, found it hard to depart, even out of a country that was hostile, and though they had endured already sufferings too great for tears and feared for the future what they might still have to suffer. There was also a general feeling of dejection and much self-condemnation. For indeed they looked like nothing else than a city in secret flight after a siege, and that no small city for in the entire throng no fewer than four myriads were on the march together. And of these, the rest all bore whatever each could that was useful, while the hoplites and the horsemen, contrary to their wont, carried their own food, some for want of attendants, others through distrust of them; for there had been desertions all along and in greatest numbers immediately on their defeat. But even so they did not carry enough, for there was no longer food in the camp. Furthermore, the rest of their misery and the equal sharing of their ills—although there was in this very sharing with many some alleviation—did not even so seem easy at the moment, especially when one considered from what splendor and boastfulness at first to what a humiliating end they had now come. For this was indeed the very greatest reversal that had ever happened to an Hellenic armament; for it so fell out that in place of having come to enslave others, they were now going away in fear lest they might rather themselves suffer this, and instead of prayers and paeans, with which they had sailed forth, were now departing for home with imprecations quite the reverse of these; going too as foot-soldiers instead of seamen, and relying upon hoplites rather than a fleet. And yet, by reason of the magnitude of the danger still impending, all these things seemed to them tolerable.

76. But Nicias, seeing the despondency of the army and the great change it had undergone, passed along the ranks and endeavored to encourage and cheer the soldiers as well as the circumstances permitted, shouting still louder in his zeal as he came to each contingent, and being desirous, by making his voice heard as far as possible, to do some good:

7.77. "Even in your present condition, Athenians and allies, you should still have hope—in the past men have been saved from even worse straits than these—and not blame yourselves too much either for your reverses or for your present unmerited miseries. I myself; who have the advantage of none of you in strength of body—nay, you see how I am afflicted by my disease—and who was once thought, perhaps, to be inferior to no one in good fortune as regards both my private life and my career in general, am now involved in the same danger as the meanest among you. And yet my life has been spent in the performance of many a religious duty toward the gods and many a just and blameless action towards men. Wherefore, in spite of all, my hope for the future is still confident, and our calamities do not frighten me as much as they might well have done. Perhaps they may even abate; for our enemies have had good fortune enough, and if we have roused the jealousy of any of the gods·by our expedition we have already been punished sufficiently. Others have ere now, we know, gone against their neighbors, and after acting as men will act, have suffered what men can bear. It is therefore reasonable that we also should now hope that the divine dispensations will be more kindly towards us—for we are now more deserving of the gods' pity than of their jealousy—and, furthermore you should, when you look upon your-selves and see what fine hoplites you are and what a multitude you are when marching in battle array, not be too greatly dismayed; nay, remember that wherever you establish yourselves you are at once a city, and that in all Sicily there is no other city which could either sustain an attack from you or drive you out if you once made a settlement anywhere. And as to the march, you yourselves must see to it that it is safe and orderly, and each one of you must have no other thought than this—that the place, wherever it may be, in which you will be forced to fight, will be, if you conquer, both your country and your fortress. And we must make haste upon our journey both night and day alike, for such supplies as we have are scanty; and if we reach some friendly place in the country of the Sicels—and we can still depend upon them because of their fear of the Syracusans—then only you may consider that you are in security. Directions have been sent ahead to the Sicels that they are to meet us and bring provisions with them. Know the whole truth, fellow-soldiers: you must of necessity be brave men, since there is no place near at hand which you can reach in safety if you are cowards; and if you escape your enemies now, the rest of you will win all that you surely long to see once more, and those who are Athenians will raise up again, however fallen, the great power of their State; for it is men that make a State, not walls nor ships devoid of men."

7.84. When day came[25] Nicias led his army forward; but the Syracusans and their allies kept attacking in the same fashion, hurling missiles and striking them down with javelins on all sides. The Athenians pushed on to the river Assinarus,[26] partly because they thought, hard pressed as they were on all sides by the attack of numerous horsemen and of the miscellaneous troops, that they would be somewhat better off if they crossed the river, and partly by reason of their weari-ness and desire for water. And when they reached it, they rushed in, no longer preserving order, but everyone eager to be himself the first to cross; and at the same time the pressure of the enemy now made the crossing difficult. For since they were obliged to move in a dense mass, they fell upon and trod one another down, and some perished at once, run through by their own spears, while others became entangled in their trappings and were carried away by the current. The Syracusans stood along the other bank of the river, which was steep, and hurled missiles down upon the Athenians, most of whom were drinking greedily and were all huddled in confusion in the hollow bed of the river. Moreover, the Peloponnesians went down to the water's edge and butchered them, especially those in the river. The water at once became foul, but was drunk all the same, although muddy and dyed with blood, and indeed was fought for by most of them.

7.85. At length, when the dead now lay in heaps one upon the other in the river,[27] and the army had perished utterly, part in the river, and part—if any got safely across—at the hands of

---

25. Eighth day of the retreat.

26. The modern Falconara, called also Fiume di Noto.

27. Thucydides is silent as to the number of the slain, but Diodorus (13.19) puts the loss at the river at 18,000 and the captured at 7,000; but it is evident that he includes the army of Demosthenes.

the cavalry, Nicias surrendered himself to Gylippus, having more confidence in him than in the Syracusans; and he bade him and the Lacedaemonians do with himself whatever they pleased, but to stop slaughtering the rest of the soldiers. Whereupon Gylippus at last gave orders to make prisoners; and those of the survivors who had not been secretly appropriated by the Syracusan soldiers—and these were many—were brought in a body to Syracuse alive. They also sent men in pursuit of the three hundred, who had got through the guards the night before, and captured them. Now that part of the army which was collected into the common stock was not large,[28] but that which was secretly taken by the soldiers was large, and all Sicily was filled with them, inasmuch as they had not been taken by capitulation, as had the force under Demosthenes. Besides, no small number had been killed; for the slaughter at the river had been very great—in fact, not inferior to any in this Sicilian war. And in the other frequent encounters which occurred on the march not a few had lost their lives. Notwithstanding all this, many escaped, some at the time, others afterwards, having become slaves and then making their escape; and the refuge for these was Catana.

7.86. When the forces of the Syracusans and their allies had been brought together, they took with them as many of the captives as they could and the booty and returned to the city. All the rest of the prisoners they had taken of the Athenians and their allies they sent down into the stone-quarries, thinking it the safest way to keep them ; but Nicias and Demosthenes they put to the sword, though against the wish of Gylippus. For he thought that it would be a glorious achievement if, in addition to his other successes, he could also bring the generals of the enemy home to the Lacedaemonians. And it so happened that the one, Demosthenes, was regarded by the Lacedaemonians as their bitterest foe, on account of what had taken place on the island of Sphacteria and at Pylos; the other, for the same reason, as a very good friend; for Nicias had eagerly desired that the Lacedaemonian prisoners taken on the island should be released, when he urged the Athenians to make peace. For these reasons the Lacedaemonians were friendly towards him, and it was not least on that account that he trusted in Gylippus and surrendered himself to him. But it was said that some of the Syracusans were afraid, seeing that they had been in communication with him, lest, if he were subjected to torture on that account, he might make trouble for them in the midst of their success ; and others, especially the Corinthians, were afraid, lest, as he was wealthy,[29] he might by means of bribes make his escape and cause them fresh difficulties; they therefore persuaded their allies and put him to death. For this reason, then, or for a reason very near to this, Nicias was put to death—a man who, of all the Hellenes of my time, least deserved to meet with such a calamity, because of his course of life that had been wholly regulated in accordance with virtue.

7.87. The prisoners in the stone-quarries were at first treated harshly by the Syracusans. Crowded as they were in large numbers in a deep and narrow place, at first the sun and the suffocating heat caused them distress, there being no roof; while the nights that followed were, on the contrary,

---

28. Not more than 1,000; for the total number of the captives was about 7,000, and of these 6,000 had belonged to the division of Demosthenes. But the full magnitude of the catastrophe is seen in the fact that eight days before the final surrender the Athenian army numbered 40,000.

29. He was worth 100 talents, according to Llysias (19.47). His property was chiefly in silver mines. He employed 1,000 slaves in his mines at Laurium.

autumnal and cold, so that the sudden change engendered illness. Besides, they were so cramped for space that they had to do everything in the same place; moreover, the dead were heaped together upon one another, some having died from wounds or because of the change in temperature or like causes, so that there was a stench that was intolerable. At the same time they were oppressed by both hunger and thirst—the Syracusans having for eight months given them each only a half-pint of water and a pint of food a day;[30] and of all the other ills which men thrown into such a place would be likely to suffer there was none that did not befall them. Now for some seventy days they lived in this way all together; then all the rest, except the Athenians and any Siceliots and Italiots that had joined the expedition, were sold. The total number of prisoners taken, though it is difficult to speak with accuracy, was nevertheless not fewer than seven thousand.

This event proved to be the greatest of all that had happened in the course of this war, and, as it seems to me, of all Hellenic events of which we have record—for the victors most splendid, for the vanquished most disastrous. For the vanquished, beaten utterly at every point and having suffered no slight ill in any respect—having met, as the saying goes, with utter destruction—land-force and fleet and everything perished, and few out of many came back home. Such was the course of events in Sicily.

Book 8.1. When the news reached Athens, even though the actual soldiers who had escaped from the action itself gave a clear report, they for long refused to believe that the armament could have been so utterly destroyed. When, however, they were convinced, they were angry with the orators who had taken part in promoting the expedition—as though they had not voted for it themselves—and they were also enraged at the oracle-mongers and soothsayers and whoever at that time by any practice of divination had led them to hope that they would conquer Sicily. Everything indeed on every side distressed them, and after what had happened they were beset with fear and utmost consternation. For having lost, both each man separately and as a state, many hoplites and horsemen and the flower of the youth, while they saw none like it left them, they were heavy of heart; and again, seeing no ships in the docks in sufficient number nor money in the treasury nor crews for the ships, they were at the moment hopeless of safety. They thought that their enemies in Sicily would sail with their fleet straight for the Peiraeus, especially as they had won so great a victory, and that their foes at home, now doubly prepared in all respects, would attack them at once with all their might both by land and by sea, and that their own allies would revolt and join them. Nevertheless it was their opinion that, as far as their present circumstances permitted, they should not give up, but should both make ready a fleet, providing timber and money from whatever source they could, and put their relations with their allies, and especially with Euboea, on a safe footing; moreover, that they should reduce the expenses of the city to an economical basis, and should select a board of elderly men who should prepare measures with reference to the present situation as there might be occasion. In the panic of the moment they were ready, as is the way with a democracy, to observe discipline in everything. And as they had determined, so they proceeded to act; and the summer ended.

---

30. The scantiness of this allowance—only half the amount of food given to slaves—is best seen by a comparison with that which was allowed the Lacedaemonians taken on the island of Sphacteria, namely, "two quarts of barley-meal for each man and a pint of wine."

Kuros. National Museum, Athens, Greece.

From Plutarch's Parallel Lives

19

Plutarch (Mestrius Plutarchus) lived in the late first and early second centuries A.D. He wrote many works on philosophy, ethics, biography, etc., but his greatest achievement was the Parallel Lives, *a series of biographies of the ancient Greeks and Romans. Twenty-three of them survive today and they remain one of the most important sources for the lives of the famous personalities of the ancient world. "His object was not to write continuous political history, but to exemplify individual virtue (or vice) in the careers of great men. Hence he gives attention especially to his heroes' education, to significant anecdotes, and to what he sees as the development or revelation of character. Much depends of course on the sources available to him, but the general pattern is maintained wherever possible: family, education, début in public life, climaxes, changes of fortune or attitude, latter years and death. The* Lives, *despite the pitfalls for the historian which have sometimes led to despair about their value as source-material, have been the main source of understanding of the ancient world for many readers from the Renaissance to the present day."[1]*

Below are selected excerpts from the lives of five of the important figures in ancient Greek history.

LYCURGUS

The Greeks believed Lycurgus was a wise old lawgiver and the founder of Sparta's peculiar social and political systems, but it is not clear when he lived, or even if he was a real person at all. Most modern historians regard him as only a legend. Nevertheless, Plutarch's Life of Lycurgus **remains one of two most important sources for ancient Sparta's constitutional and social institutions.[2]**

Reprinted by permission of the publishers and the Trustees of the Loeb Classical Library from *Plutarch: Volumes I, III, IV, VII, The Lives of Eminent Philosophers,* Loeb Classical Library Volumes L 46, 65, 80 and 99, translated by B. Perin, Cambridge, Mass.: Harvard University Press, 1914, 1916, 1919. The Loeb Classical Library® is a registered trademark of the President and Fellows of Harvard College.

1. Concerning Lycurgus the lawgiver, in general, nothing can be said which is not disputed, since indeed there are different accounts of his birth, his travels, his death, and above all, of his work as lawmaker and statesman; and there is least agreement among historians as to the times in which the man lived. . . . However, although the history of these times is such a maze, I shall try, in presenting my narrative, to follow those authors who are least contradicted, or who have the most notable witnesses for what they have written about the man. . .

8. A second, and a very bold political measure of Lycurgus, was his redistribution of the land. For there was a dreadful inequality in this regard, the city was heavily burdened with indigent and helpless people, and wealth was wholly concentrated in the hands of a few. Determined, therefore, to banish insolence and envy and crime and luxury, and those yet more deep-seated and afflictive diseases of the state, poverty and wealth, he persuaded his fellow-citizens to make one parcel of all their territory and divide it up anew, and to live with one another on a basis of entire uniformity and equality in the means of subsistence, seeking preeminence through virtue alone, assured that there was no other difference or inequality between man and man than that which was established by blame for base actions and praise for good ones.

Suiting the deed to the word, he distributed the rest of the Laconia land among the "perioikoi,"[3] or free provincials, in thirty thousand lots, and that which belonged to the city of Sparta, in nine thousand lots, to as many genuine Spartans. . . . The lot of each was large enough to produce annually seventy bushels of barley for a man and twelve for his wife, with a proportionate amount of wine and oil. Lycurgus thought that a lot of this size would be sufficient for them, since they needed sustenance enough to promote vigor and health of body, and nothing else. And it is said that on returning from a journey some time afterwards, as he traversed the land just after the harvest, and saw the heaps of grain standing parallel and equal to one another, he smiled, and said to them that were by: "All Laconia looks like a family estate newly divided among many brothers."

9. Next, he undertook to divide up their movable property also, in order that every vestige of unevenness and inequality might be removed; and when he saw that they could not bear to have it taken from them directly, he took another course, and overcame their avarice by political devices. In the first place, he withdrew all gold and silver money from currency, and ordained the use of iron money only. Then to a great weight and mass of this he gave a trifling value, so that ten minas' worth[4] required a large store-room in the house, and a yoke of cattle to transport it. When this money obtained currency, many sorts of iniquity went into exile from Lacedaemon. For who would steal, or receive as a bribe, or rob, or plunder that which could neither be concealed, nor possessed with satisfaction, nay, nor even cut to pieces with any profit? For vinegar was used, as we are told, to quench the red-hot iron, robbing it of its temper and making it worthless for any other purpose, when once it had become brittle and hard to work.

---

1. *The Oxford Classical Dictionary*, third edition, edited by Simon Hornblower and Antony Spawforth, Oxford University Press, Oxford, 1996, p. 1201

2. The other: Xenophon's *The Constitution of the Lacedaemonians*.

3. Perioikoi, "dwellers round about," was the term employed usually to describe subjects or half-citizens. Their origin and status is unclear.

4. About $200.

In the next place, he banished the unnecessary and superfluous arts. And even without such banishment most of them would have departed with the old coinage, since there was no sale for their products. For the iron money could not be carried into the rest of Greece, nor had it any value there, but was rather held in ridicule. It was not possible, therefore, to buy any foreign wares or bric-a-brac; no merchant seamen brought freight into their harbors; no rhetoric teacher set foot on Laconian soil, no vagabond soothsayer, no keeper of harlots, no gold or silver smith, since there was no money there. But luxury, thus gradually deprived of that which stimulated and supported it, died away of itself, and men of large possessions had no advantage over the poor, because their wealth found no public outlet, but had to be stored up at home in idleness. In this way it came about that such common and necessary utensils as bedsteads, chairs, and tables were most excellently made among them, and the Laconian "kothon," or drinking-cup, was in very high repute for usefulness among soldiers in active service, as Critias tells us. For its color concealed the disagreeable appearance of the water which they were often compelled to drink, and its curving lips caught the muddy sediment and held it inside, so that only the purer part reached the mouth of the drinker. For all this they had to thank their lawgiver; since their artisans were now freed from useless tasks, and displayed the beauty of their workmanship in objects of constant and necessary use.

10. With a view to attack luxury still more and remove the thirst for wealth, he introduced his third and most exquisite political device, namely, the institution of common messes, so that they might eat with one another in companies, of common and specified foods, and not take their meals at home, reclining on costly couches at costly tables, delivering themselves into the hands of servants and cooks to be fattened in the dark, like voracious animals, and ruining not only their characters but also their bodies, by surrendering them to every desire and all sorts of surfeit, which call for long sleeps, hot baths, abundant rest, and, as it were, daily nursing and tending. This was surely a great achievement, but it was a still greater one to make wealth "an object of no desire," as Theophrastus says, and even "unwealth," by this community of meals and simplicity of diet. For the rich man could neither use nor enjoy nor even see or display his abundant means, when he went to the same meal as the poor man; so that it was in Sparta alone, of all the cities under the sun, that men could have that far-famed sight, a Plutus[5] blind, and lying as lifeless and motionless as a picture. For the rich could not even dine beforehand at home and then go to the common mess with full stomachs, but the rest kept careful watch of him who did not eat and drink with them, and reviled him as a weakling, and one too effeminate for the common diet.

13. None of his laws were put into writing by Lycurgus, indeed, one of the so-called "rhetras," or decrees, forbids it. For he thought that if the most important and binding principles which conduce to the prosperity and virtue of a city were implanted in the habits and training of its citizens, they would remain unchanged and secure, having a stronger bond than compulsion in the fixed purposes imparted to the young by education, which performs the office of a law-giver for every one of them. And as for minor matters, such as business contracts, and cases where the needs vary from time to time, it was better, as he thought, not to hamper them by written constraints or fixed usages, but to suffer them, as occasion demanded, to receive such modifications

---

5. The god of wealth.

as educated men should determine. Indeed, he assigned the function of law-making wholly and entirely to education.

One of his rhetras accordingly, as I have said, prohibited the use of written laws. Another was directed against extravagance, ordaining that every house should have its roof fashioned by the axe, and its doors by the saw only, and by no other tool. For, as in later times Epaminondas is reported to have said at his own table, that such a meal did not comport with treachery, so Lycurgus was the first to see clearly that such a house does not comport with luxury and extravagance. Nor is any man so vulgar and senseless as to introduce into a simple and common house silver-footed couches, purple coverlets, gold drinking-cups, and all the extravagance which goes along with these, but one must of necessity adapt and proportion his couch to his house, his coverlets to his couch, and to this the rest of his supplies and equipment. It was because he was used to this simplicity that Leotychides the Elder, as we are told, when he was dining in Corinth, and saw the roof of the house adorned with costly panelings, asked his host if trees grew square in that country.

A third rhetra of Lycurgus is mentioned, which forbids making frequent expeditions against the same enemies, in order not to accustom such enemies to frequent defense of themselves, which would make them warlike. And this was the special grievance which they had against King Agesilaus in later times, namely, that by his continual and frequent incursions and expeditions into Boeotia he rendered the Thebans a match for the Lacedaemonians. And therefore, when Antalcidas saw the king wounded, he said: "This is a fine tuition-fee which thou art getting from the Thebans, for teaching them how to fight, when they did not wish to do it, and did not know how." Such ordinances as these were called "rhetras" by Lycurgus, implying that they came from the god and were oracles.

14. In the matter of education, which he regarded as the greatest and noblest task of the lawgiver, he began at the very source, by carefully regulating marriages and births. For it is not true that, as Aristotle says, he tried to bring the women under proper restraint, but desisted, because he could not overcome the great license and power which the women enjoyed on account of the many expeditions in which their husbands were engaged. During these the men were indeed obliged to leave their wives in sole control at home, and for this reason paid them greater deference than was their due, and gave them the title of Mistress. But even to the women Lycurgus paid all possible attention. He made the maidens exercise their bodies in running, wrestling, casting the discus, and hurling the javelin, in order that the fruit of their wombs might have vigorous root in vigorous bodies and come to better maturity, and that they themselves might come with vigor to the fullness of their times, and struggle successfully and easily with the pangs of childbirth. He freed them from softness and delicacy and all effeminacy by accustoming the maidens no less than the youths to wear tunics only in processions, and at certain festivals to dance and sing when the young men were present as spectators. There they sometimes even mocked and railed good-naturedly at any youth who had misbehaved himself; and again they would sing the praises of those who had shown themselves worthy, and so inspire the young men with great ambition and ardor. For he who was thus extolled for his valor and held in honor among the maidens, went away exalted by their praises; while the sting of their playful raillery was no less sharp than that of serious admonitions, especially as the kings and elders, together with the rest of the citizens, were all present at the spectacle.

Nor was there anything disgraceful in this scant clothing of the maidens, for modesty attended them, and wantonness was banished; nay, rather, it produced in them habits of simplicity and an ardent desire for health and beauty of body. It gave also to woman-kind a taste of lofty sentiment, for they felt that they too had a place in the arena of bravery and ambition. Wherefore they were led to think and speak as Gorgo, the wife of Leonidas, is said to have done. When some foreign woman, as it would seem, said to her: "You Spartan women are the only ones who rule their men," she answered "Yes, we are the only ones that give birth to men."

15. Moreover, there were incentives to marriage in these things—I mean such things as the appearance of the maidens without much clothing in processions and athletic contests where young men were looking on, for these were drawn on by necessity, "not geometrical, but the sort of necessity which lovers know," as Plato says. Nor was this all; Lycurgus also put a kind of public stigma upon confirmed bachelors. They were excluded from the sight of the young men and maidens at their exercises, and in winter the magistrates ordered them to march round the market-place in their tunics only, and as they marched, they sang a certain song about themselves, and its burden was that they were justly punished for disobeying the laws. Besides this, they were deprived of the honor and gracious attentions which the young men habitually paid to their elders. Therefore there was no one to find fault with what was said to Dercyllidas, reputable general though he was. As he entered a company, namely, one of the younger men would not offer him his seat, but said: "Indeed, thou hast begotten no son who will one day give his seat to me."

For their marriages the women were carried off by force, not when they were small and unfit for wedlock, but when they were in full bloom and wholly ripe. After the woman was thus carried off, the bride's-maid, so called, took her in charge, cut her hair off close to the head, put a man's cloak and sandals on her, and laid her down on a pallet, on the floor, alone, in the dark. Then the bride-groom, not flown with wine nor enfeebled by excesses, but composed and sober, after supping at his public mess-table as usual, slipped stealthily into the room where the bride lay, loosed her virgin's zone, and bore her in his arms to the marriage bed. Then, after spending a short time with his bride, he went away composedly to his usual quarters, there to sleep with the other young men. And so he continued to do from that time on, spending his days with his comrades, and sleeping with them at night, but visiting his bride by stealth and with every precaution, full of dread and fear lest any of her household should be aware of his visits, his bride also contriving and conspiring with him that they might have stolen interviews as occasion offered. And this they did not for a short time only, but long enough for some of them to become fathers before they had looked upon their own wives by daylight. Such interviews not only brought into exercise self-restraint and moderation, but united husbands and wives when their bodies were full of creative energy and their affections new and fresh, not when they were sated and dulled by unrestricted intercourse; and there was always left behind in their hearts some residual spark of mutual longing and delight.

After giving marriage such traits of reserve and decorum, he none the less freed men from the empty and womanish passion of jealous possession, by making it honorable for them, while keeping the marriage relation free from all wanton irregularities, to share with other worthy men in the begetting of children, laughing to scorn those who regard such common privileges as intolerable, and resort to murder and war rather than grant them. For example, an elderly man with a young wife, if he looked with favor and esteem on some fair and noble young man, might introduce him to her, and adopt her offspring by such a noble father as his own. And again, a worthy man who admired some woman for the fine children that she bore her husband and the modesty of her behavior as a wife, might enjoy her favors, if her husband would consent, thus planting, as it were, in a soil of beautiful fruitage, and begetting for himself noble sons, who would have the blood of noble men in their veins. For in the first place, Lycurgus did not regard sons as the peculiar property of their fathers, but rather as the common property of the state, and therefore would not have his citizens spring from random parentage, but from the best there was. In the second place, he saw much folly and vanity in what other peoples enacted for the regulation of these matters; in the breeding of dogs and horses they insist on having the best sires which money or favor can secure, but they keep their wives under lock and key, demanding that they have children by none but themselves, even though they be foolish, or infirm, or diseased; as though children of bad stock did not show their badness to those first who possessed and reared them, and children of good stock, contrariwise, their goodness. The freedom which thus prevailed at that time in marriage relations was aimed at physical and political well-being, and was far removed from the licentiousness which was afterwards attributed to their women, so much so that adultery was wholly unknown among them. And a saying is reported of one Geradas, a Spartan of very ancient type, who, on being asked by a stranger what the punishment for adulterers was among them, answered: "Stranger, there is no adulterer among us." "Suppose, then," replied the stranger, "there should be one." "A bull," said Geradas, "would be his forfeit, a bull so large that it could stretch over Mount Taygetus and drink from the river Eurotas." Then the stranger was astonished and said: "But how could there be a bull so large?" To which Geradas replied, with a smile: "But how could there be an adulterer in Sparta?" Such, then, are the accounts we find of their marriages.

16. Offspring was not reared at the will of the father, but was taken and carried by him to a place called Lesche, where the elders of the tribes officially examined the infant, and if it was well-built and sturdy, they ordered the father to rear it, and assigned it one of the nine thousand lots of land; but if it was ill-born and deformed, they sent it to the so-called Apothetae, a chasm-like place at the foot of Mount Taygetus, in the conviction that the life of that which nature had not well equipped at the very beginning for health and strength, was of no advantage either to itself or the state. On the same principle, the women used to bathe their new-born babes not with water, but with wine, thus making a sort of test of their constitutions. For it is said that epileptic and sickly infants are thrown into convulsions by the strong wine and loose their senses, while the healthy ones are rather tempered by it, like steel, and given a firm habit of body. Their nurses, too, exercised great care and skill; they reared infants without swaddling-bands, and thus left their limbs and figures free to develop; besides, they taught them to be contented and happy, not dainty about their food, nor fearful of the dark, nor afraid to be left alone, nor given to contemptible peevishness and whimpering. This is the reason why foreigners sometimes bought Spartan nurses for their children. Amycla, for instance, the nurse of the Athenian Alcibiades, is said to have been a Spartan.

And yet Alcibiades, as Plato says, had for a tutor, set over him by Pericles, one Zopyrus, who was just a common slave. But Lycurgus would not put the sons of Spartans in charge of purchased or hired tutors, nor was it lawful for every father to rear or train his son as he pleased, but as soon as they were seven years old, Lycurgus ordered them all to be taken by the state and enrolled in companies, where they were put under the same discipline and nurture, and so became accustomed to share one another's sports and studies. The boy who excelled in judgment and was most courageous in fighting, was made captain of his company; on him the rest all kept their eyes, obeying his orders, and submitting to his punishments, so that their boyish training was a practice of obedience. Besides, the elderly men used to watch their sports, and by ever and anon egging them on to mimic battles and disputes, learned accurately how each one of them was naturally disposed when it was a question of boldness and aggressiveness in their struggles.

Of reading and writing, they learned only enough to serve their turn; all the rest of their training was calculated to make them obey commands well, endure hardships, and conquer in battle. Therefore, as they grew in age, their bodily exercise was increased; their heads were close-clipped, and they were accustomed to going bare-foot, and to playing for the most part without clothes. When they were twelve years old, they no longer had tunics to wear, received one cloak a year, had hard, dry flesh, and knew little of baths and ointments; only on certain days of the year, and few at that, did they indulge in such amenities. They slept together, in troops and companies, on pallet-beds which they collected for themselves, breaking off with their hands—no knives allowed—the tops of the rushes which grew along the river Eurotas. In the winter-time, they added to the stuff of these pallets the so-called "lycophon," or *thistle-down,* which was thought to have warmth in it.

17. When the boys reached this age, they were favored with the society of lovers from among the reputable young men. The elderly men also kept close watch of them, coming more frequently to their places of exercise, and observing their contests of strength and wit, not superficially, but with the idea that they were all in a sense the fathers and tutors and governors of all the boys. In this way, at every fitting time and in every place, the boy who went wrong had someone to admonish and chastise him. Nor was this all; one of the noblest and best men of the city was appointed paedonome, or inspector of the boys, and under his directions the boys, in their several companies, put themselves under the command of the most prudent and warlike of the so-called Eirens. This was the name given to those who had been for two years out of the class of boys, and Melleirens, or *Would-be Eirens,* was the name for the oldest of the boys. This eiren, then, a youth of twenty years, commands his subordinates in their mimic battles, and in doors makes them serve him at his meals. He commissions the larger ones to fetch wood, and the smaller ones potherbs. And they steal what they fetch, some of them entering the gardens, and others creeping right slyly and cautiously into the public messes of the men; but if a boy is caught stealing, he is soundly flogged, as a careless and un-skilful thief. They steal, too, whatever food they can, and learn to be adept in setting upon people when asleep or off their guard. But the boy who is caught gets a flogging and must go hungry. For the meals allowed them are scanty, in order that they may take into their own hands the fight against hunger, and so be forced into boldness and cunning.

This is the main object of their spare diet; a secondary one is to make them grow tall. For it contributes to height of stature when the vitality is not impeded and hindered by a mass of nourishment which forces it into thickness and width, but ascends of its own lightness, and when the body grows freely and easily. The same thing seems also to conduce to beauty of form; for lean and meager habits yield more readily to the force of articulation, whereas the gross and over fed are so heavy as to resist it. Just so, we may be sure, women who take physic while they are pregnant, bear children which are lean, it may be, but well-shaped and fine, because the lightness of the parent matter makes it more susceptible to molding. However, the reason for this I must leave for others to investigate.

18. The boys make such a serious matter of their stealing, that one of them, as the story goes, who was carrying concealed under his cloak a young fox which he had stolen, suffered the animal to tear out his bowels with its teeth and claws, and died rather than have his theft detected. And even this story gains credence from what their youths now endure, many of whom I have seen expiring under the lash at the altar of Artemis Orthia.

The eiren, as he reclined after supper, would order one of the boys to sing a song, and to another would put a question requiring a careful and deliberate answer, as, for instance, "Who is the best man in the city?" or, "What think you of this man's conduct?" In this way the boys were accustomed to pass right judgments and interest themselves at the very outset in the conduct of the citizens. For if one of them was asked who was a good citizen, or who an infamous one, and had no answer to make, he was judged to have a torpid spirit, and one that would not aspire to excellence. And the answer must not only have reasons and proof given for it, but also be couched in very brief and concise language, and the one who gave a faulty answer was punished with a bite in the thumb from the eiren. Often-times, too, the eiren punished the boys in the presence of the elders and magistrates, thus showing whether his punishments were reasonable and proper or not. While he was punishing them, he suffered no restraint, but after the boys were gone, he was brought to an account if his punishments were harsher than was necessary, or, on the other hand, too mild and gentle.

The boys' lovers also shared with them in their honor or disgrace; and it is said that one of them was once fined by the magistrates because his favorite boy had let an ungenerous cry escape him while he was fighting. Moreover, though this sort of love was so approved among them that even the maidens found lovers in good and noble women, still, there was no jealous rivalry in it, but those who fixed their affections on the same boys made this rather a foundation for friendship with one another, and persevered in common efforts to make their loved one as noble as possible.

19. The boys were also taught to use a discourse which combined, pungency with grace, and condensed much observation into a few words. His iron money, indeed, Lycurgus made of large weight and small value, as I have observed, but the current coin of discourse he adapted to the expression of deep and abundant meaning with simple and brief diction, by contriving that the general habit of silence should make the boys sententious and correct in their answers. For as sexual incontinence generally produces unfruitfulness and sterility, so intemperance in talking makes discourse empty and vapid. King Agis, accordingly, when a certain Athenian decried the Spartan swords for being so short, and said that jugglers on the stage easily swallowed them, replied: "And yet we certainly reach our enemies with these daggers." And I observe that although the speech also of the Spartans seems short, yet it certainly reaches the point, and arrests the thought of the listener.

And indeed Lycurgus himself seems to have been short and sententious in his speech, if we may judge from his recorded sayings; that, for instance, on forms of government, to one who demanded the establishment of democracy in the city: "Go thou," said he, "and first establish democracy in thy household." That, again, to one who inquired why he ordained such small and inexpensive sacrifices: "That we may never omit," said he, "to honor the gods." Again, in the matter of athletic contests, he allowed the citizens to engage only in those where there was no stretching forth of hands.[6] There are also handed down similar answers which he made by letter to his fellow-citizens. When they asked how they could ward off an invasion of enemies, he answered: "By remaining poor, and by not desiring to be greater the one than the other." And when they asked about fortifying their city, he answered: "A city will be well fortified which is surrounded by brave men and not by bricks." Now regarding these and similar letters, belief and skepticism are alike difficult.

20. Of their aversion to long speeches, the following apothegms are proof. King Leonidas, when a certain one discoursed with him out of all season on matters of great concern, said: "My friend, the matter urges, but not the time." Charilaus, the nephew of Lycurgus, when asked why his uncle had made so few laws, answered: "Men of few words need few laws." Archidamidas, when certain ones found fault with Hecataeus the Sophist for saying nothing after being admitted to their public mess, answered: "He who knows how, knows also when to speak." Instances of the pungent sayings not devoid of grace, of which I spoke,[7] are the following. Demaratus, when a troublesome fellow was pestering him with ill-timed questions, and especially with the oft repeated query who was the best of the Spartans, answered at last: "He who is least like you." And Agis, when certain ones were praising the Eleians for their just and honorable conduct of the Olympic games, said: "And what great matter is it for the Eleians to practice righteousness one day in five years?" And Theopompus, when a stranger kept saying, as he showed him kindness, that in his own city he was called a lover of Sparta, remarked: "My good Sir, it were better for you to be called a lover of your own city." And Pleistoanax, the son of Pausanias, when an Athenian orator declared that the Lacedaemonians had no learning, said: "True, we are indeed the only Hellenes who have learned no evil from you." And Archidamus when some one asked him how many Spartans there were, replied: "Enough, good Sir, to keep evil men away."

And even from their jests it is possible to judge of their character. For it was their wont never to talk at random, and to let slip no speech which did not have some thought or other worth serious attention. For instance, when one of them was invited to hear a man imitate the nightingale, he said: "I have heard the bird herself." And another, on reading the epitaph:

"Tyranny's fires they were trying to quench when panoplied Ares
Slew them; Selinus looked down from her gates on their death,"

said: "The men deserved to die; they should have let the fires burn out entirely." And a youth, when some one promised to give him game-cocks that would die fighting, said, "Don't do that, but give me some of the kind that kill fighting." Another, seeing men seated on stools in a privy, said: "May I never sit where I cannot give place to an elder." The character of their apothegms, then, was such as to justify the remark that love of wisdom rather than love of bodily exercise was the special characteristic of a Spartan.

24. The training of the Spartans lasted into the years of full maturity. No man was allowed to live as he pleased, but in their city, as in a military encampment, they always had a prescribed regimen and employment in public service, considering that they belonged entirely to their country

---

6. After the manner of men begging their conquerors to spare their lives.
7. Chapter 19.

and not to themselves, watching over the boys, if no other duty was laid upon them, and either teaching them some useful thing, or learning it themselves from their elders. For one of the noble and blessed privileges which Lycurgus provided for his fellow citizens, was abundance of leisure, since he forbade their engaging in any mechanical art whatsoever, and as for money making, with its laborious efforts to amass wealth, there was no need of it at all, since wealth awakened no envy and brought no honor. Besides, the Helots[8] tilled their ground for them, and paid them the produce mentioned above.[9] Therefore it was that one of them who was sojourning at Athens when the courts were in session, and learned that a certain Athenian had been fined for idleness and was going home in great distress of mind and attended on his way by sympathetic and sorrowing friends, begged the bystanders to show him the man who had been fined for living like a freeman. So servile a thing did they regard the devotion to the mechanical arts and to money-making. And law suits, of course, vanished from among them with their gold and silver coinage, for they knew neither greed nor want, but equality in well-being was established there, and easy living based on simple wants. Choral dances and feasts and festivals and hunting and bodily exercise and social converse occupied their whole time, when they were not on a military expedition.

27. Furthermore, Lycurgus made most excellent regulations in the matter of their burials. To begin with, he did away with all superstitious terror by allowing them to bury their dead within the city, and to have memorials of them near the sacred places, thus making the youth familiar with such sights and accustomed to them, so that they were not confounded by them, and had no horror of death as polluting those who touched a corpse or walked among graves. In the second place, he permitted nothing to be buried with the dead; they simply covered the body with a scarlet robe and olive leaves when they laid it away. To inscribe the name of the dead upon the tomb was not allowed, unless it were that of a man who had fallen in war, or that of a woman who had died in sacred office. He set apart only a short time for mourning, eleven days; on the twelfth, they were to sacrifice to Demeter and cease their sorrowing. Indeed, nothing was left untouched and neglected, but with all the necessary details of life he blended some commendation of virtue or rebuke of vice; and he filled the city full of good examples, whose continual presence and society must of necessity exercise a controlling and molding influence upon those who were walking the path of honor.

This was the reason why he did not permit them to live abroad at their pleasure and wander in strange lands, assuming foreign habits and imitating the lives of peoples who were without training and lived under different forms of government. Nay more, he actually drove away from the city the multitudes which streamed in there for no useful purpose, not because he feared they might become imitators of his form of government and learn useful lessons in virtue, as Thucydides says,[10] but rather that they might not become in any wise teachers of evil. For along with strange people, strange doctrines must come in; and novel doctrines bring novel decisions, from which there must arise many feelings and resolutions which destroy the harmony of the existing political order. Therefore he thought it more necessary to keep bad manners and customs from invading and filling the city than it was to keep out infectious diseases.

---

8. State slaves, somewhat similar to medieval serfs.
9. Chapter 8.
10. See the *Funeral Oration of Pericles*, 2.39.1.

28. Now in all this there is no trace of injustice or arrogance, which some attribute to the laws of Lycurgus, declaring them efficacious in producing valor, but defective in producing righteousness. The so-called "krupteia," or *secret service*, of the Spartans, if this be really one of the institutions of Lycurgus, as Aristotle says it was, may have given Plato also this opinion of the man and his civil polity. This secret service was of the following nature. The magistrates from time to time sent out into the country at large the most discreet of the young warriors, equipped only with daggers and such supplies as were necessary. In the day time they scattered into obscure and out of the way places, where they hid themselves and lay quiet; but in the night they came down into the highways and killed every Helot whom they caught. Oftentimes, too, they actually traversed the fields where Helots were working and slew the sturdiest and best of them. So, too, Thucydides, in his *History of the Peloponnesian War*,[11] tells us that the Helots who had been judged by the Spartans to be superior in bravery, set wreaths upon their heads in token of their emancipation, and visited the temples of the gods in procession, but a little while afterwards all disappeared, more than two thousand of them, in such a way that no man was able to say, either then or afterwards, how they came by their deaths. And Aristotle in particular says also that the ephors, as soon as they came into office, made formal declaration of war upon the Helots, in order that there might be no impiety in slaying them.

And in other ways also they were harsh and cruel to the Helots. For instance, they would force them to drink too much strong wine, and then introduce them into their public messes, to show the young men what a thing drunkenness was. They also ordered them to sing songs and dance dances that were low and ridiculous, but to let the nobler kind [of music] alone. And therefore in later times, they say, when the Thebans made their expedition into Laconia,[12] they ordered the Helots whom they captured to sing the songs of Terpander, Alcman, and Spendon the Spartan; but they declined to do so, on the plea that their masters did not allow it, thus proving the correctness of the saying: "In Sparta the freeman is more a freeman than anywhere else in the world, and the slave more a slave." However, in my opinion, such cruelties were first practiced by the Spartans in later times, particularly after the great earthquake,[13] when the Helots and Messenians together rose up against them, wrought the widest devastation in their territory, and brought their city into the greatest peril. I certainly cannot ascribe to Lycurgus so abominable a measure as the "krupteia," judging of his character from his mildness and justice in all other instances. To this the voice of the god also bore witness.

29. When his principal institutions were at last firmly fixed in the customs of the people, and his civil polity had sufficient growth and strength to support and preserve itself; just as Plato says that Deity was rejoiced to see His universe come into being and make its first motion, so Lycurgus was filled with joyful satisfaction in the magnitude and beauty of his system of laws, now that it was in operation and moving along its pathway. He therefore ardently desired, so far as human forethought could accomplish the task, to make it immortal, and let it go down unchanged to future ages. Accordingly, he assembled the whole people, and told them that the provisions already made were sufficiently adapted to promote the prosperity and virtue of the state, but that

---

11. Thucydides, 4.80.
12. In 369 B.C.
13. 464 B.C.

something of the greatest weight and importance remained, which he could not lay before them until he had consulted the god at Delphi. They must therefore abide by the established laws and make no change nor alteration in them until he came back from Delphi in person; then he would do whatsoever the god thought best. When they all agreed to this and bade him set out on his journey, he exacted an oath from the kings and the elders, and afterwards from the rest of the citizens, that they would abide by the established polity and observe it until Lycurgus should come back; then he set out for Delphi.

On reaching the oracle, he sacrificed to the god, and asked if the laws which he had established were good, and sufficient to promote a city's prosperity and virtue. Apollo answered that the laws which he had established were good, and that the city would continue to be held in highest honor while it kept to the polity of Lycurgus. This oracle Lycurgus wrote down, and sent it to Sparta. But for his own part, he sacrificed again to the god, took affectionate leave of his friends and of his son, and resolved never to release his fellow-citizens from their oath, but of his own accord to put an end to his life where he was. He had reached an age in which life was not yet a burden, and death no longer a terror; when he and his friends, moreover, appeared to be sufficiently prosperous and happy. He therefore abstained from food till he died, considering that even the death of a statesman should be of service to the state, and the ending of his life not void of effect, but recognized as a virtuous deed. As for himself, since he had wrought out fully the noblest tasks, the end of life would actually be a consummation of his good fortune and happiness; and as for his fellow-citizens, he would make his death the guardian, as it were, of all the blessings he had secured for them during his life, since they had sworn to observe and maintain his polity until he should return. And he was not deceived in his expectations, so long did his city have the first rank in Hellas for good government and reputation, observing as she did for five hundred years the laws of Lycurgus, in which no one of the fourteen kings who followed him made any change, down to Agis the son of Archidamus. For the institution of the ephors did not weaken, but rather strengthened the civil polity, and though it was thought to have been done in the interests of the people, it really made the aristocracy more powerful.

30. But in the reign of Agis, gold and silver money first flowed into Sparta, and with money, greed and a desire for wealth prevailed through the agency of Lysander, who, though incorruptible himself, filled his country with the love of riches and with luxury, by bringing home gold and silver from the war, and thus subverting the laws of Lycurgus. While these remained in force, Sparta led the life, not of a city under a constitution, but of an individual man under training and full of wisdom. Nay rather, as the poets weave their tales of Heracles, how with his club and lion's skin he traversed the world chastising lawless and savage tyrants, so we may say that Sparta, simply with the dispatch-staff and cloak of her envoys, kept Hellas in willing and glad obedience, put down illegal oligarchies and tyrannies in the different states, arbitrated wars, and quelled seditions, often without so much as moving a single shield, but merely sending one ambassador, whose commands all at once obeyed, just as bees, when their leader appears, swarm together and array themselves about him. Such a surplus fund of good government and justice did the city enjoy.

Wherefore, I for one am amazed at those who declare that the Lacedaemonians knew how to obey, but did not understand how to command, and quote with approval the story of King Theopompus, who, when some one said that Sparta was safe and secure because her kings knew how to command, replied: "Nay, rather because her citizens know how to obey." For men will not consent to obey those who have not the ability to rule, but obedience is a lesson to be learned from a commander. For a good leader makes good followers, and just as the final attainment of the art of horsemanship is to make a horse gentle and tractable, so it is the task of the science of government to implant obedience in men. And the Lacedaemonians implanted in the rest of the Greeks not only a willingness to obey, but a desire to be their followers and subjects. People did not send requests to them for ships, or money, or hoplites, but for a single Spartan commander; and when they got him, they treated him with honor and reverence, as the Sicilians treated Gylippus; the Chalcidians, Brasidas; and all the Greeks resident in Asia, Lysander, Callicratidas, and Agesilaus. These men, wherever they came, were styled regulators and chasteners of peoples and magistrates, and the city of Sparta from which they came was regarded as a teacher of well-ordered private life and settled civil polity. To this position of Sparta Stratonicus would seem to have mockingly alluded when, in jest, he proposed a law that the Athenians should conduct mysteries and processions, and that the Eleians should preside at games, since herein lay their special excellence, but that the Lacedaemonians should be cudgelled if the others did amiss. This was a joke; but Antisthenes the Socratic, when he saw the Thebans in high feather after the battle of Leuctra,[14] said in all seriousness that they were just like little boys strutting about because they had thrashed their tutor.

31. It was not, however, the chief design of Lycurgus then to leave his city in command over a great many others, but he thought that the happiness of an entire city, like that of a single individual, depended on the prevalence of virtue and concord within its own borders. The aim, therefore, of all his arrangements and adjustments was to make his people free-minded, self-sufficing, and moderate in all their ways, and to keep them so as long as possible. His design for a civil polity was adopted by Plato, Diogenes, Zeno, and by all those who have won approval for their treatises on this subject, although they left behind them only writings and words. Lycurgus, on the other hand, produced not writings and words, but an actual polity which was beyond imitation, and because he gave, to those who maintain that the much talked of natural disposition to wisdom exists only in theory, an example of an entire city given to the love of wisdom, his fame rightly transcended that of all who ever founded polities among the Greeks. Therefore Aristotle says that the honors paid him in Sparta were less than he deserved, although he enjoys the highest honors there. For he has a temple, and sacrifices are offered to him yearly as to a god. It is also said that when his remains were brought home, his tomb was struck by lightning, and that this hardly happened to any other eminent man after him except Euripides, who died and was buried at Arethusa in Macedonia. The lovers of Euripides therefore regard it as a great testimony in his favor that he alone experienced after death what had earlier befallen a man who was most holy and beloved of the gods.

Some say that Lycurgus died in Cirrha; Apollothemis, that he was brought to Elis and died there; Timacus and Aristoxenus, that he ended his days in Crete; and Aristoxenus adds that his tomb is shown by the Cretans in the district of Pergamus, near the public highway. It is also said that he left an only son, Antiorus, on whose death without issue, the family became extinct. His friends and relations, however, instituted a periodical assembly in his memory, which continued

---

14. In 371 B.C., when the Thebans under Epaminondas broke the supremacy of Sparta.

to be held for many ages, and they called the days on which they came together, Lycurgidae. Aristocrates the son of Hipparchus says that the friends of Lycurgus, after his death in Crete, burned his body and scattered the ashes into the sea, and that this was done at his request, and because he wished to prevent his remains from ever being carried to Sparta, lest the people there should change his polity, on the plea that he had come back, and that they were therefore released from their oaths. This, then, is what I have to say about Lycurgus.

Solon

Solon was the Athenian equivalent of Lycurgus, a famous, wise old lawgiver. In the early sixth century B.C. there was serious discontent in Athens. Many of the poor farmers had sunk into virtual serfdom, burdened with debt to their richer neighbors. At the same time there was a demand for political rights from certain groups who had hitherto had none. Solon was considered a suitable mediator and was elected archon in 594 and given the power to reform the political, economic and social system of Athens. The following excerpts from Plutarch's Life of Solon *describe Solon's reforms.*

1. Didymus the grammarian, in his reply to Asciepiades on Solon's tables of law, mentions a remark of one Philocles, in which it is stated that Solon's father was Euphorion, contrary to the opinion of all others who have written about Solon. For they all unite in saying that he was a son of Execestides, a man of moderate wealth and influence in the city, but a member of its foremost family, being descended from Codrus. Solon's mother, according to Heracleides Ponticus, was a cousin of the mother of Peisistratus. And the two men were at first great friends, largely because of their kinship, and largely because of the youthful beauty of Peisistratus, with whom, as some say, Solon was passionately in love. And this may be the reason why, in later years, when they were at variance about matters of state, their enmity did not bring with it any harsh or savage feelings, but their former amenities lingered in their spirits, and preserved there,

"smoldering with a lingering flame of Zeus-sent fire,"[15]

the grateful memory of their love. And that Solon was not proof against beauty in a youth, and made not so bold with Love as "to confront him like a boxer, hand to hand,"[16] may be inferred from his poems. He also wrote a law forbidding a slave to practice gymnastics or have a boy lover, thus putting the matter in the category of honorable and dignified practices, and in a way inciting the worthy to that which he forbade the unworthy. And it is said that Peisistratus also had a boy lover, Charmus, and that he dedicated the statue of Love in the Academy, where the runners in the sacred torch race light their torches.

---

15. Euripides, *Bacchae*, 8.
16. The remains of solon's poetry have been collected in Bergk's *Poetae Lyrici Graeci*.

2. Solon, then, after his father had impaired his estate in sundry benevolent charities, as Hermippus tells us, might have found friends enough who were willing to aid him. But he was ashamed to take from others, since he belonged to a family which had always helped others, and therefore, while still a young man, embarked in commerce. And yet some say that he traveled to get experience and learning rather than to make money. For he was admittedly a lover of wisdom, since even when he was well on in years he would say that he "grew old ever learning many things"; and he was not an admirer of wealth, but actually says that two men are alike wealthy of whom one

". . .much silver hath,
And gold, and wide domains of wheat-bearing soil,
Horses and mules; while to the other only enough belongs
To give him comfort of food, and clothes, and shoes,
Enjoyment of child and blooming wife, when these too come,
And only years commensurate therewith are his."

However, in another place he says:

"Wealth I desire to have; but wrongfully to get it,
I do not wish. Justice, even if slow, is sure."

And there is no reason why a good statesman should either set his heart too much on the acquisition of superfluous wealth, or despise unduly the use of what is necessary and convenient. In those earlier times, to use the words of Hesiod,[17] "work was no disgrace," nor did a trade bring with it social inferiority, and the calling of a merchant was actually held in honor, since it gave him familiarity with foreign parts, friendships with foreign kings, and a large experience in affairs. Some merchants were actually founders of great cities, as Protis, who was beloved by the Gauls along the Rhone, was of Marseilles. Thales is said to have engaged in trade, as well as Hippocrates the mathematician; and Plato defrayed the expenses of his sojourn in Egypt by the sale of oil.

3. Accordingly, if Solon's way of living was expensive and profuse, and if, in his poems, he speaks of pleasure with more freedom than becomes a philosopher, this is thought to be due to his mercantile life; he encountered many and great dangers, and sought his reward therefor in sundry luxuries and enjoyments. But that he classed himself among the poor rather than the rich, is clear from these verses:

"For often evil men are rich, and good men poor;
But we will not exchange with them
Our virtue for their wealth, since one abides always,
While riches change their owners every day."

---

17. Hesiod, *Works and Days*, 311.

And he seems to have composed his poetry at first with no serious end in view, but as amusement and diversion in his hours of leisure. Then later, he put philosophic maxims into verse, and interwove many political teachings in his poems, not simply to record and transmit them, but because they contained justifications of his acts, and sometimes exhortations, admonitions, and rebukes for the Athenians. Some say, too, that he attempted to reduce his laws to heroic verse before he published them, and they give us this introduction to them:

"First let us offer prayers, to Zeus, the royal son of' Cronus,
That he may give these laws of ours success and fame."

In philosophy, he cultivated chiefly the domain of political ethics, like most of the wise men of the time; and in physics, he is very simple and antiquated, as is clear from the following verses:

"From clouds come sweeping snow and hail,
And thunder follows on the lightning's flash.
By winds the sea is lashed to storm, but if it be
Unvexed, it is of all things most amenable."

And in general, it would seem that Thales was the only wise man of the time who carried his speculations beyond the realm of the practical; the rest[18] got the name of wisdom from their excellence as statesmen.

13. But the Athenians, now that the Cylonian disturbance[19] was over and the polluted persons banished, as described, relapsed into their old disputes about the form of government, the city being divided into as many parties as there were diversities in its territory. The Hill-men favored an extreme democracy; the Plain-men an extreme oligarchy; the Shore-men formed a third party,[20] which preferred an intermediate and mixed form of government, was opposed to the other two, and prevented either from gaining the ascendancy. At that time, too, the disparity between the rich and the poor had culminated, as it were, and the city was in an altogether perilous condition; it seemed as if the only way to settle its disorders and stop its turmoils was to establish a tyranny. All the common people were in debt to the rich. For they either tilled their lands for them, paying them a sixth of the increase (whence they were called Hectemorioi and Thetes), or else they pledged their persons for debts and could be seized by their creditors, some becoming slaves at home, and others being sold into foreign countries. Many, too, were forced to sell their own children (for there was no law against it), or go into exile, because of the cruelty of the money-lenders. But the most and sturdiest of them began to band together and exhort one another not

18. The names usually given for the Seven Wise Men are: Bias of Priene, Chilon of Sparta, Cleobulus of Lindus, Periander of Corinth, Pittacus of Mitylene, Solon of Athens, and Thales of Mietus.

19. Cylon, an Athenian nobleman, with the help of a few friends seized the Acropolis with the intention of establishing a tyranny, in 632 (?). The masses, however, did not follow him, and he was besieged. He himself escaped; his friends surrendered and, though suppliants at an alter, were killed. Hence arose the "curse," which attached to those said to be responsible, especially to Megacles the archon and his family, the Alcmaeonidae.

20. The "Hill," "Plain," and "Shore" are the names of three political factions, or parties, and do not seem to necessarily denote geographic groupings, as implied by Plutarch.

to submit to their wrongs, but to choose a trusty man as their leader, set free the condemned debtors, divide the land anew, and make an entire change in the form of government.

14. At this point, the wisest of the Athenians cast their eyes upon Solon. They saw that he was the one man least implicated in the errors of the time; that he was neither associated with the rich in their injustice, nor involved in the necessities of the poor. They therefore besought him to come forward publicly and put an end to the prevailing dissensions. And yet Phanias the Lesbian writes that Solon of his own accord played a trick upon both parties in order to save the city, and secretly promised to the poor the distribution of land which they desired, and to the rich, validation of their securities. But Solon himself says that he entered public life reluctantly, and fearing one party's greed and the other party's arrogance. However, he was chosen archon [21]to succeed Philombrotus, and made mediator and legislator for the crisis, the rich accepting him readily because he was well-to-do, and the poor because he was honest. It is also said that a certain utterance of his which was current before his election, to the effect that equality bred no war, pleased both the men of substance and those who had none; the former expecting to have equality based on worth and excellence, the latter on measure and count. Therefore both parties were in high hopes; and their chief men persistently recommended a tyranny to Solon, and tried to persuade him to seize the city all the more confidently now that he had it completely in his power. Many citizens, too, who belonged to neither party, seeing that it would be a laborious and difficult matter to effect a change by means of argument and law, were not reluctant to have one man, the wisest and most just of all, put at the head of the state. Furthermore, some say that Solon got an oracle at Pytho which ran as follows

"Take your seat amidships, the pilot's task is yours;
Perform it; many in Athens are your allies."

And above all, his familiar friends chided him for being averse to absolute power because of the name of tyranny, as if the virtues of him who seized it would not at once make it a lawful sovereignty. Euboea (they argued) had formerly found this true of Tynnondas, and so had the Mitylenaeans, now that they had chosen Pittacus to be their tyrant.

None of these things shook Solon from his resolution. To his friends he said, as we are told, that a tyranny was a lovely place, but there was no way down from it. And in his poems he writes to Phocus:

". . .And if I spared my land, My native land, and unto tyranny and violence implacable
Did not set hand, polluting and disgracing my fair fame,
I'm not ashamed; in this way rather shall my name be set above
That of all other men."

From this it is clear that even before his legislation he was in high repute. And as for the ridicule which many heaped upon him for refusing the tyranny, he has written as follows:

---

21. 254 B.C.

"Solon was a shallow thinker and a man of counsel void;
When the gods would give him blessings, of his own will he refused.
When his net was full of fish, amazed, he would not pull it in,
All for lack of spirit, and because he was bereft of sense.
I had certainly been willing, for the power, and boundless wealth,
And to be tyrant over Athens no more than a single day,
Then to have a pouch flayed from me, and my lineage blotted out."

15. Thus he represents the multitude and men of low degree as speaking of him. However, though he rejected the tyranny, he did not administer affairs in the mildest possible manner, nor in the enactment of his laws did he show a feeble spirit, nor make concessions to the powerful, nor consult the pleasure of his electors; Nay, where a condition was as good as it could well be, he applied no remedy, and introduced no innovation, fearing lest, after utterly confusing and confounding the city, he should be too weak to establish it again and recompose it for the best. But those things wherein he hoped to find them open to persuasion or submissive to compulsion, these he did, "Combining both force and justice together," as he says himself. Therefore when he was afterwards asked if he had enacted the best laws for the Athenians, he replied, "The best they would receive."

Now later writers observe that the ancient Athenians used to cover up the ugliness of things with auspicious and kindly terms, giving them polite and endearing names. Thus they called harlots "companions," taxes "contributions," the garrison of a city its "guard," and the prison a "chamber." But Solon was the first, it would seem, to use this device, when he called his canceling of debts. a "disburdenment." For the first of his public measures was an enactment that existing debts should be remitted, and that in future no one should lend money on the person of a borrower. Some writers, however, and Androtion is one of them, affirm that the poor were relieved not by a canceling of debts, but by a reduction of the interest upon them, and showed their satisfaction by giving the name of" disburdenment" to this act of humanity, and to the augmentation of measures and the purchasing power of money which accompanied it. For he made the mina to consist of a hundred drachmas, which before had contained only seventy-three, so that by paying the same amount of money, but money of a lesser value, those who had debts to discharge were greatly benefited, and those who accepted such payments were no losers. But most writers agree that the "disburdenment" was a removal of all debt, and with such the poems of Solon are more in accord. For in these he proudly boasts that from the mortgaged lands

"He took away the record-stones that everywhere were planted;
Before, Earth was in bondage, now she is free."

And of the citizens whose persons had been seized for debt, some he brought back from foreign lands,

". . .uttering no longer Attic speech,
So long and far their wretched wanderings;
And some who here at home. in shameful servitude
Were held"

he says he set free.

This undertaking is said to have involved him in the most vexatious experience of his life. For when he had set out to abolish debts, and was trying to find fitting arguments and a suitable occasion for the step, he told some of his most trusted and intimate friends, namely, Conon, Cleinias, and Hipponicus, that he was not going to meddle with the land, but had determined to cancel debts. They immediately took advantage of this confidence and anticipated Solon's decree by borrowing large sums from the wealthy and buying up great estates. Then, when the decree was published, they enjoyed the use of their properties, but refused to pay the moneys due their creditors. This brought Solon into great condemnation and odium, as if he had not been imposed upon with the rest, but were a party to the imposition. However, this charge was at once dissipated by his well-known sacrifice of five talents. For it was found that he had lent so much, and he was the first to remit this debt in accordance with his law. Some say that the sum was fifteen talents, and among them is Polyzelus the Rhodian. But his friends were ever after called "chreocopidae," or *debt-cutters*.

16. He pleased neither party, however; the rich were vexed because he took away their securities for debt, and the poor still more, because he did not re-distribute the land, as they had expected, nor make all men equal and alike in their way of living, as Lycurgus did. But Lycurgus was eleventh in descent from Heracles, and had been king in Lacedaemon for many years. He therefore had great authority, many friends, and power to support his reforms in the commonwealth. He also employed force rather than persuasion, insomuch that he actually lost his eye thereby, and most effectually guaranteed the safety and unanimity of the city by making all its citizens neither poor nor rich. Solon, on the contrary, could not secure this feature in his commonwealth, since he was a man of the people and of modest station; yet he in no wise acted short of his real power, relying as he did only on the wishes of the citizens and their confidence in him. Nevertheless he gave offence to the greater part of them, who expected different results, as he himself says of them in the lines:

"Then they had extravagant thoughts of me, but now, incensed,
All look askance at me, as if I were their foe."

And yet had any other man, he says, acquired the same power:

"He had not held the people down, nor made an end
Until he had confounded all, and skimmed the cream."

Soon, however, they perceived the advantages of his measure, ceased from their private fault-finding, and offered a public sacrifice, which they called Seisactheia, or *Disburdenment*. They also appointed Solon to reform the constitution and make new laws, laying no restrictions whatever upon him, but putting everything into his hands, magistracies, assemblies, courts-of-law, and councils. He was to fix the property qualification for each of these, their numbers, and their times of meeting, abrogating and maintaining existing institutions at his pleasure.

17. In the first place, then, he repealed the laws of Draco, all except those concerning homicide, because they were too severe and their penalties too heavy. For one penalty was assigned to

almost all transgressions, namely death, so that even those convicted of idleness were put to death, and those who stole salad or fruit received the same punishment as those who committed sacrilege or murder. Therefore Demades, in later times, made a hit when he said that Draco's laws were written not with ink, but blood. And Draco himself, they say, being asked why he made death the penalty for most offences, replied that in his opinion the lesser ones deserved it, and for the greater ones no heavier penalty could be found.

18. In the second place, wishing to leave all the magistracies in the hands of the well-to-do, as they were, but to give the common people a share in the rest of the government, of which they had hitherto been deprived, Solon made an appraisement of the property of the citizens. Those who enjoyed a yearly increase of five hundred measures (wet and dry), he placed in the first class, and called them Pentakosiomedimnoi; the second class was composed of those who were able to keep a horse, or had a yearly increase of three hundred measures, and they were called Hippada Telountes, since they paid a Knight's tax; the members of the third class, whose yearly increase amounted to two hundred measures (wet and dry together), were called Zeugitai. All the rest were called Thetes they were not allowed to hold any office, but took part in the administration only as members of the assembly and as jurors. This last privilege seemed at first of no moment, but afterwards proved to be of the very highest importance, since most disputes finally came into the hands of these jurors. For even in cases which Solon assigned to the magistrates for decision, he allowed also an appeal to a popular court when any one desired it. Besides, it is said that his laws were obscurely and ambiguously worded on purpose to enhance the power of the popular courts. For since parties to a controversy could not get satisfaction from the laws, the result was that they always wanted jurors to decide it, and every dispute was laid before them, so that they were in a manner masters of the laws. And he himself claims the credit for this in the following words:

"For to the common people I gave so much power as is sufficient,
Neither robbing them of dignity, nor giving them too much;
And those who had power, and were marvelously rich,
Even for these I contrived that they suffered no harm.
I stood with a mighty shield in front of both classes,
And suffered neither of them to prevail unjustly."

Moreover, thinking it his duty to make still further provision for the weakness of the multitude, he gave every citizen the privilege of entering suit in behalf of one who had suffered wrong. If a man was assaulted, and suffered violence or injury, it was the privilege of any one who had the ability and the inclination, to indict the wrong-doer and prosecute him. The law-giver in this way rightly accustomed the citizens, as members of one body, to feel and sympathize with one another's wrongs. And we are told of a saying of his which is consonant with this law. Being asked, namely, what city was best to live in, "That city," he replied, "in which those who are not wronged, no less than those who are wronged, exert themselves to punish the wrong-doers."

19. After he had established the council of the Areopagus, consisting of those who had been archons year by year (and he himself was a member of this body, since he had been archon), he observed that the common people were uneasy and bold in consequence of their release from debt, and therefore established another council besides, consisting of four hundred men, one hundred chosen from each of the four tribes. These were to deliberate on public matters before the people did, and were not to allow any matter to come before the popular assembly without such previous deliberation. Then he made the upper council a general overseer in the state, and guardian of the laws, thinking that the city with its two councils, riding as it were at double anchor, would be less tossed by the surges, and would keep its populace in greater quiet.

Now most writers say that the council of the Areopagus, as I have stated, was established by Solon. And their view seems to be strongly supported by the fact that Draco nowhere makes any mention whatsoever of Areopagus, but always addresses himself to the "ephetai" in cases of homicide. Yet Solon's thirteenth table contains the eighth of his laws recorded in these very words "As many of the disfranchised as were made such before the archonship of Solon, shall be restored to their rights and franchises, except such as were condemned by the Areopagus, or by the ephetai, or in the prytaneium by the kings, on charges of murder or homicide, or of seeking to establish a tyranny, and were in exile when this law was published." This surely proves to the contrary that the council of the Areopagus was in existence before the archonship and legislation of Solon. For how could men have been condemned in the Areopagus before the time of Solon, if Solon was the first to give the council of the Areopagus its jurisdiction? Perhaps, indeed, there is some obscurity in the document, or some omission, and the meaning is that those who had been convicted on charges within the cognizance of those who were Areopagus and ephetai and prytanes when the law was published, should remain disfranchised, while those convicted on all other charges should recover their rights and franchises. This question, however, my reader must decide for himself.

20. Among his other laws there is a very peculiar and surprising one which ordains that he shall be disfranchised who, in time of faction, takes neither side. He wishes, probably, that a man should not be insensible or indifferent to the common weal, arranging his private affairs securely and glorying in tile fact that he has no share in the distempers and distresses of his country, but should rather espouse promptly the better and more righteous cause, share its perils and give it his aid, instead of waiting in safety to see which cause prevails. That law, too, seems absurd and ridiculous, which permits an heiress, in case the man under whose power and authority she is placed by law is himself unable to consort with her, to be married by one of his next of kin. Some, however, say that this was a wise provision against those who are unable to perform the duties of a husband, and yet, for the sake of their property, marry heiresses, and so under cover of law, do violence to nature. For when they see that the heiress can consort with whom she pleases, they will either desist from such a marriage, or make it to their shame, and be punished for their avarice and insolence. It is a wise provision, too, that the heiress may not choose her consort at large, but only from the kinsmen of her husband, that her offspring may be of his family and lineage. Conformable to this, also, is the requirement that the bride eat a quince and be shut up in a chamber with the bridegroom; and that the husband of an heiress shall approach her thrice a month without fail. For even though they have no children, still, this is a mark of esteem and affection which a man should pay to a chaste wife; it removes many of the annoyances which develop in all such cases, and prevents their being altogether estranged by their differences.

In all other marriages he prohibited dowries; the bride was to bring with her three changes of raiment, household stuff of small value, and nothing else. For he did not wish that marriage should be a matter of profit or price, but that man and wife should dwell together for the delights of love and the getting of children. Dionysius, indeed, when his mother asked him to give her in marriage to one of his citizens, said that, although he had broken the laws of the city by being its tyrant, he could not outrage the laws of nature by giving in marriage where age forbade. And so our cities should not allow this irregularity, nor tolerate unions which age forbids and love does not invite, which do not fulfill the function of marriage, and defeat its object. Nay, to an old man who is marrying a young wife, any worthy magistrate or lawgiver might say what is said to Philoctetes:[22]

"Indeed, poor wretch, thou art in fine state for marrying!"

And if he discovers a young man in the house of a rich and elderly woman, waxing fat, like a cock-partridge, in her service, he will remove him and give him to some marriageable maid that wants a husband. Thus much, then, on this head.

21. Praise is given also to that law of Solon which forbids speaking ill of the dead. For it is piety to regard the deceased as sacred, justice to spare the absent, and good policy to rob hatred of its perpetuity. He also forbade speaking ill of the living in temples, courts-of-law, public offices, and at festivals; the transgressor must pay three drachmas to the person injured, and two more into the public treasury. For never to master one's anger is a mark of intemperance and lack of training; but always to do so is difficult, and for some, impossible. And a law must regard the possibilities in the case, if its maker wishes to punish a few to some purpose, and not many to no purpose.

He was highly esteemed also for his law concerning wills. Before his time, no will could be made, but the entire estate of the deceased must remain in his family. Whereas he, by permitting a man who had no children to give his property to whom he wished, ranked friendship above kinship, and favor above necessity, and made a man's possessions his own property. On the other hand, he did not permit all manner of gifts without restriction or restraint, but only those which were not made under the influence of sickness, or drugs, or imprisonment, or when a man was the victim of compulsion or yielded to the persuasions of his wife. He thought, very rightly and properly, that being persuaded into wrong was no better than being forced into it, and he placed deceit and compulsion, gratification and affliction, in one and the same category, believing that both were alike able to pervert a man's reason.

He also subjected the public appearances of the women, their mourning and their festivals, to a law which did away with disorder and license. When they went out, they were not to wear more than three garments, they were not to carry more than an obol's worth of food or drink, nor a pannier more than a cubit high, and they were not to travel about by night unless they rode in a wagon with a lamp to light their way. Laceration of the flesh by mourners, and the use of set lamentations, and the bewailing of any one at the funeral ceremonies of another, he forbade. The sacrifice of an ox at the grave was not permitted, nor the burial with the dead of more than three changes of raiment, nor the visiting of other tombs than those of their own family, except at the time of interment. Most of these practices are also forbidden by our laws, but ours contain the

---

22. In a play of unknown authorship, not the Sophocles tragedy.

additional proviso that such offenders shall be punished by the board of censors for women, because they indulge in unmanly and effeminate extravagances of sorrow when they mourn.

22. Observing that the city was getting full of people who were constantly streaming into Attica from all quarters for greater security of living, and that most of the country was unfruitful and worthless, and that seafaring men are not wont to import goods for those who have nothing to give them in exchange, he turned the attention of the citizens to the arts of manufacture, and enacted a law that no son who had not been taught a trade should be compelled to support his father. It was well enough for Lycurgus, whose city was free from swarms of strangers, and whose country was, in the words of Euripides:

"For many large, for twice as many more than large,"

and because, above all, that country was flooded with a multitude of Helots, whom it was better not to leave in idleness, but to keep down by continual hardships and toil—it was well enough for him to set his citizens free from laborious and mechanical occupations and confine their thoughts to arms, giving them this one trade to learn and practice. But Solon, adapting his laws to the situation, rather than the situation to his laws, and observing that the land could give but a mere subsistence to those who tilled it, and was incapable of supporting an unoccupied, and leisured multitude, gave dignity to all the trades, and ordered the council of the Areopagus to examine into every man's means of livelihood, and chastise those who had no occupation.

But that provision of his was yet more severe, which, as Heracleides Ponticus informs us, relieved the sons who were born out of wedlock from the necessity of supporting their fathers at all. For he that avoids the honorable state of marriage, clearly takes a woman to himself not for the sake of children, but of pleasure; and he has his reward, in that he robs himself of all right to upbraid his sons for neglecting him, since he has made their very existence a reproach to them.

23. But in general, Solon's laws concerning women seem very absurd. For instance, he permitted an adulterer caught in the act to be killed; but if a man committed rape upon a free woman, he was merely to be fined a hundred drachmas; and if he gained his end by persuasion, twenty drachmas, unless it were with one of those who sell themselves openly, meaning of course the courtesans. For these go openly to those who offer them their price. Still further, no man is allowed to sell a daughter or a sister, unless he find that she is no longer a virgin. But to punish the same offence now severely and inexorably, and now mildly and pleasantly, making the penalty a slight fine, is unreasonable; unless money was scarce in the city at that time, and the difficulty of procuring it made these monetary punishments heavy. In the valuations of sacrificial offerings, at any rate, a sheep and a bushel of grain are reckoned at a drachma; the victor in the Isthmian games was to be paid a hundred drachmas, and the Olympic victor five hundred; the man who brought in a wolf, was given five drachmas, and for a wolf's whelp, one; the former sum, according to Demetrius the Phalerian, was the price of an ox, the latter that of a sheep. For although the prices which Solon fixes in his sixteenth table are for choice victims, and naturally many times as great as those for ordinary ones, still, even these are low in comparison with present prices. Now the Athenians were from of old great enemies of wolves, since their country was better for pasturage than for tillage. And there are those who say that their four tribes were originally named, not from the sons of Ion, but from the classes into which occupations were divided; thus the warriors

were called Hoplitai, the craftsmen Ergadeis; and of the remaining two, the farmers were called Geleontes, the shepherds and herdsmen Aigikoreis.[23]

Since the country was not supplied with water by ever-flowing rivers, or lakes, or copious springs, but most of the inhabitants used wells which had been dug, he made a law that where there was a public well within a "hippikon," a distance of four furlongs, that should be used, but where the distance was greater than this, people must try to get water of their own; if, however, after digging to a depth of ten fathoms on their own land, they could not get water, then they might take it from a neighbor's well, filling a five gallon jar twice a day; for he thought it his duty to aid the needy, not to provision the idle. He also showed great experience in the limits which he set to the planting of trees ; no one could set out a tree in a field within five feet of his neighbor's field, or, in case it was a fig-tree or an olive-tree, within nine. For these reach out farther with their roots, and injure some trees by their proximity, taking away their nourishment, and emitting an exhalation which is sometimes noxious. He that would dig a pit or a trench, must dig it at the distance of its own depth from his neighbor's; and he that would set out hives of bees, must put them three hundred feet away from those which another had already installed.

24. Of the products of the soil, he allowed oil only to be sold abroad, but forbade the exportation of others; and if any did so export, the archon was to pronounce curses upon them, or else himself pay a hundred drachmas into the public treasury. His first table is the one which contains this law. One cannot, therefore, wholly disbelieve those who say that the exportation of figs also was anciently forbidden, and that the one who showed up, or pointed out such exporters, was called a "sycophant," or *fig-shower*. He also enacted a law concerning injuries received from beasts, according to which a dog that had bitten anybody must be delivered up with a wooden collar three cubits long fastened to it; a happy device this for promoting safety.

But the law concerning naturalized citizens is of doubtful character. He permitted only those to be made citizens who were permanently exiled from their own country, or who removed to Athens with their entire families to ply a trade. This he did, as we are told, not so much to drive away other foreigners, as to invite these particular ones to Athens with the full assurance of becoming citizens; he also thought that reliance could be placed both on those who had been forced to abandon their own country, and on those who had left it with a fixed purpose. Characteristic of Solon also was his regulation of the practice of eating at the public table in the town hall, for which his word was "parasitein." The same person was not allowed to eat there often, but if one whose duty it was to eat there refused, he was punished. Solon thought the conduct of the first grasping; that of the second, contemptuous of the public interests.

25. All his laws were to have force for a hundred years, and they were written on "axones," or wooden tablets, which revolved with the oblong frames containing them. Slight remnants of these were still preserved in the Prytaneium when I was at Athens, and they were called, according to Aristotle, "kurbeis." Cratinus, also, the comic poet, somewhere says:

"By Solon, and by Draco too I make mine oath,
Whose kurbeis now are used to parch our barley-corns."

---

23. This is strained etymology to explain the ancient tribal names of Hopletes, Argadeis, Geleontes, and Aigikoreis, which are derived, in Herodotus 66, from the names of the four sons of Ion. The first has nothing to do with "hoopla," *arms*; not the second with "ergon," *work*; nor the third with "*ge*," earth; nor the fourth with "aix," *goat*.

But some say that only those tablets which relate to sacred rites and sacrifices are properly called "kurbeis," and the rest are called "axones." However that may be, the council took a joint oath to ratify the laws of Solon, and each of the "thesmothetai," or guardians of the statutes, swore separately at the herald's stone in the market-place, vowing that if he transgressed the statutes in any way, he would dedicate at Delphi a golden statue of commensurate worth.

Observing the irregularity of the month, and that the motion of the moon does not always coincide with the rising and setting of the sun, but that often she overtakes and passes the sun on the same day, he ordered that day to be called the Old and New, assigning the portion of it which preceded the conjunction to the expiring month, and the remaining portion to the month that was just beginning. He was thus the first, as it would seem, to understand Homer's verse,[24] which speaks of a day when:

"This month is waning, and the next is setting in,"

and the day following this he called the first of the month. After the twentieth he did not count the days by adding them to twenty, but by subtracting them from thirty, on a descending scale, like the waning of the moon.[25]

No sooner were the laws of Solon put into operation than some would come to him every day with praise or censure of them, or with advice to insert something into the documents, or take something out. Very numerous, too, were those who came to him with inquiries and questions about them, urging him to teach and make clear to them the meaning and purpose of each several item. He saw that to do this was out of the question, and that not to do it would bring odium upon him, and wishing to be wholly rid of these perplexities and to escape from the captiousness and censoriousness of the citizens (for "in great affairs," as he says himself, "it is difficult to please all."), he made his ownership of a vessel an excuse for foreign travel, and set sail, after obtaining from the Athenians leave of absence for ten years. In this time he hoped they would be accustomed to his laws.

29. But the people of Athens were again divided into factions while Solon was away. The Plain-men were headed by Lycurgus; the Shore-men by Megacles the son of Alcmaeon, and the Hill-men by Peisistratus. Among the last was the multitude of Thetes, who were the bitter enemies of the rich. As a consequence, though the city still observed the new laws, yet all were already expecting a revolution and desirous of a different form of government, not in hopes of an equality, but each party thinking to be bettered by the change, and to get the entire mastery of its opponents. Such was the state of affairs when Solon returned to Athens. He was revered and honored by all, but owing to his years he no longer had the strength or the ardor to speak and act in public as before. He did, however, confer privately with the chiefs of the opposing factions, endeavoring to reconcile and harmonize them, and Peisistratus seemed to pay him more heed than the others. For Peisistratus had an insinuating and agreeable quality in his address, he was ready to help the poor, and was reasonable and moderate in his enmities. Even those virtues which nature had denied

---

24 .Concerning the day when Odysseus would return to Ithaca, *Odyssey*, 14.162.

25 .Thus the twenty-first was called the tenth, the twenty-second the ninth, and so on, "of the waning month." The twenty-ninth was the second of the waning month, the thirtieth was the Old and New.

him were imitated by him so successfully that he won more confidence than those who actually possessed them. He was thought to be a cautious and order loving man, one that prized equality above all things, and would take it ill if any one disturbed the existing order and attempted a change. On these points, indeed, he completely deceived most people. But Solon quickly detected his real character, and was the first to perceive his secret designs. He did not, however, treat him as an enemy, but tried to soften and mould him by his instructions. He actually said to him and to others that if the desire for preeminence could but be banished from his soul, and his eager passion for the tyranny be cured, no other man would be more naturally disposed to virtue, or a better citizen.

Thespis was now beginning to develop tragedy, and the attempt attracted most people because of its novelty, although it was not yet made a matter of competitive contest. Solon, therefore, who was naturally fond of hearing and learning anything new, and who in his old age more than ever before indulged himself in leisurely amusement, yes, and in wine and song, went to see Thespis act in his own play, as was the custom of the ancient poets. After the spectacle, he accosted Thespis, and asked him if he was not ashamed to tell such lies in the presence of so many people. Thespis answered that there was no harm in talking and acting that way in play, whereupon Solon smote the ground sharply with his staff and said: "Soon, however, if we give play of this sort so much praise and honor, we shall find it in our solemn contracts."

30. Now when Peisistratus, after inflicting a wound upon himself, came into the market-place riding in a chariot, and tried to exasperate the populace with the charge that his enemies had plotted against his life on account of his political opinions, and many of them greeted the charge with angry cries, Solon drew near and accosted him, saying: "O son of Hippocrates, you art play-ing the Homeric Odysseus badly;[26] for when he disfigured himself it was to deceive his enemies, but you do it to mislead thy fellow-citizens." After this the multitude was ready to fight for Peisistratus, and a general assembly of the people was held. Here Ariston made a motion that Peisistratus be allowed a body-guard of fifty club-bearers, but Solon formally opposed it, and said many things which were like what he has written in his poems:

"Ye have regard indeed to the speech and words of a wily man.
Yet every one of you walks with the steps of a fox,
And in you all dwells an empty mind."

But when he saw that the poor were tumultuously bent on gratifying Peisistratus, while the rich were fearfully slinking away from any conflict with him, he left the assembly, saying that he was wiser than the one party, and braver than the other; wiser than those who did not understand what was being done, and braver than those who, though they understood it, were nevertheless afraid to oppose the tyranny. So the people passed the decree, and then held Peisistratus to no strict account of the number of his club-bearers, but suffered him to keep and lead about in pub-lic as many as he wished, until at last he seized the acropolis.

---

26. *Odyssey*, 4.244–264.

When this had been done, and the city was in an uproar, Megacles[27] straightway fled, with the rest of the Alcnaeonidae. But Solon, although he was now a very old man, and had none to support him, went nevertheless into the market-place and reasoned with the citizens, partly blaming their folly and weakness, and partly encouraging them still and exhorting them not to abandon their liberty. Then it was, too, that he uttered the famous saying, that earlier it had been easier for them to hinder the tyranny, while it was in preparation; but now it was a greater and more glorious task to uproot and destroy it when it had been already planted and was grown. No one had the courage to side with him, however, and so he retired to his own house, took his arms, and placed them in the street in front of his door, saying: "I have done all I can to help my country and its laws." From that time on he lived in quiet retirement, and when his friends urged him to fly, he paid no heed to them, but kept on writing poems, in which he heaped reproaches on the Athenians:

"If now you suffer grievously through cowardice all your own,
Cherish no wrath against the gods for this,
For you yourselves increased the usurper's power by giving him a guard,
And therefore are you now in base subjection."

31. In view of this, many warned him that the tyrant would put him to death, and asked him on what he relied. that he was so lost to all sense, to which he answered, "My old age." However, when Peisistratus had become master of the situation, he paid such court to Solon by honoring him, showing him kindness, and inviting him to his palace, that Solon actually became his counselor and approved of many of his acts. For he retained most of Solon's laws, observing them first himself, and compelling his friends to do so. For instance, he was summoned before the Areopagus on a charge of murder, when he was already tyrant, and presented himself there to make his defense in due form, but his accuser did not put in an appearance. He also made other laws himself, one of which provides that those who are maimed in war shall be maintained at the public charge. But Heracleides says that even before that Solon had caused a decree to be passed to this effect in the case of Thersippus, who had been so maimed, and that Peisistratus was following his example. Moreover, Theophrastus writes that the law against idleness, in consequence of which the country became more productive and the city more tranquil, was not made by Solon, but by Peisistratus.

Now Solon, after beginning his great work on the story or fable of the lost Atlantis, which, as he had heard from the learned men of Sais,[28] particularly concerned the Athenians, abandoned it, not for lack of leisure, as Plato says, but rather because of his old age, fearing the magnitude of the task. For that he had abundant leisure, such verses as these testify:

"But I grow old ever learning many things;"

---

27. Son of the Megacles who brought the taint of pollution upon the family (chapter 12). He had been allowed to return from banishment.

28. There is no trace of any such work of Solon's, and the attribution of it to him is probably a play of Plato's fancy.

and again:

"But now the works of the Cyprus-born goddess are dear to my soul,
Of Dionysus, too, and the Muses, which impart delights to men."

32. Plato, ambitious to elaborate and adorn the subject of the lost Atlantis, as if it were the soil of a fair estate unoccupied, but appropriately his by virtue of some kinship with Solon,[29] began the work by laying out great porches, enclosures, and courtyards, such as no story, tale, or poesy ever had before. But he was late in beginning, and his life ended before his work. Therefore the greater our delight in what he actually wrote, the greater is our distress in view of what he left undone. For as the Olympieium in the city of Athens, so the tale of the lost Atlantis in the wisdom of Plato is the only one among many beautiful works to remain unfinished.

Well, then, Solon lived on after Peisistratus had made himself tyrant, as Heracleides Ponticus states, a long time; but as Phanias of Eresos says, less than two years. For it was in the archonship of Comeas[30] that Peisistratus began his tyranny, and Phanias says that Solon died in the archonship of Hegestratus, the successor of Comeas. The story that his body was burned and his ashes scattered on the island of Salamis is strange enough to be altogether incredible and fabulous, and yet it is given by noteworthy authors, and even by Aristotle the philosopher.

PERICLES

Pericles was the effective ruler of Athens during the zenith of its power in the 440s and 430s B.C. He was responsible for the construction of the Parthenon and other buildings and he was at the center of the intellectual life of classical Athens. Not surprisingly this period is known as the "Age of Pericles." Below are excerpts from Plutarch's **Life of Pericles.**

3. Pericles was of the tribe Acamantis, of the deme Cholargus, and of the foremost family and lineage on both sides. His father, Xanthippus, who conquered the generals of the King at Mycale,[31] married Agariste, granddaughter[32] of that Cleisthenes, who, in such noble fashion, expelled the Peisistratidae and destroyed their tyranny, instituted laws, and established a constitution best suited for the promotion of harmony and safety. She, in her dreams, once fancied that she had given birth to a lion, and a few days thereafter bore Pericles. His personal appearance was unimpeachable, except that his head was rather long and out of due proportion. For this reason the images of him, almost all of them, wear helmets, because the artists, as it would seem, were not willing to reproach him with deformity. . .

---

29. Plato mentions the relationship of Critias, his maternal uncle, with solon.
30. 561–560 B.C.
31. 479 B.C.
32. Actually his niece.

7. As a young man, Pericles was exceedingly reluctant to face the people, since it was thought that in feature he was like the tyrant Peisistratus and when men well on in years remarked also that his voice was sweet, and his tongue glib and speedy in discourse, they were struck with amazement at the resemblance. Besides, since he was rich, of brilliant lineage, and had friends of the greatest influence, he feared that he might be ostracized, and so at first had naught to do with politics, but devoted himself rather to a military career, where he was brave and enterprising. However, when Aristides was dead,[33] and Themistocles in banishment,[34] and Cimon was kept by his campaigns for the most part abroad, then at last Pericles decided to devoted himself to the people, espousing the cause of the poor and the many instead of the few and the rich, contrary to his own nature, which was anything but popular. But he feared, as it would seem, to encounter a suspicion of aiming at tyranny, and when he saw that Cimon was very aristocratic in his sympathies, and was held in extraordinary affection by the party of the "Good and True," he began to court die favor of the multitude, thereby securing safety for himself, and power to wield against his rival.

Straightway, too, he made a different ordering in his way of life. On one street only in the city was he to be seen walking—the one which took him to the market-place and the council-chamber. Invitations to dinner, and all such friendly and familiar intercourse, he declined, so that during the long period that elapsed while he was at the head of the state, there was not a single friend to whose house he went to dine, except that when his kinsman Euryptolemus gave a wedding feast, he attended until the libations were made,[35] and then straightway rose up and departed. Conviviality is prone to break down and overpower the haughtiest reserve, and in familiar intercourse the dignity which is assumed for appearance's sake is very hard to maintain. Whereas, in the case of true and genuine virtue, "fairest appears what most appears," and nothing in the conduct of good men is so admirable in the eyes of strangers, as their daily walk and conversation is in the eyes of those who share it.

And so it was that Pericles, seeking to avoid the satiety which springs from continual intercourse, made his approaches to the people by intervals, as it were, not speaking on every question, nor, nor addressing the people every on occasion, but offering himself like the Salaminian trireme, as Critolaus says, for great emergencies. The rest of his policy he carried out by commissioning his friends and other public speakers. One of these, as they say, was Ephialtes, who broke down the power of the Council of the Areopagus, and so poured out for the citizens, to use the words of Plato, too much undiluted freedom," by which the people was rendered unruly, just like a horse, and, as the comic poets say, "no longer had the patience to obey the rein, but nabbed Euboea and trampled on the islands."

16. Of his power there can be no doubt, since Thucydides gives so clear an exposition of it, and the comic poets unwittingly reveal it even in their malicious gibes, calling him and his associates "new Peisistratidae," and urging him to take solemn oath not to make himself a tyrant, on the plea, forsooth, that his preeminence was incommensurate with a democracy and too oppressive. Telecleides says[36] that the Athenians had handed over to him:

---

33. Soon after 468 B.C.
34. After 472 B.C.
35. That is, until the wine for the symposium was brought in and the drinking began.
36. In a play of unknown name.

"With the cities' assessments the cities themselves, to bind or release as he pleases,
Their ramparts of stone to build up if he likes, and then to pull down again straightway,
Their treaties, their forces, their might, peace, and riches, and all the fair gifts of good fortune."

And this was not the fruit of a golden moment, nor the culminating popularity of an administration that bloomed but for a season; nay rather he stood first for forty years[37] among such men as Ephialtes, Leocrates, Myronides, Cimon, Tolmides, and Thucydides, and after the deposition of Thucydides and his ostracism, for no less than fifteen of these years did he secure an imperial sway that was continuous and unbroken, by means of his annual tenure of the office of general. During all these years he kept himself untainted by corruption, although he was not altogether indifferent to money-making; indeed, the wealth which was legally his by inheritance from his father, that it might not from sheer neglect take to itself wings and fly away, nor yet cause him much trouble and loss of time when he was busy with higher things, he set into such orderly dispensation as he thought was easiest and most exact. This was to sell his annual products all together in the lump, and then to buy in the market each article as it was needed, and so provide the ways and means of daily life. For this reason he was not liked by his sons when they grew up, nor did their wives find in him a liberal purveyor, but they murmured at his expenditure for the day merely and under the most exact restrictions, there being no surplus of supplies at all, as in a great house and under generous circumstances, but every outlay and every intake proceeding by count and measure. His agent in securing all this great exactitude was a single servant, Evangelus, who was either gifted by nature or trained by Pericles so as to surpass everybody else in domestic economy. . .

17. When the Lacedaemonians began to he annoyed by the increasing power of the Athenians, Pericles, by way of inciting the people to cherish yet loftier thoughts and to deem itself worthy of great achievements, introduced a bill to the effect that all Hellenes whether resident in Europe or in Asia, small and large cities alike, should be invited to send deputies to a council at Athens. This was to deliberate concerning the Hellenic sanctuaries which the Barbarians had burned down, concerning the sacrifices which were due to the gods in the name of Hellas in fulfillment of vows made when they were fighting with the Barbarians, and concerning the sea, that all might sail it fearlessly and keep the peace. . . But nothing was accomplished, nor did the cities come together by deputy, owing to the opposition of the Lacedaemonians, as it is said, since the effort met with its first check in Peloponnesus. I have cited this incident, however, to demonstrate the man's disposition and the greatness of his thoughts.

18. In his capacity as general, he was famous above all things for his saving caution; he neither undertook of his own accord a battle involving much uncertainty and peril, nor did he envy and imitate those who took great risks, enjoyed brilliant good fortune, and so were admired as great generals; and he was for ever saying to his fellow citizens that, so far as lay in his power, they would remain alive forever and be immortals.

So when he saw that Tolmides, son of Tolmaeus, all on account of his previous good-fortune and of the exceeding great honor bestowed upon him for his wars, was getting ready, quite inop-

---

37. Reckoning roundly from 469 to 429 B.C.

portunely, to make an incursion into Boeotia, and that he had persuaded the bravest and most ambitious men of military age to volunteer for the campaign—as many as a thousand of them, aside from the rest of his forces—he tried to restrain and dissuade him in the popular assembly, uttering then that well remembered saying, to wit, that if he would not listen to Pericles, he would yet do full well to wait for that wisest of all counselors, Time. This saving brought him only moderate repute at the time; but a few days afterwards, when word was brought that Tolmides himself was dead after defeat in battle near Coroneia,[38] and that many brave citizens were dead likewise, then it brought Pericles great repute as well as goodwill, for that he was a man of discretion arid patriotism.

19. Of all his expeditions, that to the Chersonesus[39] was held in most loving remembrance, since it proved the salvation of the Hellenes who dwelt there. Not only did he bring thither a thousand Athenian colonists and stock the cities anew with vigorous manhood, but he also belted the neck of the isthmus with defensive bulwarks from sea to sea, and so intercepted the incursions of the Thracians who swarmed about the Chersonesus, and shut out the perpetual and grievous war in which the country was all the time involved, in close touch as it was with neighboring communities of Barbarians, and full to overflowing of robber bands whose haunts were on or within its borders. But he was admired and celebrated even amongst foreigners for his circumnavigation of the Peloponnesus,[40] when he put to sea from Pegae in the Megarid with a hundred triremes. He not only ravaged a great strip of seashore, as Tolmides had done before him, but also advanced far into the interior with the hoplites from his ships, and drove all his enemies inside their walls in terror at his approach, excepting only the Sicyonians, who made a stand against him in Nemea, and joined battle with him; these he routed by main force and set up a trophy for his victory. Then from Achaia, which was friendly to him, he took soldiers on board his triremes, and proceeded with his armament to the opposite mainland, where lie sailed up the Acheloiis, overran Acarnania, shut up the people of Oeniadae behind their walls, and after ravaging and devastating their territory, went off homewards, having shown himself formidable to his enemies, but a safe and efficient leader for his fellow citizens. For nothing untoward befell, even as result of chance, those who took part in the expedition.

20. He also sailed into the Black Sea[41] with a large and splendidly equipped armament. There he effected what the Greek cities desired, and dealt with them humanely, while to the neighboring nations of Barbarians with their kings and dynasts he displayed the magnitude of his forces and the fearless courage with which they sailed wherever they pleased and brought the whole sea under their own control. He also left with the banished Sinopians thirteen ships of war and soldiers under command of Lamachus to aid them against Timesileos. When the tyrant and his adherents had been driven from the city, Pericles got a bill passed providing that six hundred volunteers of the Athenians should sail to Sinope and settle down there with the Sinopians, dividing up among themselves the houses and lands which the tyrant and his followers had formerly occupied.

---

38. 447 B.C.
39. 447 B.C.
40. 453 B.C.
41. Probably about 436 B.C.

But in other matters he did not accede to the vain impulses of the citizens, nor was he swept along with the tide when they were eager, from a sense of their great power and good fortune, to lay hands again upon Egypt and molest the realms of the King which lay along the sea. Many also were possessed already with that inordinate and auspicious passion for Sicily which was afterwards kindled into flame by such orators as Alcibiades. And some there were who actually dreamed of Tuscany and Carthage, and that not without a measure of hope, in view of the magnitude of their present supremacy and the full-flowing tide of success in their undertakings.

21. But Pericles was ever trying to restrain this extravagance of theirs, to lop off their expansive meddlesomeness, and to divert the greatest part of their forces to the guarding and securing of what they had already won. He considered it a great achievement to hold the Lacedaemonians in check, and set himself in opposition to these in every way, as he showed, above all other things, by what he did in the Sacred War.[42] The Lacedaemonians made an expedition to Delphi while the Phocians had possession of the sanctuary there, and restored it to the Delphians; but no sooner had the Lacedaemonians departed than Pericles made a counter expedition and reinstated the Phocians. And whereas the Lacedaemonians had had the "promanteia," or right of consulting the oracle in behalf of others also, which the Delphians had bestowed upon them, carved upon the forehead of the bronze wolf in the sanctuary, he secured from the Phocians this high privilege for the Athenians, and had it chiseled along the right side of the same wolf.

22. That he was right in seeking to confine the power of the Athenians within lesser Greece, was amply proved by what came to pass. To begin with, the Euboeans revolted,[43] and he crossed over to the island with a hostile force. Then straightway word was brought to him that the Megarians had gone over to the enemy, and that an army of the enemy was on the confines of Attica under the leadership of Pleistoanax, the king of the Lacedaemonians. Accordingly, Pericles brought his forces back with speed from Euboea for the war in Attica. He did not venture to join battle with hoplites who were so many, so brave, and so eager for battle, but seeing that Pleistoanax was a very young man, and that out of all his advisers he set most store by Cleandridas, whom the ephors had sent along with him, by reason of his youth, to be a guardian and an assistant to him, he secretly made trial of this man's integrity, speedily corrupted him with bribes, and persuaded him to lead the Peloponnesians back out of Attica.

When the army had withdrawn and had been disbanded to their several cities, the Lacedaemonians, in indignation, laid a heavy fine upon their king, the full amount of which he was unable to pay, and so betook himself out of Lacedaemon, while Cleandridas, who had gone into voluntary exile, was condemned to death. He was the father of that Gylippus who overcame the Athenians in Sicily. And nature seems to have imparted covetousness to the son, as it were a congenital disease, owing to which he too, after noble achievements, was caught in base practices and banished from Sparta in disgrace. This story, however, I have told at length in my life of Lysander.

23. When Pericles, in rendering his accounts for this campaign, recorded an expenditure of ten talents as "for sundry needs," the people approved it without officious meddling and without even investigating the mystery. But some writers, among whom is Theophrastus the philosopher,

---

42. About 448 B.C.
43. 446 B.C.

have stated that every year ten talents found their way to Sparta from Pericles, and that with these he conciliated all the officials there, and so staved off the war, not purchasing peace, but time, in which he could make preparations at his leisure and then carry on war all the better. However that may be, he again turned his attention to the rebels, and after crossing to Euboea with fifty ships of war and five thousand hoplites, he subdued the cities there. Those of the Chalcidians who were styled Hippobotae, or *Knights*, and who were preeminent for wealth and reputation, he banished their city, and all the Hestiaeans he removed from the country and settled Athenians in their places, treating them, and them only, thus inexorably, because they had taken an Attic ship captive and slain its crew.

24. After this, when peace had been made for thirty years between the Athenians and the Lacedaemonians, he got a decree passed for his expedition to Samos,[44] alleging against its people that, though they were ordered to break off their war against the Milesians, they were not complying.

Now, since it is thought that he proceeded thus against the Samians to gratify Aspasia, this may be a fitting place to raise the query what great art or power this woman had, that she managed as she pleased the foremost men of the state, and afforded the philosophers occasion to discuss her in exalted terms and at great length. That she was a Milesian by birth, daughter of one Axiochus, is generally agreed; and they say that it was in emulation of Thargelia, an Ionian woman of ancient times, that she made her onslaughts upon the most influential men. This Thargelia came to be a great beauty and was endowed with grace of manners as well as clever wits. Inasmuch as she lived on terms of intimacy with numberless Greeks, and attached all her consorts to the king of Persia, she stealthily sowed the seeds of Persian sympathy in the cities of Greece by means of these lovers of hers, who were men of the greatest power and influence. And so Aspasia, as some say, was held in high favor by Pericles because of her rare political wisdom. Socrates sometimes came to see her with his disciples, and his intimate friends brought their wives to her to hear her discourse, although she presided over a business that was anything but honest or even reputable, since she kept a house of young courtesans. And Aeschines[45] says that Lysicles the sheep-dealer, a man of low birth and nature, came to be the first man at Athens by living with Aspasia after the death of Pericles. And in the "Menexenus" of Plato, even though the first part of it be written in a sportive vein, there is, at any rate, thus much of fact, that the woman had the reputation of associating with many Athenians as a teacher of rhetoric. However, the affection which Pericles had for Aspasia seems to have been rather of an amatory sort. For his own wife was near of kin to him, and had been wedded first to Hipponicus, to whom she bore Callias, surnamed the Rich; she bore also, as the wife of Pericles, Xanthippus and Paralus. Afterwards, since their married life was not agreeable, he legally bestowed her upon another man, with her own consent, and himself took Aspasia, and loved her exceedingly. Twice a day, as they say, on going out and on coming in from the market-place, he would salute her with a loving kiss.

But in the comedies she is styled now the New Omphale, new Deianeira, and now Hera. Cratinus flatly called her a prostitute in these lines:

---

44. 440 B.C.

45. Aeshines the Socratic, in a dialogue entitled *Aspesia*, now lost.

"As his Hera, Aspasia was born, the child of Unnatural Lust,
A prostitute past shaming."

And it appears also that he begat from her that bastard son about whom Eupolis, in his "Demes," represented him as inquiring with these words:

"And my bastard, dose he live?"

to which Myronides replies:

"Yea, and long had been a man,
Had he not feared the mischief of his harlot-birth."

So renowned and celebrated did Aspasia become, they say, that even Cyrus, the one who went to war with the Great King for the sovereignty of the Persians, gave the name of Aspasia to that one of his concubines whom he loved best, who before was called Milto. She was a Phocaean by birth, daughter of one Hermotimus, and, after Cyrus had fallen in battle, was carried captive to the King, and acquired the greatest influence with him. These things coming to my recollection as I write, it were perhaps unnatural to reject and pass them by.

25. But to return to the war against the Samians, they accuse Pericles of getting the decree for this passed at the request of Aspasia and in the special behalf of the Milesians. For the two cities were waging their war for the possession of Priene, and the Samians were getting the better of it, and when the Athenians ordered them to stop the contest and submit the case to arbitration at Athens, they would not obey. So Pericles set sail and broke up the oligarchical government which Samos had, and then took fifty of the foremost men of the state, with as many of their children, as hostages, and sent them off to Lemons. And yet they say that every one of these hostages offered him a talent on his own account, and that the opponents of democracy in the city offered him many talents besides. And still further, Pissouthnes, the Persian satrap, who had much goodwill towards the Samians, sent him ten thousand gold staters and interceded for the city. However, Pericles took none of these bribes, but treated the Samians just as he had determined, set up a democracy and sailed back to Athens. Then the Samians at once revolted, after Pissouthnes had stolen away their hostages from Lemnos for them, and in other ways equipped them for the war. Once more, therefore, Pericles set sail against them. They were not victims of sloth, nor yet of abject terror, but full of exceeding zeal in their determination to contest the supremacy of the sea. In a fierce sea-fight which came off near an island called Tragia, Pericles won a brilliant victory, with four and forty ships outfighting seventy, twenty of which were infantry transports.

26. Close on the heels of his victorious pursuit came his seizure of the harbor, and then he laid formal siege to the Samians, who, somehow or other, still had the daring to sally forth and fight with him before their walls. But soon a second and a larger armament came from Athens, and the Samians were completely beleaguered and shut in. Then Pericles took sixty triremes and sailed out into the main sea, as most authorities say, because he wished to meet a fleet of Phoenician ships which was coming to the aid of the Samians, and fight it at as great a distance from Samos as possible; but according to Stesimbrotus, because he had designs on Cyprus, which seems in-

credible. But in any case, whichever design he cherished, he seems to have made a mistake. For no sooner had he sailed off than Melissus, the son of Ithagenes, a philosopher who was then acting as general at Samos, despising either the small number of ships that were left, or the inexperience of the generals in charge of them, persuaded his fellow-citizens to make an attack upon the Athenians. In the battle that ensued the Samians were victorious, taking many of their enemy captive, and destroying many of their ships, so that they commanded the sea and laid in large store of such necessaries for the war as they did not have before. And Aristotle says that Pericles was himself also defeated by Melissus in the sea-fight which preceded this.

The Samians retaliated upon the Athenians by branding their prisoners in the forehead with owls; for the Athenians had once branded some of them with the samaena. Now the samaena is a ship of war with a boar's head design for prow and ram, but more capacious than usual and paunch-like, so that it is a good deep-sea traveler and a swift sailor too. It got this name because it made its first appearance in Samos, where Polycrates the tyrant had some built. To these brand-marks, they say, the verse of Aristophanes made riddling reference:

"For oh! how lettered is the folk of the Samians!"

27. Be that true or not, when Pericles learned of the disaster which had befallen his fleet, he came speedily to its aid. And though Melissus arrayed his forces against him, he conquered and routed the enemy and at once walled their city in, preferring to get the upper hand and capture it at the price of money and time; rather than of the wounds and deadly perils of his fellow-citizens. And since it was a hard task for him to restrain the Athenians in their impatience of delay and eagerness to fight, he separated his whole force into eight divisions, had them draw lots, and allowed the division which got the white bean to feast and take their ease, while the others did the fighting. And this is the reason, as they say, why those who have had a gay and festive time call it a "white day"—from the white beau.

Ephorus says that Pericles actually employed siege-engines, in his admiration of their novelty, and that Artemon the engineer was with him there, who, since he was lame, and so had to be brought on a stretcher to the works which demanded his instant attention, was dubbed Periphoretus. Heracleides Ponticus, however, refutes this story out of the poems of Anacreon, in which Artemon. Periphoretus is mentioned many generations before the Samian War and its events. And he says that Artemon was very luxurious in his life, as well as weak and panic-stricken in the presence of his fears, and therefore for the most part sat still at home, while two servants held a bronze shield over his head to keep anything from falling down upon it. Whenever he was forced to go abroad, he had himself carried in a little hammock which was borne along just above the surface of the ground. On this account he was called Periphoretus.

28. After eight months the Samians surrendered, and Pericles tore down their walls, took away their ships of war, and laid a heavy fine upon them, part of which they paid at once, and part they agreed to pay at a fixed time, giving hostages therefor. To these details Duris the Samian adds stuff for tragedy, accusing the Athenians and Pericles of great brutality, which is recorded neither by Thucydides, nor Ephorus, nor Aristotle. But he appears not to speak the truth when he says, forsooth, that Pericles had the Samian trierarchs and marines brought into the market-place of Miletus and crucified there, and that then, when they had already suffered grievously for ten days, he gave orders to break their heads in with clubs and make an end of them, and then cast their bodies forth without burial rites. At all events since it is not the wont of Duris, even in cases where he has no private and personal interest, to hold his narrative down to the fundamental truth, it is all the more likely that here, in this instance, he has given a dreadful portrayal of the calamities of his country, that he might calumniate the Athenians.

When Pericles, after his subjection of Samos, had returned to Athens, he gave honorable burial to those who had fallen in the war, and for the oration which he made, according to the custom, over their tombs, he won the greatest admiration. But as he came down from the bema, while the rest of the women clasped his hand and fastened wreaths and fillets on his head, as though he were some victorious athlete, Elpinice drew nigh and said: "This is admirable in thee, Pericles, and deserving of wreaths, in that thou hast lost us many brave citizens, not in a war with Phoenicians or Medes, like my brother Cimon, but in the subversion of an allied and kindred city." On Elpinice's saving this, Pericles, with a quiet smile, it is said, quoted to her the verse of Archilochus:

"You have not else, in spite of years, perfumed yourself."[46]

Ion says that he had the most astonishingly great thoughts of himself for having subjected the Samians; whereas Agamemnon was all of ten years in taking a barbarian city, he had in nine months time reduced the foremost and most powerful people of Ionia. And indeed his estimate of himself was not unjust, nay, the war actually brought with it much uncertainty and great peril, if indeed, as Thucydides says, the city of Samos came within a very little of stripping from Athens her power on the sea.

29. After this, when the billows of the Peloponnesian War were already rising and swelling, he persuaded the people to send aid and succor to the Corcyracans[47] in their war with the Corinthians, and so to attach to themselves an island with a vigorous naval power at a time when the Peloponnesians were as good as actually at war with them. But when the people had voted to send the aid and succor, he dispatched Lacedaemonius, the son of Cimon, with only ten ships, as it were in mockery of him. Now there was much good-will and friendship on the part of the house of Cimon towards the Lacedaemonians. In order, therefore, that in no great or conspicuous achievement should be performed under the generalship of Lacedaemonius, and that he would be discredited for his pro-Spartan sympathies, Pericles gave him only a few ships, and sent him forth against his will. And in general he was prone to thwart and check the sons of Cimon, on the plea that not even in their names were they genuinely native, but rather aliens and strangers, since one of them bore the name of Lacedaemonius, another that of Thessalus, and a third that of Eleius. And they were all held to be the sons of a woman of Arcadia.

Accordingly, being harshly criticized because of these paltry ten ships, on the ground that he had furnished scanty aid and succor to the needy friends of Athens, but a great pretext for war to her accusing enemies, he afterwards sent out other ships, and more of them, to Corcyra—the ones which got there after the battle.

---

46. That is, "you are too old to meddle in affairs."
47. 433 B.C.

The Corinthians were incensed at this procedure, and denounced the Athenians at Sparta, and were joined by tile Megarians, who brought their complaint that from every market-place and from all the harbors over which the Athenians had control, they were excluded and driven away, contrary to the common law and the formal oaths of the Greeks the Aeginetans also, deeming themselves wronged and outraged, kept up a secret wailing in the ears of the Lacedaemonians, since they had not the courage to accuse the Athenians openly. At this juncture Potidaea, too, a city that was subject to Athens, although a colony of Corinth, revolted, and the siege laid to her hastened on the war all the more.

Notwithstanding all, since embassies were repeatedly sent to Athens, and since Archidamus, the king of the Lacedaemonians, tried to bring to a peaceful settlement most of the accusations of his allies and to soften their anger, it does not seem probable that the war would have come upon the Athenians for any remaining reasons, if only they could have been persuaded to rescind their decree against the Megarians and be reconciled with them. And therefore, since it was Pericles who was most of all opposed to this, and who incited the people to abide by their contention with the Megarians, he alone was held responsible for the war.

30. They say that when an embassy had come from Lacedaemon to Athens to treat of these matters, and Pericles was shielding himself behind the plea that a certain law prevented his taking down the tablet on which the decree was inscribed, Polyalces, one of the ambassadors, cried: "Well then, don't take it down, but turn the tablet to the wall surely there's no law preventing that." Clever as the proposal was, however, not one whit the more did Pericles give in. He must have secretly cherished, then, as it seems, some private grudge against the Megarians; but by way of public and open charge he accused them of appropriating to their own profane uses the sacred territory of Eleusis, and proposed a decree that a herald be sent to them, the same to go also to the Lacedaemonians with a denunciation of the Megarians. This decree, at any rate, is the work of Pericles, and aims at a reasonable and humane justification of his course. But after the herald who was sent, Anthemocritus, had been put to death through the agency of the Megarians, as it was believed, Charinus proposed a decree against them, to the effect that there be irreconcilable and implacable enmity on the part of Athens towards them, and that whosoever of the Megarians should set foot on the soil of Attica be punished with death; and that the generals, whenever they should take their ancestral oath of office, add to their oath this clause, that they would invade the Megarid twice during each succeeding year; and that Anthemocritus be buried honorably at the Thriasian gates, which are now called the Dipylum. But the Megarians denied the murder of Anthemocritus, and threw the blame for Athenian hate on Aspasia and Pericles, appealing to those far-famed and hackneyed versicles of the "Acharnians:"

"Some young Athenians in a drunken frolic
Kidnapped Simaetha, the courtesan, from Magara.
The Megarians were furious, primed themselves with garlic
Just like their fighting cocks, than came and stole
Two of Aspasia's girls to get their own back."

31. Well, then, whatever the original ground for enacting the decree—and it is no easy matter to determine this—the fact that it was not rescinded all men alike lay to the charge of Pericles.

Only, some say that he persisted in his refusal in a lofty spirit and with a clear perception of the best interests of the city, regarding the injunction laid upon it as a test of its submissiveness, and its compliance as a confession of weakness; while others hold that it was rather with a sort of arrogance and love of strife, as well as for the display of his power, that he scornfully defied the Lacedaemonians.

But the worst charge of all,[48] and yet the one which has the most vouchers, runs something like this. Pheidias the sculptor was contractor for the great statue, as I have said, and being admitted to the friendship of Pericles, and acquiring the greatest influence with him, made some enemies through the jealousy which he excited; others also made use of him to test the people and see what sort of a judge it would be in a case where Pericles was involved. These latter persuaded one Menon, an assistant of Pheidias, to take a suppliant's seat in the marketplace and demand immunity from punishment in case he should bring information and accusation against Pheidias. The people accepted the man's proposal, and formal prosecution of Pheidias was made in the assembly. Embezzlement, indeed, was not proven, for the gold of the statue, from the very start, had been so wrought upon and cast about it by Pheidias, at the wise suggestion of Pericles, that it could all be taken off and weighed, and this is what Pericles actually ordered the accusers of Pheidias to do at this time.

But the reputation of his works nevertheless brought a burden of jealous hatred upon Pheidias, and especially the fact that when he wrought the battle of the Amazons on the shield of the goddess, he carved out a figure that suggested himself as a bald old man lifting on high a stone with both hands, and also inserted a very fine likeness of Pericles fighting with an Amazon. And the attitude of the hand, which holds out a spear in front of the face of Pericles, is cunningly contrived as it were with a desire to conceal the resemblance, which is, however, plain to be seen from either side.

Pheidias, accordingly, was led away to prison, and died there of sickness; but some say of poison which the enemies of Pericles provided, that they might bring calumny upon him. And to Menon the informer, on motion of Glycon, the people gave immunity from taxation, and enjoined upon the generals to make provision for the man's safety.

32. About this time also Aspasia was put on trial for impiety, Hermippus the comic poet being her prosecutor, who alleged further against her that she received free born women into a place of assignation for Pericles. And Diopeithes brought in a bill providing for the public impeachment of such as did not believe in gods, or who taught doctrines regarding the heavens, directing suspicion against Pericles by means of Anaxagoras. The people accepted with delight these slanders, and so, while they were in this mood, a bill was passed, on motion of Dracontides, that Pericles should deposit his accounts of public moneys with the prytanes, and that the jurors should decide upon his case with ballots which had lain upon the altar of the goddess on the acropolis. But Hagnon amended this clause of the bill with the motion that the case be tried before fifteen hun-

---

48. Plutarch offers no opinion, but the *facts* do not support this charge. Other accounts suggest that Pheidias *may* have been prosecuted soon after the statue was dedicated in 438–437 B.C. and that he may have been exiled soon afterwards and died in Elis about 432 B.C.. Anaxagoras is now believed to have retired to Lampsacus nearly twenty years earlier, and Dracontides' motion was not passed until 410 B.C. and therefore had no connection with the outbreak of the war. Thucydides gives no hint that Pericles' ascendancy was being challenged in the period immediately preceding the war, but rather that the crisis strengthened it.

dred jurors in the ordinary way, whether one wanted to call it a prosecution for embezzlement and bribery, or malversation.

Well, then, Aspasia he begged off by shedding copious tears at the trial, as Aesehines says, and by entreating the jurors; and he feared for Anaxagoras so much that he sent him away from the city. And since in the case of Pheidias he had come into collision with the people, he feared a jury in his own ease, and so kindled into flame the threatening and smoldering war, hoping thereby to dissipate the charges made against him and allay the people's jealousy, inasmuch as when great undertakings were on foot, and great perils threatened, the city entrusted herself to him and to him alone, by reason of his worth and power. Such, then, are the reasons which are alleged for his not suffering the people to yield to the Lacedaemonians; but the truth about it is not clear.

33. The Lacedaemonians, perceiving that if he were deposed they would find the Athenians more pliant in their hands, ordered them to drive out the Cylonian pollution,[49] in which the family of Pericles on his mother's side was involved, as Thucydides states. But the attempt brought a result the opposite of what its makers designed, for in place of suspicion and slander, Pericles won even greater confidence and honor among the citizens than before, because they saw that their enemies hated and feared him above all other men. Therefore also, before Archidamus invaded Attica with the Peloponnesians, Pericles made public proclamation to the Athenians, that in case Archidamus, while ravaging everything else, should spare his estates, either out of regard for the friendly tie that existed between them, or with an eye to affording his enemies grounds for slander, he would make over to the city his lands and the homesteads thereon.

Accordingly, the Lacedaemonians and their allies invaded Attica with a great host under the leadership of Archidamus the king. And they advanced, ravaging the country as they went, as far as Acharnae, where they encamped, supposing that the Athenians would not tolerate it, but would fight with them out of angry pride. Pericles, however, looked upon it as a terrible thing to join battle with sixty thousand Peloponnesian and Boeotian hoplites (those who made the first invasion were as numerous as that), and stake the city itself upon the issue. So lie tried to calm down those who were eager to fight, and who were in distress at what the enemy was doing, by saying that trees, though cut and lopped, grew quickly, but if men were destroyed it was not easy to get them again. And he would not call the people together into an assembly, fearing that he would he constrained against his better judgment, but, like the helmsman of a ship, who, when a stormy wind swoops down upon it in the open sea, makes all fast, takes in sail, and exercises his skill, disregarding the tears and entreaties of the sea-sick and timorous passengers, so he shut the city up tight, put all parts of it under safe garrison, and exercised his own judgment, little heeding the brawlers and malcontents. And yet many of his friends beset him with entreaties, and many of his enemies with threats and denunciations, and choruses sang songs of scurrilous mockery, railing at his generalship for its cowardice, and its abandonment of everything to the enemy. Cleon, too, was already harassing him, taking advantage of the wrath with which the citizens regarded him to make his own way toward the leadership of the people, as these anapaestc verses of Hermippus show:

---

49. That is, the members of the Alcmaeonid family, which was involved in the stain of bloodguilt when the archon Megacles, about 636 B.C., sacrilegiously killed the followers of Cylon. See above Solon 12.1–3.

"Come now, king of the satyrs, stop waging war
With your speeches, and try a real weapon!
Though I do not believe, under all your fine talk
You have even the guts of a Teles.
For if somebody gets out a whetstone and tries
Just to sharpen so much as a pen-knife,
You start grinding your teeth and fly into a rage
As if Cleon had come up and stung you."

34. However, Pericles was moved by no such things, but gently and silently underwent the ignominy and the hatred, and, sending out an armament of a hundred ships against the Peloponnesus, did not himself sail with it, but remained behind, keeping the city under watch and ward and well in hand, until the Peloponnesians withdrew. Then, by way of soothing the multitude, who, in spite of their enemies' departure, were distressed over the war, he won their favor by distributions of moneys and proposed allotments of conquered lands; the Aeginetans, for instance, he drove out entirely, and parceled out their island among the Athenians by lot. And some consolation was to be had from what their enemies suffered. For the expedition around the Peloponnesus ravaged much territory and sacked villages and small cities, while Pericles himself, by land, invaded the Megarid and razed it all. Wherein also it was evident that though their enemies did the Athenians much harm by land, they suffered much too at their hands by sea, and therefore would not have protracted the war to such a length, but would have speedily given up, just as Pericles prophesied in the beginning, had not a terrible visitation from heaven thwarted human calculations.

For now the plague fell upon the Athenians[50] and devoured clean the prime of their youth and power. It weakened them in body and in spirit, and made them altogether wild against Pericles, so that, for all the world as the mad will attack a physician or a father, so they, in the delirium of the plague, attempted to do him harm, persuaded thereto by his enemies. These urged that the plague was caused by the crowding of the rustic multitudes together into the city, where, in the summer season, many were huddled together in small dwellings and stifling barracks, and compelled to lead a stay-at-home and inactive life, instead of being in the pure and open air of heaven as they were wont. They said that Pericles was responsible for this, who, because of the war, had poured the rabble from the country into the walled city, and then gave that mass of men no employment whatever, but suffered them, thus penned up like cattle, to fill one another full of corruption, and provided them no change or respite.

35. Desiring to heal these evils, and at the same time to inflict some annoyance upon the enemy, he manned a hundred and fifty ships of war, and, after embarking many brave hoplites and horsemen, was on the point of putting out to sea, affording great hope to the citizens, and no less fear to the enemy in consequence of so great a force. But when the ships were already manned, and Pericles had gone aboard his own trireme, it chanced that the sun was eclipsed and darkness came on, and all were thoroughly frightened, looking upon it as a great portent. Accordingly, seeing that his steersman was timorous and utterly perplexed, Pericles held up his cloak before

---

50. 430 B.C.

the man's eyes, and, thus covering them, asked him if he thought it anything dreadful, or portentous of anything dreadful. "No," said the steersman. "How then," said Pericles, "is yonder event different from this, except that it is something rather larger than my cloak which has caused the obscurity?" At any rate, this tale is told in the schools of philosophy.

Well, then, on sailing forth, Pericles seems to have accomplished nothing worthy of his preparations, but after laying siege to sacred Epidaurus, which awakened a hope that it might be captured, he had no such good fortune, because of the plague. Its fierce onset destroyed not only the Athenians themselves, but also those who, in any manner whatever, had dealings with their forces. The Athenians being exasperated against him on this account, he tried to appease and encourage them. He did not, however, succeed in allaying their wrath, nor yet in changing their purposes, before they got their hostile ballots into their hands, became masters of his fate, stripped him of his command, and punished him with a fine. The amount of this was fifteen talents, according to those who give the lowest, and fifty, according to those who give the highest figures. The public prosecutor mentioned in the records of the case was Cleon, as Idomeneus says, but according to Theophrastus it was Simmias, and Heracleides Ponticus mentions Lacratides.

36. So much, then, for his public troubles they were likely soon to cease, now that the multitude had stung him, as it were, and left their passion with their sting; but his domestic affairs were in a sorry plight, since he had lost not a few of his intimate friends during the pestilence, and had for some time been rent and torn by a family feud. The eldest of' his legitimate sons, Xanthippus, who was naturally prodigal, and had married a young and extravagant wife, the daughter of Tisander, the son of Epilycus, was much displeased at his father's exactitude in making him but a meager allowance, and that a little at a time. Accordingly, he sent to one of his father's friends and got money, pretending that Pericles bade him do it. When the friend afterwards demanded repayment of the loan, Pericles not only refused it, but brought suit against him to boot. So the young fellow, Xanthippus, incensed at this, fell to abusing his father, publishing abroad, to make men laugh, his conduct of affairs at home, and the discourses which he held with the sophists. For instance, a certain athlete had hit Epitimus the Pharsalian with a javelin, accidentally, and killed him, and Pericles, Xanthippus said, squandered an entire day discussing with Protagoras whether it was the javelin, or rather the one who hurled it, or the judges of the contests, that "in the strictest sense" ought to be held responsible for the disaster. Besides all this. the slanderous charge concerning his own wife Stesimbrotus says was sown abroad in public by Xanthippus himself, and also that the quarrel which the young man had with his father remained utterly incurable up to the time of his death—for Xanthippus fell sick and died during the plague.

Pericles lost his sister also at that time, and of his relatives and friends the largest part, and those who were most serviceable to him in his administration of the city. He did not, however, give up, nor yet abandon his loftiness and grandeur of spirit because of his calamities, nay, he was not even seen to weep, either at the funeral rites, or at the grave-of any of his connections, until indeed he lost the very last remaining one of his own legitimate sons, Paralus. Even though he was bowed down at this stroke, he nevertheless tried to persevere in his habit and maintain his spiritual greatness, but as he laid a wreath upon the dead, he was vanquished by his anguish at the sight, so that he broke out into wailing and shed a multitude of tears, although he had never done any such thing in all his life before.

37. The city made trial of its other generals and counselors for the conduct of the war, but since no one appeared to have weight that was adequate or authority that was competent for such leadership, it yearned for Pericles, and summoned him back to the assembly and the war-office.[51] He was lying dejectedly at home because of his sorrow, but was persuaded by Alcibiades and his other friends to resume his public life. When the people had apologized for their thankless treatment of him, and he had undertaken again the conduct of the state, and been elected general, he asked for a suspension of the law concerning children born out of wedlock—a law which he himself had formerly introduced—in order that the name and lineage of his house might not altogether expire through lack of succession.

The circumstances of this law were as follows. Many years before this,[52] when Pericles was at the height of his political career and had sons born in wedlock, as I have said, he proposed a law that only those should be reckoned Athenians whose parents on both sides were Athenians. And so when the king of Egypt sent a present to the People of forty thousand measures of grain, and this had to be divided up among the citizens, there was a great crop of prosecutions against citizens of illegal birth by the law of Pericles, who had up to that time escaped notice and been overlooked and many of them also suffered at the hands of informers. As a result, a little less than five thousand were convicted and sold into slavery, and those who retained their citizenship and were adjudged to be Athenians were found, as a result of this scrutiny, to be fourteen thousand and forty in number. It was, accordingly, a grave matter, that the law which had been rigorously enforced against so many should now be suspended by the very man who had introduced it, and yet the calamities which Pericles was then suffering in his family life, regarded as a kind of penalty which he had paid for his arrogance and haughtiness of old, broke down the objections of the Athenians. They thought that what he suffered was by way of retribution, and that what he asked became a man to ask and men to grant, and so they suffered him to enroll his illegitimate son in the phratry lists and to give him his own name. This was the son who afterwards conquered the Peloponnesians in a naval battle at the Arginusae islands,[53] and was put to death by the people along with his fellow-generals.

38. At this time, it would seem, the plague laid hold of Pericles, not with a violent attack, as in the case of others, nor acute, but one which, with a kind of sluggish distemper that prolonged itself through varying changes, used up his body slowly and undermined the loftiness of his spirit. Certain it is that Theophrastus, in his "Ethics," querying whether one's character follows the bent of one's fortunes and is forced by bodily sufferings to abandon its high excellence, records this fact, that Pericles, as lie lay sick, showed one of his friends who was come to see him an amulet that the women had hung round his neck, as much as to say that he was very badly off to put up with such folly as that.

Being now near his end,[54] the best of the citizens and those of his friends who survived were sitting around him holding discourse of his excellence and power, how great they had been, and estimating all his achievements and the number of his trophies—there were nine of these which

---

51. 429 B.C.
52. 452–450 B.C.
53. 406 B.C.
54. He died in the autumn of 429 B.C.

he had set up as the city's victorious general. This discourse they were holding with one another supposing that he no longer understood them but had lost consciousness. He had been attending to it all, however, and speaking out among them said he was amazed at their praising and commemorating that in him which was due as much to fortune as to himself, and which had fallen to the lot of many generals besides, instead of mentioning his fairest and greatest title to their admiration; " for," said he, "no living Athenian ever put on mourning because of me."

39. So, then, the man is to be admired not only for his reasonableness and the gentleness which he maintained in the midst of many responsibilities and great enmities, but also for his loftiness of spirit, seeing that he regarded it as the noblest of all his titles to honor that he had never gratified his envy or his passion in the exercise of his vast power, nor treated any one of his foes as a irreconcilable enemy. And it seems to me that his otherwise puerile and pompous surname is rendered unobjectionable and becoming by this one circumstance, that it was so gracious a nature and a life so pure and undefiled in the exercise of sovereign power which were called Olympian, inasmuch as we do firmly hold that the divine rulers and kings of the universe are capable only of good, and incapable of evil. In this we are not like the poets, who confuse us with their ignorant fancies, and are convicted of inconsistency by their own stories, since they declare that the place where they say the gods dwell is a secure abode and tranquil, without experience of winds and clouds, but gleaming through all the unbroken time with the soft radiance of purest light—implying that some such a manner of existence is most becoming to the blessed immortal; and yet they represent the gods themselves as full of malice and hatred and wrath and other passions which ill become even men of any sense. But this, perhaps, will he thought matter for discussion elsewhere.

The progress of events wrought in the Athenians a swift appreciation of Pericles and a keen sense of his loss. For those who, while he lived, were oppressed by a sense of his power and felt that it kept them in obscurity, straightway on his removal made trial of other orators and popular leaders, only to be led to the confession that a character more moderate than his in its solemn dignity, and more august in its gentleness, had not been created. That objectionable power of his, which they had used to call monarchy and tyranny, seemed to them now to have been a saving bulwark of the constitution, so greatly was the state afflicted by the corruption and manifold baseness which he had kept weak and groveling, thereby covering it out of sight and preventing it from becoming incurably powerful.

ALCIBIADES

"To the ancients, Alcibiades was the stock type of the sophisticated aristocrat, endowed with all possible advantages, brilliant and 'outstanding both in his vices and in his virtues' (Nepos)"[55] His extraordinary career is narrated in the following excerpts from Plutarch's Life of Alcibiades.

---

55. *Who Was Who in the Greek World*, edited by Diana Bowder, Cornell University Press, Ithaca, New Your, 1982, p.32

1. The family of Alcibiades, it is thought, may be traced back to Eurysaces, the son of Aias, as its founder; and on his mother's side he was an Alcmaeonid, being the son of Deinomache, the daughter of Megacles. His father, Cleinias, fitted out a trireme at his own cost and fought it gloriously at Artemisium.[56] He was afterwards slain at Coroneia, fighting the Boeotians, and Alcibiades was therefore reared as the ward of Pericles and Ariphron, the sons of Xanthippus, his near kinsmen.[57]

It is said, and with good reason, that the favor and affection which Socrates showed him contributed not a little to his reputation. . . As regards the beauty of Alcibiades, it is perhaps unnecessary to say aught, except that it flowered out with each successive season of his bodily growth, and made him, alike in boyhood, youth and manhood, lovely and pleasant. The saying of Euripides, that "beauty's autumn, too, is beautiful," is not always true. But it was certainly the case with Alcibiades, as with few besides, because of his excellent natural parts. Even his lisp is said to have suited his voice well, and made his speech persuasive and full of charm. Aristophanes notices this lisp of his in the verses wherein he ridicules Theorus: [58]

(Sosias) "Then Alcibiades said to me with a lisp, said he,
'Cwemabk Theoewus? What a cwaven s head he has!'"
(Xantliias) "That lisp of Alcibiades hit the mark for once!"

And Archippus, ridiculing the son of Alcibiades, says:

"He walks with utter wantonness, trailing his long robe behind him, that he may be thought the very picture of his father, yes, he slants his neck awry, and overworks the lisp."

2. His character, in later life, displayed many inconsistencies and marked changes, as was natural amid his vast undertakings and varied fortunes. He was naturally a man of many strong passions, the mightiest of which were the love of rivalry and the love of preeminence. This is clear from the stories recorded of his boyhood.

He was once hard pressed in wrestling, and to save himself from getting a fall, set his teeth in his opponent's arms, where they clutched him, and was like to have bitten through them. His adversary, letting go his hold, cried: "You bite, Alcibiades, as women do!" "Not I," said Alcibiades, "but as lions do."

While still a small boy, he was playing knuckle-bones in the narrow street, and just as it was his turn to throw, a heavy-laden wagon came along. In the first place, he bade the driver halt, since his cast lay right in the path of the wagon. The driver, however, was a boorish fellow, and paid no heed to him, but drove his team along. Whereupon, while the other boys scattered out of the way, Alcibiades threw himself flat on his face in front of the team, stretched himself out at full length, and bade the driver go on if he pleased. At this the fellow pulled up his beasts sharply, in terror; the spectators, too, were frightened, and ran with shouts to help the boy.

---

56. 480 B.C.

57. They were first cousins, once removed.

58. Aristophanes, *Wasps*, 44 ff. The lisp of Alcibiades turned his "r" into "l" and the play is on the words for *raven* and *flatterer* or *craven*.

At school, he usually paid due heed to his teachers, but he refused to play the flute, holding it to be an ignoble and illiberal thing. The use of the plectrum and the lyre, he argued, wrought no havoc with the bearing and appearance which were becoming to a gentleman; but let a man go to blowing on a flute, and even his own kinsmen could scarcely recognize his features. Moreover, the lyre blended its tones with the voice or song of its master; whereas the flute closed and barricaded the mouth, robbing its master both of voice and speech. "Flutes, then," said he, "for the sons of Thebes; they know not how to converse. But we Athenians, as our fathers say, have Athena for foundress and Apollo for patron, one of whom cast the flute away in disgust, and the other flayed the presumptuous flute-player."[59] Thus, half in jest and half in earnest, Alcibiades emancipated himself from this discipline, and the rest of the boys as well. For word soon made its way to them that Alcibiades loathed the art of flute-playing and scoffed at its disciples, and rightly, too. Wherefore the flute was dropped entirely from the program of a liberal education and was altogether despised.

4. It was not long before many men of high birth clustered about him and paid him their attentions. Most of them were plainly smitten with his brilliant youthful beauty and fondly courted him. But it was the love which Socrates had for him that bore strong testimony to the boy's native excellence and good disposition. These Socrates saw radiantly manifest in his outward person, and, fearful of the influence upon him of wealth and rank and the throng of citizens, foreigners and allies who sought to preempt his affections by flattery and favor, he was fain to protect him, and not suffer such a fair flowering plant to cast its native fruit to perdition. For there is no man whom Fortune so envelops and compasses about with the so-called good things of life that he cannot be reached by the bold and caustic reasonings of philosophy, and pierced to the heart. And so it was that Alcibiades, although he was pampered from the very first, and was prevented by the companions who sought only to please him from giving ear to one who would instruct and train him, nevertheless, through the goodness of his parts, at last saw all that was in Socrates, and clave to him, putting away his rich and famous lovers. And speedily, from choosing such an associate, and giving ear to the words of a lover who was in the chase for no unmanly pleasures, and begged no kisses and embraces, but sought to expose the weakness of his soul and rebuke his vain and foolish pride,

"He crouched, though warrior bird, like slave, with drooping wings."

And he came to think that the work of Socrates was really a kind of provision of the gods for the care and salvation of youth. Thus, by despising himself, admiring his friend, loving that friend's kindly solicitude and revering his excellence, he insensibly acquired an "image of love," as Plato says, "to match love," and all were amazed to see him eating, exercising, and tenting with Socrates, while he was harsh and stubborn with the rest of his lovers. . .

10. . . . Though great doors to public service were opened to him by his birth, his wealth, and his personal bravery in battle; and though he had many friends and followers, he thought that nothing should give him more influence with the people than the charm of his discourse. And

---

59. Athena threw away the flute because she saw her puffed and swollen checks reflected in the water of a spring. Marayas the satyr was vanquished by Apollo in a musical contest, and was flayed alive.

that he was a powerful speaker, not only do the comic poets testify, but also the most powerful of orators himself,[60] who says, in his speech "*Against Meidias,*" that Alcibiades was a most able speaker in addition to his other gifts. And if we are to trust Theophrastus, the most versatile and learned of the philosophers, Alcibiades was of all men the most capable of discovering and understanding what was required in a given case. But since he strove to find not only the proper thing to say, but also the proper words and phrases in which to say it; and since in this last regard he was not a man of large resources he would often stumble in the midst of his speech, come to a stop, and pause a while, a particular phrase eluding him. Then he would resume, and proceed with all the caution in the world.

13. On entering public life, though still a mere stripling, he immediately humbled all the other popular leaders except Phaeax, the son of Erasistratus, and Nicias, the son of Niceratus. These men made him fight hard for what he won. Nicias was already of mature years, and had the reputation of being a most excellent general; but Phaeax, like himself, was just beginning his career, and, though of illustrious parentage, was inferior to him in other ways, and particularly as a public speaker. He seemed affable and winning in private conversation rather than capable of conducting public debates. In fact, he was, as Eupolis says,

"A prince of talkers, but in speaking most incapable."

And there is extant a certain speech written by Phacax "Against Alcibiades,"[61] wherein, among other things, it is written that the city's numerous ceremonial utensils of gold and silver were all used by Alcibiades at his regular table as though they were his own. . .

14. Alcibiades was sore distressed to see Nicias no less admired by his enemies than honored by his fellow-citizens. For although Alcibiades was resident consul for the Lacedaemonians at Athens, and had ministered to their men who had been taken prisoners at Pylos,[62] still, they felt that it was chiefly due to Nicias that they had obtained peace and the final surrender of those men, and so they lavished their regard upon him. And Hellenes everywhere said that it was Pericles who had plunged them into war, but Nicias who had delivered them out of it, and most men called the peace the Peace of Nicias."[63] Alcibiades was therefore distressed beyond measure, and in his envy planned a violation of the solemn treaty. To begin with, he saw that the Argives hated and feared the Spartans and sought to be rid of them. So he secretly held out hopes to them of an alliance with Athens, and encouraged them, by conferences with the chief men of their popular party, not to fear nor yield to the Lacedaemonians, but to look to Athens and await her action, since she was now all but repentant, and desirous of abandoning the peace which she had made with Sparta.

And again, when the Lacedaemonians made a separate alliance with the Boeotians, and delivered up Panactum to the Athenians not intact, as they were bound to do by the treaty, but

---

60. Demosthenes, *Against Meidias*, 145.
61. This has come down to us among the orations of Andocides. It is clearly a fictitious speech, put by its unknown author into the mouth of Phaeax.
62. In 425 B.C.
63. Ratified in 421 B.C.

dismantled, he took advantage of the Athenians' wrath at this to embitter them yet more. He raised a tumult in the assembly against Nicias, and slandered him with accusations all too plausible. Nicias himself, he said, when he was general, had refused to capture the enemy's men who were cut off on the island of Sphacteria, and when others had captured them, he had released and given them back to the Lacedaemonians, whose favor he sought; and then he did riot persuade those same Lacedaemonians, tried friend of theirs as he was, not to make separate alliance with the Boeotians or even with the Corinthians, and yet whenever any Hellenes wished to be friends and allies of Athens, he tried to prevent it, unless it were the good pleasure of the Lacedaemonians.

Nicias was reduced to great straits by all this, but just then, by rare good fortune as it were, an embassy came from Sparta, with reasonable proposals to begin on, and with assurances that they came with full powers to adopt any additional terms that were conciliatory and just. The council received them favorably, and the people were to hold an assembly on the following day for their reception. But Alcibiades feared a peaceful outcome, and managed to secure a private conference with the embassy. When they were convened he said to them "What is the matter with you, men of Sparta? Why are you blind to the fact that the council is always moderate and courteous towards those who have dealings with it, while the people's assembly is haughty and has great ambitions? If you say to them that you are come with unlimited powers, they will lay their commands and compulsions upon you without any feeling. Come now, put away such simplicity as this, and if you wish to get moderate terms from the Athenians, and to suffer no compulsion at their hands which you cannot yourselves approve, then discuss with them what would be a just settlement of your case, assuring them that you have not full powers to act. I will cooperate with you, out of my regard for the Lacedaemonians." After this speech he gave them his oath, and so seduced them wholly away from the influence of Nicias. They trusted him implicitly, admired his cleverness and sagacity, and thought him no ordinary man.

On the following day the people convened in assembly, and the embassy was introduced to them. On being asked by Alcibiades, in the most courteous tone, with what powers they had come, they replied that they were not come with full and independent powers. At once, then, Alcibiades assailed them with angry shouts, as though he were the injured party, not they, calling them faithless and fickle men, who were come on no sound errand whatever. The council was indignant, the assembly was enraged, and Nicias was filled with consternation and shame at the men's change of front. He was unaware of the deceitful trick which had been played upon him.

15. After this fiasco on the part of the Lacedaemonians, Alcibiades was appointed general, and straightway brought the Argives, Mantineans, and Eleans into alliance with Athens.[64] The manner of this achievement of his no one approved, but the effect of it was great. It divided and agitated almost all Peloponnesus; it arrayed against the Lacedaemonians at Mantinea[65] so many warlike shields upon a single day; it set at farthest remove from Athens the struggle, with all its risks, in which, when the Lacedaemonians conquered, their victory brought them no great advantage, whereas, had they been defeated, the very existence of Sparta would have been at stake.

After this battle of Mantinea, the oligarchs of Argos, "The Thousand," set out at once to depose the popular party and make the city subject to themselves; and the Lacedaemonians came

64. 420 B.C.
65. 418 B.C.

and deposed the democracy. But the populace took up arms again and got the upper hand.[66] Then Alcibiades came and made the people's victory secure. He also persuaded them to run long walls down to the sea, and so to attach their city completely to the naval dominion of Athens. He actually brought carpenters and masons from Athens, and displayed all manner of zeal, thus winning favor and power for himself no less than for his city. In like manner he persuaded the people of Patrae to attach their city to the sea by long walls.[67] Thereupon some one said to the Patrensians: "Athens will swallow you up!" "Perhaps so," said Alcibiades, "but you will go slowly, and feet first; whereas Sparta will swallow you head first, and at one gulp."

However, he counseled the Athenians to assert dominion on land also, and to maintain in very deed the oath regularly propounded to their young warriors in the sanctuary of Agraulus. They take oath that they will regard wheat, barley, the vine, and the olive as the natural boundaries of Attica, and they are thus trained to consider as their own all the habitable and fruitful earth.

16. But all this statecraft and eloquence and lofty purpose and cleverness was attended with great luxuriousness of life, with wanton drunkenness and lewdness, with effeminacy in dress—he would trail long purple robes through the market place—and with prodigal expenditures. He would have the decks of his triremes cut away that he might sleep more softly, his bedding being slung on cords rather than spread on the hard planks. He had a golden shield made for himself, bearing no ancestral device, but an Eros armed with a thunderbolt. The reputable men of the city looked on all these things with loathing and indignation, and feared his contemptuous and lawless spirit. They thought such conduct as his tyrant-like and monstrous. How the common folk felt towards him has been well set forth by Aristophanes[68] in these words:

"It yearns for him, and hates him too, but wants him back;"

and again, veiling a yet greater severity in his metaphor:

"A lion is not to be reared within the state;
But, once you've reared him up, consult his every mood."

And indeed, his voluntary contributions of money, his support of public exhibitions, his unsurpassed munificence towards the city, the glory of his ancestry, the power of his eloquence, the comeliness and vigor of his person, together with his experience and prowess in war, made the Athenians lenient and tolerant towards everything else; they were forever giving the mildest of names to his transgressions, calling them the product of youthful spirits and ambition.

For instance, he once imprisoned the painter Agatharchus in his house until he had adorned it with paintings for him, and then dismissed his captive with a handsome present. And when Taureas was supporting a rival exhibition, he gave him a box on the ear, so eager was he for the victory. And he picked out a woman from among the prisoners of Melos to be his mistress, and reared a

66. 417 B.C.
67. 419 B.C.
68. Frogs, 1425; 1431–1432.

son she bore him. This was an instance of what they called his kindness of heart, but the execution of all the grown men of Melos[69] was chiefly due to him, since he supported the decree therefor.

Aristophon painted Nemea[70] with Alcibiades seated in her arms; whereat the people were delighted, and ran in crowds to see the picture. But the elders were indignant at this too; they said it smacked of tyranny and lawlessness. And it would seem that Archestratus, in his verdict on the painting, did not go wide of the mark when he said that Hellas could not endure more than one Alcibiades.

Timon the misanthrope once saw Alcibiades, after a successful day, being publicly escorted home from the assembly. He did not pass him by nor avoid him, as his custom was with others, but met him and greeted him, saying: "It's well you're growing so, my child; you'll grow big enough to ruin all this rabble." At this some laughed, and some railed, and some gave much heed to the saying. So undecided was public opinion about Alcibiades, by reason of the unevenness of his nature.

17. The Athenians had cast longing eyes on Sicily even while Pericles was living; and after his death they actually tried to lay hands upon it. The lesser expeditions which they sent thither from time to time, ostensibly for the aid and comfort of their allies on the island who were being wronged by the Syracusans, they regarded merely as stepping stones to the greater expedition of conquest. But the man who finally fanned this desire of theirs into flame, and persuaded them not to attempt the island any more in part and little by little, but to sail thither with a great armament and subdue it utterly, was Alcibiades; he persuaded the people to have great hopes, and he himself had greater aspirations still. Such were his hopes that he regarded Sicily as a mere beginning, and not, like the rest, as an end of the expedition. So while Nicias was trying to divert the people from the capture of Syracuse as an undertaking too difficult for them, Alcibiades was dreaming of Carthage and Libya, and, after winning these, of at once encompassing Italy and Peloponnesus. He almost regarded Sicily as the ways and means provided for his greater war. The young men were at once carried away on the wings of such hopes, and their elders kept recounting in their ears many wonderful things about the projected expedition. Many were they who sat in the palaestras and lounging-places mapping out in the sand the shape of Sicily and the position of Libya and Carthage.

Socrates the philosopher, however, and Meton the astrologer, are said to have had no hopes that any good would come to the city from this expedition; Socrates, as it is likely, because he got an inkling of the future from the divine guide who was his familiar. Meton—whether his fear of the future arose from mere calculation or from his use of some sort of divination—feigned madness, and seizing a blazing torch, was like to have set fire to his own house. Some say, however, that Meton made no pretence of madness, but actually did burn his house down in the night, and then, in the morning, came before the people begging and praying that, in view of his great calamity, his son might be released from the expedition. At any rate, he succeeded in cheating his fellow citizens, and obtained his desire.

18. Nicias was elected general against his will, and he was anxious to avoid the command most of all because of his fellow commander. For it had seemed to the Athenians that the war would go

---

69. In the summer of 416 B.C.
70. A personification of the district of Nemea, in the games of which Alcibiades had been victories.

on better if they did not send out Alcibiades unbounded, but rather tempered his rash daring with the prudent forethought of Nicias. As for the third general, Lamachus, though advanced in years, he was thought, age notwithstanding, to be no less fiery than Alcibiades, and quite as fond of taking risks in battle. During the deliberations of the people on the extent and character of the armament, Nicias again tried to oppose their wishes and put a stop to the war. But Alcibiades answered all his arguments and carried the day, and then Demostratus, the orator, formally moved that the generals have full and independent powers in the matter of the armament and of the whole war.

After the people had adopted this motion and all things were made ready for the departure of the fleet, there were some unpropitious signs and portents, especially in connection with the festival, namely, the Adonia. This fell at that time, and little images like dead folk carried forth to burial were in many places exposed to view by the women, who mimicked burial rites, beat their breasts, and sang dirges. Moreover, the mutilation of the Hermae, most of which, in a single night, had their faces and forms disfigured, confounded the hearts of many, even among those who usually set small store by such things. It was said, it is true, that Corinthians had done the deed, Syracuse being a colony of theirs, in the hope that such portents would check or stop the war. The multitude, however, were not moved by this reasoning, nor by that of those who thought the affair no terrible sign at all, but rather one of the common effects of strong wine, when dissolute youth, in mere sport, are carried away into wanton acts. They looked on the occurrence with wrath and fear, thinking it the sign of a bold and dangerous conspiracy. They therefore scrutinized keenly every suspicious circumstance, the council and the assembly convening for this purpose many times within a few days.

19. During this time Androcles, the popular leader, produced sundry aliens and slaves who accused Alcibiades and his friends of mutilating other sacred images, and of making a parody of the mysteries of Eleusis in a drunken revel. They said that one Theodorus played the part of the Herald, Pulytion that of the Torch-bearer, and Alcibiades that of the High Priest, and that the rest of his companions were there in the role of initiates, and were dubbed Mystae. Such indeed was the purport of the impeachment which Thessalus, the son of Cimon, brought in to the assembly, impeaching Alcibiades for impiety towards the Eleusinian goddesses. The people were exasperated, and felt bitterly towards Alcibiades, and Androcles, who was his mortal enemy, egged them on. At first Alcibiades was confounded. But perceiving that all the seamen and soldiers who were going to sail for Sicily were friendly to him, and hearing that the Argive and Mantinean men-at-arms, a thousand in number, declared plainly that it was all because of Alcibiades that they were making their long expedition across the seas, and that if any wrong should be done him they would at once abandon it, he took courage, and insisted on an immediate opportunity to defend himself before the people. His enemies were now in their turn dejected; they feared lest the people should be too lenient in their judgment of him because they needed him so much.

Accordingly, they devised that certain orators who were not looked upon as enemies of Alcibiades, but who really hated him no less than his avowed foes, should rise in the assembly and say that it was absurd, when a general had been appointed, with full powers, over such a vast force, and when his armament and allies were all assembled, to destroy his beckoning opportunity by casting lots for jurors and measuring out time for the case. "Nay," they said, "let him sail now, and Heaven be with him! But when the war is over, then let him come and make his defense. The laws will be the same then as now. Of course the malice in this postponement did not escape Alcibiades. He declared in the assembly that it was a terrible misfortune to be sent off at the head of such a vast force with his case still in suspense, leaving behind him vague accusations and slanders; he ought to be put to death if he did not refute them; but if he did refute them and prove his innocence, he ought to proceed against the enemy without any fear of the public informers at home.

20. He could not carry his point, however, but was ordered to set sail. So he put to sea[71] along with his fellow generals, having not much fewer than one hundred and forty triremes; fifty-one hundred men-at-arms; about thirteen hundred archers, slingers, and light-armed folk; and the rest of his equipment to correspond. On reaching Italy and taking Rhegium, he proposed a plan for the conduct of the war. Nicias opposed it, but Lamachus approved it, and so he sailed to Sicily. He secured the allegiance of Catana, but accomplished nothing further, since he was presently summoned home by the Athenians to stand his trial.

At first, as I have said, sundry vague suspicions and calumnies against Alcibiades were advanced by aliens and slaves. Afterwards, during his absence, his enemies went to work more vigorously. They brought the outrage upon the Hermae and upon the Eleusinian mysteries under one and the same design; both, they said, were fruits of a conspiracy to subvert the government, and so all who were accused of any complicity whatsoever therein were cast into prison without trial. The people were provoked with themselves for not bringing Alcibiades to trial and judgment at the time on such grave charges, and any kinsman or friend or comrade of his who fell foul of their wrath against him, found them exceedingly severe. Thucydides neglected to mention the informers by name, but others give their names as Diocleides and Teucer. For instance, Phrynichus the comic poet referred to them thus:

"Look out too, dearest Hermes, not to get a fall,
And mar your looks, and so equip with calumny
Another Diocleides bent on wreaking harm."

And the Hermes replies:

"I'm on the watch; there's Teucer, too; I would not give
A prize for tattling to an alien of his guilt."

And yet there was nothing sure or steadfast in the statements of the informers. One of them, indeed, was asked how he recognized the faces of the Hermae-defacers, and replied, "By the light of the moon." This vitiated his whole story, since there was no moon at all when the deed was done. Sensible men were troubled, but even this did not soften the people's feeling towards the slanderous stories. As they had set out to do in the beginning, so they continued, haling and casting into prison any one who was denounced.

21. Among those thus held in bonds and imprisonment for trial was Andocides the orator, whom Hellanicus the historian included among the descendants of Odysseus. He was held to be

---

71. About the middle of the summer of 415 B.C.

a foe to popular government, and an oligarch, but what most made him suspected of the mutilation of the Hermae, was the tall Hermes which stood near his house, a dedication of the Aegeid tribe. This was almost the only one among the very few statues of like prominence to remain unharmed. For this reason it is called to this day the Hermes of Andocides. Everybody gives it that name, in spite of the adverse testimony of its inscription.

Now it happened that, of all those lying in prison with him under the same charge, Andocides became most intimate and friendly with a man named Timaeus, of less repute than himself, it is true, but of great sagacity and daring. This man persuaded Andocides to turn state's evidence against himself and a few others. If he confessed—so the man argued—he would have immunity from punishment by decree of the people; whereas the result of the trial, while uncertain in all cases, was most to be dreaded in that of influential men like himself. It was better to save his life by a false confession of crime, than to die a shameful death under a false charge of that crime. One who had an eye to the general welfare of the community might well abandon to their fate a few dubious characters, if he could thereby save a multitude of good men from the wrath of the people. By such arguments of Timaeus, Andocides was at last persuaded to bear witness against himself and others. He himself received the immunity from punishment which had been decreed; but all those whom he named, excepting such as took to flight, were put to death, and Andocides added to their number some of his own household servants, that he might the better be believed.

Still, the people did not lay aside all their wrath at this point, but rather, now that they were done with the Hermae defacers, as if their passion had all the more opportunity to vent itself, they dashed like a torrent against Alcibiades, and finally dispatched the Salaminian state-galley to fetch him home. They shrewdly gave its officers explicit command not to use violence, nor to seize his person, but with all moderation of speech to bid him accompany them home to stand his trial and satisfy the people. For they were afraid that their army, in an enemy's land, would be full of tumult and mutiny at the summons. And Alcibiades might easily have effected this had be wished. For the men were cast down at his departure, and expected that the war, under the conduct of Nicias, would be drawn out to a great length by delays and inactivity, now that their goad to action had been taken away. Lamachus, it is true, was a good soldier and a brave man; but he lacked authority and prestige because he was poor.

22. Alcibiades had no sooner sailed away than he robbed the Athenians of Messana.[72] There was a party there who were on the point of surrendering the city to the Athenians, but Alcibiades knew them, and gave the clearest information of their design to the friends of Syracuse in the city, and so brought the thing to naught. Arrived at Thurii, he left his trireme and hid himself so as to escape all quest. When some one recognized him and asked, "Can you not trust your country, Alcibiades?" "In all else," he said, "but in the matter of life I wouldn't trust even my own mother not to mistake a black for a white ballot when she cast her vote." And when he afterwards heard that the city had condemned him to death, "I'll show them," he said, "that I'm alive."

His impeachment is on record, and runs as follows:

"Thessalus, son of Cimon, of the deme Laciadae, impeaches Alcibiades, son of Cleinias, of the deme Scambonidae, for committing crime against the goddesses of Eleusis, Demeter and Cora, by mimicking the mysteries and showing them forth to his companions in his own house, wear-

---

72. In September of 415 B.C.

ing a robe such as the High Priest wears when he shows forth the sacred secrets to the initiates, and calling himself High Priest, Pulytion Torch-bearer, and Theodorus, of the deme Phegaea, Herald, and hailing the rest of his companions as Mystae and Epoptac, contrary to the laws and institutions of the Eumolpidae, Heralds, and Priests of Eleusis." His case went by default, his property was confiscated, and besides that, it was also decreed that his name should be publicly cursed by all priests and priestesses. Theano, the daughter of Menon, of the deme Agraule, they say, was the only one who refused to obey this decree. She declared that she was a praying, not a cursing priestess.

23. When these great judgments and condemnations were passed upon Alcibiades, he was tarrying in Argos, for as soon as he had made his escape from Thurii, he passed over into Peloponnesus. But fearing his foes there, and renouncing his country altogether, he sent to the Spartans, demanding immunity and confidence, and promising to render them aid and service greater than all the harm he had previously done them as an enemy. The Spartans granted this request and received him among them. No sooner was he come than he zealously brought one thing to pass: they had been delaying and postponing assistance to Syracuse; he roused and incited them to send Gylippus thither for a commander, and to crush the force which Athens had there. A second thing he did was to get them to stir up the war against Athens at home; and the third, and most important of all, to induce them to fortify Deceleia.[73] This more than anything else wrought ruin and destruction to his native city.

At Sparta, he was held in high repute publicly, and privately was no less admired. The multitude was brought under his influence, and was actually bewitched, by his assumption of the Spartan mode of life. When they saw him with his hair untrimmed, taking cold baths, on terms of intimacy with their coarse bread, and supping black porridge, they could scarcely trust their eyes, and doubted whether such a man as he now was had ever had a cook in his own house, had even so much as looked upon a perfumer, or endured the touch of Milesian wool. He had, as they say, one power which transcended all others, and proved an implement of his chase for men: that of assimilating and adapting himself to the pursuits and lives of others, thereby assuming more violent changes than the chameleon. That animal, however, as it is said, is utterly unable to assume one color, namely, white; but Alcibiades could associate with good and bad alike, and found naught that he could not imitate and practice. In Sparta, he was all for bodily training, simplicity of life, and severity of countenance; in Ionia, for luxurious ease and pleasure; in Thrace, for drinking deep; in Thessaly, for riding hard; and when he was thrown with Tissaphernes the satrap, he outdid even Persian magnificence in his pomp and lavishness. It was not that he could so easily pass entirely from one manner of man to another, nor that he actually underwent in every case a change in his real character; but when he saw that his natural manners were likely to be annoying to his associates, he was quick to assume any counterfeit exterior which might in each case be suitable for them. At all events, in Sparta, so far as the outside was concerned, it was possible to say of him, "'No child of Achilles he, but Achilles himself,'[74] such a man as Lycurgus trained"; but judging

---

73. A mountain citadel of Attica, about fourteen miles from Athens towards Boeotia, commanding the Athenian plan and the shortest routes to Euboea and Boeotia. It was occupied by the Spartans in the spring of 413 B.C.

74. The first part of this passage in quotation marks is an adaptation of an iambic trimeter at some unknown poet, which Plutarch uses entire in Moals, 51.

by what he actually felt and did, one might have cried with the poet, "Tis the selfsame woman still!"[75]

For while Agis the king was away on his campaigns, Alcibiades corrupted Timaea his wife, so that she was with child by him and made no denial of it. When she had given birth to a male child, it was called Leotychides in public, but in private the name which the boy's mother whispered to her friends and attendants was Alcibiades. Such was the passion that possessed the woman. But he, in his mocking way, said he had not done this thing for a wanton insult, nor at the behest of mere pleasure, but in order that descendants of his might be kings of the Lacedaemonians. Such being the state of things, there were many to tell the tale to Agis, and he believed it, more especially owing to the lapse of time. There had been an earthquake, and he had run in terror out of his chamber and the arms of his wife, and then for ten months had had no further intercourse with her. And since Leotychides had been born at the end of this period, Agis declared that he was no child of his. For this reason Leotychides was afterwards refused the royal succession.

24. After the Athenian disaster in Sicily,[76] the Chians, Lesbians, and Cyzicenes sent embassies at the same time to Sparta, to discuss a revolt from Athens. But though the Boeotians supported the appeal of the Lesbians, and Pharnabazus that of the Cyzicenes, the Spartans, under the persuasion of Alcibiades, elected to help the Chians first of all. Alcibiades actually set sail in person and brought almost all Ionia to revolt, and, in constant association with the Lacedaemonian generals, wrought injury to the Athenians. But Agis was hostile to him because of the wrong he had suffered as a husband, and he was also vexed at the repute in which Alcibiades stood; for most of the successes won were due to him, as report had it. The most influential and ambitious of the other Spartans also were already envious and tired of him, and soon grew strong enough to induce the magistrates at home to send out orders to Ionia that he be put to death.

His stealthy discovery of this put him on his guard, and while in all their undertakings he took part with the Lacedaemonians, he sedulously avoided coming into their hands. Then, resorting to Tissaphernes, the King's satrap, for safety, he was soon first and foremost in that grandee's favor. For his versatility and surpassing cleverness were the admiration of the Barbarian, who was no straightforward man himself, but malicious and fond of evil company. And indeed no disposition could resist and no nature escape Alcibiades, so full of grace was his daily life and conversation. Even those who feared and hated him felt a rare and winning charm in his society and presence. And thus it was that Tissaphernes, though otherwise the most ardent of the Persians in his hatred of the Hellenes, so completely surrendered to the flatteries of Alcibiades as to outdo him in reciprocal flatteries. Indeed, the most beautiful park he had, both for its refreshing waters and grateful lawns, with resorts and retreats decked out in regal and extravagant fashion, he named Alcibiades; everyone always called it by that name.

25. Alcibiades now abandoned the cause of the Spartans, since he distrusted them and feared Agis, and began to malign and slander them to Tissaphernes. He advised him not to aid them very generously, and yet not to put down the Athenians completely, but rather by niggardly assis-

---

75. Euripides, Orestes, 129: spoken by Electra of Helen.
76. With these words the two years which have elapsed since the flight of Alcibiades are passed over, so far as the Sicilian expedition is concerned. This event is described by Thucydides above.

tance to straiten and gradually wear out both, and so make them easy victims for the King when they had weakened and exhausted each other. Tissaphernes was easily persuaded, and all men saw that he loved and admired his new adviser, so that Alcibiades was looked up to by the Hellenes on both sides, and the Athenians repented themselves of the sentence they had passed upon him, now that they were suffering for it. Alcibiades himself also was presently burdened with the fear that if his native city were altogether destroyed, he might come into the power of the Lacedaemonians, who now hated him.

At this time[77] almost all the forces of Athens were at Samos. From this island as their naval base of operations they were trying to win back some of their Ionian allies who had revolted, and were watching others who were disaffected. After a fashion they still managed to cope with their enemies on the sea, but they were afraid of Tissaphernes and of the fleet of one hundred and fifty Phoenician triremes which was said to be all but at hand; if this once came up, no hope of safety was left for their city. Alcibiades was aware of this, and sent secret messages to the influential Athenians at Samos, in which he held out the hope that he might bring Tissaphernes over to be their friend. He did not seek, he said, the favor of the multitude, nor trust them, but rather that of the aristocrats, in case they would venture to show themselves men, put a stop to the insolence of the people, take the direction of affairs into their own hands, and save their cause and city.

Now the rest of the aristocrats were much inclined to Alcibiades. But one of the generals, Phrynichus, of the deme Deirades, suspected (what was really the case) that Alcibiades had no more use for an oligarchy than for a democracy, but merely sought in one way or another a recall from exile, and therefore inveighed against the people merely to court now the favor of the aristocrats, and ingratiate himself with them. He therefore opposed him. When his opinion had been overborne and he was now become an open enemy of Alcibiades, he sent a secret message to Astyochus, the enemy's naval commander, bidding him beware of Alcibiades and arrest him, for that he was playing a double game. But without his knowing it, it was a case of traitor dealing with traitor. For Astyochus was much in awe of Tissaphernes, and seeing that Alcibiades had great power with the satrap, he disclosed the message of Phrynichus to them both. Alcibiades at once sent men to Samos to denounce Phrynichus. All the Athenians there were incensed and banded themselves together against Phrynichus, who, seeing no other escape from his predicament, attempted to cure one evil by another and a greater. He sent again to Astyochus, chiding him indeed for his disclosure of the former message, but announcing that he stood ready to deliver into his hands the fleet and army of the Athenians.

However, this treachery of Phrynichus did not harm the Athenians at all, because of the fresh treachery of Astyochus. This second message of Phrynichus also he delivered to Alcibiades. But Phrynichus knew all the while that he would do so, and expected a second denunciation from Alcibiades. So he got the start of him by telling the Athenians himself that the enemy were going to attack them, and advising them to have their ships manned and their camp fortified. The Athenians were busy doing this when again a letter came from Alcibiades bidding them beware of Phrynichus, since he had offered to betray their fleet to the enemy. This letter they disbelieved at the time, supposing that Alcibiades, who must know perfectly the equipment and purposes of

---

77. During the winter of 412–411 B.C.

the enemy, had used his knowledge in order to malign Phrynichus falsely. Afterwards,[78] however, when Hermon, one of the frontier guard, had smitten Phrynichus with a dagger and slain him in the open market-place, the Athenians tried the case of the dead man, found him guilty of treachery, and awarded crowns to Hermon and his accomplices.

26. But at Samos the friends of Alcibiades soon got the upper hand, and sent Peisander to Athens to change tile form of government. He was to encourage the leading men to overthrow the democracy and take control of affairs, with the plea that on these terms alone would Alcibiades make Tissaphernes their friend and ally. This was the pretence and this the pretext of those who established the oligarchy at Athens. But as soon as the so-called Five Thousand (they were really only four hundred) got the power and took control of affairs, they at once neglected Alcibiades entirely, and waged the war with less vigor, partly because they distrusted the citizens, who still looked askance at the new form of government, and partly because they thought that the Lacedaemonians, who always looked with favor on an oligarchy, would be more lenient towards them. The popular party in the city was constrained by fear to keep quiet, because many of those who openly opposed the Four Hundred had been slain. But when the army in Samos learned what had been done at home, they were enraged, and were eager to sail forthwith to the Piraeus, and sending for Alcibiades, they appointed him general, and bade him lead them in putting down the tyrants.

An ordinary man, thus suddenly raised to great power by the favor of the multitude, would have been full of complaisance, thinking that he must at once gratify them in all things and oppose them in nothing, since they had made him, instead of a wandering exile, leader and general of such a fleet and of so large an armed force. But Alcibiades, as became a great leader, felt that he must oppose them in their career of blind fury, and prevented them from making a fatal mistake. Therefore in this instance, at least, he was the manifest salvation of the city. For had they sailed off home, their enemies might at once have occupied all Ionia, the Hellespont without a battle, and the islands, while Athenians were fighting Athenians and making their own city the seat of war. Such a war Alcibiades, more than any other one man, prevented, not only persuading and instructing the multitude together, but also, taking them man by man, supplicating some and constraining others. He had a helper, too, in Thrasybulus of Steiris, who went along with him and did the shouting; for he had, it is said, the biggest voice of all the Athenians.

A second honorable proceeding of Alcibiades was his promising to bring over to their side the Phoenician ships which the King had sent out and the Lacedaemonians were expecting—or at least to see that those expectations were not realized—and his sailing off swiftly on this errand. The ships were actually seen off Aspendus, but Tissaphernes did not bring them up, and thereby played the Lacedaemonians false. Alcibiades, however, was credited with this diversion of the ships by both parties, and especially by the Lacedaemonians. The charge was that he instructed the Barbarian to suffer the Hellenes to destroy one another. For it was perfectly clear that the side to which such a naval force attached itself would rob the other altogether of the control of the sea.

27. After this the Four Hundred were overthrown,[79] the friends of Alcibiades now zealously assisting the party of the people. Then the city willingly ordered Alcibiades to come back home.

---

78. In the summer of 411 B.C., Phrynichus having been deposed from his command at Samos, and showing himself an ardent supporter of the revolutionary four Hundred at Athens.

79. They usurped the power in June of 411 B.C.; they fell in September of the same year.

But he thought he must not return with empty hands and without achievement, through the pity and favor of the multitude, but rather in a blaze of glory. So, to begin with, he set sail with a small fleet from Samos and cruised off Cnidus and Cos. There he heard that Mindarus the Spartan admiral had sailed off to the Hellespont with his entire fleet, followed by the Athenians, and so he hastened to the assistance of their generals. By chance he came up, with his eighteen triremes, at just that critical point when both parties, having joined battle with all their ships off Abydos, and sharing almost equally in victory and defeat until evening, were locked in a great struggle. The appearance of Alcibiades inspired both sides with a false opinion of his coming: the enemy were emboldened and the Athenians were confounded. But he quickly hoisted Athenian colors on his flagship and darted straight upon the victorious and pursuing Peloponnesians. Routing them, he drove them to land, and following hard after them, rammed and shattered their ships. Their crews swam ashore, and here Pharnabazus came to their aid with his infantry and fought along the beach in defense of their ships. But finally tile Athenians captured thirty of them, rescued their own, and erected a trophy of victory.

Taking advantage of a success so brilliant as this, and ambitious to display himself at once before Tissaphernes, Alcibiades supplied himself with gifts of hospitality and friendship and proceeded, at the head of an imperial retinue, to visit the satrap. His reception, however, was not what he expected. Tissaphernes had for a long time been accused by the Lacedaemonians to the King, and being in fear of the King's condemnation, it seemed to him that Alcibiades had come in the nick of time. So he arrested him and shut him up in Sardis, hoping that such an outrage upon him as this would dispel the calumnies of the Spartans.

28. After the lapse of thirty days Alcibiades ran away from his guards, got a horse from some one or other, and made his escape to Clazomenae. To repay Tissaphernes, he alleged that he had escaped with that satrap's connivance, and so brought additional calumny upon him. He himself sailed to the camp of the Athenians,[80] where he learned that Mindarus, along with Pharnabazus, was in Cyzicus. Thereupon he roused the spirits of the soldiers, declaring that they must now do sea-fighting and land-fighting and even siege-fighting, too, against their enemies, for poverty stared them in the face unless they were victorious in every way. He then manned his ships and made his way to Proconnesus, giving orders at once to seize all small trading craft and keep them under guard, that the enemy might get no warning of his approach from any source so ever.

Now it chanced that copious rain fell all of a sudden, and thunder-peals and darkness cooperated with him in concealing his design. Indeed, not only did he elude the enemy, but even the Athenians themselves had already given up all expectation of fighting, when he suddenly ordered them aboard ship and put out to sea. After a little the darkness cleared away, and the Peloponnesian ships were seen hovering off the harbor of Cyzicus. Fearing then lest they catch sight of the full extent of his array and take refuge ashore, he ordered his fellow-commanders to sail slowly and so remain in the rear, while he himself, with only forty ships, hove in sight and challenged the foe to battle. The Peloponnesians were utterly deceived, and scorning what they deemed the small numbers of their enemy, put out to meet them, and closed at once with them in a grappling fight. Presently, while the battle was raging, the Athenian reserves bore down upon their foe, who were panic stricken and took to flight.

---

80. Early in the spring of 410 B.C. The Athenians were at Cardia, a city in Thrace.

Then Alcibiades with twenty of his best ships broke though their line, put to shore, and disembarking his crews, attacked his enemy as they fled from their ships, and slew many of them. Mindarus and Pharnabazus, who came to their aid, he overwhelmed; Mindarus was slain fighting sturdily, but Pharnabazus made his escape. Many were the dead bodies and the arms of which the Athenians became masters, and they captured all their enemy's ships. Then they also stormed Cyzicus, which Pharnabazus abandoned to its fate, and the Peloponnesians in it were annihilated. Thus the Athenians not only had the Hellespont under their sure control, but even drove the Lacedaemonians at a stroke from the rest of the sea. A dispatch was captured announcing the disaster to the ephors in true laconic style: "Our ships are lost; Mindarus is gone; our men are starving we know not what to do."

29. But the soldiers of Alcibiades were now so elated and filled with pride that they disdained longer to mingle with the rest of the army, since it had often been conquered, while they were unconquered. For not long before this, Thrasyllus had suffered a reverse at Ephesus, and the Ephesians had erected their bronze trophy of victory, to the disgrace of the Athenians. This was what the soldiers of Alcibiades cast in the teeth of Thrasyllus' men, vaunting themselves and their general, and refusing to share either training or quarters in camp with them. But when Pharnabazus with much cavalry and infantry attacked the forces of Thrasyllus, who had made a raid into the territory of Abydos, Alcibiades sallied out to their aid, routed Pharnabazus, and pursued him till nightfall, along with Thrasyllus. Thus the two factions were blended, and returned to their camp with mutual friendliness and delight.

On the following day Alcibiades set up a trophy of victory and plundered the territory of Pharnabazus, no one venturing to defend it. He even captured some priests and priestesses, but let them go without ransom. On setting out to attack Chalcedon, which had revolted from Athens and received a Lacedaemonian garrison and governor, he heard that its citizens had collected all their goods and chattels out of the country and committed them for safe keeping to the Bithynians, who were their friends. So he marched to the confines of Bithynia with his army, and sent on a herald with accusations and demands. The Bithynians, in terror, gave up the booty to him, and made a treaty of friendship.

30. While Chalcedon was being walled in from sea to sea,[81] Pharnabazus came to raise the siege, and at the same time Hippocrates, the Spartan governor, led his forces out of the city and attacked the Athenians. But Alcibiades arrayed his army so as to face both enemies at once, put Pharnabazus to shameful flight, and slew Hippocrates together with many of his vanquished men.

Then he sailed in person into the Hellespont and levied moneys there. He also captured Selymbria, where he exposed himself beyond all bounds. For there was a party in the city which offered to surrender it to him, and they had agreed with him upon the signal of a lighted torch displayed at midnight. But they were forced to give this signal before the appointed time, through fear of one of the conspirators, who suddenly changed his mind. So the torch was displayed before his army was ready; but Alcibiades took about thirty men and ran to the walls, bidding the rest of his force follow with all speed. The gate was thrown open for him and he rushed into the city, his thirty men-at-arms reinforced by twenty targeteers, but he saw at once that the Selymbrians were advancing in battle array to attack him. In resistance he saw no safety, and for flight, unde-

---

81. In the spring of 409 B.C.

feated as he was in all his campaigns down to that day, he had too much spirit. He therefore bade the trumpet signal silence, and then ordered formal proclamation to be made that Selymbria must not bear arms against Athens. This proclamation made some of the Selymbrians less eager for battle, if, as they supposed, their enemies were all inside the walls; and others were mollified by hopes of a peaceful settlement. While they were thus parleying with one another, up came the army of Alcibiades. Judging now, as was really the case, that the Selymbrians were disposed for peace, he was afraid that his Thracian soldiers might plunder the city. There were many of these, and they were zealous in their service, through the favor and good will they bore Alcibiades. Accordingly, he sent them all out of the city, and then, at the plea of the Selymbrians, did their city no injury whatever, but merely took a sum of money from it, set a garrison in it, and went his way.

31. Meanwhile the Athenian generals who were besieging Chalcedon made peace with Pharnabazus on condition that they receive a sum of money, that Chalcedon be subject again to Athens, that the territories of Pharnabazus not be ravaged, and that the said Pharnabazus furnish safe escort for an Athenian embassy to the King. Accordingly, when Alcibiades came back from Selymbria, Pharnabazus demanded that he too take oath to the treaty; but Alcibiades refused to do so until Pharnabazus had taken his oath to it.

After the oaths had been taken, he went up against Byzantium, which was in revolt against Athens, and compassed the city with a wall.[82] But after Anaxilaiis, Lycurgus, and certain men besides had agreed to surrender the city to him on condition that it be not plundered, he spread abroad the story that threatening complications in Ionia called him away. Then he sailed off in broad daylight with all his ships; but in the night time stealthily returned. He disembarked with the men-at-arms under his own command, and stationed himself quietly within reach of the city's walls. His fleet, meanwhile, sailed to the harbor, and forcing its way in with much shouting and tumult and din, terrified the Byzantians by the unexpectedness of its attack, while it gave the party of Athens in the city a chance to admit Alcibiades in all security, since everybody had hurried off to the harbor and the fleet. However, the day was not won without a battle. The Peloponnesians, Boeotians and Megarians who were in garrison at Byzantium routed the ships' crews and drove them back on board again. Then, perceiving that the Athenians were inside the city, they formed in battle array and advanced to attack them. A fierce battle followed, but Alcibiades was victorious with the right wing, as well as Theramenes with the left, and they took prisoners no less than three hundred of the enemy who survived.

Not a man of the Byzantians was put to death or sent into exile after the battle, for it was on these conditions that the men who surrendered the city had acted, and this was the agreement with them; they exacted no special grace for themselves. Therefore it was that when Anaxilaits was prosecuted at Sparta for treachery, his words showed clearly that his deeds had not been disgraceful. He said that he was not a Lacedaemonian, but a Byzantian, and it was not Sparta that was in peril. Considering therefore the case of Byzantium, he saw that the city was walled up, that no help could make its way in, and that the provisions already in the city were being consumed by Peloponnesians and Boeotians, while the Byzantians were starving, together with their wives and children. He had, therefore, not betrayed the city to its enemies, but set it free from

---

82. During the winter of 409–408 B.C.

war and its horrors, therein imitating the noblest Lacedaemonians, in whose eyes the one un-qualifiedly honorable and righteous thing is their country's good. The Lacedaemonians, on hearing this, were moved with sincere respect, and acquitted the men.

32. But Alcibiades, yearning at last to see his home, and still more desirous of being seen by his fellow citizens, now that he had conquered their enemies so many times, set sail.[83] His Attic triremes were adorned all round with many shields and spoils of war; many that he had captured in battle were towed along in his wake; and still more numerous were the figure-heads he carried of triremes which had been overwhelmed and destroyed by him. There were not less than two hundred of these all together.

Duris the Samian, who claims that he was a descendant of Alcibiades, gives some additional details. He says that the oarsmen of Alcibiades rowed to the music of a flute blown by Chrysogonus the Pythian victor; that they kept time to a rhythmic call from the lips of Callipides the tragic actor; that both these artists were arrayed in the long tunics, flowing robes, and other adornment of their profession; and that the commander's ship put into the harbor with a sail of purple hue, as though, after a drinking bout, he were off on a revel. But neither Theopompus, nor Ephorus, nor Xenophon mentions these things, nor is it likely that Alcibiades put on such airs for the Athenians, to whom he was returning after he had suffered exile and many great adversities. Nay, he was in actual fear as he put into the harbor, and once in, he did not leave his trireme until, as he stood on deck, he caught sight of his cousin Euryptolemus on shore, with many other friends and kinsmen, and heard their cries of welcome.

When he landed, however, people did not deign so much as to look at the other generals whom they met, but ran in throngs to Alcibiades with shouts of welcome, escorting him on his way, and putting wreaths on his head as they could get to him, while those who could not come to him for the throng, gazed at him from afar, the elderly men pointing him out to the young. Much sorrow, too, was mingled with the city's joy, as men called to mind their former misfortunes and compared them with their present good fortune, counting it certain that they had neither lost Sicily, nor had any other great expectation of theirs miscarried if they had only left Alcibiades at the head of that enterprise and the armament therefor. For now he had taken the city when she was almost banished from the sea, when on land she was hardly mistress of her own suburbs, and when factions raged within her walls, and had raised her up from this wretched and lowly plight, not only restoring her dominion over the sea, but actually rendering her victorious over her enemies everywhere on land.

33. Now the decree for his recall had been passed before this,[84] on motion of Critias, the son of Callaeschrus, as Critias himself has written in his elegies, where he reminds Alcibiades of the favor in these words:

"Mine was the motion that brought you back; I made it in public;
Words and writing were mine; this the task I performed;
Signet and seal of words that were mine give warrant as follows."

---

83. From Samos in the spring of 408 B.C.
84. Nearly three years before, in late autumn of 411 B.C., after the overthrow of the Four Hundred.

At this time,[85] therefore, the people had only to meet in assembly, and Alcibiades addressed them. He lamented and bewailed his own lot, but had only little and moderate blame to lay upon the people. The entire mischief he ascribed to a certain evil fortune and envious genius of his own. Then he descanted at great length upon the vain hopes which their enemies were cherishing, and wrought his hearers up to courage. At last they crowned him with crowns of gold, and elected him general with sole powers by land and sea. They voted also that his property be restored to him, and that the Eumolpidae and Heralds revoke the curses wherewith they had cursed him at the command of the people. The others revoked their curses, but Theodorus the High Priest said "Nay, I invoked no evil upon him if he does no wrong to the city."

34. But while Alcibiades was thus prospering brilliantly, some were nevertheless disturbed at the particular season of his return. For he had put into harbor on the very day when the Plynteria of the goddess Athena were being celebrated. The Praxiergidae celebrate these rites on the twenty-fifth day of Thargelion, in strict secrecy, removing the robes of the goddess and covering up her image. Wherefore the Athenians regard this day as the unluckiest of all days for business of any sort. The goddess, therefore, did not appear to welcome Alcibiades with kindly favor and good will, but rather to veil herself from him and repel him. However, all things fell out as he wished, and one hundred triremes were manned for service, with which he was minded to sail off again; but a great and laudable ambition took possession of him and detained him there until the Eleusinian mysteries.

Ever since Deceleia had been fortified, and the enemy, by their presence there, commanded the approaches to Eleusis, the festal rite had been celebrated with no splendor at all, being conducted by sea. Sacrifices, choral dances, and many of the sacred ceremonies usually held on the road, when Iacchus is conducted forth from Athens to Eleusis, had of necessity been omitted. Accordingly, it seemed to Alcibiades that it would be a fine thing, enhancing his holiness in the eyes of the gods and his good repute in the minds of men, to restore its traditional fashion to the sacred festival by escorting the rite with his infantry along past the enemy by land. He would thus either thwart and humble Agis, if the king kept entirely quiet, or would fight a fight that was sacred and approved by the gods, in behalf of the greatest and holiest interests, in full sight of his native city, and with all his fellow citizens eye-witnesses of his valor.

When he had determined upon this course and made known his design to the Eumolpidae and Heralds, he stationed sentries on the heights, sent out an advance-guard at break of day, and then took the priests, mystae, and mystagogues, encompassed them with his men-at-arms, and led them over the road to Eleusis in decorous and silent array. So august and devout was the spectacle which, as general, he thus displayed, that he was hailed by those who were not unfriendly to him as High Priest, rather, and Mystagogue. No enemy dared to attack him, and he conducted the procession safely back to the city. At this he was exalted in spirit himself, and exalted his army with the feeling that it was irresistible and invincible under his command. People of the humbler and poorer sort he so captivated by his leadership that they were filled with an amazing passion to have him for their tyrant, and some proposed it, and actually came to him in solicitation of it. He was to rise superior to envy, abolish decrees and laws, and stop the mouths of the babblers

---

85. In the early spring of 408 B.C.

who were so fatal to the life of the city, that he might bear an absolute sway and act without fear of the public informer.

35. What thoughts he himself had about a tyranny, is uncertain. But the most influential citizens were afraid of it, and therefore anxious that he should sail away as soon as he could. They even voted him, besides everything else, the colleagues of his own choosing. Setting sail,[86] therefore, with his one hundred ships, and assaulting Andros, he conquered the islanders in battle, as well as the Lacedaemonians who were there, but he did not capture the city. This was the first of the fresh charges brought against him by his enemies.

And it would seem that if ever a man was ruined by his own exalted reputation, that man was Alcibiades. His continuous successes gave him such repute for unbounded daring and sagacity, that when he failed in anything, men suspected his inclination; they would not believe in his inability. Were he only inclined to do a thing, they thought, naught could escape him. So they expected to hear that the Chians also had been taken, along with the rest of Ionia. They were therefore incensed to hear that he had not accomplished everything at once and speedily, to meet their wishes. They did not stop to consider his lack of money. This compelled him, since he was fighting men who had access to the bounty in the Great King, to leave his camp frequently and sail off in quest of money for rations and wages. The final and prevailing charge against him was due to this necessity.

Lysander, who had been sent out as admiral by the Lacedaemonians, paid his sailors four obols a day instead of three, out of the moneys he received from Cyrus; while Alcibiades, already hard put to it to pay even his three obols, was forced to sail for Caria to levy money. The man whom he left in charge of his fleet, Antiochus, was a brave captain, but otherwise a foolish and low-lived fellow. Although he had received explicit commands from Alcibiades not to hazard a general engagement even though the enemy sailed out to meet him, he showed such wanton contempt of them as to man his own trireme and one other and stand for Ephesus, indulging in many shamelessly insulting gestures and cries as he cruised past the prows of the enemy's ships. At first Lysander put out with a few ships only, and gave him chase. Then, when the Athenians came to the aid of Antiochus, Lysander put out with his whole fleet, won the day, slew Antiochus himself, captured many ships and men, and set up a trophy of victory. As soon as Alcibiades heard of this, he came back to Samos, put out to sea with his whole armament, and challenged Lysander to battle. But Lysander was satisfied with his victory, and would not put out to meet him.

36. There were those who hated Alcibiades in the camp, and of these Thrasybulus,[87] the son of Thraso, his particular enemy, set sail for Athens to denounce him. He stirred up the city against him by declaring to the people that it was Alcibiades who had ruined their cause and lost their ships by his wanton conduct in office. He had handed over—so Thrasybulus said—the duties of commander to men who won his confidence merely by drinking deep and reeling off sailors' yarns, in order that he himself might be free to cruise about collecting moneys and committing excesses of drunkenness and revelry with courtesans of Abydos and Ionia, and this while the enemy's fleet lay close to him. His enemies also found ground for accusation against him in the fortress which he had constructed in Thrace, near Bisanthe. It was to serve, they said, as a refuge for him in case

---

86. Near the end of October of 408 B. C.
87. Not the illustrious commander, who was the son of Lycus. (See chapter 26.6.)

he either could not or would not live at home. The Athenians were persuaded, and chose other generals in his place, thus displaying their anger and ill-will towards him. On learning this, Alcibiades was afraid, and departed from the camp altogether, and assembling mercenary troops made war on his own account against the Thracians who acknowledge no king. He got together much money from his captives, and at the same time afforded security from barbarian inroads to the Hellenes on the neighboring frontier.

Tydeus, Menander, and Adeimantus, the generals, who had all the ships which the Athenians could finally muster in station at Aegospotami,[88] were wont to sail out at daybreak against Lysander, who lay with his fleet at Lampsacus, and challenge him to battle. Then they would sail back again, to spend the rest of the day in disorder and unconcern, since, forsooth, they despised their enemy. Alcibiades, who was near at hand, could not see such conduct with calmness or indifference, but rode up on horseback and read the generals a lesson. He said their anchorage was a bad one; the place had no harbor and no city, but they had to get their supplies from Sestos, a long way off; and they permitted their crews, whenever they were on land, to wander and scatter about at their own sweet wills, while there lay at anchor over against them an enemy which was trained to do everything silently at a word of absolute command.

37. In spite of what Alcibiades said, and in spite of his advice to change their station to Sestos, the generals paid no heed. Tydeus actually insulted him by bidding him to leave since he was not now general. So Alcibiades departed, suspecting that some treachery was on foot among them, He told his acquaintances who were escorting him out of the camp that, had he not been so grievously insulted by the generals, within a few days he would have forced the Lacedaemonians to engage them whether they wished to do so or not, or else lose their ships. Some thought that what he said was arrant boasting; but others that it was likely, since he had merely to bring up his numerous Thracian javelineers and horsemen to assault by land and confound the enemy's camp.

However, that he saw only too well the errors of the Athenians the event soon testified. Lysander suddenly and unexpectedly fell upon them, and only eight of their triremes escaped with Conon; the rest, something less than two hundred, were captured and taken away. Three thousand of their crews were taken alive and executed by Lysander. In a short time[89] he also captured Athens, burned her ships, and tore down her long walls.

Alcibiades now feared the Lacedaemonians, who were supreme on land and sea, and betook himself into Bithynia, taking booty of every sort with him, but leaving even more behind him in the fortress where he had been living. In Bithynia he again lost much of his substance, being plundered by the Thracians there, and so he determined to go up to the court of Artaxerxes. He thought to show himself not inferior to Themistocles if the King made trial of his services, and superior in his pretext for offering them. For it was not to be against his fellow countrymen, as in the case of that great man, but in behalf of his country that he would assist the King and beg him to furnish forces against a common enemy. Thinking that Pharnabazus could best give him facilities for safely making this journey up to the King, he went to him in Phrygia, and continued there with him, paying him court and receiving marks of honor from him.

---

88. With these words Plutarch's narrative leaps over the events of two and a half years, from the spring of 407 to the autumn of 405 B.C.

89. In the spring of 404 B.C., some eight months later.

38. The Athenians were greatly depressed at the loss of their supremacy. But when Lysander robbed them of their freedom too, and handed the city over to thirty men, then, their cause being lost, their eyes were opened to the course they would not take when salvation was yet in their power. They sorrowfully rehearsed all their mistakes and follies, the greatest of which they considered to be their second outburst of wrath against Alcibiades. He had been cast aside for no fault of his own; but they got angry because a subordinate of his lost a few ships disgracefully, and then they themselves, more disgracefully still, robbed the city of its ablest and most experienced general. And yet, in spite of their present plight, a vague hope still prevailed that the cause of Athens was not wholly lost so long as Alcibiades was alive. He had not, in times past, been satisfied to live his exile's life in idleness and quiet; nor now, if his means allowed, would he tolerate the insolence of the Lacedaemonians and the madness of the Thirty.

It was not strange that the multitude indulged in such dreams, when even the Thirty were moved to anxious thought and inquiry, and made the greatest account of what Alcibiades was planning and doing. Finally, Critias tried to make it clear to Lysander that as long as Athens was a democracy the Lacedaemonians could not have safe rule over Hellas; and that Athens, even though she were very peacefully and well disposed towards oligarchy, would not be suffered, while Alcibiades was alive, to remain undisturbed in her present condition. However, Lysander was not persuaded by these arguments until a dispatch-roll came from the authorities at home bidding him put Alcibiades out of the way; either because they too were alarmed at the vigor and enterprise of the man, or because they were trying to gratify Agis.

39. Accordingly, Lysander sent to Pharnabazus and bade him do this thing, and Pharnabazus commissioned Magaeus, his brother, and Sousamithras, his uncle, to perform the deed. At that time Alcibiades was living in a certain village of Phrygia, where he had Timandra the courtesan with him, and in his sleep he had the following vision. He thought he had the courtesan's garments upon him, and that she was holding his head in her arms while she adorned his face like a woman's with paints and pigments. Others say that in his sleep he saw Magaeus followers cutting off his head and his body burning. All agree in saying that he had the vision not long before his death.

The party sent to kill him did not dare to enter his house, but surrounded it and set it on fire. When Alcibiades was aware of this, he gathered together most of the garments and bedding in the house and cast them on the fire. Then, wrapping his cloak about his left arm, and drawing his sword with his right, he dashed out, unscathed by the fire, before the garments were in flames, and scattered the Barbarians, who ran at the mere sight of him. Not a man stood ground against him, or came to close quarters with him, but all held aloof and shot him with javelins and arrows. Thus he fell, and when the Barbarians were gone, Timandra took up his dead body, covered and wrapped it in her own garments, and gave it such brilliant and honorable burial as she could provide.

This Timandra, they say, was the mother of that Lais who was called the Corinthian, although she was a prisoner of war from Hyccara, a small city of Sicily. But some, while agreeing in all other details of the death of Alcibiades with what I have written, say that it was not Pharnabazus who was the cause of it, nor Lysander, nor the Lacedaemonians, but Alcibiades himself. He had corrupted a girl belonging to a certain well known family, and had her with him; and it was the brothers of this girl who, taking his wanton insolence much to heart, set fire by night to the house where he was living, and shot him down, as has been described, when he dashed out through the fire.

ALEXANDER

Alexander III (the Great) (356–323 B.C.) King of Macedon 336–323 B.C., and Persia 330–323, is one of the premier personalities of the history of Western Civilization. In only ten short years he conquered territories stretching from Greece to India and ushered in a new epoch of history, the Hellenistic Age. Shortly after his death in 323 at the young age of 33, however, his empire disintegrated into three large kingdoms and several small client states. One might think at first glance, then, that Alexander's whole life was a failure, but during the 23 centuries since his untimely death, the short life, the brilliant career and the amazing accomplishments of Alexander the Great have retained a magnetism and an absorbing interest that show no signs of fading even today. Below are selected excerpts from Plutarch's **Life of Alexander.**

2. As for the lineage of Alexander, on his father's side he was a descendant of Heracles through Caranus, and on his mother's side a descendant of Aeacus[90] through Neoptolemus;[91] this is accepted without any question. And we are told that Philip, after being initiated into the mysteries of Samothrace at the same time with Olympias, he himself being still a youth and she an orphan child, fell in love with her and betrothed himself to her at once with the consent of her brother, Arymbas. Well, then, the night before that on which the marriage was consummated, the bride dreamed that there was a peal of thunder and that a thunder-bolt fell upon her womb, and that thereby much fire was kindled, which broke into flames that traveled all about, and then was extinguished. At a later time, too, after the marriage, Philip dreamed that he was putting a seal upon his wife's womb; and the device of the seal, as he thought, was the figure of a lion. The other seers, now, were led by the vision to suspect that Philip needed to put a closer watch upon his marriage relations; but Aristander of Telmessus said that the woman was pregnant, since no seal was put upon what was empty, and pregnant of a son whose nature would be bold and lion-like. Moreover, a serpent was once seen lying stretched out by the side of Olympias as she slept, and we are told that this, more than anything else, dulled the ardor of Philip's attentions to his wife, so that he no longer came often to sleep by her side, either because he feared that some spells and enchantments might be practiced upon him by her, or because he shrank from her embraces in the conviction that she was the partner of a superior being. . .

---

90. Legendary king of the Myrmidons in Aegina. After his death he became one of the three judges of the underworld.
91. Son of Achilles and Deidameria, killed Priam when Troy was destroyed and sacrificed Poyxena. When the captives were divided among the conquerors, he had for his prize Andromache, the wife of Hector. He later married Herminone and was murdered by Orestes.

4. The outward appearance of Alexander is best represented by the statues of him which Lysippus made, and it was by this artist alone that Alexander himself thought it fit that he should be modeled. For those peculiarities which many of his successors and friends afterwards tried to imitate, namely, the poise of the neck, which was bent slightly to the left, and the inciting glance of his eyes, this artist has accurately observed. . .

But while he was still a boy his self-restraint showed itself in the fact that, although he was impetuous and violent in other matters, the pleasures of the body had little hold upon him, and he indulged in them with great moderation, while his ambition kept his spirit serious and lofty in advance of his years. For it was neither every kind of fame nor fame from every source that he courted, as Philip did, who plumed himself like a sophist on the power of his oratory, and took care to have the victories of his chariots at Olympia engraved upon his coins; nay, when those about him inquired whether he would be willing to contend in the foot race at the Olympic games, since he was swift of foot, "Yes," said he, "if I could have kings as my contestants." And in general, too, Alexander appears to have been averse to the whole race of athletes; at any rate, though he instituted very many contests, not only for tragic poets and players on the flute and players on the lyre, but also for rhapsodists, as well as for hunting of every sort and for fighting with staves, he took no interest in offering prizes either for boxing or for the pancratium.[92]

5. He once entertained the envoys from the Persian king who came during Philip's absence, and associated with them freely. He won upon them by his friendliness, and by asking no childish or trivial questions, but by enquiring about the length of the roads and the character of the journey into the interior, about the king himself, what sort of a warrior he was, and what the prowess and might of the Persians. The envoys were therefore astonished and regarded the much-talked-of ability of Philip as nothing compared with his son's eager disposition to do great things. At all events, as often as tidings were brought that Philip had either taken a famous city or been victorious in some celebrated battle, Alexander was not very glad to hear them, but would say to his comrades "Boys, my father will anticipate everything; and for me he will leave no great or brilliant achievement to be displayed to the world with your aid." For since he did not covet pleasure, nor even wealth, but excellence and fame, he considered that the more he should receive from his father the fewer would be the successes won by himself. Therefore, considering that increase in prosperity meant the squandering upon his father of opportunities for achievement, he preferred to receive from him a realm which afforded, not wealth nor luxury and enjoyment, but struggles and wars and ambitions.

In the work of caring for him, then, many persons, as was natural, were appointed to be his nurturers, tutors, and teachers, but over them all stood Leonidas, a man of stern temperament and a kinsman of Olympias. Although he did not himself shun the title of tutor, since the office afforded an honorable and brilliant occupation, yet by other people, owing to his dignity and his relationship, he was called Alexander's foster-father and preceptor. The man, however, who assumed the character and the title of tutor was Lysimachus, a native of Acarnania, who had no general refinement, but because he called himself Phoenix,[93] Alexander Achilles, and Philip Peleus, was highly regarded and held a second place.

---

92. An ancient Greek athletic contest involving both boxing and wrestling.
93. The tutor of Achilles.

6. Once upon a time Philoneicus the Thessalian brought Bucephalas, offering to sell him to Philip for thirteen talents, and they went down into the plain to try the horse, who appeared to be savage and altogether intractable, neither allowing any one to mount him, nor heeding the voice of any of Philip's attendants, but rearing up against all of them. Then Philip was vexed and ordered the horse to be led away, believing him to be altogether wild and unbroken; but Alexander, who was near by, said: "What a horse they are losing, because, for lack of skill and courage, they cannot manage him!" At first, then, Philip held his peace; but as Alexander many times let fall such words and showed great distress, he said : "Do you find fault with your elders in the belief that you know more than they do or are better able to manage a horse?"

"This horse, at any rate," said Alexander, "I could manage better than others have." "And if you should not, what penalty will you undergo for your rashness?" "Indeed," said Alexander, "I will forfeit the price of the horse." There was laughter at this, and then an agreement between father and son as to the forfeiture, and at once Alexander ran to the horse, took hold of his bridle-rein, and turned him towards the sun; for he had noticed, as it would seem, that the horse was greatly disturbed by the sight of his own shadow falling in front of him and dancing about. And after he had calmed the horse a little in this way, and had stroked him with his hand, when he saw that he was full of spirit and courage, he quietly cast aside his mantle and with a light spring safely bestrode him. Then, with a little pressure of the reins on the bit, and without striking him or tearing his mouth, he held him in hand; but when he saw that the horse was rid of the fear that had beset him, and was impatient for the course, he gave him his head, and at last urged him on with sterner tone and thrust of foot. Philip and his company were speechless with anxiety at first; but when Alexander made the turn in proper fashion and came back towards them proud and exultant, all the rest broke into loud cries, but his father, as we are told, actually shed tears of joy, and when Alexander had dismounted, kissed him, saying: "My son, seek out a kingdom equal to yourself; Macedonia has not room for you."

7. And since Philip saw that his son's nature was unyielding and that he resisted compulsion, but was easily led by reasoning into the path of duty, he himself tried to persuade rather than to command him; and because he would not wholly entrust the direction and training of the boy to the ordinary teachers of poetry and the formal studies. . . he sent for the most famous and learned of philosophers, Aristotle, and paid him a noble and appropriate tuition-fee. The city of Stageira, that is, of which Aristotle was a native, and which he had himself destroyed, he peopled again, and restored to it those of its citizens who were in exile or slavery. . .

8. Moreover, in my opinion Alexander's love of the art of healing was inculcated in him by Aristotle preeminently. For he was not only fond of the theory of medicine, but actually came to the aid of his friends when they were sick, and prescribed for them certain treatments and regimens, as one can gather from his letters. He was also by nature a lover of learning and a lover of reading. And since he thought and called the Iliad a viaticum of the military art, he took with him Aristotle's recension of the poem, called the Iliad of the Casket, and always kept it lying with his dagger under his pillow, as Onesicritus informs us; and when he could find no other books in the interior of Asia, he ordered Harpalus to send him some. So Harpalus sent him the books of Philistus, a great many of the tragedies of Euripides, Sophocles, and Aesehylus, and the dithyrambic poems of Telestus and Philoxenus. Aristotle he admired at the first, and loved him, as he himself used to say, more than he did his father, for that the one had given him life, but the other had taught him a noble life. . .

10. . . .And so when Pausanias, who had been outrageously dealt with at the instance of Attalus and Cleopatra and could get no justice at Philip's hands, slew Philip, most of the blame devolved upon Olympias, on the ground that she had added her exhortations to the young man's anger and incited him to the deed but a certain amount of accusation attached itself to Alexander also. For it is said that when Pausanias, after the outrage that he had suffered, met Alexander, and bewailed his fate, Alexander recited to him the iambic verse of the "Medeia":[94]

"The giver of the bride, the bridegroom, and the bride."

However, be did seek out the participants in the plot and punished them, and was angry with Olympias for her savage treatment of Cleopatra during his absence.[95]

11. Thus it was that at the age of twenty years Alexander received the kingdom, which was exposed to great jealousies, dire hatreds, and dangers on every hand. For the neighboring tribes of Barbarians would not tolerate their servitude, and longed for their hereditary kingdoms; and as for Greece, although Philip had conquered her in the geld, he had not had time enough to make her tame under his yoke, but had merely disturbed and changed the condition of affairs there, and then left them in a great surge and commotion, owing to the strangeness of the situation. The Macedonian counselors of Alexander had fears of the crisis, and thought he should give up the Greek states altogether and use no more compulsion there, and that he should call the revolting Barbarians back to their allegiance by mild measures and try to arrest the first symptoms of their revolutions; but he himself set out from opposite principles to win security and safety for his realm by boldness and a lofty spirit, assured that, if he were seen to abate his dignity even but a little, all his enemies would set upon him. Accordingly, he put a speedy stop to the disturbances and wars among the Barbarians by overrunning their territories with an army as far as to the river Danube, where he fought a great battle with Syrmus, the king of the Triballi, and defeated him; and on learning that the Thebans had revolted and that the Athenians were in sympathy with them, he immediately led his forces through the pass of Thermopylae, declaring that since Demosthenes had called him a boy while he was among the Illyrians and Triballians, and a stripling when he had reached Thessaly, he wished to show him that before the walls of Athens he was a man.

Arrived before Thebes,[96] and wishing to give her still a chance to repent of what she had done, he merely demanded the surrender of Phoenix and Prothytes, and proclaimed an amnesty for those who came over to his side. But the Thebans made a counter demand that he should surrender to them Philotas and Antipater, and made a counter-proclamation that all who wished to help in setting Greece free should range themselves with them; and so Alexander set his Macedonians to the work of war. On the part of the Thebans, then, the struggle was carried on with a spirit and

---

94. The *Medeia* of Euripides, 289. The context makes the verse suggest the murder of Attalus, Philip, and Cleopatra.

95. "After Philip's death Olympias killed Philip's infant son, together with his mother Cleopatra, niece of Attalus, by dragging them over a bronze vessel filled with fire." Pausanias, 8.7.5.

96. In September of 335 B.C. Plutarch makes no mention of a previous expedition of Alexander into Southern Greece, immediately after Philip's death, when he received the submission of all the Greek states except Sparta, and was made commander-in-chief of the expedition against Persia, in Philip's place.

valor beyond their powers, since they were arrayed against an enemy who was many times more numerous than they; but when the Macedonian garrison also, leaving the citadel of the Cadmeia, fell upon them in the rear, most of them were surrounded, and fell in the battle itself; and their city was taken, plundered, and razed to the ground. This was done, in the main, because Alexander expected that the Greeks would be terrified by so great a disaster and cower down in quiet, but apart from this, he also plumed himself on gratifying the complaints of his allies; for the Phocians and Plataeans had denounced the Thebans. So after separating out the priests, all who were guest-friends of the Macedonians, the descendants of Pindar,[97] and those who had voted against the revolt, he sold the rest into slavery, and they proved to be more than thirty thousand; those who had been slain were more than six thousand.

14. And now a general assembly of the Greeks was held at the Isthmus, where a vote was passed to make an expedition against Persia with Alexander, and he was proclaimed their leader. Thereupon many statesmen and philosophers came to him with their congratulations, and he expected that Diogenes of Sinope also, who was tarrying in Corinth, would do likewise. But since that philosopher took not the slightest notice of Alexander, and continued to enjoy his leisure in the suburb Craneion, Alexander went in person to see him; and he found him lying in the sun. Diogenes raised himself up a little when he saw so many persons coming towards him, and fixed his eyes upon Alexander. And when that monarch addressed him with greetings, and asked if he wanted anything, "Yes," said Diogenes, "stand a little out of my sun." It is said that Alexander was so struck by this, and admired so much the haughtiness and grandeur of the man who had nothing but scorn for him, that he said to his followers, who were laughing and jesting about the philosopher as they went away, "But verily, if I were not Alexander, I would be Diogenes." . . .

15. As to the, number of his forces, those who put it at the smallest figure mention thirty thousand foot and four thousand horse; those who put it at the highest, forty-three thousand foot and five thousand horse.[98] To provision these forces, Aristobulus says he had not more than seventy talents; Duris speaks of maintenance for only thirty days; and Onesicritus says he owed two hundred talents besides. . .

20. Now, there was in the army of Dareius a certain Macedonian who had fled from his country, Amyntas by name, and he was well acquainted with the nature of Alexander. This man, when he saw that Dareius was eager to attack Alexander within the narrow passes of the mountains, begged him to remain where he was, that he might fight a decisive battle with his vast forces against inferior numbers in plains that were broad and spacious. And when Dareius replied that he was afraid the enemy would run away before lie could get at them, and Alexander thus escape him, "Indeed," said Amyntas, "on this point, O king, you may be without fear; for he will march against you, nay, at this very moment, probably, he is on the march." Dareius would not listen to these words of Amyntas, but broke camp and marched into Cilicia, and at the same time Alexander marched into Syria against him. But having missed one another in the night, they both turned back again, Alexander rejoicing in his good fortune, and eager to meet his enemy in the passes,

---

97. "And we are told that Alexander preserved the house of Pindar the poet, and the descendants of Pindar, our of regard for Pindar." Arrian, *Anabasis*, 1.9.10.

98. "Not much more than thirty thousand foot, including light-armed troops and archers, and over five thousand horses." Arrian, *Anabasis*, 1.11.3.

while Dareius was as eager to extricate his forces from the passes and regain his former camping-ground. For he already saw that he had done wrong to throw himself into places which were rendered unfit for cavalry by sea and mountains and a river running through the middle (the Pinarus), which were broken up in many parts, and favored the small numbers of his enemy. And not only was the place for the battle a gift of Fortune to Alexander, but his generalship was better than the provisions of Fortune for his victory. For since he was so vastly inferior in numbers to the Barbarians, he gave them no opportunity to encircle him, but, leading his right wing in person, extended it past the enemy's left, got on their flank, and routed the Barbarians who were opposed to him, fighting among the foremost, so that he got a sword wound in the thigh. Chares says this wound was given him by Dareius, with whom he had a hand-to-hand combat, but Alexander, in a letter to Antipater about the battle, did not say who it was that gave him the wound; he wrote that he had been wounded in the thigh with a dagger, but that no serious harm resulted from the wound.

Although he won a brilliant victory and destroyed more than a hundred and ten thousand of his enemies, he did not capture Dareius, who got a start of four or five furlongs in his flight; but he did take the king's chariot, and his bow, before he came back from the pursuit. He found his Macedonians carrying off the wealth from the camp of the Barbarians, and the wealth was of surpassing abundance, although its owners had come to the battle in light marching order and had left most of their baggage in Damascus ; he found, too, that his men had picked out for him the tent of Dareius, which was full to overflowing with gorgeous servants and furniture, and many treasures. Straightway, then, Alexander put off his armor and went to the bath, saying: "Let us go and wash off the sweat of the battle in the bath of Dareius." "No, indeed," said one of his companions, "but rather in that of Alexander; for the property of the conquered must belong to the conqueror, and be called his." And when he saw the basins and pitchers and tubs and caskets, all of gold, and curiously wrought, while the apartment was marvelously fragrant with spices and unguents, and when he passed from this into a tent which was worthy of admiration for its size and height, and for the adornment of the couch and tables and banquet prepared for him, he turned his eyes upon his companions and said: "This, as it would seem, is to be a king."

26. . . . after his conquest of Egypt he wished to found a large and populous Greek city which should bear his name, and by the advice of his architects was on the point of measuring off and enclosing a certain site for it. Then, in the night, as he lay asleep, he saw a wonderful vision. A man with very hoary locks and of a venerable aspect appeared to stand by his side and recite these verses:

"Now, there is an island in the much-dashing sea,
In front of Egypt; Pharos is what men call it."[99]

Accordingly, he rose up at once and went to Pharos, which at that time was still an island, a little above the Canobic mouth of the Nile, but now it has been joined to the mainland by a causeway. And when he saw a site of surpassing natural advantages (for it is a strip of land like enough to a broad isthmus, extending between a great lagoon and a stretch of sea which terminates in a

---

99. *Odyssey*, 4.354.

large harbor), he said he saw now that Homer was not only admirable in other ways, but also a very wise architect, and ordered the plan of the city to be drawn in conformity with this site. There was no chalk at hand, so they took barley meal and marked out with it on the dark soil a rounded area, to whose inner arc straight lines extended so as to produce the figure of a chlamys, or military cloak, the lines beginning from the skirts (as one may say), and narrowing the breadth of the area uniformly. The king was delighted with the design; but suddenly birds from the river and the lagoon, infinite in number and of every sort and size, settled down upon the place like clouds and devoured every particle of the barley-meal, so that even Alexander was greatly disturbed at the omen.

However, the seers exhorted him to be of good cheer, since the city here founded by him would have most abundant and helpful resources and be a nursing mother for men of every nation, and so he ordered those in charge of the work to proceed with it, while he himself set out for the temple of Ammon. The journey thither was long, full of toils and hardships, and had two perils. One is the dearth of water, which leaves the traveler destitute of it for many days; the other arises when a fierce south wind smites men traveling in sand of boundless depth, as is said to have been the case with the army of Cambyses, long ago; the wind raised great billows of sand all over the plain and buried up fifty thousand men, to their utter destruction. Almost all of Alexander's followers took all these things into consideration, but it was difficult to turn him aside from any course when he had once set out upon it. . .

When Alexander had passed through the desert and was come to the place of the oracle, the prophet of Ammon gave him salutation from the god as from a father; whereupon Alexander asked him whether any of the murderers of his father had escaped him. To this the prophet answered by bidding him be guarded in his speech, since his was not a mortal father. Alexander therefore changed the form of his question, and asked whether the murderers of Philip had all been punished; and then, regarding his own empire, he asked whether it was given to him to become lord and master of all mankind. The god gave answer that this was given to him, and that Philip was fully avenged. Then Alexander made splendid offerings to the god and gave his priests large gifts of money.

This is what most writers state regarding the oracular responses; but Alexander himself in a letter to his mother, says that he received certain secret responses, which he would tell to her, and to her alone, on his return. And some say that the prophet, wishing to show his friendliness by addressing him with "O paidion," or *0 my son*, in his foreign pronunciation ended the words with "s" instead of n, and said, "O paidios," and that Alexander was pleased at the slip in pronunciation, and a story became current that the god had addressed him with "O pai Dios," or *0 son of Zeus*. . .

28. In general, he bore himself haughtily towards the Barbarians, and like one fully persuaded of his divine birth and parentage, but with the Greeks it was within limits and somewhat rarely that he assumed his own divinity. However, in writing to the Athenians concerning Samos, he said: "I cannot have given you that free and illustrious city; for you received it from him who was then your master and was called my father," meaning Philip. At a later time, however, when he had been hit by an arrow and was suffering great pain, he said: "This, my friends, that flows here, is blood, and not:

"Ichor, such as flows from the veins of the blessed gods."[100]

Once, too, there came a great peal of thunder, and all were terrified at it; whereupon Anaxarchus the sophist who was present said to Alexander: "Could you, the son of Zeus, thunder like that?" At this, Alexander laughed and said: "Nay, I do not wish to cause fear in my friends, as you would have me do, you who despise my suppers because, as you say, you see the tables furnished with fish, and not with satraps' heads." For, in fact, we are told that Anaxarchus, on seeing a present of small fish which the king had sent to Uephaestion, had uttered the speech above mentioned, as though he were disparaging and ridiculing those who undergo great toils and dangers in the pursuit of eminence and power, since in the way of enjoyments and pleasures they have little or nothing more than other men. From what has been said, then, it is clear that Alexander himself was not foolishly affected or puffed up by the belief in his divinity, but used it for the subjugation of others.

29. When he had returned from Egypt into Phoenicia,[101] he honored the gods with sacrifices and solemn processions, and held contests of dithyrambic choruses. . .

When Dareius sent to him a letter and friends, begging him to accept ten thousand talents as ransom for the captives, to hold all the territory this side of the Euphrates, to take one of his daughters in marriage, and on these terms to be his ally and friend, Alexander imparted the matter to his companions. "If I were Alexander," said Parmenio, "I would accept these terms." "And so indeed would I," said Alexander, "were I Parmenio." But to Dareius he wrote: "Come to me, and you shall receive every courtesy; but otherwise I shall march at once against you."

30. Soon, however, he repented him of this answer, when the wife of Dareius died in childbirth, and it was evident that he was distressed at this loss of opportunity to show great kindness. Accordingly, he gave the woman a sumptuous burial. One of the eunuchs of the bed-chamber who had been captured with the women, Teireos by name, ran away from the camp, made his way on horseback to Dareius, and told him of the death of his wife. Then the king, beating upon his head and bursting into lamentation, said: "Alas for the evil genius of the Persians, if the sister and wife of their king must not only become a captive in her life, but also in her death be deprived of royal burial." "Nay, O King," answered the chamberlain, "as regards her burial, and her receiving every fitting honor, you have no charge to make against the evil genius of the Persians. For neither did my mistress Stateira, while she lived, or your mother or your children, lack any of their former great blessings except the light of your countenance, which Lord Oromazdes will cause to shine again with luster; nor after her death was she deprived of any funeral adornment, nay, she was honored with the tears of enemies. For Alexander is as gentle after victory as he is terrible in battle. . ."

31. But to return to Alexander, when he had subdued all the country on this side of the Euphrates, he marched against Dareius[102] who was coming down to meet him with a million men. . . Now, the great battle against Dareius was not fought at Arbela, as most writers state, but at Gangamela. The word signifies, we are told, "camel's house," since one of the ancient kings of the

---

100. Iliad, 5.340
101. Early in 331 B.C.
102. In June of July of 331 B.C.

country, after escaping from his enemies on a swift camel, gave the animal a home here, assigning certain villages and revenues for its maintenance. It so happened that in the month Boedromion the moon suffered an eclipse,[103] about the beginning of the Mysteries at Athens, and on the eleventh night after the eclipse, the armies being now in sight of one another, Dareius kept his forces under arms, and held a review of them by torch-light; but Alexander, while his Macedonians slept, himself passed the night in front of his tent with his seer Aristander, celebrating certain mysterious sacred rites and sacrificing to the god Fear. Meanwhile the older of his companions, and particularly Parmenio, when they saw the plain between the Niphates and the Gordyaean mountains all lighted up with the barbarian fires, while an indistinguishably mingled and tumultuous sound of voices arose from their camp as if from a vast ocean, were astonished at their multitude and argued with one another that it was a great and grievous task to repel such a tide of war by engaging in broad day-light. They therefore waited upon the king when he had finished his sacrifices, and tried to persuade him to attack the enemy by night, and so to cover up with darkness the most fearful aspect of the coming struggle. But he gave them the celebrated answer, "I will not steal my victory"; whereupon some thought that he had made a vainglorious reply, and was jesting in the presence of so great a peril. Others, however, thought that he had confidence in the present situation and estimated the future correctly, not offering Dareius in case of defeat an excuse to pluck up courage again for another attempt, by laying the blame this time upon darkness and night, as he had before upon mountains, defiles, and sea. For Dareius would not give up the war for lack of arms or men when he could draw from so great a host and so vast a territory, but only when he had lost courage and hope, under the conviction brought by a downright defeat in broad daylight.

32. After the men were gone, Alexander lay down in his tent, and is said to have passed the rest of the night in a deeper sleep than usual, so that when his officers came to him in the early morning they were amazed, and on their own authority issued orders that the soldiers should first take breakfast. Then, since the occasion was urgent, Parmenio entered the tent, and standing by his couch called Alexander twice or thrice by name; and when he had thus roused him, he asked him how he could possibly sleep as if he were victorious, instead of being about to fight the greatest of all his battles. Then Alexander said with a smile: "What, pray? Do you not think that we are already victorious, now that we are relieved from wandering about in a vast and desolated country in pursuit of a Dareius who avoids a battle?" And not only before the battle, but also in the very thick of the struggle did he show himself great, and firm in his confident calculations. For in the battle the left wing under Parmenio was thrown back and in distress, when the Bactrian cavalry fell upon the Macedonians with great impetuosity and violence, and when Mazaeus sent horsemen round outside the line of battle to attack those who were guarding the Macedonian baggage. Therefore, too, Parmenio, much disturbed by both occurrences, sent messengers to Alexander telling him that camp and baggage were gone, unless he speedily sent strong reinforcements from front to rear. Now, it chanced that at that instant Alexander was about to give the signal for the onset to those under his command; but when he heard Parmenio's message, he declared that Parmenio was beside himself and had lost the use of his reason, and had forgotten in his distress that victors add the baggage of the enemy to their own, and that those who are vanquished must

---

103. September 20, 331 B.C.

not think about their wealth or their slaves, but only how they may fight gloriously and die with honor.

After sending this message to Parmenio, he put on his helmet, but the rest of his armor he had on as he came from his tent, namely, a vest of Sicilian make girt about him, and over this a breast-plate of two-ply linen from the spoils taken at Issus. His helmet was of iron, but gleamed like polished silver, a work of Theophilus; and there was fitted to this a gorget,[104] likewise of iron, set with precious stones. He had a sword, too, of astonishing temper and lightness, a gift from the king of the Citieans, and he had trained himself to use a sword for the most part in his battles. He wore a belt also, which was too elaborate for the rest of his armor; for it was a work of Helicon the ancient, and a mark of honor from the city of Rhodes, which had given it to him; this also he was wont to wear in his battles. As long, then, as he was riding about and marshalling some part of his phalanx, or exhorting or instructing or reviewing his men, he spared Bucephalas, who was now past his prime, and used another horse; but whenever he was going into action, Bucephalas would be led up, and he would mount him and at once begin the attack.

33. On this occasion, he made a very long speech to the Thessalians and the other Greeks,[105] and when he saw that they encouraged him with shouts to lead them against the Barbarians, he shifted his lance into his left hand, and with his right appealed to the gods, as Callisthenes tells us, praying them, if he was really sprung from Zeus, to defend and strengthen the Greeks. Aristander the seer, too, wearing a white mantle and having a crown of gold upon his head, rode along the ranks pointing out to them an eagle which soared above the head of Alexander and directed his flight straight against the enemy, at which sight great courage filled the beholders, and after mutual encouragement and exhortation the cavalry charged at full speed upon the enemy and the phalanx rolled on after them like a flood. But before the foremost ranks were engaged the Barbarians gave way, and were hotly pursued, Alexander driving the conquered foe towards the center of their array, where Dareius was. For from afar he was seen by Alexander through the deep ranks of the royal squadron of horse drawn up in front of him, towering conspicuous, a fine-looking man and tall, standing on a lofty chariot, fenced about by a numerous and brilliant array of horsemen, who were densely massed around the chariot and drawn up to receive the enemy. But when they saw Alexander close at hand and terrible, and driving those who fled before him upon those who held their ground, they were smitten with fear and scattered, for the most part. The bravest and noblest of them, however, slain in front of their king and falling in heaps upon one another, obstructed the Macedonians in their pursuit, weaving and twining themselves in their last agonies about riders and horses.

But Dareius, now that all the terrors of the struggle were before his eyes, and now that the forces drawn up to protect him were crowded back upon him, since it was not an easy matter to turn his chariot about and drive it away, seeing that the wheels were obstructed and entangled in the great numbers of the fallen, while the horses, surrounded and hidden away by the multitude of dead bodies, were rearing up and frightening the charioteer, forsook his chariot and his armor, mounted a mare which, as they say, had newly foaled, and took to flight. However, it is thought

---

104. A piece of armor protecting the throat.

105. Sometimes the term "Hellenes" (Greeks) excludes and sometimes it includes the Macedonians. The context must decide.

that he would not then have made his escape, had not fresh horsemen come from Parmenio summoning Alexander to his aid, on the ground that a large force of the enemy still held together there and would not give ground. For there is general complaint that in that battle Parmenio was sluggish and inefficient, either because old age was now impairing somewhat his courage, or because he was made envious and resentful by the arrogance and pomp, to use the words of Callisthenes, of Alexander's power. At the time, then, although he was annoyed by the summons, the king did not tell his soldiers the truth about it, but on the ground that it was dark and he would therefore remit further slaughter, sounded a recall; and as he rode towards the endangered portion of his army, he heard by the way that the enemy had been utterly defeated and was in flight.

34. The battle having had this issue, the empire of the Persians was thought to be utterly dissolved, and Alexander, proclaimed king of Asia, made magnificent sacrifices to the gods and rewarded his friends with wealth, estates, and provinces. And being desirous of honor among the Greeks, he wrote them that all their tyrannies were abolished and they might live under their own laws; moreover, he wrote the Plataeans specially that he would rebuild their city, because their ancestors had furnished their territory to the Greeks for the struggle in behalf of their freedom.[106] He sent also to the people of Croton in Italy a portion of the spoils, honoring the zeal and valor of their athlete Phayllus, who, in the Median wars, when the rest of the Greeks in Italy refused to help their brother Greeks, fitted out a ship at his own cost and sailed with it to Salamis, that he might have some share in the peril there. So considerate was Alexander towards every form of valor, and such a friend and guardian of noble deeds.

36. On making himself master of Susa, Alexander came into possession of forty thousand talents[107] of coined money in the palace, and of untold furniture and wealth besides. Among this they say was found five thousand talents' weight of purple from Hermione, which, although it had been stored there for a hundred and ninety years, still kept its colors fresh and lively. The reason for this, they say, is that honey was used in the purple dyes, and white olive oil in the white dyes; for these substances, after the like space of time, are seen to have a brilliancy that is pure and lustrous. Moreover, Demon says that the Persian kings had water also brought from the Nile and the Danube and stored up among their treasures, as a sort of confirmation of the greatness of their empire and the universality of their sway.

37. Persis was difficult of access, owing to the roughness of the country, and was guarded by the noblest of the Persians (for Dareius had taken to flight); but Alexander found a guide to conduct him thither by a circuit of no great extent. The man spoke two languages, since his father was a Lycian and his mother a Persian; and it was he, they say, whom the Pythian priestess had in mind when she prophesied, Alexander being yet a boy, that a "lycus," or wolf, would be Alexander's guide on his march against the Persians. In this country, then, as it turned out, there was a great slaughter of the prisoners taken; for Alexander himself writes that he gave orders to have the inhabitants butchered, thinking that this would be to his advantage; and they say that as much coined money was found there[108] as at Susa, and that it took ten thousand pairs of mules and five thousand camels to carry away the other furniture and wealth there.

---

106. In 479 B.C.
107. A talent's weight is something over fifty pounds.
108. In Persepolis.

On beholding a great statue of Xerxes which had been carelessly overthrown by a throng that forced its way into the palace, Alexander stopped before it, and accosting it as if it had been alive, said "Shall I pass on and leave you lying there, because of your expedition against the Hellenes, or, because of your magnanimity and virtue in other ways, shall I set you up again?" But finally, after communing with himself a long time in silence, he passed on. Wishing to refresh his soldiers (for it was winter time), he spent four months in that place. And it is said that when he took his seat for the first time under the golden canopy on the royal throne, Demaratus the Corinthian, a well-meaning man and a friend of Alexander's, as he had been of Alexander's father, burst into tears, as old men will, and declared that those Hellenes were deprived of great pleasure who had died before seeing Alexander seated on the throne of Dareius.

38. After this, as he was about to march forth against Dareius, it chanced that he consented to take part in a merry drinking bout of his companions, at which women also came to meet their lovers and shared in their wine and revelry. The most famous among these women was Thais, an Athenian, the mistress of Ptolemy, who was afterwards king. She, partly in graceful praise of Alexander, and partly to make sport for him, as the drinking went on, was moved to utter a speech which befitted the character of her native country, but was too lofty for one of her kind. She said, namely, that for all her hardships in wandering over Asia she was being requited that day by thus reveling luxuriously in the splendid palace of the Persians; but it would be a still greater pleasure to go in revel rout and set fire to the house of the Xerxes who burned Athens, she herself kindling the fire under the eyes of Alexander, in order that a tradition might prevail among men that the women in the train of Alexander inflicted a greater punishment upon the Persians in behalf of Hellas than all her famous commanders by sea and land. As soon as she had thus spoken, tumultuous applause arose, and the companions of the king eagerly urged him on, so that he yielded to their desires, and leaping to his feet, with a garland on his head and a torch in his hand, led them the way. The company followed with shouts and revelry and surrounded the palace, while the rest of the Macedonians who learned about it ran thither with torches and were full of joy. For they hoped that the burning and destruction of the palace was the act of one who had fixed his thoughts on home, and did not intend to dwell among Barbarians. This is the way the deed was done, according to some writers; but others say it was premeditated. However, it is agreed that Alexander speedily repented and gave orders to put out the fire.

42. . . . Now, however, he marched out against Dareius,[109] expecting to fight another battle; but when he heard that Dareius had been seized by Bessus, he sent his Thessalians home, after distributing among them a largess of two thousand talents over and above their pay. In consequence of the pursuit of Dareius, which was long and arduous (for in eleven days he rode thirty-three hundred furlongs), most of his horsemen gave out, and chiefly for lack of water. . .

43. So, then, all were alike ready and willing but only sixty, they say, were with Alexander when he burst into the camp of the enemy. There, indeed, they rode over much gold and silver that was thrown away, passed by many wagons full of women and children which were coursing hither and thither without their drivers, and pursued those who were foremost in flight, thinking that Dareius was among them. But at last they found him lying in a wagon, his body all full of javelins, at the point of death. Nevertheless, he asked for something to drink, and when he had drunk

---

109. In the spring of 330 B.C.

some cold water which Polystratus gave him, he said to him: "My man, this is the extremity of all my ill-fortune, that I receive good at your hands and am not able to return it; but Alexander will requite you for your good offices, and the gods will reward Alexander for his kindness to my mother, wife, and children; to him, through you, I give this right hand." With these words he took the hand of Polystratus and then expired. When Alexander came up, he was manifestly distressed by what had happened, and unfastening his own cloak threw it upon the body and covered it. And when, at a later time, he found Bessus, he had him rent asunder. Two straight trees were bent together and a part of his body fastened to each then when each was released and sprang vigorously back, the part of the body that was attached to it followed after. Now, however, he sent the body of Dareius, laid out in royal state, to his mother, and admitted his brother, Exathres, into the number of his Companions.

44. He himself, however, with the flower of his army, marched on into Hyrcania. Here he saw a gulf of the open sea which appeared to be as large as the Black Sea, but was sweeter than the Mediterranean. He could get no clear information about it, but conjectured that in all probability it was a stagnant overflow from the Pains Maeotis. And yet naturalists were well aware of the truth, and many years before Alexander's expedition they had set forth that this was the most northerly of four gulfs which stretch inland from the outer sea, and was called indifferently the Hyrcanian or Caspian Sea. . .

45. From thence he marched into Parthia,[110] where, during a respite from fighting, he first put on the barbaric dress, either from a desire to adapt himself to the native customs, believing that community of race and custom goes far towards softening the hearts of men; or else this was an attempt to introduce the obeisance among the Macedonians, by accustoming them little by little to put up with changes and alterations in his mode of life. However, he did not adopt the famous Median fashion of dress, which was altogether barbaric and strange, nor did he assume trousers, or sleeved vest, or tiara, but carefully devised a fashion which was midway between the Persian and the Median, more modest than the one and more stately than the other. At first he wore this only in intercourse with the Barbarians and with his companions at home, then people generally saw him riding forth or giving audience in this attire. The sight was offensive to the Macedonians, but they admired his other high qualities and thought they ought to yield to him in some things which made for his pleasure or his fame. For, in addition to all his other hardships, he had recently been shot by an arrow in the leg below the knee, so that splinters of the larger bone came out; and at another time he was smitten in the neck with a stone so severely that his eye-sight was clouded and remained so for some time. Nevertheless, he did not cease exposing himself to dangers without stint, nay, he actually crossed the river Orexartes (which he himself supposed to be the Tanais), put the Scythians to rout, and pursued them for a hundred furlongs, although he was suffering all the while from a diarrhea.

57. Alexander was now about to cross the mountains into India,[111] and since he saw that his army was by this time cumbered with much booty and hard to move, at break of day, after the baggage wagons had been loaded, he burned first those which belonged to himself and his companions, and then gave orders to set fire to those of the Macedonians. And the planning of the

---

110. In the early autumn of 330 B.C.
111. The spring of 327 B.C.

thing turned out to he a larger and more formidable matter than its execution. For it gave annoyance to a few only of the soldiers, while the most of them, with rapturous shouts and war cries, shared their necessaries with those who were in need of them, and what was superfluous they burned and destroyed with their own hands, thus filling Alexander with zeal and eagerness. Besides, he was already greatly feared, and inexorable in the chastisement of a transgressor. For instance, when a certain Menander, one of his companions, who had been put in command of a garrison, refused to remain there, he put him to death; and Orsodates, a Barbarian who had revolted from him, he shot down with his own hand. . .

58. And so it proved; for he encountered many perils in the battles which he fought and received very severe wounds; but the greatest losses which his army suffered were caused by lack of necessary provisions and severity of weather. Still, he was eager to overcome fortune by boldness and force by valor, and thought nothing invincible for the courageous, and nothing secure for the cowardly. It is said that when he was besieging the citadel of Sisimithres, which was steep and inaccessible, so that his soldiers were disheartened, he asked Oxyartes what sort of a man Sisimithres himself was in point of spirit. And when Oxyartes replied that he was most cowardly of men, "Thy words mean," said Alexander, "that we can take the citadel, since he who commands it is a weak thing" And indeed he did take the citadel by frightening Sisimithres. Again, after attacking another citadel equally precipitous, he was urging on the younger Macedonians, and addressing one who bore the name of Alexander, said: "It behooves you, at least, to be a brave man, even for your name's sake." And when the young man, fighting gloriously, fell, the king was pained beyond measure. And at another time, when his Macedonians hesitated to advance upon the citadel called Nysa because there was a deep river in front of it, Alexander, halting on the bank, cried: "Most miserable man that I am, why, pray, have I not learned to swim ?" and at once, carrying his shield, he would have tried to cross. And when, after he had put a stop to the fighting, ambassadors came from the beleaguered cities to beg for terms, they were amazed, to begin with, to see him in full armor and without an attendant; and besides, when a cushion was brought him for his use, he ordered the eldest of the ambassadors, Acuphis by name, to take it for his seat. Acuphis, accordingly, astonished at his magnanimity and courtesy, asked what he wished them to do in order to be his friends. "Your countrymen," said Alexander, "must make you their ruler, and send me a hundred of their best men." At this Acuphis laughed, and said "Nay, O King, I shall rule better if I send to you the worst men rather than the best."

59. Taxiles, we are told, had a realm in India as large as Egypt, with good pasturage, too, and in the highest degree productive of beautiful fruits. He was also a wise man in his way, and after he had greeted Alexander, said: "Why must we war and fight with one another, Alexander, if you art not come to rob us of water or of necessary sustenance, the only things for which men of sense are obliged to fight obstinately? As for other wealth and possessions, so-called, if I am your superior therein, I am ready to confer favors; but if your inferior, I will not object to thanking you for favors conferred." At this Alexander was delighted, and clasping the king's hand, said "Can you think, pray, that after such words of kindness our interview is to end without a battle? Nay, you shall not get the better of me; for I will contend against you and fight to the last with my favors, that you may not surpass me in generosity." So, after receiving many gifts and giving many more, at last he lavished upon him a thousand talents in coined money. This conduct greatly vexed Alexander's friends, but it made many of the Barbarians look upon him more kindly.

63. From thence, being eager to behold the ocean, and having built many passage-boats equipped with oars, and many rafts, he was conveyed down the rivers[114] in a leisurely course. And yet his voyage was not made without effort nor even without war, but he would land and assault the cities on his route and subdue everything. However, in attacking the, people called Malli, who are said to have been the most warlike of the Indians, he came within a little of being cut down. For after dispersing the inhabitants from the walls with missiles, he was the first to mount upon the wall by a scaling ladder, and since the ladder was broken to pieces and he was exposed to the missiles of the Barbarians who stood along the wall below, almost alone as he was, he crouched and threw himself into the midst of the enemy, and by good fortune alighted on his feet. Then, as he brandished his arms, the Barbarians thought that a shape of gleaming fire played in front of his person. Therefore at first they scattered and fled; but when they saw that he was accompanied by only two of his guards, they ran upon him, and some tried to wound him by thrusting their swords and spears through his armor as he defended himself, while one, standing a little further off, shot an arrow at him with such accuracy and force that it cut its way through his breastplate and fastened itself in his ribs at the breast. Such was the force of the blow that Alexander recoiled and sank to his knees, whereupon his assailant ran at him with drawn scimitar, while Peucestas and Limnaeus defended him. Both of them were wounded, and Limnacus was killed; but Peucestas held out, and at last Alexander killed the Barbarian. But he himself received many wounds, and at last was smitten on the neck with a cudgel, and leaned against the wall, his eyes still fixed upon his foes. At this instant his Macedonians flocked about him, caught him up, already unconscious of what was going on about him, and carried him to his tent. And straightway a report that he was dead prevailed in the camp; but when with much difficulty and pains they had sawn off the shaft of the arrow, which was of wood, and had thus succeeded at last in removing the king's breastplate, they came to the excision of the arrowhead, which was buried in one of the ribs. We are told, moreover, that it was three fingers broad and four long. Its removal, therefore, threw the king into swoons and brought him to death's door, but nevertheless he recovered. And after he was out of danger, though he was still weak and kept himself for a long time under regimen and treatment, perceiving from their tumult at his door that his Macedonians were yearning to see him, he took his cloak and went out to them. And after sacrificing to the gods he went on board ship again and dropped down the river, subduing much territory and great cities as he went.

64. He captured ten of the Gymnosophists who had done most to get Sabbas to revolt, and had made the most trouble for the Macedonians. These philosophers were reputed to be clever and concise in answering questions, and Alexander therefore put difficult questions to them, declaring that he would put to death him who first made an incorrect answer, and then the rest, in an order determined in like manner; and he commanded one of them, the oldest, to be judge in the contest. The first one, accordingly, being asked which, in his opinion, were more numerous, the living or the dead, said that the living were, since the dead no longer existed. The second, being asked whether the earth or the sea produced larger animals, said the earth did, since the sea was but a part of the earth. The third, being asked what animal was most cunning, said: "That which up to this time man has not discovered." The fourth, when asked why he had induced

---

114. Hydaspes, Acesines, and Indus.

Sabbas to revolt, replied: "Because I wished him either to live nobly or to die nobly." The fifth, being asked which, in his opinion, was older, day or night replied: "Day, by one day"; and he added, upon the king expressing amazement, that hard questions must have hard answers. Passing on, then, to the sixth, Alexander asked how a man could be most loved; "If," said the philosopher, "he is most powerful, and yet does not inspire fear." Of the three remaining, he who was asked how one might become a god instead of man, replied: "By doing something which a man cannot do"; the one who was asked which was the stronger, life or death, answered: "Life, since it supports so many ills." And the last, asked how long it were well for a man to live, answered: "Until he does not regard death as better than life." So, then, turning to the judge, Alexander bade him give his opinion. The judge declared that they had answered one worse than another. "Well, then," said Alexander, "you shall die first for giving such a verdict." "That cannot be, O King," said the judge, "unless you falsely said that you would put to death first him who answered worst."

66. His descent of the rivers to the sea consumed seven months time. And after emerging with his fleet into the ocean,[115] he sailed out to an island to which he himself gave the name of Scillustis, others that of Psiltucis. Here he landed and sacrificed to the gods, and studied the nature of the sea and of all the sea coast that was accessible. Then, after praying that no man after him might pass beyond the bounds of his expedition, he turned to go back. His fleet he ordered to go round by sea, keeping India on the right; Nearchus was appointed admiral of the fleet, Onesicritus its chief-pilot. But he himself proceeded by land through the country of the Oreites, where he was reduced to the direst straits and lost a multitude of men, so that not even the fourth part of his fighting force was brought back from India. And yet his infantry had once numbered a hundred and twenty thousand, and his cavalry fifteen thousand. But grievous diseases, wretched food, parching heats, and, worst of all, famine destroyed them, since they traversed an untilled country of men who dragged out a miserable existence, who possessed but few sheep and those of a miserable sort, since the sea-fish which they ate made their flesh unsavory and rank. It was with difficulty, then, that Alexander passed through this country in sixty days; but as soon as he reached Gedrosia he had all things in abundance, for the nearest satraps and princes had provided them.

67. Accordingly, after refreshing his forces here, he set out and marched for seven days through Carmania in a reveling rout. He himself was conveyed slowly along by eight horses, while he feasted day and night continuously with his companions on a dais built upon a lofty and conspicuous scaffolding of oblong shape; and wagons without number followed, some with purple and embroidered canopies, others protected from the sun by boughs of trees which were kept fresh and green, conveying the rest of his friends and commanders, who were all garlanded and drinking. Not a shield was to be seen, not a helmet, not a spear, but along the whole march with cups and drinking-horns and flagons the soldiers kept dipping wine from huge casks and mixing bowls and pledging one another, some as they marched along, others lying down; while pipes and flutes, stringed instruments and song, and reveling cries of women, filled every place with abundant music. Then, upon this disordered and straggling procession there followed also the sports of bacchanalian license, as though Bacchus himself were present and conducting the revel.[116] Moreover, when

---

115. In midsummer of 325 B.C.

116. According to Arrian, *Anabasis* 6.28.1, this bacchanalian procession through Carmania rests on no creditable authority.

he came to the royal palace of Gedrosia, he once more gave his army time for rest and held high festival. We are told, too, that he was once viewing some contests in singing and dancing, being well heated with wine, and that his favorite, Bagoas, won the prize for song and dance, and then, all in his festal array, passed through the theatre and took his seat by Alexander's side; at sight of which the Macedonians clapped their hands and loudly bade the king kiss the victor, until at last he threw his arms about him and kissed him tenderly.

70. . . . At Susa he brought to pass the marriage of his companions, took to wife himself the daughter of Dareins, Stateira, assigned the noblest women to his noblest men, and gave a general wedding feast for those of his Macedonians who had already contracted other marriages. At this feast, we are told, nine thousand guests reclined at supper, to each of whom a golden cup for the libations was given. All the other appointments too, were amazingly splendid, and the host paid himself the debts which his guests owed, the whole outlay amounting to nine thousand eight hundred and seventy talents. Now Antigenes, the One-eyed, had got himself enrolled as a debtor fraudulently and, on producing somebody who affirmed that he had made a loan to him at the bank, the money was paid over; then his fraud was discovered, and the king, in anger, drove him from his court and deprived him of his command. Antigenes, however, was a splendid soldier, and while he was still a young man and Philip was besieging Perinthus, though a bolt from a catapult smote him in the eye, he would not consent to have the bolt taken out nor give up fighting until he had repelled the enemy and shut them up within their walls. Accordingly, he could not endure with any complacency the disgrace that now fell upon him, but was evidently going to make away with himself from grief and despondency. So the king, fearing this, put away his wrath and ordered him to keep the money.

71. The thirty thousand boys whom he had left behind him under instruction and training were now so vigorous in their bodies and so comely in their looks, and showed besides such admirable dexterity and agility in their exercises, that Alexander himself was delighted; his Macedonians, however, were filled with dejection and fear, thinking that their king would now pay less regard to them. Therefore when he also sent the weak and maimed among them down to the sea-board, they said it was insult and abuse, after using men up in every kind of service, now to put them away in disgrace and cast them back upon their native cities and their parents, no longer the men they were when he took them. Accordingly, they bade him send them all away and hold all his Macedonians of no account, since he had these young war-dancers, with whom he could go on and conquer the world.[117] At these words of theirs Alexander was displeased, and heaped much abuse upon them in his anger, and drove them away, and committed his watches to Persians, and out of these constituted his bodyguards and attendants. When the Macedonians saw him escorted by these, while they themselves were excluded from him and treated with contumely, they were humbled; and when they reasoned the matter out they found that they had been almost mad with jealousy and rage. So finally, after coming to their senses, they went to his tent, without their arms and wearing their tunics only, and with loud cries and lamentations put themselves at his mercy, bidding him deal with them as base and thankless men. But Alexander would not see them, although his heart was softening. And the men would not desist, but for two

117. This account of the quarrel between Alexander and the Macedonians in Arrian, *Anabasis* 7.8-11, differs materially from that of Plutarch.

days and nights persisted in standing thus before his door, weeping and calling upon their master. So on the third day he came forth, and when he saw their piteous and humble plight, wept for some time then, after chiding them gently and speaking kindly to them, he dismissed those who were past service with magnificent gifts, and wrote to Antipater that at all the public contests and in the theatres they should have the foremost seats and wear garlands. He also ordained that the orphan children of those who had lost their lives in his service should receive their father's pay.

76. Moreover, in the court "Journals" there are recorded the following particular's regarding his sickness. On the eighteenth of the month Daesius[118] he slept in the bathing-room because he had a fever. On the following day, after his bath, he removed into his bed-chamber, and spent the day at dice with Medius. Then, when it was late, he took a bath, performed his sacrifices to the gods, ate a little, and had a fever through the night. On the twentieth, after bathing again, he performed his customary sacrifice; and lying in the bathing-room he devoted himself to Nearchus, listening to his story of his voyage and of the great sea. The twenty-first he spent in the same way and was still more inflamed, and during the night he was in a grievous plight, and all the following day his fever was very high. So he had his bed removed and lay by the side of the great bath, where he conversed with his officers about the vacant posts in the army, and how they might be filled with experienced men. On the twenty-fourth his fever was violent and he had to be carried forth to perform his sacrifices; moreover, he ordered his principal officers to tarry in the court of the palace, and the commanders of divisions and companies to spend the night outside. He was carried to the palace on the other side of the river on the twenty-fifth, and got a little sleep, but his fever did not abate. And when his commanders came to his bedside, he was speechless, as he was also on the twenty-sixth; therefore the Macedonians made up their minds that he was dead, and came with loud shouts to the doors of the palace, and threatened his companions until all opposition was broken down; and when the doors had been thrown open to them, without cloak or armor, one by one, they all filed slowly past his couch. During this day, too, Python and Seleucus were sent to the temple of Serapis to enquire whether they should bring Alexander thither; and the god gave answer that they should leave him where he was. And on the twenty-eighth,[119] towards evening, he died.

---

118. June 2, 323 B.C.
119. June 13, 323 B.C.

The Erechtheum Temple, Acropolis, Athens, Greece.

Plato

20

Plato (c. 429–347 B.C.) was born into an aristocratic family in Athens and became one Socrates' friends and devotees. After the death of Socrates in 399 B.C. he founded a school, known as the Academy, which survived until it was closed by Justinian in 529. We know Plato's philosophy mainly through his dialogues, in which Socrates is usually the leading protagonist. Some 25 of these dialogues survive, together with 13 letters and the Apology, a reply of Socrates to the charges for which he was put to death.

Central to Plato's philosophy is his theory of forms, or absolutes. Plato believed that all the visible, tangible things of this world are unreal and transitory, they are merely imperfect copies of the perfect and universal "forms" or "ideas" that actually exist somewhere else—in heaven, or in the mind of God, perhaps, Plato was never very clear about this. Then why did he think these forms actually exist? Because the mind perceives them. For example, we recognize a chair when we see one, although there are no two chairs in this world exactly alike, because our mind perceives what Plato called "chairness," that is, the mind perceives the ideal chair. But none of the chairs we see in this world is perfect, because they are simply corrupted copies of the ideal, the absolute, chair that exists in that other world.

In that other world there actually exists the ideal, perfect, absolute forms for all things, of which we see in this world only imperfect, corrupted copies. This led Plato to assume that there are also absolute, ideal truths, which are knowable to some men only, by correct education and moral superiority, and it follows by simple logic that once these individuals are known, it is in the interest of everyone that they be placed in charge of society, in order that they may cause society to live by the standards of these absolute truths that only they can perceive. Plato was not a democrat.

Following are excerpts from two of Plato's dialogs and an excerpt from the Apology.

PHAEDO: THE SOUL VERSUS THE BODY

"Now, how about the acquirement of pure knowledge? Is the body a hindrance or not, if it is made to share in the search for wisdom? What I mean is this: Have the sight and hearing of men any truth in them, or is it true, as the poets are always telling us, that we neither hear nor see

From *Phaedo, Volume 1*, translated by Harold North Fowler. (Cambridge, Loeb Classical Linrary, Harvard University Press, 1914).

anything accurately? And yet if these two physical senses are not accurate or exact, the rest are not likely to be, for they are inferior to these. Do you not think so?"

"Certainly I do," Crito replied.

"Then," said he, "when does the soul attain to truth? For when it tries to consider anything in company with the body, it is evidently deceived by it."

"True."

"In thought, then, if at all, something of the realities becomes clear to it?"

"Yes."

"But it thinks best when none of these things troubles it, neither hearing nor sight, nor pain nor any pleasure, but it is, so far as possible, alone by itself, and takes leave of the body, and avoiding, so far as it can, all association or contact with the body, reaches out toward the reality."

"That is true."

"In this matter also, then, the soul of the philosopher greatly despises the body and avoids it and strives to be alone by itself?"

"Evidently."

"Now how about such things as this, Simmias? Do we think there is such a thing as absolute justice, or not?"

"We certainly think there is."

"And absolute beauty and goodness."

"Of course."

"Well, did you ever see anything of that kind with your eyes?"

"Certainly not," said he.

"Or did you ever reach them with any of the bodily senses? I am speaking of all such things, as size, health, strength, and in short the essence or underlying quality of everything. Is their true nature contemplated by means of the body? Is it not rather the case that he who prepares himself most carefully to understand the true essence of each thing that he examines would come nearest to the knowledge of it?"

"Certainly."

"Would not that man do this most perfectly who approaches each thing, so far as possible, with the reason alone, not introducing sight into his reasoning nor dragging in any of the other senses along with his thinking, but who employs pure, absolute reason in his attempt to search out the pure, absolute essence of things, and who removes himself, so far as possible, from eyes and ears, and, in a word, from his whole body, because he feels that its companionship disturbs the soul and hinders it from attaining truth and wisdom? Is not this the man, Simmias, if anyone, to attain to the knowledge of reality?"

"That is true as true can be, Socrates," said Simmias.

"Then," said he, "all this must cause good lovers of wisdom to think and say one to the other something like this: 'There seems to be a short cut which leads us and our argument to the conclusion in our search that so long as we have the body, and the soul is contaminated by such an evil, we shall never attain completely what we desire, that is, the truth. For the body keeps us constantly busy by reason of its need of sustenance; and moreover, if diseases come upon it they hinder our pursuit of the truth. And the body fills us with passions and desires and fears, and all sorts of fancies and foolishness, so that, as they say, it really and truly makes it impossible for us to think at all. The body and its desires are the only cause of wars and factions and battles; for all wars arise for the sake of gaining money, and we are compelled to gain money for the sake of the body. We are slaves to its service. And so, because of all these things, we have no leisure for philosophy. But the worst of all is that if we do get a bit of leisure and turn to philosophy, the body is constantly breaking in upon our studies and disturbing us with noise and confusion, so that it prevents our beholding the truth, and in fact we perceive that, if we are ever to know anything absolutely, we must be free from the body and must behold the actual realities with the eye of the soul alone. And then, as our argument shows, when we are dead we are likely to possess the wisdom which we desire and claim to be enamored of, but not while we live. For, if pure knowledge is impossible while the body is with us, one of two thing must follow, either it cannot be acquired at all or only when we are dead; for then the soul will be by itself apart from the body, but not before. And while we live, we shall, I think, be nearest to knowledge when we avoid, so far as possible, intercourse and communion with the body, except what is absolutely necessary, and are not filled with its nature, but keep ourselves pure from it until God himself sets us free. And in this way, freeing ourselves from the foolishness of the body and being pure, we shall, I think, be with the pure and shall know of ourselves all that is pure—and that is, perhaps, the truth. For it cannot be that the impure attain the pure.' Such words as these, I think, Simmias, all who are rightly lovers of knowledge must say to each other and such must be their thoughts. Do you not agree?"

"Most assuredly, Socrates."

"Then," said Socrates, "if this is true, my friend, I have great hopes that when I reach the place to which I am going, I shall there, if anywhere, attain fully to that which has been my chief object in my past life, so that the journey which is now imposed upon me is begun with good hope; and the like hope exists for every man who thinks that his mind has been purified and made ready."

"Certainly," said Simmias.

"And does not the purification consist in this which has been mentioned long ago in our discourse, in separating, so far as possible, the soul from the body and teaching the soul the habit of collecting and bringing itself together from all parts of the body, and living, so far as it can, both now and hereafter, alone by itself, freed from the body as from fetters?"

"Certainly," said he.

"Well, then, this is what we call death, is it not, a release and separation from the body?"

"Exactly so," said he.

"But, as we hold, the true philosophers and they alone are always most eager to release the soul, and just this—the release and separation of the soul from the body—is their study, is it not?"

"Obviously."

"Then, as I said in the beginning, it would be absurd if a man who had been all his life fitting himself to live as nearly in a state of death as he could, should then be disturbed when death came to him. Would it not be absurd?"

"Of course.

"In fact, then, Simmias," said he, "the true philosophers practice dying, and death is less terrible to them than to any other men. Consider it in this way. They are in every way hostile to the body and they desire to have the soul apart by itself alone. Would it not be very foolish if they should be frightened and troubled when this very thing happens, and if they should not be glad to go to the place where there is hope of attaining what they longed for all through life—and they longed for wisdom—and of escaping from the companionship of that which they hated? When human loves or wives or sons have died, many men have willingly gone to the other world led by the hope of seeing there those whom they longed for, and of being with them; and shall he who is really in love with wisdom and has a firm belief that he can find it nowhere else than in the other world grieve when he dies and not be glad to go there? We cannot think that, my friend, if he is really a philosopher; for he will confidently believe that he will find pure wisdom nowhere else than in the other world. And if this is so, would it not be very foolish for such a man to fear death?"

"Very foolish, certainly," said he.

"Then is it not," said Socrates, "a sufficient indication, when you see a man troubled because he is going to die, that he was not a lover of wisdom but a lover of the body? And this same man is also a lover of money and of honor, one or both."

"Certainly," said he, "it is as you say.

"Then, Simmias," he continued, "is not that which is called courage especially characteristic of philosophers ?

"By all means," said he.

"And self-restraint—that which is commonly called self-restraint, which consists in not being excited by the passions and in being superior to them and acting in a seemly way—is not that characteristic of those alone who despise the body and pass their lives in philosophy?"

" Necessarily," said he.

"For," said Socrates, "if you care to consider the courage and the self-restraint of other men, you will see that they are absurd."

"How so, Socrates?"

"You know, do you not, that all other men count death among the great evils?"

"They certainly do."

"And do not brave men face death—when they do face it—through fear of greater evils?"

"That is true."

"Then all except philosophers are brave through fear. And yet it is absurd to be brave through fear and cowardice."

"Very true."

"And how about those of seemly conduct? Is their case not the same? They are self-restrained because of a kind of self-indulgence. We say, to be sure, that this is impossible, nevertheless their foolish self-restraint amounts to little more than this; for they fear that they may be deprived of certain pleasures which they desire, and so they refrain from some because they are under the sway of others. And yet being ruled by pleasures is called self-indulgence. Nevertheless they conquer pleasures because they are conquered by other pleasures. Now this is about what I said just now, that they are self-restrained by a kind of self-indulgence."

"So it seems."

". . .Now we have also been saying for a long time, have we not, that, when the soul makes use of the body for any inquiry, either through seeing or hearing or any of the other senses—for inquiry through the body means inquiry' through the senses,—then it is dragged by the body to things which never remain the same, and it wanders about and is confused and dizzy like a drunken man because it lays hold upon such things?"

"Certainly."

"But when the soul inquires alone by itself, it departs into the realm of the pure, the everlasting, the immortal and the changeless, and being akin to these it dwells always with them whenever it is by itself and is not hindered, and it has rest from its wanderings and remains always the same and unchanging with the changeless, since it is in communion therewith. And this state of the soul is called wisdom. Is it not so?"

"Socrates," said he, "what you say is perfectly right and true."

"And now again, in view of what we said before and of what has just been said, to which class do you think the soul has greater likeness and kinship?"

"I think, Socrates," said he, "that anyone, even the dullest, would agree, after this argument that the soul is infinitely more like that which is always the same than that which is not."

"And the body?"

"Is more like the other."

"Consider, then, the matter in another way. When the soul and the body are joined together, nature directs the one to serve and be ruled, and the other to rule and be master. Now this being the case, which seems to you like the divine, and which like the mortal? Or do you not think that the divine is by nature fitted to rule and lead, and the mortal to obey and serve?"

"Yes, I think so."

"Which, then, does the soul resemble?"

"Clearly, Socrates, the soul is like the divine and the body like the mortal."

"Then see, Cebes, if this is not the conclusion from all that we have said, that the soul is most like the divine and immortal and intellectual and uniform and indissoluble and ever unchanging, and the body, on the contrary, most like the human and mortal and multiform and unintellectual and dissoluble and ever changing. Can we say anything, my dear Cebes, to show that this is not so?"

"No, we cannot."

"Well then, since this is the case, is it not natural for the body to meet with speedy dissolution and for the soul, on the contrary, to be entirely indissoluble, or nearly so?"

THE APOLOGY: THE DEFENSE OF SOCRATES AT HIS TRIAL

How you, men of Athens, have been affected by my accusers, I do not know; but I, for my part, almost forgot my own identity, so persuasively did they talk; and yet there is hardly a word of truth in what they have said. But I was most amazed by one of the many lies that they told—when they said that you must be on your guard not to be deceived by me, because I was a clever speaker. For I thought it the most shameless part of their conduct that they are not ashamed be-

From *Plato, Volume 1*, translated by Harold North Fowler (Cambridge, Loeb Classical Library, 1914).

cause they will immediately be convicted by me of falsehood by the evidence of fact, when I show myself to be not in the least a clever speaker, unless indeed they call him a clever speaker who speaks the truth. . .

Now let us take up from the beginning the question, what is the accusation which has created the false prejudice against me, in which Meletus trusted when he brought this suit against me. What did those who aroused the prejudice say to arouse it? I must, as it were, read their sworn statement as if they were plaintiffs: "Socrates is a criminal and a busybody, investigating the things beneath the earth and in the heavens and making the weaker argument stronger and teaching others these same things." Something of that sort it is. For you yourselves saw these things in Aristophanes' comedy, a Socrates being carried about there, proclaiming that he was treading on air and uttering a vast deal of other nonsense, about which I know nothing, either much or little. And I say this, not to cast dishonor upon such knowledge, if anyone is wise about such matters (may I never have to defend myself against Meletus on so great a charge as that!)—but I, men of Athens, have nothing to do with these things. And I offer as witnesses most of yourselves, and I ask you to inform one another and to tell, all those of you who ever heard me conversing—and there are many such among you—now tell, if anyone ever heard me talking much or little about such matters. And from this you will perceive that such are also the other things that the multitude say about me.

But in fact none of these things are true, and if you have heard from anyone that I undertake to teach people and that I make money by it, that is not true either. Although this also seems to me to be a fine thing, if one might be able to teach people, as Gorgias of Leontini and Prodicus of Ceos and Hippias of Elis are.[1] For each of these men, gentlemen, is able to go into any one of the cities and persuade the young men, who can associate for nothing with whomever they wish among their own fellow citizens, to give up the association with those men and to associate with them and pay them money and be grateful besides.

And there is also another wise man here, a Parian,[2] who I learned was in town; for I happened to meet a man who has spent more on sophists than all the rest, Callias, the son of Hipponicus; so I asked him—for he has two sons—"Callias," said I, "if your two sons had happened to be two colts or two calves, we should be able to get and hire for them an overseer who would make them excellent in the kind of excellence proper to them; and he would be a horse-trainer or a husbandman; but now, since they are two human beings, whom have you in mind to get as overseer? Who has knowledge of that kind of excellence, that of a man and a citizen? For I think you have looked into the matter, because you have the sons. Is there anyone," said I, "or not?

---

1. These men were some of the much maligned "sophists" whom Socrates wasted no opportunity to defame. The sophists were professional "teachers of wisdom," who traveled all over Greece and beyond during the 5th century B.C. teaching philosophy and rhetoric. They asked fees and some of them amassed fortunes. After a time their teaching deteriorated, however, since they encouraged a belief in moral relativity. They were well traveled and were familiar with other moral systems—for example in Egypt brother-sister marriage was morally correct in some situations whereas the same practice was an unspeakable taboo in the Greek system. The sophists pointed out that what was correct under one system may not be under another system. This relativistic approach to morality did not set well with the Socratic belief in the absolute and perfect truth. Sophist truth was relative to time and place, therefore not absolute. Our modern word "sophisticated" has its roots (both in form and meaning) in the ancient Greek word "sophist."
2. From the island of Paros noted for its marble used extensively for sculpture in ancient times

"Certainly," said he. "Who," said I, "and where from, and what is his price for his teaching?" "Evenus," he said, "from Paros, five minae." And I called Evenus blessed, if he really had this art and taught so reasonably. I myself should be vain and put on airs, if I understood these things; but I do not understand them, men of Athens.

Now perhaps someone might rejoin: "But, Socrates, what is the trouble about you? Whence have these prejudices against you arisen? For certainly this great report and talk has not arisen while you were doing nothing more out of the way than the rest, unless you were doing something other than most people; so tell us what it is, that we may not act unadvisedly in your case." The man who says this seems to me to be right, and I will try to show you what it is that has brought about my reputation and aroused the prejudice against me. So listen. And perhaps I shall seem to some of you to be joking; be assured, however, I shall speak perfect truth to you.

The fact is, men of Athens, that I have acquired this reputation on account of nothing else than a sort of wisdom. What kind of wisdom is this? Just that which is perhaps human wisdom. For perhaps I really am wise in this wisdom; and these men, perhaps, of whom I was just speaking, might be wise in some wisdom greater than human, or I don't know what to say; for I do not understand it, and whoever says I do, is lying and speaking to arouse prejudice against me. And, men of Athens, do not interrupt me with noise, even if I seem to you to be boasting; for the word which I speak is not mine, but the speaker to whom I shall refer it is a person of weight. For of my wisdom—if it is wisdom at all—and of its nature, I will offer you the god of Delphi as a witness. You know Chaerephon, I fancy. He was my comrade from a youth and the comrade of your democratic party, and shared in the recent exile and came back with you. And you know the kind of man Chaerephon was, how impetuous in whatever he undertook. Well, once he went to Delphi and made so bold as to ask the oracle this question; and, gentlemen, don't make a disturbance at what I say; for he asked if there were anyone wiser than I. Now the Pythia[3] replied that there was no one wiser. And about these things his brother here will bear you witness, since Chaerephon is dead.

But see why I say these things; for I am going to tell you whence the prejudice against me has arisen. For when I heard this, I thought to myself: "What in the world does the god mean, and what riddle is he propounding? For I am conscious that I am not wise either much or little. What then does he mean by declaring that I am the wisest? He certainly cannot be lying, for that is not possible for him." And for a long time I was at a loss as to what he meant; then with great reluctance I proceeded to investigate him somewhat as follows.

I went to one of those who had a reputation for wisdom, thinking that there, if anywhere, I should prove the utterance wrong and should show the oracle "This man is wiser than I, but you said I was wisest." So examining this man—for I need not call him by name, but it was one of the public men with regard to whom I had this kind of experience, men of Athens—and conversing with him, this man seemed to me to seem to be wise to many other people and especially to himself, but not to be so; and then I tried to show him that he thought he was wise, but was not. As a result, I became hateful to him and to many of those present; and so, as I went away, I thought to myself, "I am wiser than this man; for neither of us really knows anything fine and good, but this man thinks he knows something when he does not, whereas I, as I do not know anything, do

---

3. The priestess of the oracle of Apollo at Delphi.

not think I do either. I seem, then, in just this little thing to be wiser than this man at any rate, that what I do not know I do not think I know either." From him I went to another of those who were reputed to be wiser than he, and these same things seemed to me to be true; and there I became hateful both to him and to many others.

After this then I went on from one to another, perceiving that I was hated, and grieving and fearing, but nevertheless I thought I must consider the god's business of the highest importance. So I had to go, investigating the meaning of the oracle, to all those who were reputed to know anything. And by the Dog, men of Athens—for I must speak the truth to you—this, I do declare, was my experience: those who had the most reputation seemed to me to be almost the most deficient, as I investigated at the god's behest, and others who were of less repute seemed to be superior men in the matter of being sensible. So I must relate to you my wandering as I performed my Herculean labors, so to speak, in order that the oracle might be proved to be irrefutable. For after the public men I went to the poets, those of tragedies, and those of dithyrambs, and the rest, thinking that there I should prove by actual test that I was less learned than they. So, taking up the poems of theirs that seemed to me to have been most carefully elaborated by them, I asked them what they meant, that I might at the same time learn something from them. Now I am ashamed to tell you the truth, gentlemen; but still it must be told. For there was hardly a man present, one might say, who would not speak better than they about the poems they themselves had composed. So again in the case of the poets also I presently recognized this, that what they composed they composed not by wisdom, but by nature and because they were inspired, like the prophets and givers of oracles; for these also say many fine things, but know none of the things they say; it was evident to me that the poets too had experienced something of this same sort. And at the same time I perceived that they, on account of their poetry, thought that they were the wisest of men in other things as well, in which they were not. So I went away from them also thinking that I was superior to them in the same thing in which I excelled the public men.

Finally then I went to the hand-workers. For I was conscious that I knew practically nothing, but I knew I should find that they knew many fine things. And in this I was not deceived; they did know what I did not, and in this way they were wiser than I. But, men of Athens, the good artisans also seemed to me to have the same failing as the poets; because of practicing his art well, each one thought he was very wise in the other most important matters, and this folly of theirs obscured that wisdom, so that I asked myself in behalf of the oracle whether I should prefer to be as I am, neither wise in their wisdom nor foolish in their folly, or to be in both respects as they are. I replied then to myself and to the oracle that it was better for me to be as I am.

Now from this investigation, men of Athens, many enmities have arisen against me, and such as are most harsh and grievous, so that many prejudices have resulted from them and I am called a wise man. For on each occasion those who are present think I am wise in the matters in which I confute someone else; but the fact is, gentlemen, it is likely that the god is really wise and by his oracle means this: "Human wisdom is of little or no value." And it appears that he does not really say this of Socrates, but merely uses my name, and makes me an example, as if he were to say: "This one of you, O human beings, is wisest, who, like Socrates, recognizes that he is in truth of no account in respect to wisdom."

. . . Now I am going to say some things to you at which you will perhaps cry out; but do not do so by any means. For know that if you kill me, I being such a man as I say I am, you will not injure me so much as yourselves; for neither Meletus nor Anytus could injure me; that would be impossible, for I believe it is not God's will that a better man be injured by a worse. He might, however, perhaps kill me or banish me or disfranchise me; and perhaps he thinks he would thus inflict great injuries upon me, and others may think so, but I do not; I think he does himself a much greater injury by doing what he is doing now—killing a man unjustly. And so, men of Athens, I am now making my defense not for my own sake, as one might imagine, but far more for yours, that you may not by condemning me err in your treatment of the gift the God gave you. For if you put me to death, you will not easily find another, who, to use a rather absurd figure of speech, attaches himself to the city as a gadfly to a horse, which, though large and well bred, is sluggish on account of his size and needs to be aroused by stinging. I think the god fastened me upon the city in some such capacity, and I go about arousing, and urging and reproaching each one of you, constantly alighting upon you everywhere the whole day long. Such another is not likely to come to you, gentlemen; but if you take my advice, you will spare me. But you, perhaps, might be angry, like people awakened from a nap, and might slap me, as Anytus advises, and easily kill me; then you would pass the rest of your lives in slumber, unless God, in his care for you, should send someone else to sting you. And that I am, as I say, a kind of gift from the god, you might understand from this; for I have neglected all my own affairs and have been enduring the neglect of my concerns all these years, but I am always busy in your interest, coming to each one of you individually like a father or an elder brother and urging you to care for virtue; now that is not like human conduct. If I derived any profit from this and received pay for these exhortations, there would be some sense in it; but now you yourselves see that my accusers, though they accuse me of everything else in such a shameless way, have not been able to work themselves up to such a pitch of shamelessness as to produce a witness to testify that I ever exacted or asked pay of anyone. For I think I have a sufficient witness that I speak the truth, namely, my poverty.

Perhaps it may seem strange that I go about and interfere in other people's affairs to give this advice in private, but do not venture to come before your assembly and advise the state. But the reason for this, as you have heard me say at many times and places, is that something divine and spiritual comes to me, the very thing which Meletus ridiculed in his indictment. I have had this from my childhood; it is a sort of voice that comes to me, and when it comes it always holds me back from what I am thinking of doing, but never urges me forward. This it is which opposes my engaging in politics. And I think this opposition is a very good thing; for you may be quite sure, men of Athens, that if I had undertaken to go into politics, I should have been put to death long ago and should have done no good to you or to myself. And do not be angry with me for speaking the truth; the fact is that no man will save his life who nobly opposes you or any other populace and prevents many unjust and illegal things from happening in the state. A man who really fights for the right, if he is to preserve his life for even a little while, must be a private citizen, not a public man.

I will give you powerful proofs of this, not mere words, but what you honor more, actions. And listen to what happened to me, that you may be convinced that I would never yield to any one, if that was wrong, through fear of death, but would die rather than yield. The tale I am going to tell you is ordinary and commonplace, but true. I, men of Athens, never held any other office in the state, but I was a member of the Boule; and it happened that my tribe held the presidency when you wished to judge collectively, not severally, the ten generals who had failed to gather up the slain after the naval battle; this was illegal, as you all agreed afterwards. At that time I was the only one of the prytanes who opposed doing anything contrary to the laws, and although the orators were ready to impeach and arrest me, and though you urged them with shouts to do so, I thought I must run the risk to the end with law and justice on my side, rather than join with you when your wishes were unjust, through fear of imprisonment or death. That was when the democracy still existed; and after the oligarchy was established, the Thirty sent for me with four others to come to the rotunda and ordered us to bring Leon the Salaminian from Salamis to be put to death. They gave many such orders to others also, because they wished to implicate as many in their crimes as they could. Then I, however, showed again, by action, not in word only, that. I did not care a whit for death if that be not too rude an expression, but that I did care with all my might not to do anything unjust or unholy. For that government, with all its power, did not frighten me into doing anything unjust, but when we came out of the rotunda, the other four went to Salamis and arrested Leon, but I simply went home; and perhaps I should have been put to death for it, if the government had not quickly been put down. Of these facts you can have many witnesses.

Do you believe that I could have lived so many years if I had been in public life and had acted as a good man should act, lending my aid to what is just and considering that of the highest importance? Far from it, men of Athens; nor could any other man. But you will find that through all my life, both in public, if I engaged in any public activity, and in private, I have always been the same as now, and have never yielded to any one wrongly, whether it were any other person or any of those who are said by my accusers to be my pupils. But I was never any one's teacher. If any one, whether young or old, wishes to hear me speaking and pursuing my mission, I have never objected, nor do I converse only when I am paid and not otherwise, but I offer myself alike to rich and poor; I ask questions, and whoever wishes may answer and hear what I say. And whether any of them turns out well or ill, I should not justly be held responsible, since I never promised or gave any instruction to any of them; but if any man says that he ever learned or heard anything privately from me, which all the others did not, be assured that he is lying.

But why then do some people love to spend much of their time with me? You have heard the reason, men of Athens; for I told you the whole truth; it is because they like to listen when those are examined who think they are wise and are not so; for it is amusing. But, as I believe, I have been commanded to do this by the God through oracles and dreams and in every way in which any man was ever commanded by divine power to do anything whatsoever. This, Athenians, is true and easily tested. For if I am corrupting some of the young men and have corrupted others, surely some of them who have grown older, if they recognize that I ever gave them any bad advice when they were young, ought now to have come forward to accuse me. Or if they did not wish to do it themselves, some of their relatives—fathers or brothers or other kinsfolk—ought now to tell the facts. And there are many of them present, whom I see; first Crito here, who is of my own age and my own deme and father of Critobulus, who is also present; then there is Lysanias the Sphettian, father of Aesehines, who is here; and also Antiphon of Cephisus, father of Epigenes. Then here are others whose brothers joined in my conversations, Nicostratus, son of Theozotides and brother of Theodotus (now Theodotus is dead, so he could not stop him by entreaties), and Paralus, son of Demodocus; Theages was his brother; and Adimantus, son of Aristo, whose brother is Plato here; and Aeantodorus, whose brother Apollodorus is present. And I can mention to you many others, some one of whom Meletus ought certainly to have produced as a witness in his speech; but if he forgot it then, let him do so now; I yield the floor to him, and let him say, if he has any such testimony. But you will find that the exact opposite is the case, gentlemen, and that they are all ready to aid me, the man who corrupts and injures their relatives, as Meletus and Anytus say. Now those who are themselves corrupted might have some motive in aiding me; but what reason could their relatives have, who are not corrupted and are already older men, unless it be the right and true reason, that they know that Meletus is lying and I am speaking the truth?

. . . And now I wish to prophesy to you, O ye who have condemned me; for I am now at the time when men most do prophesy, the time just before death. And I say to you, ye men who have slain me, that punishment will come upon you straight-way after my death, far more grievous in sooth than the punishment of death which you have meted out to me. For now you have done this to me because you hoped that you would be relieved from rendering an account of your lives, but I say that you will find the result far different. Those who will force you to give an account will be more numerous than heretofore; men whom I restrained, though you knew it not; and they will be harsher, inasmuch as they are younger, and you will be more annoyed. For if you think that by putting men to death you will prevent anyone from reproaching you because you do not act as you should, you are mistaken. That mode of escape is neither possible at all nor honorable, but the easiest and most honorable escape is not by suppressing others, but by making yourselves as good as possible. So with this prophecy to you who condemned me I take my leave.

But with those who voted for my acquittal I should like to converse about this which has happened, while the authorities are busy and before I go to the place where I must die. Wait with me so long, my friends; for nothing prevents our chatting with each other while there is time. I feel that you are my friends, and I wish to show you the meaning of this which has now happened to me. For, judges—and in calling you judges I give you your right name—a wonderful thing has happened to me. For hitherto the customary prophetic monitor always spoke to me very frequently and opposed me even in very small matters, if I was going to do anything I should not; but now, as you yourselves see, this thing which might be thought, and is generally considered, the greatest of evils has come upon me; but the divine sign did not oppose me either when I left my home in the morning, or when I came here to the court, or at any point of my speech, when I was going to say anything; and yet on other occasions it stopped me at many points in the midst of a speech; but now, in this affair, it has not opposed me in anything I was doing or saying. What then do I suppose is the reason? I will tell you. This which has happened to me is doubtless a good thing, and those of us who think death is an evil must be mistaken. A convincing proof of this has been given me; for the accustomed sign would surely have opposed me if I had not been going to meet with something good.

Let us consider in another way also how good reason there is to hope that it is a good thing. For the state of death is one of two things: either it is virtually nothingness, so that the dead has no consciousness of anything, or it is, as people say, a change and migration of the soul from this to another place. And if it is unconsciousness, like a sleep in which the sleeper does not even dream, death would be a wonderful gain. For I think if any one were to pick out that night in which he slept a dreamless sleep and, comparing with it the other nights and days of his life, were to say, after due consideration, how many days and nights in his life had passed more pleasantly than that night—I believe that not only any private person, but even the great King of Persia himself would find that they were few in comparison with the other days and nights. So if such is the nature of death, I count it a gain; for in that case, all time seems to be no longer than one night. But on the other hand, if death is, as it were, a change of habitation from here to some other place, and if what we are told is true, that all the dead are there, what greater blessing could there be, judges? For if a man when he reaches the other world, after leaving behind these who claim to be judges, shall find those who are really judges who are said to sit in judgment there, Minos[4] and Rhadamanthus,[5] and Aeacus[6] and Triptolemus,[7] and all the other demigods who were just men in their lives, would the change of habitation be undesirable? Or again, what would any of you give to meet with Orpheus[8] and Musaeus[9] and Hesiod and Homer? I am willing to die many times over, if these things are true; for I personally should find the life there wonderful, when I met Palamedes[10] or Ajax,[11] the son of Telamon, or any other men of old who lost their lives through an unjust judgment, and compared my experience with theirs. I think that would not be unpleasant. And the greatest pleasure would be to pass my time in examining and investigating the people there, as I do those here, to find out who among them is wise and who thinks he is when he is not. What price would any of you pay, judges, to examine him who led the great army against Troy, or Odysseus, or Sisyphus,[12] or countless others, both men and women, whom I might mention? To converse and associate with them and examine them would be immeasurable happiness. At any rate, the folk there do not kill people for it; since, if what we are told is true they are immortal for all future time, besides being happier in other respects than men are here.

---

4. Son of Zeus and Europa. Famous lawgiver whose laws remained in force nearly 1,000 years, with his justice, wise legislation approved by all the Greeks and all the gods.

5. Son of Zeus and Europa, broth of Minos. When he died, Zeus appointed him one of the three judges in Hades. The other two were Minos and Aeacus.

6. Son of Zeus and Aegina, a man of such high integrity that after his death Zeus appointed him one othe three judges of Hades.

7. A son of Celeus, king of Attica. He was born at Eleusis and established there the Aleusinian mysteries and festivals in honor of Demeter, the goddess of agriculture, productive soil, fruitfulness of humankind, and the guardian of marriage. After his death he was made a god.

8. The son of Apollo and Calliope. A was so masterful player of the lyre that Apollo gave him, that rivers ceased to flow, beasts forgot their wildness and mountains moved from place to place to listen to him. He married Eurydice, who died of a poisonous wound. Orpheus went to Hades and Pluto and Persephone agreed to restore Eurydice, provided that he did not look back, but he forgot his promise. Stories of his last days vary.

9. A fifth century poet who wrote a famous poem about Hero and Leander.

10. Palamedes was sent to fetch Odysseus (who was pretending insanity to avoid serving) to serve in the Trojan War. Because Palamedes perceived the deceit of Odysseus, an enmity grew up between the two. At Troy Odysseus falsely accused Palamedes and the Greeks stoned him to death.

11. After Achilles, Ajax was the bravest of the Greeks in the Trojan War. He contended with Odysseus for the armor of the dead Achilles and was so enraged because he lost that he slaughtered a whole flock of sheep because he thought they were the sons of Atreus. Then he stabbed himself.

12. Sisyphus was condemned to an unusually harsh punishment in Hades: to continuously roll a large stone to the top of a hill only to see the stone roll down again. This punishment was assessed by Zeus because Sisyphus accused Zeus of abducting Aegina, the daughter of Asopus. Zeus was, in fact, guilty of the abduction, but he punished Sisyphus for tattling to Asopus.

But you also, judges, must regard death hopefully and must bear in mind this one truth, that no evil can come to a good man either in life or after death, and God does not neglect him. So, too, this which has come to me has not come by chance, but I see plainly that it was better for me to die now and be freed from troubles. That is the reason why the sign never interfered with me, and I am not at all angry with those who condemned me or with my accusers. And yet it was not with that in view that they condemned and accused me, but because they thought to injure me. They deserve blame for that. However, I make this request of them: when my sons grow up, gentlemen, punish them by troubling them as I have troubled you; if they seem to you to care for money or anything else more than for virtue, and if they think they amount to something when they do not, rebuke them as I have rebuked you because they do not care for what they ought, and think they amount to something when they are worth nothing. If you do this, both I and my sons shall have received just treatment from you.

But now the time has come to go away. I go to die, and you to live; but which of us goes to the better lot, is known to none but God.

THE ALLEGORY OF THE CAVE

"Picture men dwelling in a sort of subterranean cavern with a long entrance open to the light on its entire width.[13] Conceive them as having their leg and necks fettered from childhood, so that they remain in the same spot, able to look forward only, and prevented by the fetters from turning their heads. Picture further the light from a fire burning higher up and at a distance behind them, and between the fire and the prisoners and above them a road along which a low wall has been built, as the exhibitors of puppet-shows have partitions before the men themselves, above which they show the puppets." "All that I see," he said. "See also, then, men carrying[14]past the wall implements of all kinds that rise above the wall, and human images and shapes of animals as well, wrought in stone and wood and every material, some of these bearers presumably speaking and others silent." "A strange image you speak of," he said, "and strange prisoners." "Like to us." I said; "for, to begin with, tell me do you think that these men would have seen anything of themselves or of one another except the shadows cast from the fire on the wall of the cave that fronted them?" "How could they," he said, "if they were compelled to hold their heads unmoved through life?" "And again, would not the same be true of the objects carried past them?" "Surely." "If then they were able to talk to one another, do you not think that they would suppose that in naming the things that they saw they were naming the passing objects?"[15] "Necessarily." "And if their prison had an echo[16] from the wall opposite them, when one of the passersby uttered a sound, do you think that they would suppose anything else than the passing shadow to be the speaker?" "By Zeus, I do not," said he. "Then in every way such prisoners would deem reality to be nothing else than the shadows of the artificial objects." "Quite inevitably," he said. "Consider, then, what would be the manner of the release and healing from these bonds and this folly if in the course of nature

Reprinted by permission of the publishers and the Trustees of the Loeb Classical Library from *Plato: Volume VI The Republic*, Loeb Classical Library Volume L 276, translated by Paul Shorey, Cambridge, Mass.: Harvard University Press, 1935. The Loeb Classical Library® is a registered trademark of the President and Fellows of Harvard College.

something of this sort should happen to them: When one was freed from his fetters and compelled to stand up suddenly and turn his head around and walk and to lift up his eyes to the light, and in doing all this felt pain and, because of the dazzle and glitter of the light, was unable to discern the objects whose shadows he formerly saw, what do you suppose would be his answer if someone told him that what he had seen before was all a cheat and an illusion, but that now, being nearer to reality and turned toward more real things, he saw more truly? And if also one should point out to him each of the passing objects and constrain him by question to say what it is, do you not think that he would be at a loss and that he would regard what he formerly saw as more real than the things now pointed out to him?"[17] "Far more real," he said.

"And if he were compelled to look at the light itself, would not that pain his eyes, and would he not turn away and flee to those things which he is able to discern and regard them as in very deed more clear and exact than the objects pointed out?" It is so," he said. "And if," said I, " someone should drag him thence by force up the ascent which is rough and steep, and not let him go before he had drawn him out into the light of the sun, do you not think that he would find it painful to be so pulled along, and would chafe at it, and when he came out into the light, that his eyes would be filled with its beams so that he would not be able to see even one of the things that we call real?" "Why, no, not immediately," he said. "Then there would be need of habituation, I take it, to enable him to see the things higher up. And at first he would most easily discern the shadows and, after that, the likenesses or reflections in water of men and other things, and later, the things themselves, and from these he would go on to contemplate the appearances in the heavens and heaven itself, more easily by night, looking at the light of the stars and the moon, than by day the sun and the sun's light"[18] "Of course." "And so, finally, I suppose, he would be

---

13. The image of the cave illustrates the contrast between the world of sense-perception and the world of thought. Instead of going above the plane of ordinary, Plato here goes below and invents a fire and shadows cast from it on the walls of a cave to correspond to the sun and the "real" objects of sense. Our "real" world becomes the symbol of Plato's ideal world. Modern fancy may read what meanings it pleases into the Platonic antithesis of the "real" and the "ideal." It has even been treated as an anticipation of the fourth dimension, but Plato never leaves an attentive and critical reader in doubt as to his own intended meaning. There may be at the most a little uncertainty as to which precise traits are intended to carry the symbolism and which are merely indispensable parts of the picture.

14. The men are merely a part of the necessary machinery of the image. Their shadows are not cast on the wall. The artificial objects correspond to the things of the sense and opinion is the divided line, and the shadows to the world of reflections.

15. As we use the word tree of the trees we see, though the reality is the idea of a tree, so they would speak of the shadows as the world, though the real reference unknown to them would be to the objects that cause the shadows, and back of the objects to the things of the "real" world of which they are copies. The general meaning, which is quite certain, is that they would suppose the shadows to be the realities. The text and the precise turn of expression are doubtful. They suppose that the names refer to the passing shadows, but (as we know) they really apply to the objects. Ideas and particulars are homonymous. Assuming a slight illogicality we can get somewhat the same meaning from the text. "Do you not think that they would identify the passing objects (which strictly speaking they do not know) with what they saw?"

16. The echo and voices merely complete the image.

17. The entire passage is an obvious allegory on the painful experience of one whose false conceit of knowledge is tested by Socratic elenchus. Elsewhere (*Meno*, 80), Plato says: "It is painful to have one's opinions set right."

18. It is probably a mistake to look for a definite symbolism in all the details of this description. There are more stages of progress than the proportion of four things calls for. All that Plato's thought requires is the general contrast between an unreal and a real world, and the goal of the rise from one to the other in the contemplation of the sun, or the idea of the good.

able to look upon the sun itself and see its true nature, not by reflections in water or phantasms of it in an alien setting,[19] but in and by itself in its own place." "Necessarily," he said. "And at this point he would infer and conclude that this it is that provides the seasons and the courses of the year and presides over all things in the visible region, and is in some sort the cause[20] of all these things that they had seen." "Obviously," he said, "that would be the next step." "Well then, if he recalled to mind his first habitation and what passed for wisdom there, and his fellow-bondsmen, do you not think that he would count himself happy in the change and pity them?" "He would indeed." "And if there had been honors and commendations among them which they bestowed on one another and prizes for the man who is quickest to make out the shadows as they pass and best able to remember their customary precedences, sequences and co-existences, and so most successful in guessing at what was to come, do you think he would be very keen about such rewards, and that he would envy and emulate those who were honored by these prisoners and lorded it among them, or that he would feel with Homer and greatly prefer while living on earth to be serf of another, a landless man, and endure anything rather than opine with them and live that life?" "Yes," he said, "I think that he would choose to endure anything rather than such a life." "And consider this also," said I, "if such a one should go down again and take his old place would he not get his eyes full of darkness, thus suddenly coming out of the sunlight?" "He would indeed." "Now if he should be required to contend with these perpetual prisoners in 'evaluating' these shadows while his vision was still dim and before his eyes were accustomed to the dark—and this time required for habituation would not be very short—would he not provoke laughter, and would it not be said of him that he had returned from his journey aloft with his eyes ruined and that it was not worth while even to attempt the ascent? And if it were possible to lay hands on and to kill the man who tried to release them and lead them up, would they not kill him?"[21]

"They certainly would," he said.

"This image then, dear Glaucon, we must apply as a whole to all that has been said, likening the region revealed through sight to the habitation of the prison, and the light of the fire in it to the power of the sun. And if you assume that the ascent and the contemplation of the things above is the soul's ascension to the intelligible region, you will not miss my surmise, since that is what you desire to hear. But God knows whether it is true.[22] But, at any rate, my dream as it appears to me is that in the region of the known the last thing to be seen and hardly seen is the idea of good, and that when seen it must needs point us to the conclusion that this is indeed the cause for all things of all that is right and beautiful, giving birth in the visible world to light, and the author of light and itself in the intelligible world being the authentic source of truth and reason, and that anyone who is to act wisely in private or public must have caught sight of this."[23] "I concur," he said, " so far as I am able." "Come then," I said, "and join me in this further thought, and do

---

19. That is, its reflection.

20. And for the idea of good as the cause of all things.

21. An obvious allusion to the fate of Socrates.

22. Plato was much less prodigal of affirmation about metaphysical ultimates than interpreters who take him myths literally have supposed.

23. This is the main point of *The Republic*: the significance of the idea of the good.

not be surprised that those who have attained to this height are not willing to occupy themselves with the affairs of men, but their souls ever feel the upward urge and the yearning for that sojourn above. For this, I take it, is likely if in this point too the likeness of our image holds." "Yes it is likely." "And again, do you think it at all strange," said I, "if a man returning from divine contemplations to the petty miseries of men cuts a sorry figure and appears most ridiculous, if, while still blinking through the gloom, and before he has become sufficiently accustomed to the environment of darkness, he is compelled in courtrooms or elsewhere to contend about the shadows of justice or the images that cast the shadows and to wrangle in debate about the notions of these things in the minds of those who have never seen justice itself?" "It would be by no means strange," he said. "But a sensible man," I said, "would remember that there are two distinct disturbances of the eyes arising from two causes, according as the shift is from light to darkness or from darkness to light, and, believing that the same thing happens to the soul too, whenever he saw a soul perturbed and unable to discern something, he would not laugh unthinkingly, but would observe whether coming from a brighter life its vision was obscured by the unfamiliar darkness, or whether the passage from the deeper dark of ignorance into a more luminous world and the greater brightness had dazzled its vision.[24] And so, only after that, he would deem the one happy in its experience and way of life and pity the other, and if it pleased him to laugh at it, his laughter would be less laughable than that at the expense of the soul that had come down from the light above." "That is a very fair statement," he said.

"Then, if this is true, our view of these matters must be this, that education is not in reality what some people proclaim it to be in their professions What they allege is that they can put true knowledge into a soul that does not possess it, as if they were inserting vision into blind eyes." "They do indeed," he said. "But our present argument indicates," said I, "that the true analogy for this indwelling power in the soul and the instrument whereby each of us apprehends is that of an eye that could not be converted to the light from the darkness except by turning the whole body. Even so this organ of knowledge must be turned around from the world of becoming together with the entire soul, like the scene-shifting periact[25] in the theatre, until the soul is able to endure the contemplation of essence and the brightest region of being. And this, we say, is the good, do we not?"[26] "Yes."

"Of this very thing, then," I said," there might be an art,[27] an art of the speediest and most effective shifting or conversion of the soul, not an art of producing vision in it, but on the assumption that it possesses vision but does not rightly direct it and does not look where it should, an art of bringing this about." "Yes, that seems likely," he said. "Then the other so-called virtues

---

24. Literally: "or whether coming from a deeper ignorance into a more luminous world, it is dazzled by the brilliance of a greater light."

25. A reference to the triangular prisms on each side of the stage. They revolved on an axis and had different scenes painted on each of their three faces.

26. Distaste for the mysticism of Plato's language should not blind us to its meaning. Plato says that men can be preached and drilled into ordinary morality, but that the degree of their intelligence is an unalterable endowment of nature. Some teachers will agree.

27. Plato often distinguishes the things that do and do not admit of reduction to an art or science.

of the soul do seem akin to those of the body.[28] For it is true that where they do not pre-exist, they are afterwards created by habit and practice. But the excellence of thought, it seems, is certainly of a more divine quality, a thing that never loses its potency, but, according to the direction of its conversion, becomes useful and beneficent, or, again, useless and harmful. Have you never observed in those who are popularly spoken of as bad, but smart men, how keen is the vision of the little soul, how quick it is to discern the things that interest it,[29] a proof that it is not a poor vision which it has, but one forcibly enlisted in the service of evil, so that the sharper its sight the more mischief it accomplishes?" "I certainly have," he said. "Observe then," said I, "that this part of such a soul, if it had been hammered from childhood, and had thus been struck free of the leaden weights, so that all virtues except wisdom could be acquired habitually to speak, of our birth and becoming, which attaching themselves to it by food and similar pleasures and gluttonies turn downwards the vision of the soul[30]—if, I say, freed from these, it had suffered a conversion towards the things that are real and true, that same faculty of the same men would have been most keen in its vision of the higher things, just as it is for the things toward which it is now turned." "It is likely," he said. " Well, then," said I, "is not this also likely and a necessary consequence of what has been said, that neither could men who are uneducated and inexperienced in truth ever adequately preside over a state, nor could those who had been permitted to linger on to the end in the pursuit of culture—the one because they have no single aim[31] and purpose in life to which all their actions, public and private, must be directed, and the others, because they will not voluntarily engage in action, believing that while still living they have been transported to the Islands of the Blest." "True," he said. "It is the duty of us, the founders, then," said I, "to compel the best natures to attain the knowledge which we pronounced the greatest, and to win to the vision of the good, to scale that ascent, and when they have reached the heights and taken an adequate view, we must not allow what is now permitted." "What is that?" "That they should linger there," I said, "and refuse to go down again among those bondsmen and share their labors and honors, whether they are of less or of greater worth." "Do you mean to say that we must do them this wrong, and compel them to live an inferior life when the better is in their power ?

"You have again forgotten, my friend," said I, "that the law is not concerned with the special happiness of any class in the state, but is trying to produce this condition in the city as a whole, harmonizing and adapting the citizens to one another by persuasion and compulsion and requiring them to impart to one another any benefit which they are severally able to bestow upon the community, and that it itself creates such men in the state, not that it may allow each to take

---

28. This then is Plato's answer (intended from the first) to the question whether virtue can be taught, also debated in the *Protagoras* and *Meno*. The intellectual virtues (to use Aristotle's term), broadly speaking, cannot be taught; they are a gift. And the highest moral virtue is inseparable from rightly directed intellectual virtue. Ordinary moral virtue is not rightly taught in democratic Athens, but comes by the grace of God. In a reformed state it could be systematically inculcated and "taught." But we need not infer that Plato did not believe in mental discipline. According to Charles Fox, *Educational Psychology,* p. 164 "The conception of mental discipline is at least as old as Plato, as may be seen from the seventh book of the *Republic.*"

29. Literally, "toward which it is turned."

30. Or "eye of the mind."

31. This is what distinguishes the Philosopher politician from the opportunist politician.

what course pleases him, but with a view to using them for the binding together of the common-wealth." "True," he said, "I did forget it." "Observe, then, Glaucon," said I, "that we shall not be wronging, either, the philosophers who arise among us, but that we can justify our action when we constrain them to take charge of the other citizens and be their guardians.[32] For we will say to them that it is natural that men of similar quality who spring up in other cities should not share in the labors there. For they grow up spontaneously from no volition of the government in the several states,[33] and it is justice that the self-grown, indebted to none for its breeding, should not be zealous either to pay to anyone the price of its nurture. But you we have engendered for yourselves and the rest of the city to be, as it were, king-bees and leaders in the hive. You have received a better and more complete education than the others, and you are more capable of sharing both ways of life. Down you must go then, each in his turn, to the habitation of the others and accustom yourselves to the observation of the obscure things there. For once habituated you will discern them infinitely better than the dwellers there,[34] and you will know what each of the 'idols' is and whereof it is a semblance, because you have seen the reality of the beautiful, the just and the good. So our city will be governed by us and you with waking minds, and not, as most cities now which are inhabited and ruled darkly as in a dream by men who fight one another for shadows and wrangle for office as if that were a great good, when the truth is that the city in which those who are to rule are least eager to hold office must needs be best administered and most free from dissension, and the state that gets the contrary type of ruler will be the opposite of this."

---

32. *Noblesse oblige.* This idea is not commonplace in our society. All wealthy people are expected, as a matter of course, to support charities and "serve the public."

33. The thought is that there are a few men naturally good in any state.

34. They must descend again into the cave. Plato insisted that philosophers must descend by turn back into the cave from which they had been released to help their former fellow-prisoners.

Aristotle 21

Aristotle (384–322 B.C.) was the son of a physician at Stagiraa in Calcidice. At the age of 17 he went to Athens and studied at Plato's Academy until Plato's death in 347 B.C. He then spent some time in Asia Minor, on Lesbos and in Macedonia as the tutor of Alexander. He returned to Athens in 355 and founded a school, the Lyceum. He died in Euboea in 322.

His philosophy was eclectic and included logic, natural science, psychology, metaphysics, theology, ethics, politics, esthetics, and rhetoric. He wrote extensively about all these subjects. His investigations typically explored the past opinions held on these subjects, pointed out the inconsistencies of these views and explained why these opinions were held in the past. Then he proposed new, more refined answers to the problems. His procedure of investigation resembled modern scientific methods. About one third of his surviving works are in the field of biology, and his successors at the Lyceum greatly expanded the knowledge of natural science.

Nearly all the works prepared for publication by Aristotle are lost. What survives are lecture materials, notes and memoranda, some of them spurious. Following are excerpts from two of his best known works: The Nicomachean Ethics *and* The Politics.

NICOMACHEAN ETHICS

1.1. Every art and every investigation, and likewise every practical pursuit or undertaking, seems to aim at some good: hence it has been well said that the Good is That at which all things aim. (It is true that that a certain variety is to be observed among the ends at which the arts and sciences aim: in some cases the activity of practicing the art is itself the end,[1] whereas in others the end is some product over and above the mere exercise of the art; and in the arts whose ends are certain things beside the practice of the arts themselves, these products are essentially superior in value to the activities.) But as there are numerous pursuits and arts and sciences, it follows that their ends are correspondingly numerous: for instance, the end of the science of medicine is health, that of the art of shipbuilding a vessel, that of strategy victory, that of domestic economy wealth.

Reprinted by permission of the publishers and the Trustees of the Loeb Classical Library from *Aritstotle: Volume XIX The Nicomachean Ethics*, Loeb Classical Library Volume L 73, translated by H. Rackham, Cambridge, Mass.: Harvard University Press, 1926. The Loeb Classical Library® is a registered trademark of the President and Fellows of Harvard College.

The Library of Celsus, Ephesus, Turkey.

Now in cases where several such pursuits are subordinate to some single faculty—as bridle-making and the other trades concerned with horses' harness are subordinate to horsemanship, and this and every other military pursuit to the science of strategy, and similarly other arts to different arts again—in all these cases, I say, the ends of the master arts are things more to be desired than all those of the arts subordinate to them; since the latter ends are only pursued for the sake of the former. (And it makes no difference whether the ends of the pursuits are the activities themselves or some other thing beside, these, as in the case of the sciences mentioned.)

1.2. If therefore among the ends at which our actions aim there be one which we wish for its own sake, while we wish the others only for the sake of this, and if we do not choose everything for the sake of something else (which would obviously result in a process *ad infinitum*, so that all desire would be futile and vain), it is clear that this one ultimate End must be the Good, and indeed the Supreme Good. Will not then a knowledge of this Supreme Good be also of great

---

1. Aristotle gives flute-playing as an instance of an art the practice of which is an end in itself, in contrast with the art of building, the end of which is the house built. *Magna Moralia*, 1211.

practical importance for the conduct of life? Will it not better enable us to attain what is fitting, like archers having a target to aim at? If this be so, we ought to make an attempt to determine at all events in outline what exactly this Supreme Good is, and of which of the theoretical or practical sciences it is the object.

Now it would be agreed that it must be the object of the most authoritative of the sciences—some science which is pre-eminently a master-craft. But such is manifestly the science of Politics; for it is this that ordains which of the sciences are to exist in states, and what branches of knowledge the different classes of the citizens are to learn, and up to what point; and we observe that even the most highly esteemed of the faculties, such as strategy, domestic economy, oratory, are subordinate to the political science. Inasmuch then as the rest of the sciences are employed by this one, and as it moreover lays down laws as to what people shall do and what things they shall refrain from doing, the end of this science must include the ends of all the others. Therefore, the Good of man must be the end of the science of Politics. For even though it be the case that the Good is the same for the individual and for the state, nevertheless, the good of the state is manifestly a greater and more perfect good, both to attain and to preserve.[2] To secure the good of one person only is better than nothing; but to secure the good of a nation or a state is a nobler and more divine achievement. This then being its aim, our investigation is in a sense the study of Politics.

1.3. Now our treatment of this science will be adequate, if it achieves that amount of precision which belongs to its subject matter. The same exactness must not be expected in all departments of philosophy alike, any more than in all the products of the arts and crafts. The subjects studied by political science are Moral Nobility[3] and Justice; but these conceptions involve much difference of opinion and uncertainty, so that they are sometimes believed to be mere conventions and to have no real existence in the nature of things. And a similar uncertainty surrounds the conception of the Good, because it frequently occurs that good things have harmful consequences: people have before now been ruined by wealth, and in other cases courage has cost men their lives. We must therefore be content if, in dealing with subjects and starting from premises thus uncertain, we succeed in presenting a broad outline of the truth: when our subjects and our premises are merely generalities, it is enough if we arrive at generally valid conclusions. Accordingly we may ask the student also to accept the various views we put forward in the same spirit; for it is the mark of an educated mind to expect that amount of exactness in each kind which the nature of the particular subject admits. It is equally unreasonable to accept merely probable conclusions from a mathematician and to demand strict demonstration from an orator.

Again, each man judges correctly those matters with which he is acquainted; it is of these that he is a competent critic. To criticize a particular subject, therefore, a man must have been trained in that subject: to be a good critic generally, he must have had an all-round education. Hence the young are not fit to be students of Political Science.[4] For they have no experience of life and con-

---

2. Or perhaps "both to ascertain and to secure."

3. This is a term of admiration applied to what is correct, especially (1) bodies well shaped and works of art or handicraft well made, and (2) actions well done; it thus means (1) beautiful, (2) morally right.

4. Quoted by Shakespeare in *Troilus and Cressida*, II, ii, 165:

Young men, whom Aristotle thought
Unfit to hear moral philosophy.

duct, and it is these that supply the premises and subject matter of this branch of philosophy. And moreover they are led by their feelings; so that they will study the subject to no purpose or advantage, since the end of this science is not knowledge but action. And it makes no difference whether they are young in years or immature in character: the defect is not a question of time, it is because their life and its various aims are guided by feeling; for to such persons their knowledge is of no use, any more than it is to persons of defective self-restraint.[5] But Moral Science may be of great value to those who guide their desires and actions by principle.

Let so much suffice by way of introduction as to the student of the subject, the spirit in which our conclusions are to be received, and the object that we set before us.

1.4. To resume, inasmuch as all studies and undertakings are directed to the attainment of some good, let us discuss what it is that we pronounce to be the aim of Politics, that is, what is the highest of all the goods that action can achieve. As far as the name goes, we may almost say that the great majority of mankind are agreed about this; for both the multitude and persons of refinement speak of it as Happiness,[6] and conceive ' the good life' or 'doing well' to be the same thing as 'being happy.' But what constitutes happiness is a matter of dispute; and the popular account of it is not the same as that given by the philosophers. Ordinary people identify it with some obvious and visible good, such as pleasure or wealth or honor—some say one thing and some another, indeed very often the same man says different things at different times: when he falls sick he thinks health is happiness, when he is poor, wealth. At other times, feeling conscious of their own ignorance, men admire those who propound something grand and above their heads; and it has been held by some thinkers that beside the many good things we have mentioned, there exists another Good, that is good in itself, and stands to all those goods as the cause of their being good.

Now perhaps it would be a somewhat fruitless task to review all the different opinions that are held. It will suffice to examine those that are most widely prevalent, or that seem to have some argument in their favor.

And we must not overlook the distinction between arguments that start from first principles and those that lead to first principles. It was a good practice of Plato to raise this question, and to enquire whether the right procedure was to start from or to lead up to the first principles, as in a race-course one may run from the judges to the far end of the track or reversely. Now no doubt it is proper to start from the known. But 'the known' has two meanings—'what is known to us,' which is one thing, and 'what is knowable in itself,' which is another. Perhaps then for us[7] at all events it is proper to start from what is known to us. This is why in order to be a competent student of the Right and Just, and in short of the topics of Politics in general, the pupil is bound to have been well trained in his habits. For the starting-point or first principle is the fact that a

---

5. The argument is, that even if the young could gain a knowledge of Ethics (which they cannot, because it requires experience of life), they would not use it as a guide to conduct, because they are led by their passions and appetites; and therefore the study is of no value for them, since Ethics, being a practical science, is only pursued for the sake of its practical application.

6. This would perhaps be more accurately rendered by "Well-being" or "Prosperity"; and it will be found that Aristotle does not interpret it as a state of feeling but as a kind of activity.

7. In contrast apparently with the school of Plato.

thing is so; if this be satisfactorily ascertained, there will be no need also to know the reason why it is so. And the man of good moral training knows first principles already, or can easily acquire them. As for the person who neither knows nor can learn, let him hear the words of Hesiod:[8]

"Best is the man who can himself advise;
He too is good who hearkens to the wise;
But who, himself being witless, will not heed
Another's wisdom, is worthless indeed."

1.7. We may now return to the Good which is the object of our search, and try to find out what exactly it can be. For good appears to be one thing in one pursuit or art and another in another: it is different in medicine from what it is in strategy, and so on with the rest of the arts. What definition of the Good then will hold true in all the arts? Perhaps we may define it as that for the sake of which everything else is done. This applies to something different in each different art—to health in the case of medicine, to victory in that of strategy, to a house in architecture, and to something else in each of the other arts; but in every pursuit or undertaking it describes the end of that pursuit or undertaking, since in all of them it is for the sake of the end that everything else is done. Hence if there be something which is the end of all the things done by human action, this will be the practicable Good—or if there be several such ends, the sum of these will be the Good. Thus by changing its ground the argument has reached the same result as before. We must attempt however to render this still more precise.

Now there do appear to be several ends at which our actions aim; but as we choose some of them—for instance wealth, or flutes, and instruments generally—as a means to something else, it is clear that not all of them are final ends; whereas the Supreme Good seems to be something final. Consequently if there be some one thing which alone is a final end, this thing—or if there be several final ends, the one among them which is the most final—will be the Good which we are seeking. In speaking of degrees of finality, we mean that a thing pursued as an end in itself is more final than one pursued as a means to something else, and that a thing never chosen as a means to anything else is more final than things chosen both as ends in themselves and as means to that thing; and accordingly a thing chosen always as an end and never as a means we call absolutely final. Now happiness above all else appears to be absolutely final in this sense, since we always choose it for its own sake and never as a means to something else; whereas honor, pleasure, intelligence, and excellence in its various forms, we choose indeed for their own sakes (since we should be glad to have each of them although no extraneous advantage resulted from it), but we also choose them for the sake of happiness, in the belief that they will be a means to our securing it. But no one chooses happiness for the sake of honor, pleasure, etc., nor as a means to anything whatever other than itself.

The same conclusion also appears to follow from a consideration of the self-sufficiency of happiness—for it is felt that the final good must be a thing sufficient in itself. The term self-sufficient, however, we employ with reference not to oneself alone, living a life of isolation, but also to one's parents and children and wife, and one's friends and fellow citizens in general, since man is by

8. *Works and Days*, 293 ff.

nature a social being.[9] On the other hand a limit has to be assumed in these relationships; for if the list be extended to one's ancestors and descendants and to the friends of one's friends, it will go on *ad infinitum*. But this is a point that must be considered later on; we take a self-sufficient thing to mean a thing which merely standing by itself alone renders life desirable and lacking in nothing, and such a thing we deem happiness to be. Moreover, we think happiness the most desirable of all good things without being itself reckoned as one among the rest;[10] for if it were so reckoned, it is clear that we should consider it more desirable when even the smallest of other good things were combined with it, since this addition would result in a larger total of good, and of two goods the greater is always the more desirable.

Happiness, therefore, being found to be something final and self-sufficient, is the End at which all actions aim.

To say however that the Supreme Good is happiness will probably appear a truism; we still require a more explicit account of what constitutes happiness. Perhaps then we may arrive at this by ascertaining what is man's function. For the goodness or efficiency of a flute-player or sculptor or craftsman of any sort, and in general of anybody who has some function or business to perform, is thought to reside in that function; and similarly it may be held that the good of man resides in the function of man, if he has a function.

Are we then to suppose that, while the carpenter and the shoemaker have definite functions or businesses belonging to them, man as such has none, and is not designed by nature to fulfill any function? Must we not rather assume that, just as the eye, the hand, the foot and each of the various members of the body manifestly has a certain function of its own, so a human being also has a certain function over and above all the functions of his particular members? What then precisely can this function be? The mere act of living appears to be shared even by plants, whereas we are looking for the function peculiar to man; we must therefore set aside the vital activity of nutrition and growth. Next in the scale will come some form of sentient life; but this too appears to be shared by horses, oxen, and animals generally. There remains therefore what may be called the practical[11] life of the rational part of man. (This part has two divisions, one rational as obedient to principle, the other as possessing principle and exercising intelligence).[12] Rational life again has two meanings; let us assume that we are here concerned with the active exercise of the rational faculty,[13] since this seems to be the more proper sense of the term. If then the function of man is the active exercise of the soul's faculties[14] in conformity with rational principle, or at all events not in dissociation from rational principle, and if we acknowledge the function of an individual and of a good individual of the same class (for instance, a harper and a good harper, and so generally with all classes) to be generically the same, the qualification of the latter's superiority in excellence being added to the function in his case (I mean that if the function of a harper is to

9. Literally "a political thing." Elsewhere, *Politics*, 1253, Aristotle says "a political animal."
10. But as including all other things as the end includes the means.
11. "Practice" for Aristotle denotes purposeful conduct of which only rational beings are capable.
12. On grounds of the Greek text, this parenthesis has been suspected as an interpretation, and perhaps should be left out and the preceding words rendered "the practical life of a rational being."
13. In contrast with the mere state of possessing the faculty.
14. Literally "activity of the soul."

play the harp, that of a good harper is to play the harp well): if this is so, and if we declare that the function of man is a certain form of life, and define that form of life as the exercise of the soul's faculties and activities in association with rational principle, and say that the function of a good man is to perform these activities well and rightly, and if a function is well performed when it is performed in accordance with its own proper excellence—from these premises it follows that the Good of man is the active exercise of his soul's faculties in conformity with excellence or virtue, or if there be several human excellences or virtues, in conformity with the best and most perfect among them. Moreover this activity must occupy a complete lifetime for one swallow does not make spring, nor does one fine day; and similarly one day or a brief period of happiness does not make a man supremely blessed and happy.

Let this account then serve to describe the Good in outline—for no doubt the proper procedure is to begin by making a rough sketch, and to fill it in afterwards. If a work has been well laid down in outline, to carry it on and complete it in detail may be supposed to be within the capacity of anybody; and in this working out of details Time seems to be a good inventor or at all events coadjutor. This indeed is how advances in the arts have actually come about, since anyone can fill in the gaps. Also the warning given above[15] a must not be forgotten; we must not look for equal exactness in all departments of study, but only such as belongs to the subject matter of each, and in such a degree as is appropriate to the particular line of enquiry. A carpenter and a geometrician both seek after a right angle, but in different ways; the former is content with that approximation to it which satisfies the purpose of his work; the latter, being a student of truth, looks for its essence or essential attributes. We should therefore proceed in the same manner in other subjects also, and not allow side issues to outweigh the main task in hand.

Nor again must we in all matters alike demand an explanation of the reason why things are what they are; in some cases it is enough if the fact that they are so is satisfactorily established. This is the case with first principles; and the fact is the primary thing—it *is* a first principle. And principles are studied—some by induction, others by perception, others by some form of habituation, and also others otherwise; so we must endeavor to arrive at the principles of each kind in their natural manner, and must also be careful to define them correctly, since they are of great importance for the subsequent course of the enquiry. The beginning is admittedly more than half of the whole,[16] and throws light at once on many of the questions under investigation.

1.13. But inasmuch as happiness is a certain activity of soul in conformity with perfect goodness, it is necessary to examine the nature of goodness. For this will probably assist us in our investigation of the nature of happiness. Also, the true statesman seems to be one who has made a special study of goodness, since his aim is to make the citizens good and law-abiding men— witness the lawgivers of Crete and Sparta, and the other great legislators of history but if the study of goodness falls within the province of Political Science, it is clear that in investigating goodness we shall be keeping to the plan which we adopted at the outset.

---

15. See 1.3.

16. The usual form of the proverb is "The beginning is half of the whole." By a sort of play on words, Aristotle transforms this, in a sense, into a general principle of science, which is a "beginning" in the sense that it is the starting point of deductive reasoning.

Now the goodness that we have to consider is clearly human goodness, since the good or happiness which we set out to seek was human good and human happiness. But human goodness means in our view excellence of soul, not excellence of body; also our definition of happiness is an activity of the soul. Now if this is so, clearly it behooves the statesman to have some acquaintance with psychology, just as the physician who is to heal the eye or the other parts of the body must know their anatomy. Indeed a foundation of science is even more requisite for the statesman, inasmuch as politics is a higher and more honorable art than medicine; but physicians of the better class devote much attention to the study of the human body. The student of politics[17] therefore as well as the psychologist must study the nature of the soul, though he will do so as an aid to politics, and only so far as is requisite for the objects of enquiry that he has in view to pursue the subject in further detail would doubtless be more laborious than is necessary for his purpose.

Now on the subject of psychology some of the teaching current in extraneous discourses[18] is satisfactory, and may be adopted here: namely that the soul consists of two parts, one irrational and the other capable of reason. (Whether these two parts are really distinct in the sense that the parts of the body or of any other divisible whole are distinct, or whether though distinguishable in thought as two they are inseparable in reality, like the convex and concave sides of a curve, is a question of no importance for the matter in hand.) Of the irrational part of the soul again one division appears to be common to all living things, and of a vegetative nature: I refer to the part that causes nutrition and growth; for we must assume that a vital faculty of this nature exists in all things that assimilate nourishment, including embryos—the same faculty being present also in the fully-developed organism (this is more reasonable than to assume a different nutritive faculty in the latter). The excellence of this faculty therefore appears to be common to all animate things and not peculiar to man; for it is believed that this faculty or part of the soul is most active during sleep, but when they are asleep you cannot tell a good man from a bad one (whence the saying that for half their lives there is no difference between the happy and the miserable). This is a natural result of the fact that sleep is a cessation of the soul from the activities on which its goodness or badness depends—except that in some small degree certain of the sense-impressions may reach the soul during sleep, and consequently the dreams of the good are better than those of ordinary men. We need not however pursue this subject further, but may omit from consideration the nutritive part of the soul, since it exhibits no specifically human excellence.

But there also appears to be another element in the soul, which, though irrational, yet in a manner participates in rational principle. In self-restrained and unrestrained people we approve their principle, or the rational part of their souls, because it urges them in the right way and exhorts them to the best course; but their nature seems also to contain another element beside that of rational principle, which combats and resists that principle. Exactly the same thing may take place in the soul as occurs with the body in a case of paralysis: when the patient wills to move his limbs to the right they swerve to the left; and similarly in unrestrained persons their impulses run

17. To Aristotle "political scientist" and "statesman" mean the same thing.
18. These "discourses" are mentioned in seven other places by Aristotle. The phrase therefore seems to denote arguments or doctrines, weather familiar in philosophic debates, or actually recorded in books, that were not peculiar to the Peripatetic school; in some case, as here, it may refer specially to the tenets of the Academy.

counter to their principle. But whereas in the body we see the erratic member, in the case of the soul we do not see it; nevertheless it cannot be doubted that in the soul also there is an element beside that of principle, which opposes and runs counter to principle (though in what sense the two are distinct does not concern us here). But this second element also seems, as we said, to participate in rational principle; at least in the self-restrained man it obeys the behest of principle—and no doubt in the temperate and brave man it is still more amenable, for all parts of his nature are in harmony with principle.

Thus we see that the irrational part, as well as the soul as a whole, is double. One division of it, the vegetative, does not share in rational principle at all; the other, the seat of the appetites and of desire in general, does in a sense participate in principle, as being amenable and obedient to it (in the sense in fact in which we speak of 'paying heed' to one's father and friends, not in the sense of the term 'rational' in mathematics)[19] And that principle can in a manner appeal to the irrational part, is indicated by our practice of admonishing delinquents, and by our employment of rebuke and exhortation generally.

If on the other hand it be more correct to speak of the appetitive part of the soul also as rational, in that case it is the rational part which, as well as the whole soul, is divided into two, the one division having rational principle in the proper sense and in itself, the other obedient to it as a child to its father.

Now virtue also is differentiated in correspondence with this division of the soul. Some forms of virtue are called intellectual virtues, others moral virtues Wisdom or intelligence and Prudence[20] are intellectual, Liberality and Temperance are moral virtues. When describing a man's moral character we do not say that he is wise or intelligent, but gentle or temperate; but a wise man also is praised for his disposition,[21] and praiseworthy dispositions we term virtues.

2.1. Virtue being, as we have seen, of two kinds, intellectual and moral, intellectual virtue is for the most part both produced and increased by instruction, and therefore requires experience and time; whereas moral or ethical virtue is the product of habit (ethos), and has indeed derived its name, with a slight variation of form, from that word. And therefore it is clear that none of the moral virtues is engendered in us by nature, for no natural property can be altered by habit. For instance, it is the nature of a stone to move downwards, and it cannot be trained to move upwards, even though you should try to train it to do so by throwing it up into the air ten thousand times; nor can fire be trained to move downwards, nor can anything else that naturally behaves

---

19. This parenthetical note on the phrase 'to have *logos*' is untranslatable, and confusing even in the Greek. According to the psychology here expounded, the intellect 'has a plan or principle,' in the sense of understanding principle, and being able to reason and make a plan: in other words, it is fully rational. The appetitive part of man's nature 'has a plan or principle' in so far as it is capable of following or obeying a principle. It happens that this relationship of following or obeying can itself be expressed by the words 'to have *logos*' in another sense of that phrase, viz. 'to take account of pay heed to.' To be precise the writer should say that the appetitive part 'has Logos (takes account of) the *Logos*.' The phrase has yet a third sense in mathematics, where "to have Logo." (*ratio*) means "to be rational" in the sense of commensurable.

20. I.e., practical, as distinguished from speculative, wisdom.

21. That is to say, Speculative Wisdom (as distinguished from Prudence or Practical Wisdom), which is therefore a virtue, though not a virtue on the narrower sense of a moral virtue. Throughout Aristotle's ethical works, praise and blame are the ordinary tests of virtue and vice.

in one way be trained into a habit of behaving in another way. The virtues[22] therefore are engendered in us neither by nature nor yet in violation of nature; nature gives us the capacity to receive them, and this capacity is brought to maturity by habit.

Moreover, the faculties given us by nature are bestowed on us first in a potential form; we exhibit their actual exercise afterwards. This is clearly so with our senses: we did not acquire the faculty of sight or hearing by repeatedly seeing or repeatedly listening, but the other way about—because we had the senses we began to use them, we did not get them by using them. The virtues on the other hand we acquire by first having actually practiced them, just as we do the arts. We learn an art or craft by doing the things that we shall have to do when we have learnt it: for instance, men become builders by building houses, harpers by playing on the harp. Similarly we become just by doing just acts, temperate by doing temperate acts, brave by doing brave acts. This truth is attested by the experience of states lawgivers make the citizens good by training them in habits of right action—this is the aim of all legislation, and if it fails to do this it is a failure; this is what distinguishes a good form of constitution from a bad one. Again, the actions from or through which any virtue is produced are the same as those through which it also is destroyed—just as is the case with skill in the arts, for both the good harpers and the bad ones are produced by harping, and similarly with builders and all the other craftsmen: as you will become a good builder from building well, so you will become a bad one from building badly. Were this not so, there would be no need for teachers of the arts, but everybody would be born a good or bad craftsman as the case might be. The same then is true of the virtues. It is by taking part in transactions with our fellow-men that some of us become just and others unjust; by acting in dangerous situations and forming a habit of fear or of confidence we become courageous or cowardly. And the same holds good of our dispositions with regard to the appetites, and anger; some men become temperate and gentle, other profligate and irascible, by actually comporting themselves in one way or the other in relation to those passions. In a word, our moral dispositions are formed as a result of the corresponding activities. Hence it is incumbent on us to control the character of our activities, since on the quality of these depends the quality of our dispositions. It is therefore not of small moment whether we are trained from childhood in one set of habits or another; on the contrary it is of very great, or rather of supreme, importance.

2.6. But it is not enough merely to define virtue generically as a disposition; we must also say what species of disposition it is. It must then be premised that all excellence has a twofold effect on the thing to which it belongs it not only renders the thing itself good, but it also causes it to perform its function well. For example, the effect of excellence in the eye is that the eye is good *and* functions well; since having good eyes means having good sight. Similarly excellence in a horse makes it a good horse, and also good at galloping, at carrying its rider, and at facing the enemy. If therefore this is true of all things, excellence or virtue in a man will be the disposition which renders him a good man and also which will cause him to perform his function well. We have already indicated what this means; but it will throw more light on the subject if we consider what constitutes the specific nature of virtue.

---

22. *Arete* is here, as often in this and the following books, employed in the limited sense of "moral excellence" or "goodness of character," i.e. virtue in the ordinary sense of the term.

Now of everything that is continuous[23] and divisible, it is possible to take the larger part, or the smaller part, or an equal part, and these parts may be larger, smaller, and equal either with respect to the thing itself or relatively to us; the equal part being a mean between excess and deficiency.[24] By the mean of the thing I denote a point equally distant from either extreme, which is one and the same for everybody; by the mean relative to us, that amount which is neither too much nor too little, and this is not one and the same for everybody. For example, let 10 be many and 2 few; then one takes the mean with respect to the thing if one takes 6; since 6 − 2 = 10 − 6, and this is the mean according to arithmetical proportion. But we cannot arrive by this method at the mean relative to us. Suppose that 10 lb. of food is a large ration for anybody and 2 lb. a small one: it does not follow that a trainer will prescribe 6 lb., for perhaps even this will be a large ration, or a small one, for the particular athlete who is to receive it; it is a small ration for a Milo,[25] but a large one for a man just beginning to go in for athletics. And similarly with the amount of running or wrestling exercise to be taken. In the same way then an expert in any art avoids excess and deficiency, and seeks and adopts the mean—the mean, that is, not of the thing but relative to us. If therefore the way in which every art or science performs its work well is by looking to the mean and applying that as a standard to its productions (hence the common remark about a perfect work of art, that you could not take from it nor add to it—meaning that excess and deficiency destroy perfection, while adherence to the mean preserves it)—if then, as we say, good craftsmen look to the mean as they work, and if virtue, like nature, is more accurate and better than any form of art, it will follow that virtue has the quality of hitting the mean. I refer to moral virtue,[26] for this is concerned with emotions and actions, in which one can have excess or deficiency or a due mean. For example, one can be frightened or bold, feel desire or anger or pity, and experience pleasure and pain in general, either too much or too little, and in both cases wrongly; whereas to feel these feelings at the right time, on the right occasion, towards the right people, for the right purpose and in the right manner, is to feel the best amount of them, which is the mean amount—and the best amount is of course the mark of virtue. And similarly there can be excess, deficiency, and the due mean in actions. Now feelings and actions are the objects with which virtue is concerned; and in feelings and actions excess and deficiency are errors, while the mean amount is praised, and constitutes success; and to be praised and to be successful are both marks of virtue. Virtue, therefore, is a mean state in the sense that it is able to hit the mean. Again, error is multiform (for evil is a form of the unlimited, as in the old Pythagorean imagery, and good of the limited), whereas success is possible in one way only (which is why it is easy to fail and difficult

---

23. I.e., without distinct parts, and so (if divisible at all, divisible at any point, as contrasted to what is "discrete," or made up of distinct parts and only divisible between them.

24. Greek comparatives, "larger," "smaller," etc., may also mean "too large," "too small," etc. and there is the same ambiguity in the words translated "excess" "and deficiency." Hence "to take an equal part with respect to the thing itself" means to take a part equal to the part left, that is to say, a half; "to take an equal part relatively to us," means to take what is a fair or suitable amount. The former is a mean as being exactly in the middle between all and none—if the thing in question is represented by a line, this is bisected at a point equidistant from its two ends; the latter is a mean in the sense of being the right amount for the recipient, and also of lying somewhere between any two other amounts that happen to be too much and too little for him.

25. A famous wrestler.

26. The formula of the mean does not apply to the intellectual virtues.

to succeed—easy to miss the target and difficult to hit it); so this is another reason why excess and deficiency are a mark of vice, and observance of the mean a mark of virtue:

"Goodness is simple, badness manifold."[27]

Virtue then is a settled disposition of the mind determining the choice of actions and emotions, consisting essentially in the observance of the mean relative to us, this being determined by principle, that is, as the prudent man would determine it.

And it is a mean state between two vices, one of excess and one of defect. Furthermore, it is a mean state in that whereas the vices either fall short of or exceed what is right in feelings and in actions, virtue ascertains and adopts the mean. Hence while in respect of its substance and the definition that states what it really is in essence virtue is the observance of the mean, in point of excellence and rightness it is an extreme.

Not every action or emotion however admits of the observance of a due mean. Indeed the very names of some directly imply evil, for instance malice, shamelessness, envy, and, of actions, adultery, theft, murder. All these and similar actions and feelings are blamed as being bad in themselves; it is not the excess or deficiency of them that we blame. It is impossible therefore ever to go right in regard to them—one must always be wrong; nor does right or wrong in their case depend on the circumstances, for instance, whether one commits adultery with the right woman, at the right time, and in the right manner; the mere commission of any of them is wrong. One might as well suppose there could be a due mean and excess and deficiency in acts of injustice or cowardice or profligacy, which would imply that one could have a medium amount of excess and of deficiency, an excessive amount of excess and a deficient amount of deficiency. But just as there can be no excess or deficiency in temperance and justice, because the mean is in a sense an extreme, so there can be no observance of the mean nor excess nor deficiency in the corresponding vicious acts mentioned above, but however they are committed, they are wrong; since, to put it in general terms, there is no such thing as observing a mean in excess or deficiency, nor as exceeding or falling short in the observance of a mean

10.7. But if happiness consists in activity in accordance with virtue, it is reasonable that it should be activity in accordance with the highest virtue; and this will be the virtue of the best part of us. Whether then this be the intellect, or whatever else it be that is thought to rule and lead us by nature, and to have cognizance of what is noble and divine, either as being itself also actually divine, or as being relatively the most divine part of us, it is the activity of this part of us in accordance with the virtue proper to it that will constitute perfect happiness; and it has been stated already that this activity is the activity of contemplation.

And that happiness consists in contemplation may be accepted as agreeing both with the results already reached and with the truth. For contemplation is at once the highest form of activity (since the intellect is the highest thing in us, and the objects with which the intellect deals are the highest things that can be known), and also it is the most continuous, for we can reflect more continuously than we can carry on any form of action. And again we suppose that happiness must contain an element of pleasure; now activity in accordance with wisdom is admittedly the most

---

27. A verse from an unknown source.

pleasant of the activities in accordance with virtue at all events it is held that philosophy or the pursuit of wisdom contains pleasures of marvelous purity and permanence, and it is reasonable to suppose that the enjoyment of knowledge is a still more pleasant occupation than the pursuit of it. Also the activity of contemplation will be found to possess in the highest degree the quality that is termed self-sufficiency; for while it is true that the wise man equally with the just man and the rest requires the necessaries of life, yet, these being adequately supplied, whereas the just man needs other persons towards whom or with whose aid he may act justly, and so likewise do the temperate man and the brave man and the others, the wise man on the contrary can also contemplate by himself, and the more so the wiser he is; no doubt he will study better with the aid of fellow-workers, but still he is the most self-sufficient of men. Also the activity of contemplation may be held to be the only activity that is loved for its own sake it produces no result beyond the actual act of contemplation, whereas from practical pursuits we look to secure some advantage, greater or smaller, beyond the action itself. Also happiness is thought to involve leisure for we do business in order that we may have leisure, and carry on war in order that we may have peace. Now the practical virtues are exercised in politics or in warfare; but the pursuits of politics and war seem to be unleisured—those of war indeed entirely so, for no one desires to be at war for the sake of being at war, nor deliberately takes steps to cause war: a man would be thought an utterly bloodthirsty character if he declared war on a friendly state for the sake of causing battles and massacres. But the activity of the politician also is unleisured, and aims at securing something beyond the mere participation in politics—positions of authority and honor, or, if the happiness of the politician himself and of his fellow-citizens, this happiness conceived as something distinct from political activity (indeed we are clearly investigating it as so distinct)[28] If then among practical pursuits displaying the virtues, politics and war stand out pre-eminent in nobility and grandeur, and yet they are unleisured, and directed to some further end, not chosen for their own sakes whereas the activity of the intellect is felt to excel in serious worth,[29] consisting as it does in contemplation, and to aim at no end beyond itself, and also to contain a pleasure peculiar to itself, and therefore augmenting its activity: and if accordingly the attributes of this activity are found to be self-sufficiency, leisuredness, such freedom from fatigue as is possible for man, and all the other attributes of blessedness: it follows that it is the activity of the intellect that constitutes complete human happiness—provided it be granted a complete span of life, for nothing that belongs to happiness can be incomplete.

Such a life as this however will be higher than the human level: not in virtue of his humanity will a man achieve it, but in virtue of something within him that is divine; and by as much as this something is superior to his composite nature, by so much is its activity superior to the exercise of the other forms of virtue. If then the intellect is something divine in comparison with man, so is the life of the intellect divine in comparison with human life. Nor ought we to obey those who enjoin that a man should have man's thoughts[30] and a mortal the thoughts of mortality,[31] but we

---

28. Probably the sentence should be curtailed to run "or in fact the happiness of himself and his fellow citizens; and happiness we are clearly investigating as something distinct from the art of politics [whose object it is]."

29. This should almost certainly be emended to "excel in leisuredness."

30. Euripides, *Fragment* 1040.

31. Pindar, *Isthmian Odes* 4.16.

ought so far as possible to achieve immortality, and do all that man may to live in accordance with the highest thing in him for though this be small in bulk, in power and value it far surpasses all the rest.

It may even be held that this is the true self of each, inasmuch as it is the dominant and better part; and therefore it would be a strange thing if a man should choose to live not his own life but the life of some other than himself.

Moreover what was said before will apply here also: that which is best and most pleasant for each creature is that which is proper to the nature of each; accordingly the life of the intellect is the best and the pleasantest life for man, inasmuch as the intellect more than anything else is man; therefore this life will be the happiest.

10.8. The life of moral virtue, on the other hand, is happy only in a secondary degree. For the moral activities are purely human: Justice, I mean, Courage and the other virtues we display in our intercourse with our fellows, when we observe what is due to each in contracts and services and in our various actions, and in our emotions also; and all of these things seem to be purely human affairs. And some moral actions are thought to be the outcome of the physical constitution, and moral virtue is thought to have a close affinity in many respects with the passions. Moreover, Prudence is intimately connected with Moral Virtue, and this with Prudence, inasmuch as the first principles which Prudence employs are determined by the Moral Virtues, and the right standard for the Moral Virtues is determined by Prudence. But these being also connected with the passions are related to our composite nature; now the virtues of our composite nature are purely human; so therefore also is the life that manifests these virtues, and the happiness that belongs to it. Whereas the happiness that belongs to the intellect is separate: so much may be said about it here, for a full discussion of the matter is beyond the scope of our present purpose.[32] And such happiness would appear to need but little external equipment, or less than the happiness based on moral virtue. Both, it may be granted, require the mere necessaries of life, and that in an equal degree (though the politician does as a matter of fact take more trouble about bodily requirements and so forth than the philosopher); for in this respect there may be little difference between them. But for the purpose of their special activities their requirements will differ widely. The liberal man will need wealth in order to do liberal actions, and so indeed will the just man in order to discharge his obligations (since mere intentions are invisible, and even the unjust pretend to wish to act justly); and the brave man will need strength if he is to perform any action displaying his virtue; and the temperate man opportunity for indulgence: otherwise how can he, or the possessor of any other virtue, show that he is virtuous? It is disputed also whether purpose or performance is the more important factor in virtue, as it is alleged to depend on both; now the perfection of virtue will clearly consist in both; but the performance of virtuous actions requires much outward equipment, and the more so the greater and more noble the actions are. But the student, so far as the pursuit of his activity is concerned, needs no external apparatus: on the contrary, worldly goods may almost be said to be a hindrance to contemplation; though it is true that, being a man and living in the society of others, he chooses to engage in virtuous action, and so will need external goods to carry on his life as a human being.

---

32. In De anima, 3.5, Aristotle distinguishes the active from the passive intellect, and pronounces the former to be "separate or separable (from matter, or the body), unmixed and impassible."

The following considerations also will show that perfect happiness is some form of contemplative activity. The gods, as we conceive them, enjoy supreme felicity and happiness. But what sort of actions can we attribute to them? Just actions? but will it not seem ridiculous to think of them as making contracts, restoring deposits and the like? Then brave actions—enduring terrors and running risks for the nobility of so doing? Or liberal actions? but to whom will they give? Besides, it would be absurd to suppose that they actually have a coinage or currency of some sort! And temperate actions—what will these mean in their case? surely it would be derogatory to praise them for not having evil desires! If we go through the list we shall find that all forms of virtuous conduct seem trifling and unworthy of the gods. Yet nevertheless they have always been conceived as, at all events, living, and therefore living actively, for we cannot suppose they are always asleep like Endymion.[33] But for a living being, if we eliminate action, and *a fortiori* creative action, what remains save contemplation? It follows that the activity of God, which is transcendent in blessedness, is the activity of contemplation; and therefore among human activities that which is most akin to the divine activity of contemplation will be the greatest source of happiness.

A further confirmation is that the lower animals cannot partake of happiness, because they are completely devoid of the contemplative activity. The whole of the life of the gods is blessed, and that of man is so in so far as it contains some likeness to the divine activity; but none of the other animals possess happiness, because they are entirely incapable of contemplation. Happiness therefore is co-extensive in its range with contemplation: the more a class of beings possesses the faculty of contemplation, the more it enjoys happiness, not as an accidental concomitant of contemplation but as inherent in it, since contemplation is valuable in itself. It follows that happiness is some form of contemplation.

But the philosopher being a man will also need external well-being, since man's nature is not self-sufficient for the activity of contemplation, but he must also have bodily health and a supply of food and other requirements. Yet if supreme blessedness is not possible without external goods, it must not be supposed that happiness will demand many or great possessions; for self-sufficiency does not depend on excessive abundance, nor does moral conduct, and it is possible to perform noble deeds even without being ruler of land and sea one can do virtuous acts with quite moderate resources. This may be clearly observed in experience: private citizens do not seem to be less but more given to doing virtuous actions than princes and potentates. It is sufficient then if moderate resources are forthcoming; for a life of virtuous activity will be essentially a happy life.

Solon also doubtless gave a good description of happiness,[34] when he said that in his opinion those men were happy who, being moderately equipped with external goods, had performed noble exploits and had lived temperately; for it is possible for a man of but moderate possessions to do what is right. Anaxagoras again does not seem to have conceived the happy man as rich or powerful, since he says that he would not be surprised if he were to appear a strange sort of person in

---

33. Endymion was the son of Zeus and Calyce. The moon goddess Artemis saw Endymion naked as he slept on Mount Latmos and was so enamored of his beauty that she came down from heaven and made love to him in his dreams. Endymion begged Zeus for perpetual youth, sleep, and immortality so he could prolong this pleasant dream forever. Artemis bore him fifty daughters and according to legend she still visits him nightly in his immortal sleep.

34. Solon in his conversation with Croesus, Herodotus 1.30–32, says that Tellus the Athenian was the happiest man he ever knew. Tellus was well off, he lived to see his children's children, and died gloriously in battle.

the eyes of the many; for most men judge by externals, which are all that they can perceive. So our theories seem to be in agreement with the opinions of the wise.

Such arguments then carry some degree of conviction; but it is by the practical experience of life and conduct that the truth is really tested, since it is there that the final decision lies. We must therefore examine the conclusions we have advanced by bringing them to the test of the facts of life. If they are in harmony with the facts, we may accept them if found to disagree, we must deem them mere theories.

And it seems likely that the man who pursues intellectual activity, and who cultivates his intellect and keeps that in the best condition, is also the man most beloved of the gods. For if, as is generally believed, the gods exercise some superintendence over human affairs, then it will be reasonable to suppose that they take pleasure in that part of man which is best and most akin to themselves, namely the intellect, and that they recompense with their favors those men who esteem and honor this most, because these care for the things dear to themselves, and act rightly and nobly. Now it is clear that all these attributes belong most of all to the wise man. He therefore is most beloved by the gods; and if so, he is naturally most happy. Here is another proof that the wise man is the happiest.

10.9. If then we have sufficiently discussed in their outlines the subjects of Happiness and of Virtue in its various forms, and also Friendship and Pleasure, may we assume that the investigation we proposed is now complete? Perhaps however, as we maintain, in the practical sciences the end is not to attain a theoretic knowledge of the various subjects, but rather to carry out our theories in action. If so, to know what virtue is is not enough; we must endeavor to possess and to practice it, or in some other manner actually ourselves to become good.

Now if discourses on ethics were sufficient in themselves to make men virtuous, "large fees and many" (as Theognis[35] says) "would they win," quite rightly, and to provide such discourses would be all that is wanted. But as it is, we see that although theories have power to stimulate and encourage generous youths, and, given an inborn nobility of character and a genuine love of what is noble, can make them susceptible to the influence of virtue, yet they are powerless to stimulate the mass of mankind to moral nobility. For it is the nature of the many to be amenable to fear but not to a sense of honor, and to abstain from evil not because of its baseness but because of the penalties it entails; since, living as they do by passion, they pursue the pleasures akin to their nature, and the things that will procure those pleasures, and avoid the opposite pains, but have not even a notion of what is noble and truly pleasant, having never tasted true pleasure. What theory then can reform the natures of men like these? To dislodge by argument habits long firmly rooted in their characters is difficult if not impossible. We may doubtless think ourselves fortunate if we attain some measure of virtue when all the things believed to make men virtuous are ours.

Now some thinkers hold that virtue is a gift of nature; others think we become good by habit, others that we can be taught to be good. Natural endowment is obviously not under our control;

---

35. Theognis, 432 ff:
If to physicians God had given
The power to cure mankind of sin,
Large fees and many would they win.

it is bestowed on those who are fortunate, in the true sense, by some divine dispensation. Again, theory and teaching are not, I fear, equally efficacious in all cases the soil must have been previously tilled if it is to foster the seed, the mind of the pupil must have been prepared by the cultivation of habits, so as to like and dislike aright. For he that lives at the dictates of passion will not hear nor understand the reasoning of one who tries to dissuade him; but if so, how can you change his mind by argument?

And, speaking generally, passion seems not to be amenable to reason, but only to force.

We must therefore by some means secure that the character shall have at the outset a natural affinity for virtue, loving what is noble and hating what is base. And it is difficult to obtain a right education in virtue from youth up without being brought up under right laws; for to live temperately and hardily is not pleasant to most men, especially when young; hence the nurture and exercises of the young should be regulated by law, since temperance and hardiness will not be painful when they have become habitual. But doubtless it is not enough for people to receive the right nurture and discipline in youth; they must also practice the lessons they have learnt, and confirm them by habit, when they are grown up. Accordingly we shall need laws to regulate the discipline of adults as well, and in fact the whole life of the people generally; for the many are more amenable to compulsion and punishment than to reason and to moral ideals. Hence some persons hold, that while it is proper for the lawgiver to encourage and exhort men to virtue on moral grounds, in the expectation that those who have had a virtuous moral upbringing will respond, yet he is bound to impose chastisement and penalties on the disobedient and ill-conditioned, and to banish the incorrigible out of the state altogether. For (they argue) although the virtuous man, who guides his life by moral ideals, will be obedient to reason, the base, whose desires are fixed on pleasure, must be chastised by pain, like a beast of burden. This indeed is the ground for the view that the pains and penalties for transgressors should be such as are most opposed to their favorite pleasures.

But to resume: if, as has been said, in order to be good a man must have been properly educated and trained, and must subsequently continue to follow virtuous habits of life, and to do nothing base whether voluntarily or involuntarily, then this will be secured if men's lives are regulated by a certain intelligence, and by a right system, invested with adequate sanctions. Now paternal authority has not the power to compel obedience, nor indeed, speaking generally, has the authority of any individual unless he be a king or the like; but law on the other hand is a rule, emanating from a certain wisdom and intelligence, that has compulsory force. Men are hated when they thwart people's inclinations, even though they do so rightly, whereas law can enjoin virtuous conduct without being invidious. But Sparta appears to be the only or almost the only state in which the lawgiver has paid attention to the nurture and exercises of the citizens; in most states such matters have been entirely neglected, and every man lives as he likes, in Cyclops fashion "laying down the law for children and for spouse."[36]

The best thing is then that there should be a proper system of public regulation; but when the matter is neglected by the community, it would seem to be the duty of the individual to assist his own children and friends to attain virtue, or even if not able to do so successfully, at all events to make this his aim. But it would seem to follow from what has been said before, that he will be

---

36. Homer, *Odyssey*, 9.114.

more likely to be successful in this if he has acquired the science of legislation. Public regulations in any case must clearly be established by law, and only good laws will produce good regulations; but it would not seem to make any difference whether these laws are written or unwritten, or whether they are to regulate the education of a single person or of a number of people, any more than in the case of music or athletics or any other form of training. Paternal exhortations and family habits have authority in the household, just as legal enactments and national customs have authority in the state, and the more so on account of the ties of relationship and of benefits conferred that unite the head of the household to its other members he can count on their natural affection and obedience at the outset. Moreover individual treatment is better than a common system, in education as in medicine. As a general rule rest and fasting are good for a fever, but they may not be best for a particular case; and presumably a professor of boxing does not impose the same style of fighting on all his pupils. It would appear then that private attention gives more accurate results in particular cases, for the particular subject is more likely to get the treatment that suits him. But a physician or trainer or any other director can best treat a particular person if he has a general knowledge of what is good for everybody, or for other people of the same kind: for the sciences deal with what is universal, as their names imply.[37] Not but what it is possible no doubt for a particular individual to be successfully treated by someone who is not a scientific expert, but has an empirical knowledge based on careful observation of the effects of various forms of treatment upon the person in question; just as some people appear to be their own best doctors, though they could not do any good to someone else. But nevertheless it would doubtless be agreed that anyone who wishes to make himself a professional and a man of science must advance to general principles, and acquaint himself with these by the proper method: for science, as we said, deals with the universal. So presumably a man who wishes to make other people better (whether few or many) by discipline, must endeavor to acquire the science of legislation—assuming that it is possible to make us good by laws. For to mould aright the character of any and every person that presents himself is not a task that can be done by anybody, but only (if at all) by the man with scientific knowledge, just as is the case in medicine and the other professions involving a system of treatment and the exercise of prudence.

Is not then the next question to consider from whom or how the science of legislation can be learnt? Perhaps, like other subjects, from the experts, namely the politicians; for we saw that legislation is a branch of political science. But possibly it may seem that political science is unlike the other sciences and faculties. In these the persons who impart a knowledge of the faculty are the same as those who practice it, for instance physicians and painters but in politics the sophists, who profess to teach the science, never practice it. It is practiced by the politicians, who would appear to rely more upon a sort of empirical shill than on the exercise of abstract intelligence; for we do not see them writing or lecturing about political principles (though this might be a more honorable employment than composing forensic and parliamentary speeches), nor yet do we notice that they have made their own sons or any others of their friends into statesmen. Yet we should expect them to have done so had they been able, for they could have bequeathed no more valuable legacy to their countries, nor is there any quality they would choose for themselves, and therefore for those nearest to them, to possess, in preference to political capacity. Not that expe-

---

37. That is, medicine is the "science of healing" not the "science of healing Brown or Jones."

rience does not seem to contribute considerably to political success; otherwise men would never have become statesmen merely through practical association with politics; so it would appear that those who aspire to a scientific knowledge of politics require practical experience as well as study. On the other hand those sophists who profess to teach politics are found to be very far from doing so successfully. In fact they are absolutely ignorant of the very nature of the science and of the subjects with which it deals; otherwise they would not class it as identical with, or even inferior to, the art of rhetoric. Nor would they imagine that it is easy to frame a constitution by making a collection of such existing laws as are reputed to be good ones, on the assumption that one can then select the best among them; as if even this selection did not call for understanding, and as if to judge correctly were not a very difficult task, just as much as it is for instance in music. It is only the experts in an art who can judge correctly the productions of that art, and who understand the means and the method by which perfection is attained, and know which elements harmonize with which; amateurs may be content if they can discern whether the general result produced is good or bad, for example in the art of painting. Laws are the product, so to speak, of the art of politics; how then can a mere collection of laws teach a man the science of legislation, or make him able to judge which of them are the best? We do not see men becoming expert physicians from a study of medical handbooks. Yet medical writers attempt to describe not only general courses of treatment, but also methods of cure and modes of treatment for particular sorts of patients, classified according to their various habits of body; and their treatises appear to be of value for men who have had practical experience, though they are useless for the novice. Very possibly therefore collections of laws and constitutions may be serviceable to students capable of studying them critically, and judging what measures are valuable or the reverse, and what kind of institutions are suited to what national characteristics. But those who peruse such compilations without possessing a trained faculty cannot be capable of judging them correctly, unless they do so by instinct, though they may very likely sharpen their political intelligence.

Politics

1.1. Every state is as we see a sort of partnership, and every partnership is formed with a view to some good (since all the actions of all mankind are done with a view to what they think to be good). It is therefore evident that, while all partnerships aim at some good, the partnership that is the most supreme of all and includes all the others does so most of all, and aims at the most supreme of all goods; and this is the partnership entitled the state, the political association. Those[38] then who think that the natures of the statesman, the royal ruler, the head of an estate aid the master of a family are the same, are mistaken; they imagine that the difference between these various forms of authority is one of greater and smaller numbers, not a difference in kind—that is, that the ruler over a few people is a master, over more the head of an estate, over more still a statesman or royal ruler, as if there were no difference between a large household and a small city; and also

Reprinted by permission of the publishers and the Trustees of the Loeb Classical Library from *Aristotle: Volume XXI, Politics*, Loeb Classical Library Volumes L 264, translated by H. Rackham, Cambridge, Mass.: Harvard University Press, 1932. The Loeb Classical Library® is a registered trademark of the President and Fellows of Harvard College.

as to the statesman and the royal ruler, they think that one who governs as sole head is royal, and one who, while the government follows the principles of the science of royalty, takes turns to govern and be governed is a statesman; but these views are not true. And a proof of what we assert will appear if we examine the question in accordance with our regular method of investigation. In every other matter it is necessary to analyze the composite whole down to its uncompounded elements (for these are the smallest parts of the whole); so too with the state, by examining the elements of which it is composed we shall better discern in relation to these different kinds of rulers what is the difference between them, and whether it is possible to obtain any scientific precision in regard to the various statements made above.

In this subject as in others the best method of investigation is to study things in the process of development from the beginning. The first coupling together of persons then to which necessity gives rise is that between those who are unable to exist without one another, namely the union of female and male for the continuance of the species (and this not of deliberate purpose, but with man as with the other animals and with plants there is a natural instinct to desire to leave behind one another being of the same sort as oneself), and the union of natural ruler and natural subject for the sake of security (for one that can foresee with his mind is naturally ruler and naturally master, and one that can do these things with his body is subject and naturally a slave; so that master and slave have the same interest). Thus the female and the slave are by nature distinct (for nature makes nothing as the cutlers make the Delphic knife, in a niggardly way, but one thing for one purpose; for so each tool will be turned out in the finest perfection, if it serves not many uses but one). Yet among barbarians the female and the slave have the same rank; and the cause of this is that barbarians have no class of natural rulers, but with them the conjugal partnership is a partnership of female slave and male slave. Hence the saying of the poets:

"Tis meant that Greeks should rule barbarians" [39]

implying that barbarian and slave are the same in nature. From these two partnerships then is first composed the household, and Hesiod[40] was right when he wrote:

"First and foremost a house and a wife and an ox for the plowing:"

for the ox serves instead of a servant for the poor. The partnership therefore that comes about in the course of nature for everyday purposes is the "house," the persons whom Charondas[41] speaks of as "meal-tub-fellows" and the Cretan Epimenides[42] as "manger-fellows."

---

38. Socrates and Plato.
39. Euripides, *Iphigwnia Aulidensis*, 1400.
40. Hesiod, *Work and Days*, 405.
41. A lawgiver of Catana in Sicily, 6th century B.C. or earlier.
42. A poet and prophet invited to Athens in 596 B.C. to purify it of plague.

On the other hand the primary partnership made up of several households for the satisfaction of not mere daily needs is the village. The village according to the most natural account seems to be a colony from[43] a household, formed of those whom some people speak of as "fellow-nurslings," sons and sons' sons.[44] It is owing to this that our cities were at first under royal sway and that foreign races are so still, because they were made up of parts that were under royal rule; for every household is under the royal rule of its eldest member, so that the colonies from the household were so too, because of the kinship of their members. And this is what Homer means:

"And each one gives law
To sons and eke to spouses" [45]

for his Cyclopes live in scattered families; and that is the way in which people used to live in early times. Also this explains why all races speak of the gods as ruled by a king, because they themselves too are some of them actually now so ruled and in other cases used to be of old; and as men imagine the gods in human form, so also they suppose their manner of life to be like their own

The partnership finally composed of several villages is the city-state; it has at last attained the limit of virtually complete self-sufficiency, and thus, while it comes into existence for the sake of life, it exists for the good life. Hence every city-state exists by nature, inasmuch as the first partnerships so exist; for the city-state is the end of the other partnerships, and nature is an end, since that which each thing is when its growth is completed we speak of as being the nature of each thing, for instance of a man, a horse, a household. Again, the object for which a thing exists, its end, is its chief good; and self-sufficiency is an end, and a chief good. From these things therefore it is clear that the city-state is a natural growth, and that man is by nature a political animal, and a man that is by nature and not merely by fortune citiless is either low in the scale of humanity or above it (like the "clanless, lawless, heartless" man reviled by Homer,[46] for he is by nature citiless and also a lover of war) inasmuch as he resembles an isolated piece at checkers. And why man is a political animal in a greater measure than any bee or any gregarious animal is clear. For nature, as we declare, does nothing without purpose; and man alone of the animals possesses speech. The mere voice, it is true, can indicate pain and pleasure, and therefore is possessed by the other animals as well (for their nature has been developed so far as to have sensations of what is painful and pleasant and to signify those sensations to one another), but speech is designed to indicate the advantageous and the harmful, and therefore also the right and the wrong; for it is the special property of man in distinction from the other animals that he alone has perception of good and bad and right and wrong and the other moral qualities, and it is partnership in these things that makes a household and a city-state.

Thus also the city-state is prior in nature to the household and to each of us individually. For the whole must necessarily be prior to the part; since when the whole body is destroyed, foot or

---

43. Perhaps the Greek should be altered to give "consists of colonies from."
44. The words "sons and dons' sons" are probably an interpolated note.
45. Homer, Odyssey, 9.114, of the Cyclopes.
46. Homer, *Iliad*, 9.63.

hand will not exist except in an equivocal sense, like the sense in which one speaks of a hand sculptured in stone as a hand; because a hand in those circumstances will be a hand spoiled,[47] and all things are defined by their function and capacity, so that when they are no longer such as to perform their function they must not be said to be the same things, but to bear their names in an equivocal sense. It is clear therefore that the state is also prior by nature to the individual; for if each individual when separate is not self-sufficient, he must be related to the whole state as other parts are to their whole, while a man who is incapable of entering into partnership, or who is so self-sufficing that he has no need to do so, is no part of a state, so that he must be either a lower animal or a god.

Therefore the impulse to form a partnership of this kind is present in all men by nature; but the man who first united people in such a partnership was the greatest of benefactors. For as man is the best of the animals when perfected, so he is the worst of all when sundered from law and justice. For unrighteousness is most pernicious when possessed of weapons, and man is born possessing weapons for the use of wisdom and virtue, which it is possible to employ entirely for the opposite ends. Hence when devoid of virtue man is the most unscrupulous and savage of animals, and the worst in regard to sexual indulgence and gluttony. Justice on the other hand is an element of the state; for judicial procedure, which means the decision of what is just, is the regulation of the political partnership.

1.2. And now that it is clear what are the component parts of the state, we have first of all to discuss household management; for every state is composed of households. Household management falls into departments corresponding to the parts of which the household in its turn is composed; and the household in its perfect form consists of slaves and freemen. The investigation of everything should begin with its smallest parts, and the primary and smallest parts of the household are master and slave, husband and wife, father and children; we ought therefore to examine the proper constitution and character of each of these three relationships, I mean that of mastership, that of marriage[48] (there is no exact term denoting the relation uniting wife and husband), and thirdly the progenitive relationship (this too has not been designated by a special name). Let us then accept these three relationships that we have mentioned. There is also a department which some people consider the same as household management and others the most important part of it, and the true position of which we shall have to consider:

I mean what is called the art of getting wealth.[49]

Let us begin by discussing the relation of master and slave, in order to observe the facts that have a bearing on practical utility, and also in the hope that we may be able to obtain something better than the notions at present entertained, with a view to a theoretic knowledge of the subject. For some thinkers hold the function of the master to be a definite science, and moreover think that household management, mastership, statesmanship and monarchy are the same thing, as we said at the beginning of the treatise; others however maintain that for one man to be another man's master is contrary to nature, because it is only convention that makes the one a slave

---

47. Or, "a hand thus spoiled will not be a hand at all."

48 The Greek word properly denotes the marriage ceremony, not the married state.

49. No English word covers all the associations of the Greek, which means "dealing in things," i.e. goods, property, money, and so "business."

and the other a freeman and there is no difference between them by nature, and that therefore it is unjust, for it is based on force.

Since therefore property is a part of a household and the art of acquiring property a part of household management (for without the necessaries even life, as well as the good life,[50] is impossible), and since, just as for the definite arts it would be necessary for the proper tools to be forthcoming if their work is to be accomplished, so also the manager of a household must have his tools, and of tools some are lifeless and others living (for example, for a helmsman the rudder is a lifeless tool and the look-out man a live tool—for an assistant in the arts belongs to the class of tools), so also an article of property is a tool for the purpose of life, and property generally is a collection of tools, and a slave is a live article of property. And every assistant is as it were a tool that serves for several tools; for if every tool could perform its own work when ordered, or by seeing what to do in advance, like the statues of Daedalus[51] in the story, or the tripods of Hephaestus which the poet says "enter self-moved the company divine,"[52] if thus shuttles wove and quills played harps of themselves, master-craftsmen would have no need of assistants and masters no need of slaves. Now the tools mentioned are instruments of production, whereas an article of property is an instrument of action;[53] for from a shuttle we get something else beside the mere use of the shuttle, but from a garment or a bed we get only their use. And also inasmuch as there is a difference in kind between production and action, and both need tools, it follows that those tools also must possess the same difference. But life is doing things, not making things; hence the slave is an assistant in the class of instruments of action.

And the term "article of property" is used in the same way as the term "part:" a thing that is a part is not only a part of another thing but absolutely belongs to another thing, and so also does an article of property. Hence whereas the master is merely the slave's master and does not belong to the slave, the slave is not merely the slave of the master but wholly belongs to the master.

These considerations therefore make clear the nature of the slave and his essential quality one who is a human being belonging by nature not to himself but to another is by nature a slave, and a person is a human being belonging to another if being a man he is an article of property, and an article of property is an instrument for action separable from its owner. But we must next consider whether or not anyone exists who is by nature of this character, and whether it is advantageous and just for anyone to be a slave, or whether on the contrary all slavery is against nature. And it is not difficult either to discern the answer by theory or to learn it empirically. Authority and subordination are conditions not only inevitable but also expedient; in some cases things are marked out from the moment of birth to rule or to be ruled. And there are many varieties both of rulers and of subjects (and the higher the type of the subjects, the loftier is the nature of the authority exercised over them, for example to control a human being is a higher thing than to tame a wild beast; for the higher the type of the parties to the performance of a function, the higher is the function, and when one party rules and another is ruled, there is a function performed between them)—because in every composite thing, where a plurality of parts, whether

---

50. "As well as the good life" is probably an interpolation.
51. This legendary sculptor first represented the eyes as open and the limbs in motion, so his statures had to be chained to prevent them from running away.
52. Homer, *Iliad*, 18.369.
53. I.e. with it we do not *make* something but *do* something (e.g. wear a dress, lie in bed).

continuous or discrete, is combined to make a single common whole, there is always found a ruling and a subject factor, and this characteristic of living things is present in them as an outcome of the whole of nature, since even in things that do not partake of life there is a ruling principle, as in the case of a musical scale. However, this matter perhaps belongs to an investigation lying somewhat outside our subject. But in the first place an animal consists of soul and body, of which the former is by nature the ruling and the latter the subject factor. And to discover what is natural we must study it preferably in things that are in a natural state, and not in specimens that are degenerate. Hence in studying man we must consider a man that is in the best possible condition in regard to both body and soul, and in him the principle stated will clearly appear—since in those that are bad or in a bad condition it might be thought that the body often rules the soul because of its vicious and unnatural condition. But to resume—it is in a living creature, as we say, that it is first possible to discern the rule both of master and of statesman the soul rules the body with the sway of a master, the intelligence the appetites with constitutional or royal rule and in these examples it is manifest that it is natural and expedient for the body to be governed by the soul and for the emotional part to be governed by the intellect, the part possessing reason, whereas for the two parties to be on an equal footing or in the contrary positions is harmful in all cases. Again, the same holds good between man and the other animals tame animals are superior in their nature to wild animals, yet for all the former it is advantageous to be ruled by man, since this gives them security. Also, as between the sexes, the male is by nature superior and the female inferior, the male ruler and the female subject. And the same must also necessarily apply in the case of mankind generally therefore all men that differ as widely as the soul does from the body and the human being from the lower animal (and this is the condition of those whose function is the use of the body and from whom this is the best that is forthcoming)—these are by nature slaves, for whom to be governed by this kind of authority is advantageous, inasmuch as it is advantageous to the subject things already mentioned. For he is by nature a slave who is capable of belonging to another (and that is why he does so belong), and who participates in reason so far as to apprehend it but not to possess it; for the animals other than man are subservient not to reason, by apprehending it, but to feelings. And also the usefulness of slaves diverges little from that of animals; bodily service for the necessities of life is forthcoming from both, from slaves and from domestic animals alike. The intention of nature therefore is to make the bodies also of freemen and of slaves different—the latter strong for necessary service, the former erect and unserviceable for such occupations, but serviceable for a life of citizenship (and that again divides into the employments of war and those of peace); though as a matter of fact often the very opposite comes about—slaves have the bodies of freemen and freemen the souls only; since this is certainly clear, that if freemen were born as distinguished in body as are the statues of the gods, everyone would say that those who were inferior deserved to be these men's slaves; and if this is true in the case of the body, there is far more just reason for this rule being laid down in the case of the soul, but beauty of soul is not so easy to see as beauty of body. It is manifest therefore that there are cases of people of whom some are freemen and the others slaves by nature, and for these slavery is an institution both expedient and just.

But at the same time it is not difficult to see that those who assert the opposite are also right in a manner. The fact is that the terms "slavery" and "slave" are ambiguous; for there is also such a thing as a slave or a man that is in slavery by law, for the law is a sort of agreement under which the things conquered in war are said to belong to their conquerors. Now this conventional right is arraigned by many jurists just as a statesman is impeached for proposing an unconstitutional measure; they say that it is monstrous if the person powerful enough to use force, and superior in power, is to have the victim of his force as his slave and subject; and even among the learned some hold this view, though others hold the other. But the reason of this dispute and what makes the theories overlap is the fact that in a certain manner virtue when it obtains resources has in fact very great power to use force, and the stronger party always possesses superiority in something that is good, so that it is thought that force cannot be devoid of goodness, but that the dispute is merely about the justice of the matter (for it is due to the one party holding that the justification of authority is good-will, while the other identifies justice with the mere rule of the stronger); because obviously if these theories be separated apart, the other theories have no force or plausibility at all, implying that the superior in goodness has no claim to rule and be master. But some persons, doing their best to cling to some principle of justice (for the law is a principle of justice), assert that the enslavement of prisoners of war is just; yet at the same time they deny the assertion, for there is the possibility that wars may be unjust in their origin and one would by no means admit that a man that does not deserve slavery can be really a slave—otherwise we shall have the result that persons reputed of the highest nobility are slaves and the descendants of slaves if they happen to be taken prisoners of war and sold. Therefore they do not mean to assert that Greeks themselves if taken prisoners are slaves, but that barbarians are. Yet when they say this, they are merely seeking for the principles of natural slavery of which we spoke at the outset; for they are compelled to say that there exist certain persons who are essentially slaves everywhere and certain others who are so nowhere. And the same applies also about nobility: our nobles consider themselves noble not only in their own country but everywhere, but they think that barbarian noblemen are only noble in their own country—which implies that there are two kinds of nobility and of freedom, one absolute and the other relative, as Helen says in Theodectes:[54]

"But who would dare to call me menial,
The scion of a twofold stock divine?"

Yet in so speaking they make nothing but virtue and vice the distinction between slave and free, the noble and the base-born; for they assume that just as from a man springs a man and from brutes a brute, so also from good parents comes a good son; but as a matter of fact nature frequently while intending to do this is unable to bring it about.

It is clear therefore that there is some reason for this dispute, and that in some instances it is not the case that one set are slaves and the other freemen by nature; and also that in some instances such a distinction does exist, when slavery for the one and mastership for the other are advantageous, and it is just and proper for the one party to be governed and for the other to govern by the form of government for which they are by nature fitted, and therefore by the exercise of mastership, while to govern badly is to govern disadvantageously for both parties (for the same thing is advantageous for a part and for the whole body or the whole soul, and the slave is a part of the master—he is, as it were, a part of the body, alive but yet separated from it; hence there is

---

54. A tragic poet and friend of Aristotle.

a certain community of interest and friendship between slave and master in cases when they have been qualified by nature for those positions, although when they do not hold them in that way but by law and by constraint of force the opposite is the case).

And even from these considerations it is clear that the authority of a master over slaves is not the same as the authority of a magistrate in a republic, nor are all forms of government the same, as some assert. Republican government controls men who are by nature free, the master's authority men who are by nature slaves; and the government of a household is monarchy (since every house is governed by a single ruler), whereas statesmanship is the government of men free and equal. The term "master" therefore denotes the possession not of a certain branch of knowledge but of a certain character, and similarly also the terms "slave" and "freeman." Yet there might be a science of mastership and a slave's science—the latter being the sort of knowledge that used to be imparted by the professor at Syracuse (for there used to be a man there who for a fee gave lessons to servants in their ordinary duties); and indeed there might be more advanced scientific study of such matters, for instance a science of cookery and the other such kinds of domestic service—for different servants have different functions, some more honorable and some more menial, and as the proverb says:

"Slave before slave and master before master."[55]

The slave's sciences then are all the various branches of domestic work; the master's science is the science of employing slaves—for the master's function consists not in acquiring slaves but in employing them. This science however is one of no particular importance or dignity : the master must know how to direct the tasks which the slave must know how to execute. Therefore all people rich enough to be able to avoid personal trouble have a steward who takes this office, while they themselves engage in politics or philosophy. The science of acquiring slaves is different both from their ownership and their direction—that is, the just acquiring of slaves being like a sort of warfare or hunting. Let this then stand as our definition of slave and master.

2.5. Hippodamus[56] son of Euryphon, a Milesian (who invented the division of cities into blocks and cut up Piraeus, and who also became somewhat eccentric in his general mode of life owing to a desire for distinction, So that Some people thought that he lived too fussily, with a quantity of hair[57] and expensive ornaments, and also a quantity of cheap yet warm clothes not only in winter but also in the summer periods, and who wished to be a man of learning in natural science generally), was the first man not engaged in politics who attempted to speak on the subject of the best form of constitution. His system was for a city with a population of ten thousand, divided into three classes; for he made one class of artisans, one of farmers, and the third the class that fought for the state in war and was the armed class. He divided the land into three parts, one sacred, one public and one private: sacred land to supply the customary offerings to the gods, common land to provide the warrior class with food, and private land to be owned by the farmers. He thought that there are only three divisions of the law, since the matters about which lawsuits

---

55. Probably from a comedy of Aristotle's contemporary Philemon.
56. Architect and town-planer, c. 475 B.C.
57. At Sparta men wore their hair long, but at Athens this was a mark of a dandy.

take place are three in number—outrage, damage, homicide. He also proposed to establish one supreme court of justice, to which were to be carried up all the cases at law thought to have been decided wrongly, and this court he made to consist of certain selected elders. He held that the verdicts in the courts ought not to be given by ballot, but that each juryman should bring a tablet on which if he found a simple verdict of guilty he should write the penalty, and if simply not guilty leave a blank, but if he found the prisoner guilty on some counts but not on others he should state this; for the present state of the law he thought unsatisfactory, since it forces jurors to commit perjury by giving either the one verdict or the other. He proposed a law that those who discovered something of advantage to the state should receive honor, and that the children of those who died in war should have their maintenance from the state, in the belief that this had never yet been provided by law among other people—but as a matter of fact this law exists at present both at Athens and in others of the cities. The governing officials were all to be chosen by the assembly of the people, and this he made to consist of the three classes of the city; and the officials elected were to superintend the business of the community and the affairs of foreign residents and of orphans. These then are the greatest number and the most noteworthy of the provisions in the system of Hippodamus. But doubt might be raised first of all about the division of the general mass of the citizens. The artisans, the farmers and the military class all participate in the government, though the farmers have not got arms and the artisans neither arms nor land, which makes them almost the slaves of those who possess the arms. Therefore for them to share in all the offices is impossible (for it is inevitable that both military commanders and civic guards and in general the most important offices should be appointed from those that have the arms); but if they do not share in the government of the state, how is it possible for them to be friendly towards the constitution? But it may be said that the ruling class as possessing the arms is bound to be stronger than both classes. But this is not easy if they are not numerous; and if this be the case, why should the other classes participate in the government and control the appointment of the rulers?[58] Again, what use are the farmers to the state? Artisans there must necessarily be (for every state requires artisans), and they can make a living as in the other states from the practice of their craft; but as for the farmers, although it would have been reasonable for them to be a portion of the state if they provided the class possessing the arms with its food, as it is they have private land of their own and farm it for themselves. And again, if the common land from which those who fight for the state are to have their food is to be farmed by themselves, the military class would not be different from the agricultural, but the legislator intends it to be; while if the cultivators of the common land are to be a different set of people from both those who cultivate the private farms and the soldiers, this will be yet a fourth section of the state, holding no part in it but quite estranged from the government. But yet if one is to make those who cultivate the private and the common land the same people, the amount of the produce from the farms which each man will cultivate will be scanty for two households, and moreover why are they not both to take food for themselves and to supply it to the soldiers direct from the land and from the same allotments? All these points therefore involve much confusion. Also the law about trials is unsatisfactory—the permission for a qualified verdict though the charge in the indictment is unqualified,

---

58. As military posts must be filled by the military class, civilians will feel excluded and be disaffected; and the military class may not be strong enough to control them. Better, then, not to give full citizenship to civilians.

and the conversion of the juror into an arbitrator. A qualified verdict is practicable in an arbitration even when there are several arbitrators, for they confer with one another about their verdict; but it is not practicable in the law-courts, in fact the contrary to this is provided for by most lawgivers, who prohibit consultation between the jurymen. Then the verdict will inevitably be a confused one when the juror thinks that the defendant is liable for damages but not in so large an amount as the plaintiff claims; for the plaintiff will sue for twenty minae and the juror will adjudge ten minae (or the former some larger and the latter some smaller sum), and another juror five minae, and yet another four (and they obviously make fractions like this), while others will award the whole sum, and others nothing; what then will be the method of counting the votes? Again, nobody compels the juror to commit perjury who, as the indictment has been drawn in simple form, gives a simple verdict of acquittal or condemnation, if he gives it justly; for the juror who gives a verdict of acquittal does not give judgment that the defendant owes nothing, but that he does not owe the twenty minae for which he is sued; it is only the juror who gives a verdict condemning the defendant when he does not think that he owes twenty minae who commits perjury. As for the view that an honor ought to be awarded to those who invent something advantageous to the state, legislation to this effect is not safe, but only specious to the ear; for it involves malicious prosecutions and, it may even happen, constitutional upheavals. And the matter leads to another problem and a different inquiry: some persons raise the question whether to alter the traditional laws, supposing another law is better, is harmful or advantageous to states. Hence it is not easy to give a speedy agreement to the above proposal to honor reformers, if really it is disadvantageous to alter the laws; and a revolutionary legal or constitutional proposal in the interest of the community is quite possible. And since we have made mention of this question, it will be better if we set out a few further details about it, for, as we said, it involves difficulty. And it might be thought that it would be better for alteration to take place; at all events in the other fields of knowledge this has proved beneficial—for example, medicine has been improved by being altered from the traditional system, and gymnastic training, and in general all the arts and faculties; so that since statesmanship also is to be counted as one of these, it is clear that the same thing necessarily holds good in regard to it as well. And it might be said that a sign of this has occurred in the actual events of history, for (one might argue) the laws of ancient times were too simple and uncivilized: the Hellenes, for instance, used both to carry arms and to purchase their wives from one another, and all the survivals of the customs of antiquity existing anywhere are utterly foolish, as for example at Cyme there is a law relating to trials for murder, that if the prosecutor on the charge of murder produces a certain number of his own relatives as witnesses, the defendant is guilty of the murder. And in general all men really seek what is good, not what was customary with their forefathers; and it is probable that primitive mankind, whether sprung from the earth[59] or the survivors of some destructive cataclysm, were just like ordinary foolish people, as indeed is actually said of the earth-born race, so that would be absurd for us to abide by their notions. Moreover even written codes of law may with advantage not be left unaltered. For just as in the other arts as well, so with the structure of the state it is impossible that it should have been framed aright in all its details for it must of necessity be couched in general terms, but our actions deal with particular things. These considerations then do seem to show that it is proper

---

59. Hesiod, *Works and Days*, 676 ff.

for some laws sometimes to be altered. But if we consider the matter in another way, it would seem to be a thing that needs much caution. For in cases when the improvement would be small, while it is a bad thing to accustom men to repeal the laws lightly, it is clear that some mistakes both of the legislator and of the magistrate should be passed over; for the people will not be as much benefited by making an alteration as they will be harmed by becoming accustomed to distrust their rulers. Also the example from the case of the arts is fallacious, as to change the practice of an art is a different thing from altering a law; for the law has no power to compel obedience beside the force of custom, and custom only grows up in long lapse of time, so that lightly to change from the existing laws to other new laws is to weaken the power of the law. Again even if alteration of the laws is proper, are all the laws to be open to alteration, and in every form of constitution, or not? And is any chance person to be competent to introduce alterations or only certain people? For there is a great difference between these alternatives. Therefore let us abandon this inquiry for the present, since it belongs to other occasions.

3.6. But it is a matter of question what ought to be the sovereign power in the state. Clearly it must be either the multitude, or the rich, or the good, or the one man who is best of all, or a tyrant. But all of these arrangements appear to involve disagreeable consequences. For instance, if the poor take advantage of their greater numbers to divide up the property of the rich, is not this unjust? No, it may be said, for it was a resolution made by the supreme authority in just form. Then what must be pronounced to be the extreme of injustice? And again, when everybody is taken into account, suppose the majority share out among themselves the property of the minority, it is manifest that they are destroying the state; but assuredly virtue does not destroy its possessor, and justice is not destructive of the state, so that it is clear that this principle also cannot be just. Also it follows from it that all the actions done by a tyrant are just, for his use of force is based upon superior strength, as is the compulsion exerted by the multitude against the rich. But is it just that the minority and the rich should rule? Suppose therefore they also act in the same way and plunder and take away the property of the multitude, is this just? If it is, so also is the plunder of the rich by the multitude. It is clear therefore that all these things are bad and not just. But ought the good to rule, and be in control of all classes? If so, then it follows that all the other classes will be dishonored,[60] if they are not honored by holding the offices of government; for we speak of offices as honors, and if the same persons are always in office the rest must necessarily be excluded from honor. But is it better for the most virtuous individual to be the ruler? But that is still more oligarchical, for the people excluded from honor will be more numerous. But perhaps some one would say that in any case it is a bad thing for a human being, having in his soul the passions that are the attributes of humanity, to be sovereign, and not the law. Suppose therefore that law is sovereign, but law of an oligarchic or democratic nature, what difference will it make as regards the difficulties that have been raised? For the results described before will come about just the same.

Most of these points therefore must be discussed on another occasion; but the view that it is more proper for the multitude to be sovereign than the few of greatest virtue might be thought to be explicable, arid to raise some difficulty but probably to be true. For it is possible that the many, though not individually good men, yet when they come together may be better, not individually

---

60. Technical term for disfranchisement and loss of civil rights.

but collectively, than those who are so, just as public dinners to which many contribute are better than those supplied at one man's cost; for where there are many, each individual, it may be argued, has some portion of virtue and wisdom, and when they have come together, just as the multitude becomes a single man with many feet and many hands and many senses, so also it becomes one personality as regards the moral and intellectual faculties. This is why the general public is a better judge of the works of music and those of the poets, because different men can judge a different part of the performance, and all of them all of it. But the superiority of good men over the mass of men individually, like that of handsome men, so it is said, over plain men and of the works of the painter's art over the real objects, really consists in this, that a number of scattered good points have been collected together into one example; since if the features be taken separately, the eye of one real person is more beautiful than that of the man in the picture, and some other feature of somebody else. It is not indeed clear whether this collective superiority of the many compared with the few good men can possibly exist in regard to every democracy and every multitude, and perhaps it may be urged that it is manifestly impossible in the case of some— for the same argument would also apply to animals, yet what difference is there, practically, between some multitudes and animals?—but nothing prevents what has been said from being true about some particular multitude. One might therefore employ these considerations to solve not only the previously stated difficulty but also the related question, over what matters is the authority of the freemen, the mass of the citizens, to extend (using that expression to denote those who are not rich nor possessed of any distinguishing excellence at all)? For it is not safe for them to participate in the highest offices (for injustice and folly would inevitably cause them to act unjustly in some things and to make mistakes in others), but yet not to admit them and for them not to participate is an alarming situation, for when there are a number of persons without political honors and in poverty, the city then is bound to be full of enemies. It remains therefore for them to share the deliberative and judicial functions. For this reason Solon and certain other lawgivers appoint the common citizens to the election of the magistrates and the function of calling them to audit, although they do not allow them to hold office singly. For all when assembled together have sufficient discernment, and by mingling with the better class are of benefit to the state, just as impure food mixed with what is pure makes the whole more nourishing than the small amount of pure food alone;[61] but separately the individual is immature in judgment. This arrangement of the constitution is however open to question in the first place on the ground that it might be held that the best man to judge which physician has given the right treatment is the man that is himself capable of treating and curing the patient of his present disease, and this is the man who is himself a physician; and that this is the case similarly with regard to the other arts and crafts. Hence just as a court of physicians must .judge the work of a physician, so also all other practitioners ought to be called to account before their fellows. But physician means both the ordinary practitioner, and the master of the craft, and thirdly, the man who has studied medicine as part of his general education (for in almost all the arts there are some such students, and we assign the right of judgment just as much to cultivated amateurs as to experts). Further the same might be thought to hold good also of the election of officials, for to elect rightly is a task for experts—for example, it is for experts in the science of mensuration to elect a land-surveyor and for experts in

---

61. I.e., especially, bran mixed with pure flower.

navigation to choose a pilot; for even though in some occupations and arts some laymen also have a voice in appointments, yet they certainly do not have more voice than the experts. Hence according to this argument the masses should not be put in control over either the election of magistrates or their audit. But perhaps this statement is not entirely correct, both for the reason stated above, in case the populace is not of too slavish a character (for although each individual separately will be a worse judge than the experts, the whole of them assembled together will be better or at least as good judges), and also because about some things the man who made them would not be the only nor the best judge, in the case of professionals whose products come within the knowledge of laymen also: to judge a house, for instance, does not belong only to the man who built it, but in fact the man who uses the house (that is, the householder) will be an even better judge of it, and a steersman judges a rudder better than a carpenter, and the diner judges a banquet better than the cook.

This difficulty then might perhaps be thought to be satisfactorily solved in this way. But there is another one connected with it: it is thought to be absurd that the base should be in control over more important matters than the respectable; but the audits and elections of magistrates are a very important matter, yet in some constitutions, as has been said, they are assigned to the common people, for all such matters are under the control of the assembly, yet persons of a low property-assessment and of any age take part in the assembly and the council and sit on juries, whereas treasury officials, generals and the holders of the highest magistracies are drawn from among persons of large property. Now this difficulty also may be solved in a similar way; for perhaps these regulations also are sound, since it is not the individual juryman or councilor or member of the assembly in whom authority rests, but the court, the council and the people, while each of the individuals named (I mean the councilor, the members of assembly and the juryman) is a part of those bodies. Hence justly the multitude is sovereign in greater matters, for the popular assembly, the council and the jury-court are formed of a number of people, and also time assessed property of all these members collectively is more than that of the magistrates holding great offices individually or in small groups.

Let these points therefore be decided in this manner. But the difficulty first mentioned[62] proves nothing else so clearly as that it is proper for the laws when rightly laid down to be sovereign, while the ruler or rulers in office should have supreme powers over matters as to which the laws are quite unable to pronounce with precision because of the difficulty of making a general rule to cover all cases. We have not however yet ascertained at all what particular character a code of laws correctly laid down ought to possess, but the difficulty raised at the start still remains; for necessarily the laws are good or bad, just or unjust, simultaneously with and similarly to the constitutions of states (though of course it is obvious that the laws are bound to be adapted to the constitution); yet if so, it is clear that the laws in conformity with the correct constitutions must necessarily be just and those in conformity with the divergent forms of constitution unjust.

3.9. And perhaps it is well after the subjects that have been discussed to pass over to consider royal government; for we pronounce this to be one of the correct constitutions. And it has to be considered whether it is advantageous for a city or a country that is to be well administered to be ruled by a king, or whether it is not so but some other constitution is more expedient, or whether

---

62. That under any plan some hardships will result.

royal rule is expedient for some states and not for others. But it is needful to decide first whether there is only one sort of kingship or whether it has several varieties.

Now it is at all events easy to discern that kingship includes several kinds, and that the mode of government is not the same in all. For the kingship in the Spartan constitution, which is held to be a typical royalty of the kind guided by law, does not carry sovereignty in all matters, though when a king goes on a foreign expedition he is the leader in all matters relating to the war; and also matters relating to religion have been assigned to the kings. This kingship therefore is a sort of military command vested in generals with absolute powers and held for life; for the king has not authority to put a subject to death, except in some emergency, as in ancient times kings on their military expeditions could kill an offender out of hand, as Homer proves, for Agamemnon endured being reviled in the assemblies but when they were on an expedition had authority to put a man to death: at all events he says:

"But whomsoever I see far from the fray . . .
Shall have no hope to fly from dogs and vultures,
For death is in my hands!"[63]

This then is one sort of kingship, a lifelong generalship, and some of the kingships of this kind are hereditary, others elective; and by its side there is another sort of monarchy, examples of which are kingships existing among some of the barbarians. The power possessed by all of these resembles that of tyrannies, but they govern according to law and are hereditary; for because the barbarians are more servile in their nature than the Greeks, and the Asiatics than the Europeans, they endure despotic rule without any resentment. These kingships therefore are for these reasons of a tyrannical nature, but they are secure because they are hereditary and rule by law. Also their bodyguard is of a royal and not a tyrannical type for the same reason; for kings are guarded by the citizens in arms, whereas tyrants have foreign guards, for kings rule in accordance with law and over willing subjects, but tyrants rule over unwilling subjects, owing to which kings take their guards from among the citizens but tyrants have them to guard against the citizens. These then are two kinds of monarchy; while another is that which existed among the ancient Greeks, the type of rulers called *aesymnetae*. This, to put it simply, is an elective tyranny, and it differs from the monarchy that exists among barbarians not in governing without the guidance of law but only in not being hereditary. Some holders of this type of monarchy ruled for life, others until certain fixed limits of time or until certain undertakings were ended, as for example the people of Mitylene once elected Pittacus[64] to resist the exiles under the leadership of Antimenides and the poet Alcaeus. That they elected Pittacus as tyrant is proved by Alcaeus in one of his catches; for he rebukes the people because:

"The base-born Pittacus they did set up
As tyrant of the meek and luckless city,
And all did greatly praise him."

---

63. Homer, Iliad, 2.391, but the last line is not in our Homer.
64. Pittacus held office 587–579 B.C. He was one of the Seven Sages. Antimenides and Alcaeus were brothers.

These monarchies therefore now and in the past are of the nature of tyrannies because they are autocratic, but of the nature of kingships because they are elective and rule over willing subjects. A fourth class of royal monarchy consists of the hereditary legal kingships over willing subjects in the heroic period. For because the first of the line had been benefactors of the multitude in the arts or in war, or through having drawn them together or provided them with land, these kings used to come to the throne with the consent of the subjects and hand it on to their successors by lineal descent. And they had supreme command in war and control over all sacrifices that were not in the hands of the priestly class, and in addition to these functions they were judges in lawsuits; some gave judgment not on oath and some on oath—the I oath was taken by holding up the scepter. These kings then of ancient times used to govern continuously in matters within the city and in the country and across the frontiers; but later on when gradually the kings relinquished some of their powers and had others taken from them by the multitudes, in the cities in general only the sacrifices were left to the kings,[65] while where anything that deserves the name of royalty survived the kings only had the command in military expeditions across the frontiers.

4.1. In all the arts and the sciences that are not merely sectional but that in relation to some one class of subject are complete, it is the function of a single art or science to study what is suited to each class, for instance what sort of gymnastic exercise is beneficial for what sort of bodily frame, and what is the best sort (for the best must naturally suit the person of the finest natural endowment and equipment), and also what one exercise taken by all is the best for the largest number (for this is also a question for gymnastic science), and in addition, in case someone desires a habit of body and a knowledge of athletic exercises that are not the ones adapted to him, it is clearly the task of the trainer and gymnastic master to produce this capacity[66] also just as much; and we notice this also happening similarly in regard to medicine, and ship-building, and the making of clothes, and every other craft. Hence it is clear that in the case of the constitution as well it is the business of the same science to study which is the best constitution and what character it must have to be the most ideal if no external circumstance stands in the way, and what constitution is adapted to what people (since for many it is doubtless impossible to attain the best one, so that the good lawgiver and the true statesman must be acquainted with both the form of constitution that is the highest absolutely and that which is best under assumed conditions), and also thirdly the form of constitution based on a certain supposition (for he must be also capable of considering both how some given constitution could be brought into existence originally and also in what way having been brought into existence it could be preserved for the longest time: I mean for example if it has befallen some state not only not to possess the best constitution and to be unprovided even with the things necessary for it, but also not to have the constitution that is practicable under the circumstances but an inferior one); and beside all these matters he must ascertain the form of constitution most suited to all states, since most of those who make pronouncements about the constitution, even if the rest of what they say is good, entirely miss the points of practical utility. For it is proper to consider[67] not only what is the best constitution but also what is the one possible of achievement, and likewise also what is the one

---

65. The monarchy was reduced to a priesthood at Cyrene (Herodotus, 4.161) and at Ephesus.
66. I.e. a bodily bearing and athletic skill that are not the ones most suited to the pupil's particular physique.
67. The fourfold classification given just before is repeated in rather loose terms in this sentence.

that is easier and more generally shared by all states. But as it is, some students inquire which is the highest form of all even though requiring much material equipment,[68] while those who rather state some general form sweep aside the constitutions actually existing and praise that of Sparta or some other; but the proper course is to bring forward an organization of such a sort that men will easily be persuaded and be able in the existing circumstances to take part in it, since to reform a constitution is no less a task than to frame one from the beginning, just as to re-learn a science is just as hard as to learn it originally; in addition therefore to the things mentioned the student of politics must also be able to render aid to the constitutions that exist already, as was also said before. But this is impossible if he does not know how many kinds of constitution there are; but at present some people think that there is only one kind of democracy and one kind of oligarchy, but this is not true. Hence he must take in view the different varieties of the constitutions, and know how many there are and how many are their combinations. And after this it needs this same discrimination also to discern the laws that are the best, and those that are suited to each of the forms of constitution. For the laws should be laid down, and all people lay them down, to suit the constitutions—the constitutions must not be made to suit the laws; for a constitution is the regulation of the offices of the state in regard to the mode of their distribution and to the question what is the sovereign power in the state and what is the object of each community, but laws are distinct from the principles of the constitution, and regulate how the magistrates are to govern and to guard against those who transgress them. So that clearly it is necessary to be in possession of the different varieties of each form of constitution, and the number of these, even for the purpose of legislation; for it is impossible for the same laws to be expedient for all oligarchies or democracies if there are really several kinds of them, and not one sort of democracy or oligarchy only.

4.2. And inasmuch as in our first inquiry about the forms of the constitution we classified the right constitutions as three, kingship, aristocracy and constitutional government, and the deviations from these as three, tyranny from kingship, oligarchy from aristocracy and democracy from constitutional government, and about aristocracy and kingship we have spoken (for to study the best constitution is the same thing as to speak about the forms that bear those names, since each of them means a system based on the qualification of virtue equipped with means), and as also the question what constitutes the difference between aristocracy and kingship and when a royal government is to be adopted has been decided before, it remains to discuss the form of constitution designated by the name common to them all,[69] and the other forms, oligarchy, democracy and tyranny. Now it is manifest also which of these deviations[70] is the worst and which the second worst. For necessarily the deviation from the first and most divine must be the worst,[71] and kingship must of necessity either possess the name only, without really being kingship, or be based on the outstanding superiority of the man who is king; so that tyranny being the worst form must

---

68. The word originally denoted the duty of the wealthy citizen holding the Choregus (a leader of a dramatic chorus in ancient Greece) to supply dresses, etc., for the chorus and actors in a drama.

69. Which denotes not only a constitution of any form, but also (like our term "constitutional government") a particular form, that is, republic.

70. The three forms of constitution just mentioned.

71. A Socratic notion: "the men of the best natural gifts, when uneducated, are the worst." Xenophon, *Memorabilia*, 4.1.3.

be the one farthest removed from constitutional government, and oligarchy must be the second farthest (for aristocracy is widely separated from that constitution), while democracy must be the most moderate. An account of their relative merits has indeed already been given also by one of the former writers,[72] though not on the same principle as ours; for he inclined to judge that there were good varieties of all the forms, for instance a good sort of oligarchy and so on, and that democracy was the worst among these, but the best among the bad varieties, whereas we say that the deviations are wholly wrong, and that it is not right to speak of one form of oligarchy as better than another, but only as less bad. But let us for the present dismiss the question of a classification of this nature. Our business is first to distinguish how many different forms of the constitutions there are, assuming that there do exist several kinds of democracy and of oligarchy; next, which form is most general, and which most desirable after the best constitution, and also if there exists some other form that is aristocratic in nature and well constructed but not fitted to the largest number of cities, which this is; next, which of the other forms too is desirable for what people (since probably for some democracy is necessary more than oligarchy, and for others oligarchy more than democracy); and after this, in what way should one proceed who wishes to set up these constitutions, I mean the various forms of democracy and of oligarchy; and finally, when as far as possible we have concisely touched upon all these questions, we must endeavor to review what are the agencies that destroy and what are those that preserve constitutions generally and each variety of constitution in particular, and what are the causes by which it is most natural for these events to be brought about.

4.3. Now the reason of there being several forms of constitution is that every city has a considerable number of parts. For in the first place we see that all the cities are composed of households, and then again that of this multitude some must necessarily be rich and some poor and some between the two, and also of the rich and the poor the former class is heavy-armed and the latter without armor. And we see that one portion of the common people is agricultural, another engaged in trade and another mechanic. And the upper classes have distinctions also corresponding to their wealth and the amounts of their property (for example in a stud of horses—for it is not easy to rear horses without being rich, and this is why in ancient times there were oligarchies in all the states whose strength lay in their cavalry, and they used to use horses for their wars against their neighbors, as for instance did the Eretrians and Chalcidians and the people of Magnesia on the Macander and many of the other Asiatic peoples). Moreover in addition to differences in wealth there is the difference of birth, and that in regard to virtue, and indeed any other similar distinction that in the discussion of aristocracy has been stated to constitute a part of the state (for there we distinguished how many necessary parts there are of which every state must consist); for sometimes all of these parts participate in the constitution and sometimes a smaller or a larger number of them. It is clear therefore that there must necessarily be several forms of constitution differing in kind from one another, inasmuch as these parts differ in kind among themselves. For a constitution means the arrangement of the magistracies, and these all people distribute either according to the power of those who share political rights, or according to some common equality between them, I mean for example between the poor or between the rich, or some equality common to

---

72. Plato, *Politicus*, 302 ff.

them both.[73] It follows therefore that there are as many forms of constitution as there are modes of arrangement according to the superiorities and the differences of the sections. But the forms mostly are thought to be two—just as in the case of the winds we speak of some as north and some as south and regard the rest as deviations from these,[74] so also of constitutions there are held to be two forms, democracy and oligarchy; for men reckon aristocracy as a kind of oligarchy because it is oligarchy of a sort, and what is called constitutional government as democracy, just as in the case of the winds they reckon the west wind as a kind of north wind and the east wind as a kind of south wind. And the case is similar with musical modes, as some people say for there too they posit two kinds, the Dorian mode and the Phrygian, and call the other scales some of them Dorian and the others Phrygian. For the most part therefore they are accustomed to think in this way about the constitutions; but it is truer and better to class them as we did, and assuming that there are two well constructed forms, or else one, to say that the others are deviations, some from the well blended constitution and the others from the best one, the more tense and masterful constitutions being oligarchic and the relaxed and soft ones demotic.

But it is not right to define democracy, as some people are in the custom of doing now, merely as the constitution in which the multitude is sovereign (for even in oligarchies and everywhere the majority is sovereign) nor oligarchy as the constitution in which a few are sovereign over the government. For if the whole number were thirteen hundred, and a thousand of these were rich and did not give the three hundred poor a share in the government although they were free-born and like themselves in all other respects, no one would say that this people was governed democratically; and similarly also if there were few poor, but these more powerful than the rich who were more numerous, no one would call such a government a democracy either, if the other citizens being rich had no share in the honors. Rather therefore ought we to say that it is a democracy when the free are sovereign and an oligarchy when the rich are, but that it comes about that the sovereign class in a democracy is numerous and that in an oligarchy small because there are many men of free birth and few rich. For otherwise, suppose people assigned the offices by height, as some persons[75] say is done in Ethiopia, or by beauty, that would be an oligarchy, because both the handsome and the tall are few in number. Nevertheless it is not enough to define these constitutions even by wealth and free birth only; but inasmuch as there are more elements than one both in democracy and in oligarchy, we must add the further distinction that nether is it a democracy if the free[76] being few govern the majority who are not of free birth, as for instance at Apollonia on the Ionian Gulf and at Thera (for in each of these cities the offices of honor were filled by the specially noble families who had been the first settlers of the colonies, and these were few out of many), nor is it a democracy[77] if the rich rule because they are in a majority, as in ancient times at Colophon (for there the majority of the population owned large property before the war against the Lydians took place), but it is a democracy when those who are free are in the

---

73. This clause looks like an interpolation.
74. Aristotle refers to this view in *Meteorologica*, 364, saying that the west winds are classed with the north and the east winds with the south, because wind from the setting sun is cooler and from the rising sun warmer. He notes that north and south winds are the most frequent; this may have suggested the idea that they were the typical winds.
75. Herodotus, 3.20.
76. Those of citizen birth.
77. Perhaps the Greek should be altered here to give "an oligarchy."

majority and have sovereignty over the government, and an oligarchy when the rich and more well born are few and sovereign.

It has then been stated that there are several forms of constitution, and what is the cause of this; but let us take the starting-point that was laid down before and say that there are more forms than those mentioned, and what these forms are, and why they vary. For we agree that every state possesses not one part but several. Therefore just as, in the case we intended to obtain a classification of animals, we should first define the properties necessarily belonging to every animal (for instance some of the sense-organs, and the machinery for masticating and for receiving food, such as a mouth and a stomach, and in addition to these the locomotive organs of the various species), and if there were only so many necessary parts, but there were different varieties of these (I mean for instance certain various kinds of mouth and stomach and sensory organs, and also of the locomotive parts as well), the number of possible combinations of these variations will necessarily produce a variety of kinds of animals (for it is not possible for the same animal to have several different sorts of mouth, nor similarly of ears either), so that when all the possible combinations of these are taken they will all produce animal species, and there will be as many species of the animal as there are combinations of the necessary parts: so in the same way also we shall classify the varieties of the constitutions that have been mentioned. For states also are composed not of one but of several parts, as has been said often. One of these parts therefore is the mass of persons concerned with food who are called farmers, and second is what is called the mechanic class (and this is the group engaged in the arts without which it is impossible for a city to be inhabited, and some of these arts are indispensably necessary, while others contribute to luxury or noble living), and third is a commercial class (by which I mean the class that is engaged in selling and buying and in wholesale and retail trade), and fourth is the class of manual laborers, and the fifth class is the one to defend the state in war, which is no less indispensable than the others if the people are not to become the slaves of those who come against them for surely it is quite out of the question that it should be proper to give the name of state to a community that is by nature a slave, for a state is self-sufficient, but that which is a slave is not self-sufficient. Therefore the statement made in the *Republic*[78] is witty but not adequate. For Socrates says that the most necessary elements of which a state is composed are four, and he specifies these as a weaver, a farmer, a shoemaker and a builder; and then again he adds, on the ground that these are not self-sufficient, a copper-smith and the people to look after the necessary live-stock, and in addition a merchant and a retail trader. These elements together constitute the full complement of his first city, implying that every city is formed for the sake of the necessaries of life and not rather for the sake of what is noble, and that it has equal need of both shoemakers and farmers; but the warrior class he does not assign to it until as the territory is increased and comes into contact with that of the neighbors they are brought into war. But yet even among the four partners or whatever their number be there must necessarily be some body to assign justice and to judge their claims; inasmuch therefore as one would count the soul of an animal to be more a part of it than the body, so also the factors in states corresponding to the soul must be deemed to be parts of them more than those factors which contribute to necessary utility,—the former being the military class and the class that plays a part in judicial justice, and in addition to these the deliberative class, deliberation being a function of

---

78. Plato, *Republic*, 2.369.

political intelligence. And it makes no difference to the argument whether these functions are held by special classes separately or by the same persons; for it often happens for the same men to be both soldiers and farmers. Hence inasmuch as both groups of classes[79] must be counted parts of the state, it is clear that the heavy-armed soldiery at any rate[80] must be a part of the state. And a seventh class is the one that serves the community by means of its property, the class that we call the rich. And an eighth is the class of public servants, that is, those who serve in the magistracies, inasmuch as without rulers it is impossible for a city to exist; it is therefore necessary that there should be some men who are able to govern and who render this service to the state either continuously or in turn. And there remain the classes which we happen to have defined just before, the deliberative class and the one that judges the claims of litigants. If therefore it is proper for the states to have these functions performed, and well and justly performed, it is necessary for there also to be some men possessing virtue in the form of political excellence. Now as to the other capacities many people think that it is possible for them to be possessed in combination, for example for the same men to be the soldiers that defend the state in war and the farmers that till the land and the artisans, and also the councilors and judges, and indeed all men claim to possess virtue and think themselves capable of filling most of the offices of state; but it is not possible for the same men to be poor and rich. Hence these seem to be in the fullest sense the parts of the state, the rich and the poor. And also the fact that the rich are usually few and the poor many makes these two among the parts of the state appear as opposite sections; so that the superior claims of these classes are even made the guiding principles upon which constitutions are constructed, and it is thought that there are two forms of constitution, democracy and oligarchy.

4.4. That there are then several forms of constitution, and the reasons for this have been stated before; let us now say that there are several varieties both of democracy and of oligarchy. And this is clear even from what has been said already. For there are several classes both of the people and of those called the notables; for instance classes of the people are, one the farmers, another the class dealing with the arts and crafts, another the commercial class occupied in buying and selling and another the one occupied with the sea—and this is divided into the classes concerned with naval warfare, with trade, with ferrying passengers and with fishing (for each of these classes is extremely numerous in various places, for instance fishermen at Tarentum and Byzantium, navy men at Athens the mercantile class at Aegina and Chios, and the ferryman class at Tenedos), and in addition to these the hand-working class and the people possessing little substance so that they cannot live a life of leisure, also those that are not free men of citizen parentage on both sides, and any other similar class of common people; while among the notables wealth, birth, virtue, education, and the distinctions that are spoken of in the same group as these, form the classes.

The first kind of democracy therefore is the one which receives the name chiefly in respect of equality. For the law of this sort of democracy ascribes equality to the state of things in which the poor have no more prominence than the rich, and neither class is sovereign, but both are alike; for assuming that freedom is chiefly found in a democracy, as some persons suppose, and also equality, this would be so most fully when to the fullest extent all alike share equally in the government. And since the people are in the majority, and a resolution passed by a majority is

---

79. The first four classes and the military and judicial.
80. Lower grades of soldiers may be excluded from citizenship, e.g. the rowers of the triemes.

paramount, this must necessarily be a democracy. This therefore is one kind of democracy, where the offices are held on property-qualifications, but these low ones, although it is essential that the man who acquires the specified amount should have the right to hold office, and the man who loses it should not hold office. And another kind of democracy is for all the citizens that are not open to challenge[81] to have a share in office, but for the law to rule; and another kind of democracy is for all to share in the offices on the mere qualification of being a citizen, but for the law to rule. Another kind of democracy is where all the other regulations are the same, but the multitude is sovereign and not the law; and this comes about when the decrees of the assembly over-ride the law. This state of things is brought about by the demagogues; for in the states under democratic government guided by law a demagogue does not arise, but the best classes of citizens are in the most prominent position; but where the laws are not sovereign, then demagogues arise; for the common people become a single composite monarch, since the many are sovereign not as individuals but collectively. Yet what kind of democracy Homer[82] means by the words "no blessing is the lordship of the many"—whether he means this kind or when those who rule as individuals are more numerous, is not clear. However, a people of this sort, as being monarch, seeks to exercise monarchic rule through not being ruled by the law, and becomes despotic, so that flatterers are held in honor. And a democracy of this nature is comparable to the tyrannical form of monarchy, because their spirit is the same, and both exercise despotic control over the better classes, and the decrees voted by the assembly are like the commands issued in a tyranny, and the demagogues and the flatterers are the same people or a corresponding class, and either set has the very strongest influence with the respective ruling power, the flatterers with the tyrants and the demagogues with democracies of this kind. And these men cause the resolutions of the assembly to be supreme and not the laws, by referring all things to the people; for they owe their rise to greatness to the fact that the people is sovereign over all things while they are sovereign over the opinion of the people, for the multitude believes them. Moreover those who bring charges against the magistrates say that the people ought to judge the suits, and the people receive the invitation gladly, so that all the magistracies are put down. And it would seem to be a reasonable criticism to say that such a democracy is not a constitution at all; for where the laws do not govern there is no constitution, as the law ought to govern all things while the magistrates control particulars, and we ought to judge this to be constitutional government; if then democracy really is one of the forms of constitution, it is manifest that an organization of this kind, in which all things are administered by resolutions of the assembly, is not even a democracy in the proper sense, for it is impossible for a voted resolution to be a universal rule.

Let this be our discussion of the different kinds of democracy.

4.5. Of the kinds of oligarchy, one is for the magistracies to be appointed from property assessments so high that the poor who are the majority have no share in the government, but for the man who acquires the requisite amount of property to be allowed to take part in it; another is when the magistracies are filled from high assessments and the magistrates themselves elect to fill vacancies (so that if they do so from all the citizens of this assessment, this appears rather to be of the nature of an aristocracy, but if from a particular section of them, it is oligarchical); an-

---

81. I.e. on the score of birth.
82. Homer, *Iliad*, 2.204.

other variety of oligarchy is when son succeeds father in office; and a fourth kind is when the hereditary system just mentioned exists and also the magistrates govern and not the law. This among oligarchies is the form corresponding to tyranny among monarchies and to the form of democracy about which we spoke last among democracies, and indeed oligarchy of this sort has the special name of dynasty.[83]

So many therefore are the kinds of oligarchy and of democracy; but it must not escape notice that in many places it has come about that although the constitution as framed by the laws is not democratic, yet owing to custom and the social system it is democratically administered, and similarly by a reverse process in other states although the legal constitution is more democratic, yet by means of the social system and customs it is carried on rather as an oligarchy. This occurs chiefly after alterations of the constitutions have taken place; for the people do not change over to the new system immediately but are content at the first stages to gain small advantages from the other party, so that the previously existing laws continue although power is in the hands of the party that changed the constitution.

And that these various kinds of democracy and oligarchy exist is manifest from the actual things that have been said. For necessarily either all the parts of the population that have been mentioned must have a share in the government, or some and not others. When therefore the farmer class and the class possessed of moderate property is sovereign over the government, they govern according to laws for they have a livelihood if they work, but are not able to be at leisure, so that they put the law in control and hold the minimum of assemblies necessary; and the other persons have the right to take part when they have acquired the property assessment fixed by the laws, so that to take part in the government is open to all who have got that amount of property; since for it not to be open to everybody on any terms at all is a characteristic of oligarchy, but then on the other hand it is impossible for it to be open to them to have leisure if there are no revenues.[84] This then is one kind of democracy for these reasons. Another kind is due to the distinction that comes next: it is possible that all the citizens not liable to objection on the score of birth may have the right to take part in the assembly, but may actually take part only when they are able to be at leisure; hence in a democracy of this nature the laws govern because there is no revenue. A third kind is when all those who are free men have the right to take part in the government yet do not do so because of the aforesaid reason, so that it follows that in this form of democracy also the law governs. And a fourth kind of democracy is the one that has been the last in point of time to come into existence in the states. Because the states have become much greater than the original ones and possess large supplies of revenue, while all the citizens have a share in the government because of the superiority of the multitude, all actually take part in it and exercise their citizenship because even the poor are enabled to be at leisure by receiving pay. Indeed the multitude in this kind of state has a very great deal of leisure, for they are not hampered at all by the care of

---

83. Government controlled by a few powerful families. See Thucydides, 3.62.4, where the Thebans say, "In those days our state was not governed by an oligarchy that granted equal justice to all, nor yet by a democracy; the power was in the hands of a small cabal, than which nothing is more opposed to the law or to true political order, or more nearly resembles a tyranny."

84. I.e. revenues from abroad; the poor can only attend often if paid for attendance, and this can only be financed if the state has income from tribute or foreign property, as at Athens during the period of the empire.

their private affairs, but the rich are, so that often they take no part in the assembly nor in judging lawsuits. Owing to this the multitude of the poor becomes sovereign over the government, instead of the laws. Such in number and in nature are the kinds of democracy that these causes necessarily bring into existence. To turn to the varieties of oligarchy, when more men possess property, but less of it and not a very large amount, this is the first form of oligarchy; for they allow the man that acquires property the right to participate, and because there is a large number of persons participating in the government it necessarily follows that not the men but the law is sovereign (for the farther removed they are from monarchy, and as they have not so much property as to be idle and neglect it, nor yet so little as to be kept at the expense of the state, they are compelled to call upon the law to rule instead of ruling themselves). But then if the owners of the properties are fewer than those who owned them previously, and own more, the second form of oligarchy comes into being; for as they become stronger they claim to have a larger share, and therefore they themselves select those from among the rest of the citizens who go into the government, but as they are not yet strong enough to rule without law they make the law conform with this.[85] And if they carry matters further by becoming fewer and holding larger properties, there comes about the third advance in oligarchy, which consists in their keeping the offices in their own hands, but under a law enacting that they are to be hereditary. And when finally they attain very great pre-eminence by their wealth and their multitude of friends, a dynasty of this nature is near to monarchy, and men become supreme instead of the law; and this is the fourth kind of oligarchy, the counterpart of the last kind of democracy.

Furthermore[86] there are two constitutions by the side of democracy and oligarchy, one[87] of which is counted by everybody and has been referred to as one of the four forms of constitution (and the four meant are monarchy, oligarchy, democracy and fourth the form called aristocracy), but there is a fifth, entitled by the common name of them all (for it is called constitutional government), but as it does not often occur it is overlooked by those who try to enumerate the forms of constitution, and they use the four names only (as does Plato) in the list of constitutions. Now the name of aristocracy is indeed properly given to the constitution that we discussed in our first discourses (for it is right to apply the name "aristocracy"—"government of the best"—only to the constitution of which the citizens are best in virtue absolutely and not merely good men in relation to some arbitrary standard, for under it alone the same person is a good man and a good citizen absolutely, whereas those who are good under the other constitutions are good relatively to their own form of constitution); nevertheless there are also some constitutions that have differences both in comparison with oligarchically governed states and with what is termed constitutional government, inasmuch as in them they elect the officials not only by wealth but also by goodness; this form of constitution differs from both and is called aristocratic. For even in the states that do not pay any public attention to virtue there are nevertheless some men that are held in high esteem and are thought worthy of respect. Where then the constitution takes in view wealth and virtue as well as the common people, as for instance at Carthage, this is of the

---

85. I.e. they legalize the recruiting of the ruling class by cooption; or the words may mean "they make the law ruler."
86. We now pass from the varieties of Oligarchy and of Democracy to those of the other actually existing constitutions, Aristocracy so-called and Constitutional Government.
87. I.e. aristocracy.

nature of an aristocracy; and so also are the states, in which the constitution, like that of Sparta, takes in view two of these things only, virtue and the common people, and there is a mingling of these two factors, democracy and virtue. These then are two kinds of aristocracy beside the first, which is the best constitution, and a third kind is those instances of what is called constitutional government that incline more in the direction of oligarchy.

4.11. And again, let us speak about the points that come next, both generally and with reference to each constitution separately, taking their appropriate starting-point. All forms of constitution then have three factors in reference to which the good lawgiver has to consider what is expedient for each constitution; and if these factors are well ordered the constitution must of necessity be well ordered, and the superiority of one constitution over another necessarily consists in the superiority of each of these factors. Of these three factors one is, what is to be the body that deliberates about the common interests, second the one connected with the magistracies, that is, what there are to be and what matters they are to control, and what is to be the method of their election, and a third is, what is to be the judiciary.

The deliberative factor is sovereign about war and peace and the formation and dissolution of alliances, and about laws, and about sentences of death and exile and confiscation of property, and about the audits of magistrates. And necessarily either all these decisions must be assigned to all the citizens, or all to some of them (for instance to some one magistracy or to several), or different ones to different magistracies, or some of them to all the citizens and some to certain persons.

For all the citizens to be members of the deliberative body and to decide all these matters is a mark of a popular government, for the common people seek for equality of this nature. But there are several modes of such universal membership. One is for the citizens to serve in rotation and not all in a body (as is enacted in the constitution of the Milesian Telecles,[88] and in other constitutions also the boards of magistrates deliberate in joint assemblies but all the citizens enter into the magistracies from the tribes or from the very smallest sections of the citizen-body in rotation until office has gone through the whole body), and for there to be joint assemblies only to consider legislation and reforms of the constitution and to hear the reports submitted by the magistrates. Another mode is for all to assemble in a body, but only for the purpose of electing magistrates, enacting laws, considering the declaration of war and the conclusion of peace and holding the audit of magistrates, but for all other matters to be considered by the magistrates appointed to deal with each respectively and elected by suffrage or by lot from all the citizens. Another mode is for the citizens to meet about the magistracies and the audits and in order to deliberate about declaring war and concluding an alliance, but for all other matters to be dealt with by the magistrates, elected by suffrage in as many cases as circumstances allow,[89] and such magistracies are all those which must of necessity be filled by experts. A fourth mode is for all to meet in council about all matters, and for the magistracies to decide about nothing but only to make preliminary decisions; this is the mode in which democracy in its last form is administered at the present day—the form of democracy which we pronounce to correspond to dynastic oligarchy and to tyrannical monarchy. These modes then are all of them democratic. On the other hand for some persons to deliberate upon all matters is oligarchic. But this also has several varia-

---

88. Otherwise unknown.
89. I.e. in an advanced democracy.

tions. For when the members of the deliberative body are elected on comparatively moderate property qualifications, and the eligible persons are comparatively numerous because of the moderateness of the qualification, and when they do not make changes in things in which the law forbids it but follow the law, and when anybody acquiring the property qualification is allowed to become a member, a constitution of this sort is indeed an oligarchy, but one of the nature of constitutional government, because of its moderation. When on the other hand not everybody thus qualified participates in deliberation but only certain persons previously chosen by election, and these govern in accordance with law as in the former case, this is oligarchical; and also when the deliberative officials are elected by co-optation, and when the office is hereditary and has supreme control over the laws, this system is bound to be oligarchical. But when certain persons control certain matters, for instance when all the citizens control decisions as to war and peace and the audit of officials while everything else is controlled by magistrates and these are elected by vote, not by lot, the constitution is an aristocracy; while if some matters are controlled by magistrates elected by vote and others by magistrates chosen by lot, and this either directly or from a list previously selected by vote, or if magistrates elected by vote and by lot sit in a joint body, some of these regulations are features of an aristocratic constitution and others of constitutional government itself.

We have then in this way distinguished the different kinds of deliberative body in relation to the forms of constitution, and each form of constitution carries on the administration in accordance with the distinction stated. But for a democracy of the form that at the present day is considered to be democracy in the fullest degree (and I mean one of the sort in which the people is sovereign even over the laws) it is advantageous for the improvement of its deliberative function for it to do the same as is done in oligarchies in the matter of the law-courts (for they enact a fine to compel the attendance on juries of those whom they want to attend, whereas democratic states institute payment for attendance for the benefit of the poor), and also to do this in respect of the assemblies (for they will deliberate better when all are deliberating jointly, the common people when with the notables and these when with the masses), and it is also advantageous for those who deliberate to be elected by vote or by lot equally from the different sections, and, if the men of the people far exceed the political class in number, it is advantageous either not to give pay to all but only to as many as are commensurate with the number of the notables, or to discard by lot those who exceed this number. In oligarchies on the other hand it is advantageous either to co-opt some persons from the multitude, or to institute an office like the one that exists in certain constitutional governments under the name of Preliminary Councilors or Guardians of the Law,[90] and deal with the matters about which these officials have held a preliminary deliberation (for thus the common people will have a share in deliberation and will not have the power to abolish any part of the constitution), and then for the people by their vote either to confirm or at all events not to pass anything contrary to the resolutions brought before them, or to allow all to take part in debate but only the magistrates to frame resolutions; and in fact it is proper to do just the opposite of what takes place in constitutionally governed states; for the common people ought to be given power to vote the rejection of a measure, but not to vote its ratification, but it

---

90. There were *probouloi* at Corinth as well as a *boule* and an *ecclesia*; and *nomophulaces* at Sparta, Athens and elsewhere: At Athens they sat with *prytaneis* of the *boule* and ecclesia to check illegal procedure.

should be referred back to the magistrates. In constitutional governments the procedure is the reverse; the few are competent to vote the rejection of a resolution but are not competent to vote its ratification, this being always referred back to the most numerous body.

5.8. It remains to speak of monarchy, the causes that destroy it and the natural means of its preservation. And the things that happen about royal governments and tyrannies are almost similar to those that have been narrated about constitutional governments. For royal government corresponds with aristocracy, while tyranny is a combination of the last form of oligarchy and of democracy and for that very reason it is most harmful to its subjects, inasmuch as it is a combination of two bad things, and is liable to the deviations and errors that spring from both forms of constitution. And these two different sorts of monarchy have their origins from directly opposite sources; royalty has come into existence for the assistance of the distinguished against the people, and a king is appointed from those distinguished by superiority in virtue or the actions that spring from virtue, or by superiority in coming from a family of that character, while a tyrant is set up from among the people and the multitude to oppose the notables, in order that the people may suffer no injustice from them. And this is manifest from the facts of history. For almost the greatest number of tyrants have risen, it may be said, from being demagogues, having won the people's confidence by slandering the notables. For some tyrannies were set up in this manner when the states had already grown great, but others that came before them arose from kings departing from the ancestral customs and aiming at a more despotic rule, and others from the men elected to fill the supreme magistracies (for in old times the peoples used to appoint the popular officials and the sacred embassies[91] for long terms of office), and others from oligarchies electing some one supreme official for the greatest magistracies. For in all these methods they had it in their power to effect their purpose easily, if only they wished, because they already possessed the power of royal rule in the one set of cases and of their honorable office in the other, for example Phidon in Argos[92] and others became tyrants when they possessed royal power already, while the Ionian tyrants[93] and Phalaris[94] rose from offices of honor, and Panaetius at Leontini and Cypselus at Corinth and Pisistratus[95] at Athens and Dionysius[96] at Syracuse and others in the same manner from the position of demagogue. Therefore, as we said, royalty is ranged in correspondence with aristocracy, for it goes by merit, either by private virtue or by family or by services or by a combination of these things and ability. For in every instance this honor fell to men after they had conferred benefit or because they had the ability to confer benefit on their cities or their nations, some having prevented their enslavement in war, for instance Codrus,[97] others having set them free, for instance Cyrus,[98] or having settled or acquired territory, for instance the kings of Sparta and Macedon and the Molossians.[99] And a king wishes to be a guardian, to protect the owners of

---

91. Official missions to religious games and to oracles.
92. Perhaps c. 750 B.C.
93. E.g. Thrasybulus, tyrant of Miletus, 612 B.C.
94. Tyrant of Agrigentum 572 B.C.
95. Tyrant at Athens. 546–527 B.C.
96. Dionysius the elder, tyrant of Syracuse 405–367 B.C.
97. The usual tradition was that Codrus was already king when he saved Athens by sacrificing his life.
98. Cyrus liberated Persia from the Median empire in 559 B.C.
99. Neoptolemus, son of Achilles, conquered the Molossi and became their king.

estates from suffering injustice and the people from suffering insult, but tyranny, as has repeatedly been said, pays regard to no common interest unless for the sake of its private benefit; and the aim of tyranny is what is pleasant, that of royalty what is noble. Hence even in their requisitions money is the aim of tyrants but rather marks of honor that of kings; and a king's bodyguard consists of citizens, a tyrant's of foreign mercenaries. And it is manifest that tyranny has the evils of both democracy and oligarchy; it copies oligarchy in making wealth its object (for inevitably that is the only way in which the tyrant's bodyguard and his luxury can be kept up) and in putting no trust in the multitude (which is why they resort to the measure of stripping the people of arms, and why ill-treatment of the mob and its expulsion from the city and settlement in scattered places is common to both forms of government, both oligarchy and tyranny), while it copies democracy in making war on the notables and destroying them secretly and openly and banishing them as plotting against it and obstructive to its rule. For it is from them that counter movements actually spring, some of them wishing themselves to rule, and others not to be slaves. Hence comes the advice of Periander to Thrasybulus, his docking of the prominent corn stalks, meaning that the prominent citizens must always be made away with.

Therefore, as was virtually stated,[100] the causes of revolutions in constitutional and in royal governments must be deemed to be the same; for subjects in many cases attack monarchies because of unjust treatment and fear and contempt, and among the forms of unjust treatment most of all because of insolence, and sometimes the cause is the seizure of private property. Also the objects aimed at by the revolutionaries in the ease both of tyrannies and of royal governments are the same as in revolts against constitutional government; for monarchs possess great wealth and great honor, which are desired by all men. And in some cases the attack is aimed at the person of the rulers, in others at their office. Risings provoked by insolence are aimed against the person; and though insolence has many varieties, each of them gives rise to anger, and when men are angry they mostly attack for the sake of revenge, not of ambition. For example the attack on the Pisistratidae took place because they outraged Harmodius's sister and treated Harmodius with contumely (for Harmodius attacked them because of his sister and Aristogiton because of Harmodius, and also the plot was laid against Periander the tyrant in Ambracia because when drinking with his favorite he asked him if he was yet with child by him), and the attack on Philip by Pausanias[101] was because he allowed him to be insulted by Attalus and his friends, and that on Amyntas the Little[102] by Derdas because he mocked at his youth, and the attack of the eunuch on Evagoras of Cyprus was for revenge, for he murdered him as being insulted, because Evagoras's son had taken away his wife. And many risings have also occurred because of shameful personal indignities committed by certain monarchs. One instance is the attack of Crataeas on Archelaus;[103] for he was always resentful of the association, so that even a smaller excuse became sufficient, or

---

100. This has not been stated, but can be inferred from what preceeds.

101. A Macedonian youth of family, who murdered Philip in 336 B.C. Attalus was the uncle of Philip's second wife Cleopatra.

102. Perhaps the adjective should be transferred to Derdas and expunged as an interpolated note. The persons referred to are uncertain.

103. King of Macedon 413–399 B.C. Euripides went to reside at hie court in 408 B.C. and died there 406 B.C. at the age of 75.

perhaps it was because he did not give him the hand of one of his daughters after agreeing to do so, but gave the elder to the king of Elimea when hard pressed in a war against Sirras and Arrabacus, and the younger to his son Amyntas, thinking that thus Amyntas would be least likely to quarrel with his son by Cleopatra; but at all events Crataeas's estrangement was primarily caused by resentment because of the love affair. And Hellanocrates of Larisa also joined in the attack for the same reason; for because while enjoying his favors Archelaus would not restore him to his home although he had promised to do so, he thought that the motive of the familiarity that had taken place had been insolence and not passionate desire. And Pytho and Heraclides of Aenus made away with Cotys[104] to avenge their father, and Adamas revolted from Cotys because he had been mutilated by him when a boy, on the ground of the insult. And also many men when enraged by the indignity of corporal chastisement have avenged the insult by destroying or attempting to destroy its author, even when a magistrate or member of a royal dynasty. For example when the Penthilidae at Mitylene[105] went about striking people with their staves Megacles with his friends set on them and made away with them, and afterwards Smerdis when he had been beaten and dragged out from his wife's presence killed Penthilus. Also Decamnichus took a leading part in the attack upon Archelaus, being the first to stir on the attackers; and the cause of his anger was that he had handed him over to Euripides the poet to flog, Euripides being angry because he had made a remark about his breath smelling. And many others also for similar reasons have been made away with or plotted against. And similarly also from the motive of fear; for this was one of the causes we mentioned in the case of monarchies, as also in that of constitutional governments; for instance Artapanes[106] killed Xerxes fearing the charge about Darius, because he had hanged him when Xerxes had ordered him not to, but he had thought that he would forgive him because he would forget, as he had been at dinner. And other attacks on monarchs have been on account of contempt, as somebody killed Sardanapallus[107] when he saw him combing his hair with his women (if this story told by the narrators of legends is true—and if it did not happen with Sardanapallus, it might quite well be true of somebody else), and Dion attacked the younger Dionysius[108] because he despised him, when he saw the citizens despising him and the king himself always drunk. And contempt has led some even of the friends of monarchs to attack them, for they despise them for trusting them and think they will not be found out. And contempt is in a manner the motive of those who attack monarchs thinking that they are able to seize the government; for they make the attempt with a light heart, feeling that they have the power and because of their despising the danger, as generals commanding the armies attack their monarchs; for instance Cyrus attacked Astyages[109] when he despised both his mode of life and his power, because his power had waned and he himself was living luxuriously, and the Thracian Seuthes attacked Amadocus[110] when he was his general. Others again attack monarchs for more than one of these

---

104. King of Thrace 382–358 B.C.
105. The ruling family in the early oligarchy there, claiming descent from Penthilus, an illegitimate son of Orestes.
106. Captain of Xerxes' body guard.
107. Last king of the Assyrian empire at Nineveh.
108. Dionysius II, son of Dionysius the elder, tyrant of Syracuse 367–356 and 346–343 B.C.
109. The last king of Media, reigned 594–559 B.C.
110. Both these Thracian kings became allies of Athens in 390 B.C., but the event referred may be later.

motives, for instance both because they despise them and for the sake of gain, as Mithridates[111] attacked Ariobarzanes. And it is men of bold nature and who hold a military office with monarchs who most often make the attempt for this reason; for courage possessing power is boldness, and they make their attacks thinking that with courage and power they will easily prevail. But with those whose attack is prompted by ambition the motive operates in a different way from those spoken of before; some men attack tyrants because they see great profits and great honors belonging to them, but that is not the reason that in each ease leads the persons who attack from motives of ambition to resolve on the venture; those others are led by the motive stated, but these attack monarchs from a wish to gain not monarchy but glory, just as they would wish to take part in doing any other uncommon deed that makes men famous and known to their fellows. But those who make the venture from this motive are very few indeed in number, for underlying it there must be an utter disregard of safety, if regard for safety is not to check the enterprise; they must always have present in their minds the opinion of Dion, although it is not easy for many men to have it; Dion marched with a small force against Dionysius, saying that his feeling was that, whatever point he might be able to get to, it would be enough for him to have had that much share in the enterprise—for instance, if it should befall him to die as soon as he had just set foot in the country, that death would satisfy him.

And one way in which tyranny is destroyed, as is each of the other forms of constitution also, is from without, if some state with an opposite constitution is stronger (for the wish to destroy it will clearly be present in such a neighbor because of the opposition of principle, and all men do what they wish if they have the power)—and the constitutions opposed to tyranny are, on the one hand democracy, which is opposed to it as (in Hesiod's phrase[112]) "potter to potter," because the final form of democracy is tyranny, and on the other hand royalty and aristocracy are opposed to tyranny because of the opposite nature of their constitutional structure (owing to which the Spartans put down a very great many tyrannies, and so did the Syracusans at the period when they were governed well). But one way is from within itself, when the partners in it fall into discord, as the tyranny of the family of Gelo[113] was destroyed, and in modern times[114] that of the family of Dionysius—Gelo's, when Thrasybulus the brother of Hiero paid court to the son of Gelo and urged him into indulgences in order that he himself might rule, and the son's connections banded together a body of confederates in order that the tyranny might not be put down entirely but only Thrasybulus, but their confederates seizing the opportunity expelled them all; Dionysius was put down by Dion, his relative, who got the people on to his side and expelled him, but was afterwards killed. There are two causes that chiefly lead men to attack tyranny, hatred and contempt; the former, hatred, attaches to tyrants always, but it is their being despised that causes their downfall in many cases. A proof of this is that most of those that have won tyrannies have also kept their offices to the end, but those that have inherited them almost all lose them at once; for they live a life of indulgence, and so become despicable and also give many opportunities to their attackers. And also anger must be counted as an element in the hatred felt

---

111. Perhaps Mithridates II, who succeeded his father Ariobarzanes as satrap of Pontus in 336 B.C.
112. Hesiod, *Works and Days*, 25, "two of a trade never agree."
113. Tyrant Of Syracuse 485–478 B.C., succeeded by his brother Hiero who died in 467 B.C. Gelo's son is unknown.
114. 356 B.C., a good many years before this book was written.

for them, for in a way it occasions the same actions. And often it is even more active than hatred, since angry men attack more vigorously because passion does not employ calculation (and insolence most frequently causes men to be led by their angry tempers, which was the cause of the fall of the tyranny of the Pisistratidae and many others), but hatred calculates more; for anger brings with it an element of pain, making calculation difficult, but enmity is not accompanied by pain. And to speak summarily, all the things that we have mentioned as causing the downfall of unmixed and extreme oligarchy and of the last form of democracy must be counted as destructive of tyranny as well, since extreme oligarchy and democracy are in reality divided a tyrannies. Royal government on the other hand is very seldom destroyed by external causes, so that it is long lasting; but in most cases its destruction arises out of itself. And it is destroyed in two ways, one when those who participate in it quarrel, and another when the kings try to administer the government too tyrannically, claiming to exercise sovereignty in more things and contrary to the law. Royal governments do not occur any more now, but if ever monarchies do occur they are rather tyrannies, because royalty is government over willing subjects but with sovereignty over greater matters, but men of equal quality are numerous and no one is so outstanding as to fit the magnitude and dignity of the office so that for this reason the subjects do not submit willingly, and if a man has made himself ruler by deception or force, then this is thought to be a tyranny. In cases of hereditary royalty we must also set down as a cause of their destruction, in addition to those mentioned, the fact that hereditary kings often become despicable, and that although possessing not the power of a tyrant but the dignity of a king they commit insolent outrages; for the deposition of kings used to be easy, since a king will at once cease to be king if his subjects do not wish him to be, whereas a tyrant will still be tyrant even though his subjects do not wish it.

These causes then and others of the same nature are those that bring about the destruction of monarchies.

5.9. On the other hand it is clear that monarchies, speaking generally, are preserved in safety as a result of the opposite causes to those by which they are destroyed. But taking the different sorts of monarchy separately—royalties are preserved by bringing them into a more moderate form; for the fewer powers the kings have, the longer time the office in its entirety must last, for they themselves become less despotic and more equal to their subjects in temper, and their subjects envy them less. For this was the cause of the long persistence of the Molossian royalty, and that of Sparta has continued because the office was from the beginning divided into two halves, and because it was again limited in various ways by Theopompus,[115] in particular by his instituting the office of the ephors to keep a check upon it; for by taking away some of the kings' power he increased the permanence of the royal office, so that in a manner he did not make it less but greater. This indeed as the story goes is what he said in reply to his wife, when she asked if he felt no shame in bequeathing the royal power to his sons smaller than he had inherited it from his father: "Indeed I do not," he is said to have answered, "for I hand it on more lasting."

Tyrannies on the other hand are preserved in two extremely opposite ways. One of these is the traditional way and the one in which most tyrants administer their office. Most of these ordinary safeguards of tyranny are said to have been instituted by Periander[116] of Corinth, and also many

---

115. King of Sparta c. 770–790 B.C.
116. Tyrant of Corinth c. 626–585 B.C.

such devices may be borrowed from the Persian empire. These are both the measures mentioned some time back to secure the safety of a tyranny as far as possible—the lopping off of outstanding men and the destruction of the proud—and also the prohibition of common meals and club-fellowship and education and all other things of this nature, in fact the close watch upon all things that usually engender the two emotions of pride and confidence, and the prevention of the formation of study circles and other conferences for debate,[117] and the employment of every means that will make people as much as possible unknown to one another (for familiarity increases mutual confidence); and for the people in the city to be always visible and to hang about the palace-gates (for thus there would be least concealment about what they are doing, and they would get into a habit of being humble from always acting in a servile way); and all the other similar devices of Persian and barbarian tyranny (for all have the same effect); and to try not to be uninformed about any chance utterances or actions of any of the subjects, but to have spies like the women called "provocatrices" at Syracuse and the "sharp-ears" that used to be sent out by Hiero wherever there was any gathering or conference (for when men are afraid of spies of this sort they keep a check on their tongues, and if they do speak freely are less likely not to be found out); and to set men at variance with one another and cause quarrels between friend and friend and between the people and the notables and among the rich. And it is a device of tyranny to make the subjects poor, so that a guard[118] may not be kept, and also that the people being busy with their daily affairs may not have leisure to plot against their ruler. Instances of this are the pyramids in Egypt and the votive offerings of the Cypselids,[119] and the building of the temple of Olympian Zeus by the Pisistratidae[120] and of the temples at Samos, works of Polycrates[121] (for all these undertakings produce the same effect, constant occupation and poverty among the subject people) and the levying bf taxes, as at Syracuse (for in the reign of Dionysius a the result of taxation used to be that in five years men had contributed the whole of their substance). Also the tyrant is a stirrer-up of war, with the deliberate purpose of keeping the people busy and also of making them constantly in need of a leader. Also whereas friends are a means of security to royalty, it is a mark of a tyrant to be extremely distrustful of his friends, on the ground that, while all have the wish, these chiefly have the power. Also the things that occur in connection with the final form of democracy are all favorable to tyranny—dominance of women in the homes, in order that they may carry abroad reports against the men, and lack of discipline among the slaves, for the same reason; for slaves and women do not plot against tyrants, and also, if they prosper under tyrannies, must feel well disposed to them, and to democracies as well (for the common people also wishes to be sole ruler). Hence also the flatterer is in honor with both—with democracies the demagogue (for the demagogue is a flatterer of the people), and with the tyrants those who associate with them humbly, which is the task of flattery. In fact owing to this tyranny is a friend

---

117. These phrases cover Plato's gatherings in the Academy, Aristotle's in the Peripatos of the Lyceum, and other meetings for the intellectuals use of leisure in gymnasia, palestrae and leschae.

118. Apparently this means a citizen force side by side with the tyrant's mercenaries; a variant gives "in order that the (tyrant's) guard may be kept."

119. Cypselus and his son Periander dedicated a colossal statue to Zeus at Olympia and other monuments there and at Delphi.

120. Pisitratus is said to have begun the temple of Olympian Zeus at Athens, not finished till the time of Hadrian.

121. Tyrant of Samos, d. 522 B.C.

of the base; for tyrants enjoy being flattered, but nobody would ever flatter them if he possessed a free spirit—men of character love their ruler, or at all events do not flatter him. And the base are useful for base business, for nail is driven out by nail, as the proverb goes.[122] And it is a mark of a tyrant to dislike anyone that is proud or free-spirited; for the tyrant claims for himself alone the right to bear that character, and the man who meets his pride with pride and shows a free spirit robs tyranny of its superiority and position of mastery; tyrants therefore hate the proud as undermining their authority. And it is a mark of a tyrant to have men of foreign extraction rather than citizens as guests at table and companions, feeling that citizens are hostile but strangers make no claim against him.[123] These and similar habits are characteristic of tyrants and preservative of their office, but they lack no element of baseness. And broadly speaking, they are all included under three heads for tyranny aims at three things, one to keep its subjects humble (for a humble-spirited man would not plot against anybody), second to have them continually distrust one another (for a tyranny is not destroyed until some men come to trust each other, owing to which tyrants also make war on the respectable, as detrimental to their rule not only because of their refusal to submit to despotic rule, but also because they are faithful to one another and to the other citizens, and do not inform against one another nor against the others); and the third is lack of power for political action (since nobody attempts impossibilities, so that nobody tries to put down a tyranny if he has not power behind him). These then in fact are the three aims to which the plans of tyrants are directed; for all the measures taken by tyrants one might class under these principles—some are designed to prevent mutual confidence among the subjects, others to curtail their power, and others to make them humble-spirited.

Such then is the nature of one method by which security is obtained for tyrannies. The other tries to operate in a manner almost the opposite of the devices mentioned. And it can be ascertained from considering the downfall of royal governments. For just as one mode of destroying royalty is to make its government more tyrannical, so a mode of securing tyranny is to make it more regal, protecting one thing only, its power, in order that the ruler may govern not only with the consent of the subjects but even without it; for if he gives up this, he also gives up his position as tyrant. But while this must stand as a fundamental principle, in all his other actions real or pretended he should cleverly play the part of royalty. The first step is to be careful of the public funds, not squandering presents such as the multitudes resent, when tyrants take money from the people themselves while they toil and labor in penury and lavish it on mistresses and foreigners and craftsmen, and also rendering account of receipts and expenditure, as some tyrants have done already (for this careful management would make a ruler seem a steward of the state and not a tyrant, and he need not be afraid of ever being at a loss for funds while he is master of the state; on the contrary, for those tyrants who go abroad on foreign campaigns this is actually more expedient than to leave their money there collected into one sum, for there is less fear of those guarding it making an attempt on power; since for tyrants campaigning abroad the keepers of the treasury are more to be feared than the citizens, for the citizens go abroad with him but the others stay at home). Secondly he must be seen to collect his taxes and benevolences for purposes of

---

122. The proverb usually meant driving out something by a thing of the same kind ("set a thief to catch a thief"), not as here the execution of evil designs by appropriate agents.
123. I.e. they do not claim to be respected as equals.

administration and to meet his occasional requirements for military emergencies, and generally must pose as guardian and steward as it were of a public fund and not a private estate. And his bearing must not be harsh but dignified, and also such as to inspire not fear but rather respect in those who encounter him, though this is not easy to achieve if he is a contemptible personality; so that even if he neglects the other virtues he is bound to cultivate military valor, and to make himself a reputation as a soldier. And furthermore not only must he himself be known not to outrage any of his subjects, either boy or girl, but so also must everybody about him, and also their wives must similarly show respect towards the other women, since even the insolences of women have caused the fall of many tyrannies. And in regard to bodily enjoyments he must do the opposite of what some tyrants do now (for they not only begin their debaucheries at daybreak and carry them on for many days at a time, but also wish to be seen doing so by the public, in order that people may admire them as fortunate and happy), but best of all he must be moderate in such matters, or if not, he must at all events avoid displaying his indulgences to his fellows (for not the sober man but the drunkard is easy to attack and to despise, not the wakeful man but the sleeper). And he must do the opposite of almost all the things mentioned some time back, for he must lay out and adorn the city as if he were a trustee and not a tyrant. And further he must be seen always to be exceptionally zealous as regards religious observances (for people are less afraid of suffering any illegal treatment from men of this sort, if they think that their ruler has religious scruples and pays regard to the gods, and also they plot against him less, thinking that he has even the gods as allies), though he should not display a foolish religiosity. And he must pay such honor to those who display merit in any matter that they may think that they could never be more honored by the citizens if they were independent; and honors of this kind he should bestow in person, but inflict his punishments by the agency of other magistrates and law-courts. And it is a protection common to every sort of monarchy to make no one man great, but if necessary to exalt several (for they will keep watch on one another), and if after all the ruler has to elevate an individual, at all events not take a man of bold spirit (for such a character is most enterprising in all undertakings); and if he thinks fit to remove somebody from his power, to do this by gradual stages and not take away the whole of his authority at once. And again he should carefully avoid all forms of outrage, and two beyond all, violent bodily punishments and outrage of the young. And this caution must especially be exercised in relation to the ambitious, for while to be slighted in regard to property annoys the lovers of wealth, slights that involve dishonor are what men of honorable ambition and high character resent. Hence the tyrant should either not consort with men of this kind, or appear to inflict his punishments paternally and not because of contempt, and to indulge in the society of the young for reasons of passion, not because he has the power, and in general he should buy off what are thought to be dishonors by greater honors. And among those who make attempts upon the life of a ruler the most formidable and those against whom the greatest precaution is needed are those that are ready to sacrifice their lives if they can destroy him. Hence the greatest care must be taken to guard against those who think that insolent outrage is being done either to themselves or to those who happen to be under their care; for men attacking under the influence of anger are reckless of themselves, as Heraclitus[124] also observed when he said that anger is hard to combat because it buys its wish with life. And since states con-

---

124. A philosopher of Ephesus, flourished c. 513 B.C.

sist of two parts, the poor people and the rich, the most important thing is for both to think that they owe their safety to the government and for it to prevent either from being wronged by the other, but whichever class is the stronger, this must be made to be entirely on the side of the government, as, if this support for the tyrant's interests is secured, there is no need for him to institute a liberation of slaves or a disarming of the citizens, for one of the two parts of the state added to his power will be enough to make him and them stronger than their attackers. But to discuss each of such matters separately is superfluous for the thing to aim at is clear, that it is necessary to appear to the subjects to be not a tyrannical ruler but a steward and a royal governor, and not an appropriator of wealth but a trustee, and to pursue the moderate things of life and not its extravagances, and also to make the notables one's comrades and the many one's followers. For the result of these methods must be that not only the tyrant's rule will be more honorable and more enviable because he will rule nobler subjects and not men that have been humiliated, and will not be continually hated and feared, but also that his rule will endure longer, and moreover that he himself in his personal character will be nobly disposed towards virtue, or at all events half virtuous, and not base but only half base.

Nevertheless oligarchy and tyranny are less lasting than any of the constitutional governments. For the longest-lived was the tyranny at Sicyon, that of the sons[125] of Orthagoras and of Orthagoras himself, and this lasted a hundred years.[126] The cause of this was that they treated their subjects moderately and in many matters were subservient to the laws, and Cleisthenes because he was a warlike man was not easily despised, and in most things they kept the lead of the people by looking after their interests. At all events it is said that Cleisthenes placed a wreath on the judge who awarded the victory away from him, and some say that the statue of a seated figure in the market place is a statue of the man who gave this judgment. And they say that Pisistratus also once submitted to a summons for trial before the Areopagus. And the second longest is the tyranny at Corinth, that of the Cypselids,[127] for even this lasted seventy-three and a half years, as Cypselus was tyrant for thirty years, Periander for forty-four,[128] and Psammetichus son of Gordias for three years. And the reasons for the permanence of this tyranny also are the same: Cypselus was a leader of the people and continuously throughout his period of office dispensed with a bodyguard; and although Periander became tyrannical, yet he was warlike. The third longest tyranny is that of the Pisistratidae at Athens, but it was not continuous; for while Pisistratus a was tyrant he twice fled into exile, so that in a period of thirty-three years he was tyrant for seventeen years out of the total, and his sons for eighteen years, so that the whole duration of their rule was thirty-five years. Among the remaining tyrannies is the one connected with Hiero and Gelo at Syracuse, but even this did not last many years, but only eighteen in all, for Gelo after being tyrant for seven years ended his life in the eighth, and Hiero ruled ten years, but Thrasybulus was expelled after ten months. And the usual tyrannies have all of them been of quite short duration.

The causes therefore of the destruction of constitutional governments and of monarchies and those again of their preservation have almost all of them been discussed.

---

125. Actually "descendants;" Cleisthenes was his grandson.
126. From 670 B.C.
127. From 655 B.C.
128. The Greek may be corrected to "forty four and a half" to give the stated total.

8.1. Now nobody would dispute that the education of the young requires the special attention of the lawgiver. Indeed the neglect of this in states is injurious to their constitutions; for education ought to be adapted to the particular form of constitution, since the particular character belonging to each constitution both guards the constitution generally and originally establishes it—for instance the democratic spirit promotes democracy and the oligarchic spirit oligarchy; and a better spirit always produces a better constitution. Moreover in regard to all the faculties and crafts certain forms of preliminary education and training in their various operations are necessary, so that manifestly this is also requisite in regard to the actions of virtue. And inasmuch as the end for the whole state is one, it is manifest that education also must necessarily be one and the same for all and that the superintendence of this must be public, and not on private lines, in the way in which at present each man superintends the education of his own children, teaching them privately, and whatever special branch of knowledge he thinks fit. But matters of public interest ought to be under public supervision; at the same time also we ought not to think that any of the citizens belongs to himself, but that all belong to the state, for each is a part of the state, and it is natural for the superintendence of the several parts to have regard to the superintendence of the whole. And one might praise the Spartans in respect of this, for they pay the greatest attention to the training of their children, and conduct it on a public system.

It is clear then that there should be legislation about education and that it should be conducted on a public system. But consideration must be given to the question, what constitutes education and what is the proper way to be educated. At present there are differences of opinion as to the proper tasks to be set; for all peoples do not agree as to the things that the young ought to learn, either with a view to virtue or with a view to the best life, nor is it clear whether their studies should be regulated more with regard to intellect or with regard to character. And confusing questions arise out of the education that actually prevails, and it is not at all clear whether the pupils should practice pursuits that are practically useful, or morally edifying, or higher accomplishments—for all these views have won the support of some judges; and nothing is agreed as regards the exercise conducive to virtue, for, to start with, all men do not honor the same virtue, so that they naturally hold different opinions in regard to training in virtue.

Three Greek Poets 22

MIMNERMUS: FRAGMENTS

Mimnermus was from Ionia and has been labeled the "inventor of elegy." The ancient Alexandrians knew of two books of poetry by him, but only brief fragments survive. His appeal as a love poet, and the nostalgia of the passing of youth, come across naturally and clearly in the verses below.

What life is there, what pleasure without golden Aphrodite?
May I die when I no longer care about secret intrigues,
persuasive gifts, and the bed,
those blossoms of youth that men and women find alluring.
But when painful old age comes on,
which makes even a handsome man ugly,
grievous cares wear away his heart
and he derives no joy from looking upon the sunlight;
he is hateful to boys and women hold him in no honor.
So harsh has the god made old age.

We are like the leaves which the flowery season of spring brings forth,
when they quickly grow beneath the rays of the sun;
like them we delight in the flowers of youth for an arm's length of time,
knowing neither the bad nor the good that comes from the gods.
But the dark spirits of doom stand beside us,
one holding grievous old age as the outcome, the other death.
Youth's fruit is short-lived, lasting as long as the sunlight spreads over the earth.[1]
And when the end of this season passes by,
straightway death is better than life.

For many are the miseries that beset one's heart.
Sometimes a man's estate wastes away and a painful life of poverty is his;
another in turn lacks sons
and longing for them most of all he goes beneath the earth to Hades;
another has soul-destroying illness.
There is no one to whom Zeus does not give a multitude of ills.

For the Sun's lot is toil every day
and there is never any respite for him and his horses,
from the moment rose-fingered Dawn leaves Oceanus
and goes up into the sky.
A lovely bed, hollow, forged by the hands of Hephaestus,
of precious gold and winged, carries him, as he sleeps soundly,
over the waves on the water's surface from the place of the Hesperides[2]
to the land of the Ethiopians,[3]
where his swift chariot and horses stand[4] until early-born Dawn comes.
There the son of Hyperion mounts his other vehicle.

THEOGNIS

Theognis is the only elegist for which there is a corpus of work surviving in its original manuscript tradition. It consists of about 1,400 verses, but it is almost certainly a composite of two or three anthologies of elegiac excerpts, Theognis being only one of many poets included. Scholars have identified some 308 verses as definitely by Theognis, though some of the rest may be his. Drinking and merry-making are frequent themes, but some pieces are reflective and philosophic.

1–4
O lord, son of Leto, child of Zeus,[5]
I will never forget you at the beginning or at the end,
but I will ever sing of you first, last, and in between;
and do you give ear to me and grant me success.

---

1. I.e., for a day.
2. Daughters of the night who garded the golden apples of the far west.
3. Here a mythical people located in the far east.
4. It is unclear whether Mimnermus assumes that the Sun had a new chariot and horses every day or that they somehow hot back to the east while the sun slept. The poet does not suggest that they were also in the "bed."
5. Apollo

5–10

Lord Phoebus, when the august goddess Leto gave birth to you,
fairest of the immortals, as she clasped the palm-tree
with her slender arms beside the circular lake,[6]
all Delos was filled from end to end with an ambrosial aroma,
the vast earth beamed,
and the deep expanse of the white-capped sea rejoiced.

11–14

Artemis, slayer of wild beasts, daughter of Zeus,
for whom Agamemnon set up a temple[7]
when he was preparing to sail on his swift ships to Troy,
give ear to my prayer and ward off the evil death-spirits.
For you, goddess, this is a small thing, but for me it is critical.[8]

15–18

Muses and Graces, daughters of Zeus,
who came once to the wedding of Cadmus[9] and sang the lovely verse,
"What is beautiful is loved, what is not beautiful is not loved."
This is the verse that went through your immortal lips.

133–142

No one, Cyrnus, is responsible on his own for ruin or profit,
but it is the gods who give both.
Nor does anyone know in his heart whether his toil
will turn out well or badly in the end.
For often a man who thought he would fail succeeds
and a man who thought he would succeed fails.
No one has at hand everything he wants,
since the constraints of grievous helplessness hold him back.
We mortals have vain thoughts, not knowledge;
it is the gods who bring everything to pass according to their own intent.

183–192

We seek out rams and asses and horses that are purebred, Cyrnus,
and everyone wishes that they mount (females) of good stock;
but a noble man does not mind marrying the base daughter of a base father

---

6. Actually a pond used as a reservoir.

7. According to Pausanias 1.43.1 Agamemnon set up this temple in Megara when he went there to persuade Calchas to accompany him to Troy.

8. The author, identified by Aristotle as Theognis, is presumably about to go on a voyage and is praying to Artemis in her capacity as the protector of seafarers.

9. The wedding in Thebes of Cadmus and Harmonia, daughter of Ares and Aphrodite, was attended by the gods.

if the latter gives him a lot of money,
and a woman does not refuse to be the wife of a base man who is rich,
but she wants a wealthy man instead of one who is noble.
It is money people honor;
one who is noble marries the daughter of one who is base
and one who is base marries the daughter of one who is noble.
Wealth has mixed up blood.
And so, Polypaides, do not be surprised that the townsmen's stock is becoming enfeebled,
since what is noble is mixing with what is base.

271–278

The gods have given mortal men an equal share of other things, accursed old age and youth,
but there is something that is the worst and most grievous of all things in human life,
including death and every kind of sickness,
(namely, that) whenever you have raised sons,
provided everything that is fitting,
and stored up wealth (for them) after much bitter suffering,
they hate their father, pray for his death,
and loathe him as if he were a beggar at the door.

373–400

Dear Zeus, I'm surprised at you.
You are lord over all, you alone have great power and prestige,
you know well the mind and heart of every man,
and your rule, king, is the highest of all.
How then, son of Cronus, does your mind bear to hold sinners
and the just man in the same esteem,
whether the mind of men is disposed to prudent discretion
or to wanton outrage, when they yield to unjust acts?
Have no rules been set by divinity for mortals,
is there no path along which one can go and please the immortals?
[Some people rob and steal quite shamelessly,][10]
but for all that they have a prosperity free from harm,
while others who refrain from wicked deeds nevertheless get poverty,
the mother of helplessness, despite their love of justice,
poverty which leads men's hearts astray to sinful action,
impairing their wits under the force of necessity.
Against his will a man brings himself to endure much that is shameful,
yielding to need which teaches many bad ways,
including lies, deceit, and deadly strife, even though he is unwilling.

---

10. Suggestion for the contents of the lacuna (M.L. West, *Studies in Greek Elegy and Iambus*, Berlin, 1974).

There is no ill comparable to need, for it gives birth to painful helplessness.
In poverty, whenever need takes hold,
both the base man and he who is much better are brought to light.
For the latter's mind has its thoughts on justice
and straight judgment is ever implanted in his breast,
while the former's mind does not go along with either bad times or good.[11]
The noble man must bring himself to endure both, to respect his friends,
and to shun false oaths that bring ruin to men. . . .
carefully, avoiding the wrath of the immortals.

429–438

It is easier to beget and rear a man than to put good sense in him.
No one has yet devised a means whereby one has made the fool wise
and a noble man out of one who is base.
If the god had granted this power to the Asclepiads,[12]
to cure men's baseness and muddled wits,
they would be earning many a handsome fee.
And if good sense could be made and placed in a man,
there would never be a base son of a noble father,
since he would heed words of wisdom.
But you will never make the base man noble through teaching.

511–522

You've crossed the deep sea, Clearistus,[13]
and come here penniless, poor fellow, to one who's penniless.
But I'll provide the best of what there is,
and if any friend of yours comes along,
recline as suits your degree of friendship.[14]
I'll not hold back anything of what I have
nor bring in more from elsewhere to entertain you.
I'll stow under the benches at the side of your ship, Clearistus,
such as I have and the gods provide.
And if anyone asks how I live, reply to him as follows:
"Poorly by good standards, but quite well by poor standards,[15]
and so he doesn't fail one friend of the family,
but is unable to offer entertainment to more."

---

11. The may be textual corruption here, but perhaps the meaning is that the base man cannot accommodate himself to either bad or good fortune.

12. Literally, "descendants of Asclepius," the god of healing, but here simply "physicians."

13. Identity unknown.

14. Seating arrangements were very important at the symposium, or formal banquet.

15. More literally, "compared to one who lives well, he lives poorly, but compared to one who lives poorly, he lives well."

903–930

He who watches over his spending according to his means
is held in the highest esteem by men of understanding.
For if it were possible to see the end of life,
how much one was destined to complete before passing into Hades,
it would be reasonable for the man who expected a longer period of life
to be more sparing, so that he might have livelihood.
But as things are, it's impossible.
Because of this I am greatly saddened, torn at heart, and of two minds.
I'm standing at the crossroads, with two ways ahead of me,
and deliberating which of them to choose,
whether to spend nothing and wear away my life in misery
or to live a life of pleasure, accomplishing little.
For I have seen one who was sparing
and though wealthy never gave his belly the food of a freeman,
but he went down to the house of Hades before spending his money(?)
and some chance person got his property;
as a result he toiled to no purpose
and did not give (his money) to whomever he wished.
And I have seen another who gratifying his belly squandered his money,
having delighted his heart with the eating of sweet food;
he begs from all his friends, wherever he sees any.
So, Democles, it is best of all to spend according to one's means and to be careful.
For you won't give another the fruit of your labors after a life of toil
nor will you be a beggar and endure slavery.
Not even if you reach old age will all your means run out.
In such a generation as this it's best to have money.
For if you are wealthy, many are your friends, but few if you are poor,
and you are no longer the same worthy man you once were.

SAPPHO

Sappho of Lesbos is perhaps antiquity's greatest love poet, especially admired by a society where women rarely achieved renown. She lived around 600 B.C., but very little is known about her life, except for the speculation that survives. Poetry dedicated to her companions focus almost entirely on her love for one of them. Her poetry is simple and personal, her control of words and themes are the mark of artistic genius.

Before Their Time

Six birthdays of mine had passed when the bones of my parent,
gathered from the pyre,
drank before their time my tears.[16]

The Fairest Thing on Earth

Some say a host of cavalry,
others of infantry,
and others of ships,
is the most beautiful thing on the black earth,
but I say it is whatsoever a person loves.

It is perfectly easy to make this understood by everyone:
for she who far surpassed mankind in beauty, Helen,
left her most noble husband and went sailing off to Troy
with no thought at all for her child or dear parents,
but (love) led her astray . . . lightly . .

(and she?) has reminded me now of Anactoria who is not here;
I would rather see her lovely walk and the bright sparkle of her face
than the Lydians' chariots and armed infantry. . .[17]

My Trembling Heart

He seems as fortunate as the gods to me, the man who sits opposite you
and listens nearby to your sweet voice and lovely laughter.
Truly that sets my heart trembling in my breast.
For when I look at you for a moment,
then it is no longer possible for me to speak;
my tongue has broken,
at once a subtle fire has stolen beneath my flesh,
I see nothing with my eyes, my ears hum,
sweat pours from me, a trembling seizes me all over,
I am greener than grass,
and it seems to me that I am little short of dying.
But all can be endured, since . . .[18]

---

16. Quoted by Ovid, Heroides, 15.61.
17. Fragment from a papyrus, P. Oxy. 1231.
18 .Quoted by Longinus, *On Sublimity*, 10.1–3.

To an Uneducated Woman

But when you die you will lie there,
and afterwards there will never be any recollection of you
or any longing for you since you have no share in the roses of Pieria;[19]
unseen in the house of Hades also, flown from our midst,
you will go to and fro among the shadowy corpses.[20]

The Sweetest Apple

As the sweet-apple reddens on the bough-top,
on the top of the topmost bough;
the apple-gatherers have forgotten it
—no they have not forgotten it entirely,
but they could not reach it.[21]

The Purple Hyacinth

Like the wild hyacinth flower,
Which on the hills is found,
And which the passing feet of shepherds
Forever tear and wound,
Until the purple blossom is trodden into the ground.[22]

The Moon Has Set

The silver moon has set
and the Pleiades are gone;
half the long night is spent, and yet,
I lie alone.[23]

---

19. In Macedonia; birthplace of the Muses.
20. Quoted by Stobaeus, Anthology, 3.4.12.
21. Quoted by Syrianus , *Hermogenes*, 1.1.
22. Quoted by Demetrius, *De Elocutione*, 106.
23. Quoted in Hephaestion, *Handbook on Metres*, 11.5.

Chapter 4

Ancient Rome

Scene from the Ara Pacis Augustae, the Alter of the Augustan Peace, Mother Earth,
or a personification of Italy, with two children on her lap. The Ara Pacis, Rome.

Livy: From the Founding of the City

23

Livy (Titus Livius, c. 64B.C.–c. A.D. 12) was a native of Patavium (Padua). He was a Romanized Celt who wrote the first great history of Rome in Latin, Ab urbe condita (From the Foundation of the City). *It contained 142 books and recorded Roman history down to 9 B.C. Only 35 books survive, however. His purpose was to use history as means of moral education. In his preface Livy says that he wishes to record the great achievements of the Romans, the sovereigns of the world, and to teach by example noble conduct and virtue. This attitude is, of course, rather in conflict with the point of view of much of modern historical thought, which seems most concerned with exposing the depravity of human nature, but Livy has, nevertheless, exerted great influence on historiography. Because so much historical writing is overwhelmingly negative and pessimistic, reading Livy can be quite refreshing.*

THE RAPE OF LUCRETIA

The first age of Roman history is the Kingdom, the period between the traditional founding of Rome in 753 B.C. by the legendary Romulus and the establishment of the Republic, traditionally dated in 509 B.C. The history of this age is shrouded in legend and myth. At least some of Romulus' six successors were historical figures. The last king of Rome, the tyrannical Tarquinius Superbus ("the Proud"), was overthrown by an oligarchic revolution and the aristocratic patrician class set up a republic. That event also was surrounded by legend and romance. Livy recorded it as history in the excerpt below.

1.56. Being intent upon completing the temple, the king called in workmen from every quarter of Etruria, and used for this purpose not only the state funds but laborers drawn from the commons. This work was far from light in itself, and was added to their military service. Yet the plebeians felt less abused at having to build with their own hands the temples of the gods, than

---

From *Livy, Volume I*, translated by B.O. Foster, Ph.D. (Cambridge, Loeb Classical Library, Harvard University Press, 1919).

they did when they came to be transferred to other tasks also, which, while less in show, were yet rather more laborious. I mean the erection of seats in the circus, and the construction underground of the Great Sewer, as a receptacle for all the off-scourings of the City—two works for which the new splendor of these days has scarcely been able to produce a match. After making the plebeians toil at these hard tasks, the king felt that a populace which had now no work to do was only a burden to the City; he wished, moreover, by sending out settlers, to extend the frontiers of his dominions. He therefore sent colonists to Signia and Circei, to safeguard the City by land and sea.

While he was thus occupied, a terrible portent appeared. A snake glided out of a wooden pillar, causing fright and commotion in the palace. As for the king himself, his heart was not so much struck with sudden terror as filled with anxious forebodings. Now for public prodigies none but Etruscan soothsayers were wont to be employed, but this domestic apparition, as he regarded it, so thoroughly alarmed him that he determined to send to Delphi, the most famous oracle in the world; and, not daring to trust the oracle's reply to anybody else, he sent two of his sons, through strange lands, as they were then, and over stranger seas, to Greece. Titus and Arruns were the ones who went; and, to bear them company, Lucius Junius Brutus was sent too, the son of Tarquinia, sister of the king, a young man of a very different mind from that which he pretended to bear. Having heard that the leading men of the state, and among them his own brother, had been put to death by his uncle, he determined to leave nothing in his disposition which the king might justly fear, nor anything in his fortune to covet, resolving to find safety in contempt, where justice afforded no protection. He therefore deliberately assumed the appearance of stupidity, and permitted himself and his property to become the spoil of the king; he even accepted the surname Brutus,[1] that behind the screen afforded by this title the great soul which was to free the Roman People might bide its time unseen. He it was who was then taken by the Tarquinii to Delphi, more as a butt than as a comrade; and he is said to have carried a golden staff enclosed within one of cornel wood, hollowed out to receive it, as a gift to Apollo, and a roundabout indication of his own character. When they came there, and had carried out their father's instructions, a desire sprang up in the hearts of the youths to find out which one of them should be king at Rome. From the depths of the cavern this answer, they say, was returned "The highest power at Rome shall be his, young men, who shall be first among you to kiss his mother." The Tarquinii, anxious that Sextus, who had been left in Rome, might know nothing of the answer and have no share in the rule, gave orders that the incident should be kept strictly secret; as between themselves, they decided by lot which should be first, upon their return to Rome, to give their mother a kiss. Brutus thought the Pythian utterance had another meaning; pretending to stumble, he fell and touched his lips to Earth, evidently regarding her as the common mother of all mortals. They then returned to Rome, where preparations for war with the Rutuli were being pushed with the greatest vigor.

1.57. Ardea belonged to the Rutuli, who were a nation of commanding wealth, for that place and period. This very fact was the cause of the war, since the Roman king was eager not only to enrich himself, impoverished as he was by the splendor of his public works, but also to appease with booty the feeling of the common people; who, besides the enmity they bore the monarch

---

1. Literally "Dullard."

for other acts of pride, were especially resentful that the king should have kept them employed so long as artisans and doing the work of slaves. An attempt was made to capture Ardea by assault. Having failed in this, the Romans invested the place with entrenchments, and began to beleaguer the enemy. Here in their permanent camp, as is usual with a war not sharp but long drawn out, furlough was rather freely granted, more freely however to the leaders than to the soldiers; the young princes for their part passed their idle hours together at dinners and drinking bouts. It chanced, as they were drinking in the quarters of Sextus Tarquinius, where Tarquinius Collatinus, son of Egerius, was also a guest, that the subject of wives came up. Every man fell to praising his own wife with enthusiasm, and, as their rivalry grew hot, Collatinus said that there was no need to talk about it, for it was in their power to know, in a few hours' time, how far the rest were excelled by his own Lucretia. "Come! If the vigor of youth is in us let us mount our horses and see for ourselves the disposition of our wives. Let every man regard as the surest test what meets his eyes when the woman's husband enters unexpected." They were heated with wine. "Agreed" they all cried, and clapping spurs to their horses were off for Rome. Arriving there at early dusk, they thence proceeded to Collatia, where Lucretia was discovered very differently employed from the daughters-in-law of the king. These they had seen at a luxurious banquet, whiling away the time with their young friends; but Lucretia, though it was late at night, was busily engaged upon her wool, while her maidens toiled about her in the lamplight as she sat in the hall of her house. The prize of this contest in womanly virtues fell to Lucretia. As Collatinus and the Tarquinii approached, they were graciously received, and the victorious husband courteously invited the young princes to his table. It was there that Sextus Tarquinius was seized with a wicked desire to debauch Lucretia by force; not only her beauty, but her proved chastity as well, provoked him. However, for the present they ended the boyish prank of the night and returned to the camp.

1.58. When a few days had gone by, Sextus Tarquinius, without letting Collatinus know, took a single attendant and went to Collatia. Being kindly welcomed, for no one suspected his purpose, he was brought after dinner to a guest-chamber. Burning with passion, he waited till it seemed to him that all about him was secure and everybody fast asleep; then, drawing his sword, he came to the sleeping Lucretia. Holding the woman down with his left hand on her breast, he said, "Be still, Lucretia! I am Sextus Tarquinius. My sword is in my hand. Utter a sound, and you die!" In affright the woman started out of her sleep. No help was in sight, but only imminent death. Then Tarquinius began to declare his love, to plead, to mingle threats with prayers, to bring every resource to bear upon her woman's heart. When he found her obdurate and not to be moved even by fear of death, he went farther and threatened her with disgrace, saying that when she was dead he would kill his slave and lay him naked by her side, that she might be said to have been put to death in adultery with a man of base condition. At this dreadful prospect her resolute modesty was overcome, as if with force, by his victorious lust; and Tarquinius departed, exulting in his conquest of a woman's honor. Lucretia, grieving at her great disaster, dispatched the same message to her father in Rome and to her husband at Ardea: that they should each take a trusty friend and come; that they must do this and do it quickly, for a frightful thing had happened. Spurius Lucretius came with Publius Valerius, Volesus' son. Collatinus brought Lucius Junius Brutus, with whom he chanced to be returning to Rome when he was met by the messenger from his wife. Lucretia they found sitting sadly in her chamber. The entrance of her friends brought the tears to her eyes, and to her husband's question, "Is all well?" she replied, " Far from it for what can be well with a woman when she has lost her honor? The print of a strange man, Collatinus, is in your bed. Yet my body only has been violated; my heart is guiltless, as death shall be my witness. But pledge your right hands and your words that the adulterer shall not go unpunished. Sextus Tarquinius is he that last night returned hostility for hospitality, and armed with force brought ruin on me, and on himself no less—if you are men—when he worked his pleasure with me." They give their pledges, every man in turn. They seek to comfort her, sick at heart as she is, by diverting the blame from her who was forced to the doer of the wrong. They tell her it is the mind that sins, not the body; and that where purpose has been wanting there is no guilt. "It is for you to determine," she answers, "what is due to him; for my own part, though I acquit myself of the sin, I do not absolve myself from punishment; not in time to come shall ever unchaste woman live through the example of Lucretia." Taking a knife which she had concealed beneath her dress, she plunged it into her heart, and sinking forward upon the wound, died as she fell. The wail for the dead was raised by her husband and her father.

1.59. Brutus, while the others were absorbed in grief, drew out the knife from Lucretia's wound, and holding it up, dripping with gore, exclaimed, "By this blood, most chaste until a prince wronged it, I swear, and I take you, gods, to witness, that I will pursue Lucius Tarquinius Superbus and his wicked wife and all his children, with sword, with fire, aye with whatsoever violence I may; and that I will suffer neither them nor any other to be king in Rome!" The knife he then passed to Collatinus, and from him to Lucretius and Valerius. They were dumbfounded at this miracle. Whence came this new spirit in the breast of Brutus? As he bade them, so they swore. Grief was swallowed up in anger; and when Brutus summoned them to make war from that very moment on the power of the kings, they followed his lead. They carried out Lucretia's corpse from the house and bore it to the market-place, where men crowded about them, attracted, as they were bound to be, by the amazing character of the strange event and its heinousness. Every man had his own complaint to make of the prince's crime and his violence. They were moved, not only by the father's sorrow, but by the fact that it was Brutus who chided their tears and idle lamentations and urged them to take up the sword, as befitted men and Romans, against those who had dared to treat them as enemies. The boldest of the young men seized their weapons and offered themselves for service, and the others followed their example. Then, leaving Lucretia's father to guard Collatia, and posting sentinels so that no one might announce the rising to the royal family, the rest, equipped for battle and with Brutus in command, set out for Rome. Once there, wherever their armed band advanced it brought terror and confusion; but again, when people saw that in the van were the chief men of the state, they concluded that whatever it was it could be no meaningless disturbance. And in fact there was no less resentment at Rome when this dreadful story was known than there had been at Collatia. So from every quarter of the City men came running to the Forum. No sooner were they there than a crier summoned the people before the Tribune of the Celeres,[2] which office Brutus then happened to be holding. There he made a speech by no means like what might have been expected of the mind and the spirit which he had feigned up to that day. He spoke of the violence and lust of Sextus Tarquinius, of the shameful defilement of Lucretia and her deplorable death, of the bereavement of Tricipitinus, in whose eyes the

---

2. The office is obscure, but it probably included both military and civil functions: command of the cavalry, and presidency of the assembly and the senate.

death of his daughter was not so outrageous and deplorable as was the cause of her death. He reminded them, besides, of the pride of the king himself and the wretched state of the commons, who were plunged into ditches and sewers and made to clear them out. The men of Rome, he said, the conquerors of all the nations round about, had been transformed from warriors into artisans and stone-cutters. He spoke of the shameful murder of King Tullius, and how his daughter had driven her accursed chariot over her father's body, and he invoked the gods who punish crimes against parents. With these and, I fancy, even fiercer reproaches, such as occur to a man in the very presence of an outrage, but are far from easy for an historian to reproduce, he inflamed the people, and brought them to abrogate the king's authority and to exile Lucius Tarquinius, together with his wife and children. Brutus himself then enrolled the juniors, who voluntarily gave in their names, and arming them set out for the camp at Ardea to arouse the troops against the king. The command at Rome he left with Lucretius, who had been appointed Prefect of the City by the king, some time before. During this confusion Tullia fled from her house, cursed wherever she went by men and women, who called down upon her the furies that avenge the wrongs of kindred.

THE STRUGGLE OF THE ORDERS

The constitution of the Roman Republic was the product of over three centuries of struggle and compromise between the various social and political factions of the Roman body politic. One of the first compromises which had to be worked out was between the patricians and the plebeians. At the beginning of the Republic, in 509 B.C., the patricians, the aristocratic upper class, controlled the government in every aspect. They alone could be elected to office or serve as priests of the state religion and they enjoyed a monopoly of political power, even though they constituted far less than five percent of the citizen body. Thus, during the early Republic the plebs were economically and politically oppressed by the aristocratic patricians. The first step in the "struggle of the orders," as the Roman called this conflict between the two classes of citizens, was the creation of the tribal assembly and the office of the tribune of the people. The Latin historian Levy here describes the "first secession of the plebs," in 494 B.C.

The First Secession of the Plebs (494 B.C.)

2.32. Thereupon the senators became alarmed, fearing that if the army should be disbanded there would again be secret gatherings and conspiracies. And so, although the levy had been held by order of the dictator, yet because the men had been sworn in by the consuls they regarded the troops as bound by their oath, and, under the pretext that the Aequi had recommenced hostili-

From *Livy, Volume I*, translated by B.O. Foster, Ph.D. (Cambridge, Loeb Classical Library, Harvard University Press, 1919).

ties, gave orders to lead the legions out of the City. This brought the revolt to a head. At first, it is said, there was talk of killing the consuls, that men might thus be freed from their oath; but when it was explained to them that no sacred obligation could be dissolved by a crime, they took the advice of one Sicinius, and without orders from the consuls withdrew to the Sacred Mount, which is situated across the river Anio, three miles from the City. . . There, without any leader, they fortified their camp with stockade and trench, and continued quietly, taking nothing but what they required for their subsistence, for several days, neither receiving provocation nor giving any. There was a great panic in the City, and mutual apprehension caused the suspension of all activities. The plebeians, having been abandoned by their friends, feared violence at the hands of the senators; the senators feared the plebeians who were left behind in Rome, being uncertain whether they had rather they stayed or went. Besides, how long would the seceding multitude continue peaceable? What would happen next if some foreign war should break out in the interim? Assuredly no hope was left save in harmony amongst the citizens, and this they concluded they must restore to the state by fair means or foul. They therefore decided to send as an ambassador to the commons Agrippa Menenius, an eloquent man and dear to the plebeians as being one of themselves by birth.[3] On being admitted to the camp he is said merely to have related the following apologue, in the quaint and uncouth style of that age: In the days when man's members did not all agree amongst themselves, as is now the case, but had each its own ideas and a voice of its own, the other parts thought it unfair that they should have the worry and the trouble and the labor of providing everything for the belly, while the belly remained quietly in their midst with nothing to do but to enjoy the good things which they bestowed upon it; they therefore conspired together that the hands should carry no food to the mouth, nor the mouth accept anything that was given it, nor the teeth grind up what they received. While they sought in this angry spirit to starve the belly into submission, the members themselves and the whole body were reduced to the utmost weakness. Hence it had become clear that even the belly had no idle task to perform, and was no more nourished than it nourished the rest, by giving out to all parts of the body that by which we live and thrive, when it has been divided equally amongst the veins and is enriched with digested food—that is, the blood. Drawing a parallel from this to show how like was the internal dissension of the bodily members to the anger of the plebs against the Fathers, he prevailed upon the minds of his hearers.

2.33. Steps were then taken towards harmony, and a compromise was effected on these terms the plebeians were to have magistrates of their own, who should be inviolable, and in them should lie the right to aid the people against the consuls, nor should any senator be permitted to take this magistracy. And so they chose two "tribunes of the people," Gaius Licinius and Lucius Albinus. These appointed three others to be their colleagues. Amongst the latter, Sicinius, the promoter of the revolt, was one, as all agree; the identity of the other two is less certain. Some hold that there were only two tribunes elected on the Sacred Mount, and that the law of inviolability was enacted there.[4]

---

3. If Menenius was a plebeian, it is improbable that he was also, as Livy implies, a senator.

4. In either case the number was five from the year 471 till it was raised to ten in the year 457.

THE SECOND SECESSION OF THE PLEBS (449 B.C.)

The next step in the struggle of the orders resolved one of the principal grievances of the plebeians, which was that the law was customary and known only to the patricians, who as magistrates used their exclusive knowledge to oppress the common people. After prolonged agitation by the tribunes of the plebs ten commissioners (decemviri) were appointed in 451 B.C. to codify the law. They were given absolute powers and no consuls were elected while the board was in office, and even the tribunate of the plebs was suspended. The decemviri compiled ten tables of laws, and the next year a second commission was elected, which added two more, thus making the famous Twelve Tables, the basic legal code of the Roman republic.

The second board of decemviri abused their absolute powers and tried to prolong their office without re-election. The result was the second secession of the plebs. This passage from Livy's history describes the subsequent settlement. The right of appeal was confirmed. The tribunes of the plebs were restored and the suspension of the office prohibited. Their sacrosanctity, which had depended on an oath of the plebs, was reaffirmed by a law. The third main point of the settlement was that plebiscites, resolutions proposed by the tribunes and passed by an assembly of the plebs, should have the force of law, binding the patricians also. The historicity of this measure has been doubted, since it was re-enacted in 339 and 287 B.C. But it may well be, as with the law of appeal, that the patricians refused to implement the law and that it was thus necessary to re-enact it.

3.52. Having learned from Marcus Duillius, who had been a plebeian tribune, that nothing was coming of the endless bickering of the senate, the commons quitted the Aventine for the Sacred Mount, since Duillius assured them that not until the patricians beheld the City deserted would they feel any real concern; the Sacred Mount would remind them of the firmness of the plebs, and they would know whether it were possible or not that affairs should be reduced to harmony without the restoration of the tribunician power. Marching out by the Via Nomentana, then called Ficulensis, they pitched their camp on the Sacred Mount, having imitated the good behavior of their fathers and made no depredations. Following the army came the plebeian civilians; nor did any one who was of an age to go hold back. They were attended a little way forth by their wives and children, who inquired pathetically to whose protection they were leaving them, in that City where neither chastity nor liberty was sacred.

Now that all Rome was desolate with an unwonted loneliness, and there was nobody in the Forum but a few old men, and it appeared, particularly when the Fathers had been summoned to

From *Livy, Volume II*, translated by B.O. Foster, Ph.D. (Cambridge, Loeb Classical Library, Harvard University Press, 1922).

the senate-house, quite deserted, there were many others besides Horatius and Valerius who remonstrated. "What will you wait for, Conscript Fathers?" they cried out. "If the decemvirs persist in their obstinacy, will you suffer everything to go to wrack and ruin? Pray what is that authority, decemvirs, to which you cling with such tenacity? Is it to roofs and walls you will render judgment? Are you not ashamed that your lictors should be seen in the Forum in almost larger numbers than the other citizens? What do you mean to do if the enemy should come to the City? What if, by and bye, the plebs, finding us unmoved by their secession, come with sword in hand? Do you wish the downfall of the City to be the end of your rule? And yet, either we must have no plebs, or we must have plebeian tribunes. We will sooner dispense with patrician magistrates than they with plebeian. It was a new and untried power when they extorted it from our fathers: now that they have once been captivated by its charm, they would be even less willing to forgo it, especially when we on our side do not so temper the exercise of our authority that they stand in no need of help." As these reproaches were flung at them from every quarter, the decemvirs were overborne by the consensus of opinion and gave assurances that they would submit, since it was thought best, to the authority of the senate. They had but this one request to make—which was also a warning—that their persons might be protected from men's hate, and that their blood might not be the means of accustoming the plebs to punish senators.

3.53. Valerius and Horatius were then sent to bring back the plebs and adjust all differences, on such terms as might seem good to them; and they were also instructed to secure the decemvirs against the anger and violence of the people. Having proceeded to the camp, they were received with great rejoicings by the plebs, as undoubted champions of liberty both in the beginning of the disturbance and in the sequel. In recognition of this they were thanked on their arrival, Icilius speaking on behalf of the multitude. And it was Icilius too who, when terms were discussed and the commissioners inquired what the plebeians demanded, made such requests, in pursuance of an understanding already reached before the arrival of the envoys, that it was apparent they based their hope more on equity than on arms. For the recovery of the tribunician power and the appeal were the things they sought—things which had been the help of the plebs before the election or decemvirs;—and that it should not be held against any man that he had incited the soldiers or the people to recover their liberties by secession. Only in regard to the punishment of the decemvirs was their demand a harsh one; for they thought it just that the decemvirs should be delivered up to them, and threatened to burn them alive. To these proposals the commissioners replied: "The demands which have been prompted by your judgment are so right that they ought to have been accorded you voluntarily; for you seek in them guarantees of liberty, not of a license to make attacks on others. But your anger calls for pardon rather than indulgence, seeing that hatred of cruelty is driving you headlong into cruelty, and almost before you are free yourselves you are wishing to lord it over your adversaries. Will the time never come when our state shall rest from punishments visited either by the patricians on the Roman plebs or by the plebs on the patricians? A shield is what you need more than a sword. It is enough and more than enough for a lowly citizen when he lives in the enjoyment of equal rights in the state, neither inflicting an injury nor receiving one. Even if you are one day to make yourselves dreaded, when you have got back your magistrates and laws and possess authority to put us on trial for our lives and fortunes, you shall then give judgment in accord with the merits of each particular case for the present it is enough to regain your liberty."

3.54. When the people all consented that they should do as they saw fit, the envoys assured them that they would settle matters and presently return. So they departed and explained to the Fathers the demands of the plebs. The other decemvirs, when they found that, contrary to their expectation, no mention was made of any punishment of themselves, made no objection to anything: Appius, hard-hearted, knowing himself peculiarly unpopular, and measuring other men's hatred of himself by his own of them, exclaimed, "I am not unaware of the lot which threatens me. I perceive that the attack upon us is only being postponed till arms are handed over to our adversaries. Hatred must have its offering of blood. I too am willing to relinquish the decemvirate." A decree was passed by the senate that the decemvirs should abdicate the magistracy at the earliest possible moment; that Quintus Furius, the Pontifex Maximus, should hold an election of plebeian tribunes; and that no one should be made to suffer for the secession of the soldiers and the plebs.

Having so decreed the senate adjourned and the decemvirs went before the people and laid down their office, to the great delight of all. These events were reported to the plebs, the envoys being accompanied by all the people left in the City. The multitude was met by another joyful throng from the camp, and they exchanged congratulations on the restoration of freedom and harmony to the state. The commissioners addressed the people as follows:

"Prosperity, favor, and good fortune to you and the Republic! Return to your native City, to your homes, to your wives, and your children; but let the self-restraint you have shown here, where no man's farm has been violated, though so many things were useful and necessary to so great a multitude, be preserved when you return to the City. Go to the Aventine, whence you set out. There in the auspicious place where you first laid the foundations of your liberty, you shall choose tribunes of the plebs. The Pontifex Maximus will be at hand to hold the election." With loud applause and great alacrity the people showed their approval of all that had been said. They pulled up their standards from the place and set out for Rome, vying with those whom they met in joyful demonstrations. Armed, they proceeded in silence through the City to the Aventine. There the Pontifex Maximus at once held the assembly, and they elected tribunes of the plebs; first of all Lucius Verginius; then Lucius Icilius and Publius Numitorius, Verginia's great-uncle, the instigators of the secession; then Gaius Sicinius, son of the man who is related to have been the first plebeian tribune chosen on the Sacred Mount; and Marcus Duillius, who had filled the tribuneship with distinction before the decemvirs were appointed, and had not failed the plebs in their contentions with the decemvirs. Then, more by reason of their promise than for any deserts of theirs, they elected Marcus Titinius, Marcus Pomponius, Gaius Apronius, Appius Villius, and Gaius Oppius. As soon as they had taken office, Lucius Icilius proposed to the people, and they so voted, that no man should suffer for the secession from the decemvirs. Immediately a bill that consuls should be elected subject to appeal was offered by Marcus Duillius and was carried. These matters were all transacted by the assembly of the plebs, in the Flaminian Meadows, which men now call the Flaminian Circus.

3.55. Then, through an interrex, they elected to the consulship Lucius Valerius and Marcus Horatius, who at once assumed office. Their administration was favorable to the people, without in any way wronging the patricians, though not without offending them; for whatever was done to protect the liberty of the plebs they regarded as a diminution of their own strength. To begin with, since it was virtually an undecided question whether the patricians were legally bound by plebiscites, they carried a statute in the centuriate assembly enacting that what the plebs should order in the tribal organization should be binding on the people—a law which provided the rogations of the tribunes with a very sharp weapon. Next they not only restored a consular law about the appeal, the unique defense of liberty, which had been overthrown by the decemviral power, but they also safeguarded it for the future by the solemn enactment of a new law, that no one should declare the election of any magistrate without appeal, and that he who should so declare might be put to death without offence to law or religion, and that such a homicide should not be held a capital crime. And having sufficiently strengthened the plebs, by means of the appeal on the one hand and the help of the tribunes on the other, they revived, in the interest of the tribunes themselves, the principle of their sacrosanctity (which was a thing that had now come to be well-nigh forgotten) by restoring certain long-neglected ceremonies; and they rendered those magistrates inviolate, not merely on the score of religion but also by a statute, solemnly enacting that he who should hurt the tribunes of the plebs, the aediles,[5] or the decemviral judges[6] should forfeit his head to Jupiter, and that his possessions should be sold at the temple of Ceres, Liber, and Libera. Expounders of the law deny that any one is sacrosanct by virtue of this statute, but maintain that the man who has injured any of these officials is solemnly forfeited to Jupiter; hence the aedile may be arrested and imprisoned by the greater magistrates, an act which, though it be unlawful—for he is thereby injured who, according to this statute, may not be injured—is nevertheless a proof that the aedile is not regarded as sacrosanct; whereas the tribunes are sacrosanct in consequence of the ancient oath taken by the plebs, when they first created this magistracy.[7] There were some who taught that by this same Horatian law the consuls also were protected, and the praetors, inasmuch as they were created under the same auspices as the consuls; for the consul was called "judge." But this interpretation is refuted by the fact that it was not yet the custom in those days for the consul to be called "judge," but "praetor." Such were the consular laws. The practice was also instituted by the same consuls that the decrees of the senate should be delivered to the aediles of the plebs at the temple of Ceres. Up to that time they were wont to be suppressed or falsified, at the pleasure of the consuls. Marcus Duillius, the tribune of the plebs, then proposed to the plebs, and they so decreed, that whosoever should leave the plebs without tribunes and whosoever should declare the election of a magistrate without appeal should be scourged and beheaded. All these measures, though they were passed against the will of the patricians, were yet not opposed by them, since, so far, no one person had been singled out for attack.

3.56. Then, when the tribunician power and the liberty of the plebs were firmly established, the tribunes, believing that it was now safe to proceed against individuals and that the time was ripe for doing so, selected Verginius to bring the first accusation and Appius to be defendant. When Verginius had cited Appius to appear, and the latter, attended by a crowd of young patri-

---

5. The plebian aediles, two in number, elected by the plebeians to assist the tribunes, as the quaestors did the consuls, and take charge of the achieves of the plebs, kept in the temple of Cares.

6. These *decemviri stlitibus iudicandis* judged cases involving liberty or citizenship.

7. The legal experts seem to have held that there was a distinction between the status of the tribunes and that of the aediles based on the belief that the former had been given *sacrosanctitas* at the time their office and that of the aediles was established, and that any violation of their persons automatically made the violator an outlaw (*sacer*);whereas it was necessary for an aedile to bring suit against the higher magistrate and convict him of the violation before the man became *sacer*.

cians, had come down into the Forum, there was instantly revived in the minds of all the recollection of that most wicked power, as soon as they caught sight of the man himself and his satellites. Then Verginius said, "Oratory was invented for doubtful matters; and so I shall neither waste time in arraigning before you the man from whose cruelty you freed yourselves with arms, nor shall I suffer him to add to his other crimes the impudence of defending himself.[8] I therefore pardon you, Appius Claudius, all the impious and wicked deeds which you dared, during two years, to heap one upon another; on one charge only, unless you shall name a referee to establish your innocence of having illegally assigned custody of a free person to him who claimed her as his slave, I shall order you to be taken to prison." Neither in the protection of the tribunes nor in the decision of the people had Appius anything to hope; yet he called upon the tribunes, and when none of them would stay proceedings, and he had been arrested by an officer, he cried, "I appeal." The sound of this word, the one safeguard of liberty, coming from that mouth by which, shortly before, a free person had been given into the custody of one who claimed her as a slave, produced a hush. And while the people muttered, each man to himself, that there were gods after all, who did not neglect the affairs of men; and that pride and cruelty were receiving their punishment, which though late was nevertheless not light—that he was appealing who had nullified appeal; that he was imploring the protection of the people who had trodden all the rights of the people under foot; that he was being carried off to prison, deprived of his right to liberty, who had condemned the person of a free citizen to slavery—the voice of Appius himself was heard amidst the murmurs of the assembly, beseeching the Roman People to protect him. He reminded them of the services his forefathers had rendered the state in peace and in war; of his own unfortunate affection for the Roman plebs, in consequence of which he had given up his consulship—in order to make the laws equal for all—with great offence to the patricians—of the laws he had himself drawn up,[9] which were still standing while their author was being dragged off to prison. For the rest, when he should be given an opportunity to plead his cause, he would try what would come of his own peculiar services and shortcomings; at present he asked that, in accordance with the common right of citizenship, he be permitted, being a Roman citizen and under accusation, to speak, and to be judged by the Roman People. He did not so fear men's malice as to have no hope in the justice and pity of his fellow citizens. But if he was to be imprisoned, his cause unheard, he appealed once more to the tribunes of the plebs, and warned them not to imitate those whom they hated. And if the tribunes should confess that they were bound by the same agreement which they charged the decemvirs with having entered into, not to hear an appeal, he still appealed to the people, and invoked the laws, both consular and tribunician, which had been enacted concerning appeals that very year. For who, he asked, should make an appeal, if a man who had not been condemned, whose cause had not been heard, might not do so? What humble plebeian would find protection in the laws, if they afforded none to Appius Claudius? His own case would show whether the new statutes had established tyranny or freedom, and whether the appeal to the tribunes and that to the people against the injustice of magistrates had been merely a parade of meaningless forms, or had been really granted.

---

8. Verginius did not mean to deprive Appius of the right to speak eventually in his own defense, but merely to abridge the preliminary hearing. He therefore proposed a *sponsio* to determine the guilt or innocence of Appius on one essential point.
9. The Twelve Tables.

3.57. Against this plea Verginius asserted that Appius Claudius alone was beyond the pale of the laws and of the rights of citizens and men. He bade his hearers look on the tribunal, the stronghold of all crimes, where that man, as perpetual decemvir, deadly foe to their fortunes, their persons, and their lives, threatening them all with rods and axes, despising gods and men, backed by executioners instead of lictors, had began to turn his thoughts from rapine and murder to lust; and, in full sight of the Roman People, had torn a free maiden from her father's arms, as though she had been a captive taken in war, and bestowed her as a gift upon his pimp and client —the tribunal where, by his tyrannical decree and wicked judgments, he had armed a father's right hand against his daughter; where, as they were lifting up the body of the dying girl, he had ordered her betrothed and her uncle to be haled to prison—more moved by the disappointing of his pleasure than by her death. For Appius too had been built that prison which he was wont to call the home of the Roman plebs. Accordingly, though he should again and repeatedly appeal, he would himself again and repeatedly challenge him to prove before a referee that he had not adjudged a free citizen to the custody of one who claimed her as a slave. Should he refuse to go before a referee, he bade him be led to jail, as one found guilty. Though none raised his voice in disapproval, there were yet profound misgivings on the part of the plebs when he was cast into prison, since they saw in the punishment of so great a man a sign that their own liberty was already grown excessive. The tribune appointed a day for the continuance of the trial.

Meanwhile from the Latins and the Hernici came envoys to congratulate the Romans upon the harmony subsisting between the patricians and the plebs; and to commemorate it they brought a gift for Jupiter Optimus Maximus, to the Capitol. This was a golden crown, of no great weight, for their states were not rich, and they observed the worship of the gods with piety rather than magnificence. From these same envoys came the information that the Aequi and the Volsci were making strenuous preparations for war. The consuls were therefore bidden to divide the commands between them. To Horatius fell the campaign against the Sabines; to Valerius that against the Aequi. When they had proclaimed a levy for these wars, the plebs showed so much good-will that not only the juniors but also a great number of volunteers who had served their time presented themselves for enrolment, with the result that not alone in numbers but in the quality of the troops as well, owing to the admixture of veterans, the army was stronger than usual. Before they left the City, the consuls had the decemviral laws, which are known as the Twelve Tables, engraved on bronze, and set them up in a public place. Some authors say that the aediles, acting under orders from the tribunes, performed this service.

The Goddess Isis. Capitoline Museum, Rome.

Polybius: The Constitution of the Roman

24

The Greek historian Polybius (c. 200–c. 120 B.C.) gives us a unique view of ancient Rome. He became a prominent politician in his native Achaea, which pursued an independent policy toward Rome. But independence was not possible in the face of Roman expansion. Ultimately, in 167 B.C., Rome took 1,000 political prisoners back to Italy as hostages to insure the good behavior of the Greeks. Polybius was one of them and he lived with the Scipio family, one of the most famous political families of Rome, until 151, when the surviving detainees were released.

During his confinement in Italy, Polybius became familiar with Roman society and institutions. His friendship with the Scipios gave him access to the achieves and libraries of Rome and he also met and interviewed visiting ambassadors and dignitaries from others states. Indeed, as he learned more about the Romans, he developed a deep admiration for them and eventually became convinced they were destined to rule the Mediterranean world, including his Greek homeland. In fact, he thought this might not be such a bad idea, since the Greeks had not demonstrated much ability to rule themselves very well over the centuries. But Polybius realized that the Greeks at this point really did not know much about these Romans, so he decided to explain them to the Greeks by writing their history from the its early beginnings down to his own time. Thus his history was written in Greek primarily for a Greek audience, which gives it a unique point of view.

Polybius attributed Rome's greatness to the superior character of its citizens and to its stable political institutions. In this excerpt from his history he describes the constitution of the Roman Republic.

6.2 I am aware that some will wonder why I have deferred until the present occasion my account of the Roman constitution, thus being obliged to interrupt the due course of my narrative. Now, that I have always regarded this account as one of the essential parts of my whole design, I have, I am sure, made evident in numerous passages and chiefly in the prefatory remarks dealing with the fundamental principles of this history, where I said that the best and most valuable result I aim at is that readers of my work may gain a knowledge how it was and by virtue of what peculiar political institutions that in less than fifty-three years nearly the whole world was overcome and fell under the single dominion of Rome, a thing the like of which had never happened before. Having made up my mind to deal with the matter, I found no occasion more suitable than the present for turning my attention to the constitution and testing the truth of what I am about to say on the subject. For just as those who pronounce in private on the characters of bad or good men, do not, when they really resolve to put their opinion to the test, choose for investigation those periods of their life which they passed in composure and repose, but seasons when they were afflicted by adversity or blessed with success, deeming the sole test of a perfect man to be the power of bearing high-mindedly and bravely the most complete reverses of fortune, so it should be in our judgment of states. Therefore, as I could not see any greater or more violent change in the fortunes of the Romans than this which has happened in our own times, I reserved my account of the constitution for the present occasion. . . .

What chiefly attracts and chiefly benefits students of history is just this—the study of causes and the consequent power of choosing what is best in each case. Now the chief cause of success or the reverse in all matters is the form of a state's constitution; for springing from this, as from a fountain-head, all designs and plans of action not only originate, but reach their consummation.

ON THE FORMS OF STATES

6.3. In the case of those Greek states which have often risen to greatness and have often experienced a complete change of fortune, it is an easy matter both to describe their past and to pronounce as to their future. For there is no difficulty in reporting the known facts, and it is not hard to foretell the future by inference from the past. But about the Roman state it is neither at all easy to explain the present situation owing to the complicated character of the constitution, nor to foretell the future owing to our ignorance of the peculiar features of public and private life at Rome in the past. Particular attention and study are therefore required if one wishes to attain a clear general view of the distinctive qualities of their constitution.

Most of those whose object it has been to instruct us methodically concerning such matters, distinguish three kinds of constitutions, which they call kingship, aristocracy, and democracy. Now we should, I think, be quite justified in asking them to enlighten us as to whether they represent these three to be the sole varieties or rather to be the best; for in either case my opinion is that they are wrong. For it is evident that we must regard as the best constitution a combination of all these three varieties, since we have had proof of this not only theoretically but by actual experience, Lycurgus having been the first to draw up a constitution—that of Sparta—on this principle. Nor on the other hand can we admit that these are the only three varieties; for we have witnessed monarchical and tyrannical governments, which while they differ very widely from kingship, yet bear a certain resemblance to it, this being the reason why monarchs in general falsely assume and use, as far as they can, the regal title. There have also been several oligarchical constitutions which seem to bear some likeness to aristocratic ones, though the divergence is, generally, as wide as possible. The same holds good about democracies.

6 4. The truth of what I say is evident from the following considerations. It is by no means every monarchy which we can call straight off a kingship, but only that which is voluntarily accepted by the subjects and where they are governed rather by an appeal to their reason than by

fear and force. Nor again can we style every oligarchy an aristocracy, but only that where the government is in the hands of a selected body of the most just and wisest men. Similarly that is no true democracy in which the whole crowd of citizens is free to do whatever they wish or purpose, but when, in a community where it is traditional and customary to reverence the gods, to honor our parents, to respect our elders, and to obey the laws, the will of the greater number prevails, this is to be called a democracy. We should therefore assert that there are six kinds of governments, the three above mentioned which are in everyone's mouth and the three which are naturally allied to them, I mean monarchy, oligarchy, and mob-rule. Now the first of these to come into being is monarchy, its growth being natural and unaided; and next arises kingship derived from monarchy by the aid of art and by the correction of defects. Monarchy first changes into its vicious allied form, tyranny; and next, the abolishment of both gives birth to aristocracy. Aristocracy by its very nature degenerates into oligarchy; and when the commons inflamed by anger take vengeance on this government for its unjust rule, democracy comes into being ; and in due course the license and lawlessness of this form of government produces mob-rule to complete the series. The truth of what I have just said will be quite clear to anyone who pays due attention to such beginnings, origins, and changes as are in each case natural. For he alone who has seen how each form naturally arises and develops, will be able to see when, how, and where the growth, perfection, change, and end of each are likely to occur again. And it is to the Roman constitution above all that this method, I think, may be successfully applied, since from the outset its formation and growth have been due to natural causes.

6.5. Perhaps this theory of the natural transformations into each other of the different forms of government is more elaborately set forth by Plato and certain other philosophers; but as the arguments are subtle and are stated at great length, they are beyond the reach of all but a few. I therefore will attempt to give a short summary of the theory, as far as I consider it to apply to the actual history of facts and to appeal to the common intelligence of mankind. For if there appear to be certain omissions in my general exposition of it, the detailed discussion which follows will afford the reader ample compensation for any difficulties now left unsolved.

What then are the beginnings I speak of and what is the first origin of political societies? When owing to floods, famines, failure of crops or other such causes there occurs such a destruction of the human race as tradition tells us has more than once happened, and as we must believe will often happen again, all arts and crafts perishing at the same time, then in the course of time, when springing from the survivors as from seeds men have again increased in numbers and just like other animals form herds—it being a matter of course that they too should herd together with those of their kind owing to their natural weakness—it is a necessary consequence that the man who excels in bodily strength and in courage will lead and rule over the rest. We observe and should regard as a most genuine work of nature this very phenomenon in the case of the other animals which act purely by instinct and among whom the strongest are always indisputably the masters—I speak of bulls, boars, cocks, and the like. It is probable then that at the beginning men lived thus, herding together like animals and following the lead of the strongest and bravest, the ruler's strength being here the sole limit to his power and the name we should give his rule being monarchy.

But when in time feelings of sociability and companionship begin to grow in such gatherings of men, then kingship has struck root; and the notions of goodness, justice, and their opposites begin to arise in men.

6.6. The manner in which these notions come into being is as follows. Men being all naturally inclined to sexual intercourse, and the consequence of this being the birth of children, whenever one of those who have been reared does not on growing up show gratitude to those who reared him or defend them, but on the contrary takes to speaking ill of them or ill treating them, it is evident that he will displease and offend those who have been familiar with his parents and have witnessed the care and pains they spent on attending to and feeding their children. For seeing that men are distinguished from the other animals by possessing the faculty of reason, it is obviously improbable that such a difference of conduct should escape them, as it escapes the other animals: they will notice the thing and be displeased at what is going on, looking to the future and reflecting that they may all meet with the same treatment. Again when a man who has been helped or succored when in danger by another does not show gratitude to his preserver, but even goes to the length of attempting to do him injury, it is clear that those who become aware of it will naturally be displeased and offended by such conduct, sharing the resentment of their injured neighbor and imagining themselves in the same situation. From all this there arises in everyone a notion of the meaning and theory of duty, which is the beginning and end of justice. Similarly, again, when any man is foremost in defending his fellows from danger, and braves and awaits the onslaught of the most powerful beasts, it is natural that he should receive marks of favor and honor from the people, while the man who acts in the opposite manner will meet with reprobation and dislike. From this again some idea of what is base and what is noble and of what constitutes the difference is likely to arise among the people; and noble conduct will be admired and imitated because it is advantageous, while base conduct will be avoided. Now when the leading and most powerful man among the people always throws the weight of his authority on the side of the notions on such matters which generally prevail, and when in the opinion of his subjects he apportions rewards and penalties according to desert, they yield obedience to him no longer because they fear his force, but rather because their judgment approves him; and they join in maintaining his rule even if he is quite enfeebled by age, defending him with one consent and battling against those who conspire to overthrow his rule. Thus by insensible degrees the monarch becomes a king, ferocity and force having yielded the supremacy to reason.

6.7. Thus is formed naturally among men the first notion of goodness and justice, and their opposites this is the beginning and birth of true kingship. For the people maintain the supreme power not only in the hands of these men themselves, but in those of their descendants, from the conviction that those born from and reared by such men will also have principles like to theirs. And if they ever are displeased with the descendants, they now choose their kings and rulers no longer for their bodily strength and brute courage, but for the excellency of their judgment and reasoning powers, as they have gained experience from actual facts of the difference between the one class of qualities and the other. In old times, then, those who had once been chosen to the royal office continued to hold it until they grew old, fortifying and enclosing fine strongholds with walls and acquiring lands, in the one case for the sake of the security of their subjects and in the other to provide them with abundance of the necessities of life. And while pursuing these aims, they were exempt from all vituperation or jealousy, as neither in their dress nor in their food and drink did they make any great distinction, but lived very much like everyone else, not keeping apart from the people. But when they received the office by hereditary succession and found their safety now provided for, and more than sufficient provision of food, they gave way to their appetites owing to this superabundance, and came to think that the rulers must be distinguished from their subjects by a peculiar dress, that there should be a peculiar luxury and variety in the dressing and serving of their viands, and that they should meet with no denial in the pursuit of their amours, however lawless. These habits having given rise in the one case to envy and offence and in the other to an outburst of hatred and passionate resentment, the kingship changed into a tyranny; the first steps towards its overthrow were taken by the subjects, and conspiracies began to be formed. These conspiracies were not the work of the worst men, but of the noblest, most high-spirited, and most courageous, because such men are least able to brook the insolence of princes.

6.8. The people now having got leaders, would combine with them against the ruling powers for the reasons I stated above; kingship and monarchy would be utterly abolished, and in their place aristocracy would begin to grow. For the commons, as if bound to pay at once their debt of gratitude to the abolishers of monarchy, would make them their leaders and entrust their destinies to them. At first these chiefs gladly assumed this charge and regarded nothing as of greater importance than the common interest, administering the private and public affairs of the people with paternal solicitude. But here again when children inherited this position of authority from their fathers, having no experience of misfortune and none at all of civil equality and liberty of speech, and having been brought up from the cradle amid the evidences of the power and high position of their fathers, they abandoned themselves some to greed of gain and unscrupulous moneymaking, others to indulgence in wine and the convivial excess which accompanies it, and others again to the violation of women and the rape of boys; and thus converting the aristocracy into an oligarchy aroused in the people feelings similar to those of which I just spoke, and in consequence met with the same disastrous end as the tyrant.

6.9. For whenever anyone who has noticed the jealousy and hatred with which they are regarded by the citizens, has the courage to speak or act against the chiefs of the state he has the whole mass of the people ready to back him. Next, when they have either killed or banished the oligarchs, they no longer venture to set a king over them, as they still remember with terror the injustice they suffered from the former ones, nor can they entrust the government with confidence to a select few, with the evidence before them of their recent error in doing so. Thus the only hope still surviving unimpaired is in themselves, and to this they resort, making the state a democracy instead of an oligarchy and assuming the responsibility for the conduct of affairs. Then as long as some of those survive who experienced the evils of oligarchical dominion, they are well pleased with the present form of government, and set a high value on equality and freedom of speech. But when a new generation arises and the democracy falls into the hands of the grandchildren of its founders, they have become so accustomed to freedom and equality that they no longer value them, and begin to aim at pre-eminence; and it is chiefly those of ample fortune who fall into this error. So when they begin to lust for power and cannot attain it through themselves or their own good qualities, they ruin their estates, tempting and corrupting the people in every possible way. And hence when by their foolish thirst for reputation they have created among the masses an appetite for gifts and the habit of receiving them, democracy in its turn is abolished and changes into a rule of force and violence. For the people, having grown accustomed to feed at the expense of others and to depend for their livelihood on the property of others, as soon as they find a leader who is enterprising but is excluded from the honors of office by his penury, institute the rule of violence; and now uniting their forces massacre, banish, and plunder, until they degenerate again into perfect savages and find once more a master and monarch.

Such is the cycle of political revolution, the course appointed by nature in which constitutions change, disappear, and finally return to the point from which they started. Anyone who clearly perceives this may indeed in speaking of the future of any state be wrong in his estimate of the time the process will take, but if his judgment is not tainted by animosity or jealousy, he will very seldom be mistaken as to the stage of growth or decline it has reached, and as to the form into which it will change. And especially in the case of the Roman state will this method enable us to arrive at a knowledge of its formation, growth, and greatest perfection, and likewise of the change for the worse which is sure to follow some day. For, as I said, this state, more than any other, has been formed and has grown naturally, and will undergo a natural decline and change to its contrary. The reader will be able to judge of the truth of this from the subsequent parts of this work.

6.10. At present I will give a brief account of the legislation of Lycurgus, a matter not alien to my present purpose. Lycurgus had perfectly well understood that all the above changes take place necessarily and naturally, and had taken into consideration that every variety of constitution which is simple and formed on one principle is precarious, as it is soon perverted into the corrupt form which is proper to it and naturally follows on it. For just as rust in the case of iron and wood-worms and ship-worms in the case of timber are inbred pests, and these substances, even though they escape all external injury, fall a prey to the evils engendered in them, so each constitution has a vice engendered in it and inseparable from it. In kingship it is despotism, in aristocracy oligarchy, and in democracy the savage rule of violence; and it is impossible, as I said above, that each of these should not in course of time change into this vicious form. Lycurgus, then, foreseeing this, did not make his constitution simple and uniform, but united in it all the good and distinctive features of the best governments, so that none of the principles should grow unduly and be perverted into its allied evil, but that, the force of each being neutralized by that of the others, neither of them should prevail and outbalance another but that the constitution should remain for long in a state of equilibrium like a well-trimmed boat, kingship being guarded from arrogance by the fear of the commons, who were given a sufficient share in the government, and the commons on the other hand not venturing to treat the kings with contempt from fear of the elders, who being selected from the best citizens would be sure all of them to be always on the side of justice; so that that part of the state which was weakest owing to its subservience to traditional custom, acquired power and weight by the support and influence of the elders. The consequence was that by drawing up his constitution thus he preserved liberty at Sparta for a longer period than is recorded elsewhere.

Lycurgus then, foreseeing, by a process of reasoning, whence and how events naturally happen, constructed his constitution untaught by adversity, but the Romans while they have arrived at the same final result as regards their form of government, have not reached it by any process of reasoning, but by the discipline of many struggles and troubles, and always choosing the best by the light of the experience gained in disaster have thus reached the same result as Lycurgus, that is to say, the best of all existing constitutions.

ON THE ROMAN CONSTITUTION AT ITS PRIME

6.11. From the crossing of Xerxes to Greece . . . and for thirty years after this period, it was always one of those polities which was an object of special study, and it was at its best and nearest to perfection at the time of the Hannibalic war, the period at which I interrupted my narrative to deal with it. Therefore now that I have described its growth, I will explain what were the conditions at the time when by their defeat at Cannae the Romans were brought face to face with disaster. . . .

The three kinds of government that I spoke of above all shared in the control of the Roman state. And such fairness and propriety in all respects was shown in the use of these three elements for drawing up the constitution and in its subsequent administration that it was impossible even for a native to pronounce with certainty whether the whole system was aristocratic, democratic, or monarchical. This was indeed only natural. For if one fixed one's eyes on the power of the consuls, the constitution seemed completely monarchical and royal; if on that of the senate it seemed again to be aristocratic; and when one looked at the power of the masses, it seemed clearly to be a democracy. The parts of the state falling under the control of each element were and with a few modifications still are as follows.

6.12. The consuls, previous to leading out their legions, exercise authority in Rome over all public affairs, since all the other magistrates except the tribunes are under them and bound to obey them, and it is they who introduce embassies to the senate. Besides this it is they who consult the senate on matters of urgency, they who carry out in detail the provisions of its decrees. Again as concerns all affairs of state administered by the people it is their duty to take these under their charge, to summon assemblies, to introduce measures, and to preside over the execution of the popular decrees. As for preparation for war and the general conduct of operations in the field, here their power is almost uncontrolled; for they are empowered to make what demands they choose on the allies, to appoint military tribunes, to levy soldiers and select those who are fittest for service. They also have the right of inflicting, when on active service, punishment on anyone under their command; and they are authorized to spend any sum they decide upon from the public funds, being accompanied by a quaestor who faithfully executes their instructions. So that if one looks at this part of the administration alone, one may reasonably pronounce the constitution to be a pure monarchy or kingship. I may remark that any changes in these matters or in others of which I am about to speak that may be made in present or future times do not in any way affect the truth of the views I here state.

6.13. To pass to the senate. In the first place it has the control of the treasury, all revenue and expenditure being regulated by it. For with the exception of payments made to the consuls, the quaestors are not allowed to disburse for any particular object without a decree of the senate. And even the item of expenditure which is far heavier and more important than any other—the outlay every five years by the censors on public works, whether constructions or repairs—is under the control of the senate, which makes a grant to the censors for the purpose. Similarly crimes committed in Italy which require a public investigation, such as treason, conspiracy, poisoning, and assassination, are under the jurisdiction of the senate. Also if any private person or community in Italy is in need of arbitration or indeed claims damages or requires succor or protection, the senate attends to all such matters. It also occupies itself with the dispatch of all embassies sent to countries outside of Italy for the purpose either of settling differences, or of offering friendly advice, or indeed of imposing demands, or of receiving submission, or of declaring war; and in like manner with respect to embassies arriving in Rome it decides what reception and what answer should be given to them. All these matters are in the hands of the senate, nor have the people anything whatever to do with them. So that again to one residing in Rome during the absence of the consuls the constitution appears to be entirely aristocratic; and this is the conviction of many Greek states and many of the kings, as the senate manages all business connected with them.

6.14. After this we are naturally inclined to ask what part in the constitution is left for the people, considering that the senate controls all the particular matters I mentioned, and, what is most important, manages all matters of revenue and expenditure, and considering that the consuls again have uncontrolled authority as regards armaments and operations in the field. But nevertheless there is a part and a very important part left for the people. For it is the people which alone has the right to confer honors and inflict punishment, the only bonds by which kingdoms and states and in a word human society in general are held together. For where the distinction between these is overlooked or is observed but ill applied, no affairs can be properly administered. How indeed is this possible when good and evil men are held in equal estimation? It is by the people, then, in many cases that offences punishable by a fine are tried when the accused have held the highest office; and they are the only court which may try on capital charges. As regards the latter they have a practice which is praiseworthy and should be mentioned. Their usage allows those on trial for their lives when found guilty liberty to depart openly, thus inflicting voluntary exile on themselves, if even only one of the tribes that pronounce the verdict has not yet voted. Such exiles enjoy safety in the territories of Naples, Praeneste, Tibur, and other *civitates foederatae*. Again it is the people who bestow office on the deserving, the noblest reward of virtue in a state; the people have the power of approving or rejecting laws, and what is most important of all, they deliberate on the question of war and peace. Further in the case of alliances, terms of peace, and treaties, it is the people who ratify all these or the reverse. Thus here again one might plausibly say that the people's share in the government is the greatest, and that the constitution is a democratic one.

6.15. Having stated how political power is distributed among the different parts of the state, I will now explain how each of the three parts is enabled, if they wish, to counteract or co-operate with the others. The consul, when he leaves with his army invested with the powers I mentioned, appears indeed to have absolute authority in all matters necessary for carrying out his purpose; but in fact he requires the support of the people and the senate, and is not able to bring his operations to a conclusion without them. For it is obvious that the legions require constant supplies, and without the consent of the senate, neither corn, clothing, nor pay can be provided; so that the commander's plans come to nothing, if the senate chooses to be deliberately negligent and obstructive. It also depends on the senate whether or not a general can carry out completely his conceptions and designs, since it has the right of either superseding him when his year's term of office has expired or of retaining him in command. Again it is in its power to celebrate with pomp and to magnify the successes of a general or on the other hand to obscure and belittle them. For the processions they call triumphs, in which the generals bring the actual spectacle of their achievements before the eyes of their fellow-citizens, cannot be properly organized and sometimes even cannot be held at all, unless the senate consents and provides the requisite funds. As for the people it is most indispensable for the consuls to conciliate them, however far away from home they may be; for, as I said, it is the people which ratifies or annuls terms of peace and treaties, and what is most important, on laying down office the consuls are obliged to account for their actions to the people. So that in no respect is it safe for the consuls to neglect keeping in favor with both the senate and the people.

6.16. The senate again, which possesses such great power, is obliged in the first place to pay attention to the commons in public affairs and respect the wishes of the people, and it cannot carry out inquiries into the most grave and important offenses against the state, punishable with death, and their correction, unless the *senatus consultum* is confirmed by the people. The same is the case in matters which directly affect the senate itself. For if anyone introduces a law meant to deprive the senate of some of its traditional authority, or to abolish the precedence and other distinctions of the senators or even to curtail them of their private fortunes, it is the people alone which has the power of passing or rejecting any such measure. And what is most important is that if a single one of the tribunes interposes, the senate is unable to decide finally about any matter, and cannot even meet and hold sittings; and here it is to be observed that the tribunes are always obliged to act as the people decree and to pay every attention to their wishes. Therefore for all these reasons the senate is afraid of the masses and must pay due attention to the popular will.

6.17. Similarly, again, the people must be submissive to the senate and respect its members both in public and in private. Through the whole of Italy a vast number of contracts, which it would not be easy to enumerate, are given out by the censors for the construction and repair of public buildings, and besides this there are many things which are farmed, such as navigable rivers, harbors, gardens, mines, lands, in fact everything that forms part of the Roman dominion. Now all these matters are undertaken by the people, and one may almost say that everyone is interested in these contracts and the work they involve. For certain people are the actual purchasers from the censors of the contracts, others are the partners of these first, others stand surety for them, others pledge their own fortunes to the state for this purpose. Now in all these matters the senate is supreme. It can grant extension of time; it can relieve the contractor if any accident occurs; and if the work proves to be absolutely impossible to carry out it can liberate him from his contract. There are in fact many ways in which the senate can either benefit or injure those who manage public property, as all these matters are referred to it. What is even more important is that the judges in most civil trials, whether public or private, are appointed from its members, where the action involves large interests. So that all citizens being at the mercy of the senate, and looking forward with alarm to the uncertainty of litigation, are very shy of obstructing or resisting its decisions. Similarly everyone is reluctant to oppose the projects of the consuls as all are generally and individually under their authority when in the field.

6.18. Such being the power that each part has of hampering the others or co-operating with them, their union is adequate to all emergencies, so that it is impossible to find a better political system than this. For whenever the menace of some common danger from abroad compels them to act in concord and support each other, so great does the strength of the state become, that nothing which is requisite can be neglected, as all are zealously competing in devising means of meeting the need of the hour, nor can any decision arrived at fail to be executed promptly, as all are co-operating both in public and in private to the accomplishment of the task they have set themselves; and consequently this peculiar form of constitution possesses an irresistible power of attaining every object upon which it is resolved. When again they are freed from external menace, and reap the harvest of good fortune and affluence which is the result of their success, and in the enjoyment of this prosperity are corrupted by flattery and idleness and wax insolent and overbearing, as indeed happens often enough, it is then especially that we see the state providing itself a remedy for the evil from which it suffers. For when one part having grown out of proportion to the others aims at supremacy and tends to become too predominant, it is evident that, as for the reasons above given none of the three is absolute, but the purpose of the one can be counterworked and thwarted by the others, none of them will excessively outgrow the others or treat them with contempt. All in fact remains *in statu quo,* on the one hand, because any aggressive impulse is sure to be checked and from the outset each estate stands in dread of being interfered with by the others.

Plutarch: From the Parallel Lives

25

Below are excerpts from four of Plutarch's biographies of famous Romans from his Parallel Lives (see the introduction to Plutarch's readings in Chapter 3).

MARCUS CATO (THE ELDER)

The early Romans attributed their success to the character and stability of their society, qualities represented by the mos majorum, literally "the customs of our ancestors." This concept represented the tradition of the subordination of the individual citizen to family, state and gods. But Roman success and expansion outside of Italy, especially after the Second Punic War, brought them into contact with the peoples of the Hellenistic east. The influx of Greek influences, in particular, effected every aspect of Roman society, from its political process, to its intellectual life, from its social structure, to its religious beliefs.

Marcus Porcius Cato (Cato the Elder, 234–149 B.C.) was a politician and orator of immense fame. He always sought to project an image of himself as a conservative defender of the old traditional Roman values against the dangerous influences from the east, i.e. Greece. But the portrait of Cato given here by Plutarch portrays him as a complex man with many sides to his personality.

1. The family of Marcus Cato, it is said, was of Tusculan origin, though he lived, previous to his career as soldier and statesman, on an inherited estate in the country of the Sabines. His ancestors commonly passed for men of no note whatever, but Cato himself extols his father, Marcus, as a brave man and good soldier. He also says that his grandfather, Cato, often won prizes for

soldierly valor, and received from the state treasury, because of his bravery, the price of five horses which had been killed under him in battle. The Romans used to call men who had no family distinction, but were coming into public notice through their own achievements, "new men," and such they called Cato. But he himself used to say that as far as office and distinction went, he was indeed new, but having regard to ancestral deeds of valor, he was oldest of the old. His third name was not Cato at first, but Priscus. Afterwards he got the surname of Cato for his great abilities. The Romans call a man who is wise and prudent, *catus.*

As for his outward appearance, he had reddish hair, and keen gray eyes, as the author of the well known epigram ill-naturedly gives us to understand:

—Red-haired, snapper and biter, his gray eyes flashing defiance,
Porcius, come to the shades, back will be thrust by their Queen.

His bodily habit, since he was addicted from the very first to labor with his own hands, a temperate mode of life, and military duties, was very serviceable, and disposed alike to vigor and health. His discourse—a second body, as it were, and, for the use of a man who would live neither obscurely nor idly, an instrument with which to perform not only necessary, but also high and noble services—this he developed and perfected in the villages and towns about Rome, where he served as advocate for all who needed him, and got the reputation of being, first a zealous pleader, and then a capable orator. Thenceforth the weight and dignity of his character revealed themselves more and more to those who had dealings with him; they saw that he was bound to be a man of great affairs, and have a leading place in the state. For he not only gave his services in legal contests without fee of any sort, as it would seem, but did not appear to cherish even the repute won in such contests as his chief ambition. Nay, he was far more desirous of high repute in battles and campaigns against the enemy, and while he was yet a mere stripling, had his breast covered with honorable wounds. He says himself that he made his first campaign when he was seventeen years old, at the time when Hannibal was consuming Italy with the flames of his successes.[1]

In battle, he showed himself effective of hand, sure and steadfast of foot, and of a fierce countenance. With threatening speech and harsh cries he would advance upon the foe, for he rightly thought, and tried to show others, that often-times such action terrifies the enemy more than the sword. On the march, he carried his own armor on foot, while a single attendant followed in charge of his camp utensils. With this man, it is said, he was never wroth, and never scolded him when he served up a meal, nay, he actually took hold himself and assisted in most of such preparations, provided he was free from his military duties. Water was what he drank on his campaigns, except that once in a while, in a raging thirst, he would call for vinegar, or, when his strength was failing, would add a little wine.

2. Near his fields was the cottage which had once belonged to Manius Curius, a hero of three triumphs. To this he would often go, and the sight of the small farm and the mean dwelling led him to think of their former owner, who, though he had become the greatest of the Romans, had subdued the most warlike nations, and driven Pyrrhus out of Italy, nevertheless tilled this little patch of ground with his own hands and occupied this cottage, after three triumphs. Here it was

---

1. 217 B.C.

that the ambassadors of the Samnites once found him seated at his hearth cooking turnips, and offered him much gold; but he dismissed them, saying that a man whom such a meal satisfied had no need of gold, and for his part he thought that a more honorable thing than the possession of gold was the conquest of its possessors. Cato would go away with his mind full of these things, and on viewing again his own house and lands and servants and mode of life, would increase the labors of his hands and lop off his extravagancies.

When Fabius Maximus took the city of Tarentum,[2] it chanced that Cato, who was then a mere stripling, served under him, and being lodged with a certain Nearchus, of the sect of the Pythagoreans, he was eager to know of his doctrines. When he heard this man holding forth as follows, in language which Plato also uses, condemning pleasure as "the greatest incentive to evil," and the body as "the chief detriment to the soul, from which she can release and purify herself only by such reasonings as most do wean and divorce her from bodily sensations," he fell still more in love with simplicity and restraint. Further than this, it is said, he did not learn Greek till late in life, and was quite well on in years when he took to reading Greek books; then he profited in oratory somewhat from Thucydides, but more from Demosthenes. However, his writings are moderately embellished with Greek sentiments and stories, and many literal translations from the Greek have found a place among his maxims and proverbs.

4. The influence which Cato's oratory won for him waxed great, and men called him a Roman Demosthenes; but his manner of life was even more talked about and noised abroad. For his oratorical ability only set before young men a goal which many already were striving eagerly to attain; but a man who wrought with his own hands, as his fathers did, and was contented with a cold breakfast, a frugal dinner, simple raiment, and a humble dwelling—one who thought more of not wanting the superfluities of life than of possessing them—such a man was rare. The commonwealth had now grown too large to keep its primitive integrity; the sway over many realms and peoples had brought a large admixture of customs, and the adoption of examples set in modes of life of every sort. It was natural, therefore, that men should admire Cato, when they saw that, whereas other men were broken down by toils and enervated by pleasures, he was victor over both, and this too, not only while he was still young and ambitious, but even in his hoary age, after consulship and triumph. Then, like some victorious athlete, he persisted in the regimen of his training, and kept his mind unaltered to the last.

He tells us that he never wore clothing worth more than a hundred drachmas; that he drank, even when he was praetor or consul, the same wine as his slaves; that as for fish and meats, he would buy thirty asses' worth[3] for his dinner from the public stalls, and even this for the city's sake, that he might not live on bread alone, but strengthen his body for military service; that he once fell heir to an embroidered Babylonian robe, but sold it at once; that not a single one of his cottages had plastered walls; that he never paid more than fifteen hundred drachmas for a slave, since he did not want them to be delicately beautiful, but sturdy workers, such as grooms and herdsmen, and these he thought it his duty to sell when they got old, instead of feeding them when they were useless ; and that in general, he thought nothing cheap that one could do without, but that what one did not need, even if it cost but a penny, was dear; also that he bought

2. 209 B.C.
3. The ass corresponded to a penny.

lands where crops were raised and cattle herded, not those where lawns were sprinkled and paths swept.

5. These things were ascribed by some to the man's parsimony; but others condoned them in the belief that he lived in this contracted way only to correct and moderate the extravagance of others. However, for my part, I regard his treatment of his slaves like beasts of burden, using them to the uttermost, and then, when they were old, driving them off and selling them, as the mark of a very mean nature, which recognizes no tie between man and man but that of necessity. And yet we know that kindness has a wider scope than justice. Law and justice we naturally apply to men alone; but when it comes to beneficence and charity, these often flow in streams from the gentle heart, like water from a copious spring, even down to dumb beasts. A kindly man will take good care of his horses even when they are worn out with age, and of his dogs, too, not only in their puppy-hood, but when their old age needs nursing.

While the Athenians were building the Parthenon, they turned loose for free and unrestricted pasturage such mules as were seen to be most persistently laborious. One of these, they say, came back to the works of its own accord, trotted along by the side of its fellows under the yoke, which were dragging the wagons up to the Acropolis, and even led the way for them, as though exhorting and inciting them on. The Athenians passed a decree that the animal be maintained at the public cost as long as it lived. Then there were the mares of Cimon, with which he won three victories at Olympia; their graves are near the tombs of his family. Dogs also that have been close and constant companions of men, have often been buried with honor. Xanthippus, of olden time, gave the dog which swam along by the side of his trireme to Salamis, when the people were abandoning their city, honorable burial on the promontory which is called to this day Cynossema, or Dog's Mound.

We should not treat living creatures like shoes or pots and pans, casting them aside when they are bruised and worn out with service, but, if for no other reason, for the sake of practice in kindness to our fellow men, we should accustom ourselves to mildness and gentleness in our dealings with other creatures. I certainly would not sell even an ox that had worked for me, just because he was old, much less an elderly man, removing him from his habitual place and customary life, as it were from his native land, for a paltry price, useless as he is to those who sell him and as he will be to those who buy him. But Cato, exulting as it were in such things, says that he left in Spain even the horse which had carried him through his consular campaign, that he might not tax the city with the cost of its transportation. Whether, now, these things should be set down to greatness of spirit or littleness of mind, is an open question.

18. Cato[4] was rather bitterly censured for his treatment of Lucius, the brother of Scipio, whom, though he had achieved the honor of a triumph, he expelled from the equestrian order. He was thought to have done this as an insult to the memory of Scipio Africanus. But he was most obnoxious to the majority of his enemies because he lopped off extravagance in living. This could not be done away with outright, since most of the people were already infected and corrupted by it, and so he took a roundabout way. He had all apparel, equipages, jewelry, furniture and plate, the value of which in any case exceeded fifteen hundred drachmas, assessed at ten times its worth,

---

4. Cato was elected censor is 184 B.C. He was severe in his review of the roll of the senate, removing several high ranking senators. He also imposed high taxation on items he considered luxuries.

wishing by means of larger assessments to make the owners' taxes also larger. Then he laid a tax of three on every thousand asses thus assessed, in order that such property holders, burdened by their charges, and seeing that people of equal wealth who led modest and simple lives paid less into the public treasury, might desist from their extravagance. As a result, both classes were incensed against him, both those who endured the taxes for the sake of their luxury, and those no less who put away their luxury because of the taxes. For most men think themselves robbed of their wealth if they are prevented from displaying it, and that display of it is made in the superfluities, not in the necessaries of life. This, we are told, is what most astonished Ariston the philosopher, namely, that those possessed of the superfluities of life should be counted happy, rather than those well provided with life's necessary and useful things. Scopas the Thessalian, when one of his friends asked for something of his which was of no great service to him, with the remark that he asked for nothing that was necessary and useful, replied: "And yet my wealth and happiness are based on just such useless and superfluous things." Thus the desire for wealth is no natural adjunct of the soul, but is imposed upon it by the false opinions of the outside world.

19. However, Cato paid not the slightest heed to his accusers, but grew still more strict. He cut off the pipes by which people conveyed part of the public water supply into their private houses and gardens; he upset and demolished all buildings that encroached on public land; he reduced the cost of public works to the lowest, and forced the rent of public lands to the highest possible figure. All these things brought much odium upon him. Titus Flamininus headed a party against him which induced the Senate to annul as useless the outlays and payments which he had authorized for temples and public works, and incited the boldest of the tribunes to call him to account before the people and fine him two talents. The Senate also strongly opposed the erection of the basilica which he built at the public cost below the council-house in the Forum, and which was called the Basilica Porcia.

Still, it appears that the people approved of his censorship to an amazing extent. At any rate, after erecting a statue to his honor in the temple of Health, they commemorated in the inscription upon it, not the military commands nor the triumph of Cato, but, as the inscription may be translated, the fact "that when the Roman state was tottering to its fall, he was made censor, and by helpful guidance, wise restraints, and sound teachings, restored it again." And yet, before this time he used to laugh at those who delighted in such honors, saying that, although they knew it not, their pride was based simply on the work of statuaries and painters, whereas his own images, of the most exquisite workmanship, were borne about in the hearts of his fellow citizens. And to those who expressed their amazement that many men of no fame had statues, while he had none, he used to say: "I would much rather have men ask why I have no statue, than why I have one." In short, he thought a good citizen should not even allow himself to be praised, unless such praise was beneficial to the commonwealth.

And yet of all men he has heaped most praises upon himself. He tells us that men of self-indulgent lives, when rebuked for it, used to say: "We ought not to be blamed; we are no Catos." Also that those who imitated some of his practices and did it clumsily, were called "left-handed Catos." Also that the Senate looked to him in the most dangerous crises as seafarers to their helmsman, and often, if he was not present, postponed its most serious business. These boasts of his are confirmed, it is true, by other witnesses, for he had great authority in the city, alike for his life, his eloquence, and his age.

20. He was also a good father, a considerate husband, and a household manager of no mean talent, nor did he give only a fitful attention to this, as a matter of little or no importance. Therefore I think I ought to give suitable instances of his conduct in these relations. He married a wife who was of gentler birth than she was rich, thinking that, although the rich and the high-born may be alike given to pride, still, women of high birth have such a horror of what is disgraceful that they are more obedient to their husbands in all that is honorable. He used to say that the man who struck his wife or child, laid violent hands on the holiest of holy things. Also that he thought it more praiseworthy to be a good husband than a great senator, nay, there was nothing else to admire in Socrates of old except that he was always kind and gentle in his intercourse with a shrewish wife and stupid sons. After the birth of his son, no business could be so urgent, unless it had a public character, as to prevent him from being present when his wife bathed and swaddled the babe. For the mother nursed it herself, and often gave suck also to the infants of her slaves, that so they might come to cherish a brotherly affection for her son. As soon as the boy showed signs of understanding, his father took him under his own charge and taught him to read, although he had an accomplished slave, Chilo by name, who was a school-teacher, and taught many boys. Still, Cato thought it not right, as he tells us himself, that his son should be scolded by a slave, or have his ears tweaked when he was slow to learn, still less that he should be indebted to his slave for such a priceless thing as education. He was therefore himself not only the boy's reading teacher, but his tutor in law, and his athletic trainer, and he taught his son not merely to hurl the javelin and fight in armor and ride the horse, but also to box, to endure heat and cold, and to swim lustily through the eddies and billows of the Tiber. His History of Rome, as he tells us himself, he wrote out with his own hand and in large characters, that his son might have in his own home an aid to acquaintance with his country's ancient traditions. He declares that his son's presence put him on his guard against indecencies of speech as much as that of the so-called Vestal Virgins, and that he never bathed with him. This, indeed, would seem to have been a general custom with the Romans, for even fathers-in-law avoided bathing with their sons-in-law, because they were ashamed to uncover their nakedness. Afterwards, however, when they had learned from the Greeks their freedom in going naked, they in their turn infected the Greeks with the practice even when women were present.

So Cato wrought at the fair task of molding and fashioning his son to virtue, finding his zeal blameless, and his spirit answering to his good natural parts. But since his body was rather too delicate to endure much hardship, he relaxed somewhat in his favor the excessive rigidity and austerity of his own mode of life. But his son, although thus delicate, made a sturdy soldier, and fought brilliantly under Paulus Aemilius in the battle against Perseus.[5] On that occasion his sword either was smitten from his hand or slipped from his moist grasp. Distressed at this mishap, he turned to some of his companions for aid, and supported by them rushed again into the thick of the enemy. After a long and furious struggle, he succeeded in clearing the place, and found the sword at last among the many heaps of arms and dead bodies where friends and foes alike lay piled upon one another. Paulus, his commander, admired the young man's exploit, and there is still extant a letter written by Cato himself to his son, in which he heaps extravagant praise upon him for this honorable zeal in recovering his sword. The young man afterwards married Tertia, a

---

5. Pydna, 168 B.C.

daughter of Paulus and a sister of the younger Scipio, and his admission into such a family was due no less to himself than to his father. Thus Cato's careful attention to the education of his son bore worthy fruit.

21. He owned many domestics, and usually bought those prisoners of war who were young and still capable of being reared and trained like whelps or colts. Not one of his slaves ever entered another man's house unless sent thither by Cato or his wife, and when such an one was asked what Cato was doing, he always answered that he did not know. A slave of his was expected either to be busy about the house, or to be asleep, and he was very partial to the sleepy ones. He thought these gentler than the wakeful ones, and that those who had enjoyed the gift of sleep were better for any kind of service than those who lacked it. In the belief that his slaves were led into most mischief by their sexual passions, he stipulated that the males should consort with the females at a fixed price, but should never approach any other woman.

At the outset, when he was still poor and in military service, he found no fault at all with what was served up to him, declaring that it was shameful for a man to quarrel with a domestic over food and drink. But afterwards, when his circumstances were improved and he used to entertain his friends and colleagues at table, no sooner was the dinner over than he would flog those slaves who had been remiss at all in preparing or serving it. He was always contriving that his slaves should have feuds and dissensions among themselves; harmony among them made him suspicious and fearful of them. He had those who were suspected of some capital offence brought to trial before all their fellow servants, and, if convicted, put to death.

However, as he applied himself more strenuously to making money, he came to regard agriculture as more entertaining than profitable, and invested his capital in business that was safe and sure. He bought ponds, hot springs, districts given over to fullers, pitch factories, land with natural pasture and forest, all of which brought him in large profits, and " could not," to use his own phrase, " be ruined by Jupiter." He used to loan money also in the most disreputable of all ways, namely, on ships, and his method was as follows. He required his borrowers to form a large company, and when there were fifty partners and as many ships for his security, he took one share in the company himself, and was represented by Quintio, a freedman of his, who accompanied his clients in all their ventures. In this way his entire security was not imperiled, but only a small part of it. and his profits were large. He used to lend money also to those of his slaves who wished it, and they would buy boys with it, and after training and teaching them for a year, at Cato's expense, would sell them again. Many of these boys Cato would retain for himself, reckoning to the credit of the slave the highest price bid for his boy. He tried to incite his son also to such economies, by saying that it was not the part of a man, but of a widow woman, to lessen his substance. But that surely was too vehement a speech of Cato's, when he went so far as to say that a man was to be admired and glorified like a god if the final inventory of his property showed that he had added to it more than he had inherited.

22. When he was now well on in years, there came as ambassadors from Athens to Rome,[6] Carneades the Academic, and Diogenes the Stoic philosopher, to beg the reversal of a certain decision against the Athenian people, which imposed upon them a fine of five hundred talents. The people of Oropus had brought the suit, the Athenians had let the case go by default, and the

---

6. 155 B.C.

Sicyonians had pronounced judgment against them. Upon the arrival of these philosophers, the most studious of the city's youth hastened to wait upon them, and became their devoted and admiring listeners. The charm of Carneades especially, which had boundless power, and a fame not inferior to its power, won large and sympathetic audiences, and filled the city, like a rushing mighty wind, with the noise of his praises. Report spread far and wide that a Greek of amazing talent, who disarmed all opposition by the magic of his eloquence, had infused a tremendous passion into the youth of the city, in consequence of which they forsook their other pleasures and pursuits and were "possessed" about philosophy. The other Romans were pleased at this, and glad to see their young men lay hold of Greek culture and consort with such admirable men. But Cato, at the very outset, when this zeal for discussion came pouring into the city, was distressed, fearing lest the young men, by giving this direction to their ambition, should come to love a reputation based on mere words more than one achieved by martial deeds. And when the fame of the visiting philosophers rose yet higher in the city, and their first speeches before the Senate were interpreted, at his own instance and request, by so conspicuous a man as Gaius Acilius, Cato determined, on some decent pretext or other, to rid and purge the city of them all. So he rose in the Senate and censured the magistrates for keeping in such long suspense an embassy composed of men who could easily secure anything they wished, so persuasive were they. "We ought," he said, "to make up our minds one way or another, and vote on what the embassy proposes, in order that these men may return to their schools and lecture to the sons of Greece, while the youth of Rome give ear to their laws and magistrates, as heretofore."

23. This he did, not, as some think, out of personal hostility to Carneades, but because he was wholly averse to philosophy, and made mock of all Greek culture and training, out of patriotic zeal. He says, for instance, that Socrates was a mighty prattler, who attempted, as best he could, to be his country's tyrant, by abolishing its customs, and by enticing his fellow citizens into opinions contrary to the laws. He made fun of the school of Isocrates, declaring that his pupils kept on studying with him till they were old men, as if they were to practice their arts and plead their cases before Minos in Hades. And seeking to prejudice his son against Greek culture, he indulges in an utterance all too rash for his years, declaring, in the tone of a prophet or a seer, that Rome would lose her empire when she had become infected with Greek letters. But time has certainly shown the emptiness of this ill-boding speech of his, for while the city was at the zenith of its empire, she made every form of Greek learning and culture her own.

It was not only Greek philosophers that he hated, but he was also suspicious of Greeks who practiced medicine at Rome. He had heard, it would seem, of Hippocrates' reply when the Great King of Persia consulted him, with the promise of a fee of many talents, namely, that he would never put his skill at the service of Barbarians who were enemies of Greece. he said all Greek physicians had taken a similar oath, and urged his son to beware of them all. He himself, lie said, had written a book of recipes, which he followed in the treatment and regimen of any who were sick in his family. He never required his patients to fast, but fed them on greens, or bits of duck, pigeon, or hare. Such a diet, he said, was light and good for sick people, except that it often causes dreams. By following such treatment and regimen he said he had good health himself, and kept his family in good health.

25. He composed speeches, then, on all sorts of subjects, and histories, and as for farming, he followed it in earnest when he was young and poor—indeed, he says he then had only two ways

of getting money, farming and frugality—but in later life he was only a theoretical and fancy farmer. He also composed a book on farming, in which he actually gave recipes for making cakes arid preserving fruit, so ambitious was he to be superior and peculiar in everything. The dinners, too, which he gave in the country, were quite plentiful. He always asked in congenial country neighbors, and made merry with them, and not only did those of his own age find in him an agreeable and much desired companion, but also the young. For he was a man of large experience, who had read and heard much that was well worth repeating. He held the table to be the very best promoter of friendship, and at his own, the conversation turned much to the praise of honorable and worthy citizens, greatly to the neglect of those who were worthless and base. About such Cato suffered no table-talk, either by way of praise or blame.

26. The last of his public services is supposed to have been the destruction of Carthage. It was Scipio the Younger who actually brought the task to completion,[7] but it was largely in consequence of the advice and counsel of Cato that the Romans undertook the war. It was on this wise. Cato was sent[8] on an embassy to the Carthaginians and Masinissa the Numidian, who were at war with one another, to inquire into the grounds of their quarrel. Masinissa had been a friend of the Roman people from the first, and the Carthaginians had entered into treaty relations with Rome after the defeat which the elder Scipio had given them. The treaty deprived them of their empire, and imposed a grievous money tribute upon them. Cato, however, found the city by no means in a poor and lowly state, as the Romans supposed, but rather teeming with vigorous fighting men, overflowing with enormous wealth, filled with arms of every sort and with military supplies, and not a little puffed up by all this. He therefore thought it no time for the Romans to be ordering and arranging the affairs of Masinissa and the Numidians, but that unless they should repress a city which had always been their malignant foe, now that its power was so incredibly grown, they would be involved again in dangers as great as before. Accordingly, he returned with speed to Rome, and advised the Senate that the former calamitous defeats of the Carthaginians had diminished not so much their power as their foolhardiness, and were likely to render them in the end not weaker, but more expert in war; their present contest with Numidia was but a prelude to a contest with Rome, while peace and treaty were mere names wherewith to cover their postponement of war till a fit occasion offered.

27. In addition to this, it is said that Cato contrived to drop a Libyan fig in the Senate, as he shook out the folds of his toga, and then, as the senators admired its size and beauty, said that the country where it grew was only three days' sail from Rome. And in one thing he was even more savage, namely, in adding to his vote on any question whatsoever these words: "In my opinion, Carthage must be destroyed." Publius Scipio Nasica, on the contrary, when called upon for his vote, always ended his speech with this declaration: "In my opinion, Carthage must be spared." He saw, probably, that the Roman people, in its wantonness, was already guilty of many excesses, and in the pride of its prosperity, spurned the control of the Senate, and forcibly dragged the whole state with it, whithersoever its mad desires inclined it. He wished, therefore, that the fear of Carthage should abide, to curb the boldness of the multitude like a bridle, believing her not strong enough to conquer Rome, nor yet weak enough to be despised. But this was precisely what

---

7. 146 B.C.
8. 150 B.C.

Cato dreaded, when the Roman people was inebriated and staggering with its power, to have a city which had always been great, and was now but sobered and chastened by its calamities, for ever threatening them. Such external threats to their sovereignty ought to be done away with altogether, he thought, that they might be free to devise a cure for their domestic failings.

In this way Cato is said to have brought to pass the third and last war against Carthage,[9] but it had no sooner begun than he died,[10] having first prophesied of the man who was destined to end it. This man was then young, but as tribune in the army, he was giving proofs of judgment and daring in his engagements with the enemy. Tidings of this came to Rome, and Cato is said to have cried on hearing them:

"Only he has wits, but the rest are fluttering shadows."[11]

This utterance of Cato's, Scipio speedily confirmed by his deeds. Cato left one son by his second wife, whose surname, as we have already remarked, was Salonius; and one grandson by the son who died before him. Salonius died in the praetorship, but the son whom he left, Marcus, came to be consul. This Marcus was the grandfather of Cato the philosopher, who was the best and most illustrious man of his time.

TIBERIUS GRACCHUS

By the year 133 B.C. the Roman state had overcome all adversaries and was rich, proud and powerful. But its success overseas was not without severe social and political cost at home. Expansion created power blocks and pressure groups which threatened to tear apart the very fabric of the republic. Overseas conquest funneled unprecedented wealth into Italy and created a new class of wealthy citizens known as the equites. *The* equites *are usually thought of as the business class of ancient Rome. And in fact this class did conduct most of the commercial activity of Rome, since senators were forbidden by law to engage in business—their wealth was supposed to be derived from land ownership. When the Romans who made their fortunes out in the provinces returned to Italy, they invested their new wealth in land, because land was the most honorable form of wealth and land ownership aided these* **nouveau riche** *in their attempts to gain entrance into the senatorial class.*

During the invasion of Hannibal's army, large numbers of Italian farmers were forced to desert their farms and migrate to the cities for protection. After the war, the rising equites *and senatorial class bought up this vacant land and formed it*

From *Plutarch: Plutarch's Lives, Volume X*, translated by Beradotte Perrin (Cambridge, Loeb Classical Library, Harvard University Press, 1921).

into large estates, called latifundia, which they farmed with large gangs of slaves. Large numbers of slaves were imported from overseas as a result of Rome's successful imperialism, because prisoners of war were the chief source of slaves in the ancient world.

Now the class of proletarii, poor Roman citizens who possessed no property at all, began to increase dramatically, while the peasant farmer class, the mainstay of the republic and the backbone of the army, began to disappear altogether. Small land owners formed the manpower pool for the Roman army—without them all the gains of imperialism would be lost. Two young Roman aristocrats, the brothers Tiberius and Gaius Gracchus, attempted to solve this problem, and of course, in the process to carve out lucrative political careers for themselves.

1. . . . [Tiberius and Gaius] were sons of Tiberius Gracchus, who, although he had been censor at Rome, twice consul, and had celebrated two triumphs, derived his more illustrious dignity from his virtue. Therefore, after the death of the Scipio[12] who conquered Hannibal, although Tiberius had not been his friend, but actually at variance with him, he was judged worthy to take Scipio's daughter Cornelia in marriage. We are told, moreover, that he once caught a pair of serpents on his bed, and that the soothsayers, after considering the prodigy, forbade him to kill both serpents or to let both go, but to decide the fate of one or the other of them, declaring also that the male serpent, if killed, would bring death to Tiberius, and the female, to Cornelia. Tiberius, accordingly, who loved his wife, and thought that since she was still young and he was older it was more fitting that he should die, killed the male serpent, hut let the female go. A short time afterwards, as the story goes, he died,[13] leaving Cornelia with twelve children by him.

Cornelia took charge of the children and of the estate, and showed herself so discreet, so good a mother, and so magnanimous, that Tiberius was thought to have made no bad decision when he elected to die instead of such a woman. For when Ptolemy[14] the king offered to share his crown with her and sought her hand in marriage, she refused him, and remained a widow. In this state she lost most of her children, but three survived; one daughter, who married Scipio the Younger, and two sons, Tiberius and Gaius, whose lives I now write. These sons Cornelia reared with such scrupulous care that although confessedly no other Romans were so well endowed nature, they were thought to owe their virtues more to education than to nature.

2. Now, just as, in spite of the likeness between Castor and Pollux as they are represented in sculpture and painting, there is a certain difference of shape between the boxer and the runner,

9. 151–146 B.C.

10. 149 B.C.

11. Odyssey, 10.495

12. 183 B.C.

13. He was consul for the second time in 163 B.C. The year of his death is unknown. This story is told and commented on by Cicero in *De divinatione* 1.18.36; 2.29.62.

14. Probably Ptolemy VI, surnamed Philometor, king of Egypt 181–146 B.C.

so in the case of these young Romans, along with their strong resemblance to one another in bravery and self-command, as well as in liberality, eloquence, and magnanimity, in their actions and political careers great unlikenesses blossomed out, as it were, and came to light. Therefore I think it not amiss to set these forth before going further.

In the first place, then, as regards cast of features and look and bearing, Tiberius was gentle and sedate while Gaius was high strung and vehement, so that even when haranguing the people the one stood composedly in one spot, while the other was the first Roman to walk about upon the rostra and pull his toga off his shoulder as he spoke. So Cleon the Athenian is said to have been the first of the popular orators to strip away his mantle and smite his thigh. In the second place, the speech of Gaius was awe-inspiring and passionate to exaggeration, while that of Tiberius was more agreeable and more conducive to pity. The style also of Tiberius was pure and elaborated to a nicety, while that of Gaius was persuasive and ornate. So also as regards their table and mode of life, Tiberius was simple and plain, while Gaius, although temperate and austere as compared with others, in contrast with his brother was ostentatious and fastidious. Hence men like Drusus found fault with him because he bought silver dolphins at twelve hundred and fifty drachmas the pound. Again, their tempers were no less different than their speech. Tiberius was reasonable and gentle, while Gaius was harsh and fiery, so that against his better judgment he was often carried away by anger as he spoke, raising his voice to a high pitch and uttering abuse and losing the thread of his discourse. Wherefore, to guard against such digressions, he employed an intelligent servant, Licinius, who stood behind him when he was speaking, with a sounding instrument for giving the tones of the voice their pitch. Whenever this servant noticed that the voice of Gaius was getting harsh and broken with anger, he would give out a soft key-note, on hearing which Gaius would at once remit the vehemence of his passion and of his speech, grow gentle, and show himself easy to recall.

8. Of the territory which the Romans won in war from their neighbors, a part they sold, and a part they made common land, and assigned it for occupation to the poor and indigent among the citizens, on payment of a small rent into the public treasury. And when the rich began to offer larger rents and drove out the poor, a law was enacted forbidding the holding by one person of more than five hundred acres of land. For a short time this enactment gave a check to the rapacity of the rich, and was of assistance to the poor, who remained in their places on the land which they had rented and occupied the allotment which each had held from the outset. But later on the neighboring rich men, by means of fictitious personages, transferred these rentals to themselves, and finally held most of the land openly in their own names. Then the poor, who had been ejected from their land, no longer showed themselves eager for military service, and neglected the bringing up of children, so that soon all Italy was conscious of a dearth of freemen, and was filled with gangs of forting slaves, by whose aid the rich cultivated their estates, from which they had driven away the free citizens. An attempt was therefore made to retify this evil. and by Gaius Laelius the comrade of Scipio; but the men of influence opposed his measures, and he, fearing the disturbance which might ensue, desisted, and received the surname of *Wise* or *Prudent*.[15] Tiberius, however, on being elected tribune of the people, took the matter directly in hand. He was incited to this step, as most writers say, by Diophanes the rhetorician and Blossius the phi-

15. For the Latin word "*sapiens*" would seem to have either meaning.

losopher. Diophanes was an exile from Mitylene, but Blossius was a native Italian from Cumae, had been an intimate friend of Antipater of Tarsus at Rome, and had been honored by him with the dedication of philosophical treatises. But some put part of the blame upon Cornelia the mother of Tiberius, who often reproached her sons because the Romans still called her the mother-in-law of Scipio, but not yet the mother of the Gracchi. Others again say that a certain Spurius Postumius was to blame. He was of the same age as Tiberius, and a rival of his in reputation as an advocate; and when Tiberius came back from his campaign and found that his rival had far outstripped him in reputation and influence and was an object of public admiration, he determined, as it would seem, to outdo him by engaging in a bold political measure which would arouse great expectations among the people. But his brother Gaius, in a certain pamphlet,[16] has written that as Tiberius was passing through Tuscany on his way to Numantia, and observed the dearth of inhabitants in the country, and that those who tilled its soil or tended its flocks there were imported barbarian slaves, he then first conceived the public policy which was the cause of countless ills to the two brothers. However, the energy and ambition of Tiberius were most of all kindled by the people themselves who posted writings on porticos, house walls, and monuments, calling upon him to recover for the poor the public land.

9. He did not, however, draw up his law by himself, but took counsel with the citizens who were foremost in virtue and reputation, among whom were Crassus the pontifex maximus, Mucius Scaevola the jurist, who was then consul, and Appius Claudius, his father-in-law. And it is thought that a law dealing with injustice and rapacity so great was never drawn up in milder and gentler terms. For men who ought to have been punished for their disobedience and to have surrendered with payment of a fine the land which they were illegally enjoying, these men it merely ordered to abandon their unjust acquisitions upon being paid their value, and to admit into ownership of them such citizens as needed assistance. But although the rectification of the wrong was so considerate, the people were satisfied to let bygones be bygones if they could be secure from such wrong in the future: the men of Wealth and substance, however, were led by their greed to hate the law, and by their wrath and contentiousness to hate the law-giver, and tried to dissuade the people by alleging that Tiberius was a re-distribution of land for the confusion of the body politic, and was stirring up a general revolution.

But they accomplished nothing; for Tiberius, striving to support a measure which was honorable and just with an eloquence that would have adorned even a meaner cause, was formidable and invincible, whenever, with the people crowding around the rostra, he took his stand there and pleaded for the poor. "The wild beasts that roam over Italy," he would say "have every one of them a cave or lair to lurk in; but the men who fight and die for Italy enjoy the common air and light, indeed, but nothing else; houseless and homeless they wander about with their wives and children. And it is with lying lips that their imperators exhort the soldiers in their battles to defend sepulchers and shrines from the enemy; for not a man of them has an hereditary altar, not one of all these many Romans an ancestral tomb, but they fight and die to support others in wealth and luxury, and though they are styled masters of the world, they have not a single clod of earth that is their own."

---

16. Probably a political pamphlet in the form of a letter.

10. Such words as these, the product of a lofty spirit and genuine feeling, and falling upon the ears of a people profoundly moved and fully aroused to the speaker's support, no adversary of Tiberius could successfully withstand. Abandoning therefore all counter-pleading, they addressed themselves to Marcus Octavius, one of the popular tribunes, a young man of sober character, discreet, and an intimate companion of Tiberius. On this account Octavius at first tried to hold himself aloof, out of regard for Tiberius; but he was forced from his position, as it were, by the prayers and supplications of many influential men, so that he set himself in opposition to Tiberius and staved off the passage of the law. Now, the decisive power is in the hands of the tribune who interposes his veto; for the wishes of the majority avail nothing if one tribune is in opposition. Incensed at this procedure, Tiberius withdrew his considerate law, and introduced this time one which was more agreeable to the multitude and more severe against the wrongdoers, since it simply ordered them to vacate without compensation the land which they had acquired in violation of the earlier laws.

Almost every day, therefore, there were forensic contests between Tiberius and Octavius, in which, as we are told, although both strove together with the utmost earnestness and rivalry, neither abused the other or let fall a single word about the other which anger made unseemly. For not only "in Bacchic revelries," as it appears, but also in the exercise of rivalry and wrath, a noble nature and a sound training restrain and regulate the mind. Moreover, when Tiberius observed that Octavius himself was amenable to the law as a large holder of the public land, he begged him to remit his opposition, promising to pay him the value of the land out of his own means, although these were not splendid. But Octavius would not consent to this, and therefore Tiberius issued an edict forbidding all the other magistrates to transact any public business until such time as the vote should be cast either for or against his law. He also put is private seal upon the temple of Saturn in order that the quaestors might not take any money from its treasury or pay any into it, and he made proclamation that a penalty would be imposed upon such praetors as disobeyed, so that all magistrates grew fearful and ceased performing their several functions. Thereupon tile men of property put on the garb of mourning and went about the forum in pitiful and lowly guise; but in secret they plotted against the life of Tiberius and tried to raise a band of assassins to take him off, so that Tiberius on his part—and everybody knew it—wore a concealed short-sword such as brigands use (the name for it is "*dolo*").

11. When the appointed day was come and Tiberius was summoning the people to the vote, the voting urns were stolen away by the party of the rich, and great confusion arose. However, the supporters of Tiberius were numerous enough to force the issue, and were banding together for this purpose when Manlius and Fulvius, men of consular dignity, fell down before Tiberius, clasped his hands, and with tears besought him to desist. Tiberius, conscious that the future was now all but desperate, and moved by respect for the men, asked them what they would have him do. They replied that they were not competent to advise in so grave a crisis, and urged him with entreaties to submit the case to the senate. To this Tiberius consented.

But the senate in its session accomplished nothing, owing to the prevailing influence of the wealthy class in it, and therefore Tiberius resorted to a measure which was illegal and unseemly, the ejection of Octavius from his office; but he was unable in any other way to bring his law to the vote. In the first place, however, he begged Octavius in public, addressing him with kindly words and clasping his hands, to give in and gratify the people, who demanded only their just rights, and would receive only a trifling return for great toils and perils. But Octavius rejected the petition, and therefore Tiberius, after premising that, since they were colleagues in office with equal powers and differed on weighty measures, it was impossible for them to complete their term of office without open war, said he saw only one remedy for this, and that was for one or the other of them to give up his office. Indeed, he urged Octavius to put to the people a vote on his own case first, promising to retire at once to private life if this should be the will of the citizens. But Octavius was unwilling, and therefore Tiberius declared that he would put the case of Octavius unless Octavius should change his mind upon reflection.

12. With this understanding, he dissolved the assembly for that day; but on the following day, after the people had come together, he mounted the rostra and once more attempted to persuade Octavius. When, however, Octavius was not to be persuaded, Tiberius introduced a law depriving him of his tribuneship, and summoned the citizens to cast their votes upon it at once. Now, there were five and thirty tribes, and when seventeen of them had cast their votes, and the addition of one more would make it necessary for Octavius to become a private citizen, Tiberius called a halt in the voting, and again entreated Octavius, embracing and kissing him in the sight of the people, and fervently begging him not to allow himself to be dishonored, and not to attach to a friend responsibility for a measure so grievous and severe.

On hearing these entreaties, we are told, Octavius was not altogether untouched or unmoved; his eyes filled with tears and he stood silent for a long time. But when he turned his gaze towards the men of wealth and substance who were standing in a body together, his awe of them, as it would seem, and his fear of ill repute among them, led him to take every risk with boldness and bid Tiberius do what he pleased. And so the law was passed, and Tiberius ordered one of his freedmen to drag Octavius from the rostra; for Tiberius used his freedmen as officers, and this made the sight of Octavius dragged along with contumely a more pitiful one. Moreover, the people made a rush at him, and though the men of wealth ran in a body to his assistance and spread out their hands against the crowd, it was with difficulty that Octavius was snatched away and safely rescued from the crowd; and a trusty servant of his who stood in front of his master and protected him, had his eyes torn out, against the protest of Tiberius, who, when he perceived what was going on, ran down with great haste to appease the tumult.

13. After this the agrarian law was passed and three men were chosen for the survey and distribution of the public land, Tiberius himself, Appius Claudius his father-in-law, and Gaius Gracchus his brother, who was not at Rome, but was serving under Scipio in the expedition against Numantia. These measures were carried out by Tiberius quietly and without opposition, and, besides, he procured the election of a tribune in the place of Octavius. The new tribune was not a man of rank or note, but a certain Mucius, a client of Tiberius. The aristocrats, however, who were vexed at these proceedings and feared the growing power of Tiberius, heaped insult upon him in the senate. When he asked for the customary tent at public expense, for his use when dividing up the public land, they fixed his daily allowance for expenses at nine obols.[17] These things were done on motion of Publius Nasica, who surrendered completely to his hatred of Tiberius. For he was a very large holder of public land, and bitterly resented his being forced to give it up.

---

17. That is, in Roman money, nine *sestertii*, equivalent perhaps to about forty cents.

But people were all the more inflamed; and when a friend of Tiberius died suddenly and his body broke out all over with evil spots, they ran in throngs to the man's funeral, crying out that he had been poisoned to death, and they carried the bier themselves, and stood by at the last ceremonies. And their suspicions of poison were thought to be not without reason. For the dead body burst open and a great quantity of corrupt humors gushed forth, so that the flame of the funeral pyre was extinguished. And when fresh fire was brought, again the body would not burn, until it was carried to another place, where, after much trouble, the fire at last took hold of it. Upon this, Tiberius, that he might exasperate the multitude still more, put on a garb of mourning, brought his children before the assembly, and begged the people to care for them and their mother, saying that he despaired of his own life.

14. And now Attalus Philometor died,[18] and Eudemus of Pergamum brought to Rome the king's last will and testament, by which the Roman people was made his heir. At once Tiberius courted popular favor by bringing in a bill which provided that the money of King Attalus, when brought to Rome, should be given to the citizens who received a parcel of the public land, to aid them in stocking and tilling their farms. And as regard to the cities which were included in the kingdom of Attalus, he said it did not belong to the senate to deliberate about them, but he himself would submit a pertinent resolution to the people. By this proceeding he gave more offence than ever to the senate; and Pompeius, rising to speak there, said that he was a neighbor of Tiberius, and therefore knew that Eudemus of Pergamum had presented Tiberius with a royal diadem and purple robe, believing that he was going to be king in Rome. Moreover, Quintus Metellus upbraided Tiberius with the reminder that whenever his father, during his censorship, was returning home after a supper, the citizens put out their lights, for fear they might be thought to be indulging immoderately in entertainments and drinking bouts, whereas Tiberius himself was lighted on his way at night by the neediest and most reckless of the populace. Titus Annius, too, a man of no high character or sobriety, but held to be invincible in arguments carried on by question and answer, challenged Tiberius to a judicial wager, solemnly asserting that he had branded with infamy his colleague, who was sacred and inviolable by law. As many senators applauded this speech, Tiberius dashed out of the senate-house, called the people together, and ordered Annius to be brought before them, with, the intention of denouncing him. But Annius, who was far inferior to Tiberius both in eloquence and in reputation, had recourse to his own particular art, and called upon Tiberius to answer a few questions before the argument began. Tiberius assented to this and silence was made, whereupon Annius said " If you wish to heap insult upon me and degrade me, and I invoke the aid of one of your colleagues in office, and he mount the rostra to speak in my defense, and you fly into a passion, come, will you deprive that colleague of his office?" At this question, we are told, Tiberius was so disconcerted that, although he was of all men most ready in speech and most vehement in courage, he held his peace.

15. For the present, then, he dissolved the assembly; but perceiving that the course he had taken with regard to Octavius was very displeasing, not only to the nobles, but also to the multitude (for it was thought that the high and honorable dignity of the tribunate, so carefully guarded up to that time, had been insulted and destroyed), he made a lengthy speech before the people, a few of the arguments of which it will not be our of place to lay before the reader, that he may get

---

18. 133 B.C.

a conception of the man's subtlety and persuasiveness. A tribune, he said, was sacred and inviolable, because he was consecrated to the people and was a champion of the people, "If then," said Tiberius, "he should change about, wrong the people, maim its power, and rob it of the privilege of noting, he has by his own acts deprived himself of his honorable office by not fulfilling the conditions on which he received it; for otherwise there would be no interference with a tribune even though he should try to demolish the Capitol or set fire to the naval arsenal. If a tribune does these things, he is a bad tribune; but if he annuls the power of the people, he is no tribune at all. It is not a monstrous thing that a tribune should have power to hale a consul to prison, while the people cannot deprive a tribune of his power when he employs it against the very ones who bestowed it? For consul and tribune alike are elected by the people. And surely the kingly office, besides comprehending in itself every civil function, is also consecrated to the Deity by the performance of the most solemn religious rites; and yet Tarquin was expelled by the city for his wrong doing, and because of one man's insolence the power which had founded Rome and descended from father to son was overthrown. Again, what institution at Rome is so holy and venerable as that of the virgins who tend and watch the undying fire? And yet if one of these breaks her vows, she is buried alive; for when they sin against the gods they do not preserve that inviolable character which is given them for their service to the gods. Therefore it is not just that a tribune who wrongs the people should retain that inviolable character which is given him for service to the people, since he is destroying the very power which is the source of his own power. And surely, if it is right for him to be made tribune by a majority of the votes of the tribes, it must be even more right for him to be deprived of his tribuneship by unanimous vote. And again, nothing is so sacred and inviolate as objects consecrated to the gods; and yet no one has hindered the people from using such objects, or moving them, or changing their position in such manner as may be desired. It is therefore permissible for the people to transfer the tribunate also, as a consecrated thing, from one man to another. And that the office is not inviolable or irremovable is plain from the fact that many times men holding it resign it under oath of disability, and of their own accord beg to be relieved of it."

16. Such were the chief points in the justification of his course which Tiberius made. And now his friends, observing the threats and the hostile combination against him, thought that he ought to be made tribune for the following year. Once more, therefore Tiberius sought to win the favor of the multitude by fresh laws, reducing the time of military service, granting appeal to the people from the verdicts of the judges, adding to the judges, who at that time were composed of senators only, an equal number from the equestrian order, and in every way at length trying to maim the power of the senate from motives of anger and contentiousness rather than from calculations of justice and the public good. And when, as the voting was going on, the friends' of Tiberius perceived that their opponents were getting the better of the contest, since all the people were not present, in the first place they resorted to abuse of his fellow tribunes, and so protracted the time; next, they dismissed the assembly, and ordered that it should convene on the following day. Then Tiberius, going down into the forum, at first supplicated the citizens in a humble manner and with tears in his eyes, next, he declared he was afraid that his enemies would break into his house by night and kill him, and thereby so wrought upon his hearers that great numbers of them took up their station about his house and spent the night there on guard.

17. At break of day there came to the house the man who brought the birds with which auspices are taken, and threw food before them. But the birds would not come out of the cage, with the exception of one, though the keeper shook the cage right hard; and even the one that came out would not touch the food, but raised its left wing, stretched out its leg, and then ran back into the cage. This reminded Tiberius of an omen that had happened earlier, he had a helmet which he wore in battle, exceptionally adorned and splendid; into this serpents crawled unnoticed, laid eggs there and hatched them out. For this reason Tiberius was all the more disturbed by the signs from the birds. But nevertheless he set out, on learning that the people were assembled on the Capitol; and before he got out of the house, he stumbled against the threshold, The blow was so severe that the nail of his great toe was broken and the blood ran out through his shoe. He had gone on but a little way when ravens were seen fighting on the roof of a house to his left hand and though there were many people, as was natural. passing by, a stone dislodged by one of the ravens fell at the foot of Tiberius himself. This caused even the boldest of his followers to pause; but Blossius of Cumae, who was present, said it would be a shame and a great disgrace if Tiberius, a son of Gracchus, a grandson of Scipio African us, and a champion of the Roman people, for fear of a raven should refuse to obey the summons of his fellow citizens; such shameful conduct, moreover, would not be made a mere matter of ridicule by his enemies, but they would decry him to the people as one who was at last giving himself the airs of a tyrant. At the same time also many of his friends on the Capitol came running to Tiberius with urgent appeals to hasten thither, since matters there were going well. And in fact things turned out splendidly for Tiberius at first; as soon as he came into view the crowd raised a friendly shout, and as he came up the hill they gave him a cordial welcome and ranged themselves about him, that no stranger might approach.

18. But after Mucius began once more to summon the tribes to the vote, none of the customary forms could be observed because of the disturbance that arose on the outskirts of the throng, where there was crowding back and forth between the friends of Tiberius and their opponents, who were striving to force their way in and mingle with the rest. Moreover, at this juncture Fulvius Flaccus, a senator, posted himself in a conspicuous place, and since it was impossible to make his voice heard so far, indicated with his hand that he wished to tell Tiberius something meant for his ear alone. Tiberius ordered the crowd to part for Flavius, who made his way up to him with difficulty, and told him that at a session of the senate the party of the rich, since they could not prevail upon the consul to do so, were purposing to kill Tiberius themselves, and for this purpose had under arms a multitude of their friends and slaves.

19. Tiberius, accordingly, reported this to those who stood about him, and they at once girded up their togas, and breaking in pieces the spear-shafts with which the officers keep back the crowd, distributed the fragments among themselves, that they might defend themselves against their assailants. Those who were farther off, however, wondered at what was going on and asked what it meant. Where upon Tiberius put his hand to his head, making this visible sign that his life was in danger, since the questioners could not heart his voice. But his opponents, on seeing this, ran to the senate and told that body that Tiberius was asking for a crown; and that his putting his hand to his head was a sign having that meaning. All the senators, of course, were greatly disturbed, and Nasica demanded that the consul should come to the rescue of the state and put down the tyrant. The consul replied with mildness that he would resort to no violence and would put no citizen to death without a trial; if, however, the people, under persuasion or compulsion from

Tiberius, should vote anything that was unlawful, he would not regard this vote as binding. Thereupon Nasica sprang to his feet and said "Since, then, the chief magistrate betrays the state, do you who wish to succor the laws follow me." With these words he covered his head with the skirt of his toga and set out for the Capitol. All the senators who followed him wrapped their togas about their left arms and pushed aside those who stood in their path, no man opposing them, in view of their dignity, but all taking to flight and trampling upon one another.

Now, the attendants of the senators carried clubs and staves which they had brought from home; but the senators themselves seized the fragments and legs of the benches that were shattered by the crowd in its flight, and went up against Tiberius, at the same time smiting those who were drawn up to protect him. Of these there was a rout and a slaughter and as Tiberius himself turned to fly, someone laid hold of his garments. So he let his toga go and fled in his tunic. But he stumbled and fell to the ground among some bodies that lay in front of him. As he strove to rise to his feet, he received his first blow, as everybody admits, from Publius Satyreius, one of his colleagues, who smote him on the head with the leg of a bench; to the second blow claim was made by Lucius Rufus, who plumed himself upon it as upon some noble deed. And of the rest more than three hundred were slain by blows from sticks and stones, but not one by the sword.

20. This is said to have been the first sedition at Rome, since the abolition of royal power, to end in bloodshed and the death of citizens; the rest, though neither trifling nor raised for trifling objects, were settled by mutual concessions, the nobles yielding from fear of the multitude, and the people out of respect for the senate. And it was thought that even on this occasion Tiberius would have given way without difficulty had persuasion been brought to bear upon him, and would have yielded still more easily if his assailants had not resorted to wounds and bloodshed; for his adherents numbered not more than three thousand. But the combination against him would seem to have arisen from the hatred and anger of the rich rather than from the pretexts which they alleged; and there is strong proof of this in their lawless and savage treatment of his dead body. For they would not listen to his brother's request that he might take up the body and bury it by night, but threw it into the river along with the other dead. Nor was this all; they banished some of his friends without a trial and others they arrested and put to death. Among these Diophanes the rhetorician also perished. A certain Gaius Villius they shut up in a cage, and then put in vipers and serpents, and in this way killed him. Blossius of Cumae was brought before the consuls, and when he was asked about what had passed, he admitted that he had done everything at the bidding of Tiberius. Then Nasica said to him, "What, then, if Tiberius had ordered you to set fire to the Capitol?" Blossius at first replied that Tiberius would not have given such an order; but when the same question was put to him often and by many persons, he said: "If such a man as Tiberius had ordered such a thing, it would also have been right for me to do it; for Tiberius would not have given such an order if it had not been for the interest of the people." Well, then, Blossius was acquitted, and afterwards went to Aristonicus[19] in Asia, and when the cause of Aristonicus was lost, slew himself.

21. But the senate, trying to conciliate the people now that matters had gone so far, no longer opposed the distribution of the public land, and proposed that the people should elect a commissioner in place of Tiberius. So they took a ballot and elected Publius Crassus, who was a relative

---

19. The pretender to the throne of Attalus Philometer. He was defeated and taken prisoner by the Romans in 130 B.C.

of Gracchus; for his daughter Licinia was the wife of Gaius Gracchus. And yet Cornelius Nepos says that it was not the daughter of Crassus, but of the Brutus who triumphed over the Lusitanians, whom Gaius married; the majority of writers, however, state the matter as I have done. Moreover, since the people felt bitterly over the death of Tiberius and were clearly awaiting an opportunity for revenge, and since Nasica was already threatened with prosecutions, the senate, fearing for his safety, voted to send him to Asia, although it had no need of him there. For when people met Nasica, they did not try to hide their hatred of him, but grew savage and cried out upon him wherever he chanced to be, calling him an accursed man and a tyrant, who had defiled with the murder of an inviolable and sacred person the holiest and most awe-inspiring of the city's sanctuaries. And so Nasica stealthily left Italy, although he was bound there by the most important and sacred functions; for he was pontifex maximus. He roamed and wandered about in foreign lands ignominiously, and after a short time ended his life at Pergamum. Now, it is no wonder that the people so much hated Nasica, when even Scipio Africanus, than whom no one would seem to have been more justly or more deeply loved by the Romans, came within a little of forfeiting and losing the popular favor because, to begin with, at Numantia, when he learned of the death of Tiberius, he recited in a loud voice the verse of' Homer:[20]

"So perish also all other's who on such wickedness venture,"

and because, in the second place, when Gaius and Fulvius asked him in an assembly of the people what he thought about the death of Tiberius, he made a reply which showed his dislike of the measures advocated by him. Consequently the people began to interrupt him as he was speaking, a thing which they had never done before, and Scipio himself was thereby led on to abuse the people. Of these matters I have written circumstantially in my Life of Scipio.[21]

GAIUS GRACCHUS

To an even greater degree than Tiberius, Gaius attempted to return the government of Rome to the people.

1. Gaius Gracchus, at first, either because he feared his enemies, or because he wished to bring odium upon them, withdrew from the forum and lived quietly by himself, like one who was humbled for the present and for the future intended to live the same inactive life, so that some were actually led to denounce him for disliking and repudiating his brother's political measures. And he was also quite a stripling, for he was nine years younger than his brother, and Tiberius was not yet thirty when he died. But as time went on he gradually showed a disposition that was averse to idleness, effeminacy. Wine-bibbing, and money-making; and by preparing his oratory to waft him as on swift pinions to public life, he made it clear that he was not going to remain

From *Plutarch: Plutarch's Lives, Volume X*, translated by Beradotte Perrin (Cambridge, Loeb Classical Library, Harvard University Press, 1921).

quiet; and in defending Vettius, a friend of his who was under prosecution, he had the people about him inspired and frantic with sympathetic delight, and made the other orators appear to he no better than children, Once more, therefore, the nobles began to be alarmed, and there was much talk among them about not permitting Gaius to he made tribune.

By accident, however, it happened that the lot tell on him to go to Sardinia as quaestor for Orestes the consul.[22] This gave pleasure to his enemies, and did not annoy Gaius. For he was fond of war, and quite as well trained for military service as for pleading in the courts. Moreover, he still shrank from public life and the rostra, but was unable to resist the calls to this career which came from the people and his friends. He was therefore altogether satisfied with this opportunity of leaving the city. And yet a strong opinion prevails that he was a demagogue pure and simple, and far more eager than Tiberius to win the favor of the multitude. But this is not the truth nay, it would appear that he was led by a certain necessity rather than by his own choice to engage in public matters. And Cicero the orator also relates that Gaius declined all office and had chosen to live a quiet life, but that his brother appeared to him in a dream and addressed him, saving: "Why, pray, do you hesitate, Gaius? There is no escape; one life is fated for us both, and one death, as champions of the people."

2. After reaching Sardinia, then, Gaius gave proof of every excellence, and far surpassed all the other young men in conflicts with the enemy, in just dealings with the subject peoples, and in the good will and respect which he showed towards his commander, while in self-restraint, frugality, and industry, he excelled even his elders. The winter in Sardinia proved to be rigorous and unhealthy, and the Roman commander made a requisition upon the cities of clothing for his soldiers, whereupon the cities sent to Rome and begged to be relieved from the exaction. The senate granted their petition and ordered the commander to get clothing for his soldiers in some other way. The commander was at a loss what to do, and the soldiers were suffering; so Gaius made a circuit of the cities and induced them of their own free will to send clothing and other assistance to the Romans. This was reported to Rome, where it was thought to be a prelude to a struggle for popular favor, and gave fresh concern to the senate. So, to begin with, when ambassadors of King Micipsa came from Africa, and announced that out of regard for Gaius Gracchus the king had sent grain to the Roman commander in Sardinia, the senators were displeased and turned them away. In the second place, they passed a decree that fresh troops should be sent to relieve the soldiers in Sardinia, but that Orestes should remain, with the idea that Gaius also would remain with him by virtue of his office. But Gaius, when this came to his ears, straightway sailed off in a passion, and his unexpected appearance in Rome not only was censured by his enemies, but also made the people think it strange that he, quaestor as he was, had left his post before his commander. However, when he was denounced before the censors. he begged leave to speak, and wrought such a change in the opinions of his hearers that he left the court with the reputation of having been most grossly wronged. For he said that he had served in the army twelve years, although other men were required to serve there only ten, and that he had continued to serve as quaestor under his commander for more than two years, although the law permitted him to come back after a year. He was the

20. *Odyssey*, 1.47, Athena of Aegisthus.
21. One of the lost biographies.
22. 126 B.C.

only man in the army, he said, who had entered the campaign with a full purse and left it with an empty one; the rest had drunk up the wine which they took into Sardinia, and had come back to Rome with their wine-jars full of' gold and silver.

3. After this, other fresh charges and indictments were brought against him, on the ground that he had caused the allies to revolt and had been privy to the conspiracy at Fregellae,[23] information of which was brought to Rome. But he cleared himself of all suspicion, and having established his entire innocence, immediately began a canvass for the tribuneship. All the men of note, without exception, were opposed to him, but so great a throng poured into the city from the country and took part in the elections that many could not be housed, and since the Campus Martius could not accommodate the multitude, they gave in their voices from the house-tops and tilings. So far, however, did the nobility prevail against the people and disappoint the hopes of Gaius that he was not returned first, as he expected, but fourth. But after entering upon his office[24] he was at once first of all the tribunes, since he had an incomparable power in oratory, and his affliction gave him great boldness of speech in bewailing the fate of his brother. For to this subject he would bring the people round on every pretext, reminding them of what had happened in the case of Tiberius, and contrasting the conduct of their ancestors, who went to war with the people of Falerii on behalf of Genucius, a tribune whom they had insulted, and condemned Gaius Veturius to death because he was the only man who would not make way for a tribune passing through the forum. "But before your eyes," he said, "these men beat Tiberius to death with clubs, and his dead body was dragged from the Capitol through the midst of the city to be thrown into the Tiber; moreover, those of his friends who were caught were put to death without trial. And yet it is ancient usage among us that if anyone who is arraigned on a capital charge does not answer to his summons, a trumpeter shall go to the door of this man's house in the morning and summon him forth by sound of trumpet, and until this has been done the judges shall not vote on his case. So careful and guarded were the men of old in capital cases."

4. Having first stirred up the people with such words as these (and he had a very loud voice, and was most vigorous in his speaking), he introduced two laws, one providing that if the people had deprived any magistrate of his office, such magistrate should not he allowed to hold office a second time; and another providing that if any magistrate had banished a citizen without trial, such magistrate should be liable to public prosecution. Of these laws, one had the direct effect of branding with infamy Marcus Octavius, who had been deposed from the tribunate by Tiberius; and by the other Popillius was affected, for as praetor he had banished the friends of Tiberius. Popillius, indeed, without standing his trial, fled out of Italy; but the other law was withdrawn by Gaius himself, who said that he spared Octavius at the request of his mother Cornelia. The people were pleased at this and gave their consent, honoring Cornelia no less on account of her sons than because of her father; indeed, in after times they erected a bronze statue of her, bearing the inscription:

"Cornelia, Mother of the Gracchi." There are on record also many things which Gaius said about her in the coarse style of forensic speech, when he was attacking one of his enemies: "What," said he, "do you abuse Cornelia, who gave birth to Tiberius?" And since the one who had uttered

---

23. Fregellae revolted and was destroyed in 125 B.C.
24. For the year 121 B.C., ten years after Tiberius had entered upon the same office.

the abuse was charged with effeminate practices, "With what effrontery," said Gaius, "can you compare yourself with Cornelia? Have you borne such children as she did? And verily all Rome knows that she refrained from commerce with men longer than you have, though you are a man." Such was the bitterness of his language, and many similar examples can be taken from his writings.

5. Of the laws which he proposed by way of gratifying the people and overthrowing the senate, one was agrarian, and divided the public land among the poor citizens; another was military, and ordained that clothing should be furnished to the soldiers at the public cost, that nothing should be deducted from their pay to meet this charge, and that no one under seventeen should be enrolled as a soldier; another concerned the allies, and gave the Italians equal suffrage rights with Roman citizens; another related to the supplies of grain, and lowered the market price to the poor and another dealt with the appointment of judges. This last law most of all curtailed the power of the senators; for they alone could serve as judges in criminal cases, and this privilege made them formidable both to the common people and to the equestrian order. The law of Gracchus, however, added to the membership of the senate, which was three hundred, three hundred men from the equestrian order, and made service as judges a prerogative of the whole six hundred. In his efforts to carry this law Gaius is said to have shown remarkable earnestness in many ways, and especially in this, that whereas all popular orators before him had turned their faces towards the senate and that part of the forum called the "*comitium*," he now set a new example by turning towards the other part of the forum as he harangued the people, and continued to do this from that time on, thus by a slight deviation and change of attitude stirring up a great question, and to a certain extent changing the constitution from an aristocratic to a democratic form; for his implication was that. speakers ought to address themselves to the people, and not to the senate.

6. The people not only adopted this law, but also entrusted to its author the selection of the judges who were to come from the equestrian order, so that he found himself invested with something like monarchical power, and even the senate consented to follow his counsel. But when he counseled them, it was always in support of measures befitting their body; as, for instance, the very equitable and honorable decree concerning the grain which Fabius the pro-praetor sent to the city from Spain. Gaius induced the Senate to sell the grain and send the money back to the cities of Spain, and further, to censure Fabius for making his government of the province intolerably burdensome to its inhabitants. This decree brought Gaius great reputation as well as popularity in the provinces.

He also introduced bills for sending out colonies, for constructing roads, and for establishing public granaries, making himself director and manager of all these undertakings, and showing no weariness in the execution of all these different and great enterprises; nay, he actually carried out each one of them with an astonishing speed and power of application, as if it were his sole business, so that even those who greatly hated and feared him were struck with amazement at the powers of achievement and accomplishment which marked all that be did. And as for the multitude, they were astonished at the very sight, when they beheld him closely attended by a throng of contractors, artificers, ambassadors, magistrates, soldiers, and literary men, with all of whom he was on easy terms, preserving his dignity while showing kindliness, and rendering properly to every man the courtesy which was due from him, whereby he set in the light of malignant slanderers those who stigmatized him as threatening or utterly arrogant or violent. Thus he was a more skilful popular leader in his private intercourse with men and in his business transactions than in his speeches from the rostra.

7. But he busied himself most earnestly with the construction of roads, laying stress upon utility as well as upon that which conduced to grace and beauty. For his roads were carried straight through the country without deviation, and had pavements of quarried stone, and substructures of tight-rammed masses of sand. Depressions were tilled up, all intersecting torrents or ravines were bridged over, and both sides of the roads were of equal and corresponding height, so that the work had everywhere an even and beautiful appearance. In addition to all this, he measured off every road by miles (the Roman mile falls a little short of eight furlongs) and planted stone pillars in the ground to mark the distances. Other stones, too, he placed at smaller intervals from one another on both sides of the road, in order that equestrians might be able to mount their horses from them and have no need of assistance.

8. Since the people extolled him for all these services and were ready to show him any token whatsoever of their good will, he said to them once in a public harangue that he was going to ask a favor of them, which, if granted, he should value supremely, but if it were refused, he should find no fault with them. This utterance was thought to be a request for a consulship, and led everybody to expect that he would sue for a consulship and a tribuneship at the same time. But when the consular elections were at hand and everybody was on the tip-toe of expectation, he was seen leading Gaius Fannius down into the Campus Martius and joining in the canvass for him along with his friends. This turned the tide strongly in favor of Fannius. So Fannius was elected consul, and Gaius tribune for the second time, though he was not a candidate and did not canvass for the office; but the people were eager to have it so.

However, he soon saw that the senate was hostile to him out and out, and that the good will of Fannius towards him had lost its edge, and therefore again began to attach the multitude to himself by other laws, proposing to send colonies to Tarenturn and Capua, and inviting the Latins to a participation in the Roman franchise. But the senate, tearing that Gracchus would become altogether invincible, made a new and unusual attempt to divert the people from him; they vied with him, that is, in courting the favor of the people, and granted their wishes contrary to the best interests of the state. For one of the colleagues of Gaius was Livius Drusuus, a man who was not inferior to any Roman either in birth or rearing, while in character, eloquence, and wealth he could vie with those who were most honored and influential in consequence of these advantages. To this man, accordingly, the nobles had recourse, and invited him to attack Gaius and league himself with them against him, not resorting to violence or coming into collision with the people, but administering his office to please them and making them concessions where it would have been honorable to incur their hatred.

9. Livius, accordingly, put his influence as tribune at the service of the senate to this end, and drew up laws which aimed at what was neither honorable nor advantageous; nay, he had the emulous eagerness of the rival demagogues of comedy to achieve one thing, namely, to surpass Gaius in pleasing and gratifying the people.[25] In this way the senate showed most plainly that it was not displeased with the public measures of Gaius, but rather was desirous by all means to

---

25. An allusion to the rival demagogues in the *Knights* of Aristophanes.

humble or destroy the man himself. For when Gaius proposed to found two colonies, and these composed of the most respectable citizens. they accused him of truckling to the people; but when Livius proposed to found twelve, and to send out to each of them three thousand of the needy citizens, they supported him. With Gaius, because he distributed public land among the poor for which every man of them was required to pay a rental into the public treasury, they were angry, alleging that he was seeking thereby to win favor with the multitude; but Livius met with their approval when he proposed to relieve the tenants even from this rental. And further, when Gaius proposed to bestow upon the Latins equal rights of suffrage, he gave offence; but when Livius brought in a bill forbidding that any Latin should be chastised with rods even during military service, he had the senates support. And indeed Livius himself, in his public harangues. always said that he introduced these measures on the authority of the senate, which desired to help the common people; and this in fact was the only advantage which resulted from his political measures. For the people became more amicably disposed towards the senate; and whereas before this they had suspected and hated the nobles, Livius softened and dissipated their remembrance of past grievances and their bitter feelings by alleging that it was the sanction of the nobles which had induced him to enter upon his course of conciliating the people and gratifying the wishes of the many.

12. On returning to Rome, in the first place Gaius changed his residence from the Palatine hill to the region adjoining the forum, which he thought more democratic, since most of the poor and lowly had come to live there; in the next place, he promulgated the rest of his laws, intending to get the peoples vote upon them. But when a throng came together from all parts of Italy for his support, the senate prevailed upon the consul Fannius to drive out of the city all who were not Romans. Accordingly a strange and unusual proclamation was made, to the effect that none of the allies and friends of Rome should appear in the city during those days; whereupon Gaius published a counter edict in which he denounced the consul, and promised the allies his support, in case they should remain there. He did not, however, give them his support, but when he saw one of his comrades and guest-friends dragged off by the lictors of Fannius, he passed by without giving him any help, either because he feared to give a proof that his power was already on the decline, or because he was unwilling, as he said, by his own acts to afford his enemies the occasions which they sought for a conflict at close quarters.

Moreover, it chanced that he had incurred the anger of his colleagues in office, and for the following reason. The people were going to enjoy an exhibition of gladiators in the forum, and most of the magistrates had constructed seats for the show round about, and were offering them for hire. Gaius ordered them to take down these seats, in order that the poor might be able to enjoy the spectacle from those places without paying hire. But since no one paid any attention to his command, he waited till the night before the spectacle, and then, taking all the workmen whom he had under his orders in public contracts, he pulled down the seats, and when day came he had the place all clear for the people. For this proceeding the populace thought him a man, but his colleagues were annoyed and thought him reckless and violent. It was believed also that this conduct cost him his election to the tribunate for the third time, since, although he got a majority of the votes, his colleagues were unjust and fraudulent in their proclamation and returns. This, however, was disputed. But he took his failure overmuch to heart, and what is more, when his enemies were exulting over him, he told them, it is said, with more boldness than was fitting, that they were laughing with sardonic laughter, and were not aware of the great darkness that enveloped them in consequence of his public measures.

13. The enemies of Gaius also effected the election of Opimius as consul, and then proceeded to revoke many of the laws which Gaius had secured and to meddle with the organization of the colony at Carthage. This was by way of irritating Gaius, that he might furnish ground for resentment, and so be got rid of. At first he endured all this patiently, but at last, under the instigations of his friends, and especially of Fulvius, he set out to gather a fresh body of partisans for opposition to the consul. Here, we are told, his mother also took active part in his seditious measures, by secretly hiring from foreign parts and sending to Rome men who were ostensibly reapers; for to this matter there are said to have been obscure allusions in her letters to her son. Others, however, say that Cornelia was very much displeased with these activities of her son.

Be that as it may, on the day when Opimius and his supporters were going to annul the laws, the Capitol had been occupied by both factions since earliest morning, and after the consul had offered sacrifice, one of his servants, Quintus Antyllins, as he was carrying from one place to another the entrails of the victims, said to the partisans of Fulvius: "Make way for honest citizens, you rascals" Some say, too, that along with this speech Antyllius bared his arm and waved it with an insulting gesture. At any rate he was killed at once and on the spot, stabbed with large writing styles said to have been made for just such a purpose. The multitude were completely confused by the murder, but it produced an opposite state of mind in the leaders of the two factions. Gaius was distressed, and upbraided his followers for having given their enemies ground for accusing them which had long been desired; but Opimius, as though he had got something for which he was waiting, was elated, and urged the people on to vengeance.

14. A shower of rain fell just then, and the assembly was dissolved; but early next morning the consul called the senate together indoors and proceeded to transact business, while others placed the body of Antyllius without covering upon a bier, and carried it, as they had agreed to do, through tile forum and past the senate house, with wailings and lamentations. Opimius knew what was going on, but pretended to be surprised, so that even the senators went out into the forum. After the bier had been set down in the midst of the throng, the senators began to inveigh against what they called a heinous and monstrous crime, but the people were moved to hatred and abuse of the oligarchs, who, they said, after murdering Tiberius Gracchus on the Capitol with their own hands, tribune that he was, had actually flung away his dead body besides; whereas Antyllius, a mere servant, who perhaps had suffered more than he deserved, but was himself chiefly to blame for it, had been laid out in the forum, and was surrounded by the Roman senate, which shed tears and shared in the obsequies of a hireling fellow, to tile end that the sole remaining champion of the people might be done away with. Then the senators went back into the senate house, where they formally enjoined upon the consul Opirnius to save the city as best he could[26] and to put down the tyrants.

The consul therefore ordered the senators to take up arms, and every member of the equestrian order was notified to bring next morning two servants fully armed; Fulvius, on the other hand, made counter preparations and got together a rabble, but Gaius, as he left the forum, stopped

---

26. The formal decree of martial law, the *senatus consultum ultimum*.

in front of his father's statue, gazed at it for a long time without uttering a word, then burst into tears, and with a groan departed. Many of those who saw this were moved to pity Gaius; they reproached themselves for abandoning and betraying him, and went to his house, and spent the night at his door, though not in the same manner as those who were guarding Fulvius. For these passed the whole time in noise and shouting, drinking, and boasting of what they would do, Fulvius himself being the first to get drunk, and saying and doing much that was unseemly for a man of his years; but the followers of Gaius, feeling that they faced a public calamity, kept quiet and were full of concern for the future, and passed the night sleeping and keeping watch by turns.

16. When all were assembled together, Fulvius, yielding to the advice of Gaius, sent the younger of his Sons with a herald's wand into the forum. The young man was very fair to look upon; and now, in a decorous attitude, modestly, and with tears in his eyes, he addressed conciliatory words to the consul and the senate. Most of his audience, then, were not disinclined to accept his terms of peace; but Opimius declared that the petitioners ought not to try to persuade the senate by word of messenger; they should rather come down and surrender themselves for trial, like citizens amenable to the laws, and then beg for mercy; he also told the young man plainly to come back again on these terms or not come back at all. Gaius, accordingly, as we are told, was willing to come and try to persuade the senate; but no one else agreed with him, and so Fulvius sent his son again to plead in their behalf as before. But Opimius, who was eager to join battle, at once seized the youth and put him under guard, and then advanced on the party of Fulvius with numerous men-at-arms and Cretan archers. And it was the archers who, by discharging their arrows and wounding their opponents, were most instrumental in throwing them into confusion. After the rout had taken place, Fulvius fled for refuge into an unused bath, where he was shortly discovered and slain, together with his elder son. Gaius, however, was not seen to take any part in the battle, but in great displeasure at what was happening he withdrew into the temple of Diana. There he was minded to make away with himself, but was prevented by his most trusty companions, Pomponius and Licinius; for they were at hand, and took away his sword, and urged him to flight again. Then, indeed, as we are told, he sank upon his knees, and with hands outstretched towards the goddess prayed that the Roman people, in requital for their great in gratitude and treachery, might never cease to be in servitude; for most of them were manifestly changing sides, now that proclamation of immunity had been made.

17. So then, as Gaius fled, his foes pressed hard upon him and were overtaking him at the wooden bridge over the Tiber, but his two friends bade him go on, while they themselves withstood his pursuers, and, fighting there at the head of the bridge, would suffer no man to pass, until they were killed. Gaius had with him in his flight a single servant, by name Philocrates; and though all the spectators, as at a race, urged Gaius on to greater speed, not a man came to his aid, or even consented to furnish him with a horse when he asked for one, for his pursuers were pressing close upon him. He barely succeeded in escaping into a sacred grove of the Furies, and there fell by the hand of Philocrates, who then slew himself upon his master. According to some writers, however, both were taken alive by the enemy, and because the servant had thrown his arms about his master, no one was able to strike the master until the slave had first been dispatched by the blows of many. Someone cut off the head of Gaius, we are told, and was carrying it along, but was robbed of it by a certain friend of Opimius, Septimuleius; for proclamation had been made at the beginning of the battle that an equal weight of gold would be paid the men who brought

the head of Gaius or Fulvius. So Septimuleius stuck the head of Gaius on a spear and brought it to Opimius, and when it was placed in a balance it weighed seventeen pounds and two thirds, since Septimuleius, besides showing himself to be a scoundrel, had also perpetrated a fraud; for he had taken out the brain and poured melted lead in its place. But those who brought the head of Fulvius were of the obscurer sort, and therefore got nothing. The bodies of Gaius and Fulvius and of the other slain were thrown into the Tiber, and they numbered three thousand; their property was sold and the proceeds paid into the public treasury. Moreover, their wives were forbidden to go into mourning, and Licinnia, the wife of Gaius, was also deprived of her marriage portion. Most cruel of all, however, was the treatment of the younger son of Fulvius, who had neither lifted a hand against the nobles nor been present at the fighting. but had come to effect a truce before the battle and had been arrested; after the battle he was slain. However, what vexed the people more than this or anything else was the erection of a temple of Concord by Opimius;[27] for it was felt that he was priding himself and exulting and in a manner celebrating a triumph in view of all this slaughter of citizens. Therefore at night, beneath the inscription on the temple, somebody carved this verse—"A work of mad discord produces a temple of Concord."

18. And yet this Opimius, who was the first consul to exercise the power of a dictator, and put to death without trial, besides three thousand other citizens, Gaius Gracchus and Fulvius Flaccus, of whom one had been consul and had celebrated a triumph, while the other was the foremost man of his generation in virtue and reputation—this Opimius could not keep his hands from fraud, but when he was sent as ambassador to Jugurtha the Numidian was bribed by him, and after being convicted must shamefully of corruption, he spent his old age in infamy, hated and abused by the people, a people which was humble and cowed at the time when the Gracchi fell, but soon afterwards showed how much it missed them and longed for them. For it had statues of the brothers made and set up in a conspicuous place, consecrated the places where they were slain, and brought thither offerings of all the first-fruits of the seasons, nay, more, many sacrificed and fell down before their statues every day, as though they were visiting the shrines of gods.

19. And further, Cornelia is reported to have borne all her misfortunes in a noble and magnanimous spirit, and to have said of the sacred places where her sons had been slain that they were tombs worthy of the dead which occupied them. She resided on the promontory called Misenum, and made no change in her customary way of living. She had many friends, and kept a good table that she might show hospitality, for she always had Greeks and other literary men about her, and all the reigning kings interchanged gifts with her. She was indeed very agreeable to her visitors and associates when she discoursed to them about the life and habits of her father Africanus, but most admirable when she spoke of her sons without grief or tears, and narrated their achievements and their fate to all enquirers as if she were speaking of men of the early days of Rome. Some were therefore led to think that old age or the greatness of her sorrows had impaired her mind and made her insensible to her misfortunes, whereas, really, such persons themselves were insensible how much help in the banishment of grief mankind derives from a noble nature and from honorable birth and rearing, as well as of the fact that while Fortune often prevails over virtue when it endeavors to ward off evils, she cannot rob virtue of the power to endure those evils with calm assurance.

---

27. Opimius restored the temple of Concord which had been built by Camillus.

THE ASSASSINATION OF JULIUS CAESAR

Caesar's open autocratic rule and trampling underfoot of the republican institutions (see The Life of Caesar by Suetonius below) was a grave insult to Rome's upper class and turned on him and committed one of the most famous political assassination of ancient times. This excerpt from Plutarch's biography of Caesar describes that event.

57. However, the Romans gave way before the good fortune of the man and accepted the bit, and regarding the monarchy as a respite from the evils of the civil wars, they appointed him dictator for life. This was confessedly a tyranny, since the monarchy, besides the element of irresponsibility, now took on that of permanence. It was Cicero who proposed the first honors for him in the senate, and their magnitude was, after all, not too great for a man; but others added excessive honors and vied with one another in proposing them, thus rendering Caesar odious and obnoxious even to the mildest citizens because of the pretension and extravagance of what was decreed for him. It is thought, too, that the enemies of Caesar no less than his flatterers helped to force these measures through, in order that they might have as many pretexts as possible against him and might be thought to have the best reasons for attempting his life. For in all other ways, at least, after the civil wars were over, he showed himself blameless; and certainly it is thought not inappropriate that the temple of Clemency was decreed as a thank-offering in view of his mildness. For he pardoned many of those who had fought against him, and to some he even gave honors and offices besides, as to Brutus and Cassius, both of whom were now praetors. The statues of Pompey, too, which had been thrown down, he would not suffer to remain so, but set them up again, at which Cicero said that in setting up Pompey's statues Caesar firmly fixed his own. When his friends thought it best that he should have a body-guard, and many of them volunteered for this service, he would not consent, saying that it was better to die once for all than to be always expecting death. And in the effort to surround himself with men's good will as the fairest and at the same time the securest protection, he again courted the people with banquets and distributions of grain, and his soldiers with newly planted colonies, the most conspicuous of which were Carthage and Corinth. The earlier capture of both these cities, as well as their present restoration, chanced to fall at one and the same time.[28]

58. As for the nobles, to some of them he promised consulships and praetorships in the future, others he appeased with sundry other powers and honors, and in all he implanted hopes, since he ardently desired to rule over willing subjects. Therefore, when Maximus the consul died, he appointed Caninius Revilius consul for the one day still remaining of the term of office. To him, as we are told, many were going with congratulations and offers of escort, whereupon Cicero said: "Let us make haste, or else the man's consulship will have expired."

Caesar's many successes, however, did not divert his natural spirit of enterprise and ambition to the enjoyment of what he had laboriously achieved, but served as fuel and incentive for future

From *Plutarch: Plutarch's Lives, Volume VII*, translated by Beradotte Perrin (Cambridge, Loeb Classical Library, Harvard University Press, 1919).

achievements, and begat in him plans for greater deeds and a passion for fresh glory, as though he had used up what he already had. What he felt was therefore nothing else than emulation of himself, as if he had been another man, and a sort of rivalry between what he had done and what he purposed to do. For he planned and prepared to make an expedition against the Parthians; and after subduing these and marching around the Euxine by way of Hyrcania, the Caspian sea, and the Caucasus, to invade Scythia; and after overrunning the countries bordering on Germany and Germany itself, to come back by way of Gaul to Italy, and so to complete this circuit of his empire, which would then be bounded on all sides by the ocean. During this expedition, moreover, he intended to dig through the isthmus of Corinth, and had already put Anienus in charge of this work; he intended also to divert the Tiber just below the city into a deep channel, give it a bend towards Circeium, and make it empty into the sea at Terracina, thus contriving for merchantmen a safe as well as an easy passage to Rome; and besides this, to convert the marshes about Pomentinum and Setia into a plain which many thousands of men could cultivate; and further, to build moles which should barricade the sea where it was nearest to Rome, to clear away the hidden dangers on the shore of Ostia, and then construct harbors and roadsteads sufficient for the great fleets that would visit them. And all these things were in preparation.

59. The adjustment of the calendar, however, and the correction of the irregularity in the computation of time, were not only studied scientifically by him, but also brought to completion, and proved to be of the highest utility. For not only in very ancient times was the relation of the lunar to the solar year in great confusion among the Romans, so that the sacriticial feasts and festivals, diverging gradually, at last fell in opposite seasons of the year, but also at this time people generally had no way of computing the actual solar year;[29] the priests alone knew the proper time, and would suddenly and to everybody's surprise insert the intercalary month called Mercedonius. Numa the king is said to have been the first to intercalate this month, thus devising a slight and short-lived remedy for the error in regard to the sidereal and solar cycles, as I have said in his Life. But Caesar laid the problem before the best philosophers and mathematicians, and out of the methods of correction which were already at hand compounded one of his own which was more accurate than any. This the Romans use down to the present time, and are thought to be less in error than other peoples as regards the inequality between the lunar and solar years. However, even this furnished occasion for blame to those who envied Caesar and disliked his power. At any rate, Cicero the orator, we are told, when some one remarked that Lyra would rise on the morrow, said: "Yes, by decree," implying that men were compelled to accept even this dispensation.

60. But the most open and deadly hatred towards him was produced by his passion for the royal power. For the multitude this was a first cause of hatred, and for those who had long smothered their hate, a most specious pretext for it. And yet those who were advocating this honor for Caesar actually spread abroad among the people a report that from the Sibylline books it appeared that Parthia could be taken if the Romans went up against it with a king, but otherwise could not be assailed; and as Caesar was coming down from Alba into the city they ventured to hail him as

---

28. Both cities were captured in 146 B.C. and both were restored in 44 B.C.

29. At this time the Roman calendar was more than two months ahead of the solar year. Caesar's reform went into effect in 46 B.C.

king. But at this the people were confounded, and Caesar, disturbed in mind, said that his name was not King, but Caesar, and seeing that his words produced an universal silence, he passed on with no very cheerful or contented looks. Moreover, after sundry extravagant honors had been voted him in the senate, it chanced that he was sitting above the rostra, and as the praetors and consuls drew near, with the whole senate following them, he did not rise to receive them, but as if he were dealing with mere private persons, replied that his honors needed curtailment rather than enlargement. This vexed not only the senate, but also the people, who felt that in the persons of the senators the state was insulted, and in a terrible dejection they went away at once, all who were not obliged to remain, so that Caesar too, when he was aware of his mistake, immediately turned to go home, and drawing back his toga from his neck, cried in loud tones to his friends that he was ready to offer his throat to any one who wished to kill him. But afterwards he made his disease[30] an excuse for his behavior, saying that the senses of those who are thus afflicted do not usually remain steady when they address a multitude standing, but are speedily shaken and whirled about, bringing on giddiness and insensibility. However, what he said was not true; on the contrary, he was very desirous of rising to receive the senate; but one of his friends, as they say, or rather one of his flatterers, Cornelius Balbus, restrained him, saying: "Remember that you are Caesar, and permit yourself to be courted as a superior."

61. There was added to these causes of offence his insult to the tribunes. It was, namely, the festival of the Lupercalia, of which many write that it was anciently celebrated by shepherds, and has also some connection with the Arcadian Lycaea. At this time many of the noble youths and of the magistrates run up and down through the city naked, for sport and laughter striking those they meet with shaggy thongs. And many women of rank also purposely get in their way, and like children at school present their hands to be struck, believing that the pregnant will thus be helped to an easy delivery, and the barren to pregnancy. These ceremonies Caesar was witnessing, seated upon the rostra on a golden throne, arrayed in triumphal attire. And Antony was one of the runners in the sacred race; for he was consul. Accordingly, after he had dashed into the forum and the crowd had made way for him, he carried a diadem, round which a wreath of laurel was tied, and held it out to Caesar. Then there was applause, not loud, but slight and preconcerted. But when Caesar pushed away the diadem, all the people applauded; and when Antony offered it again, few, and when Caesar declined it again, all, applauded. The experiment having thus failed, Caesar rose from his seat, after ordering the wreath to be carried up to the Capitol; but then his statues were seen to have been decked with royal diadems. So two of the tribunes, Flavius and Maryllus, went up to them and pulled off the diadems, and after discovering those who had first hailed Caesar as king, led them off to prison. Moreover, the people followed the tribunes with applause and called them Brutuses, because Brutus was the man who put an end to the royal succession and brought the power into the hands of the senate and people instead of a sole ruler. At this, Caesar was greatly vexed, and deprived Maryllus and Flavius of their office, while in his denunciation of them, although he at the same time insulted the people, he called them repeatedly Brutes and Cymaeans.[31]

---

30. Epilepsy.
31. The word "brutus" in Latin signified stupid and the people of Cyme, in Asia Minor, were celebrated for their stupidity.

62. Under these circumstances the multitude turned their thoughts towards Marcus Brutus, who was thought to be a descendant of the elder Brutus on his father's side, on his mother's side belonged to the Servilii, another illustrious house, and was a son-in-law and nephew of Cato. The desires which Brutus felt to attempt of his own accord the abolition of the monarchy were blunted by the favors and honors that he had received from Caesar. For not only had his life been spared at Pharsalus after Pornpey's flight, and the lives of many of his friends at his entreaty, but also he had great credit with Caesar. He had received the most honorable of the praetorships for the current year, and was to be consul three years later, having been preferred to Cassius, who was a rival candidate. For Caesar, as we are told, said that Cassius urged the more just claims to the office, but that for his own part he could not pass Brutus by. Once, too, when certain persons were actually accusing Brutus to him, the conspiracy being already on foot, Caesar would not heed them, but laying his hand upon his body said to the accusers "Brutus will wait for this shriveled skin," implying that Brutus was worthy to rule because of his virtue, but that for the sake of ruling he would not become a thankless villain. Those, however, who were eager for the change, and fixed their eyes on Brutus alone, or on him first, did not venture to talk with him directly, but by night they covered his praetorial tribune and chair with writings, most of which were of this sort "You art asleep, Brutus," or, "You art not Brutus." When Cassius perceived that the ambition of Brutus was somewhat stirred by these things, he was more urgent with him than before, and pricked him on, having himself also some private grounds for hating Caesar; these I have mentioned in the Life of Brutus. Moreover, Caesar actually suspected him, so that he once said to his friends: "What, think you, dose Cassius want? I like him not over much, for he is much too pale." And again, we are told that when Antony and Dolabella were accused to him of plotting revolution, Caesar said: "I am not much in fear of these fat, long haired fellows, but rather of those pale, thin ones," meaning Brutus and Cassius.

63. But destiny, it would seem, is not so much unexpected as it is unavoidable, since they say that amazing signs and apparitions were seen. Now, as for lights in the heavens, crashing sounds borne all about by night, and birds of omen coining down into the forum, it is perhaps not worth while to mention these precursors of so great an event; but Strabo the philosopher says that multitudes of men all on fire were seen rushing up, and a soldier's slave threw from his hand a copious flame and seemed to the spectators to be burning, but when the flame ceased the man was uninjured; he says, moreover, that when Caesar himself was sacrificing, the heart of the victim was not to be found, and the prodigy caused fear, since in the course of nature, certainly, an animal without a heart could not exist. The following story, too, is told by many. A certain seer warned Caesar to be on his guard against a great peril on the day of the month of March which the Romans call the Ides; and when the day had come and Caesar was on his way to the senate-house, he greeted the seer with a jest and said: "Well, the Ides of March are come," and the seer said to him softly: "Aye, they are come, but they are not gone." Moreover, on the day before, when Marcus Lepidus was entertaining him at supper, Caesar chanced to be signing letters, as his custom was, while reclining at table, and the discourse turned suddenly upon the question what sort of death was the best; before any one else could answer Caesar cried out: "That which is unexpected." After this, while he was sleeping as usual by the side of his wife, all the windows and doors of the chamber flew open at once, and Caesar, confounded by the noise and the light of the moon shining down upon him, noticed that Calpurnia was in a deep slumber, but was uttering indistinct words and inarticulate groans in her sleep; for she dreamed, as it proved, that she was holding her murdered husband in her arms and bewailing him.

Some, however, say that this was not the vision which the woman had; but that there was attached to Caesar's house to give it adornment and distinction, by vote of the senate, a gable ornament, as Livy says, and it was this which Calpurnia in her dreams saw torn down, and therefore, as she thought, wailed and wept. At all events, when the day came, she begged Caesar, if it was possible, not to go out, but to postpone the meeting of the senate; if, however, he had no concern at all for her dreams, she besought him to enquire by other modes of divination and by sacrifices concerning the future. And Caesar also, as it would appear, was in some suspicion and fear. For never before had he perceived in Calpurnia any womanish superstition, but now he saw that she was in great distress. And when the seers also, after many sacrifices, told him that the omens were unfavorable, he resolved to send Antony and dismiss the senate.

64. But at this juncture Decimus Brutus, surnamed Albinus, who was so trusted by Caesar that he was entered in his will as his second heir, but was partner in the conspiracy of the other Brutus and Cassius, fearing that if Caesar should elude that day, their undertaking would become known, ridiculed the seers and chided Caesar for laying himself open to malicious charges on the part of the senators, who would think themselves mocked at; for they had met at his bidding, and were ready and willing to vote as one man that he should be declared king of the provinces outside of Italy, and might wear a diadem when he went anywhere else by land or sea; but if some one should tell them at their session to be gone now, but to come back again when Calpurnia should have better dreams, what speeches would be made by his enemies, or who would listen to his friends when they tried to show that this was not slavery and tyranny? But if he was fully resolved (Albinus said) to regard the day as inauspicious, it was better that he should go in person and address the senate, and then postpone its business. While saying these things Brutus took Caesar by the hand and began to lead him along. And he had gone but a little way from his door when a slave belonging to some one else, eager to get at Caesar, but unable to do so for the press of numbers about him, forced his way into the house, gave himself into the hands of Calpurnia, and bade her keep him secure until Caesar came back, since he had important matters to report to him.

65. Furthermore, Artemidorus, a Cnidian by birth, a teacher of Greek philosophy, and on this account brought into intimacy with some of the followers of Brutus, so that he also knew most of what they were doing, came bringing to Caesar in a small roll the disclosures which he was going to make; but seeing that Caesar took all such rolls and handed them to his attendants, he came quite near, and said: "Read this, Caesar, by yourself, and speedily; for it contains matters of importance and of concern to you." Accordingly, Caesar took the roll and would have read it, but was prevented by the multitude of people who engaged his attention, although he set out to do so many times, and holding in his hand and retaining that roll alone, he passed on into the senate. Some, however, say that another person gave him this roll, and that Artemidorus did not get to him at all, but was crowded away all along the route.

66. So far, perhaps, these things may have happened of their own accord; the place, however, which was the scene of that struggle and murder, and in which the senate was then assembled, since it contained a statue of Pompey and had been dedicated by Pompey as an additional ornament to his theatre, made it wholly clear that it was the work of some heavenly power which was

calling and guiding the action thither. Indeed, it is also said that Cassius, turning his eyes toward the statue of Pompey before the attack began, invoked it silently, although he was much addicted to the doctrines of Epicurus;[32] but the crisis, as it would seem, when the dreadful attempt was now close at hand, replaced his former cool calculations with divinely inspired emotion.

Well, then, Antony, who was a friend of Caesar's and a robust man, was detained outside by Brutus Albinus, who purposely engaged him in a lengthy conversation; but Caesar went in, and the senate rose in his honor. Some of the partisans of Brutus took their places round the back of Caesar's chair, while others went to meet him, as though they would support the petition which Tillius Cimber presented to Caesar in behalf of his exiled brother, and they joined their entreaties to his and accompanied Caesar up to his chair, But when, after taking his seat, Caesar continued to repulse their petitions, and, as they pressed upon him with greater importunity, began to show anger towards one and another of them, Tillius seized his toga with both hands and pulled it down from his neck. This was the signal for the assault. It was Casca who gave him the first blow with his dagger, in the neck, not a mortal wound, nor even a deep one, for which he was too much confused, as was natural at the beginning of a deed of great daring; so that Caesar turned about, grasped the knife, and held it fast. At almost the same instant both cried out, the smitten man in Latin: "Accursed Casca, what are you doing?" and the smiter, in Greek, to his brother: "Brother, help!"

So the affair began, and those who were not privy to the plot were filled with consternation and horror at what was going on; they dared not fly, nor go to Caesar's help, nay, nor even utter a word. But those who had prepared themselves for the murder bared each of them his dagger, and Caesar, hemmed in on all sides, whichever way he turned confronting blows of weapons aimed at his face and eyes, driven hither and thither like a wild beast, was entangled in the hands of all; for all had to take part in the sacrifice and taste of the slaughter. Therefore Brutus also gave him one blow in the groin. And it is said by some writers that although Caesar defended himself against the rest and darted this way and that and cried aloud, when he saw that Brutus had drawn his dagger, he pulled his toga down over his head and sank, either by chance or because pushed there by his murderers, against the pedestal on which the statue of Pompey stood. And the pedestal was drenched with his blood, so that one might have thought that Pompey himself was presiding over this vengeance upon his enemy, who now lay prostrate at his feet, quivering from a multitude of wounds. For it is said that he received twenty-three; and many of the conspirators were wounded by one another, as they struggled to plant all those blows in one body.

67. Caesar thus done to death, the senators, although Brutus came forward as if to say something about what had been done, would not wait to hear him, but burst out of doors and fled, thus filling the people with confusion and helpless fear, so that some of them closed their houses, while others left their counters and places of business and ran, first to the place to see what had happened, then away from the place when they had seen. Antony and Lepidus, the chief friends of Caesar, stole away and took refuge in the houses of others. But Brutus and his partisans, just as they were, still warm from the slaughter, displaying their daggers bare, went all in a body out of the senate house and marched to the Capitol, not like fugitives, but with glad faces and full of confidence, summoning the multitude to freedom, and welcoming into their ranks the most dis-

---

32. These discouraged belief in superhuman powers.

tinguished of those who met them. Some also joined their number and went up with them as though they had shared in the deed, and laid claim to the glory of it, of whom were Gaius Octavius and Lentulus Spinther. These men, then, paid the penalty for their imposture later, when they were put to death by Antony and the young Caesar, without even enjoying the fame for the sake of which they died, owing to the disbelief of their fellow men. For even those who punished them did not exact a penalty for what they did, but for what they wished they had done.

On the next day Brutus came down and held a discourse, and the people listened to what was said without either expressing resentment at what had been done or appearing to approve of it; they showed, however, by their deep silence, that while they pitied Caesar, they respected Brutus. The senate, too, trying to make a general amnesty and reconciliation, voted to give Caesar divine honors and not to disturb even the most insignificant measure which he had adopted when in power; while to Brutus and his partisans it distributed provinces and gave suitable honors, so that everybody thought that matters were decided and settled in the best possible manner.

68. But when the will of Caesar was opened and it was found that he had given every Roman citizen a considerable gift, and when the multitude saw his body carried through the forum all disfigured with its wounds, they no longer kept themselves within the restraints of order and discipline, but after heaping round the body benches, railings, and tables from the forum, they set fire to them and burned it there; then, lifting blazing brands on high, they ran to the houses of the murderers with intent to burn them down, while others went every whither through the city seeking to seize the men themselves and tear them to pieces. Not one of these came in their way, but all were well barricaded. There was a certain Cinna, however, one of the friends of Caesar, who chanced, as they say, to have seen during the previous night a strange vision. He dreamed, that is, that he was invited to supper by Caesar, and that when he excused himself, Caesar led him along by the hand, although he did not wish to go, but resisted. Now, when he heard that they were burning the body of Caesar in the forum, he rose up and went thither out of respect, although he had misgivings arising from his vision, and was at the same time in a fever. At sight of him, one of the multitude told his name to another who asked him what it was, and he to another, and at once word ran through the whole throng that this man was one of the murderers of Caesar. For there was among the conspirators a man who bore this same name of Cinna, and assuming that this man was he, the crowd rushed upon him and tore him in pieces among them. This more than anything else made Brutus and Cassius afraid, and not many days afterwards they withdrew from the city. What they did and suffered before they died, has been told in the Life of Brutus.

69. At the time of his death Caesar was fully fifty-six years old, but he had survived Pompey not much more than four years, while of the power and dominion which he had sought all his life at so great risks, and barely achieved at last, of this he had reaped no fruit but the name of it only, and a glory which had awakened envy on the part of his fellow citizens. However, the great guardian genius of the man, whose help he had enjoyed through life, followed upon him even after death as an avenger of his murder, driving and tracking down his slayers over every land and sea until not one of them was left, but even those who in any way whatsoever either put hand to the deed or took part in the plot were punished.

Among events of man's ordering, the most amazing was that which befell Cassius; for after his defeat at Philippi he slew himself with that very dagger which he had used against Caesar; and among events of divine ordering, there was the great comet, which showed itself in great splendor for seven nights after Caesar's murder, and then disappeared; also, the obscuration of the sun's rays. For during all that year its orb rose pale and without radiance, while the heat that came down from it was slight and ineffectual, so that the air in its circulation was dark and heavy owing to the feebleness of the warmth that penetrated it, and the fruits, imperfect and half ripe, withered away and shriveled up on account of the coldness of the atmosphere. But more than anything else the phantom that appeared to Brutus showed that the murder of Caesar was not pleasing to the gods; and it was on this wise. As he was about to take his army across from Abydos to the other continent, he was lying down at night, as his custom was, in his tent, not sleeping, but thinking of the future; for it is said that of all generals Brutus was least given to sleep, and that he naturally remained awake a longer time than anybody else. And now he thought he heard a noise at the door, and looking towards the light of the lamp, which was slowly going out, he saw a fearful vision of a man of unnatural size and harsh aspect. At first he was terrified, but when he saw that the visitor neither did nor said anything, but stood in silence by his couch, he asked him who he was. Then the phantom answered him "I am your evil genius, Brutus, and you shall see me at Philippi." At the time, then, Brutus said courageously "I shall see you;" and the heavenly visitor at once went away. Subsequently, however, when arrayed against Antony and Caesar at Philippi, in the first battle he conquered the enemy in his front, routed and scattered them, and sacked the camp of Caesar; but as he was about to fight the second battle, the same phantom visited him again at night, and though it said nothing to him, Brutus understood his fate, and plunged headlong into danger. He did not fall in battle, however, but after the rout retired to a crest of ground, put his naked sword to his breast (while a certain friend, as they say, helped to drive the blow home), and so died.

Head of Constantine, a fragment of the colossal stature from the basilica of Constantine.
Capitoline Museum, Rome.

Suetonius, Julius Caesar

Caesar was controversial and baffling, even to his own contemporaries, and he has remained so down to the present day. It is true that he enriched himself from the proceeds of his military campaigns and political success, but in this he was no different from the other politicians of his age (or any other age). After he became the master of the Roman world, he showed too little regard for the Roman republican forms. That was a grievous fault, and he paid for it with his life (see Plutarch's Assassination of Caesar *above). But on the other hand, he had an unequaled reputation for magnanimity and forgiveness toward his enemies— a very un-Roman trait. In the civil wars, for example, he always set free the opposing generals whom he captured, and given the opportunity, he undoubtedly would have done the same for Pompey. And no one can question Caesar's charismatic leadership qualities. His soldiers were ready to follow him anywhere and fight for him with amazing tenacity and discipline. Below are selected excerpts from Suetonius'* Life of Julius Caesar. *As with all of the biographies of Suetonius, it is full of gossip and unsubstantiated rumors.*

40. Then turning his attention to the reorganization of the state, he reformed the calendar, which the negligence of the pontiff's had long since so disordered, through their privilege of adding months or days at pleasure, that the harvest festivals did not come in summer nor those of the vintage in the autumn; and he adjusted the year to the sun's course by making it consist of three hundred and sixty-five days, abolishing the intercalary month,[1] and adding one day every fourth year. . .

41. He filled the vacancies in the senate, enrolled additional patricians, and increased the number of praetors, aediles, and quaestors, as well as of the minor officials; he reinstated those who had been degraded by official action of the censors or found guilty of bribery by verdict of the jurors. He shared the elections with the people on this basis: that except in the case of the consulship, half of the magistrates should be appointed by the people's choice, while the rest should be those whom he had personally nominated. And these he announced in brief notes like the following, circulated in each tribe: "Caesar the Dictator to this or that tribe. I commend to you so and so, to hold their positions by your votes." He admitted to office even the sons of those who had been

---

1. The year had previously consisted of 355 days, and the deficiency of about eleven days was made up by inserting an intercalary month of twenty-two days after February.

proscribed. He limited the right of serving as jurors to two classes, the equestrian and senatorial orders, disqualifying the third class, the tribunes of the treasury.[2]

He made the enumeration of the people neither in the usual manner nor place, but from street to street aided by the owners of blocks of houses, and reduced the number of those who received grain at public expense from three hundred and twenty thousand to one hundred and fifty thousand. And to prevent the calling of additional meetings at any future time for purposes of enrolment, he provided that the places of such as died should be filled each year by the praetors from those who were not on the list.

42. Moreover, to keep up the population of the city, depleted as it was by the assignment of eighty thousand citizens to colonies across the sea, he made a law that no citizen older than twenty or younger than forty, who was not detained by service in the army, should be absent from Italy for more than three successive years; that no senator's son should go abroad except as the companion of a magistrate or on his staff; and that those who made a business of grazing should have among their herdsmen at least one-third who were men of free birth. He conferred citizenship on all who practiced medicine at Rome, and on all teachers of the liberal arts, to make them more desirous of living in the city and to induce others to resort to it.

As to debts, he disappointed those who looked for their cancellation, which was often agitated, but finally decreed that the debtors should satisfy their creditors according to a valuation of their possessions at the price which they had paid for them before the civil war, deducting from the principal whatever interest had been paid in cash or pledged through bankers; an arrangement which wiped out about a fourth part of their indebtedness. He dissolved all guilds, except those of ancient foundation. He increased the penalties for crimes; and inasmuch as the rich involved themselves in guilt with less hesitation because they merely suffered exile, without any loss of property, he punished murderers of freemen by the confiscation of all their goods, as Cicero writes, and others by the loss of one-half.

43. He administered justice with the utmost conscientiousness and strictness. Those convicted of extortion he even dismissed from the senatorial order. He annulled the marriage of an ex-praetor, who had married a woman the very day after her divorce, although there was no suspicion of adultery. He imposed duties on foreign wares. He denied the use of litters and the wearing of scarlet robes or pearls to all except to those of a designated position and age, and on set days. In particular he enforced the law against extravagance, setting watchmen in various parts of the market, to seize and bring to him dainties which were exposed for sale in violation of the law; and sometimes he sent his lictors and soldiers to take from a dining room any articles which had escaped the vigilance of his watchmen, even after they had been served.

44. In particular, for the adornment and convenience of the city, also for the protection and extension of the Empire, he formed more projects and more extensive ones every day: first of all, to rear a temple to Mars, greater than any in existence, filling up and leveling the pool in which he had exhibited the sea-fight, and to build a theatre of vast size, sloping down from the Tarpeian rock; to reduce the civil code to fixed limits, and of the vast and prolix mass of statutes to include only the best and most essential in a limited number of volumes; to open to the public the greatest possible libraries of Greek and Latin books, assigning to Marcus Varro the charge of procuring

---

2. Plebeians, who collected the *tributum* and paid the soldiers, apparently heads of the tribes.

and classifying them; to drain the Pomptine marshes; to let out the water from Lake Fucinus; to make a highway from the Adriatic across the summit of the Apennines as far as the Tiber; to cut a canal through the Isthmus; to check the Dacians, who had poured into Pontus and Thrace; then to make war on the Parthians by way of Lesser Armenia, but not to risk a battle with them until he had first tested their mettle.

All these enterprises and plans were cut short by his death. But before I speak of that, it will not be amiss to describe briefly his personal appearance, his dress, his mode of life, and his character, as well as his conduct in civil and military life.

45. He is said to have been tall of stature, with a fair complexion, shapely limbs, a somewhat full face, and keen black eyes; sound of health, except that towards the end he was subject to sudden fainting fits and to nightmare as well. He was twice attacked by the falling sickness[3] during his campaigns. He was somewhat overnice in the care of his person, being not only carefully trimmed and shaved, but even having superfluous hair plucked out, as some have charged; while his baldness was a disfigurement which troubled him greatly, since he found that it was often the subject of the gibes of his detractors. Because of it he used to comb forward his scanty locks from the crown of his head, and of all the honors voted him by the senate and people there was none which he received or made use of more gladly than the privilege of wearing a laurel wreath at all times. They say, too, that he was remarkable in his dress; that he wore a senator's tunic[4] with fringed sleeves reaching to the wrist, and always had a girdle[5] over it, though rather a loose one; and this, they say, was the occasion of Sulla's mot, when he often warned the nobles to keep an eye on the ill-girt boy.

46. He lived at first in the Subura in a modest house, but after he became pontifex maximus, in the official residence on the Sacred Way. Many have written that he was very fond of elegance and luxury; that having laid the foundations of a country house on his estate at Nemi and finished it at great cost, he tore it all down because it did not suit him in every particular, although at the time he was still poor and heavily in debt; and that he carried tessellated and mosaic floors about with him on his campaigns.

47. They say that he was led to invade Britain by the hope of getting pearls, and that in comparing their size he sometimes weighed them with his own hand; that he was always a most enthusiastic collector of gems, carvings, statues, and pictures by early artists; also of slaves of exceptional figure and training at enormous prices, of which he himself was so ashamed that he forbade their entry in his accounts.

50. That he was unbridled and extravagant in his intrigues is the general opinion, and that he seduced many illustrious women, among them Postumia, wife of Servius Sulpicius, Lollia, wife of Aulus Gabinius, Tertulla, wife of Marcus Crassus, and even Gnaeus Pompey's wife Mucia. At all events there is no doubt that Pompey was taken to task by the elder and the younger Curio, as well as by many others, because through a desire for power he had afterwards married the daugh-

---

3. Epilepsy, called *morbus comitialis*, because an attack was regarded as sufficient cause for the postponement of elections, or other public business. Sometimes a seizure was feigned for political reasons.

4. *Latus clavus*, the broad purple strip, is also applied to the tunic with the broad strip. All senators had the right to wear this; the peculiarity of Caesar's case consisted in the long fringed sleeves.

5. While it was commonly worn with the ordinary tunic, it was not usual to wear one with the *latus clavus*. The looseness of the girdle was an additional peculiarity.

ter of a man on whose account he divorced a wife who had borne him three children, and whom he had often referred to with a groan as an Aegisthus. But beyond all others Caesar loved Servilia, the mother of Marcus Brutus, for whom in his first consulship he bought a pearl costing six million sesterces. During the civil war, too, besides other presents, he knocked down some fine estates to her in a public auction at a nominal price, and when some expressed their surprise at the low figure, Cicero wittily remarked: " It's a better bargain than you think, for there is a third off" And in fact it was thought that Servilia was prostituting her own daughter Tertia to Caesar.

51. That he did not refrain from intrigues in the provinces is shown in particular by this couplet, which was also shouted by the soldiers in his Gallic triumph:

"Men of Rome, keep close your consorts, here's a bald adulterer.
Gold in Gaul you spent in dalliance, which you borrowed here in Rome."

52. He had love affairs with queens too, including Eunoe the Moor, wife of Bogudes, on whom, as well as on her husband, he bestowed many splendid presents, as Naso writes; but above all with Cleopatra, with whom he often feasted until daybreak, and he would have gone through Egypt with her in her state barge almost to Aethiopia, had not his soldiers refused to follow him. Finally he called her to Rome and did not let her leave until he had ladened her with high honors and rich gifts, and he allowed her to give his name to the child which she bore. In fact, according to certain Greek writers, this child was very like Caesar in looks and carriage. Mark Antony declared to the senate that Caesar had really acknowledged the boy, and that Gaius Matius, Gaius Oppius, and other friends of Caesar knew this. Of these Gaius Oppius, as if admitting that the situation required apology and defense, published a book, to prove that the child whom Cleopatra fathered on Caesar was not his. Helvius Cinna, tribune of the commons, admitted to several that he had a bill drawn up in due form, which Caesar had ordered him to propose to the people in his absence, making it lawful for Caesar to marry what wives he wished, and as many as he wished, "for the purpose of begetting children." But to remove all doubt that he had an evil reputation both for shameless vice and for adultery, I have only to add that the elder Curio in one of his speeches calls him "every woman's man and every man's woman."

53. That he drank very little wine not even his enemies denied. There is a saying of Marcus Cato that Caesar was the only man who undertook to overthrow the state when sober. Even in the matter of food Gaius Oppius tells us that he was so indifferent, that once when his host served stale oil instead of fresh, and the other guests would have none of it, Caesar partook even more plentifully than usual, not to seem to charge his host with carelessness or lack of manners.

54. Neither when in command of armies nor as a magistrate at Rome did he show a scrupulous integrity; for as certain men have declared in their memoirs, when he was proconsul in Spain,[6] he not only begged money from the allies, to help pay his debts, but also attacked and sacked some towns of the Lusitanians although they did not refuse his terms and opened their gates to him on his arrival. In Gaul he pillaged shrines and temples of the gods filled with offerings, and oftener sacked towns for the sake of plunder than for any fault. In consequence he had more gold than he knew what to do with, and offered it for sale throughout Italy and the provinces at the

---

6. Caesar was really propraetor, but proconsul is sometimes used of the governor of a province, regardless of his rank.

rate of three thousand sesterces the pound.[7] In his first consulship he stole three thousand pounds of gold from the Capitol, replacing it with the same weight of gilded bronze. He made alliances and thrones a matter of barter, for he extorted from Ptolemy alone in his own name and that of Pompey nearly six thousand talents, while later on he met the heavy expenses of the civil wars and of his triumphs and entertainments by the most bare faced pillage and sacrilege.

55. In eloquence and in the art of war he either equaled or surpassed the fame of their most eminent representatives. After his accusation of Dolabella, he was without question numbered with the leading advocates. At all events when Cicero reviews the orators in his *Brutus,* he says that he does not see to whom Caesar ought to yield the palm, declaring that his style is elegant as well as transparent, even grand and in a sense noble. Again in a letter to Cornelius Nepos he writes thus of Caesar: "Come now, what orator would you rank above him of those who have devoted themselves to nothing else? Who has cleverer or more frequent epigrams? Who is either more picturesque or more choice in diction?" He appears, at least in his youth, to have imitated the manner of Caesar Strabo, from whose speech entitled "For the Sardinians" he actually transferred some passages word for word to a trial address[8] of his own. He is said to have delivered himself in a high-pitched voice with impassioned action and gestures, which were not without grace. . .

65. He valued his soldiers neither for their personal character nor their fortune, but solely for their prowess, and he treated them with equal strictness and indulgence; for he did not curb them everywhere and at all times, but only in the presence of the enemy. Then he required the strictest discipline, not announcing the time of a march or a battle, but keeping them ready and alert to be led on a sudden at any moment where ever he might wish. He often called them out even when there was no occasion for it, especially on rainy days and holidays. And warning them every now and then that they must keep close watch on him, he would steal away suddenly by day or night and make a longer march than usual, to tire out those who were tardy in following.

66. When they were in a panic through reports about the enemy's numbers, he used to rouse their courage not by denying or discounting the rumors, but by falsely exaggerating the true danger. For instance, when the anticipation of Juba's coming filled them with terror, he called the soldiers together and said "Let me tell you that within the next few days the king will be here with ten legions, thirty thousand horsemen, a hundred thousand light armed troops, and three hundred elephants. Therefore some of you may as well cease to ask further questions or make surmises and may rather believe me, since I know all about it. Otherwise, I shall surely have them shipped on some worn out craft and carried off to whatever lands the wind may blow them."

67. He did not take notice of all their offences or punish them by rule, but he kept a sharp look out for deserters and mutineers, and chastised them most severely, shutting his eyes to other faults. Sometimes, too, after a great victory he relieved them of all duties and gave them full license to revel, being in the habit of boasting that his soldiers could fight well even when reeking of perfumes. In the assembly he addressed them not as "soldiers," but by the more flattering term "comrades," and he kept them in fine trim, furnishing them with arms inlaid with silver and gold, both for show and to make them hold the faster to them in battle, through fear of the greatness

---

7. Apparently about two thirds of the usual price.

8. I.e a speech in which he competed with other advocates for the right to conduct a prosecution.

of the loss. Such was his love for them that when he heard of the disaster to Titurius, he let his hair and beard grow long, and would not cut them until he had taken vengeance.

68. In this way he made them most devoted to his interests as well as most valiant. When he began the civil war, every centurion of each legion proposed to supply a horseman from his own savings, and the soldiers one and all offered their service without pay and without rations, the richer assuming the care of the poorer. Throughout the long struggle not one deserted and many of them, on being taken prisoner, refused to accept their lives, when offered them on the condition of consenting to serve against Caesar. They bore hunger and other hardships, both when in a state of siege and when besieging others, with such fortitude, that when Pompey saw in the works at Dyrrachium a kind of bread made of herbs, on which they were living, he said that he was fighting wild beasts; and he gave orders that it be put out of sight quickly and shown to none of his men, for fear that the endurance and resolution of the foe would break their spirit.

How valiantly they fought is shown by the fact that when they suffered their sole defeat before Dyrrachium, they insisted on being punished, and their commander felt called upon rather to console than to chastise them. In the other battles they overcame with ease countless forces of the enemy, though decidedly fewer in number themselves. Indeed one cohort of the sixth legion, when set to defend a redoubt, kept four legions of Pompey at bay for several hours, though almost all were wounded by the enemy's showers of arrows, of which a hundred and thirty thousand were picked up within the ramparts. And no wonder, when one thinks of the deeds of individual soldiers, either of Cassius Scaeva the centurion, or of Gaius Acilius of the rank and file, not to mention others. Scaeva, with one eye gone, his thigh and shoulder wounded, and his shield bored through in a hundred and twenty places, continued to guard the gate of a fortress put in his charge. Acilius in the sea-fight at Massilia grasped the stern of one of the enemy's ships, and when his right hand was lopped off, rivaling the famous exploit of the Greek hero Cynegirus, boarded the ship and drove the enemy before him with the boss of his shield.

73. On the other hand he never formed such bitter enmities that he was not glad to lay them aside when opportunity offered. Although Gaius Memmius had made highly caustic speeches against him, to which he had replied with equal bitterness, he went so far as to support Memmius afterwards in his suit for the consulship. When Gaius Calvus, after some scurrilous epigrams, took steps through his friends towards a reconciliation, Caesar wrote to him first and of his own free will. Valerius Catullus, as Caesar himself did not hesitate to say, inflicted a lasting stain on his name by the verses about Mamurra; yet when he apologized, Caesar invited the poet to dinner that very same day, and continued his usual friendly relations with Catullus's father.

74. Even in avenging wrongs he was by nature most merciful, and when he got hold of the pirates who had captured him, he had them crucified, since he had sworn beforehand that he would do so, but ordered that their throats be cut first. He could never make up his mind to harm Cornelius Phagites, although when he was sick and in hiding, the man had waylaid him night after night, and even a bribe had barely saved him from being handed over to Sulla. The slave Philemon, his amanuensis, who had promised Caesar's enemies that he would poison him, he merely punished by death, without torture. When summoned as a witness against Publius Clodius, the paramour of his wife Pompeia, charged on the same count with sacrilege, Caesar declared that he had no evidence, although both his mother Aurelia and his sister Julia had given the same jurors a faithful account of the whole affair; and on being asked why it was then that he

had put away his wife, he replied: "Because I maintain that the members of my family should be free from suspicion, as well as from accusation."

75. He certainly showed admirable self-restraint and mercy, both in his conduct of the civil war and in the hour of victory. While Pompey announced that he would treat as enemies those who did not take up arms for the government, Caesar gave out that those who were neutral and of neither party should be numbered with his friends. He freely allowed all those whom he had made centurions on Pompey's recommendation to go over to his rival. When conditions of surrender were under discussion at Ilerda, and friendly intercourse between the two parties was constant, Afranius and Petreius, with a sudden change of purpose, put to death all of Caesar's soldiers whom they found in their camp but Caesar could not bring himself to retaliate in kind. At the battle of Pharsalus he cried out, "Spare your fellow citizens," and afterwards allowed each of his men to save any one man he pleased of the opposite party. And it will be found that no Pompeian lost his life except in battle, save only Afranius and Faustus, and the young Lucius Caesar; and it is believed that not even these men were slain by his wish, even though the two former had taken up arms again after being pardoned, while Caesar had not only cruelly put to death the dictator's slaves and freedmen with fire and sword, but had even butchered the wild beasts which he had procured for the entertainment of the people. At last, in his later years, he went so far as to allow all those whom he had not yet pardoned to return to Italy, and to hold magistracies and the command of armies: and he actually set up the statues of Lucius Sulla and Pompey, which had been broken to pieces by the populace. After this, if any dangerous plots were formed against him, or slanders uttered, he preferred to quash rather than to punish them. Accordingly, he took no further notice of the conspiracies which were detected, and of meetings by night, than to make known by proclamation that he was aware of them; and he thought it enough to give public warning to those who spoke ill of him, not to persist in their conduct, bearing with good nature the attacks on his reputation made by the scurrilous volume of Aulus Caecina and the abusive lampoons of Pitholaus.

76. Yet after all, his other actions and words so turn the scale, that it is thought that he abused his power and was justly slain. For not only did he accept excessive honors, such as an uninterrupted consulship, the dictatorship for life, and the censorship of public morals, as well as the forename Imperator, the surname of Father of his Country, a statue among those of the kings, and a raised couch in the orchestra;[9] but he also allowed honors to be bestowed on him which were too great for mortal man: a golden throne in the House and on the judgment seat; a chariot and litter[10] in the procession at the circus; temples, altars, and statues beside those of the gods; a special priest, an additional college of the Luperci, and the calling of one of the months by his name. In fact, there were no honors which he did not receive or confer at pleasure.

He held his third and fourth consulships in name only, content with the power of the dictatorship conferred on him at the same time as the consulships. Moreover, in both years he substituted two consuls for himself for the last three months, in the meantime holding no elections except for tribunes and plebeian aediles, and appointing praefects instead of the praetors, to manage the affairs of the city during his absence. When one of the consuls suddenly died the day before the

---

9. At the theater.
10. For carrying his statue among those of the gods.

Kalends of January, he gave the vacant office for a few hours to a man who asked for it. With the same disregard of law and precedent he named magistrates for several years to come, bestowed the emblems of consular rank on ten ex-praetors, and admitted to the House men who had been given citizenship, and in some cases half-civilized Gauls. He assigned the charge of the mint and of the public revenues to his own slaves, and gave the oversight and command of the three legions which he had left at Alexandria to a favorite of his called Ruflo, son of one of his freedmen.

77. No less arrogant were his public utterances, which Titus Ampius records: that the state was nothing, a mere name without body or form; that Sulla did not know his A. B. C. when he laid down his dictatorship; that men ought now to be more circumspect in addressing him, and to regard his word as law. So far did he go in his presumption, that when a soothsayer once reported direful inwards without a heart, he said: "They will be more favorable when I wish it; it should not be regarded as a portent, if a beast has no heart."

78. But it was the following action in particular that roused deadly hatred against him. When the Senate approached him in a body with many highly honorary decrees, he received them before the temple of Venus Genetrix without rising. Some think that when he attempted to get up, he was held back by Cornelius Balbus; others, that he made no such move at all, but on the contrary frowned angrily on Gaius Trebatius when he suggested that he should rise. And this action of his seemed the more intolerable, because when he himself in one of his triumphal processions rode past the benches of the tribunes, he was so incensed because a member of the college, Pontius Aquila by name, did not rise, that he cried: "Come then, Aquila. take back the republic from me, you tribune;" and for several days he would not make a promise to any one without adding, "That is, if Pontius Aquila will allow me."

79. To an insult which so plainly showed his contempt for the Senate he added an act of even greater insolence; for at the Latin Festival, as he was returning to the city, amid the extravagant and unprecedented demonstrations of the populace, someone in the press placed on his statue a laurel wreath with a white fillet tied to it;[11] and when Epidius Marullus and Caesetius Flavus, tribunes of the commons, gave orders that the ribbon be removed from the wreath and the man taken off to prison, Caesar sharply rebuked and deposed them, either offended that the hint at regal power had been received with so little favor, or, as he asserted, that he had been robbed of the glory of refusing it. But from that time on he could not rid himself of the odium of having aspired to the title of monarch, although he replied to the commons, when they hailed him as king, "I am Caesar and no king," and at the Lupercalia, when the consul Antony several times attempted to place a crown upon his head as he spoke from the rostra, he put it aside and at last sent it to the Capitol, to be offered to Jupiter Optimus Maximus. Nay, more, the report had spread in various quarters that he intended to move to Ilium or Alexandria, taking with him the resources of the state, draining Italy by levies, and leaving the charge of the city to his friends; also that at the next meeting of the Senate Lucius Cotta would announce as the decision of the Fifteen,[12] that inasmuch as it was written in the books of fate that the Parthians could be conquered only by a king, Caesar should he given that title.

---

11. The white fillet was an emblem of royalty.
12. The college of fifteen priests in charge of the Sybilline Books.

80. It was this that led the conspirators to hasten in carrying out their designs, in order to avoid giving their assent to this proposal.

Therefore the plots which had previously been formed separately, often by groups of two or three, were united in a general conspiracy, since even the populace no longer were pleased with present conditions, but both secretly and openly rebelled at his tyranny and cried out for defenders of their liberty. On the admission of foreigners to the Senate, a placard was posted: "God bless the Commonwealth! let no one consent to point out the House to a newly made senator." The following verses too were sung everywhere

"Caesar led the Gauls in triumph, led them to the senate house;
Then the Gauls put off their breeches, and put on the laticlave."

When Quintus Maximus, whom he had appointed consul in his place for three months, was entering the theatre, and his lictor called attention to his arrival in the usual manner, a general shout was raised: "He's no consul!" At the first election after the deposing of Caesetius and Marullus, the tribunes, several votes were found for their appointment as consuls. Some wrote on the base of Lucius Brutus' statue, "Oh, that you were still alive;" and on that of Caesar himself:

"First of all was Brutus consul, since he drove the kings from Rome;
Since this man drove out the consuls, he at last is made our king."

More than sixty joined the conspiracy against him, led by Gaius Cassius and Marcus and Decimus Brutus. At first they hesitated whether to form two divisions at the elections in the Campus Martius, so that while some hurled him from the bridge[13] as he summoned the tribes to vote, the rest might wait below and slay him; or to set upon him in the Sacred Way or at the entrance to the theatre. When, however, a meeting of the Senate was called for the Ides of March in the Hall of Pompey, they readily gave that time and place the preference.

---

13. The *pons suffragiorum*, a temporary bridge of planks over which the voters passed one by one to cast their ballots.

Perseus with Head of Medusa. Ostia museum, Italy.

Dio Cassius: 27
Maecenas' Advice to Augustus

When Octavian returned to Rome after defeating Mark Antony and Cleopatra and annexing Egypt, he was the master of the Roman world. The most pressing problem he had to face was the one that had defeated his adoptive father, Julius Caesar: how to rule Rome without seeming to be an autocrat; without so deeply insulting the Roman nobility that they would turn on him and assassinate him as they had Caesar.

Octavian cleverly solved this problem by restoring the appearance, by reconstructing the façade of the Roman republic, but yet retaining all the real power of the state in his own hands. This was accomplished by a series of institutional reforms known to history as "constitutional settlements," which created a monarchy behind a republican image. In the process Octavian assumed the title "Augustus." According to Suetonius Augustus expressed the "desire to be known as the author of the best possible constitution."

The historian Dio Cassius (c. 163–after 229), writing over two centuries later, attempted to describe the nature of the "best constitution" for the Roman Empire. Dio placed his description in the mouth of Maecenas, one of Augustus' trusted advisors. Of course, Dio's ideal constitution was the imperial monarchy, the government of his own time, which produced the pax Romana, the "peace of Rome," which was the longest period of prosperity and peace the Mediterranean basin has ever experienced. This extraordinary speech from Dio's Roman History is given below.

"....¹Hence, if you feel any concern at all for your country, for which you have fought so many wars and would so gladly give even your life, reorganize it and regulate it in the direction of greater moderation. For while the privilege of doing and saving precisely what one pleases becomes, in the case of sensible persons, if you examine the matter, a cause of the highest happiness to them all, yet in the case of the foolish it becomes a cause of disaster. For this reason he who offers this privilege to the foolish is virtually putting a sword in the hands of a child or a madman but he who offers it to the prudent is not only preserving all their other privileges but is also saving these men themselves even in spite of themselves. Therefore I ask you not to fix your gaze upon the specious terms applied to these things and thus be deceived, but to weigh carefully

From *Dio Cassius, Roman History, Volume VI*, translated by Earnest Cary, Ph.D. (Cambridge, Loeb Classical Library, Harvard University Press, 1917).

the results which come from the things themselves and then put an end to the insolence of the populace and place the management of public affairs in the hands of yourself and the other best citizens, to the end that the business of deliberation may be performed by the most prudent and that of ruling by those best fitted for command, while the work of serving in the army for pay is left to those who are strongest physically and most needy. In this way each class of citizens will zealously discharge the duties which devolve upon them and will readily render to one another such services as are due, and will thus be unaware of their inferiority when one class is at a disadvantage as compared with another, and all will gain the true democracy and the freedom which does not fail. For the boasted freedom of the mob proves in experience to be the bitterest servitude of the best element to the other and brings upon both a common destruction; whereas this freedom of which I speak everywhere prefers for honor the men of prudence, awarding at the same time equality to all according to their deserts, and thus gives happiness impartially to all who enjoy this liberty.

"For I would not have you think that I am advising you to enslave the people and the senate and then set up a tyranny. This is a thing I should never dare suggest to you nor would you bring yourself to do it. The other course, however, would be honorable and expedient both for you and for the city—that you should yourself, in consultation with the best men, enact all the appropriate laws, without the possibility of any opposition or remonstrance to these laws on the part of any one from the masses;[2] that you and your counselors should conduct the wars according to your own wishes, all other citizens rendering instant obedience to your commands; that the choice of the officials should rest with you and your advisers; and that you and they should also determine the honors and the punishments. The advantage of all this would be that whatever pleased you in consultation with your peers would immediately become law; that our wars against our enemies would be waged with secrecy and at the opportune time; that those to whom any task was entrusted would be appointed because of their merit and not as the result of the lot or rivalry for office; that the good would be honored without arousing jealousy and the bad punished without causing rebellion. Thus whatever business was done would most likely to be managed in the right way, instead of being referred to the popular assembly, or deliberated upon openly, or entrusted to partisan delegates, or exposed to the danger of ambitious rivalry; and we should be happy in the enjoyment of the blessings which are vouchsafed to us, instead of being embroiled in hazardous wars abroad or in unholy civil strife. For these are the evils found in every democracy—the more powerful men, namely, in reaching out after the primacy and hiring the weaker, turn everything upside down—but they have been most frequent in our country, and there is no other way to put a stop to them than the way I propose. And the evidence is, that we have now for a long time been engaged in wars and civil strife. The cause is the multitude of our population and the magnitude of the business of our government; for the population embraces men of every kind, in respect both to race and to endowment, and both their tempers and their desires are manifold; and the business of the state has become so vast that it can be administered only with the greatest difficulty.

---

1. A number of lines at the beginning of this speech are missing.
2. Probably a reference to the tribunes.

"Witness to the truth of my words is borne by our past. For while we were but few in number and differed in no important respect from our neighbors, we got along well with our government and subjugated almost all Italy; but ever since we were led outside the peninsula and crossed over to many continents and many islands, filling the whole sea and the whole earth with our name and power, nothing good has been our lot. At first it was only at home and within our walls that we broke up into factions and quarreled, but afterwards we even carried this plague out into the legions. Therefore our city, like a great merchantman manned with a crew of every race and lacking a pilot, has now for many generations been rolling and plunging as it has drifted this way and that in a heavy sea, a ship as it were without ballast. Do not, then, allow her to be longer exposed to the tempest; for you see that she is waterlogged. And do not let her be pounded to pieces upon a reef for her timbers are rotten and she will not be able to hold out much longer. But since the gods have taken pity on her and have set you over her as her arbiter and overseer, prove not false to her, to the end that, even as now she has revived a little by your aid, so she may survive in safety for the ages to come.

"Now I think you have long since been convinced that I am right in urging you to give the people a monarchical government; if this is the case, accept the leadership over them readily and with enthusiasm—or rather do not throw it away. For the question we are deliberating upon is not whether we shall take something, but whether we shall decide not to lose it and by so doing incur danger into the bargain. Who, indeed, will spare you if you thrust the control of the state into the hands of the people, or even if you entrust it to some other man, seeing that there are great numbers whom you have injured, and that practically all these will lay claim to the sovereignty, and yet no one of them will wish either that you should go unpunished for what you have done or that you should be allowed to survive as his rival? Pompey, for example, once he had given up the supreme power, became the object of scorn and of secret plotting and consequently lost his life when he was unable to regain his power. Caesar also, your father, lost not only his position but also his life for doing precisely what you are proposing to do. And Marius and Sulla would certainly have suffered a like fate had they not died first. And yet some say that Sulla, fearing this very fate, forestalled it by making away with himself;[3] at any rate, much of his legislation began to be undone while he was yet alive. Therefore you also must expect that there will be many a man who will prove a Lepidus to you and many a man who will prove a Sertorius, a Brutus, or a Cassius.

"Looking, then, at these facts and reflecting upon all the other considerations involved, do not abandon yourself and your country merely in order to avoid giving the impression to some that you deliberately sought the office. For, in the first place, even if men do suspect this, the ambition is not inconsistent with human nature and the risk involved is a noble one. Again, what man is there who does not know the circumstances which constrained you to assume your present position? Hence, if there be any fault to find with these compelling circumstances, one might with entire justice lay it upon your father's murderers. For if they had not slain him in so unjust and pitiable a fashion, you would not have taken up arms, would not have gathered your legions, would not have made your compact with Antony and Lepidus, and would not have had to defend yourself against these men themselves. That you were right, however, and were justified in

---

3. This tradition is found only here.

doing all this, no one is unaware. Therefore, even if some slight error has been committed, yet we cannot at this time with safety undo anything that has been done. Therefore, for our own sake and for that of the state let us obey Fortune, who offers you the sole rulership. And let us be very grateful to her that she has not only freed us from our domestic troubles, but has also placed in your hands the organization of the state, to the end that you, by bestowing due care upon it, may prove to all mankind that those troubles were stirred up and that mischief wrought by other men, whereas you are an upright man.

"And do not, I beg you, be afraid of the magnitude of the empire. For the greater its extent, the more numerous are the salutary elements it possesses; also, to guard anything is far easier than to acquire it. Toils and dangers are needed to win over what belongs to others, but a little care suffices to retain what is already yours. Moreover, you need not be afraid, either, that you will not live quite safely in that office and enjoy all the blessings which men know, provided that you will consent to administer it as I shall advise you. And do not think that I am shifting the discussion from the subject in hand if I speak to you at considerable length about the office. For of course my purpose in doing this will be, not to hear myself talk, but that you may learn by a strict demonstration that it is both possible and easy, for a man of sense at least, to rule well and without danger.

"I maintain, therefore, that you ought first and foremost to choose and select with discrimination the entire senatorial body, inasmuch as some who have not been fit have, on account of our dissensions, become senators. Such of them as possess any excellence you ought to retain, but the rest you should erase from the roll. Do not, however, get rid of any good man because of his poverty, but even give him the money he requires. In the place of those who have been dropped introduce the noblest, the best, and the richest men obtainable, selecting them not only from Italy but also from the allies and the subject nations. In this way you will have many assistants for yourself and will have in safe keeping the leading men from all the provinces; thus the provinces, having no leaders of established repute, will not begin rebellions, and their prominent men will regard you with affection because they have been made sharers in your empire.

"Take these same measures in the case of the knights also, by enrolling in the equestrian order such men as hold second place in their several districts as regards birth, excellence and wealth. Register as many new members in both classes as you please, without being over particular on the score of their number. For the more men of repute you have as your associates, the easier you will find it, for your own part, to administer everything in time of need and, so far as your subjects are concerned, the more easily will you persuade them that you are not treating them as slaves or as in any way inferior to us, but that you are sharing with them, not only all the other advantages which we ourselves enjoy, but also the chief magistracy as well, and thus make them as devoted to that office as if it were their own. And so far am I from retracting this last statement as rashly made, that I declare that the citizens ought every one actually to be given a share in the government, in order that, being on an equality with us in this respect also, they may be our faithful allies, living as it were in a single city, namely our own, and considering that this is in very truth a city, whereas their own homes are but the countryside and villages.

"But regarding this matter we shall at a later time examine more carefully the question of what measures should be taken to prevent our granting the people every privilege at once. As for the matter of eligibility for office, now, we should put men on the roll of knights when they are eighteen years old, for at that age their physical soundness and their mental fitness can best be discerned; but we should not enroll them in the senate until they are twenty-five years old. For is it not disgraceful, and indeed hazardous, to entrust the public business to men younger than this, when we never commit our private affairs to any one before he has reached this age? After they have served as quaestors and aediles or tribunes, let them be praetors when they reach the age of thirty. For it is my opinion that these offices, and that of consul, are the only ones at home which you ought to fill by election, and these merely out of regard for the institutions of our fathers and to avoid the appearance of making a complete change in the constitution. But make all the appointments yourself and do not any longer commit the filling of one or another of these offices either to the plebs or to the people,[4] for they will quarrel over them, or to the senate, for the senators will use them to further their private ambitions. And do not maintain the traditional powers of these offices, either, for fear history may repeat itself, but preserve the honor attaching to them, at the same time abating their influence to such an extent that, although you will be depriving the office of none of its prestige, you will still be giving no opportunity to those who may desire to stir up a rebellion. Now this will be accomplished if you assign them on appointment chiefly to home affairs and do not permit any of them to have armed forces during their term of office or immediately afterward, but only after the lapse of some time, as much as you think sufficient in each instance. In this way they will never be put in command of legions while still enjoying the prestige of their official titles and thus be led to stir up rebellions, and after they have been private citizens for a time they will be of milder disposition. Let these magistrates conduct such of the festivals as naturally belong to their office, and let them all severally sit as judges in all kinds of cases except homicide during their tenure of office in Rome. Courts should be established, to be sure, with the other senators and knights as members, but final authority should rest with these magistrates.

"As for the prefect of the city, men should be appointed to that office who are leading citizens and have previously passed through the appropriate offices; it should be the prefect's duty, not to govern merely when the consuls are out of town, but in general to be at all times in charge of the affairs of the city, and to decide the cases which come to him from all the other magistrates I have mentioned, whether on appeal or for review, together with those which involve the death penalty; and his jurisdiction should extend, not only to those who live in the city, except such as I shall name, but also to those who dwell outside the city for a distance of one hundred miles.

"Let still another magistrate be chosen, this man also from the class described, whose duties shall be to pass upon and supervise all matters pertaining to the families, property, and morals both of the senators and of the knights, alike of the men and of their wives and children. He should personally correct such behavior as deserves no punishment, yet if neglected becomes the cause of many evils; but about the more important matters of misconduct he should confer with you. For the officer to whom these duties are assigned should be a senator, and in fact the best one after the prefect of the city, rather than one of the knights. As for the title of his office, he would naturally receive one derived from your censorial functions (for it is certainly appropriate that you should be in charge of the censuses), and be called sub-censor.[5] Let these two, the city

---

4. I.e. to the *concilium plebes* or the *comitia*, the assembly.

5. In practice there were six of them—three to nominate senators and three to hold review of the *equites* (knights).

prefect and the sub-censor, hold office for life, unless one of them becomes demoralized in some way or is incapacitated by sickness or old age. For no harm could result from their holding office for life, since the one would be entirely without armed forces and the other would have but few soldiers and would be acting for the most part under your eyes; whereas the effect of the yearly tenure would be that they would shrink from offending any one and would be afraid to act with energy, since they would be looking ahead to their own retirement to private life and to the exercise of the power of the office by others. They should also draw a salary, not only to compensate them for the loss of their leisure but also to enhance the prestige of their office.

"This is the opinion I have to give you in regard to these officials. As for those who have served as praetors, let them hold some office among the subject nations (before they have been praetors I do not think they should have this privilege, but they ought first to serve for one or two terms as lieutenants to the ex-praetors just mentioned); then they should next hold office as consuls, provided that they have proved satisfactory officials to the end of their terms, and after that they should receive the more important governorships. I advise you, namely, to arrange these positions as follows. Take Italy as a whole (I mean the part of it which is more than one hundred miles from the city), and all the rest of the territory which owns our sway, the islands and the continents, and divide it into districts, in each case according to races and nations, and take also all the cities that are strong and independent enough to be ruled by one governor with full powers. Then station soldiers in them and send out as governor to each district or independent city one of the ex-consuls, who shall have general charge, and two of the ex-praetors. One of the latter, fresh from the city, should be put in charge of all matters pertaining to persons in private life and of the commissary; the other, a man who has had special training for this work, will administer the public business of the cities and will have command of the soldiers, except in cases that involve disfranchisement or death. Such cases, of course, should be referred to the ex-consul who is governor, and to him alone, except where the persons involved are centurions recruited from the levies or private persons of prominence in their respective communities; as for both these classes, do not allow anybody but yourself to punish them, lest they come to fear some of these officials to such an extent as to take measures, on occasion, against you as well as against them. As for my suggestion that the second of the ex-praetors should be put in charge of the soldiers, it is to be understood as follows if only a small body of troops is serving abroad in the military posts or at home in a single post, my proposal is satisfactory; but if two citizen legions are wintering in the same province (and more than this number I should not advise you to trust to one commander), it will no doubt be necessary for both the ex-praetors to hold the command over them, each having charge of one, and for each to have his share of authority similarly in matters affecting either the state or private citizens. Let the ex-consul, accordingly, [have] these [duties], and let him also decide the cases which come to him on appeal and those which are referred to him by the praetors for review. And do not be surprised that I recommend to you the dividing of Italy also into these administrative districts. It is large and populous, and so cannot possibly be well administered by the magistrates in the city for a governor ought always to be present in the district he governs, and no duties should be laid upon our city magistrates which they cannot perform.

"Let all these men to whom the commands outside the city are assigned receive salaries, the more important officers more, the less important less, and those between an intermediate amount. For they cannot live in a foreign land upon their own resources, nor should they indulge, as they do now, in unlimited and indefinite expenditure. They should hold office not less than three years, unless they are guilty of misconduct, nor more than five. The reason is that offices held for only one year or for short periods merely teach the officials their hare duties and then dismiss them before they can put any of their acquired knowledge into use, while, on the other hand, the longer terms of many years duration somehow have the effect, in many cases, of filling the officials with conceit and encouraging them to rebellion. Hence, again, I think that the more important posts ought in no case to be given consecutively to the same man. For it makes no difference whether a man is governor in the same province or in several in succession, if he holds office for a period longer than is advisable; besides, appointees improve when there is an interval between their incumbencies during which they return home and resume the life of ordinary citizens.

"As regards the senators, therefore, I declare that they ought to discharge the duties named and in the way described. Of the knights the two best should command the bodyguard which protects you, for it is hazardous to entrust it to one man, and sure to lead to confusion to entrust it to more than two. Therefore let the number of these prefects be two, in order that, if one of them feel indisposed, you may still not lack a person to guard you. And men should be appointed to this office who have served in many military campaigns and have, besides, held many administrative positions. And they should have command both of the Pretorians and of all the other soldiers in Italy, with power even to put to death any of them who do wrong, with the exception of the centurions and of those in general who have been assigned to the staffs of magistrates of senatorial rank. For these soldiers should be tried by the senatorial magistrates themselves, in order that the latter, by virtue of the authority they would thus possess of dealing out punishments to them as well as honors, may be able to command their unhesitating support. Over all the other soldiers in Italy, however, the prefects I have mentioned should be in command, having lieutenants under them, and likewise over the Caesarians, both those who are in attendance upon you and such of the others as are of any account. These duties will be both fitting and sufficient for them to discharge, for if they have more responsibilities assigned to them than they are able to carry satisfactorily, there is danger that they may have no time for the essential things, or, if they have, may prove incompetent to exercise oversight over all their duties. These prefects also should hold office for life, like the prefect of the city and the sub-censor. Let another official be appointed to be commander of the night watch and still another to be commissioner of grain and of the market in general, both of them from the equestrian order and the best men after the prefects, and let them hold their posts for a definite term, like the magistrates elected from the senatorial class. The management of the public funds, also—I mean both those of the people and those of the empire, not only in Rome but also in the rest of Italy and outside Italy—should be entirely in the hands of the knights, and they, as well as all the other members of the equestrian order who are charged with an administrative position, should be on salary, greater or less in proportion to the dignity and importance of their duties. The reason for the second part of this suggestion is that it is not possible for the knights, since they are poorer than the senators, to meet their expenditures out of their own means, even when their duties keep them in Rome, and for the first point, that it is neither practicable nor to your interest that the same men should be given authority over both the troops and the public funds. And, furthermore, it is well that the whole business of the empire should be transacted by a number of agents, in order that many may at the same time receive the benefits and gain experience in public affairs; for in this way your subjects, reaping a manifold enjoyment of the common blessings, will be more favorably disposed towards you, and you will have at your disposal in the largest measure those who are at any particular time the best men for all urgent needs. One official of the equestrian order is sufficient for each branch of the fiscal service in the city, and, outside the city, for each province, each one of them to have as many subordinates, drawn from the knights and from your own freedmen, as the needs of the case demand; for you need to associate with the officials such assistants in order that your service may offer a prize for merit, and that you may not lack those from whom you may learn the truth, even contrary to their wishes, in case any irregularity is committed.

"If any of the knights, after passing through many branches of the service, distinguishes himself enough to become a senator, his age ought not to hinder him at all from being enrolled in the senate. Indeed, some knights should be received into the senate, even if they have seen service only as company commanders in the citizen legions, except such as have served in the rank and file. For it is both a shame and a reproach that men of this sort, who have carried faggots and charcoal, should be found on the roll of the senate; but in the case of knights who began their service with the rank of centurion, there is nothing to prevent the most notable of them from belonging to the senate.

"With regard, then, to the senators and the knights, this is the advice I have to give you—yes, and this also, that while they are still children they should attend the schools, and when they come out of childhood into youth they should turn their minds to horses and to arms, and have paid public teachers in each of these departments. In this way from their very boyhood they will have had both instruction and practice in all that they will themselves be required to do on reaching manhood, and will thus prove more serviceable to you for every undertaking. For the best ruler— the ruler who is worth anything—should not only perform himself all the duties which devolve upon him, but should make provision for the rest also, that they may become as excellent as possible. And this title can be yours, not if you allow them to do whatever they please and then censure those who err, but if, before any mistakes are made, you give them instruction in everything the practice of which will render them more useful both to themselves and to you, and if you afford nobody any excuse whatever, either wealth or nobility of birth or any other attribute of excellence, for affecting indolence or effeminacy or any other behavior that is counterfeit. For many persons, fearing that, by reason of some such advantage, they may incur jealousy or danger, do many things that are unworthy of themselves, expecting by such behavior to live in greater security. As a consequence, not only do they, on their part, become objects of pity as being victims of injustice in precisely this respect, that men believe that they are deprived of the opportunity of leading upright lives, but their ruler also, on his part, suffers not only a loss, in that he is robbed of men who might have been good, but also ill-repute, because he is blamed for the others' condition. Therefore never permit this thing to happen, and have no fear, on the other hand, that anyone who has been reared and educated as I propose will ever venture upon a rebellion. On the contrary, it is the ignorant and licentious that you should suspect; for it is such persons who are easily influenced to do absolutely any and every thing, even the most disgraceful and outrageous, first toward themselves and then toward others, whereas those who have been well reared and educated do not deliberately do wrong to any one else and least of all to the one who has cared for their rearing and education. If, however, one of these does show himself wicked and ungrateful, you have merely to refuse to entrust him with any position of such a kind as will enable him to do any mischief; and if even so he rebels, let him be convicted and punished. You need not, I assure yon, be afraid that anyone will blame you for this, provided that you carry out all my injunctions. For in taking vengeance on the wrongdoer you will be guilty of no sin, any more than the physician is who resorts to cautery and surgery; but all men will assuredly say that the offender has got his deserts, because, after partaking of the same rearing and education as the rest, he plotted against you.

"Let this be your procedure, then, in the case of the senators and the knights. A standing army also should be supported, drawn from the citizens, the subject nations, and the allies, its size in the several provinces being greater or less according as the necessities of the case demand; and these troops ought always to be under arms and to engage in the practice of warfare continually. They should have winter quarters constructed for them at the most advantageous points, and should serve for a stated period, so that a portion of life may still be left for them between their retirement from service and old age. The reason for such a standing army is this: far removed as we are from the frontiers of tile empire, with enemies living near our borders on every side, we are no longer able at critical times to depend upon expeditionary forces; and if, on the other hand, we permit all the men of military age to have arms and to practice warfare, they will always be the source of seditions and civil wars. If, however, we prevent them from all making arms their profession and afterwards need their aid in war, we shall be exposed to danger, since we shall never have anything but inexperienced and untrained soldiers to depend upon. For these reasons I give it as my opinion that, while in general the men of military age should have nothing to do with arms and walled camps during their lives, the hardiest of them and those most in need of a livelihood should be enlisted as soldiers and given a military training. For they will fight better if they devote their time to this one business, and the rest will find it easier to carry on their farming, seafaring, and the other pursuits appropriate to peace, if they are not compelled to take part in military expeditions but have others to act as their defenders. Thus the most active and vigorous element of the population, which is generally obliged to gain its livelihood by brigandage, will support itself without molesting others, while all the rest will live without incurring dangers.

"From what source, then, is the money to be provided for these soldiers and for the other expenses that will of necessity be incurred? I shall explain this point also, prefacing it with a brief reminder that even if we have a democracy we shall in any case, of course, need money. For we cannot survive without soldiers, and men will not serve as soldiers without pay. Therefore let us not be oppressed by the idea that the necessity of raising money belongs only to a monarchy, and let us not be led by that consideration to turn our backs upon this form of government, but let us assume in our deliberations that, under whatever form of government we shall live, we shall certainly be constrained to secure funds. My proposal, therefore, is that you shall first of all sell the property that belongs to the state—and I observe that this has become vast on account of the wars—reserving only a little that is distinctly useful or necessary to you; and that you lend out all the money thus realized at a moderate rate of interest. In this way not only will the land be put under cultivation, being sold to owners who will cultivate it themselves, but also the latter will acquire a capital and become more prosperous, while the treasury will gain a permanent revenue that will suffice for its needs. In the second place, I advise you to make an estimate of the revenues from this source and of all the other revenues which can with certainty be derived from the mines or any other source, and then to make and balance against this a second estimate of all the expenses, not only those of the army, but also of all those which contribute to the well-being of a state, and furthermore of those which will necessarily be incurred for unexpected campaigns and the other needs which are wont to arise in an emergency. The next step is to provide for any deficiency by levying an assessment upon absolutely all property which produces any profit for its possessors, and by establishing a system of taxes among all the peoples we rule. For it is but just and proper that no individual or district be exempt from these taxes, inasmuch as they are to enjoy the benefits derived from the taxation as much as the rest. And you should appoint tax-collectors to have supervision of this business in each district, and cause them to exact the entire amount that falls due during the term of their supervision from all the sources of revenue. This plan will not only render the work of collection easier for these officials, but will in particular benefit the tax-payers, inasmuch, I mean, as these will bring in what they owe in the small installments appointed, whereas now, if they are remiss for a brief period, the entire sum is added up and demanded of them in a single payment.

"I am not unaware that some will object if this system of assessments and taxes is established. But I know this, too—that if they are subjected to no further abuses and are indeed convinced that all these contributions of theirs will make for their own security and for their fearless enjoyment of the rest of their property, and that, again, the larger part of their contributions will be received by none but themselves, as governors, procurators, or soldiers, they will be exceedingly grateful to you, since they will be giving but a slight portion of the abundance from which they derive the benefit without having to submit to abuses. Especially will this be true if they see that you live temperately and spend nothing foolishly. For who, if he saw that you were quite frugal in your expenditures for yourself and quite lavish in those for the commonwealth, would not willingly contribute, believing that your wealth meant his own security and prosperity?

"So far as funds are concerned, therefore, a great abundance would be supplied from these sources. And I advise you to conduct as follows the administration of such matters as have not yet been mentioned. Adorn this capital with utter disregard of expense and make it magnificent with festivals of every kind. For it is fitting that we who rule over many people should surpass all men in all things, and brilliance of this sort, also, tends in a way to inspire our allies with respect for us and our enemies with terror. The affairs of the other cities you should order in this fashion: In the first place, the populace should have no authority in any matter, and should not be allowed to convene in any assembly at all; for nothing good would come out of their deliberations and they would always be stirring up a good deal of turmoil. Hence it is my opinion that our populace here in Rome, for that matter, should not come together either as a court or to hold the elections, or indeed in any meeting whose object is to transact business. In the second place, the cities should not indulge in public buildings unnecessarily numerous or large, nor waste their resources on expenditures for a large number and variety of public games, lest they exhaust themselves in futile exertions and be led by unreasonable rivalries to quarrel among themselves. They ought, indeed, to have their festivals and spectacles—to say nothing of the Circensian games held here in Rome—but not to such an extent that the public treasury or the estates of private citizens shall be ruined thereby, or that any stranger resident there shall be compelled to contribute to their expense, or that maintenance for life shall be granted to every one without exception who has won a victory in a contest. For it is unreasonable that the well-to-do should be put under compulsion to spend their money outside their own countries; and as for the competitors in the games, the prizes which are offered in each event are enough, unless a man wins in the Olympian or Pythian games or in some contest here in Rome. For these are the only victors who ought to receive their maintenance, and then the cities will not be wearing themselves out to no purpose nor will any athlete go into training except those who have a chance of winning; the rest will be able to follow some occupation that will be more profitable both to themselves and to the commonwealth. This is my opinion about these matters. But as to the horse races in connection with which there are no gymnastic contests, I think that no city but Rome should be permitted to have them, the object being to prevent the wanton dissipation of vast sums of money and to keep the populace from becoming deplorably crazed over such a sport, and, above all, to give those who are serving in the army an abundant supply of the best horses. It is for these reasons, therefore, that I would altogether forbid the holding of such races anywhere else than here in Rome; as to the other games, I have proposed to keep them within bounds, in order that each community, by putting upon an inexpensive basis its entertainments for both eye and ear, may live with greater moderation and less factious strife.

"None of the cities should be allowed to have its own separate coinage or system of weights and measures; they should all be required to use ours. They should send no embassy to you, unless its business is one that involves a judicial decision; they should rather make what representations they will to their governor and through him bring to your attention such of their petitions as he shall approve. In this way they will be spared expense and be prevented from resorting to crooked practices to gain their object; and the answers they receive will be uncontaminated by their agents and will involve no expense or red tape.

"Moreover (to pass to other matters), it seems to me that you would be adopting the best arrangement if you should, in the first place, introduce before the senate the embassies which come from the enemy and from those under treaty with us, whether kings or democracies; for, among other considerations, it is both awe inspiring and calculated to arouse comment for the impression to prevail that the senate has full authority in all matters and for all men to be fully aware that those envoys who are unfair in their dealings will have many to oppose them. In the second place, you would do well to have all your legislation enacted by the senate, and to enforce no measure whatever upon all the people alike except the decrees of this body. In this way the dignity of the empire would be more securely established and the judgments rendered in accordance with the laws would instantly be free from all dispute or uncertainty in the eyes of all the people. In the third place, it would be well in the case of the members of the senatorial order who are actually members of the senate,[6] their children, and their wives, if ever they are charged with a serious offence for which the penalty on conviction would be disfranchisement, exile, or even death, that you should bring the matter before the Senate without prejudgment against the accused, and should commit to that body the entire decision uninfluenced by your opinion. The purpose of this is, that the guilty, thus tried by a jury consisting solely of their peers, may be punished without there being any resentment against you, and that the others, seeing this, may mend their ways through fear of being publicly pilloried themselves.

"These suggestions have to do only with those offences regarding which laws have been established and judgments are rendered in accordance with these laws. For as to a charge that some

---

6. As distinguished from those of the senatorial order who have not yet gained admission to the senate.

one has vilified you or in some other way has used unseemly language regarding you, I would have you neither listen to the accuser nor follow up the accusation. For it is disgraceful for you to believe that any one has wantonly insulted you if you are indeed doing no wrong and are but conferring benefits upon all, and it is only those who are ruling badly who believe such things; for they draw evidence from their own conscience of the credibility of the alleged slanders. And it is, furthermore, a dangerous thing even to show anger at such imputations (for if they are true, it were better not to be angry, and if their are false, it were better to pretend not to be angry), since many a man in times past has, by adopting this course, caused to be circulated against himself scandals far more numerous and more difficult to bear. This, then, is my advice concerning those who are accused of calumniating you; for you should be superior to any insult and too exalted to be reached by it, and you should never allow yourself even to imagine, or lead others to imagine, that it is possible for any one to treat you with contumely, since you desire that men shall think of you, as they do of the gods, that your sanctity is inviolable. If, however, any one is accused of plotting against you (and such a thing might also happen), refrain, in his case also, from either giving judgment yourself or prejudging the charge (for it is absurd that the same man should be both accuser and judge), but bring him before the senate and let him plead his defense there, and, if he is convicted, punish him, moderating the sentence as far as possible, in order that belief in his guilt may be fostered. For most men are very reluctant to believe that an unarmed man is plotting against one who is armed; and the only way you can win them to the belief is by showing, so far as possible, neither resentment nor the desire to exact the utmost when you inflict the penalty. But I make an exception to this rule in the case of a commander of an army who openly revolts; for of course it is fitting that such an one should not be tried at all, but chastised as a public enemy.

"These matters, then, should be referred by you to the senate, and also those others which are of the greatest importance to the state. For interests which are shared in common should be administered in common. Besides, it is doubtless a quality implanted by nature in all men that they take delight in any marks of esteem received from a superior which imply that they are his equals, and that they not only approve of all decisions made by another in consultation with themselves, as being their own decisions, but also submit to them as having been imposed by their own free choice. Therefore I say that such business ought to be brought before the senate. Furthermore, all the senators alike, that is, all who are present, should vote on all other matters but when one of their own number is accused, not all of them should do so, unless the one who is on trial is not yet sitting as a senator or is still in the ranks of the ex-quaestors. For it is absurd that one who has not yet been a tribune or an aedile should cast a vote against men who have held those offices or, worse yet, that any one of the latter should vote against men who have been praetors, or one of these last against men who have been consuls. Rather, let the ex-consuls alone have authority to render decisions in the case of all senators, and let the rest of the senators vote only in the cases of senators of a rank equal or inferior to their own.

"But do you judge by yourself alone the cases which come to you on appeal or reference from the higher officials and the procurators, from the prefect of the city, the sub-censor, and from the prefects in charge respectively of the grain supply and the night-watch. For none of these should have such absolute jurisdiction and final authority that an appeal cannot be made from him. Do you, therefore, pass upon these cases and those which involve knights and centurions recruited from the levies and the foremost private citizens, when they are defendants on a charge punishable by death or disfranchisement. For such cases should be committed to you alone, and for the reasons mentioned no one else should judge them solely upon his own responsibility. Indeed, in the rendering of decisions generally you should be brought into consultation, invariably by the senators and knights of highest rank and also, as occasion calls for one or another, by the other senators who are ex-consuls and ex-praetors, the object being twofold: that you on your part may first become more intimately acquainted with their characters and may then be able to put them to the right kind of employment, and that they, on their part, may first become familiar with your habits of mind and your plans before they go out to govern the provinces. Do not, however, ask for a public expression of their opinion on any matter that requires an unusually careful consideration, lest they hesitate to speak freely, since in giving their opinions they follow their superiors in rank; make them, rather, write their opinions on tablets. These you should read in private, that they may become known to no one else, and should then order the writing to be erased forthwith. For the best way for you to get at each man's precise opinion would be to give him the certainty that his vote cannot be detected among the rest.

"Moreover, for your judicial work and your correspondence, to help you attend to the decrees of the states and the petitions of private individuals, and for all other business which belongs to the administration of the empire, you must have men chosen from the knights to be your helpers and assistants. For all the details of administration will move along more easily in this way, and you will neither err through relying upon your own judgment nor become exhausted through relying upon your own efforts. Grant to every one who wishes to offer you advice, on any matter whatever, the right to speak freely and without fear of the consequences; for if you are pleased with what he says you will be greatly benefited, and if you are not convinced it will do you no harm. Those who win your favorable opinion for their suggestions you should both commend and honor, since you yourself will gain credit through their discoveries; but do not treat with disrespect or criticize those who fail of your approval, since it is their intentions that you should consider, and their lack of success should not call forth your censure. Guard against this same mistake in matters of warfare, also; give way neither to anger against a man for an unintentional misfortune nor to jealousy for a piece of good fortune, that all may zealously and gladly incur danger for your sake, confident that if they meet with any reverse they will not be punished for it and that if they gain success they will not have snares laid for them. There have been many, at any rate, who through fear of jealousy on the part of those in power have chosen to accept defeat rather than achieve success, and as a result have gained safety for themselves while inflicting the loss upon their rulers. Therefore, since you yourself stand to reap the major part of the fruits of both outcomes, the failures as well as the successes, you should never consent to become jealous, nominally of others, but really of yourself.

"Whatever you wish your subjects to think and do, this you should always say and do yourself. In this way you will be educating them, rather than intimidating them through the punishments prescribed by the laws. The former policy inspires zeal, the latter fear; and one finds it easier to imitate that which is good when he sees it actually practiced than to avoid that which is evil when he hears it forbidden by mere words. Be scrupulous yourself in all your actions, showing no mercy to yourself, in the full assurance that all men will forthwith learn of whatever you say or do. For you will live as it were in a theatre in which the spectators are the whole world; and it will not be possible for you to escape detection if you make even the most trivial mistake. Indeed, you will never be alone, but always in the company of many when you do anything; and since the remainder of mankind somehow take the keenest delight in prying into the conduct of their rulers, if once they ascertain that you are recommending to them one course but are yourself taking another, instead of fearing your threats they will imitate your actions.

"You should, of course, supervise the lives of your subjects, but do not scrutinize them with too much rigor. Sit in judgment upon all offences reported to you by others, but act as if you were not even aware of offences concerning which no one has made accusation—except in the case of trespasses against the public interest. These ought, of course, to receive proper attention, even if no one files a charge; but as to private shortcomings, while you should indeed have knowledge of them, in order that you may avoid making a mistake some day by employing an unsuitable person as your agent in some matter, yet you should not go so far as to convict those who are guilty of them. For human nature often tempts men to commit many a violation of the law, and if you were to prosecute such offences rigorously, you would leave unpunished few or none of the offenders; but if in a kindly spirit you mix reasonableness with the prescriptions of the law, you may succeed in bringing the offenders to their senses. The law, you know, though it of necessity makes its punishments severe, cannot always conquer nature. And so in the case of some men, if they think that their sins have not been discovered, or if they have been reproved but not unduly, they reform, either because they feel disgraced at having been found out, or because their self-respect keeps them from falling again; whereas, if they have been publicly exposed and have lost all sense of shame, or have been chastised unduly, they overturn and trample under foot all the conventions of the law and become wholly slaves to the impulses of nature. Therefore it is neither easy to punish offenders invariably in all cases nor is it seemly to allow them in particular cases to flaunt their wickedness openly.

"Now this is the way I advise you to deal with men's shortcomings, with the exception of those persons who are utterly incorrigible; and you should honor their good actions even beyond the merits of the deeds themselves. For you can best induce men to refrain from evil ways by kindness, and to desire better ways by liberality. You need have no fear that you will ever lack either money or the other means of rewarding those who do good deeds. On the contrary, I fancy that those who will deserve your favors will prove far too few, seeing that you hold empire over so vast an extent of land and sea. Nor need you fear that any who have received your benefactions will ever act ungratefully; for nothing so captivates and conciliates a man, be he foreigner or foe, as being not only the object of no wrongs but, in addition, the recipient of kindness.

"As regards your subjects, then, you should so conduct yourself, in my opinion. So far as you yourself are concerned, permit no exceptional or prodigal distinction to be given you, through word or deed, either by the senate or by any one else. For whereas the honor which you confer upon others lends glory to them, yet nothing can be given to you that is greater than what you already possess, and, besides, no little suspicion of insincerity would attach to its giving. No subject, you see, is ever supposed to vote any such distinction to his ruler of his own free will, and since all such honors as a ruler receives he must receive from himself, he not only wins, no commendation for the honor but becomes a laughing stock besides. You must therefore depend upon your good deeds to provide for you any additional splendor. And you should never permit gold or silver images of yourself to be made, for they are not only costly but also invite destruction and last only a brief time; but rather by your benefactions fashion other images in the hearts of your people, images which will never tarnish or perish. Neither should you ever permit the raising of a temple to you; for the expenditure of vast sums of money on such objects is sheer waste. (This money would better be used for necessary objects; for wealth which is really wealth is gathered, not so much by getting largely, as by saving largely.) Then, again, from temples comes no enhancement of one's glory. For it is virtue that raises many men to the level of gods, and no man ever became a god by popular vote. Hence, if you are upright as a man and honorable as a ruler, the whole earth will be your hallowed precinct, all cities your temples, and all men your statues, since within their thoughts you will ever be enshrined and glorified. As for those, on the contrary, who administer their realms in any other way, such honors not only do not lend holiness to them, even though shrines are set apart for them in all their cities, but even bring a greater reproach upon them, becoming, as it were, trophies of their baseness and memorials of their injustice; for the longer these temples last, the longer abides the memory of their infamy. Therefore, if you desire to become in very truth immortal, act as I advise; and, furthermore, do you not only yourself worship the Divine Power everywhere and in every way in accordance with the traditions of our fathers, but compel all others to honor it. Those who attempt to distort our religion with strange rites you should abhor and punish, not merely for the sake of the gods (since if a man despises these he will not pay honor to any other being), but because such men, by bringing in new divinities in place of the old, persuade many to adopt foreign practices, from which spring up conspiracies, factions, and cabals, which are far from profitable to a monarchy. Do not, therefore, permit anybody to be an atheist or a sorcerer. Soothsaying, to be sure, is a necessary art, and you should by all means appoint some men to be diviners and augurs, to whom those will resort who wish to consult them on any matter but there ought to be no workers in magic at all. For such men, by speaking the truth sometimes, but generally falsehood, often encourage a great many to attempt revolutions. The same thing is done also by many who pretend to be philosophers; hence I advise you to be on your guard against them, too. Do not, because you have had experience of good and honorable men like Areius and Athenodorus, believe that all the rest who claim to be philosophers are like them; for infinite harm, both to communities and to individuals, is worked by certain men who but use this profession as a screen.

"Now you should be wholly inclined to peace, so far as your purpose is concerned and your desire for nothing more than you now possess, but as regards your military preparations you should be distinctly warlike, in order that, if possible, no one may either wish or attempt to wrong you, but if he should, that he may be punished easily and instantly. And inasmuch as it is necessary, for these and other reasons, that there shall be persons who are to keep eyes and ears open to anything which affects your imperial position, in order that you may not be unaware of any situation that requires measures of precaution or correction, you should have such agents, but remember that you should not believe absolutely everything they say, but should carefully investigate their reports. For there are many who, from various motives—either because they hate others or covet their possessions, or because they want to do a favor to some one else, or because they have demanded money from some one and have not obtained it—bring false charges against the persons concerned, pretending that they are engaged in sedition or are planning or saying something prejudicial to the ruler. Therefore one ought not to give heed to them forthwith or readily, but rather should prove everything they say. For if you are too slow in placing your trust in one of these men, you will suffer no great harm, but if you are too hasty you may possibly make a mistake which you cannot repair.

"Now it is both right and necessary for you to honor the good who are associated with you, both your freedmen and the rest; for this course will bring you credit and a large measure of security. They should not, however, acquire excessive power, but should all be rigorously kept under discipline, so that you shall never be brought into discredit by them. For everything they do, whether good or ill, will be set to your account, and you will yourself be considered by the world to be of a character akin to the conduct which you do not object to in them.

"As regards the men of power and influence, then, you should not permit them to overreach others, nor yet, on the other hand, to be blackmailed by others; neither let the mere fact that a man possesses power be imputed to him as a crime even though he commit no offence. But in the case of the masses, vindicate them vigorously when they are wronged and be not too ready to give heed to accusations against them; but make the accused persons' actions alone and by themselves the object of your scrutiny, neither harboring suspicion against whatever is superior nor placing your trust in whatever is inferior. Honor those who are diligent and those who by their skill devise something useful, but abhor those who are slothful or who busy themselves with trivial things, in order that your subjects, cleaving to the former by reason of your emoluments and holding themselves aloof from the latter by reason of your punishments, may become, as you desire, more competent in respect to their private affairs and more serviceable in respect to the interests of the state.

"It is well to make the number of disputes on the part of private citizens as few as possible and to render as expeditious as possible their settlement; but it is most important to restrain the rash enterprises of communities, and if they are attempting to coerce others or to go beyond their capacity or means in any undertaking or expenditure, to forbid it, even though in their petitions they invoke blessings upon the empire and pray for your welfare and good fortune. It is important also to eradicate their mutual enmities and rivalries, and not to permit them to assume empty titles or to do anything else that will bring them into strife with others. And all will readily yield obedience to you, both individuals and communities, in this and in every other matter, provided that you make no exceptions whatever to this rule as a concession to anybody; for the uneven application of laws nullifies even those which are well established. Consequently you ought not to allow your subjects even to ask you, in the first place, for what you are not going to give them, but should compel them strenuously to avoid at the outset this very practice of petitioning for what is prohibited.

"So much for these things. And I counsel you never to make full use of your power against your subjects as a body, nor to consider it any curtailment of your power if you do not actually put into effect all the measures you are in a position to enforce but the greater your ability to do all you desire, the more eager you should be to desire in all things only what it is fitting you should desire. Always question your own heart in private whether it is right or not to do a given thing, and what you should do or refrain from doing to cause men to love you, with the purpose of doing the one and avoiding the other. For do not imagine that men will think you are doing your duty if only you hear no word of censure passed upon you; neither must you expect that any man will so abandon his senses as to reproach you openly for anything you do. No one will do this, no matter how flagrantly he has been wronged; on the contrary, many are compelled even to commend their oppressors in public, though they must struggle to keep from showing their resentment. But the ruler must get at the disposition of his subjects, not by what they say, but by what they in all likelihood think.

"These are the things I would have you do—these and others of like nature; for there are many which I must pass over, since it is impossible to include them all in a single discussion. There is, however, one statement which will serve as a summary with respect both to what has been said and to what has been left unsaid: if you of your own accord do all that you would wish another to do if he became your ruler, you will err in nothing and succeed in everything, and in consequence you will find your life most happy and utterly free from danger. For how can men help regarding you with affection as father and savior, when they see that you are orderly and upright in your life, successful in war though inclined to peace; when you refrain from insolence and greed; when you meet them on a footing of equality, do not grow rich yourself while levying tribute on them, do not live in luxury yourself while imposing hardships upon them, are not licentious yourself while reproving licentiousness in them—when, instead of all this, your life is in every way and manner precisely like theirs? Therefore, since you have in your own hands a mighty means of protection—that you never do wrong to another—be of good courage and believe me when I tell you that you will never become the object of hatred or of conspiracy. And since this is so, it follows of necessity that you will also lead a happy life; for what condition is happier, what more blissful, than, possessing virtue, to enjoy all the blessings which men can know and to be able to bestow them upon others?

"Think upon these things and upon all that I have told you, and be persuaded of me, and let not this fortune slip which has chosen you from all mankind and has set you up as their ruler. For, if you prefer the monarchy in fact but fear the title of 'king' as being accursed, you have but to decline this title and still be sole ruler under the appellation of 'Caesar.' And if you require still other epithets, your people will give you that of '*imperator*' as they gave it to your father; and they will pay reverence to your august position by still another term of address, so that you will enjoy fully the reality of the kingship without the odium which attaches to the name of 'king.'"

Tacitus, Scenes From the Early Reign of Tiberius: the Germanicus Affair

28

Publius Grainelius Tacitus (56/7–117) was a native of Gaul. He was famous for his oratorical skills, became a senator under Vespasian, obtained the rank of consul in 97. He wrote Agricola (On the Life of Julius Agricola) *and* Germania (On the Origins and Country of the Germans)*, but his most famous works were his* Histories *(a history of the Julio-Claudian emperors from the death of Augustus to the Death of Nero) and* Annals *(the reigns of the Flavian emperors, Vespasian, Titus and Domitian).*

The selections below, taken from his Histories*, are glimpses into the early reign of Tiberius, the second of the Julio-Claudian emperors. Ruling the Roman Empire was a difficult task under the best of conditions, and Tiberius came to the throne with several handicaps, the most obvious of which was the fact that he was not a Julian and the soldiers gave him their loyalty with reluctance.*

1.1. Rome at the beginning was ruled by kings. Freedom and the consulship were established by Lucius Brutus. Dictatorships were held for a temporary crisis. The power of the decemvirs did not last beyond two years, nor was the consular jurisdiction of the military tribunes of long duration. The despotisms of Cinna and Sulla were brief; the rule of Pompeius and of Crassus soon yielded before Caesar; the arms of Lepidus and Antonius before Augustus; who, when the world was wearied by civil strife,[1] subjected it to empire under the title of "Prince."[2] But the successes and reverses of the old Roman people have been recorded by famous historians; and fine intellects were not wanting to describe the times of Augustus, till growing sycophancy scared them away. The histories of Tiberius, Gaius, Claudius, and Nero, while they were in power, were falsified through terror, and after their death were written under the irritation of a recent hatred. Hence my purpose is to relate a few facts about Augustus—more particularly his last acts, then the reign of Tiberius, and all which follows, without either bitterness or partiality, from any motives to which I am far removed.

Credit: Tacitus, *The Annals* Translation: Brodribb, W. J. (William Jackson), 1829–1905 and Church, Alfred John, 1829–1912

1.2. When after the destruction of Brutus and Cassius there was no longer any army of the Republic, when Pompeius was crushed in Sicily,[3] and when, with Lepidus pushed aside and Antony slain, even the Julian faction had only Caesar left to lead it, then, dropping the title of triumvir, and giving out that he was a Consul, and was satisfied with a tribune's authority for the protection of the people, Augustus won over the soldiers with gifts, the populace with cheap grain, and all men with the sweets of repose, and so grew greater by degrees, while he concentrated in himself the functions of the Senate, the magistrates, and the laws. He was wholly unopposed, for the boldest spirits had fallen in battle, or in the proscription, while the remaining nobles, the readier they were to be slaves, were raised the higher by wealth and promotion, so that, aggrandized by revolution, they preferred the safety of the present to the dangerous past. Nor did the provinces dislike that condition of affairs, for they distrusted the government of the Senate and the people, because of the rivalries between the leading men and the rapacity of the officials, while the protection of the laws was unavailing, as they were continually deranged by violence, intrigue, and finally by corruption.

1.3. Augustus meanwhile, as supports to his despotism, raised to the pontificate and curule aedileship Claudius Marcellus, his sister's son, while a mere stripling, and Marcus Agrippa, of humble birth, a good soldier, and one who had shared his victory, to two consecutive consulships, and as Marcellus soon afterwards died, he also accepted him as his son–in–law. Tiberius Nero and Claudius Drusus, his stepsons, he honored with imperial tides, although his own family was as yet undiminished. For he had admitted the children of Agrippa, Gaius and Lucius, into the house of the Caesars; and before they had yet laid aside the dress of boyhood he had most fervently desired, with an outward show of reluctance, that they should be entitled "princes of the youth," and be consuls-elect. When Agrippa died, and Lucius Caesar as he was on his way to our armies in Spain, and Gaius while returning from Armenia, still suffering from a wound, were prematurely cut off by destiny, or by their step-mother Livia's treachery, Drusus too having long been dead, Tiberius remained alone of the stepsons, and in him everything tended to center. He was adopted as a son, as a colleague in empire and a partner in the tribunician power, and paraded through all the armies, no longer through his mother's secret intrigues, but at her open suggestion. For she had gained such a hold on the aged Augustus that he drove out as an exile into the island of Planasia, his only grandson, Agrippa Postumus, who, though devoid of worthy qualities, and having only the brute courage of physical strength, had not been convicted of any gross offence. And yet Augustus had appointed Germanicus, Drusus' offspring, to the command

---

1. The principal dates for the opening sentences are 753 B.C. Foundation of Rome; 509 B.C. Consulate of L. Brutus; 451–450 B.C. (with part of 449 B.C.) Decemvirate; 445 B.C. Institution of *Tribuni militum consulari potesstate* (found with little interruption from 408 to 367 B.C.); 87–84 B.C. Four Consulates of Cinna; 82–79 B.C. Dictatorship of Sulla; 53 B.C. Battle of Carrhae and death of Crassus: 48 B.C. Battle of Pharsalia and death of Pompey (in Egypt): 36 B.C. Lepidus divested of his powers by Octavian; 31 B.C. Defeat of Antony at Actium; 27 B.C. Octavian receives the title of Augustus.

2. This rendering of the Latin *princeps* is generally so convenient as to be inevitable, but the reader should be careful to strip the English word of its monarchical connotation. To Roman ears it simply meant "first citizen," or "first among equals."

3. Sextus Pompey (younger son of Gnaeus Pompey), defeated by Agrippa Augustus' general) in a naval battle off Pelorum, Sicily, in 36 B.C.

of eight legions on the Rhine, and required Tiberius to adopt him, although Tiberius had a son, now a young man, in his house; but he did it that he might have several safeguards to rest on. He had no war at the time on his hands except against the Germans, which was rather to wipe out the disgrace of the loss of Quintilius Varus[4] and his army than out of an ambition to extend the empire, or for any adequate recompense. At home all was tranquil, and there were magistrates with the same titles; there was a younger generation, sprung up since the victory of Actium, and even many of the older men had been born during the civil wars. How few were left who had seen the republic!

1.4. Thus the State had been revolutionized, and there was not a vestige left of the old sound morality. Stripped of equality, all looked up to the commands of a sovereign without the least apprehension for the present, while Augustus in the vigor of life, could maintain his own position, that of his house, and the general tranquility. When in advanced old age, he was worn out by a sickly frame, and the end was near and new prospects opened, a few spoke in vain of the blessings of freedom, but most people dreaded and some longed for war. The popular gossip of the large majority fastened itself variously on their future masters. "Agrippa was savage, and had been exasperated by insult, and neither from age nor experience in affairs was equal to so great a burden. Tiberius Nero was of mature years, and had established his fame in war, but he had the old arrogance inbred in the Claudian family, and many symptoms of a cruel temper, though they were repressed, now and then broke out. He had also from earliest infancy been reared in an imperial house; consulships and triumphs had been heaped on him in his younger days; even in the years which, on the pretext of seclusion he spent in exile at Rhodes, he had had no thoughts but of wrath, hypocrisy, and secret sensuality. There was his mother too with a woman's caprice. They must, it seemed, be subject to a female and to two striplings besides, who for a while would burden, and some day rend asunder the State."

1.5. While these and like topics were discussed, the infirmities of Augustus increased, and some suspected guilt on his wife's part. For a rumor had gone abroad that a few months before he had sailed to Planasia on a visit to Agrippa, with the knowledge of some chosen friends, and with one companion, Fabius Maximus; that many tears were shed on both sides, with expressions of affection, and that thus there was a hope of the young man being restored to the home of his grandfather. This, it was said, Maximus had divulged to his wife Marcia, she again to Livia. All was known to Caesar, and when Maximus soon afterwards died, by a death some thought to be self-inflicted, there were heard at his funeral wailings from Marcia, in which she reproached herself for having been the cause of her husband's destruction. Whatever the fact was, Tiberius as he was just entering Illyricum was summoned home by an urgent letter from his mother, and it has not been thoroughly ascertained whether at the city of Nola he found Augustus still breathing or quite lifeless. For Livia had surrounded the house and its approaches with a strict watch, and favorable bulletins were published from time to time, till, provision having been made for the demands of the crisis, one and the same report told men that Augustus was dead and that Tiberius Nero was master of the State.[5]

---

4. Husband of a great-niece of Augustus, destroyed, with three legions, by the Germans in the forest of Westphalia, 9 A.D.

5. August 19, 14 A.D.

1.6. The first crime of the new reign was the murder of Postumus Agrippa. Though he was surprised and unarmed, a centurion of the firmest resolution dispatched him with difficulty. Tiberius gave no explanation of the matter to the Senate; he pretended that there were directions from his father ordering the tribune in charge of the prisoner not to delay the slaughter of Agrippa, whenever he should himself have breathed his last. Beyond a doubt, Augustus had often complained of the young man's character, and had thus succeeded in obtaining the sanction of a decree of the Senate for his banishment. But he never was hard-hearted enough to destroy any of his kinsfolk, nor was it credible that death was to be the sentence of the grandson in order that the stepson might feel secure. It was more probable that Tiberius and Livia, the one from fear, the other from a stepmother's enmity, hurried on the destruction of a youth whom they suspected and hated. When the centurion reported, according to military custom, that he had executed the command, Tiberius replied that he had not given the command, and that the act must be justified to the Senate.

As soon as Sallustius Crispus who shared the secret (he had, in fact, sent the written order to the tribune) knew this, fearing that the charge would be shifted on himself, and that his peril would be the same whether he uttered fiction or truth, he advised Livia not to divulge the secrets of her house or the counsels of friends, or any services performed by the soldiers, nor to let Tiberius weaken the strength of imperial power by referring everything to the Senate, for "the condition," he said, "of holding empire is that an account cannot be balanced unless it be rendered to one person."

1.7. Meanwhile at Rome people plunged into slavery—consuls, senators, knights. The higher a man's rank, the more eager his hypocrisy, and his looks the more carefully studied, so as neither to betray joy at the decease of one emperor nor sorrow at the rise of another, while he mingled delight and lamentations with his flattery. Sextus Pompeius and Sextus Apuleius, the consuls, were the first to swear allegiance to Tiberius Caesar, and in their presence the oath was taken by Seius Strabo and Gaius Turranius, respectively the commander of the praetorian cohorts and the superintendent of the grain supplies. Then the Senate, the soldiers and the people did the same. For Tiberius would inaugurate everything with the consuls, as though the ancient constitution remained, and he hesitated about being emperor. Even the proclamation by which he summoned the senators to their chamber, he issued merely with the title of Tribune, which he had received under Augustus. The wording of the proclamation was brief, and in a very modest tone. "He would," it said, "provide for the honors due to his father, and not leave the lifeless body, and this was the only public duty he now claimed."

As soon, however, as Augustus was dead, he had given the watchword to the praetorian cohorts, as commander-in-chief. He had the guard under arms, with all the other adjuncts of a court; soldiers attended him to the forum; soldiers went with him to the Senate House. He sent letters to the different armies, as though supreme power was now his, and showed hesitation only when he spoke in the Senate. His chief motive was fear that Germanicus, who had at his disposal so many legions, such vast auxiliary forces of the allies, and such wonderful popularity,[6] might prefer the possession to the expectation of empire. He looked also at public opinion, wishing to

---

6. Germanicus was descended from Augustus and was a Julian, while Tiberius was a Claudian with no Julian ancestry, only the adopted son of Augustus.

have the credit of having been called and elected by the State rather than of having crept into power through the intrigues of a wife and a senile act of adoption. It was subsequently understood that he assumed a wavering attitude, to test likewise the temper of the nobles. For he would twist a word or a look into a crime and treasure it up in his memory.

1.8. On the first day of the Senate he allowed nothing to be discussed but the funeral of Augustus, whose will, which was brought in by the Vestal Virgins,[7] named as his heirs Tiberius and Livia. The latter was to be admitted into the Julian family with the name of Augusta; next in expectation were the grand and great-grandchildren. In the third place, he had named the chief men of the State, most of whom he hated, simply out of ostentation and to win credit with posterity. His legacies were not beyond the scale of a private citizen, except a bequest of forty-three million five hundred thousand sesterces "to the people and populace of Rome," of one thousand to every praetorian soldier, and of three hundred to every man in the legionary cohorts[8] composed of Roman citizens.

Next followed a deliberation about funeral honors. Of these the most imposing were thought fitting. The procession was to be conducted through "the gate of triumph," on the motion of Gallus Asinius; the titles of the laws passed, the names of the nations conquered by Augustus were to be borne in front, on that of Lucius Arruntius. Messala Valerius further proposed that the oath of allegiance to Tiberius should be yearly renewed, and when Tiberius asked him whether it was at his bidding that he had brought forward this motion, he replied that he had proposed it spontaneously, and that in whatever concerned the State he would use only his own discretion, even at the risk of offending. This was the only style of adulation which yet remained. The Senators unanimously exclaimed that the body ought to be borne on their shoulders to the funeral pile. The emperor left the point to them with disdainful moderation, he then admonished the people by a proclamation not to indulge in that tumultuous enthusiasm which had distracted the funeral of the Divine Julius, or express a wish that Augustus should be burnt in the Forum instead of in his appointed resting-place in the Campus Martius.[9]

On the day of the funeral soldiers stood round as a guard, amid much ridicule from those who had either themselves witnessed or who had heard from their parents of the famous day when slavery was still something fresh, and freedom had been re-sought in vain, when the slaying of Caesar, the Dictator, seemed to some the vilest, to others, the most glorious of deeds. "Now," they said, "an aged sovereign, whose power had lasted long, who had provided his heirs with abundant means to coerce the State, requires forsooth the defense of soldiers that his burial may be undisturbed."

1.9. Then followed much talk about Augustus himself, and many expressed an idle wonder that the same day marked the beginning of his assumption of empire and the close of his life, and, again, that he had ended his days at Nola in the same house and room as his father Octavius. People extolled too the number of his consulships, in which he had equaled Valerius Corvus and

---

7. Wills and other important legal documents were traditionally deposited with the Vestal Virgins for safe keeping.

8. Cohorts (normally of Italian volunteers) attached to no particular legion, but otherwise on a parity with the legionaries. Over thirty of them have been traced in the imperial age.

9. The Mausoleum, which he had built in his sixth consulate (28 B.C.) in the northern part of the Campus Martius, between the Flaminian Road and the Tiber.

Gaius Marius combined,[10] the continuance for thirty-seven years of the tribunician power, the title of Imperator twenty-one times earned, and his other honors which had either frequently repeated or were wholly new. Sensible men, however, spoke variously of his life with praise and censure. Some said "that dutiful feeling towards a father, and the necessities of the State in which laws had then no place, drove him into civil war, which can neither be planned nor conducted on any right principles. He had often yielded to Antony, while he was taking vengeance on his father's murderers, often also to Lepidus. When the latter sank into feeble senility and the former had been ruined by his profligacy, the only remedy for his distracted country was the rule of a single man. Yet the State had been organized under the name neither of a kingdom nor a dictatorship, but under that of a prince. The ocean and remote rivers were the boundaries of the empire; the legions, provinces, fleets, all things were linked together; there was law for the citizens; there was respect shown to the allies. The capital had been embellished on a grand scale; only in a few instances had he resorted to force, simply to secure general tranquility."

1.10. It was said, on the other hand, "that filial duty and State necessity were merely assumed as a mask. It was really from a lust of sovereignty that he had excited the veterans by bribery, had, when a young man and a subject, raised an army, seduced the legions of a consul,[11] and feigned an attachment to the faction of Pompeius. Then, when by a decree of the Senate he had usurped the high functions and authority of Praetor when Hirtius and Pansa were slain[12]— whether they were destroyed by the enemy, or Pansa by poison infused into a wound, Hirtius by his own soldiers and Caesar's treacherous machinations—·he at once possessed himself of both their armies, wrested the consulate from a reluctant Senate, and turned against the State the arms with which he had been entrusted against Antony. Citizens were proscribed, lands assigned,[13] without so much as the approval of those who executed these deeds. Even granting that the deaths of Cassius and of the Bruti were sacrifices to a hereditary enmity (though duty requires us to waive private feuds for the sake of the public welfare), still Pompeius had been deluded by the phantom of peace,[14] and Lepidus by the mask of friendship. Subsequently, Antony had been lured on by the treaties of Tarentum and Brundisium,[15] and by his marriage with the sister, and paid by his death the penalty of a treacherous alliance. No doubt, there was peace after all this, but it was a peace stained with blood; there were the disasters of Lollius[16] and Varus, the murders at Rome of the Varro, Egnatius, and Iullus."[17]

---

10. Thirteen (=6+7)

11. The legions of Antony in 44 B.C.

12. Mutina, 44 B.C. "The rumor gained currency that both had perished by his agency: so that with Antony in flight and the commonwealth bereft of its consuls, he might as sole victor seize the command of three armies" (Suetonius, Augustus, 11).

13. To the soldiers.

14. The treaty of Misenum between Octavian, Antony, and Sextus Pompey (39 B.C.); not kept, and followed the next year by war.

15. The Treaty of Brundisium (practically dividing the Roman world between Octavian and Antony), 40 B.C.: Tarentine, 37 B.C.

16. Defeated with the loss of an eagle in Germany, 16 B.C.

17. Varro Murena and Egnatius Rufus, executed for conspiracy in 23 B.C. and 19 B.C. respectively; Iullus Antonius, son of the triumvir, compelled to suicide in 2 B.C. for adultery with Julia.

The domestic life too of Augustus was not spared. "Nero's wife had been taken from him, and there had been the farce of consulting the pontiffs, whether, with a child conceived and not yet born, she could properly marry.[18] There were the excesses of Quintus Tedius and Vedius Pollio;[19] last of all, there was Livia, a curse to the State as a mother, a curse to the house of the Caesars as a stepmother.[20] No honor was left for the gods, when Augustus chose to be himself worshipped with temples and statues, like those of the deities, and with flamens and priests. He had not even adopted Tiberius as his successor out of affection or any regard to the State, but, having thoroughly seen his arrogant and savage temper, he had sought glory for himself by a contrast of extreme wickedness." For, in fact, Augustus, a few years before, when he was a second time asking from the Senate the tribunician power for Tiberius, though his speech was complimentary, had thrown out certain hints as to his manners, style, and habits of life, which he meant as reproaches, while he seemed to excuse. However, when his obsequies had been duly performed, a temple with a religious ritual was decreed him.

1.11. After this all prayers were addressed to Tiberius. He, on his part, urged various considerations, the greatness of the empire, his distrust of himself. "Only," he said, "the intellect of the Divine Augustus was equal to such a burden. Called as he had been by him to share his anxieties, he had learnt by experience how exposed to fortune's caprices was the task of universal rule. Consequently, in a state which had the support of so many great men, they should not put everything on one man, as many, by uniting their efforts would more easily discharge public functions." There was more grand sentiment than good faith in such words. Tiberius's language even in matters which he did not care to conceal, either from nature or habit, was always hesitating and obscure, and now that he was struggling to hide his feelings completely, it was all the more involved in uncertainty and doubt. The Senators, however, whose only fear was lest they might seem to understand him, burst into complaints, tears, and prayers. They raised their hands to the gods, to the statue of Augustus, and to the knees of Tiberius, when he ordered a document[21] to be produced and read. This contained a description of the resources of the State, of the number of citizens and allies under arms, of the fleets, subject kingdoms, provinces, taxes, direct and indirect, necessary expenses and customary bounties. All these details Augustus had written with his own hand, and had added a clause, that the empire should be confined to its present limits, either from fear or out of jealousy.

1.12. Meantime, while the Senate stooped to the most abject supplication, Tiberius happened to say that although he was not equal to the whole burden of the State, yet he would undertake the charge of whatever part of it might be entrusted to him. Thereupon Asinius Gallus said, "I ask you, Caesar, what part of the State you wish to have entrusted to you?" Confounded by the

---

18. Livia's first husband was Tiberius Claudius Nero. She was pregnant with Tiberius at the time she divorced Nero and married Augustus.

19. A Roman equestrian of obscure origins and great wealth, said to have thrown slaves to his lampreys: a friend of Augustus.

20. Because, in the one capacity, she had borne Tiberius, and, in the other, was credited (by rumor only) with procuring the deaths of Gaius and Lucius Caesar.

21. One of the three left by Augustus: the first dealing with his own funeral arrangements; the second (known in part from the *Monumentum Ancyranum*), a record of his achievements; the third (meant here), a *breviarium totius imperii* (Suetonius, *Augustus*, 101)

sudden inquiry he was silent for a few moments; then, recovering his presence of mind, he replied that it would by no means become his modesty to choose or to avoid in a case where he would prefer to be wholly excused. Then Gallus again, who had inferred anger from his looks, said that the question had not been asked with the intention of dividing what could not be separated, but to convince him by his own admission that the body of the State was one, and must be directed by a single mind. He further spoke in praise of Augustus, and reminded Tiberius himself of his victories, and of his admirable deeds for many years as a civilian. Still, he did not thereby soften the emperor's resentment, for he had long been detested from an impression that, as he had married Vipsania, daughter of Marcus Agrippa, who had once been the wife of Tiberius, he aspired to be more than a citizen, and kept up the arrogant tone of his father, Asinius Pollio.

1.13. Next, Lucius Arruntius, who differed but little from the speech of Gallus, gave like offence, though Tiberius had no old grudge against him, but simply mistrusted him, because he was rich and daring, had brilliant accomplishments, and corresponding popularity. For Augustus, when in his last conversations he was discussing who would refuse the highest place, though sufficiently capable, who would aspire to it without being equal to it, and who would unite both the ability and ambition, had described Marcus Lepidus as able but contemptuously indifferent, Gallus Asinius as ambitious and incapable, Lucius Arruntius as not unworthy of it, and, should the chance be given him, sure to make the venture. About the two first there is a general agreement, but instead of Arruntius some have mentioned Cneius Piso, and all these men, except Lepidus, were soon afterwards destroyed by various charges through the contrivance of Tiberius.[22] Quintus Haterius too and Mamercus Scaurus ruffled his suspicious temper, Haterius by having said, "How long, Caesar, will you suffer the State to be without a head?" Scaurus by the remark that there was a hope that the Senate's prayers would not be fruitless, seeing that he had not used his right as Tribune to veto the motion of the Consuls. Tiberius instantly broke out into invective against Haterius; Scaurus, with whom he was far more deeply displeased, he passed over in silence. Wearied at last by the assembly's clamorous importunity and the urgent demands of individual Senators, he gave way by degrees, not admitting that he undertook empire, but yet ceasing to refuse it and to be entreated. It is known that Haterius having entered the palace to ask pardon, and thrown himself at the knees of Tiberius as he was walking, was almost killed by the soldiers, because Tiberius fell forward, accidentally or from being entangled by the suppliant's hands. Yet the peril of so great a man did not make him relent, till Haterius went with entreaties to Augusta, and was saved by her very earnest intercessions.

1.14. Great too was the Senate's sycophancy to Augusta. Some would have her styled "parent"; others "mother of the country," and a majority proposed that to the name of Caesar should be added "son of Julia." The emperor repeatedly asserted that there must be a limit to the honors paid to women, and that he would observe similar moderation in those bestowed on himself, but annoyed at the invidious proposal, and indeed regarding a woman's elevation as a slight to himself, he would not allow so much as a lictor to be assigned her, and forbade the erection of an altar in memory of her adoption,[23] and any like distinction. But for Germanicus Caesar he asked

---

22. This assertion is hardly born out by Tacitus himself. In the case of Piso, it runs counter to his whole narrative; in that of Arruntius, he half acquits Tiberius in Book 4, 47; while thirteen years were to elapse before the arrest of Gallus, and sixteen before his execution.

23. I.e. her adoption into the Julian family as provided in Augustus' will.

proconsular powers,[24] and envoys were dispatched to confer them on him, and also to express sympathy with his grief at the death of Augustus. The same request was not made for Drusus, because he was consul elect and present at Rome.[25] Twelve candidates were named for the praetorship, the number which Augustus had handed down, and when the Senate urged Tiberius to increase it, he bound himself by an oath not to exceed it.

1.15. It was then for the first time that the elections were transferred from the Campus Martius to the Senate. For up to that day, though the most important rested with the emperor's choice, some were settled by the partialities of the tribes. Nor did the people complain of having the right taken from them, except in mere idle talk, and the Senate, being now released from the necessity of bribery and of degrading solicitations, gladly upheld the change, Tiberius confining himself to the recommendation of only four candidates who were to be nominated without rejection or canvass. Meanwhile the tribunes of the people asked leave to exhibit at their own expense games to be named after Augustus and added to the Calendar as the Augustales. Money was, however, voted from the treasury, and though the use of the triumphal robe in the circus was prescribed, it was not allowed them to ride in a chariot. Soon the annual celebration was transferred to the praetor, to whose lot fell the administration of justice between citizens and foreigners.

1.33. Meantime Germanicus, while, as I have related, he was collecting the taxes of Gaul, received news of the death of Augustus. He was married to the granddaughter of Augustus, Agrippina, by whom he had several children, and though he was himself the son of Drusus, brother of Tiberius, and grandson of Augusta, he was troubled by the secret hatred of his uncle and grandmother, the motives for which were the more venomous because unjust. For the memory of Drusus was held in honor by the Roman people, and they believed that had he obtained empire, he would have restored freedom. Hence they regarded Germanicus with favor and with the same hope. He was indeed a young man of unassuming temper, and of wonderful kindliness, contrasting strongly with the proud and mysterious reserve that marked the conversation and the features of Tiberius. Then, there were feminine jealousies, Livia feeling a stepmother's bitterness towards Agrippina, and Agrippina herself too being rather excitable, only her purity and love of her husband gave a right direction to her otherwise imperious disposition.

1.34. But the nearer Germanicus was to the highest hope, the more laboriously did he exert himself for Tiberius, and he made the neighboring Sequani and all the Belgic states swear obedience to him. On hearing of the mutiny in the legions, he instantly went to the spot, and met them outside the camp, eyes fixed on the ground, and seemingly repentant. As soon as he entered the entrenchments, confused murmurs became audible. Some men, seizing his hand under pretence of kissing it, thrust his fingers into their mouths, that he might touch their toothless gums; others showed him their limbs bowed with age. He ordered the throng which stood near him, as it seemed a promiscuous gathering, to separate itself into its military companies. They replied that they would hear better as they were. The standards were then to be advanced, so that thus at least the cohorts might be distinguished. The soldiers obeyed reluctantly. Then beginning with

---

24. Not the ordinary proconsular *imperium* of the governor of a senatorial province, but a renewal of the imperium *maius* in Gaul and Germany, which he had held for three years.

25. For as consul designate, and present, he would have been placed in the invidious position of voting first on the question of his own preferment.

a reverent mention of Augustus, he passed on to the victories and triumphs of Tiberius, dwelling with especial praise on his glorious achievements with those legions in Germany.[26] Next, he extolled the unity of Italy, the loyalty of Gaul, the entire absence of turbulence or strife. He was heard in silence or with but a slight murmur.

1.35. As soon as he touched on the mutiny and asked what had become of soldierly obedience, of the glory of ancient discipline, whither they had driven their tribunes and centurions, they all bared their bodies and taunted him with the scars of their wounds and the marks of the lash. And then with confused exclamations they spoke bitterly of the prices of exemptions, of their scanty pay, of the severity of their tasks, with special mention of the entrenching, the parapet making, the conveyance of fodder, building-timber, firewood, and whatever else had to be procured from necessity, or as a check on idleness in the camp. The fiercest clamor arose from the veteran soldiers, who, as they counted their thirty campaigns or more, implored him to relieve worn-out men, and not let them die under the same hardships, but have an end of such harassing service, and repose without beggary. Some even claimed the legacy of the Divine Augustus, with words of good omen for Germanicus,[27] and, should he wish for empire, they showed themselves abundantly willing. Thereupon, as though he were contracting the pollution of guilt, he leapt impetuously from the tribunal. The men opposed his departure with their weapons, threatening him repeatedly if he would not go back. But Germanicus protesting that he would die rather than cast off his loyalty, plucked his sword from his side, raised it aloft and was plunging it into his breast, when those nearest him seized his hand and held it by force. The remotest and most densely crowded part of the throng, and, what almost passes belief, some, who came close up to him, urged him to strike the blow, and a soldier, by name Calusidius, offered him a drawn sword, saying that it was sharper than his own. Even in their fury, this seemed to them a savage act and one of evil precedent, and there was a pause during which Caesar's friends hurried him into his tent.

1.36. There they took counsel how to heal matters. For news was also brought that the soldiers were preparing the dispatch of envoys who were to draw the upper army into their cause; that the capital of the Ubii[28] was marked out for destruction, and that hands with the stain of plunder on them would soon be daring enough for the pillage of Gaul. The alarm was heightened by the knowledge that the enemy was aware of the Roman mutiny, and would certainly attack if the Rhine bank were undefended. Yet if the auxiliary troops and allies were to be armed against the retiring legions, civil war was in fact begun. Severity would be dangerous; profuse liberality would be scandalous. Whether all or nothing were conceded to the soldiery, the State was equally in jeopardy. Accordingly, having weighed their plans one against each other, they decided that a letter should be written in the prince's name, to the effect that full discharge was granted to those who had served in twenty campaigns; that there was a conditional release for those who had served sixteen, and that they were to be retained under a standard with immunity from everything except actually keeping off the enemy; that the legacies which they had asked, were to be paid and doubled.

---

26. Tiberius—the foremost Roman general after the death of Augustus—operated against the Germans, first in 9–8 B.C., then in A.D. 4–5, and finally, after the Varian disaster, in A.D. 9–11.
27. The implication is that they considered Germanicus the lawful heir.
28. Cologne.

1.37. The soldiers perceived that all this was invented for the occasion, and instantly pressed their demands. The discharge from service was quickly arranged by the tribunes. Payment was put off till they reached their respective winter quarters. The men of the fifth and twenty-first legions refused to go till in the summer-camp where they stood the money was made up out of the purses of Germanicus himself and his friends, and paid in full. The first and twentieth legions were led back by their officer Caecina to the canton of the Ubii, marching in disgrace, since sums of money which had been extorted from the general were carried among the eagles and standards. Germanicus went to the Upper Army, and the second, thirteenth, and sixteenth legions, without any delay, accepted from him the oath of allegiance. The fourteenth hesitated a little, but their money and the discharge were offered even without their demanding it.

1.38. Meanwhile there was an outbreak among the Chauci, begun by some veterans of the mutinous legions on garrison duty. They were quelled for a time by the instant execution of two soldiers. Such was the order of Mennius, the camp prefect, more as a salutary warning than as a legal act. Then, when the commotion increased, he fled and having been discovered, as his hiding place was now unsafe, he borrowed a resource from audacity. "It was not," he told them, "the camp prefect, it was Germanicus, their general, it was Tiberius, their emperor, whom they were insulting." At the same moment, overawing all resistance, he seized the standard, faced round towards the river bank, and exclaiming that whoever left the ranks, he would hold as a deserter, he led them back into their winter quarters, disaffected indeed, but cowed.

1.39. Meanwhile envoys from the Senate had an interview with Germanicus, who had now returned, at the Altar of the Ubii.[29] Two legions, the first and twentieth, with veterans discharged and serving under a standard, were there in winter quarters. In the bewilderment of terror and conscious guilt they were penetrated by an apprehension that persons had come at the Senate's orders to cancel the concessions they had extorted by mutiny. And as it is the way with a mob to fix any charge, however groundless, on some particular person, they reproached Manatius Plancus, an ex–consul and the chief envoy, with being the author of the Senate's decree. At midnight they began to demand the imperial standard kept in Germanicus's quarters,[30] and having rushed together to the entrance, burst the door, dragged Caesar from his bed, and forced him by menaces of death to give up the standard. Then roaming through the camp streets, they met the envoys, who on hearing of the tumult were hastening to Germanicus. They loaded them with insults, and were on the point of murdering them, Plancus especially, whose high rank had deterred him from flight. In his peril he found safety only in the camp of the first legion. There clasping the standards and the eagle, he sought to protect himself under their sanctity.[31] And had not the eagle-bearer, Calpurnius, saved him from the worst violence, the blood of an envoy of the Roman people, an occurrence rare even among our foes, would in a Roman camp have stained the altars of the gods. At last, with the light of day, when the general and the soldiers and the whole affair were clearly recognized, Germanicus entered the camp, ordered Plancus

---

29. The deputation is that sent out to confer the *proconsulare imperium* (chapter 1.14 above): the Alter was at Cologne, dedicated to Augustus, and serving apparently as a center of the imperial cult to the whole of Roman Germany.

30. The veterans, like Germanicus, are presumably quartered not in camp, but in the town. They demand their *vexillum* as the symbol and guarantee of their status, in case the motives of the deputation should prove sinister.

31. The standards and eagles were sacrosanct and adored as such.

to be conducted to him, and received him on the tribunal. He then upbraided them with their fatal infatuation, revived not so much by the anger of the soldiers as by that of heaven, and explained the reasons of the envoys' arrival. On the rights of ambassadors, on the dreadful and undeserved peril of Plancus, and also on the disgrace into which the legion had brought itself, he dwelt with the eloquence of pity, and while the throng was confounded rather than appeased, he dismissed the envoys with an escort of auxiliary cavalry.

1.40. Amid the alarm all condemned Germanicus for not going to the Upper Army, where he might find obedience and help against the rebels. "Enough and more than enough blunders," they said, "had been made by granting discharges and money, indeed, by conciliatory measures. Even if Germanicus held his own life cheap, why should he keep a little son and a pregnant wife among madmen who outraged every human right? Let these, at least, be restored safely to their grandsire and to the State." When his wife spurned the notion, protesting that she was a descendant of the Divine Augustus and could face peril with no degenerate spirit, he at last embraced her and the son of their love with many tears, and after long delay compelled her to depart. Slowly moved along a pitiable procession of women, a general's fugitive wife with a little son in her bosom, her friends' wives weeping round her, as with her they were dragging themselves from the camp. Not less sorrowful were those who remained.

1.41. There was no appearance of the triumphant general about Germanicus, and he seemed to be in a conquered city rather than in his own camp, while groans and wailings attracted the ears and looks even of the soldiers. They came out of their tents, asking "what was that mournful sound? What meant the sad sight? Here were ladies of rank, not a centurion to escort them, not a soldier, no sign of a prince's wife, none of the usual retinue. Could they be going to the Treveri,[32] to be subjects of the foreigner?" Then they felt shame and pity, and remembered his father Agrippa, her grandfather Augustus, her father-in-law Drusus, her own glory as a mother of children, her noble purity. And there was her little child too, born in the camp, brought up amid the tents of the legions, whom they used to call in soldiers' fashion, Caligula,[33] because he often wore the shoe so called, to win the men's goodwill. But nothing moved them so much as jealousy towards the Treveri. They entreated, stopped the way, that Agrippina might return and remain, some running to meet her, while most of them went back to Germanicus. He, with a grief and anger that were yet fresh, thus began to address the throng around him:

1.42. "Neither wife nor son are dearer to me than my father and the State. But he will surely have the protection of his own majesty, the empire of Rome that of our other armies. My wife and children whom, were it a question of your glory, I would willingly expose to destruction, I now remove to a distance from your fury, so that whatever wickedness is thereby threatened, may be expiated by my blood only, and that you may not be made more guilty by the slaughter of a great-grandson of Augustus, and the murder of a daughter-in-law of Tiberius. For what have you not dared, what have you not profaned during these days? What name shall I give to this gathering? Am I to call you soldiers, you who have beset with entrenchments and arms your

32. A Gallic tribe whose capital was modern Trèves.
33. "Little *caliga*"—the bob-nailed military (and rustic) boot, not worn by officers above the rank of centurion, and therefore regarded by the private soldier as typifying his vocation. The tradition that Caligula was actually born in camp is refuted by Suetonius, *Caligula*, 8.

general's son, or citizens, when you have trampled under foot the authority of the Senate? Even the rights of public enemies, the sacred character of the ambassador, and the law of nations have been violated by you. The Divine Julius once quelled an army's mutiny with a single word by calling those who were renouncing their military obedience 'citizens.'[34] The Divine Augustus cowed the legions who had fought at Actium with one look of his face.[35] Though I am not yet what they were, still, descended as I am from them, it would be a strange and unworthy thing should I be spurned by the soldiery of Spain or Syria. First and twentieth legions,[36] you who received your standards from Tiberius, you, men of the twentieth who have shared with me so many battles and have been enriched with so many rewards, is not this a fine gratitude with which you are repaying your general? Are these the tidings which I shall have to carry to my father when he hears only joyful intelligence from our other provinces, that his own recruits, his own veterans are not satisfied with discharge or pay; that here only centurions are murdered, tribunes driven away, envoys imprisoned, camps and rivers stained with blood, while I am myself dragging on a precarious existence amid those who hate me?

1.43. "Why, on the first day of our meeting, why did you, my friends, wrest from me, in your blindness, the steel which I was preparing to plunge into my breast? Better and more loving was the act of the man who offered me the sword. At any rate I should have perished before I was as yet conscious of all the disgraces of my army, while you would have chosen a general who though he might allow my death to pass unpunished would avenge the death of Varus and his three legions. Never indeed may heaven suffer the Belgae, though they proffer their aid, to have the glory and honor of having rescued the name of Rome and quelled the tribes of Germany. It is your spirit, Divine Augustus, now received into heaven, your image, father Drusus, and the remembrance of you, which, with these same soldiers who are now stimulated by shame and ambition, should wipe out this blot and turn the wrath of civil strife to the destruction of the foe. You too, in whose faces and in whose hearts I perceive a change, if only you restore to the Senate their envoys, to the emperor his due allegiance, to myself my wife and son, do you stand aloof from pollution and separate the mutinous from among you. This will be a pledge of your repentance, a guarantee of your loyalty."

1.44. Thereupon, as suppliants confessing that his reproaches were true, they implored him to punish the guilty, pardon those who had erred, and lead them against the enemy. And he was to recall his wife, to let the nursling of the legions return and not be handed over as a hostage to the Gauls. As to Agrippina's return, he made the excuse of her approaching confinement[37] and of winter. His son, he said, would come, and the rest they might settle themselves. Away they hurried hither and thither, altered men, and dragged the chief mutineers in chains to Gaius Caetronius commander of the first legion, who tried and punished them one by one in the following fashion. In front of the throng stood the legions with drawn swords. Each accused man

---

34. "Citizens," as opposed to soldiers: the occasion was the mutiny of the tenth legion in 47 B.C. a dubious story runs that long afterwards Severus Alexander repeated the device at Antioch.

35. At Brindisi, in the winter of 30 B.C. But Germanicus (or Tacitus) seems to embellish the facts.

36. The scene is in the camp of the first legion, to which Germanicus addresses his direct appeal. The twentieth, one of those raised, possibly by Tiberius himself, to cope with the great Pannonian revolt of A.D. 6, is more remote in thought.

37. The child, in all probability, was still-born.

was on a raised platform and was pointed out by a tribune. If they shouted out that he was guilty, he was thrown headlong and cut to pieces. The soldiers gloated over the bloodshed as though it gave them absolution. Nor did Caesar check them, seeing that without any order from himself the same men were responsible for all the cruelty and all the odium of the deed. The example was followed by the veterans, who were soon afterwards sent into Raetia,[38] nominally to defend the province against a threatened invasion of the Suevi[39] but really that they might tear themselves from a camp stamped with the horror of a dreadful remedy no less than with the memory of guilt. Then the general revised the list of centurions. Each, at his summons, stated his name, his rank, his birthplace, the number of his campaigns, what brave deeds he had done in battle, his military rewards, if any. If the tribunes and the legion commended his energy and good behavior, he retained his rank; where they unanimously charged him with rapacity or cruelty, he was dismissed the service.

1.45. Quiet being thus restored for the present, a no less formidable difficulty remained through the turbulence of the fifth and twenty-first legions, who were in winter quarters sixty miles away at Old Camp, as the place was called. These, in fact, had been the first to begin the mutiny, and the most atrocious deeds had been committed by their hands. Undaunted by the punishment of their comrades, and unmoved by their contrition, they still retained their resentment. Caesar accordingly proposed to send an armed fleet with some of our allies down the Rhine, resolved to make war on them should they reject his authority.

1.46. At Rome, meanwhile, when the result of affairs in Illyricum was not yet known, and men had heard of the commotion among the German legions, the citizens in alarm reproached Tiberius for the hypocritical irresolution with which he was befooling the senate and the people, feeble and disarmed as they were, while the soldiery were all the time in revolt, and could not be quelled by the yet imperfectly matured authority of two striplings. "He ought to have gone himself and confronted with his imperial majesty those who would have soon yielded, when they once saw a sovereign of long experience, who was the supreme dispenser of rigor or of bounty. Could Augustus, with the feebleness of age on him, so often visit Germany, and is Tiberius, in the vigor of life,[40] to sit in the Senate and criticize its members' words? He had taken good care that there should be slavery at Rome; he should now apply some soothing medicine to the spirit of soldiers, that they might be willing to endure peace."

1.47. Notwithstanding these remonstrances, it was the inflexible purpose of Tiberius not to quit the headquarters of empire or to imperil himself and the State. Indeed, many conflicting thoughts troubled him. The army in Germany was the stronger; that in Pannonia the nearer; the first was supported by all the strength of Gaul; the latter menaced Italy. Which was he to prefer, without the fear that those whom he slighted would be infuriated by the affront? But his sons might alike visit both, and not compromise the imperial dignity, which inspired the greatest awe at a distance. There was also an excuse for mere youths referring some matters to their father,

---

38. The province, which included on the north the frontier district of Vindelicia, comprised the upper valleys of the Danube and Inn, the Grisons, Tyrol , and part of Bavaria.

39. A group of tribes, east of the Elbe and north of the Danube, which constituted the kingdom of Marbod.

40. The rhetoric is more effective than accurate, since the latest expeditions of Augustus which can possibly be brought under the description in the text are dated in 16 B.C. and 8 B.C. At the time of the latter, he was fifty-four years of age, and Tiberius was now fifty-six.

with the possibility that he could conciliate or crush those who resisted Germanicus or Drusus. What resource remained, if they despised the emperor? However, as if on the eve of departure, he selected his attendants, provided his camp equipage, and prepared a fleet; then winter and matters of business were the various pretexts with which he amused, first, sensible men, then the populace, last, and longest of all, the provinces.

1.48. Meanwhile Germanicus, though he had concentrated his army and prepared vengeance against the mutineers, thought that he ought still to allow them an interval, in case they might, with the late warning before them, regard their safety. He sent a dispatch to Caecina, which said that he was on the way with a strong force, and that, unless they forestalled his arrival by the execution of the guilty, he would resort to an indiscriminate massacre. Caecina read the letter confidentially to the eagle and standard bearers, and to all in the camp who were least tainted by disloyalty, and urged them to save the whole army from disgrace, and themselves from destruction. "In peace," he said, "the merits of a man's case are carefully weighed; when war bursts on us, innocent and guilty alike perish." Upon this, they sounded those whom they thought best for their purpose, and when they saw that a majority of their legions remained loyal, at the commander's suggestion they fixed a time for falling with the sword on all the vilest and foremost of the mutineers. Then, at a mutually given signal, they rushed into the tents, and butchered the unsuspecting men, none but those in the secret knowing what was the beginning or what was to be the end of the slaughter.

1.49. The scene was a contrast to all civil wars which have ever occurred. It was not in battle, it was not from opposing camps, it was from those same dwellings where day saw them at their common meals, night resting from labor, that they divided themselves into two factions, and showered on each other their missiles. Uproar, wounds, bloodshed, were everywhere visible; the cause was a mystery. All else was at the disposal of chance. Even some loyal men were slain, for, on its being once understood who were the objects of fury, some of the worst mutineers too had seized on weapons. Neither commander nor tribune was present to control them; the men were allowed license and vengeance to their heart's content. Soon afterwards Germanicus entered the camp, and exclaiming with a flood of tears, that this was destruction rather than remedy, ordered the bodies to be burnt.

Even then their savage spirit was seized with desire to march against the enemy, as an atonement for their frenzy, and it was felt that the ghosts of their fellow soldiers could be appeased only by exposing such impious breasts to honorable scars. Caesar followed up the enthusiasm of the men, and having bridged over the Rhine, he sent across it 12,000 from the legions, with twenty-six allied cohorts, and eight squadrons of cavalry, whose discipline had been without a stain during the mutiny.

1.50. There was exultation among the Germans, not far off, as long as we were detained by the public mourning for the loss of Augustus, and then by our dissensions. But the Roman general in a forced march, cut through the Caesian forest and the line of delimitation which had been begun by Tiberius,[41] and pitched his camp on this line, his front and rear being defended by

---

41. With the Caesian Forest and the Tiberian *limes* alike unidentified, and the locality of the Marsi unknown (according to Strabo, 290, they had anticipated deportation into Gaul), the topography of Germanicus' raid must remain as obscure to the modern reader as it doubtless was to Tacitus.

entrenchments, his flanks by timber barricades. He then penetrated some forest passes but little known, and, as there were two routes, he deliberated whether he should pursue the short and ordinary route, or that which was more difficult unexplored, and consequently unguarded by the enemy. He chose the longer way, and hurried on every remaining preparation, for his scouts had brought word that among the Germans it was a night of festivity, with games, and one of their grand banquets. Caecina had orders to advance with some light cohorts, and to clear away any obstructions from the woods. The legions followed at a moderate interval. They were helped by a night of bright starlight, reached the villages of the Marsi, and threw their pickets round the enemy, who even then were stretched on beds or at their tables, without the least fear, or any sentries before their camp, so complete was their carelessness and disorder; and of war indeed there was no apprehension. Peace it certainly was not—merely the languid and heedless ease of half intoxicated people.

1.51. Caesar, to spread devastation widely, divided his eager legions into four columns, and ravaged a space of fifty miles with fire and sword. Neither sex nor age moved his compassion. Everything, sacred or profane, the temple too of Tanfana,[42] as they called it, the special resort of all those tribes, was levelled to the ground. There was not a wound among our soldiers, who cut down a half asleep, an unarmed, or a straggling foe. The Bructeri, Tubantes, and Usipetes, were roused by this slaughter, and they beset the forest passes through which the army had to return. The general knew this, and he marched, prepared both to advance and to fight. Part of the cavalry, and some of the auxiliary cohorts led the van; then came the first legion, and, with the baggage in the center, the men of the twenty-first closed up the left, those of the fifth, the right flank. The twentieth legion secured the rear, and, next, were the rest of the allies. Meanwhile the enemy moved not till the army began to defile in column through the woods, then made slight skirmishing attacks on its flanks and van, and with his whole force charged the rear. The light cohorts were thrown into confusion by the dense masses of the Germans, when Caesar rode up to the men of the twentieth legion, and in a loud voice exclaimed that this was the time for wiping out the mutiny. "Advance," he said, "and hasten to turn your guilt into glory." This fired their courage, and at a single dash they broke through the enemy, and drove him back with great slaughter into the open country. At the same moment the troops of the van emerged from the woods and fortified a camp. After this their march was uninterrupted, and the soldiery, with the confidence of recent success, and forgetful of the past, were placed in winter quarters.

1.52. The news was a source of joy and also of anxiety to Tiberius. He rejoiced that the mutiny was crushed, but the fact that Germanicus had won the soldiers' favor by lavishing money, and promptly granting the discharge, as well as his fame as a soldier, annoyed him. Still, he brought his achievements under the notice of the Senate, and spoke much of his greatness in language elaborated for effect, more so than could be believed to come from his inmost heart. He bestowed a briefer praise on Drusus, and on the termination of the disturbance in Illyricum, but he was more earnest, and his speech more hearty. And he confirmed, too, in the armies of Pannonia all the concessions of Germanicus.

---

42. The "temple" was probably a consecrated grove and alter.

1.53. That same year Julia ended her days.[43] For her profligacy she had formerly been confined by her father Augustus in the island of Pandateria, and then in the town of the Rhegium on the shores of the straits of Sicily. She had been the wife of Tiberius while Gaius and Lucius Caesar were in their glory, and had disdained him as an unequal match. This was Tiberius's special reason for retiring to Rhodes. When he obtained the empire, he left her in banishment and disgrace, deprived of all hope after the murder of Postumus Agrippa,[44] and let her perish by a lingering death of destitution, with the idea that an obscurity would hang over her end from the length of her exile. He had a like motive for cruel vengeance on Sempronius Gracchus, a man of noble family, of shrewd understanding, and a perverse eloquence, who had seduced this same Julia when she was the wife of Marcus Agrippa. And this was not the end of the intrigue. When she had been handed over to Tiberius, her persistent paramour inflamed her with disobedience and hatred towards her husband; and a letter which Julia wrote to her father, Augustus, inveighing against Tiberius, was supposed to be the composition of Gracchus. He was accordingly banished to Cercina, where he endured an exile of fourteen years. Then the soldiers who were sent to slay him, found him on a promontory, expecting no good. On their arrival, he begged a brief interval in which to give by letter his last instructions to his wife Alliaria, and then offered his neck to the executioners, dying with a courage not unworthy of the Sempronian name, which his degenerate life had dishonored. Some have related that these soldiers were not sent from Rome, but by Lucius Asprenas, proconsul of Africa, on the authority of Tiberius, who had vainly hoped that the infamy of the murder might be shifted on Asprenas.

Even though the campaigns in Germany were something less than totally successful, in May of the year 17, Tiberius recalled Germanicus to Rome to celebrate a triumph. It was a case of ending a war simply by declaring victory. Germanicus was then assigned to the East with special powers to deal with unrest there. Cornelius Piso, an old friend of Tiberius, was appointed governor of Syria as a kind of check on Germanicus' impetuousness. But enmity soon developed between the two men and a conflict resulted.

2.69. Germanicus meanwhile, as he was returning from Egypt, found that all his directions to the legions and to the various cities had been repealed or reversed. This led to grievous insults on Piso, while he as savagely assailed the prince. Piso then resolved to quit Syria. Soon he was detained there by the failing health of Germanicus, but when he heard of his recovery, while people were paying the vows they had offered for his safety, he went attended by his lictors, drove away the victims placed by the altars with all the preparations for sacrifice, and the festal gathering of the populace of Antioch. Then he left for Seleucia and awaited the result of the illness which

---

43. Daughter of Augustus by Scribonia, his first wife, and his only child (born 39 B.C., died 14 A.D.); married in 25 B.C. to her first cousin M. Marcellus, and upon his death without issue, two years later, to M. Vipsanius Agrippa, by whom she had three sons, Gaius and Lucius Caesar and Agrippa Postumus, with two daughters, Julia and Germanicus' wife Agrippina; transferred after Agrippa's death to Tiberius (11 B.C.), who was compelled to divorce his wife Vipsania for the occasion. She was disgraced and exiled in 2 B.C.

44. The implication is that she saw no hope from her son-in-law Germanicus.

had again attacked Germanicus. The terrible intensity of the malady was increased by the belief that he had been poisoned by Piso. And certainly there were found hidden in the floor and in the walls disinterred remains of human bodies, incantations and spells, and the name of Germanicus inscribed on leaden tablets,[45] half burnt cinders smeared with blood,[46] and other horrors by which in popular belief souls are devoted to the infernal deities. Piso too was accused of sending emissaries to note curiously every unfavorable symptom of the illness.

2.70. Germanicus heard of all this with anger, no less than with fear. "If my doors," he said, "are to be besieged, if I must gasp out my last breath under my enemies' eyes, what will then be the lot of my most unhappy wife, of my infant children?[47] Poisoning seems tedious; he is in eager haste to have the sole control of the province and the legions. But Germanicus is not yet fallen so low, nor will the murderer long retain the reward of the fatal deed." He then addressed a letter to Piso, renouncing his friendship, and, as many also state, ordered him to quit the province. Piso without further delay weighed anchor, slackening his course that he might not have a long way to return should Germanicus' death leave Syria open to him.

2.71. For a brief space the prince's hopes rose; then his frame became exhausted, and, as his end drew near, he spoke as follows to the friends by his side: "Were I succumbing to nature, I should have just ground of complaint even against the gods for thus tearing me away in my youth by an untimely death from parents, children, country. Now, cut off by the wickedness of Piso and Plancina,[48] I leave to your hearts my last entreaties. Describe to my father and brother, torn by what persecutions, entangled by what plots, I have ended by the worst of deaths the most miserable of lives. If any were touched by my bright prospects, by ties of blood, or even by envy towards me while I lived, they will weep that the once prosperous survivor of so many wars has perished by a woman's treachery. You will have the opportunity of complaint before the Senate, of an appeal to the laws. It is not the chief duty of friends to follow the dead with unprofitable laments, but to remember his wishes, to fulfill his commands. Tears for Germanicus even strangers will shed; vengeance must come from you, if you loved the man more than his fortune. Show the people of Rome her who is the granddaughter of the Divine Augustus, as well as my consort; set before them my six children. Sympathy will be on the side of the accusers, and to those who screen themselves under infamous orders belief or pardon will be refused." His friends clasped the dying man's right hand, and swore that they would sooner lose life than revenge.

2.72. He then turned to his wife and implored her by the memory of her husband and by their common offspring to lay aside her high spirit, to submit herself to the cruel blows of fortune, and not, when she returned to Rome, to enrage by political rivalry those who were stronger than herself. This was said openly; other words were whispered, pointing, it was supposed, to his fears from Tiberius. Soon afterwards he expired, to the intense sorrow of the province and of the neighboring peoples. Foreign nations and kings grieved over him, so great was his courtesy to

---

45. The tablets were employed in the ancient and almost ubiquitous rite of defixion, which consisted essentially of running a nail or needle through the effigy or the name of the person marked for destruction.
46. Half burned human remains from the funeral pyre.
47. In addition to the infant Julia, Caligula was with him.
48. The wife of Piso, whom Tacitus portrays as a kind of a mirror image, or opposite character, of Germanicus' wife Agrippina.

allies, his humanity to enemies. He inspired reverence alike by look and voice, and while he maintained the greatness and dignity of the highest rank, he had escaped the hatred that waits on arrogance.

2.73. His funeral, though it lacked the family statues and procession, was honored by panegyrics and a commemoration of his virtues. Some there were who, as they thought of his beauty, his age, and the manner of his death, the vicinity too of the country where he died, likened his end to that of Alexander the Great.[49] Both had a graceful person and were of noble birth; neither had much exceeded thirty years of age, and both fell by the treachery of their own people in strange lands.[50] But Germanicus was gracious to his friends, temperate in his pleasures, the husband of one wife, with only legitimate children. He was too no less a warrior, though rashness he had none, and, though after having cowed Germany by his many victories, he was hindered from crushing it into subjection. Had he had the sole control of affairs, had he possessed the power and title of a king, he would have attained military glory as much more easily as he had excelled Alexander in clemency, in self-restraint, and in all other virtues. As to the body which, before it was burnt, lay bare in the forum at Antioch, its destined place of burial, it is doubtful whether it exhibited the marks of poisoning. For men according as they pitied Germanicus and were prepossessed with suspicion or were biased by partiality towards Piso, gave conflicting accounts.

3.1. Without pausing in her winter voyage Agrippina arrived at the island of Corcyra,[51] facing the shores of Calabria. There she spent a few days to compose her mind, for she was wild with grief and knew not how to endure. Meanwhile on hearing of her arrival, all her intimate friends and several officers, every one indeed who had served under Germanicus, many strangers too from the neighboring towns, some thinking it respectful to the emperor, and still more following their example, thronged eagerly to Brundisium, the nearest and safest landing place for a voyager.

As soon as the fleet was seen on the horizon, not only the harbor and the adjacent shores, but the city walls too and the roofs and every place which commanded the most distant prospect were filled with crowds of mourners, who incessantly asked one another, whether, when she landed, they were to receive her in silence or with some utterance of emotion. They were not agreed on what befitted the occasion when the fleet slowly approached, its crew, not joyous as is usual, but wearing all a studied expression of grief. When Agrippina descended from the vessel with her two children, clasping the funeral urn, with eyes riveted to the earth, there was one universal groan. You could not distinguish kinsfolk from strangers, or the laments of men from those of women; only the attendants of Agrippina, worn out as they were by long sorrow, were surpassed by the mourners who now met them, fresh in their grief.

3.2. The emperor had dispatched two praetorian cohorts with instructions that the magistrates of Calabria, Apulia, and Campania were to pay the last honors to his son's memory. Accordingly tribunes and centurions bore Germanicus' ashes on their shoulders. They were preceded by the standards unadorned and the faces reversed. As they passed colony after colony, the populace in black, the knights in their state robes, burnt vestments and perfumes with other

---

49. Alexander was a year younger at the time of his death.
50. The rumor of the poising of Alexander may be found in Plutarch, *Alexander*, 77.
51. Corfu.

usual funeral adjuncts, in proportion to the wealth of the place. Even those whose towns were out of the route, met the mourners, offered victims and built altars to the dead, testifying their grief by tears and wailings. Drusus went as far as Tarracina[52] with Claudius, brother of Germanicus, and had been at Rome. Marcus Valerius and Caius Aurelius, the consuls, who had already entered on office, and a great number of the people thronged the road in scattered groups, every one weeping as he felt inclined. Flattery there was none, for all knew that Tiberius could scarcely dissemble his joy at the death of Germanicus.

3.3. Tiberius and Augusta refrained from showing themselves, thinking it below their dignity to shed tears in public, or else fearing that, if all eyes scrutinized their faces, their hypocrisy would be revealed. I do not find in any historian or in the daily register that Antonia,[53] Germanicus's mother, rendered any conspicuous honor to the deceased, though besides Agrippina, Drusus, and Claudius, all his other kinsfolk are mentioned by name. She may either have been hindered by illness, or with a spirit overpowered by grief she may not have had the heart to endure the sight of so great an affliction. But I can more easily believe that Tiberius and Augusta, who did not leave the palace, kept her within, that their sorrow might seem equal to hers, and that the grandmother and uncle might be thought to follow the mother's example in staying at home.

3.4. The day on which the remains were consigned to the tomb of Augustus, was now desolate in its silence, now distracted by lamentations. The streets of the city were crowded; torches were blazing throughout the Campus Martius. There the soldiers under arms,[54] the magistrates without their symbols of office, the people in the tribes, were all incessantly exclaiming that the commonwealth was ruined, that not a hope remained, too boldly and openly to let one think that they remembered their rulers. But nothing impressed Tiberius more deeply than the enthusiasm kindled in favor of Agrippina, whom men spoke of as the glory of the country, the sole surviving offspring of Augustus, the solitary example of the old times, while looking up to heaven and the gods they prayed for the safety of her children and that they might outlive their oppressors.

3.5. Some there were who missed the grandeur of a state funeral, and contrasted the splendid honors conferred by Augustus on Drusus, the father of Germanicus. "Then the emperor himself," they said, "went in the extreme rigor of winter as far as Ticinum,[55] and never leaving the corpse entered Rome with it. Round the funeral bier were ranged the images of the Claudii and the Julii; there was weeping in the forum,[56] and a panegyric before the rostra; every honor devised by our ancestors or invented by their descendants was heaped on him. But as for Germanicus, even the customary distinctions due to any noble had not fallen to his lot. Granting that his body, because of the distance of tie journey, was burnt in any fashion in foreign lands,

---

52. An old coastal town of Latium on the Appian Way, some 60 miles from Rome.

53. The younger of the two daughters of Antony by Augustus' sister, Octavia; born about 36 B.C.; wife of Drusus, the brother of Tiberius; she survived till the reign of Caligula.

54. On ordinary occasions the Guards in the capital wore the toga, not the military *sagum*, and carried sword and spear, but neither shield, helmet, not breastplate.

55. In modern Pavia. Drusus died in Germany in 9 B.C. and Tiberius posted on a celebrated journey of 200 miles, to his death bed. The corpse was met by Augustus at Ticinum and born to Rome.

56. The oration in the Forum was delivered by Tiberius himself; Augusta spoke in the Flaminian Circus, according to Dio Cassius, 55.2. Tacitus, however, as usual chooses to record only facts that cast a bad reflection of Tiberius.

still all the more honors ought to have been afterwards paid him, because at first chance had denied them. His brother[57] had gone but one day's journey to meet him; his uncle, not even to the city gates. Where were all those usages of the past, the image at the head of the bier, the lays composed in commemoration of worth, the eulogies and laments, or at least the semblance of grief?"

3.6. All this was known to Tiberius, and, to silence popular talk, he reminded the people in a proclamation that many eminent Romans had died for their country and that none had been honored with such passionate regret. This regret was a glory both to himself and to all, provided only a due mean were observed; for what was becoming in humble homes and communities, did not befit princely personages and an imperial people. Tears and the solace found in mourning were suitable enough for the first burst of grief; but now they must brace their hearts to endurance, as in former days the Divine Julius after the loss of his only daughter,[58] and the Divine Augustus when he was bereft of his grandchildren,[59] had thrust away their sorrow. There was no need of examples from the past, showing how often the Roman people had patiently endured the defeats of armies, the destruction of generals, the total extinction of noble families. Princes were mortal; the State was everlasting. Let them then return to their usual pursuits, and, as the shows of the festival of the Great Goddess were at hand,[60] even resume their amusements.

3.7. The period of mourning then ceased, and men went back to their occupations. Drusus was sent to the armies of Illyricum, amidst an universal eagerness to exact vengeance on Piso, and ceaseless complaints that he was meantime roaming through the delightful regions of Asia and Achaia, and was weakening the proofs of his guilt by an insolent and artful procrastination. It was indeed widely rumored that the notorious poisoner Martina, who, as I have related, had been dispatched to Rome by Cneius Sentius, had died suddenly at Brundisium; that poison was concealed in a knot of her hair, and that no symptoms of suicide were discovered on her person.[61]

3.8. Piso meanwhile sent his son on to Rome with a message intended to pacify the emperor, and then made his way to Drusus, who would, he hoped, be not so much infuriated at his brother's death as kindly disposed towards himself in consequence of a rival's removal. Tiberius, to show his impartiality, received the youth courteously, and enriched him with the liberality he usually bestowed on the sons of noble families. Drusus replied to Piso that if certain insinuations were true, he must be foremost in his resentment, but he preferred to believe that they were false and groundless, and that Germanicus' death need be the ruin of no one. This he said openly, avoiding anything like secrecy. Men did not doubt that his answer prescribed him by Tiberius, inasmuch as one who had generally all the simplicity and candor of youth, now had recourse to the artifices of old age.

---

57. Since the movements of Claudius were negligible, this must refer to Germanicus' brother by adoption, Drusus.

58. Daughter of Caesar and Cornelia: born 82 or 82 B.C.; married to Pompey in 59 B.C.; died five years later.

59. Gaius and Lucius Caesar.

60. April 4–10. The Games, mainly theatrical, were in honor of the Great Mother, Cybele: They were instituted near the end of the Second Punic War.

61. The gossips reasoned that Piso had, beyond doubt, forced Martina to poison herself: but , if her drugs could kill without leaving a trace on her body, then obviously it was idle to debate, in the case of Germanicus, whether the corpse had shown evidence of poising.

3.9. Piso, after crossing the Dalmatian sea[62] and leaving his ships at Ancona, went through Picenum and along the Flaminian road,[63] where he overtook a legion which was marching from Pannonia to Rome and was then to garrison Africa. It was a matter of common talk how he had repeatedly displayed himself to the soldiers on the road during the march. From Narnia, to avoid suspicion or because the plans of fear are uncertain, he sailed down the Nar, then down the Tiber, and increased the fury of the populace by bringing his vessel to shore at the tomb of the Caesars. In broad daylight, when the river bank was thronged, he himself with a numerous following of dependents, and Plancina with a retinue of women, moved onward with joy in their countenances. Among other things which provoked men's anger was his house towering above the forum, gay with festal decorations, his banquets and his feasts, about which there was no secrecy, because the place was so public.

3.10. Next day, Fulcinius Trio asked the consul's leave to prosecute Piso.[64] It was contended against him by Vitellius and Veranius and the others who had been the companions of Germanicus, that this was not Trio's proper part, and that they themselves meant to report their instructions from Germanicus, not as accusers, but as deponents and witnesses to facts. Trio, abandoning the prosecution on this count, obtained leave to accuse Piso's previous career, and the emperor was requested to undertake the inquiry. This even the accused did not refuse, fearing, as he did, the bias of the people and of the Senate; while Tiberius, he knew, was resolute enough to despise report, and was also entangled in his mother's complicity. Truth too would be more easily distinguished from perverse misrepresentation by a single judge, where a number would be swayed by hatred and ill will. Tiberius was not unaware of the formidable difficulty of the inquiry and of the rumors by which he was himself assailed. Having therefore summoned a few intimate friends, he listened to the threatening speeches of the prosecutors and to the pleadings of the accused, and finally referred the whole case to the Senate.

3.11. Drusus meanwhile, on his return from Illyricum, though the Senate had voted him an ovation for the submission of Maroboduus and the successes of the previous summer, postponed the honor and entered Rome. Then the defendant sought the advocacy of Lucius Arruntius, Marcus Vinicius, Asinius Gallus, Aeserninus Marcellus and Sextus Pompeius, and on their declining for different reasons, Marcus Lepidus, Lucius Piso, and Livineius Regulus became his counsel, amid the excitement of the whole country, which wondered how much fidelity would be shown by the friends of Germanicus, on what the accused rested his hopes, and how far Tiberius would repress and hide his feelings. Never were the people more keenly interested; never did they indulge themselves more freely in secret whispers against the emperor or in the silence of suspicion.

---

62. The Adriatic.

63. The great highway running from Rome to Ariminum (Rimini). Piso strikes westward through northern Picenum, joins the via Flaminis in Umbria, and follows it in company with the legion as far as Narnia (now Narni). Then to avoid the appearance of tampering with the soldiers, he descends the Nar (Nera) by boat until its confluence with the Tiber, and so proceeds by water to Rome.

64. Before the senate. The case might have gone: (1) before a praetor and jury; (2) before the consuls and the senate; (3) before a private court of the emperor, assisted by an informal board of advisors. Actually, it comes before Tiberius, who naturally decides to transfer the responsibility to the senate.

3.12. On the day the Senate met, Tiberius delivered a speech of studied moderation. "Piso," he said, "was my father's representative[65] and friend, and was appointed by myself, on the advice of the Senate, to assist Germanicus in the administration of the East. Whether he there had provoked the young prince by willful opposition and rivalry, and had rejoiced at his death or wickedly destroyed him, is for you to determine with minds unbiased. Certainly if a subordinate oversteps the bounds of duty and of obedience to his commander, and has exulted in his death and in my affliction, I shall hate him and exclude him from my house, and I shall avenge a personal quarrel without resorting to my power as emperor. If however a crime is discovered which ought to be punished, whoever the murdered man may be, it is for you to give just reparation both to the children of Germanicus and to us, his parents.

"Consider this too, whether Piso dealt with the armies in a revolutionary and seditious spirit; whether he sought by intrigue popularity with the soldiers; whether he attempted to repossess himself of the province by arms, or whether these are falsehoods which his accusers have published with exaggeration. As for them, I am justly angry with their intemperate zeal. For to what purpose did they strip the corpse and expose it to the pollution of the vulgar gaze, and circulate a story among foreigners that he was destroyed by poison, if all this is still doubtful and requires investigation? For my part, I sorrow for my son and shall always sorrow for him; still I would not hinder the accused from producing all the evidence which can relieve his innocence or convict Germanicus of any unfairness, if such there was. And I implore you not to take as proven charges alleged, merely because the case is intimately bound up with my affliction. Do you, whom ties of blood or your own true heartedness have made his advocates, help him in his peril, every one of you, as far as each man's eloquence and diligence can do so. To like exertions and like persistency I would urge the prosecutors. In this, and in this only, will we place Germanicus above the laws, by conducting the inquiry into his death in this house instead of in the forum, and before the Senate instead of before a bench of judges. In all else let the case be tried as simply as others. Let no one heed the tears of Drusus or my own sorrow, or any stories invented to our discredit."

3.13. Two days were then assigned for the bringing forward of the charges, and after six days' interval, the prisoner's defense was to occupy three days. Thereupon Fulcinius Trio began with some old and irrelevant accusations about intrigues and extortion during Piso's government of Spain. This, if proved, would not have been fatal to the defendant, if he cleared himself as to his late conduct, and, if refuted, would not have secured his acquittal, if he were convicted of the greater crimes. Next, Servaeus, Veranius, and Vitellius, all with equal earnestness, Vitellius with striking eloquence, alleged against Piso that out of hatred of Germanicus and a desire of revolution he had so corrupted the common soldiers by license and oppression of the allies that he was called by the vilest of them "father of the legions" while on the other hand to all the best men, especially to the companions and friends of Germanicus, he had been savagely cruel. Lastly, he had, they said, destroyed Germanicus himself by sorceries and poison, and hence came those ceremonies and horrible sacrifices made by himself and Plancina; then he had threatened the State with war, and had been defeated in battle, before he could be tried as a prisoner.

3.14. On all points but one the defense broke down. That he had tampered with the soldiers, that his province had been at the mercy of the vilest of them, that he had even insulted his chief,

---

65. As the governor of Hither Spain.

he could not deny. It was only the charge of poisoning from which he seemed to have cleared himself. This indeed the prosecutors did not adequately sustain by merely alleging that at a banquet given by Germanicus, his food had been tainted with poison by the hands of Piso who sat next above him. It seemed absurd to suppose that he would have dared such an attempt among strange servants, in the sight of so many bystanders, and under Germanicus's own eyes. And, besides, the defendant offered his slaves to the torture, and insisted on its application to the attendants on that occasion. But the judges for different reasons were merciless: the emperor,[66] because war had been made on a province, the Senate because they could not be sufficiently convinced that there had been no treachery about the death of Germanicus. . . .[67]

At the same time shouts were heard from the people in front of the Senate House, threatening violence if he escaped the verdict of the Senators. They had actually dragged Piso's statues to the Gemonian stairs,[68] and were breaking them in pieces, when by the emperor's order they were rescued and replaced. Piso was then put in a litter and attended by a tribune of one of the Praetorian cohorts, who followed him, so it was variously rumored, to guard his person or to be his executioner.

3.15. Plancina was equally detested, but had stronger influence. Consequently it was considered a question how far the emperor would be allowed to go against her. While Piso's hopes were in suspense, she offered to share his lot, whatever it might be, and in the worst event, to be his companion in death. But as soon as she had secured her pardon through the secret intercessions of Augusta, she gradually withdrew from her husband and separated her defense from his. When the prisoner saw that this was fatal to him, he hesitated whether he should still persist, but at the urgent request of his sons braced his courage and once more entered the Senate. There he bore patiently the renewal of the accusation, the furious voices of the Senators, savage opposition indeed from every quarter, but nothing daunted him so much as to see Tiberius, without pity and without anger, resolutely closing himself against any inroad of emotion. He was conveyed back to his house, where, seemingly by way of preparing his defense for the next day, he wrote a few words, sealed the paper and handed it to a freedman. Then he bestowed the usual attention on his person; after a while, late at night, his wife having left his chamber, he ordered the doors to be closed, and at daybreak was found with his throat cut and a sword lying on the ground.

3.16. I remember to have heard old men say that a document was often seen in Piso's hands, the substance of which he never himself divulged, but which his friends repeatedly declared contained a letter from Tiberius with instructions referring to Germanicus, and that it was his intention to produce it before the Senate and upbraid the emperor, had he not been deluded by vain promises from Sejanus.[69] Nor did he perish, they said, by his own hand, but by that of one sent to be

---

66. As a member of the senate he was necessarily one of the judges.
67. There is a gap in the text at this point, evidently of considerable length. It must have contained a mention of the adjournment of the trial, followed by a second hearing. The correspondence, demanded by the accusers and refused by the defendant and the emperor alike, can hardly have been other than letters from Piso and Plancina to Tiberius and Augusta.
68. A flight of stairs leading from the Capital to the Forum Romanum, on which the bodies of criminals garroted in the *carcer* were exposed before being consigned to the Tiber.
69. The praetorian prefect and confidant of Tiberius.

his executioner. Neither of these statements would I positively affirm; still it would not have been right for me to conceal what was related by those who lived up to the time of my youth.

The emperor, assuming an air of sadness, complained in the Senate that the purpose of such a death was to bring odium on himself. . . .[70] and he asked with repeated questionings how Piso had spent his last day and night. Receiving answers which were mostly judicious, though in part somewhat incautious, he read out a note written by Piso, nearly to the following effect: "Crushed by a conspiracy of my foes and the odium excited by a lying charge, since my truth and innocence find no place here, I call the immortal gods to witness that towards you Caesar, I have lived loyally, and with like dutiful respect towards your mother. And I implore you to think of my children, one of whom, Gneius is in no way implicated in my career, whatever it may have been, seeing that all this time he has been at Rome, while the other, Marcus Piso, dissuaded me from returning to Syria. Would that I had yielded to my young son rather than he to his aged father! And therefore I pray the more earnestly that the innocent may not pay the penalty of my wickedness. By forty-five years of obedience, by my association with you in the consulate,[71] as one who formerly won the esteem of the Divine Augustus, your father, as one who is your friend and will never hereafter ask a favor, I implore you to save my unhappy son." About Plancina he added not a word.

3.17. Tiberius after this acquitted the young Piso of the charge of civil war on the ground that a son could not have refused a father's orders, compassionating at the same time the high rank of the family and the terrible downfall even of Piso himself, however he might have deserved it. For Plancina he spoke with shame and conscious disgrace, alleging in excuse the intercession of his mother, secret complaints against whom from all good men were growing more and more vehement. "So it was the duty of a grandmother," people said, "to look a grandson's murderess in the face, to converse with her and rescue her from the Senate. What the laws secure on behalf of every citizen, had to Germanicus alone been denied. The voices of a Vitellius and Veranius had bewailed a Caesar, while the emperor and Augusta had defended Plancina. She might as well now turn her poisonings, and her devices which had proved so successful, against Agrippina and her children, and thus sate this exemplary grandmother and uncle with the blood of a most unhappy house."

Two days were frittered away over this mockery of a trial, Tiberius urging Piso's children to defend their mother. While the accusers and their witnesses pressed the prosecution with rival zeal, and there was no reply, pity rather than anger was on the increase. Aurelius Cotta, the consul, who was first called on for his vote (for when the emperor put the question, even those in office went through the duty of voting), held that Piso's name ought to be erased from the public register, half of his property confiscated, half given up to his son, Gneius Piso, who was to change his first name;[72] that Marcus Piso, be stripped of his rank, with an allowance of five million

---

70. Another gap in the text. Since it is natural to suppose that both this lacuna and the not inconsiderable one above are due to the mutilation of the same leaf in the archetype, this loss is probably also considerable.

71. He was consul with Tiberius in 7 B.C.

72. He appears to have taken the name of "Lucius," and to be rightly identified with Lucius Calpurnius Piso, consul in A.D. 27.

sesterces, should be banished for ten years,[73] Plancina's life being spared in consideration of Augusta's intercession.

3.18. Much of the sentence was mitigated by the emperor. The name of Piso was not to be struck out of the public register, since that of Marcus Antonius who had made war on his country,[74] and that of Julius Antonius[75] who had dishonored the house of Augustus, still remained. Marcus Piso too he saved from degradation, and gave him his father's property, for he was firm enough, as I have often related, against the temptation of money, and now for very shame at Plancina's acquittal, he was more than usually merciful. Again, when Valerius Messalinus and Caecina Severus proposed respectively the erection of a golden statue in the temple of Mars the Avenger and of an altar to Vengeance, he interposed, protesting that victories over the foreigner were commemorated with such monuments, but that domestic woes ought to be shrouded in silent grief.

There was a further proposal of Messalinus, that Tiberius, Augusta, Antonia, Agrippina and Drusus ought to be publicly thanked for having avenged Germanicus. He omitted all mention of Claudius. Thereupon he was pointedly asked by Lucius Asprenas before the Senate, whether the omission had been intentional, and it was only then that the name of Claudius was added. For my part, the wider the scope of my reflection on the present and the past, the more am I impressed by their mockery of human plans in every transaction. Clearly, the very last man marked out for empire by public opinion, expectation and general respect was he whom fortune was holding in reserve as the emperor of the future.

---

73. The milder form of banishment, retaining his civic rights and property.
74. In 44 B.C. and 32 B.C. His name was actually cancelled from the public monuments, but was restored, presumably in the later years of Augustus' reign.
75. Son of Mark Antony, compelled to suicide in 2 B.C. for adultery with Julia.

Pliny the Younger, Selected Letters of a Roman Senator

29

Pliny the Younger (Gaius Plinius Caecilius Secundus, c. 61–112) was a member of the municipal aristocracy of Como. His family connections and good education enabled him to pursue a career that allowed him to proceed smoothly up the political latter to the praetorship in 93 and the consulship in 100. He became governor of Bithynia in 110 and probably died there while in office in 112. Three of his writings survive: the Panegyric, a formal thanksgiving for his consulship made before an invited audience; Nine books of letters to his friends, containing 247 letters; and one book of correspondence with the emperor Trajan, containing 14 letters before his governorship of Bithynia and 107 letters from the province. His letters give us an unprecedented view of the life of a busy imperial bureaucrat in general and a look into the personal life of an ancient upper class Roman in particular. In addition, the letters are written in a literary style that makes them interesting and entertaining to read.

1.6. To Cornelius Tacitus (the Historian): The Boar Hunter

You will laugh (and you are quite welcome) when I tell you that your old acquaintance is turned sportsman, and has taken three noble boars. "What!" you exclaim, "Pliny!"—*Even he*. However, I indulged at the same time my beloved inactivity; and, whilst I sat at my nets, you would have found me, not with boar spear or javelin, but pencil and tablet, by my side. I mused and wrote, being determined to return, if with my hands empty, at least with my memorandums full. Believe me, this way of studying is not to be despised: it is wonderful how the mind is stirred and quickened into activity by brisk bodily exercise. There is something, too, in the solemnity of the venerable woods with which one is surrounded, together with that profound silence which is

Credit: Pliny the Younger. *Letters*, translated by William Melmoth; revised by F. C. T. Bosanquet. Vol. IX, Part 4. The Harvard Classics. New York: P.F. Collier & Son, 1909–14

observed on these occasions, that forcibly disposes the mind to meditation. So for the future, let me advise you, whenever you hunt, to take your tablets along with you, as well as your basket and bottle, for be assured you will find Minerva no less fond of traversing the hills than Diana. Farewell.

1.12. To Calestrius Tiro: On the Death of a Friend

I have suffered the heaviest loss; if that word be sufficiently strong to express the misfortune which has deprived me of so excellent a man. Corellius Rufus is dead; and dead, too, by his own act! A circumstance of great aggravation to my affliction: as that sort of death which we cannot impute either to the course of nature, or the hand of Providence, is, of all others, the most to be lamented. It affords some consolation in the loss of those friends whom disease snatches from us that they fall by the general destiny of mankind; but those who destroy themselves leave us under the inconsolable reflection, that they had it in their power to have lived longer. It is true, Corellius had many inducements to be fond of life; a blameless conscience, high reputation, and great dignity of character, besides a daughter, a wife, a grandson, and sisters, and, amidst these numerous pledges of happiness, faithful friends. Still, it must be admitted he had the highest motive (which to a wise man will always have the force of destiny) urging him to this resolution. He had long been tortured by so tedious and painful a complaint that even these inducements to living on, considerable as they are, were overbalanced by the reasons on the other side. In his thirty-third year (as I have frequently heard him say) he was seized with the gout in his feet. This was hereditary; for diseases, as well as possessions, are sometimes handed down by a sort of inheritance. A life of sobriety and continence had enabled him to conquer and keep down the disease while he was still young; latterly, as it grew upon him with advancing years, he had to manfully bear it, suffering meanwhile the most incredible and undeserved agonies; for the gout was now not only in his feet, but had spread itself over his whole body. I remember, in Domitian's reign, paying him a visit at his villa, near Rome. As soon as I entered his chamber, his servants went out: for it was his rule never to allow them to be in the room when any intimate friend was with him; nay, even his own wife, though she could have kept any secret, used to go too. Casting his eyes round the room, "Why," he exclaimed, "do you suppose I endure life so long under these cruel agonies? It is with the hope that I may outlive, at least for one day, that villain." Had his bodily strength been equal to his resolution, he would have carried his desire into practical effect. God heard and answered his prayer; and when he felt that he should now die a free, un-enslaved Roman, he broke through those other great, but now less forcible, attachments to the world. His malady increased; and, as it now grew too violent to admit of any relief from temperance, he resolutely determined to put an end to its uninterrupted attacks, by an effort of heroism. He had refused all sustenance during four days, when his wife, Hispulla, sent our common friend Geminius to me, with the melancholy news that Corellius was resolved to die; and that neither her own entreaties nor her daughter's could move him from his purpose; I was the only person left who could reconcile him to life. I ran to his house with the utmost precipitation. As I approached it, I met a second messenger from Hispulla, Julius Atticus, who informed me there was nothing to be hoped for now, even from me, as he seemed more hardened than ever in his purpose. He had said, indeed, to his physician, who pressed him to take some nourishment, "'Tis resolved": an expression which, as it raised my admiration of the greatness of his soul, so it does my grief for the loss of him. I keep thinking what a friend, what a man, I am deprived of. That he had reached his sixty-seventh year, an age which even the strongest seldom exceed, I well know; that he is released from a life of continual pain; that he has left his dearest friends behind him, and (what was dearer to him than all these) the state in a prosperous condition: all this I know. Still I cannot forbear to lament him, as if he had been in the prime and vigor of his days; and I lament him (shall I own my weakness?) on my own account. And—to confess to you as I did to Calvisius, in the first transport of my grief—I sadly fear, now that I am no longer under his eye, I shall not keep so strict a guard over my conduct. Speak comfort to me then, not that *he was old, he was infirm*: all this I know; but by supplying me with some reflections that are new and resistless, which I have never heard, never read, anywhere else. For all that I have heard, and all that I have read, occur to me of themselves; but all these are by far too weak to support me under so severe an affliction. Farewell.

1.14. To Junius Mauricus: An Arranged Marriage

You desire me to look out a proper husband for your niece: it is with justice you enjoin me that office. You know the high esteem and affection I bore that great man, her father, and with what noble instructions he nurtured my youth, and taught me to deserve those praises he was pleased to bestow upon me. You could not give me, then, a more important, or more agreeable, commission; nor could I be employed in an office of higher honor, than that of choosing a young man worthy of being father of the grandchildren of Rusticus Arulenus; a choice I should be long in determining, were I not acquainted with Minutius Aemilianus, who seems formed for our purpose. He loves me with all that warmth of affection which is usual between young men of equal years (as indeed I have the advance of him but by a very few), and reveres me at the same time, with all the deference due to age; and, in a word, he is no less desirous to model himself by my instructions than I was by those of yourself and your brother.

He is a native of Brixia, one of those provinces in Italy which still retain much of the old modesty, frugal simplicity, and even rusticity, of manner. He is the son of Minutius Macrinus, whose humble desires were satisfied with standing at the head of the equestrian order: for though he was nominated by Vespasian in the number of those whom that prince dignified with the praetorian office, yet, with an inflexible greatness of mind, he resolutely preferred an honorable repose to the ambitious, shall I call them, or exalted, pursuits, in which we public men are engaged. His grandmother, on the mother's side, is Serrana Procula, of Patavium:[1] you are no stranger to the character of its citizens; yet Serrana is looked upon, even among these correct people, as an exemplary instance of strict virtue. Acilius, his uncle, is a man of almost exceptional gravity, wisdom, and integrity. In short, you will find nothing throughout his family unworthy of yours. Minutius himself has plenty of vivacity, as well as application, together with a most amiable and becoming modesty. He has already, with considerable credit, passed through the offices of quaestor, tribune, and praetor; so that you will be spared the trouble of soliciting for him those honorable employ-

---

1. Padua

ments. He has a fine, well bred countenance, with a ruddy, healthy complexion, while his whole person is elegant and comely and his mien graceful and senatorian: advantages, I think, by no means to be slighted, and which I consider as the proper tribute to virgin innocence. I think I may add that his father is very rich. When I contemplate the character of those who require a husband of my choosing, I know it is unnecessary to mention wealth; but when I reflect upon the prevailing manners of the age, and even the laws of Rome, which rank a man according to his possessions, it certainly claims *some* regard; and, indeed, in establishments of this nature, where children and many other circumstances are to be duly weighed, it is an article that well deserves to be taken into the account. You will be inclined, perhaps, to suspect that affection has had too great a share in the character I have been drawing, and that I have heightened it beyond the truth; but I will stake all my credit, you will find everything far beyond what I have represented. I love the young fellow indeed (as he justly deserves) with all the warmth of a most ardent affection; but for that very reason I would not ascribe more to his merit than I know it will bear. Farewell.

1.15. To Septimius Clarus: A Missed Dinner Engagement

Ah! you are a pretty fellow! You make an engagement to come to supper and then never appear. Justice shall be exacted—you shall reimburse me to the very last penny the expense I went to on your account; no small sum, let me tell you. I had prepared, you must know, a lettuce apiece, three snails, two eggs, and a barley cake, with some sweet wine and snow (the snow most certainly I shall charge to your account, as a rarity that will not keep). Olives, beet-root, gourds, onions, and a thousand other dainties equally sumptuous. You should likewise have been entertained either with an interlude, the rehearsal of a poem, or a piece of music, whichever you preferred; or (such was my liberality) with all three. But the oysters, sows' bellies, sea-urchins, and dancers from Cadiz of a certain—I know not who, were, it seems, more to your taste. You shall give satisfaction; how, shall at present be a secret.

Oh! you have behaved cruelly, grudging your friend—I had almost said yourself—and upon second thoughts I do say so—in this way: for how agreeably should we have spent the evening, in laughing, trifling, and literary amusements! You may sup, I confess, at many places more splendidly; but nowhere with more unconstrained mirth, simplicity, and freedom: only make the experiment, and if you do not ever after excuse yourself to your other friends, to come to me, always put me off to go to them. Farewell.

1.21. To Plinius Paternus: The Purchase of Slaves

As I rely very much upon the soundness of your judgment, so I do upon the goodness of your eyes: not because I think your discernment very great (for I don't want to make you conceited), but because I think it as good as mine: which, it must be confessed, is saying a great deal. Joking apart, I like the look of the slaves which were purchased for me on your recommendation very well; all I further care about is, that they be honest: and for this I must depend upon their characters more than their countenances. Farewell.

2.11. To Voconius Romanus: The Death of Verginius Rufus

Rome has not for many years beheld a more magnificent and memorable spectacle than was lately exhibited in the public funeral of that great, illustrious, and no less fortunate man, Verginius Rufus. He lived thirty years after he had reached the zenith of his fame. He read poems composed in his honor, he read histories of his achievements, and was himself witness of his fame among posterity. He was thrice raised to the dignity of consul, that he might at least be the highest of subjects, who[2] had refused to be the first of princes, this friend of mankind[3] was in quiet possession of the empire, it seems as if Providence had purposely preserved him to these times, that he might receive the honor of a public funeral. He reached his eighty-fourth year, in full tranquility and universally revered, having enjoyed strong health during his lifetime, with the exception of a trembling in his hands, which, however, gave him no pain. His last illness, indeed, was severe and tedious, but even that circumstance added to his reputation. As he was practicing his voice with a view of returning his public acknowledgements to the emperor, who had promoted him to the consulship, a large volume he had taken into his hand, and which happened to be too heavy for so old a man to hold standing up, slid from his grasp. In hastily endeavoring to recover it, his foot slipped on the smooth pavement, and he fell down and broke his thigh-bone, which being clumsily set, his age as well being against him, did not properly unite again. The funeral obsequies paid to the memory of this great man have done honor to the emperor, to the age, and to the bar. The consul Cornelius Tacitus[4] pronounced his funeral oration and thus his good fortune was crowned by the public applause of so eloquent an orator. He has departed from our midst, full of years, indeed, and of glory; as illustrious by the honors he refused as by those he accepted. Yet still we shall miss him and lament him, as the shining model of a past age; I, especially, shall feel his loss, for I not only admired him as a patriot, but loved him as a friend. We were of the same province, and of neighboring towns, and our estates were also contiguous. Besides these accidental connections, he was left my guardian, and always treated me with a parent's affection. Whenever I offered myself as a candidate for any office in the state, he constantly supported me with his interest; and although he had long since given up all such services to friends, he would kindly leave his retirement and come to give me his vote in person. On the day on which the priests nominate those they consider most worthy of the sacred office[5] he constantly proposed

---

2. "Verginius Rufus was governor of Upper Germany at the time of the revolt of Julius Vindex in Gaul, A. D. 68. The soldiers of Verginius wished to raise him to the empire, but he refused the honor, and marched against Vindex, who perished before Vesontio. After the death of Nero, Verginius supported the claims of Galba, and accompanied him to Rome. Upon Otho's death, the soldiers again attempted to proclaim Verginius emperor, and in consequence of his refusal of the honor, he narrowly escaped with his life."

3. Nerva.

4. The historian.

5. Namely, of augurs. "This college, as regulated by Sulla, consisted of fifteen, who were all persons of the first distinction in Rome; it was a priesthood for life, of a character indelible, which no crime or forfeiture could efface; it was necessary that every candidate should be nominated to the people by two augurs, who gave a solemn testimony upon oath of his dignity and fitness for that office." Middleton's *Life of Cicero*, p. 147.

me. Even in his last illness, apprehending the possibility of the senate's appointing him one of the five commissioners for reducing the public expenses, he fixed upon me, young as I am, to bear his excuses, in preference to so many other friends, elderly men too, and of consular rank and said to me, "Had I a son of my own, I would entrust you with this matter." And so I cannot but lament his death, as though it were premature, and pour out my grief into your bosom; if indeed one has any right to grieve, or to call it death at all, which to such a man terminates his mortality, rather than ends his life. He lives, and will live on for ever; and his fame will extend and be more celebrated by posterity, now that he is gone from our sight. I had much else to write to you but my mind is full of this. I keep thinking of Verginius: I see him before me: I am for ever fondly yet vividly imagining that I hear him, am speaking to him, embrace him. There are men amongst us, his fellow-citizens, perhaps, who may rival him in virtue; but not one that will ever approach him in glory. Farewell.

2.13. TO NERATIUS PRISCUS: RECOMMENDATION FOR VOCONIUS ROMANUS

As I know you eagerly embrace every opportunity of obliging me, so there is no man whom I had rather be under an obligation to. I apply to you, therefore, in preference to anyone else, for a favor which I am extremely desirous of obtaining. You, who are commander-in-chief of a very considerable army, have many opportunities of exercising your generosity; and the length of time you have enjoyed that post must have enabled you to provide for all your own friends. I hope you will now turn your eyes upon some of mine: as indeed they are but a few. Your generous disposition, I know, would be better pleased if the number were greater, but one or two will suffice my modest desires; at present I will only mention Voconius Romanus. His father was of great distinction among the Roman knights, and his father-in-law, or, I might more properly call him, his second father (for his affectionate treatment of Voconius entitles him to that appellation), was still more conspicuous. His mother was one of the most considerable ladies of Upper Spain: you know what character the people of that province bear, and how remarkable they are for their strictness of their manners. As for himself, he lately held the post of flamen.[6] Now, from the time when we were first students together, I have felt very tenderly attached to him. We lived under the same roof, in town and country, we joked together, we shared each other's serious thoughts: for where indeed could I have found a truer friend or pleasanter companion than he? In his conversation, and even in his very voice and countenance, there is a rare sweetness; as at the bar he displays talents of a high order; acuteness, elegance, ease, and skill: and he writes such letters too that were you to read them you would imagine they had been dictated by the Muses themselves. I have a very great affection for him, as he has for me. Even in the earlier part of our lives, I warmly embraced every opportunity of doing him all the good services which then lay in my power, as I

---

6. Any Roman priest devoted to the service of one particular god was designated *flamen*, receiving a distinguishing epithet from the deity to whom he ministered. The office was understood to last for life; but a flamen might be compelled to resign for a breach of duty, or even on account of the occurrence of an ill-omened accident while discharging his functions. Pliny himself was *flamen divi Titi* in Cumun.

have lately obtained for him from our most gracious prince[7] the privilege[8] granted to those who have three children: a favor which, though Caesar very rarely bestows, and always with great caution, yet he conferred, at my request, in such a manner as to give it the air and grace of being his own choice. The best way of showing that I think he deserves the kindnesses he has already received from me is by increasing them, especially as he always accepts my services so gratefully as to deserve more. Thus I have shown you what manner of man Romanus is, how thoroughly I have proved his worth, and how much I love him. Let me entreat you to honor him with your patronage in a way suitable to the generosity of your heart, and the eminence of your station. But above all let him have your affection; for though you were to confer upon him the utmost you have in your power to bestow, you can give him nothing more valuable than your friendship. That you may see he is worthy of it, even to the closest degree of intimacy, I send you this brief sketch of his tastes, character, his whole life, in fact. I should continue my intercessions in his behalf, but that I know you prefer not being pressed, and I have already repeated them in every line of this letter: for to show a good reason for what one asks is true intercession, and of the most effectual kind. Farewell.

2.17. TO CEUSINIUS GALLUS: HIS HOUSE AT LAURENTINE

You are surprised that I am so fond of my Laurentine, or (if you prefer the name) my Laurens: but you will cease to wonder when I acquaint you with the beauty of the villa, the advantages of its situation, and the extensive view of the sea-coast. It is only seventeen miles from Rome; so that when I have finished my business in town, I can pass my evenings here after a good, satisfactory day's work. There are two different roads to it: if you go by that of Laurentum, you must turn off at the fourteenth mile-stone; if by Astia, at the eleventh. Both of them are sandy in places, which makes it a little heavier and longer by carriage, but short and easy on horseback. The landscape affords plenty of variety, the view in some places being closed in by woods, in others extending over broad meadows, where numerous flocks of sheep and herds of cattle, which the severity of the winter has driven from the mountains, fatten in the spring warmth, and on the rich pasturage.

My villa is of a convenient size without being expensive to keep up. The entrance hall [A] in front is plain, but not mean, through which you enter porticoes shaped into the form of the letter D, enclosing a small but cheerful courtyard [B]. These make a splendid retreat for bad weather, not only as they are shut in with windows, but particularly as they are sheltered by a projection of the roof. From the middle of these porticoes you pass into a bright, pleasant inner court [C], and

---

7. Trajan.

8. The *ius trium liberorum* provided that every citizen of Rome who had three children should be excused from all troublesome offices where he lived. It also removed bars on inheriting, permitted offices to be held before the statutory age, and allowed priority in holding office and being assigned a province.

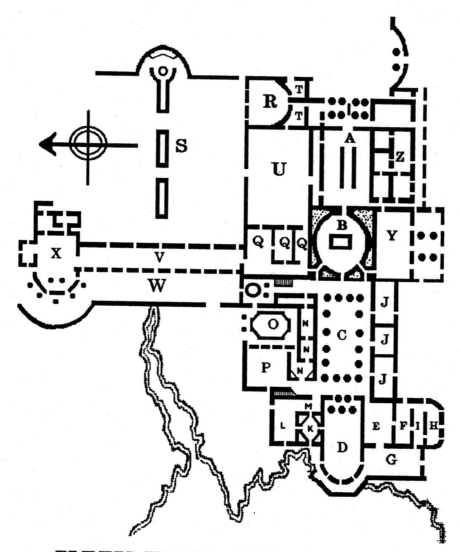

PLINY'S HOUSE AT LAURENTUM

A. Entrance Hall
B. Courtyard
C. Inner Hall
D. Dining Room
E. Bedroom
G. Gymnasium
H. Bedroom
I. Bedroom
J. Slaves' Rooms
K. Bedroom
L. Small Dining Room

M. Rooms and Antechambers
N. Bathrooms
O. Heated Swimming Pool
P. Ball Court
Q. Suite With Upper Story
R. Dining Room With Stores Above
S. Garden With Vine Pergoda
T. Rooms Behind Dining Room
U. Kitchen Garden
V. Covered Arcade
W. Terrace
X. Pliny's Private Suite
Y-Z Kitchens and Storerooms

out of that into a handsome dinning-hall running out towards the seashore [D]; so that when there is a south-west breeze, it is gently washed with the waves, which spend themselves at its base. On every side of this hall there are either folding doors or windows equally large, by which means you have a view from the front and the two sides of three different seas, as it were: from the back you see the middle court, the portico, and the area; and from another point you look through the portico into the courtyard, and out upon the woods and distant mountains beyond.

On the left hand of this hall, a little farther from the sea, lies a large bed-room [E], and beyond that, a second of a smaller size [F], which has one window to the rising and another to the setting sun: this as well has a view of the sea, but more distant and agreeable. The angle formed by the projection of the dining-room with this bed-room retains and intensifies the warmth of the sun, and this forms our winter quarters and family gymnasium [O], which is sheltered from all the winds except those which bring on clouds, but the clear sky comes out again before the warmth has gone out of the place.[9] Adjoining this angle is a room forming the segment of a circle, the windows of which are so arranged as to get the sun all through the day: in the walls are contrived a sort of cases, containing a collection of authors who can never be read too often [H]. Next to this is a bed-room [I], connected with it by a raised passage furnished with pipes, which supply, at a wholesome temperature, and distribute to all parts of this room, the heat they receive. The rest of this side of the house is appropriated to the use of my slaves and freedmen [J]. but most of the rooms in it are respectable enough to put my guests into.

In the opposite wing is a most elegant, tastefully fitted-up bed-room [K]; next to which lies another, which you may call either a large bed-room or a modified dining-room [L]; it is very warm and light, not only from the direct rays of the sun, but by their reflection from the sea. Beyond this is a bed-room with an ante-room [M], the height of which renders it cool in summer, its thick walls warm in winter, for it is sheltered, every way, from the winds. To this apartment another ante-room is joined by one common wall. From thence you enter into the wide and spacious cooling-room belonging to the bath, from the opposite walls of which two curved basins are thrown out, so to speak [N]; which are more than large enough if you consider that the sea is close at hand. Adjacent to this is the anointing-room, then the sweating-room, and beyond that the bath-heating room: adjoining are two other little bath-rooms, elegantly rather than sumptuously fitted up: annexed to them is a warm bath of wonderful construction, in which one can swim and take a view of the sea at the same time [O]. Not far from this stands the tennis-court [P], which lies open to the warmth of the afternoon sun. From thence you go up a sort of turret which has two rooms below, with the same number above, besides a dining-room commanding a very extensive look out on to the sea [Q], the coast, and the beautiful villas scattered along the shore line. At the other end is a second turret, containing a room that gets the rising and setting sun. Behind this is a large store-room and granary, and underneath, a spacious dining-room [R], where only the murmur and break of the sea can be heard, even in a storm: it looks out upon the garden, and the *gestatio*[10] running round the garden.

The *gestatio* is bordered round with box shrub, and, where that is decayed, with rosemary: for the box, wherever sheltered by the buildings, grows plentifully, but where it lies open and ex-

---

9. Laurentum was primarily a winter residence.
10. A drive way.

posed to the weather and spray from the sea, though at some distance from the latter, it quite withers up. Next the *gestatio*, and running along inside it, is a shady vine pergota[11] [S], the path of which is so soft and easy to the tread that you may walk bare-foot upon it. The garden is chiefly planted with fig and mulberry trees, to which this soil is as favorable as it is averse from all others. Here is a dining-room, which, though it stands away from the sea, enjoys the garden view which is just as pleasant: two apartments run round the back part of it [T], the windows of which look out upon the entrance of the villa, and into a fine kitchen garden [U].

From here extends an enclosed portico [V] which, from its great length, you might take for a public one. It has a range of windows on either side, but more on the side facing the sea, and fewer on the garden side, and these, single windows and alternate with the opposite rows. In calm, clear weather these are all thrown open; but if it blows, those on the weather side are closed, whilst those away from the wind can remain open without any inconvenience. Before this enclosed portico lies a terrace fragrant with the scent of violets [W], and warmed by the reflection of the sun from the portico, which, while it retains the rays, keeps away the northeast wind; and it is as warm on this side as it is cool on the side opposite: in the same way it is a protection against the wind from the southwest; and thus, in short, by means of its several sides, breaks the force of the winds, from whatever quarter they may blow. These are some of its winter advantages; they are still more appreciable in the summertime; for at that season it throws a shade upon the terrace during the whole of the forenoon, and upon the adjoining portion of the *gestatio* and garden in the afternoon, casting a greater or less shade on this side or on that as the day increases or decreases. But the portico itself is coolest just at the time when the sun is at its hottest, that is, when the rays fall directly upon the roof. Also, by opening the windows you let in the western breezes in a free current, which prevents the place getting oppressive with close and stagnant air.

At the upper end of the terrace and portico stands a detached garden building [X], which I call my favorite; my favorite indeed, as I put it up myself. It contains a very warm winter room, one side of which looks down upon the terrace, while the other has a view of the sea, and both lie exposed to the sun. The bed-room opens on to the covered portico by means of folding doors, while its window looks out upon the sea. On that side next the sea, and facing the middle wall, is formed a very elegant little recess, which, by means of transparent[12] windows and a curtain drawn to or aside, can be made part of the adjoining room, or separated from it. It contains a couch and two chairs: as you lie upon this couch, from where your feet are you get a peep of the sea; looking behind, you see the neighboring villas, and from the head you have a view of the woods: these three views may be seen either separately, from so many different windows, or blended together in one. Adjoining this is a bed-room, which neither the servants' voices, the murmuring of the sea, the glare of lightning, nor daylight itself can penetrate, unless you open the windows. This profound tranquility and seclusion are occasioned by a passage separating the wall of this room from that of the garden, and thus, by means of this intervening space, every noise is drowned. Annexed to this is a tiny stove-room, which, by opening or shutting a little aperture, lets out or

---

11. Not a vineyard for producing grapes; Pliny makes his wine in Tuscany.

12. Windows made of a transparent stone called *lapis specularis* (mica), which was first found in Hispania Citerior, and afterwards in Cyprus, Cappadocia, Sicily, and Africa; but the best came from Spain and Cappadocia. It was easily split into the thinnest sheets. Windows made of this stone were called *specularia*.

retains the heat from underneath, according as you require. Beyond this lie a bed-room and ante-room, which enjoy the sun, though obliquely indeed, from the time it rises till the afternoon. When I retire to this garden summer-house, I fancy myself a hundred miles away from my villa, and take especial pleasure in it at the feast of the Saturnalia,[13] when, by the license of that festive season, every other part of my house resounds with my servants' mirth: thus I neither interrupt their amusement nor they my studies. Amongst the pleasures and conveniences of this situation, there is one drawback, and that is, the want of running water; but then there are wells about the place, or rather springs, for they lie close to the surface. And, altogether, the quality of this coast is remarkable; for dig where you may, you meet, upon the first turning up of the ground, with a spring of water, quite pure, not in the least salt, although so near the sea. The neighboring woods supply us with all the fuel we require, the other necessaries Ostia furnishes. Indeed, to a moderate man, even the village[14] (between which and my house there is only one villa) would supply all ordinary requirements. It has three public baths, which are a great convenience if it happen that friends come in unexpectedly, or make too short a stay to allow time for preparing my own. The whole coast is very pleasantly sprinkled with villas either in rows or detached, which, whether looking at them from the sea or the shore, present the appearance of so many different cities. The strand is, sometimes, after a long calm, perfectly smooth, though, in general, through the storms driving the waves upon it, it is rough and uneven. I cannot boast that our sea is plentiful in choice fish; however, it supplies us with excellent soles and prawns; but as to other kinds of provisions, my villa aspires to excel even inland countries, particularly in milk: for the cattle come up there from the meadows in large numbers, in pursuit of water and shade.

Tell me, now, have I not good reason for living in, staying in, loving, such a retreat, which if you feel no appetite for, you must be morbidly attached to town? And I only wish you would feel inclined to come down to it, that to so many charms with which my little villa abounds, it might have the very considerable addition of your company to recommend it. Farewell.

3.5. TO BAEBIUS MACER: CATALOG OF PLINY THE ELDER'S BOOKS

It gives me great pleasure to find you such a reader of my uncle's works as to wish to have a complete collection of them, and to ask me for the names of them all. I will act as an index then, and you shall know the very order in which they were written, for the studious reader likes to know this. The first work of his was a treatise in one volume, "On the Use of the Dart by Cavalry"; this he wrote when in command of one of the cavalry corps of our allied troops, and is drawn

---

13. A feast held in honor of the god Saturn, which began on the 19th of December, and continued for seven days. It was a time of general rejoicing, particularly among the slaves, who had at this season the privilege of taking great liberties with their masters.
14. Viscus Augustanus. See Meiggs, *Roman Ostia*, p. 69, and map, p. 112.

up with great care and ingenuity. "The Life of Pomponius Secundus,"[15] in two volumes. Pomponius had a great affection for him, and he thought he owed this tribute to his memory. "The History of the Wars in Germany," in twenty books, in which he gave an account of all the battles we were engaged in against that nation. A dream he had while serving in the army in Germany first suggested the design of this work to him. He imagined that Drusus Nero[16] (who extended his conquest very far into the country, and there lost his life) appeared to him in his sleep, and entreated him to rescue his memory from oblivion. Next comes a work entitled "The Student," in three parts, which from their length spread into six volumes: a work in which are discussed the earliest length training and subsequent education of the orator. "Questions of Grammar and Style," in eight books, written in the latter part of Nero's reign, when the tyranny of the times made it dangerous to engage in literary pursuits requiring freedom and elevation of tone. He has completed the history which Aufidius Bassus[17] left unfinished, and has added to it thirty books. And lastly he has left thirty-seven books on "Natural History," a work of great compass and learning, and as full of variety as nature herself. You will wonder how a man as busy as he was could find time to compose so many books, and some of them too involving such care and labor. But you will be still more surprised when you hear that he pleaded at the bar for some time, that he died in his sixty-sixth year, that the intervening time was employed partly in the execution of the highest official duties, partly in attendance upon those emperors who honored him with their friendship. But he had a quick apprehension, marvelous power of application, and was of an exceedingly wakeful temperament. He always began to study at midnight at the time of the feast of Vulcan, not for the sake of good luck, but for learning's sake; in winter generally at one in the morning, but never later than two, and often at twelve.[18] He was a most ready sleeper, insomuch that he would sometimes, while in the midst of his studies, fall off and then wake up again. Before day-break he used to wait upon Vespasian (who also used his nights for transacting business), and then proceed to execute the orders he had received. As soon as he returned home, he gave what time was left to study. After a short and light refreshment at noon (agreeably to the good old custom of our ancestors) he would frequently in the summer, if he was disengaged from business, lie down and bask in the sun; during which time some author was read to him, while he took notes and made extracts, for every book he read he made extracts out of, indeed it was a maxim of his, that "no

---

15. A poet to whom Quintilian assigns the highest rank, as a writer of tragedies, among his contemporaries (10.100.1.98). Tacitus also speaks of him in terms of high appreciation (Annals, 5.8).

16. Stepson of Augustus and brother to Tiberius. An amiable and popular prince. He died at the close of his third campaign, from a fracture received by falling from his horse.

17. A historian under Augustus and Tiberius. He wrote part of a history of Rome, which was continued by the elder Pliny; also an account of the German war, to which Quintilian makes allusion (Inst. 10.103), pronouncing him, as a historian, "estimable in all respects, yet in some things failing to do himself justice."

18. The distribution of time among the Romans was very different from ours. They divided the night into four equal parts, which they called *watches*, each three hours in length; and part of these they devoted either to the pleasures of the table or to study. The natural day they divided into twelve hours, the first beginning with sunrise, and the last ending with sunset; by which means their hours were of unequal length, varying according to the different seasons of the year. The time for business began with sunrise, and continued to the fifth hour, being that of lunch, which with them was only a slight repast. From there to the seventh hour was a time of repose; a custom which still prevails in Italy. The eighth hour was employed in bodily exercises; after which they constantly bathed, and from there went to dinner.

book was so bad but some good might be got out of it." When this was over, he generally took a cold bath, then some light refreshment and a little nap. After this, as if it had been a new day, he studied till dinner time, when a book was again read to him, which he would take down running notes upon. I remember once, his reader having mispronounced a word, one of my uncle's friends at the table made him go back to where the word was and repeat it again; upon which my uncle said to his friend, "Surely you understood it?" Upon his acknowledging that he did, "Why, then," said he, "did you make him go back again? We have lost more than ten lines by this interruption." Such an economist he was of time! In the summer he used to rise from dinner at daylight, and in winter as soon as it was dark: a rule he observed as strictly as if it had been a law of the state. Such was his manner of life amid the bustle and turmoil of the town: but in the country his whole time was devoted to study, excepting only when he bathed. In this exception I include no more than the time during which he was actually in the bath; for all the while he was being rubbed and wiped, he was employed either in hearing some book read to him or in dictating himself. In going about anywhere, as though he were disengaged from all other business, he applied his mind wholly to that single pursuit. A shorthand writer constantly attended him, with book and tablets, who, in the winter, wore a particular sort of warm gloves, that the sharpness of the weather might not occasion any interruption to my uncle's studies: and for the same reason, when in Rome, he was always carried in a chair. I recollect his once taking me to task for walking. "You need not," he said, "lose these hours." For he thought every hour gone that was not given to study. Through this extraordinary application he found time to compose the several treatises I have mentioned, besides one hundred and sixty volumes of extracts which he left me in his will, consisting of a kind of commonplace, written on both sides, in very small hand, so that one might fairly reckon the number considerably more. He used himself to tell us that when he was comptroller of the revenue in Spain, he could have sold these manuscripts to Largius Licinus for four hundred thousand sesterces, and then there were not so many of them. When you consider the books he has read, and the volumes he has written, are you not inclined to suspect that he never was engaged in public duties or was ever in the confidence of his prince? On the other hand, when you are told how indefatigable he was in his studies, are you not inclined to wonder that he read and wrote no more than he did? For, on one side, what obstacles would not the business of a court throw in his way? And on the other, what is it that such intense application might not effect? It amuses me then when I hear myself called a studious man, who in comparison with him am the merest idler. But why do I mention myself, who am diverted from these pursuits by numberless affairs both public and private? Who amongst those whose whole lives are devoted to literary pursuits would not blush and feel himself the most confirmed of sluggards by the side of him? I see I have run out my letter farther than I had originally intended, which was only to let you know, as you asked me, what works he had left behind him. But I trust this will be no less acceptable to you than the books themselves, as it may, possibly, not only excite your curiosity to read his works, but also your emulation to copy his example, by some attempts of a similar nature. Farewell.

3.14. To Publius Acilius: Revolt of Slaves

The atrocious treatment that Largius Macedo, a man of praetorian rank, lately received at the hands of his slaves is so extremely tragical that it deserves a place rather in public history than in a private letter; though it must at the same time be acknowledged there was a haughtiness and severity in his behavior towards them which showed that he little remembered, indeed almost entirely forgot, the fact that his own father had once been in that station of life. He was bathing at his Formian Villa, when he found himself suddenly surrounded by his slaves; one seizes him by the throat, another strikes him on the mouth, whilst others trampled upon his breast, stomach, and even other parts which I need not mention. When they thought the breath must be quite out of his body, they threw him down upon the heated pavement of the bath, to try whether he was still alive, where he lay outstretched and motionless, either really insensible or only feigning to be so, upon which they concluded him to be actually dead. In this condition they brought him out, pretending that he had got suffocated by the heat of the bath. Some of his more trusty servants received him, and his mistresses came about him shrieking and lamenting. The noise of their cries and the fresh air, together, brought him a little to himself; he opened his eyes, moved his body, and showed them (as he now safely might) that he was not quite dead. The murderers immediately made their escape; but most of them have been caught again, and they are after the rest. He was with great difficulty kept alive for a few days, and then expired, having, however, the satisfaction of finding himself as amply revenged in his lifetime as he would have been after his death. Thus you see to what affronts, indignities, and dangers we are exposed. Lenity and kind treatment are no safeguard; for it is malice and not reflection that arms such ruffians against their masters. So much for this piece of news. And what else? What else? Nothing else, or you should hear it, for I have still paper, and time too (as it is holiday time with me) to spare for more, and I can tell you one further circumstance relating to Macedo, which now occurs to me. As he was in a public bath once, at Rome, a remarkable, and (judging from the manner of his death) an ominous, accident happened to him. A slave of his, in order to make way for his master, laid his hand gently upon a Roman knight, who, turning suddenly round, struck, not the slave who had touched him, but Macedo, so violent a blow with his open palm that he almost knocked him down. Thus the bath by a kind of gradation proved fatal to him; being first the scene of an indignity he suffered, afterwards the scene of his death. Farewell.

3.16. To Maecilius Nepos: A Faithful Wife and Mother

I have constantly observed that amongst the deeds and sayings of illustrious persons of either sex, some have made more noise in the world, whilst others have been really greater, although less talked about; and I am confirmed in this opinion by a conversation I had yesterday with Fannia. This lady is a granddaughter to that celebrated Arria who animated her husband to meet death, by her own glorious example. She informed me of several particulars relating to Arria, no less heroic than this applauded action of hers, though taken less notice of, and I think you will be as surprised to read the account of them as I was to hear it. Her husband, Caecina Paetus, and her son, were both attacked at the same time with a fatal illness, as was supposed; of which the son died, a youth of remarkable beauty, and as modest as he was comely, endeared indeed to his parents no less by his many graces than from the fact of his being their son. His mother prepared his funeral and conducted the usual ceremonies so privately that Paetus did not know of his death. Whenever she came into his room, she pretended her son was alive and actually better: and as often as he enquired after his health, would answer, "He has had a good rest, and eaten his food with quite an appetite." Then when she found the tears she had so long kept back, gushing forth in spite of herself, she would leave the room, and having given vent to her grief, return with dry eyes and a serene countenance, as though she had dismissed every feeling of bereavement at the door of her husband's chamber. I must confess it was a brave action[19] in her to draw the steel, plunge it into her breast, pluck out the dagger, and present it to her husband with that ever memorable, I had almost said that divine, expression, "Paetus, it is not painful." But when she spoke and acted thus, she had the prospect of glory and immortality before her; how far greater, without the support of any such animating motives, to hide her tears, to conceal her grief, and cheerfully to act the mother, when a mother no more!

Scribonianus had taken up arms in Illyricum against Claudius, where he lost his life, and Paetus, who was of his party, was brought a prisoner to Rome. When they were going to put him on board ship, Arria besought the soldiers that she might be permitted to attend him: "For surely," she urged, "you will allow a man of consular rank some servants to dress him, attend to him at meals, and put his shoes on for him; but if you will take me, I alone will perform all these offices." Her request was refused; upon which she hired a fishing boat, and in that small vessel followed the ship. On her return to Rome, meeting the wife of Scribonianus in the emperor's palace, at the time when this woman voluntarily gave evidence against the conspirators—"What," she exclaimed, "shall I hear you even speak to me, you, on whose bosom your husband, Scribonianus, was murdered, and yet you survive him?"—an expression which plainly shows that the noble manner in which she put an end to her life was no unpremeditated effect of sudden passion. Moreover, when Thrasea, her son-in-law, was endeavoring to dissuade her from her purpose of destroying herself, and, amongst other arguments which he used, said to her, "Would you then advise your daughter to die with me if my life were to be taken from me?" "Most certainly I would," she replied, "if she had lived as long, and in as much harmony with you, as I have with my Paetus." This answer greatly increased the alarm of her family, and made them watch her for the future more narrowly; which when she perceived, "It is of no use," she said, "you may oblige me to effect my death in a more painful way, but it is impossible you should prevent it." Saying this, she sprang from her chair, and running her head with the utmost violence against the wall, fell down, to all appearance, dead; but being brought to herself again, "I told you," she said, "if you would not suffer me to take an easy path to death, I should find a way to it, however hard."

---

19. The following is the story, as related by several of the ancient historians: Paetus, having joined Scribonianus, who was in arms, in Illyricum, against Claudius, was taken after the death of Scribonianus, and condemned to death. Arria, having, in vain, solicited his life, persuaded him to destroy himself, rather than suffer the ignominy of falling by the executioner's hands; and, in order to encourage him to an act, to which, it seems, he was not particularly inclined, she set him the example in the manner Pliny relates.

Now, is there not, my friend, something much greater in all this than in the so-much-talked-of "Paetus, it is not painful," to which these led the way? And yet this last is the favorite topic of fame, while all the former are passed over in silence. Whence I cannot but infer, what I observed at the beginning of my letter, that some actions are more celebrated, whilst others are really greater.

3.19. To Calvisius Rufus: Request for Advice

I must have recourse to you, as usual, in an affair which concerns my finances. An estate adjoining my land, and indeed running into it, is for sale. There are several considerations strongly inclining me to this purchase, while there are others no less weighty deterring me from it. Its first recommendation is the beauty which will result from uniting this farm to my own lands; next, the advantage as well as pleasure of being able to visit it without additional trouble and expense; to have it superintended by the same steward, and almost by the same sub-agents, and to have one villa to support and embellish, the other just to keep in common repair. I take into this account furniture, housekeepers, fancy-gardeners, artificers, and even hunting apparatus, as it makes a very great difference whether you get these altogether into one place or scatter them about in several. On the other hand, I don't know whether it is prudent to expose so large a property to the same climate, and the same risks of accident happening; to distribute one's possessions about seems a safer way of meeting the caprice of fortune, besides, there is something extremely pleasant in the change of air and place, and the going about between one's properties. And now, to come to the chief consideration: the lands are rich, fertile, and well watered, consisting chiefly of meadow, vineyard, and wood, while the supply of building timber and its returns, though moderate, still, keep at the same rate. But the soil, fertile as it is, has been much impoverished by not having been properly looked after. The person last in possession used frequently to seize and sell the stock, by which means, although he lessened his tenants' arrears for the time being, yet he left them nothing to go on with and the arrears ran up again in consequence. I shall be obliged, then, to provide them with slaves, which I must buy, and at a higher than the usual price, as these will be good ones; for I keep no fettered slaves[20] myself, and there are none upon the estate. For the rest, the price, you must know, is three millions of sesterces. It has formerly gone for five millions, but owing partly to the general hardness of the times, and partly to its being thus stripped of tenants, the income of this estate is reduced, and consequently its value. You will be inclined perhaps to enquire whether I can easily raise the purchase-money? My estate, it is true, is almost entirely in land, though I have some money out at interest; but I shall find no difficulty in borrowing any sum I may want. I can get it from my wife's mother, whose purse I may use with the same freedom as my own; so that you need not trouble yourself at all upon that point, should you have no other objections, which I should like you very carefully to consider: for, as in everything else, so, particularly in matters of economy, no man has more judgment and experience than yourself. Farewell.

---

20. The Romans used to employ their criminals as slaves in the lower offices of husbandry, such as plowing, etc.

4.1. To Calpurnius Fabatus, His Wife's Grandfather

You have long desired a visit from your granddaughter[21] accompanied by me. Nothing, be assured, could be more agreeable to either of us; for we equally wish to see you, and are determined to delay that pleasure no longer. For this purpose we are already packing up, and hastening to you with all the speed the roads will permit. We shall make only one short stop, for we intend turning a little out of our way to go into Tuscany: not for the sake of looking upon our estate, and into our family concerns, which we can postpone to another opportunity, but to perform an indispensable duty. There is a town near my estate, called Tifernum-on-the-Tiber,[22] which, with more affection than wisdom, put itself under my patronage when I was yet a youth. These people celebrate my arrival among them, express the greatest concern when I leave them, and have public rejoicings whenever they hear of my preferments. By way of requiting their kindnesses (for what generous mind can bear to be excelled in acts of friendship?) I have built a temple in this place, at my own expense, and as it is finished, it would be a sort of impiety to put off its dedication any longer. So we shall be there on the day on which that ceremony is to be performed, and I have resolved to celebrate it with a general feast. We may possibly stay on there for all the next day, but shall make so much the greater haste in our journey afterwards. May we have the happiness to find you and your daughter in good health! In good spirits I am sure we shall, should we get to you safely. Farewell.

4.10. To Statius Sabinus: Freedom for a Slave

Your letter informs me that Sabina, who appointed you and me her heirs, though she has nowhere expressly directed that Modestus shall have his freedom, yet has left him a legacy in the following words: "I give, etc.—To Modestus, whom I have ordered to have his freedom": upon which you desire my opinion. I have consulted skilful lawyers upon the point, and they all agree Modestus is not entitled to his liberty, since it is not *expressly* given, and consequently that the legacy is void, as being bequeathed to a slave.[23] But it evidently appears to be a mistake in the testatrix; and therefore I think we ought to act in this case as though Sabina had directed, in so many words, what, it is clear, she had ordered. I am persuaded you will go with me in this opinion, who so religiously regard the will of the deceased, which indeed where it can be discovered will always be law to honest heirs. Honor is to you and me as strong an obligation as the compulsion of law is to others. Let Modestus then enjoy his freedom and his legacy as fully as if Sabina had observed all the requisite forms, as indeed they effectually do who make a judicious choice of their heirs. Farewell.

---

21. Calpurnia, Pliny's wife.
22. Now Citta di Castello.
23. A slave was incapable of property; and, therefore, whatever he acquired became the right of his master.

4.19. To Calpurnia Hispulla, His Wife's Aunt

As you are a model of all virtue, and loved your late excellent brother, who had such a fondness for you, with an affection equal to his own; regarding too his daughter[24] as your child, not only showing her an aunt's tenderness, but supplying the place of the parent she had lost; I know it will give you the greatest pleasure and joy to hear that she proves worthy of her father, her grandfather, and yourself. She possesses an excellent understanding together with a consummate prudence, and gives the strongest evidence of the purity of her heart by her fondness of her husband. Her affection for me, moreover, has given her a taste for books, and my productions, which she takes a pleasure in reading, and even in getting by heart, are continually in her hands. How full of tender anxiety is she when I am going to speak in any case, how rejoiced she feels when it is got through! While I am pleading, she stations persons to inform her from time to time how I am heard,[25] what applauses I receive, and what success attends the case. When I recite my works at any time, she conceals herself behind some curtain, and drinks in my praises with greedy ears. She sings my verses too, adapting them to her lyre, with no other master but love, that best of instructors, for her guide. From these happy circumstances I derive my surest hopes that the harmony between us will increase with our days, and be as lasting as our lives. For it is not my youth or person, which time gradually impairs; it is my honor and glory that she cares for. But what less could be expected from one who was trained by your hands, and formed by your instructions; who was early familiarized under your roof with all that is pure and virtuous, and who learnt to love me first through your praises? And as you revered my mother with all the respect due even to a parent, so you kindly directed and encouraged my tender years, presaging from that early period all that my wife now fondly imagines I really am. Accept therefore of our mutual thanks, mine for your giving me her, hers for your giving her me; for you have chosen us out, as it were, for each other. Farewell.

5.5. To Novius Maximus: A Dream Come True

I am deeply afflicted with the news I have received of the death of Fannius; in the first place, because I loved one so eloquent and refined, in the next, because I was accustomed to be guided by his judgment—and indeed he possessed great natural acuteness, improved by practice, rendering him able to see a thing in an instant. There are some circumstances about his death, which aggravate my concern. He left behind him a will which had been made a considerable time before his decease, by which it happens that his estate is fallen into the hands of those who had incurred his displeasure, whilst his greatest favorites are excluded. But what I particularly regret is, that he has left unfinished a very noble work in which he was employed. Notwithstanding his full practice at the bar, he had begun a history of those persons who were put to death or banished by Nero, and completed three books of it. They are written with great elegance and precision,

---

24. Calpurnia, Pliny's wife.
25. Women were not allowed to attend court or other public functions.

the style is pure, and preserves a proper medium between the plain narrative and the historical: and as they were very favorably received by the public, he was the more desirous of being able to finish the rest. The hand of death is ever, in my opinion, too untimely and sudden when it falls upon such as are employed in some immortal work. Those who abandon themselves to pleasure, who have no outlook beyond the present hour, put an end every day to all motives for living, but those who look forward to posterity, and endeavor to transmit their names with honor to future generations by their works—to such, death is always immature, as it still snatches them from amidst some unfinished design. Fannius, long before his death, had a presentiment of what has happened: he dreamed one night that as he was lying on his couch, in an undress, all ready for his work, and with his desk, as usual in front of him, Nero entered, and placing himself by his side, took up the three first books of this history, which he read through and then departed. This dream greatly alarmed him, and he regarded it as an intimation that he should not carry on his history any farther than Nero had read, and so the event has proved. I cannot reflect upon this accident without lamenting that he was prevented from accomplishing a work which had cost him so many toilsome vigils, as it suggests to me, at the same time, reflections on my own mortality, and the fate of my writings: and I am persuaded the same apprehensions alarm you for those in which you are at present employed. Let us then, my friend, while life permits, exert all our endeavors, that death, whenever it arrives, may find as little as possible to destroy. Farewell.

5.16. To Aefelanus Marcellinus: The Death of a Young Girl

I write this to you in the deepest sorrow: the youngest daughter of my friend Fundanus is dead! I have never seen a more cheerful and more lovable girl, or one who better deserved to have enjoyed a long, I had almost said an immortal, life! She was scarcely fourteen,[26] and yet there was in her a wisdom far beyond her years, a matronly gravity united with girlish sweetness and virgin bashfulness. With what an endearing fondness did she hang on her father's neck! How affectionately and modestly she used to greet us, his friends! With what a tender and deferential regard she used to treat her nurses, tutors, teachers, each in their respective offices! What an eager, industrious, intelligent reader she was! She took few amusements, and those with caution. How self-controlled, how patient, how brave she was under her last illness! She complied with all the directions of her physicians; she spoke cheerful, comforting words to her sister and her father; and when all her bodily strength was exhausted, the vigor of her mind sustained her. That indeed continued even to her last moments, unbroken by the pain of a long illness, or the terrors of approaching death; and it is a reflection which makes us miss her, and grieve that she has gone from us, the more. Oh, melancholy, untimely loss, too truly! She was engaged to an excellent young man; the wedding day was fixed, and we were all invited. How our joy has been turned into sorrow! I cannot express in words the inward pain I felt when I heard Fundanus himself (as grief is ever finding out fresh circumstances to aggravate its affliction) ordering the money he

---

26. Municia Marcella. Her age is given on her grave marker, ILS 1030, as 12 years 11 months and 7 days.

had intended laying out upon clothes, pearls, and jewels for her marriage, to be employed in frankincense, ointments, and perfumes for her funeral. He is a man of great learning and good sense, who has applied himself from his earliest youth to the deeper studies and the fine arts, but all the maxims of fortitude which he has received from books, or advanced himself, he now absolutely rejects, and every other virtue of his heart gives place to all a parent's tenderness. You will excuse, you will even approve, his grief, when you consider what he has lost. He has lost a daughter who resembled him in character no less than in face and expression, and was her father's living image in a wonderful way.

So, if you should think proper to write to him upon the subject of so reasonable a grief, let me remind you not to use the rougher arguments of consolation, and such as seem to carry a sort of reproof with them, but those of kind and sympathizing humanity. Time will render him more open to the dictates of reason: for as a fresh wound shrinks back from the hand of the surgeon, but by degrees submits to, and even seeks of its own accord, the means of its cure, so a mind under the first impression of a misfortune shuns and rejects all consolations, but at length desires and is lulled by their gentle application. Farewell.

5.19. To Valerius Paulinus; Kindness to His Freedman

As I know the humanity with which you treat your own servants, I have less reserve in confessing to you the indulgence I show to mine. I have ever in my mind that line of Homer's: "Who swayed his people with a father's love"[27] and this expression of ours, "father of a family." But were I harsher and harder than I really am by nature, the ill state of health of my freedman Zosimus (who has the stronger claim upon my tenderness, in that he now stands in more especial need of it) would be sufficient to soften me. He is a good, honest fellow, attentive in his services, and well-read; but his chief talent, and indeed his distinguishing qualification, is that of a comedian, in which he highly excels. His pronunciation is distinct, correct in emphasis, pure, and graceful: he has a very skilled touch, too, upon the lyre, and performs with better execution than is necessary for one of his profession. To this I must add, he reads history, oratory, and poetry, as well as if these had been the sole objects of his study. I am the more particular in enumerating his qualifications, to let you see how many agreeable services I receive from this one servant alone. He is indeed endeared to me by the ties of a long affection, which are strengthened by the danger he is now in. For nature has so formed our hearts that nothing contributes more to incite and kindle affection than the fear of losing the object of it: a fear which I have suffered more than once on his account. Some years ago he strained himself so much by too strong an exertion of his voice, that he spit blood, upon which account I sent him into Egypt;[28] from whence, after a long absence, he lately returned with great benefit to his health. But having again exerted himself for several days together beyond his strength, he was reminded of his former malady by a slight return of his cough, and a spitting of blood. For this reason I intend to send him to your farm at

---

27. Odyssey, 2.47.
28. The Roman physicians used to send their patients in consumptive cases into Egypt, particularly to Alexandria.

Forum-Julii,[29] having frequently heard you mention it as a healthy air, and recommend the milk of that place as very salutary in disorders of his nature. I beg you would give directions to your people to receive him into your house, and to supply him with whatever he may have occasion for: which will not be much, for he is so sparing and abstemious as not only to abstain from delicacies, but even to deny himself the necessaries his ill state of health requires. I shall furnish him towards his journey with what will be sufficient for one of his moderate requirements, who is coming under your roof. Farewell.

6.4. TO CALPURNIA, HIS WIFE

Never was business more disagreeable to me than when it prevented me not only from accompanying you when you went into Campania for your health, but from following you there soon after; for I want particularly to be with you now, that I may learn from my own eyes whether you are growing stronger and stouter, and whether the tranquility, the amusements, and plenty of that charming country really agree with you. Were you in perfect health, yet I could ill support your absence; for even a moment's uncertainty of the welfare of those we tenderly love causes a feeling of suspense and anxiety: but now your sickness conspires with your absence to trouble me grievously with vague and various anxieties. I dread everything, fancy everything, and, as is natural to those who fear, conjure up the very things I most dread. Let me the more earnestly entreat you then to think of my anxiety, and write to me every day, and even twice a day: I shall be more easy, at least while I am reading your letters, though when I have read them, I shall immediately feel my fears again. Farewell.

6.7. TO CALPURNIA, HIS WIFE

You kindly tell me my absence very sensibly affects you, and that your only consolation is in conversing with my works, which you frequently substitute in my stead. I am glad that you miss me; I am glad that you find some rest in these alleviations. In return, I read over your letters again and again, and am continually taking them up, as if I had just received them; but, alas! this only stirs in me a keener longing for you; for how sweet must *her* conversation be whose letters have so many charms! Let me receive them, however, as often as possible, notwithstanding there is still a mixture of pain in the pleasure they afford me. Farewell.

---

29. In Gallia Narbonensis, now Frejus, in Provence, the southern part of France.

7.10. TO LUCCEIUS ALBINUS: VERGINIUS RUFUS REMEMBERED

I was lately at Alsium,[30] where my mother-in-law has a villa which once belonged to Verginius Rufus.[31] The place renewed in my mind the sorrowful remembrance of that great and excellent man. He was extremely fond of this retirement, and used to call it *the nest of his old age*. Whichever way I looked, I missed him, I felt his absence. I had an inclination to visit his monument; but I repented having seen it, afterwards: for I found it still unfinished, and this, not from any difficulty residing in the work itself, for it is very plain, or rather indeed slight; but through the neglect of him to whose care it was entrusted. I could not see without a concern, mixed with indignation, the remains of a man, whose fame filled the whole world, lie for ten years after his death without an inscription, or a name. He had, however, directed that the divine and immortal action of his life should be recorded upon his tomb in the following lines:

"Here Rufus lies, who Vindex' arms withstood,
Not for himself, but for his country's good."

But faithful friends are so rare, and the dead so soon forgotten, that we shall be obliged ourselves to build even our very tombs, and anticipate the office of our heirs. For who is there that has no reason to fear for himself what we see has happened to Verginius, whose eminence and distinction, while rendering such treatment more shameful, so, in the same way, make it more notorious? Farewell.

6.16. TO CORNELIUS TACITUS: THE DESTRUCTION OF POMPEII

Your request that I would send you an account of my uncle's death, in order to transmit a more exact relation of it to posterity,[32] deserves my acknowledgments; for, if this accident shall be celebrated by your pen, the glory of it, I am well assured, will be rendered for ever illustrious. And notwithstanding he perished by a misfortune, which, as it involved at the same time a most beautiful country in ruins, and destroyed so many populous cities, seems to promise him an everlasting remembrance; notwithstanding he has himself composed many and lasting works; yet I am persuaded, the mentioning of him in your immortal writings, will greatly contribute to render his name immortal. Happy I esteem those to be to whom by provision of the gods has been granted the ability either to do such actions as are worthy of being related or to relate them in a manner

---

30. Now Alzia, not far from Como.
31. See letter 2.11 above.
32. Presumably in the second half of the Histories, planned to cover the reigns of Titus and Domitian. The eruption took place in 79.

worthy of being read; but peculiarly happy are they who are blessed with both these uncommon talents: in the number of which my uncle, as his own writings and your history will evidently prove, may justly be ranked. It is with extreme willingness, therefore, that I execute your commands; and should indeed have claimed the task if you had not enjoined it.

He was at that time with the fleet under his command at Misenum.[33] On the 24th of August, about one in the afternoon, my mother desired him to observe a cloud which appeared of a very unusual size and shape. He had just taken a turn in the sun,[34] and, after bathing himself in cold water, and making a light luncheon, gone back to his books: he immediately arose and went out upon a rising ground from whence he might get a better sight of this very uncommon appearance. A cloud, from which mountain was uncertain, at this distance (but it was found afterwards to come from Mount Vesuvius), was ascending, the appearance of which I cannot give you a more exact description of than by likening it to that of a pine tree,[35] for it shot up to a great height in the form of a very tall trunk, which spread itself out at the top into a sort of branches; occasioned, I imagine, either by a sudden gust of air that impelled it, the force of which decreased as it advanced upwards, or the cloud itself, being pressed back again by its own weight, expanded in the manner I have mentioned; it appeared sometimes bright and sometimes dark and spotted, according as it was either more or less impregnated with earth and cinders. This phenomenon seemed to a man of such learning and research as my uncle extraordinary and worth further looking into. He ordered a light vessel to be got ready, and gave me leave, if I liked, to accompany him. I said I had rather go on with my work; and it so happened, he had himself given me something to write out.

As he was coming out of the house, he received a note from Rectina, the wife of Bassus, who was in the utmost alarm at the imminent danger which threatened her; for her villa lying at the foot of Mount Vesuvius, there was no way of escape but by sea; she earnestly entreated him therefore to come to her assistance. He accordingly changed his first intention, and what he had begun from a philosophical, he now carries out in a noble and generous spirit. He ordered the galleys to be put to sea, and went himself on board with an intention of assisting not only Rectina, but the several other towns which lay thickly strewn along that beautiful coast. Hastening then to the place from whence others fled with the utmost terror, he steered his course direct to the point of danger, and with so much calmness and presence of mind as to be able to make and dictate his observations upon the motion and all the phenomena of that dreadful scene. He was now so close to the mountain that the cinders, which grew thicker and hotter the nearer he approached, fell into the ships, together with pumice-stones, and black pieces of burning rock: they were in danger too not only of being aground by the sudden retreat of the sea, but also from the vast fragments which rolled down from the mountain, and obstructed all the shore. Here he stopped to consider

---

33. On the northern arm of the Bay of Naples.
34. The Romans used to lie or walk naked in the sun, after anointing their bodies with oil, which was esteemed as greatly contributing to health, and therefore daily practiced by them. This custom, however, of anointing themselves, is inveighed against by the satirists as in the number of their luxurious indulgences: but since we find the elder Pliny here, and the amiable Spurinna in a former letter, practicing this method, we cannot suppose the thing itself was esteemed unmanly, but only when it was attended with some particular circumstances of an over refined delicacy.
35. Pliny is thinking of the umbrella pine of the Mediterranean.

whether he should turn back again; to which the pilot advising him, "Fortune," said he, "favors the brave; steer to where Pomponianus is." Pomponianus was then at Stabiae,[36] separated by a bay, which the sea, after several insensible windings, forms with the shore. He had already sent his baggage on board; for though he was not at that time in actual danger, yet being within sight of it, and indeed extremely near, if it should in the least increase, he was determined to put to sea as soon as the wind, which was blowing dead inshore, should go down. It was favorable, however, for carrying my uncle to Pomponianus, whom he found in the greatest consternation: he embraced him tenderly, encouraging and urging him to keep up his spirits, and, the more effectually to soothe his fears by seeming unconcerned himself, ordered a bath to be got ready, and then, after having bathed, sat down to supper with great cheerfulness, or at least (what is just as heroic) with every appearance of it. Meanwhile broad flames shone out in several places from Mount Vesuvius, which the darkness of the night contributed to render still brighter and clearer. But my uncle, in order to soothe the apprehensions of his friend, assured him it was only the burning of the villages, which the country people had abandoned to the flames: after this he retired to rest, and it is most certain he was so little disquieted as to fall into a sound sleep: for his breathing, which, on account of his corpulence, was rather heavy and sonorous, was heard by the attendants outside. The court which led to his apartment being now almost filled with stones and ashes, if he had continued there any time longer, it would have been impossible for him to have made his way out. So he was awoke and got up, and went to Pomponianus and the rest of his company, who were feeling too anxious to think of going to bed. They consulted together whether it would be most prudent to trust to the houses, which now rocked from side to side with frequent and violent concussions as though shaken from their very foundations; or fly to the open fields, where the calcined stones and cinders, though light indeed, yet fell in large showers, and threatened destruction. In this choice of dangers they resolved for the fields: as resolution which, while the rest of the company were hurried into by their fears, my uncle embraced upon cool and deliberate consideration. They went out then, having pillows tied upon their heads with napkins; and this was their whole defense against the storm of stones that fell round them. It was now day everywhere else, but there a deeper darkness prevailed than in the thickest night; which, however, was in some degree alleviated by torches and other lights of various kinds. They thought proper to go farther down upon the shore to see if they might safely put out to sea, but found the waves still running extremely high, and boisterous. There my uncle, laying himself down upon a sail cloth, which was spread for him, called twice for some cold water, which he drank, when immediately the flames, preceded by a strong whiff of sulfur, dispersed the rest of the party, and obliged him to rise. He raised himself up with the assistance of two of his servants, and instantly fell down dead; suffocated, as I conjecture, by some gross and noxious vapor, having always had a weak throat, which was often inflamed. As soon as it was light again, which was not till the third day after this melancholy accident, his body was found entire, and without any marks of violence upon it, in the dress in which he fell, and looking more like a man asleep than dead.

During all this time my mother and I, who were at Misenum—but this has no connection with your history, and you did not desire any particulars besides those of my uncle's death; so I

---

36. Four miles south of Pompeii, now called Castelamare, in the Bay of Naples.

will end here, only adding that I have faithfully related to you what I was either an eye-witness of myself or received immediately after the accident happened, and before there was time to vary the truth. You will pick out of this narrative whatever is most important: for a letter is one thing, a history another; it is one thing writing to a friend, another thing writing to the public. Farewell.

6.20. To Cornelius Tacitus: The Destruction of Pompeii (continued)

The letter which, in compliance with your request, I wrote to you concerning the death of my uncle has raised, it seems, your curiosity to know what terrors and dangers attended me while I continued at Misenum; for there, I think, my account broke off: "Though my mind shrinks from remembering, my tongue shall tell."[37]

My uncle having left us, I spent such time as was left on my studies (it was on their account indeed that I had stayed behind), till it was time for my bath. After which I went to supper, and then fell into a short and uneasy sleep. There had been noticed for many days before a trembling of the earth, which did not alarm us much, as this is quite an ordinary occurrence in Campania; but it was so particularly violent that night that it not only shook but actually overturned, as it would seem, everything about us. My mother rushed into my chamber, where she found me rising, in order to awaken her. We sat down in the open court of the house, which occupied a small space between the buildings and the sea. As I was at that time but eighteen years of age, I know not whether I should call my behavior, in this dangerous juncture, courage or folly; but I took up Livy, and amused myself with turning over that author, and even making extracts from him, as if I had been perfectly at my leisure. Just then, a friend of my uncle's, who had lately come to him from Spain, joined us, and observing me sitting by my mother with a book in my hand, reproved her for her calmness, and me at the same time for my careless security: nevertheless I went on with my author.

Though it was now morning,[38] the light was still exceedingly faint and doubtful; the buildings all around us tottered, and though we stood upon open ground, yet as the place was narrow and confined, there was no remaining without imminent danger: we therefore resolved to quit the town. A panic-stricken crowd followed us, and (as to a mind distracted with terror every suggestion seems more prudent than its own) pressed on us in dense array to drive us forward as we came out. Being at a convenient distance from the houses, we stood still, in the midst of a most dangerous and dreadful scene. The chariots, which we had ordered to be drawn out, were so agitated backwards and forwards, though upon the most level ground, that we could not keep them steady, even by supporting them with large stones. The sea seemed to roll back upon itself, and to be driven from its banks by the convulsive motion of the earth; it is certain at least the shore was considerably enlarged, and several sea animals were left upon it. On the other side, a black and

---

37. *Aeneid* 1.12
38. August 25.

dreadful cloud, broken with rapid, zigzag flashes, revealed behind it variously shaped masses of flame: these last were like sheet-lightning, but much larger.

Upon this our Spanish friend, whom I mentioned above, addressing himself to my mother and me with great energy and urgency: "If your brother," he said, "if your uncle be safe, he certainly wishes you may be so too; but if he perished, it was his desire, no doubt, that you might both survive him: why therefore do you delay your escape a moment?" We could never think of our own safety, we said, while we were uncertain of his. Upon this our friend left us, and withdrew from the danger with the utmost precipitation.

Soon afterwards, the cloud began to descend, and cover the sea. It had already surrounded and concealed the island of Capri and the promontory of Misenum. My mother now besought, urged, even commanded me to make my escape at any rate, which, as I was young, I might easily do; as for herself, she said, her age and slowness rendered all attempts of that sort impossible; however, she would willingly meet death if she could have the satisfaction of seeing that she was not the occasion of mine. But I absolutely refused to leave her, and, taking her by the hand, compelled her to go with me. She complied with great reluctance, and not without many reproaches to herself for retarding my flight. The ashes now began to fall upon us, though in no great quantity. I looked back; a dense, dark mist seemed to be following us, spreading itself over the country like a cloud. "Let us turn out of the high road," I said, "while we can still see, for fear that, should we fall in the road, we should be pressed to death in the dark, by the crowds that are following us." We had scarcely sat down when night came upon us, not such as we have when the sky is cloudy, or when there is no moon, but that of a room when it is shut up, and all the lights put out. You might hear the shrieks of women, the screams of children, and the shouts of men; some calling for their children, others for their parents, others for their husbands, and seeking to recognize each other by the voices that replied; one lamenting his own fate, another that of his family; some wishing to die, from the very fear of dying; some lifting their hands to the gods; but the greater part convinced that there were now no gods at all, and that the final endless night of which we have heard had come upon the world.[39] Among these there were some who augmented the real terrors by others imaginary or willfully invented. I remember some who declared that one part of Misenum had fallen, that another was on fire; it was false, but they found people to believe them. It now grew rather lighter, which we imagined to be rather the forerunner of an approaching burst of flames (as in truth it was) than the return of day: however, the fire fell at a distance from us: then again we were immersed in thick darkness, and a heavy shower of ashes rained upon us, which we were obliged every now and then to stand up to shake off, otherwise we should have been crushed and buried in the heap. I might boast that, during all this scene of horror, not a sigh, or expression of fear, escaped me, had not my support been grounded in that miserable, though mighty, consolation, that all mankind were involved in the same calamity, and that I was perishing with the world itself. At last this dreadful darkness was dissipated by degrees, like a cloud or smoke; the real day returned, and even the sun shone out, though with a lurid light, as when an eclipse is coming on. Every object that presented itself to our eyes (which were extremely weakened) seemed changed, being covered deep with ashes as if with snow. We returned to Misenum,

---

39. The Stoic and Epicurean philosophers held that the world was to be destroyed by fire, and all things fall again into original chaos; not excepting even the gods themselves from the destruction of this general conflagration.

where we refreshed ourselves as well as we could, and passed an anxious night[40] between hope and fear; though, indeed, with a much larger share of the latter: for the earthquake still continued, while many frenzied persons ran up and down heightening their own and their friends' calamities by terrible predictions. However, my mother and I, notwithstanding the danger we had passed, and that which still threatened us, had no thoughts of leaving the place, till we could receive some news of my uncle

And now, you will read this narrative without any view of inserting it in your history, of which it is not in the least worthy; and, indeed, you must put it down to your own request if it should appear not worth even the trouble of a letter. Farewell.

6.24. To Calpurnius Macer: A Faithful Wife

How much does the fame of human actions depend upon the station of those who perform them! The very same conduct shall be either applauded to the skies or entirely overlooked, just as it may happen to proceed from a person of conspicuous or obscure rank. I was sailing lately upon our lake,[41] with an old man of my acquaintance, who desired me to observe a villa situated upon its banks, which had a chamber overhanging the water. "From that room," said he, "a woman of our city threw herself and her husband." Upon enquiring into the cause, he informed me, "That her husband having been long afflicted with an ulcer in those parts which modesty conceals, she prevailed with him at last to let her inspect the sore, assuring him at the same time that she would most sincerely give her opinion whether there was a possibility of its being cured. Accordingly, upon viewing the ulcer, she found the case hopeless, and therefore advised him to put an end to his life: she herself accompanying him, even leading the way by her example, and being actually the means of his death; for tying herself to her husband, she plunged with him into the lake." Though this happened in the very city where I was born, I never heard it mentioned before; and yet that this action is taken less notice of than that famous one of Arria's,[42] is not because it was less remarkable, but because the person who performed it was more obscure. Farewell.

7.5. To Calpurnia, His Wife

You will not believe what a longing for you possesses me. The chief cause of this is my love; and then we have not grown used to being apart. So it comes to pass that I lie awake a great part of the night, thinking of you; and that by day, when the hours return at which I was wont to visit you, my feet take me, as it is so truly said, to your chamber, but not finding you there I return, sick and sad at heart, like an rejected lover. The only time that is free from these torments is when I am being worn out at the bar, and in the suits of my friends. Judge you what must be my life when I find my repose in toil, my solace in wretchedness and anxiety. Farewell.

---

40. August 25–26
41. The lake Larius.
42. See letter 3.16 above.

7.26. To Valerius Maximus: The Virtue of Illness

The lingering disorder of a friend of mine gave me occasion lately to reflect that we are never so good as when oppressed with illness. Where is the sick man who is either solicited by avarice or inflamed with lust? At such a season he is neither a slave of love nor the fool of ambition; wealth he utterly disregards, and is content with ever so small a portion of it, as being upon the point of leaving even that little. It is then he recollects there are gods, and that he himself is but a man: no mortal is then the object of his envy, his admiration, or his contempt; and the tales of slander neither raise his attention nor feed his curiosity: his dreams are only of baths and fountains. These are the supreme objects of his cares and wishes, while he resolves, if he should recover, to pass the remainder of his days in ease and tranquility, that is, to live innocently and happily. I may therefore lay down to you and myself a short rule, which the philosophers have endeavored to inculcate at the expense of many words, and even many volumes; that "we should try and realize in health those resolutions we form in sickness." Farewell.

8.16. To Plinius Paternus: Treatment of Slaves

The sickness lately in my family, which has carried off several of my servants, some of them, too, in the prime of their years, has been a great affliction to me. I have two consolations, however, which, though by no means equivalent to such a grief, still are consolations. One is, that as I have always readily manumitted my slaves, their death does not seem altogether immature, if they lived long enough to receive their freedom: the other, that I have allowed them to make a kind of will,[43] which I observe as religiously as if they were legally entitled to that privilege. I receive and obey their last requests and injunctions as so many authoritative commands, suffering them to dispose of their effects to whom they please; with this single restriction, that they leave them to someone in my household, for to slaves the house they are in is a kind of state and commonwealth, so to speak. But though I endeavor to acquiesce under these reflections, yet the same tenderness which led me to show them these indulgences weakens and gets the better of me. However, I would not wish on that account to become harder: though the generality of the world, I know, look upon losses of this kind in no other view than as a diminution of their property, and fancy, by cherishing such an unfeeling temper, they show a superior fortitude and philosophy. Their fortitude and philosophy I will not dispute. But humane, I am sure, they are not; for it is the very criterion of true manhood to feel those impressions of sorrow which it endeavors to resist, and to admit not to be above the want of consolation. But perhaps I have detained you too long upon this subject, though not so long as I would. There is a certain pleasure even in giving vent to one's grief; especially when we weep on the bosom of a friend who will approve, or, at least, pardon, our tears. Farewell.

---

43. A slave could acquire no property, and consequently was incapable by law of making a will.

9.6. To Calvisus Rufus: No Interest in the Races

I have spent these several days past, in reading and writing, with the most pleasing tranquility imaginable. You will ask, "How that can possibly be in the midst of Rome?" It was the time of celebrating the Circensian games: an entertainment for which I have not the least taste. They have no novelty, no variety to recommend them, nothing, in short, one would wish to see twice. It does the more surprise me therefore that so many thousand people should be possessed with the childish passion of desiring so often to see a parcel of horses gallop, and men standing upright in their chariots. If, indeed, it were the swiftness of the horses, or the skill of the men that attracted them, there might be some pretence of reason for it. But it is the colors[44] they like; it is the dress that takes their fancy. And if, in the midst of the course and contest, the different parties were to change colors, their different partisans would change sides, and instantly desert the very same men and horses whom just before they were eagerly following with their eyes, as far as they could see, and shouting out their names with all their might. Such mighty charms, such wondrous power reside in the color of a paltry tunic! And this not only with the common crowd (more contemptible than the dress they espouse), but even with serious-thinking people. When I observe such men thus insatiably fond of so silly, so low, so uninteresting, so common an entertainment, I congratulate myself on my indifference to these pleasures: and am glad to employ the leisure of this season upon my books, which others throw away upon the most idle occupations. Farewell

9.36. To Fuscus Salinator: A Day's Routine in Tuscany

You want to know how I portion out my day, in my summer villa at Tuscany? I get up just when I please; generally about sunrise, often earlier, but seldom later than this. I keep the shutters closed, as darkness and silence wonderfully promote meditation. Thus free and abstracted from those outward objects which dissipate attention, I am left to my own thoughts; nor suffer my mind to wander with my eyes, but keep my eyes in subjection to my mind, which, when they are not distracted by a multiplicity of external objects, see nothing but what the imagination represents to them. If I have any work in hand, this is the time I choose for thinking it out, word for word, even to the minutest accuracy of expression. In this way I compose more or less, according as the subject is more or less difficult, and I find myself able to retain it. I then call my secretary, and, opening the shutters, dictate to him what I have put into shape, after which I dismiss him, then call him in again, and again dismiss him. About ten or eleven o'clock (for I do not observe one fixed hour), according to the weather, I either walk upon my terrace or in the covered por-

---

44. The performers at these games were divided into companies, distinguished by the particular color of their dress; the principal of which were the white, the red, the blue, and the green. Accordingly the spectators favored one or the other color, as humor and caprice inclined them. In the reign of Justinian a tumult arose in Constantinople, occasioned merely by a contention among the partisans of these several colors, wherein no less than 30,000 men lost their lives. With the riots in sports arenas constantly in the news today, one is inclined to contemplate how little human nature has changed.

tico, and there I continue to meditate or dictate what remains upon the subject in which I am engaged. This completed, I get into my chariot, where I employ myself as before, when I was walking, or in my study; and find this change of scene refreshes and keeps up my attention. On my return home, I take a little nap, then a walk, and after that repeat out loud and distinctly some Greek or Latin speech, not so much for the sake of strengthening my voice as my digestion;[45] though indeed the voice at the same time is strengthened by this practice. I then take another walk, am anointed, do my exercises, and go into the bath. At dinner, if I have only my wife or a few friends with me, some author is read to us; and after supper we are entertained either with music or an interlude. When that is finished, I take my walk with my family, among whom I am not without some scholars. Thus we pass our evenings in varied conversation; and the day, even when at the longest, steals imperceptibly away. Upon some occasions I change the order in certain of the articles above mentioned. For instance, if I have studied longer or walked more than usual, after my second sleep, and reading a speech or two aloud, instead of using my chariot I get on horseback; by which means I ensure as much exercise and lose less time. The visits of my friends from the neighboring villages claim some part of the day; and sometimes, by an agreeable interruption, they come in very seasonably to relieve me when I am feeling tired. I now and then amuse myself with hunting, but always take my tablets into the field, that, if I should meet with no game, I may at least bring home something.[46] Part of my time too (though not so much as they desire) is allotted to my tenants; whose rustic complaints, along with these city occupations, make my literary studies still more delightful to me. Farewell.

OFFICIAL LETTERS

10.37. Pliny to the Emperor Trajan: An Aqueduct for Nicomedia

The citizens of Nicomedia, Sir, have expended 3,318,000 sesterces in building an aqueduct; but, not being able to finish it, the works are entirely falling to ruin. They made a second attempt in another place, where they laid out 200,000. But this likewise is discontinued; so that, after having been at an immense charge to no purpose, they must still be at further expense, in order to be accommodated with water. I have examined a fine spring from whence the water may be conveyed over arches (as was attempted in their first design) in such a manner that the higher as well as level and low parts of the city may be supplied. There are still remaining a very few of the old arches; and the square stones, moreover, employed in the former building, may be used in turning the new arches. I am of opinion part should be raised with brick, as that will be the easier and cheaper material. But that this work may not meet with the same ill success as the former, it will be necessary to send here an architect, or someone skilled in the construction of this kind of waterworks. And I will venture to say, from the beauty and usefulness of the design, it will be an erection well worthy the splendor of your times.

---

45. By the regimen which Pliny here follows, one would imagine, if he had not told us who were his physicians, that the celebrated Celsus was in the number. That author expressly recommends reading aloud, and afterwards walking, as beneficial in disorders of the stomach.
46. See letter 1.6 above.

10.38. Trajan to Pliny

Care must be taken to supply the city of Nicomedia with water; and that business, I am well persuaded, you will perform with all the diligence you ought. But really it is no less incumbent upon you to examine by whose misconduct it has happened that such large sums have been thrown away upon this, lest they apply the money to private purposes, and the aqueduct in question, like the preceding, should be begun, and afterwards left unfinished. You will let me know the result of your inquiry.

10.43. Pliny to the Emperor Trajan: Expenses of the City of Byzantium

Upon examining into the public expenses of the city of Byzantium, which, I find, are extremely great, I was informed, Sir, that the appointments of the ambassador whom they send yearly to you with their homage, and the decree which passes in the senate upon that occasion, amount to 12,000 sesterces. But knowing the generous maxims of your government, I thought proper to send the decree without the ambassador, that, at the same time they discharged their public duty to you, their expense incurred in the manner of paying it might be lightened. This city is likewise taxed with the sum of 3,000 sesterces towards defraying the expense of an envoy, whom they annually send to compliment the governor of Moesia: this expense I have also directed to be spared. I beg, Sir, you would deign either to confirm my judgment or correct my error in these points, by acquainting me with your sentiments.

10.44. Trajan to Pliny

I entirely approve, my dearest Pliny, of your having excused by Byzantines that expense of 12,000 sesterces in sending an ambassador to me. I shall esteem their duty as sufficiently paid, though I only receive the act of their senate through your hands. The governor of Moesia must likewise excuse them if they compliment him at a less expense.

10.96. Pliny to the Emperor Trajan: The Trial of Christians

It is my invariable rule, Sir, to refer to you in all matters where I feel doubtful; for who is more capable of removing my doubts, or informing my ignorance?

Having never been present at any trials[47] concerning those who profess Christianity,[48] I am unacquainted not only with the nature of their crimes, or the measure of their punishment, but how far it is proper to enter into an examination concerning them. Whether, therefore, any difference is usually made with respect to ages, or no distinction is to be observed between the young and the adult; whether repentance entitles them to a pardon, or, if a man has been once a Chris-

---

47. The term *cognitio* indicates this was a formal trial presided over by the holder of *imperium*, assisted by a *consilium*, or advisory council.

48. Although Pliny had a long and distinguished career behind him as a lawyer and high ranking civil servant in the imperial bureaucracy, he had never witnessed a trial of Christians. This is strong evidence that the persecution of Christians was not extensive and wide spread during this period.

tian, it avails him nothing to desist from his error; whether the very profession of Christianity, unattended with any criminal act, or only the crimes themselves inherent in the name of Christian[49] are punishable; on all these points I am in great doubt.

In the meanwhile, the method I have observed towards those who have been brought before me as Christians is this: I asked them whether they were Christians; if they admitted it, I repeated the question twice, and threatened them with punishment; if they persisted, I ordered them to be at once punished: for I was persuaded, whatever the nature of their opinions might be, a stubborn and inflexible obstinacy certainly deserved correction. There were others also brought before me possessed with the same fanaticism, but being Roman citizens,[50] I directed them to be sent to Rome.

But this crime spreading (as is usually the case) while it was actually under prosecution, several instances of the same nature occurred. An anonymous pamphlet was laid before me containing a charge against several persons, who upon examination denied they were Christians, or had ever been so. They repeated after me an invocation to the gods, and offered religious rites with wine and incense before your statue (which for that purpose I had ordered to be brought, together with those of the gods), and even reviled the name of Christ: whereas there is no forcing, it is said, those who are really Christians into any of these compliances: I thought it proper, therefore, to discharge them.

Some among those who were accused by a witness in person at first confessed themselves Christians, but immediately after denied it; the rest owned indeed that they had been of that number formerly, but had now (some above three, others more, and a few above twenty years ago) renounced that error. They all did reverence before your statue and the images of the gods, uttering imprecations at the same time against the name of Christ. They affirmed the whole of their guilt, or their error, was, that they met on a stated day before it was light,[51] and addressed a form of prayer to Christ, as to a divinity, binding themselves by a solemn oath, not for the purposes of any wicked design, but never to commit any fraud, theft, or adultery, never to falsify their word, nor deny a trust when they should be called upon to deliver it up; after which it was their custom to separate, and then reassemble, to eat in common a harmless meal. From this custom, however, they desisted after the publication of my edict, by which, according to your commands, I forbade the meeting of any assemblies. After receiving this account, I judged it so much the more necessary to endeavor to extract the real truth, by putting two female slaves to the torture, who were

---

49. *Nomen Christionum*, "the name of Christian.". Action taken by the Romans against foreign cults was usually directed against their associated *flagitia* (scandalous conduct); Pliny's concern here is with what the Christians apologists called *accusatio nominis*, i.e. membership in the cult, and Trajan in his reply approves of this approach. The Roman law against certain foreign cults is vaguely analogous to the modern U.S. law against organized crime—being a member of such a group is, in itself, illegal and considered a threat to society.

50. It was one of the privileges of Roman citizenship, secured by the Sempronian law, that a citizen could not be convicted of a capital crime except by the suffrage of the people; which seems to have been still so far in force as to make it necessary to send the persons here mentioned to Rome. St. Paul exercised this right.

51. The exact form of the services of the early church is unclear. Their morning service seems to be one of prayer and reading, the evening one the combined Eucharist and *Agape*. It is the latter that comes under the ban on *collegia*.

said to officiate[52] in their religious rites: but all I could discover was evidence of an absurd and extravagant superstition. I deemed it expedient, therefore, to adjourn all further proceedings, in order to consult you. For it appears to be a matter highly deserving your consideration, more especially as great numbers must be involved in the danger of these prosecutions, which have already extended, and are still likely to extend, to persons of all ranks and ages, and of both sexes. In fact, this contagious superstition is not confined to the cities only, but has spread its infection among the neighboring villages and country. Nevertheless, it still seems possible to restrain its progress. The temples, at least, which were once almost deserted, begin now to be frequented; and the sacred rites, after a long intermission, are again revived; while there is a general demand for the victims, which till lately found very few purchasers. From all this it is easy to conjecture what numbers might be reclaimed if a general pardon were granted to those who shall repent of their error.

10.97. Trajan to Pliny

You have adopted the right course, my dearest Pliny, in investigating the charges against the Christians who were brought before you. It is not possible to lay down any general rule for all such cases. Do not go out of your way to look for them. If indeed they should be brought before you, and the crime is proved, they must be punished;[53] with the restriction, however, that where the party denies he is a Christian, and shall make it evident that he is not, by invoking the gods, let him (notwithstanding any former suspicion) be pardoned upon his repentance. Anonymous pamphlets ought not to be received in any sort of prosecution. It is introducing a very dangerous precedent, and is quite foreign to the spirit of our age.

---

52. These women, it is supposed, exercised the same office as Phoebe, mentioned by St. Paul, whom he styles deaconess of the church. Their business was to tend the poor and sick, and other charitable offices; as also to assist at the ceremony of female baptism, for the more discreet performance of that rite.

53. That is, the charge must be properly made against the individuals by *delatio* and a trial held before the governor, in open court and defendants afforded the full protection of the law. There are to be no mass prosecutions. Note, however, that Trajan never answers Pliny's original question on the extent of the punishments.

If we impartially examine this prosecution of the Christians, we shall find it to have been grounded on the ancient constitution of the state, and not to have proceeded from a cruel or arbitrary temper in Trajan. The Roman law was a prohibition against innovation in the public worship; and we find the magistrates, during the old republic, frequently intervened in cases of that nature. Valerius Maximus has collected some instances to that purpose, and Livy mentions it as an established principle of the earlier ages of the commonwealth, to guard against the introduction of foreign ceremonies of religion, except when this was accomplished under the auspices of the government, as in the case of the introduction of the worship of Cybele in the second century B.C.

It was an old and fixed maxim likewise of the Roman government not to suffer any unlicensed assemblies of the people. From hence it seems evident that the Christians had rendered themselves obnoxious not so much to Trajan as to the *ancient* and *settled* laws of the state, by introducing a foreign worship, and assembling themselves without authority.